W9-ANG-874

THE
Modern Reader's Guide to
THE BIBLE

Revised Edition

THE
Modern Reader's Guide to
THE BIBLE

Harold H. Watts

Purdue University

HARPER & BROTHERS

Publishers *New York*

The Modern Reader's Guide to the Bible, Revised Edition

Printed in the United States of America

Library of Congress catalog card number: 58-11586

CONTENTS

Conclusion

CHARTS

INTRODUCTION: *Prospectus of Study*

THE BIBLE has been, for many centuries, a prime subject for study, inside and outside colleges and universities. How the Bible is studied, the avenues along which the understanding of the student approaches the edifice that is the Bible, is subject to wide variation. All these avenues are sincerely planned and faithfully executed means of approach. Each avenue is designed to conduct the learner to an edifice which is ranging, miscellaneous, and—like some old English country-house—a testimonial to centuries of construction. Each avenue of study has been laid out because of a conviction that some earlier approach—acceptable and indeed normative in an earlier century—does not give the beginning student a proper view of the vast and even sprawling mansion that he is on the point of entering; and he may, because of an incorrect or inadequate initial view of the Bible, wander through its rooms with a false impression of their separate excellence and, more important, a misconception of their relation to the general plan of the structure.

Earlier centuries said that the awareness that should be utterly central to study of the Bible was that it was the ultimate word of God; the Old Testament was chiefly interesting to a Christian, at any rate, because it was the antechamber to the more soaring halls of the New Testament. Later approaches set up a different emphasis. In the late nineteenth century "higher" and "lower" criticism directed readers' attention not to the ultimate architect of the holy book—deity itself—but to a long succession of human artificers, nameless and named, who had put antechambers and halls together. Thus, certain passageways and side chambers spoke of human confusion and uncertainty; the Bible was viewed not as one structure emerging flawless from the mind of the Great Architect but was, instead, the precious creation of a company of mortal artisans who had their separate triumphs and who did not hesitate to remedy the errors of their predecessors. Thus viewed, the Bible is a "library" of ancient literature—a "library" that is commended and studied, as are other classics, with an emphasis on the aesthetic and humane elements embodied in the Judeo-Christian sacred book. Slightly differently, the Bible is allowed to become part of a survey of ancient culture and is permitted to cast light on the early emergence of significant cultural patterns in the Fertile Crescent and Egypt as well as in Palestine itself. Or more than passing reference to the religious experience of the Hebrews is made in courses of comparative religion, ethnology, and anthropology. In short, a basic change in estimate of the Bible—an estimate which regards it as the word of man as well as the word of God—has given rise to several ways of initial study.

All of these approaches are likely to arouse interest and respect, and none of them should be ignored in a course on the Bible or in a guide (as this book is) to initial undergraduate study of the Bible. But each one of the approaches is incomplete and gives only a partial answer to the question in the minds of most students who elect to study the Bible. That question—the writer knows from experience—takes these forms: Why is the Bible an important book? What qualities does it possess that have given it a unique role to play in the history of Western culture?

To say that there is a great deal of music or many a painting linked in meaning with the Bible, or to say that the history of Western ideas is eviscerated if one is ignorant of the Bible, is to give an incomplete answer. The Bible indeed manifests many similarities to secular literature and secular history; and the gulf separating it from them should not be wider than necessary. But that a gulf still exists, that the collection of books we call the Bible has played a peculiar role in Western history, should not be overlooked.

It is one of the intentions of this guide to give an exact, continuous description of the gap that (as a matter of historical fact) sets the Scriptures apart from other bodies of literature. It will, however, be obvious to readers that the writer does not ignore what literary taste, ethnology, archaeology, and other disciplines of study tell us about the Bible. But these approaches sometimes pass by the essential point: What is it (to use terms supplied by initial student curiosity) that gave the Bible power to command a unique position in our culture for centuries?

As suggested, opinions vary a great deal. They run from the view that divine fiat set the Bible apart from other bodies of literature to the somewhat opposed assertion that the claim of the Bible to uniqueness rests on the fact that it is a means, a special combination of forces—literary, historical, and ethnological—which mingled to produce Hebrew and Christian literature. It is not the purpose of this guide to indicate decisively the proper answer to this question; rather, it is to provide the student with materials which he can employ in framing his own reply to the questions in his mind: What sort of book is the Bible? What are its just claims on the attention and study of a twentieth-century person?

A glance at the table of contents will indicate that these materials are kept in strict subordination to the conventional progress of a reader through the Bible. But their recurrence should serve to remind the student that, whatever the genre he happens to be reading, there are elements of continuity behind the variety that first meets the eye. It is true that the Scriptures can be classified (and *are* classified in this guide) as history, poetry, fiction, and drama. It is just as true that the various literary forms to be seen in the Bible all carry a mark binding them to each other more closely than, say, drama and fiction are bound to each other in our own culture. What this mark is, each reader must decide. But any initial study of the Bible that ignores the special sort of tension or awareness displayed by these ancient historians, prophets, and poets is an incomplete study. Students will, I am sure, identify this mark in differing ways. An orthodox student may decide that the assertion of the Hebrews and early Christians that they were people specially favored by God is, when all is said and done, a just assertion. An agnostic reader may decide, quite as sincerely, that the Hebrews were a people dominated to a peculiar degree by certain assumptions about their collective destiny. Either judgment is a recognition that special qualities endow the Bible with a unity beneath its variety. Either judgment—aided in part by the materials made easily accessible by this guide—represents an answer to the question which most undergraduates ask: What manner of book *is* this book?

Further, an effort to answer this question does not rule out other approaches. Rather, it gives them a focus, a meeting place. The variety of materials used in the exposition in the guide is an indication that none of the main approaches has been knowingly avoided. But none has been regarded as self-contained; whatever one's point of departure, one is drawn into the main orbit of speculation. Simultaneously—if possible—one must recognize that the Bible is literature, that it is a monument in the history of culture and inspires other monuments, that it is a record of many levels of religious belief, that it displays the workings of "laws" of religious psychology which specialists have noted outside the Judeo-Christian tradition as well as within it. But above and beyond all these recognitions, the student is encouraged to make his reckoning of the special essence that pervades the Bible and that has given it a commanding position in Western culture.

No book on the Bible can be complete, and an introduction should certainly not be. I wish, however, to point to useful items in this guide. Much attention is given to literature of the intertestamental period; this allows one to put emphasis on the considerable continuity of religious forms and patterns of thought throughout the Bible. There is also a summary of the discovery of the Dead Sea Scrolls and the questions they raise about the backgrounds of

Christianity. These and other aids remind us that the Bible is intensely alive in two obvious senses: its intrinsic vitality is great and various; and just as great and various, after 2000 years, is its power to incite men to an estimate and reinterpretation—an estimate and reinterpretation that, curiously, often swerves from Biblical man to modern man.

HAROLD H. WATTS

Purdue University
May, 1958

THE
Modern Reader's Guide to
THE BIBLE

CHAPTER I

On Reading the Bible

I

A STAGE play of past years was entitled *The Voice of the Turtle.* The plot of the play may be summarized as "boy meets girl in wartime." When the curtain descended on the expected tableau at the end of the second act, two balcony critics went to work. The young women agreed that they liked the play, and for several minutes they canvassed the merits of the play and the production. Sensing a certain reserve in her companion, one critic said: "Why, Elsie, the play has everything! Or don't you think so?" Elsie hesitated, and then she said grudgingly: "Not quite everything." When she was asked to name the lack, she answered bitterly, "Well, I certainly haven't heard that turtle yet."

Elsie's trouble is not an unusual one. She had never read—or had forgotten—certain sections of the Bible. In *The Song of Solomon,* the man cries to his beloved: "Rise up, my love, my fair one, and come away. For lo, the winter is past, the rain is over and gone. The flowers appear on earth; the time of the singing of birds is come, and the voice of the turtle is heard in our land" (*Song of Solomon* 2:10-12). The "turtle" or the "turtledove" of the King James translation is one of the many birds whose mating songs inspire both ancient and modern lovers. Elsie and her friend, doubtless, were puzzled a few years before when they discovered no trained animals in *The Little Foxes;* two verses farther on in *The Song of Solomon* appears the verse that could have aided them: "Take us the foxes, the little foxes, that spoil the vines: for our vines have tender grapes." This is a verse which, more freely rendered, is quite relevant to Lillian Hellman's play: "A curse on the sneaks, the sly foxes, who spoil our vines, our good plans."

It would be putting the cart before the horse to argue that study of the Bible is "worth while" because it makes a person more knowing and saves him from asking why Hardy called one of his novels

The Laodiceans—the Laodiceans whom St. John rebuked because they blew neither hot nor cold. The reader who wishes to exercise his ingenuity at this point can turn to *I Corinthians,* Chapter 13, and to the Sermon on the Mount (*Matthew,* chaps. 5-7), and he will quickly have a long list of titles. It is a list that, with a sense of surprise, he will keep adding to as he reads elsewhere in the Bible. He will find the "valley of decision" in *Ezekiel;* he will find the "blood of the lamb" in *Revelation;* and there is scarcely a story in *Genesis* that has not become a seed in some author's fertile mind.[1]

To be sure, it is incorrect to regard the Bible as a quarry for titles and subjects. Nevertheless, if a person in the process of education has a degree of cultivation as his goal, he will find that it is simply impossible to move with ease and security in the confines of Western art and culture without a good acquaintance with the Bible. Certainly artists, poets, and musicians take knowledge of the Bible as much for granted as they do an acquaintance with Greek and Roman civilization. From Bach onward—to go back no earlier—familiarity with the Biblical sources of musical inspiration is a part of intelligent listening to music. Bach's *St. Matthew Passion* is the crucifixion story according to the account given in the Gospel of Matthew, and Bach counts on a familiarity with the stages in Christ's agony that the modern listener does not always have. Similarly, enjoyment of the fierce choruses of the priests of Baal is less if the hearer of Mendelssohn's *Elijah* is ignorant of the grandiose contest between Hebrew prophet and pagan priesthood that inspired the mad chants. The stories of Samson and Delilah and of Salome have inspired operas and dramas; and, as someone observed satirically, there is

[1] Works with titles inspired by phrases in the Bible: *The Walls of Jericho, Giants in the Earth, The Sun Also Rises, The Lord Is a Man of War, The Pure in Heart, The Salt of the Earth, The Lilies of the Field, Within the Cup, A Few Figs from Thistles, Sounding Brass.*

Novels that treat Biblical subjects: Mann's *Joseph and His Brothers,* Asch's *The Nazarene* and *The Apostle,* Byrne's *Brother Saul,* Werfel's *Hearken unto Thy Voice,* Schmidt's *David the King.*

Works that express specifically Christian doctrines: Merezhkovski's *Peter and Alexis,* Mauriac's *Viper's Tangle,* Bernanos' *Diary of a Country Priest,* Dostoevski's *Crime and Punishment* and *The Brothers Karamazoff,* Tolstoy's *Resurrection.*

scarcely a verse of the gospel story that has not given wings to a musical pen.

Nor is it possible to make much progress in the areas of visual art without the Biblical knowledge which painters and sculptors presuppose. Part of the confusion experienced by visitors to galleries in this country and in Europe comes from a failure to be well acquainted with Biblical narrative. Gallery-goers are likely to encounter innumerable young women who carry a tray surmounted by a gory head and innumerable young men who have caught a fish in the company of an angel; and the gallery is bare indeed that does not display a young woman who has imprudently begun bathing in a stream without discovering two elderly men lurking in the bushes. The sightseer who has also read the Apocryphal books of the Bible knows that he is in the company of Judith and the head of Holofernes, Tobit and his angel, and Susannah and the wicked elders. The person who wishes to make headway with Italian and Flemish primitives or with El Greco is likely to find that a detour through the Bible is really the shortest distance between two points.

Finally, the reader of literature needs the Bible not only to identify the sources of the titles of novels and poems but as a constant companion, since it was the constant companion of many of the poets and novelists the student admires and tries to understand. That this is so receives direct testimony when we observe the innumerable dramas and poems and novels that have a Biblical story as their point of departure. The great French dramatist Racine, for example, would have had only Greek and Roman materials to put into his plays if he had lacked the Bible: his *Esther* and *Athalie* are brilliant illustrations of the ancient Hebrew stories—illustrations, doubtless, that tell us more about Racine than they do about the ancient Hebrews. Nevertheless, the student is not in a very good position to assess what Racine has done unless he is familiar with what the dramatist has put his hand to: *The Book of Esther* and the evil deeds of Athaliah that are recounted in *II Kings*. Similarly, one of the greatest novels of our own day, Thomas Mann's *Joseph and His Brothers*, takes on a sharper meaning if read with constant reference to the bare, simple materials in *Genesis* that Mann is interpreting and adorning.

But the narrative materials do not constitute the only endowment that all Western literature has had from the ancient Hebrew Scriptures. When Marcel Proust called a section of *Remembrance of Things Past* "Cities of the Plain," he was referring not only to the wicked cities, Sodom and Gomorrah, that the Lord wipes out in *Genesis* but to the whole system of right and wrong that the two cities ignored. This system is a composite of the insights of the Hebrew prophets and the later Christian teachers. It has been present in our culture for many centuries, and it has set before men, ordinary men as well as poets, certain problems that are often pondered if never solved. Is man free to choose between good and evil? After his choice is made is he able to pursue the good entirely under his own power? If he needs help in his pursuit of the good, does God provide it? Through what channels does any such power come? The Hebrew and Christian answers to these questions, as we come to see what they are, may or may not satisfy. But what is beyond debate is that these answers—in the way they are put as well as in the specific teachings they assert—have conditioned the minds of Europeans and Americans for many centuries, men as various as Dante and Pascal on one hand and Thomas Hardy and Samuel Butler on the other. It is easy to see the importance of acquaintance with the Bible if one is to understand Dante and Pascal, for both men judged they were in the service of God. It is less obvious—but nonetheless certain—that what the later Hardy and Butler arrive at is often determined by the very questions that the Bible offered to Dante and Pascal. Hardy's strong belief in a blind, malicious fate is partly his protest against certain Christian beliefs. Butler's cynicism about the Victorian Christianity he knew is partly a result of his knowledge of what Christianity professed to offer to all men.

But all of these are immediately practical reasons for being interested in the Bible. The determination to ferret out, in the Bible, the source or inspiration of a great deal that is of cultural importance in Western civilization can lead one to profitable discoveries. Nevertheless, this kind of curiosity is likely to terminate in the pleased exclamation: "Is that in the Bible too!" A much more important task will remain untouched. Some people will go no farther than to see that the Bible has been and still is one of the most influential collections of literature in the world. A person who is at all curious will be quite eager to find out why the Bible has been able to command the devotion of the obscure as well as arouse the enthusiasm and ingenuity of the great. It is thanks to the obscure readers of the King James translation that the sayings of Jesus and phrases from *The Book of Psalms* or *Proverbs* have become part and parcel of the language we speak.

All this is testimony to the fact that the Bible has cast a shadow in which the imaginations of generations of men have sought security and guidance. It underlines the necessity that should, in the study of the Bible, occupy the first place. What manner of book (or books) is it that touches us at many and unexpected points? Is it possible to read this book in a way that will reveal to us the sources of strength that give it its command over the hearts and minds of men?

II

What a person gets from the Bible depends on the preconceptions with which he begins his study. Certain expectations, not wrong but misleading or incomplete, can keep him from responding to sorts of excellence just as important as those which he is determined to find. The error of narrowing down what one expects to find does not, of course, appear only in the reading of the Scriptures. In taking up a novel which a friend has mentioned, one is likely to look for the qualities his friend has extolled and pass over qualities even more important. He may read *The Grapes of Wrath* for its social criticism or *Crime and Punishment* for the duel between Raskolnikov and the Inspector. So doing, he does not read these novels badly, but he reads them incompletely. He may even—as with *Crime and Punishment*—miss the key to the book's power to survive.

The Bible is often read in a way that allows a person to miss or evade the power that this collection of books has had to dominate men's imaginations. One may determine "to read the Bible straight through," three chapters each weekday and five on Sunday; and he usually abandons the project somewhere in *Exodus* when he runs afoul of the dietary regulations of the Hebrews. A devout member of a certain religious sect may read the Bible a great deal more—but chiefly to find illustration or confirmation of the set of religious doctrines which have been taught him by his catechism and in sermons. Superstitious people, having heard that the Bible is unlike all other books, degrade it to the function of a "dream book" and open it at random in hope of finding a verse that will give them a clue to the immediate future. (A little girl so used the Bible and was horror-struck when her finger landed on this verse: "And Elijah the Tishbite, who was of the inhabitants of Gilead . . ." She read no farther; the mere name "Tishbite" filled her with painful dread.) Often, when the Bible becomes the subject for formal study, it endures another degradation, and knowledge of the Bible is made to consist of an ability to repeat the names of the kings of Israel and Judah. Indeed, the power of the Bible to survive these sorts of treatment may be an incidental indication of its greatness—and its complexity also.

The greatness lies in not just one factor which improper reading isolates. It lies in the complex interrelation of many factors. The Bible is history, it is poetry, it is prophecy, and it is an approach to philosophy. It is these things sometimes at once and more frequently successively. In these circumstances, it resembles other collections of literature. If the Bible is, indeed "The Book," it is a book apart because beneath its surface variety a certain relationship of the many factors to each other persists; the work of many men, in prose and poetry, is subordinated to one question: What guides man's destiny?

In light of this, the frequent assertion that the Bible—the Old Testament in particular—is simply a "library" of Hebrew literature and as such deserves our respect because it contains many good books cannot be accepted as final; for it is one more assertion about the Bible that will blot out elements the reader ought not to miss.

Our present conception of what a library is does not provide us with a complete description of what the Bible is. Today a man's library consists of a collection of books that answer to the vagaries of his taste. He likes fiction, poetry, and books of travel; so that is what we find in his bookcase. And a public library aspires to the inclusion of the greatest variety of material its funds will allow. The Bible—the Hebrew and early Christian "library"—must be distinguished from both these modern collections of books. It does not reflect the taste of one man or a household; it is the memorial to the maturing preoccupations of a people—preoccupations that took fifteen hundred years or more to unfold. And it is not, despite the effect of miscellany it may convey—the omnibus collection presented in a modern card catalogue. As we shall see, the preoccupations of the Jews and the early Christians led them to reject as well as accept. Before the canons—the lists of accepted writings—were set up, there was winnowing as well as gathering. A modern library, public or private, contains chaff as well as wheat. There is no chaff in the Bible. This is not to say that the modern student is bound to find all the Bible includes to his taste. But he is not to reject a portion without asking: "In what way did *this* book offer nourishment to the preoccupations that selected and formed the Bible?"

III

Perhaps no approach to the Bible is free from limitations. But the least limiting would seem to be to ask what these Hebrew-Christian preoccupations were, to make out what they concerned. Then, whether a section we would classify as history, fiction, or poetry is being read, a person may ask: "In what way did this particular book, whatever its incidental charms, satisfy the preoccupations that both created and organized the Bible?"

The closely related preoccupations stem from one dominating one. This we may identify as *a preoccupation with "the Other."* Some persons might at once ask: "Why not say 'a preoccupation with God'?" The difficulty with the second phrase is that a study of the

Bible should begin by being a simple description of what one finds. The term "God" (for most readers) refers to a rather precise collection of ideas concerned with a being all-knowing, all-powerful, a person that is spirit rather than body. Further, it is a collection of ideas that comes late in the development one follows in the Bible. These ideas about deity the devout person will naturally regard as the completest statement man is able to make about his creator; the same ideas the student of comparative religions will simply identify as a cluster of concepts characteristic of what he calls "high religions." But both the devout person and the student of comparative religions might agree that the developed ideas which we sum up in the word "God" are somewhat removed from the simple, uncomplex insights about what shapes man's destiny encountered at the outset of the Bible. Thus, we may call the phrase "the Other" a minimum definition of the insights that later achieve precise definitions—and maximum complexity—in the dogmatic statements about God found in the writings of theologians and philosophers.

What is—in minimum definition—"the Other" with which the Bible is preoccupied? *"The Other" is that which men feel is beyond their control.* This force has as its chief attribute some degree of power; this power may either oppose man's efforts to survive or aid them. Whether it aids or hinders, "the Other" cannot be regarded with indifference. The fate of a man or a tribe depends too much on that which cannot be directly and obviously controlled. This primitive or early preoccupation with the "unchancy" is difficult for us to share as we read the Bible. Because of the comforts and the physical security of modern life, because we today think we have a good control over nature, we may perhaps look with condescension on men who located "the Other" at a well, in a tree, or in a growing field. We are likely to locate "the Other" elsewhere: in the subconscious, in the collective society to which we belong, in the mysterious complex of events which we call "history," or in an elaborately defined deity. But the contrast between our location of "the Other" and the location allotted this force by the early Hebrews should not blind us to a necessary initial perception: the modern and the ancient insights are alike in that they are expressions of a sense of dependence. Whenever man has a keen sense of being dependent, of not being entirely the master of a situation, he becomes concerned with "the Other." Early man "projects" this concern into physical objects, stones or trees or hills; and this sort of "projection" seems to us both crass and transparent. We have, as suggested, substitute locations for what the Hebrews found at a ford or a holy hill; the race, the nation, and the subconscious are, quite often, contemporary embodiments of what we feel is important and, in varying degrees, beyond our control.

IV

Students of religion have made an effort to write a descriptive history of man's early intuitions of "the Other." They have found that early man located the force he could not understand but had to reckon with in oak trees, in certain oddly shaped rocks, and at places where important events occurred. Some students, following Tylor, have argued that the process by which inanimate objects are endowed with life and awful power—a process summed up in the term *animism*—is the root of all religion. Others have supposed that religion had its start with man's awed attention to the thunder that reverberates from the mountaintop, to the sun that comes back each day, to the moon that controls the tides and measures the passage of time (*nature worship*). Still others, observing the religious practice called *totemism*—the veneration of an animal peculiar to one tribe—have felt that religion has its source in man's reverent response to the pressure of the group, a pressure that finds objective expression in an animal worshiped by the tribe and sometimes eaten in a sacrificial feast.

It can be suggested that a common element in these various efforts to find the root of human religious activity is provided by the definition of "the Other" as that which lies outside man and has power to aid or hinder human activity. "That which lies outside" may be a field spirit that makes the yams grow; it may be the genius of a ford that allows a man to cross a dangerous river; it may be the moon, which governs the tides and the mysterious life of woman as well; or it may be a projection of the tribe, another "greater than oneself." At least, so far as the Bible goes, it seems reasonable to suggest that these various explanations or descriptions of the origin of religion need not be mutually exclusive. Rather do these and similar theories isolate and describe aspects of a continuing process that commanded the attention of the Hebrew imagination: the creation and refining of speculation about "the Other." At successive points, evidence for one theory or another emerges. One may suspect animism in the veneration of the holy stone at Bethel and the trees under which holy stones and jewelry are deposited. One can suspect traces of totemism in the story of Moses' brazen serpent and in the dietary prohibitions of the Hebrews; and perhaps nature worship lurks in the Psalmist's many descriptions of God's effects of thunder and storm.

In short, the theories framed by anthropologists about early religion cast light on the initial forms of the Hebrews' guiding preoccupation since such studies tell us how "the Other" is "projected" by people other than the early Hebrews. But "the Other" (as an object of speculation) survives the advances of knowledge that put an end to totemism, nature worship, and animism. What was once in the stone, on the hill, or in the animal figure comes to be "projected" elsewhere. It turns up supported by elaborate theologies and philosophies, and it is even thought to lurk (we have suggested) in the depths of the subconscious. Yet the minimal definition—power that surpasses man and with which man, whether for good or evil, has to reckon—remains a part of any definition of deity or vital force, however sophisticated.

Particularly because it is a full record of a good many of these changes—from early "projections" to rather late ones—does the "library" that is the Bible remain a subject worthy of study. We know that when modern "primitive" people come in contact with Western culture, their "projections" of "the Other" (e.g., totemism or animism) simply collapse; the gap between the early "projection" and the late—the late being simply the mixture of mercantilism and Christianity brought in by the trader and the missionary—is too great for the primitive imagination to bridge. The Bible is a full record of how a people bridged almost as great a gap. They succeeded where the modern Trobriander fails. To be sure, the gap between the early Hebrew worship and the "high religion" of the great prophets and the New Testament did not have to be bridged all at once. The Hebrews did not face the problem of discarding overnight a primitive "projection" of "the Other" and adopting a sophisticated one. But, even with these admitted advantages, the Hebrew people achieved a religious journey that is unique in our culture. (Hindu religion presents as great an achievement, if not an identical one.)

Orthodox Hebrews tend to regard that journey as having ended in the definitive insights of the prophets or in those insights as developed and commented on in the Talmud; and orthodox Christians like to regard the "projection" of "the Other" to be found in the definitions of St. Paul and later theologians as final for them. Thus, to a Christian or (in part) to a Jew, the Bible as a record of a long-sustained effort to perceive "the Other" and define it has unique significance. To a person who is neither of these, the Bible as the creation of a "god-conscious" people still has a very special interest. For the writers of the Bible not only defined "the Other"; they created, as products of their central scrutiny, other "values" that are esteemed throughout Western culture. The dignity of man, the perception of the endless struggle of good and evil, the nature of law itself—these and other topics still regarded as worthy objects of discussion had, for our culture, one of their chief origins in the Bible, that long dialogue between the Hebrew people and the force from which they could not detach themselves.

V

How this force was defined and redefined, how the dignity of man and other topics just mentioned are incidental to this age-long process of redefinition—all this lies open to the eyes of the curious student as he reads the Bible. This book will endeavor to direct attention to the unity that lies beneath the multiplicity of the Hebrew "library." But before analysis begins, it is well to note some of the consequences of the prevailing Hebrew preoccupation that must be observed at point after point of the specific analysis.

The first consequence is that human experience, in the Bible, is always conceived of as surrounded by what anthropologists often call *mana.* This term had its origin in Polynesian religion and referred there to all the workings of the unknown with which man has to reckon. It, like the phrase "the Other," is a very inclusive term and does not presuppose too precisely what sort of force is being manifested in a particular display of mana. Mana is simply the permanent possibility of benefit or harm to man inhering in various aspects of his experience. It may lurk in objects or places (animism), in the ordinary revolutions of sun and moon, in wind and sea (nature worship), in the symbol of one's tribe and of other tribes (totemism), or in some person—a witch doctor or shaman—who has "captured" a supply of mana from another source and can use it for his own patients' benefit. Whether this mana rises from many sources (as in animism, or, for that matter, polytheism) or from a few or one (as in totemism and early Hebrew religion) is not a topic on which those who recognize the mana and seek to use it profitably are likely to speculate. Mana is *there.* It is particularly the aspect of "the Other" which counts, which makes for success or failure in a man's life or a tribe's survival, which makes a sacred place or object operative and, consequently, something to be reckoned with.

There are a few other circumstances for the reader of the Bible to reckon with—circumstances at odds, perhaps, with expectations that he is likely to bring to his study of the development of any religion. These expectations are doubtless the result of a study of biology, of recent history, and of the general growth of ideas. From a study of these fields of knowledge—or at least from a preliminary survey of them—one is likely to form the following impressions: (1) There is an "evolutionary" process to be observed in man's mental and spiritual history as well as in the development of animate and inanimate nature. (2) Since the popularized version of the story of physical evolution suggests that there has been an undeviating development of nature from the simple and "lower" to the complex and "higher" forms of physical life, a person is likely to approach his study, in the Bible, of a particular section of human thought with an analogous expectation. Here too he expects to find, in religious thought and practice, a straight-line progress from the simple to the complex, from something "lower" (e.g., animistic or totemistic) to something "higher" (e.g., ethical theism). This expectation draws additional strength from what he has been taught to see in the development of man's mind at much later stages of Western thought; for here again he has been made to see a constant shift from the naïve concepts of early ages to the mature and rationally based concepts of later times. These, in brief, are the expectations that a person is likely to have as he begins his adult study of the Bible, a book dominated (it has been suggested) by a certain sort of attention, a preoccupation with man's relation to "the Other." Such expectations the Bible will disappoint. (It may well create and gratify others.)

The Bible does not record a straight-line development of human insight. One should not expect an orderly growth from the least complex forms of awareness of "the Other" to the most complex. It is false to suggest that the procession of religious experience which we can follow in the Bible will satisfy a sophisticated person who desires, shall we say, to perceive a growth revealing first the seeds of religion and then their expansion and unfolding until they are crowned by the blossom and finally the fruit, a "high religion." What is logically distasteful is nevertheless true: that seed, blossom, and fruit coexist. We cannot—as we follow the fortunes of the Hebrew struggle with religious awareness—assume that when a new stage appears (e.g., the activity of the great prophets) the earlier stages have been left behind. The prophets may speak for ethical monotheism, but they will continue to be involved in forecasting events and performing feats of sympathetic magic that ought, logically considered, to belong to seedtime and not to the time of the blossom.

That there is, in the Biblical record, this constant effect of falling back into earlier stages, of failing to grasp the consequence of a new insight upon all departments of the religious life, will doubtless be offensive to those who approach the Bible with a conception of what it ought to display to the mature student. The Bible does not reveal any straight-line progression; it reveals rather a set of spirals of which one can say that the later arcs do not entirely coincide with the earlier ones. And the hasty student must not conclude that growth and change are not at work because he does not find the neat development suggested to him by his contact with biology (the orderly passage from amoeba to vertebrate) or by his introductory studies of the history of thought in the passage from medieval to Renaissance speculation. (Teachers of biology and philosophy would probably admit that they have been simplifying their field for purposes of expository clearness; the regressions, circlings, and spirals in biological unfolding and in the history of ideas are not unlike those we shall observe in the Bible.)

The student is likely to be unprepared for another fact, since (again) he is most familiar with sections of history in which advance and change result from conscious experimentation and intellectual analysis—from, that is, what is often called the work of the discursive reason. For the most part, the story of the Hebrew religious awareness is acted out with discursive reason off the stage or (at a few points to be noted later) on the stage in a distinctly subordinate role. *The chief role is played by what we call "intuition."* If the student understands this, he will at the outset suspend certain sorts of judgment that are suitable to a perception of the relation between Locke and Berkeley or to an estimate of the arguments of Karl Marx in support of dialectical materialism. The student is certainly aware that such an attitude is not suitable to an approach to the tortured landscapes and figures of El Greco or to the enjoyment of the protracted yearnings of a symphony by Sibelius. A person recognizes the kind of statement he has to deal with in El Greco and Sibelius, and in many poets. It is a statement in color, sound, or words of what seems to have come to the artist by a flash of insight or intuition—of what has, in the first place, appeared to the artist as true on the basis of feeling and tension, not (as often with a philosopher) on the basis of discursive reason, of sustained and often cold analysis. We recognize these differences between reason and intuition, but we do not feel impelled to stigmatize as false the painting or the poem that intuition has produced; and we may have gone so far as to discover behind the impressive façade of logic and precise terminology thrown up by many a philosophic system intuitions as brilliant and unsupported as those which we see in El Greco's pictures of Toledo. Similarly, the Bible is a complex collection of intuitions; the kind of knowledge it offers us should not, by that circumstance alone, be put out of court. Knowledge intuitively arrived at is, it is plain, usually disorderly; it is composed of what has been given by a series of flashes. But the claim of these flashes upon our attention, of these sudden and irresistible perceptions as to what God is and as to what man and man's destiny are, is not canceled when we observe that the flashes are isolated, that they often (logically) cancel each other. Such claims—to repeat—are not canceled unless we are willing to deny that the later intuitions of artists and poets, intuitions for which modern culture has considerable reverence, are (because they have a similar nature) invalid. This is a denial that most modern persons hesitate to make; whatever their desire for regularity and order in a subject of study such as physics or mathematics, they grant that they wish to remain responsive to painting and music and poetry, activities that have—as does the Bible—a different rationale.

The rationale of the Bible—the circlings, the returns, the repetitions of insights along with their growth in depth and complexity—then, is one that the student must be prepared to move with. Certain subordinate observations flow from this central perception that the whole experience compended by the Bible is dominated by intuition and not by discursive reason. First, as already suggested, *formal philosophy* (or something similar) *is either off-stage or plays a subordinate role.* Its customary absence has already been explained; the kind of on-stage existence it enjoys must be briefly predicted. Philosophy stalks the apocryphal *Wisdom of Solomon,* it guides St. John's account of Christ, it is manipulated by St. Paul as he labors at the founding of the Christian Church. How important is it even here? Its employment is, first, an indication that the sophisticated writers just mentioned feel a need to implement or defend their insights, either because of contact with Greek culture or because of an inner awareness that there are times when assertion is not enough. (For the great prophets, for Jesus as represented in the first three Gospels, for the John of the Apocalypse, assertion of insight is enough.) But—and here is a point beyond which our writers do not go and beyond which many a professional philosopher seems to go—the discipline of philosophy may serve to order, to make explicit and perhaps logically intelligible what was given by intuition or insight. On the other hand, it is not allowed to alter the content of the immediately given insight. This, some students may feel, is a limitation that should not be imposed, even in the Bible, upon the "spirit of philosophy," for to them that phrase is closely allied to another, "the free power of inquiry." Whether they are right is beside the point of our present inquiry, which attempts to define —rather than to pass judgment on—the role played by "the spirit of philosophy" in parts of the Judeo-Christian experience.

Finally, we must perceive that another modern expression, "fields of knowledge," has only slight light to cast on the Bible as a repository of ancient knowledge. We arrive at many sorts of our knowledge by discrimination and differentiation; the Hebrew arrived at his "knowledge" by a series of intuitive perceptions, of immediate awarenesses. Since what intuition presents is—at least to these early knowers—irreducible, something to accept and not something to discriminate, *whatever was given in religious experience coexists with whatever else is given.* And it coexists on one level of authority and power. To be sure, as we study the Bible, we shall, for purposes of comprehension, group and discriminate. But we must always do so with a full awareness that what we distinguish variously as theology, morality, eschatology, and so forth had a unitary existence for the men who made and preserved the Bible. The Bible was a record of knowledge (or, preferably for them, of "wisdom"); it did not offer to the devout reader "fields of knowledge." It is hard for us to read the Bible with a full sense of how the Hebrew equivalents of what we distinguish as law, economics, private morality, and theology had no independent existence. For all insights, however we may now tabulate them, came from one source and were one aspect of the impact of "the Other" upon the Hebrew imagination. All insights, whatever the logical disorder and contradiction we have to note, had equal authority. They were to be set down; they were not to be allotted to separate sciences or "fields of knowledge." This too is a recognition that the student must be willing to accept as he begins his study of the Bible.

One hears, in matters religious, of the importance of an "act of faith." An "act of faith"—comparatively slight but quite real—is demanded of the mature student who wants, as a minimum, to confront the Judeo-Christian experience successfully. He must be willing to suppose that a mode of experience predominantly intuitive is not necessarily inferior to what he considers his own present mode of experience: one predominantly rational. He must, specifically, be willing to reckon with some of the consequences of the intuitive mode of experience just noted. This is not to prejudge the value of the study of the Bible; it is simply to indicate some of the conditions under which that study can go forward at all.[2]

[2] The text quoted throughout this book is that of the King James translation. The objections to use of this text are cogent. In the centuries since the appearance of the King James translation (1611) great advances in Biblical scholarship have been made, and better ancient texts than those upon which the King James translators depended have been discovered. A reader who is puzzled by the archaic elements in the King James translation or by passages which are not clear does well to read with one of the excellent modern translations; in the past half-century excellent translations have been made by James Moffat, Edgar J. Goodspeed, and Ronald A. Knox. (See Appendix.)

The reasons for using the King James translation are also very strong. The superior literary or esthetic qualities of the old translation will soon manifest themselves upon any reading of parallel passages from the early and the recent translations. Further, the King James phrasings of many key religious ideas are the ones that have become "classic" for speakers and writers of English; they are flesh of our language's flesh and bone of its bone. This book uses the King James renderings; but, when proper, reference is made to the comments of modern scholarship on various King James renderings. As the context of many a subsequent discussion will indicate, the great translation into English is viewed in light that comes from various modern disciplines of Biblical study.

THE OLD TESTAMENT

CHAPTER II

The World in Which Hebrew History Grew

THE books in the Bible from *Genesis* to *Nehemiah* are usually called "history." The term is correctly applied, for this section of the Bible is indeed the history of the Hebrew people, or that portion of it that they thought worth preserving and systematizing. But we are likely to be disappointed and confused if we expect that "history" as conceived of by this ancient and distant culture is what "history" amounts to for us. We are accustomed to the efforts of our professional historians—our Charles Beards and Douglas Freemans—and have derived from our reading of them certain criteria which cannot be applied automatically to *Genesis* and the other books of Bible history. A history of the Civil War, for example, represents many hours spent in libraries, where the modern historian has read all the available accounts, eyewitness and second-hand, of a given event or train of events. The historian has noted where the various accounts agree and where they differ, and he is careful to give us, as he writes his own account of the surrender of Lee to Grant, an indication as to what is fact, what is prudent supposition, and what is mere wild rumor. In short, he thinks it is his chief duty to reconstruct, so far as possible, the chain of events as it actually took place.

With this criterion in mind, many readers of the historical books of the Bible are likely to ask, along with the Victorian agnostics on whom it suddenly dawned that "sacred history" was a very peculiar kind of history indeed: "Is 'sacred history' history at all?" The person who says it is not bases his reply on several observations. He observes that the Bible is full of impossible events: Jacob wrestles all night with an angel; Noah's ark is filled with two of each sort of animal; Elijah's command causes soaked wood to burst into flame. The critical reader notices manifest inaccuracies of observation and editing. Two lists of the descendants of Adam (*Genesis*

4:17-26 and chap. 5) repeat certain names and leave other names out. The person who comes direct from study of modern history wonders why the Hebrew historian did not put these two lists together or reconcile their inconsistencies. Further, the lack of care in the use of sources, the omission of materials that are of deep historical interest to us, the report of long addresses and conversations that took place under conditions making their recording most unlikely—all these and other objections come quickly to our minds. The literal person is likely to say: "This is not history at all. It is legend."

A more accurate and a more imaginative answer is: It is legend, but it is also history. Instructed by historians who have Congressional Libraries to work in, we suppose that there is only one way to write history, and that anything in a record of the past that goes counter to what a fact-finding modern observer could set down is "legendary." We do not see that our adjective may well be applied indiscriminately to several sorts of materials. The legendary event may perhaps never have happened at all, like the Greek story about the unseating of Cronus by Zeus. It may amount to an effort to explain religious practices, like the account of Jacob's wrestle with the angel, during which a sinew of the Hebrew hero is strained. The *Genesis* account ends: "Therefore the children of Israel eat not of the sinew which shrank, which is upon the hollow of the thigh, unto this day: because he [the angel] touched the hollow of Jacob's thigh in the sinew that shrank" (*Genesis* 32:32). Or the event may have happened but has been so twisted and changed by centuries of retelling that the account we read is unlikely to have any close relation to what actually took place. The wanderings of Abraham take him from "Ur of the Chaldees" near the Persian Gulf to Haran near the source of the Euphrates; later travels take him as far south as Egypt. Some doubt that Abraham, a single personage, made this great journey and believe that the tales told of the wanderings of the Hebrew patriarch represent confused recollections of the extensive migrations of the early Hebrews. That popular imagination can transform actual events and personages we can see even in the preservation of our own history. A modern historian like Lloyd Lewis writes a book called *Myths After Lincoln* to show how, in a generation or so, the real Lincoln and his actual career were transformed into a pious and romantic tale often far removed from the facts. To be sure, it is the intent of the serious modern historian and biographer, whenever he takes up the Civil War or the life of Lincoln, to strip the legend away; what is left will supposedly be the truth about an era or a person. To such a mind, and to our minds instructed by his, all that is legendary is the enemy of historical truth, and the sound historical narrative is that which has been purged of incredible events, of theological explanations, and of heroes who are larger than life.

But we have to recognize as we turn to ancient historical records —and the Hebrew record is but one of these—that the legendary narrative was the expression of the view that early man took of the past of his tribe, his nation, or of all mankind. Even so sober an inquirer as Thucydides (*c.* 460-*c.* 400 B.C.) reports long conversations not because he has a record of what was said but because in his judgment an invented report of the exchange of words at a crucial meeting would clarify that meeting. The older Greek historian, Herodotus (484?-425? B.C.) wins some modern approbation for the travels that he undertook to gather materials for his history of the Persian wars; but he has been called a credulous old woman for his often indiscriminate mingling of the (in our eyes) possible or probable—a list of kings or an account of a raid—with the impossible —the miraculous origin of a people or the miraculous preservation of a hero by a friendly god. Indeed, as we read these early historians, we tend to discriminate what may have happened from what obviously did not. We say, for example, that the contest of Zeus with Father Cronus is a "record" of the Dorian invasion of Greece (*c.* 1200 B.C. and onward) and the conquest of the earlier Mycenean culture and its god Cronus, and we take pleasure in insisting that the battle between Zeus and Cronus did not take place. Of the early English poem *Beowulf* we say: "Of course, Beowulf never killed Grendel in Heorot, but the poem is an interesting testimony to cultural interchange among various Teutonic tribes."

There is nothing wrong, to be sure, in this sort of reading of ancient record; it is a reading that supposes one can winnow a kernel of historical fact from a mountain of legendary chaff. But it ignores ancient record for what it is: an account of the past that does not draw our line between the legendary and the historical. It transforms ancient records from works unified by certain preoccupations into interesting rubbish heaps where archaeologists, historians, and students of language may rummage for a precious object, a fact, that the ancient historians may have let slip in almost by oversight. But such a reading, with an emphasis on drawing a line between the possible and the impossible, encourages the unwary person to suppose that when he has numbered the trees he knows the contour of the forest. It encourages him to believe, in the case of Hebrew narrative, that when he has identified the places mentioned and related the stories to what archaeologists can tell him about the ancient cultures involved he has uncovered a secret unknown to the framers of the books of history. Actually, the contour of the forest, the collection of preoccupations, has escaped him; and he will never grasp that contour so long as he works only at distinguishing fact from legend in the old stories. No one supposes that a person reads Dante's *Divine Comedy* well if he goes no farther than identifying the various Guelphs and Ghibellines in hell or on the mountain of purgatory; nor is study of Shakespeare's references to contemporary events a study of Shakespeare. Similarly, the modern reader does not read the early historical books of the Bible well if he believes it is his chief duty to perceive the modicum of fact concealed in the legendary aggregate. He must make a necessary concession: that there are other ways of looking at the past than the one we employ today, and that these other ways can also produce what we call "history."

The Hebrew "other way" is an expression of a "mental set" we have already noted: The Hebrews did not differentiate knowledge into fields. This mental habit is certainly apparent in their attitude toward the history of the origin, the wanderings, the triumphs, and the bitter defeats of their race. What we would regard as fairly reliable historical knowledge (the old chronicles of the kings of

Judah or "the Wars of Jasher") is not differentiated from less reliable knowledge (the older stories of the wanderings of the people in the wilderness under the leadership of Moses, and the tales of the perilous times of the "judges" when the Hebrew people were getting their foothold in the "promised land"). Nor did the Hebrew mind draw a line between this less reliable knowledge and the still more mist-enshrouded reports about Abraham and Noah. Finally, this mind was undaunted when it came to the reports, most legendary and mythological of all, that had to do with the origin of the very structure of the universe itself. All this material, from the most "mythical" to the most nearly historical in the modern sense, wins from the Hebrew historians the same kind of credence—absolute credence. Thus, whatever kind of credence the modern reader gives to the various events and figures he meets in *Genesis,* he reads the "sacred history" improperly if he does not perceive that, to its writers, Adam and Eve are just as historical as David and Ahab. The Hebrew historians who put the books into their present shape were primarily interested in establishing the *continuity* of past Hebrew history. They were not aware that in doing so they mingled what could be an object of fairly exact knowledge, the careers of the kings of Israel and Judah, with what could not be such an object: the origin of separate peoples as "explained" in the story of Ham, Shem, and Japheth; the origin of different languages in the story of the tower of Babel; the origin of different cultural patterns touched on in the story of Cain the tiller of the soil and Abel the shepherd; and finally, the origin of the earth itself as given in the opening chapters of *Genesis.*

True, a serious reading should not ignore the warnings that modern historians would make: From a modern point of view, Hebrew history is neither fish nor fowl. But a reader should not let such warnings rob him of the perception that in these ancient books is a special sort of record, with pretensions that modern histories avoid: pretensions of giving a *continuous, self-sufficient account of a people.* A modern historian works in an opposite way, unless he is an Arnold Toynbee or Oswald Spengler and tries to take the entire human past for his oyster. He isolates a certain period, and his account of it presumes that the reader has read other histories of closely related periods and of more distant cultures. Not so the Hebrew historians. They were raising a definitive edifice, *the* history of *the* people. When their work was done, the writing of the history was done. For their record was a complete, self-contained, and supposedly self-explanatory account of what had happened in history.

And what had indeed happened as these historians saw it? One phenomenon, simple enough to state but requiring fifteen hundred years and more of history to illustrate and many rolls of skin to set down properly. It was the unfolding relation between the Hebrew people and "the Other." If the Hebrew sacred history is continuous and self-sufficient, it is so because of this preoccupation. The historians are concerned with presenting enough of Hebrew history to illustrate the interest in the continuous and special manifestation of "the Other" that had chosen to fix its attention on Abraham and his descendants.

To read the stretch of books from *Genesis* to *Nehemiah* unmindful of this basic preoccupation is to lose hold of the unity to which the obvious variety is partly subordinate. To be sure, one can still take aesthetic pleasure in the naïveté of some narratives and the high skill displayed in others. To our taste, there is a crude charm in the account of the first meeting of Rebekah and Isaac:

> And Rebekah lifted up her eyes, and when she saw Isaac, she lighted off the camel. For she had said unto the servant, What man is this that walketh in the field to meet us? And the servant had said, It is my master: therefore she took a vail and covered herself. . . . And Isaac brought her into his mother Sarah's tent, and took Rebekah, and she became his wife; and he loved her: and Isaac was comforted after his mother's death. (*Genesis* 24:64-67.)

The very absence of the overtones of romantic sentiment is for us a source of pleasure. Pleasure too we can find in the grim ferocity of the phrases that tell of the latter end of the wicked Queen Jezebel. "And when Jehu was come to Jezreel, Jezebel heard of it; and she painted her face, and tired her head, and looked out at a window." After a heated exchange, Jezebel is thrown down from the window by "two or three eunuchs" who act on the suggestion of Jehu. Yet, after he has enjoyed his triumph, Jehu says, as though he has just recalled *noblesse oblige:* "Go, see now this cursed woman, and bury her: for she is a king's daughter" (*II Kings* 9:31-34). As in this narrative, so in the narratives of Deborah and David and Elijah and innumerable others the constant juxtaposition of violence and dignity can stir a jaded modern taste. Nor is sheer narrative skill, the power to compel and delight, ever long absent. No one is likely to contend that the great cumulative effect of the complex accounts of Joseph and David was produced by accident.

But such perceptions about the historical books come easily. To cultivate only them and ignore the need to identify and watch for the basic preoccupations of the historians is to reduce "sacred history" to a thing of shreds and patches. Shreds and patches there are, some gorgeous and some dun; and the materials came from many sources—from older cultures and from different levels of Hebrew culture. But all these patches are so pieced together as to compose a single new length of material. Although not entirely seamless, this material deserves better treatment than being ripped apart into its component parts. The loss against which the reader of "sacred history" must guard is that of failing to see—as he takes delight in such purple passages as the address of Ruth to Naomi (*Ruth* 1:16, 17) or David's lament for the death of his rebellious son Absalom (*II Samuel* 18:33)—that the writers and compilers were embarked upon a single task: to illuminate the interrelation of man and his various ideas about deity. In the historical books, this task is executed in no abstract way; it is done by means of employing tales that come from very different sources—from old nomads seated around campfires, from much more recent court records. There is little discussion, in these sections, of the abstract ideas that may be formed about "the Other." Instead, there is a rich display of what, in terms of concrete event, "the Other" has been able to accomplish for the heroes of the Hebrew race.

Such is the clue to guide us through what is, confessedly, a labyrinth. Perhaps it is well to remind ourselves that we Americans would, for our history, possess a similar labyrinth if the following conditions prevailed: if we lacked early written records for crucial periods of our history and if, for example, our knowledge of what happened before the presidency of General Grant was no more than a compilation of word-of-mouth tradition about Washington, Jefferson, and Lincoln. (We should probably discover that Jefferson was Washington's brother and that Lincoln was Washington's son.) Our history would further resemble Hebrew history if we lacked abundance of writing materials so that records had to be economically set down and could not be multiplied *ad libitum.* The resemblance would be very close if the compiling and shaping of our records were in the hands of a small group of men who wished to show that, in their account of the entire stretch of American history, a certain party and a certain version of "the American way of life" were the correct ones. The omissions in such a record, the compressions, the conflict between what happened and what ideally ought to have happened—it is easy to imagine all these. But in place of typical American convictions about the "manifest destiny" of our nation—convictions that would organize an account of our past all at the expense of "historical accuracy" and in the service of a certain ideal vision of what we were and are—we have, as we read Hebrew history, to reckon with a slightly different set of convictions. The Hebrews had, to be sure, their version of Theodore Roosevelt's "manifest destiny." But they felt, a little more keenly than do we, its dependence on a will inscrutable and arbitrary to a degree, the will of a creature that they called by various names such as El (the Lord), Jehovah or Yahwe, and (much later) "Father."[1]

[1] Scholars point out that a transliteration into English such as Yahwe, Yahweh, or Yahveh is much more accurate than the conventional Jehovah and is to be preferred. The English form combines the consonants of the sacred name, the "tetragrammaton" YHWH, with the vowels of a word often substituted for the

All this is a promise of what we shall see when we have finished a survey of the books of history. Hebrew historical record has at its core an awareness that events are saturated with the working of the will of "the Other" as well as with the workings of human desires. This is an awareness that the modern historian, naturally, is careful to avoid. A part of this ancient attention to past events is a result of the conditions under which they took place and were recorded. The books were not written in a vacuum. They were created and then systematized by groups of people over a period of fifteen hundred years or more, people who faced certain geographical and historical conditions that intensified the effort to see the past as more than a jumble of chance events. A person whose lines are fallen in pleasant places need not search the record of his past life to see there the favor of god or fate. But the Hebrew lines did not fall in pleasant places; and their mounting miseries doubled their determination to discover a fundamental coherence in their past which transformed a fate not unlike that of other ancient peoples who won temporary prominence and then faded away into a fate unlike anything else man had yet known. It was a fate that put in the shadow the great nations of Egypt, Assyria, and Babylon. No other people had been chosen by a deity to be his "peculiar treasure"; this, the Hebrew historians were determined to read from the materials at hand.

From our point of view, the Hebrew tale-tellers and historians were the articulate part of a people that occupied a tough historical spot. It is part of the truth about Hebrew history to say that geographical and historical necessities intensified the assertions that the Hebrew people had a place in the sun, had a god the peer and more than the peer of Marduk of Babylon and Amon-Ra of Egypt, had a historical experience more full of meaning than the events set down by the court chroniclers of Babylon, Nineveh, and Thebes.

name, Adonai or "lord." The English form is no older than the time of the Reformation (*c.* 1520). Modern efforts to popularize the correct transliteration have been partially successful, and the reader should be aware that the term Jehovah of the King James translation has the strong sanction of tradition and English using piety, but not that of modern scholarship.

What was once overlooked by readers of the Bible or was unknown to them was the fact that the Bible is not as old a book as we are tempted to think. Because it gives an account of the entire history of the world as it appeared to early man, we are likely to

CHART 1. The World of Old Testament Times

	EGYPT	THE HEBREWS		FERTILE CRESCENT
3100	Fourth Dynasty: age of the Pyramids			
3000	Fifth Dynasty: sun worship			
2800	Sixth Dynasty			
2700	End of Egyptian Old Kingdom			
2600	Asiatics invade Egypt			
2400	Middle Kingdom: predominantly feudal		2360	Lugal-zaggisi of Erech claims rule from Mediterranean to Persian Gulf
			2360-2305	Sargon, founder of Semitic kingdom of Agade
			2300	Naram-Sin of Agade: stele of victory
			2300	Gudea of Lagash
2200	Prominence of the god Amon		2100	Dynasty of Ur: law codes
			1800	First Dynasty of Babylon
2100	War in Palestine		1728-1686	Hammurabi: lawgiver
		Abraham?	1600	Hittite raid on Accad
1675-1567	Hyksos invasion: the "Shepherd kings"	Joseph?	1400	Non-Semitic Kassites conquer Babylon
			1400	Assyria overlord of the Semites of the middle Euphrates

think that the Hebrew stories and the culture they express belong to the dawn of human history. This is not so. When *Genesis* took its final form, dawn was over and morning was well advanced. If we think of history as an endless torch race in which a burning brand is passed on from exhausted runners to fresh and vigorous ones, we must recognize that the Hebrew nation played the part of the fresh and vigorous runners. They were not present at the lighting of the flame; instead, they took from the feeble hands of old Egypt and the less feeble hands of peoples in Mesopotamia the torch that still provides some light for what we call civilized nations.

The Hebrew people found as they passed from a nomad stage to a settled mode of life that there are advantages and disadvantages to being late-comers in the history of civilization. They were keenly aware of the disadvantages and felt a need to assert the superiority of their god, of the laws which he had created, and of the events in which he had displayed himself. But the advantages were also great; the Hebrews came onto the stage of history when older cultures already existed and had perfected laws and social patterns. Certain concepts about God and law had already demonstrated their excellence or weakness. As someone has said: Later peoples are not greater than earlier peoples, but they can see farther; they stand on the shoulders of earlier men.

Thus the cultural situation of the Hebrews was much to their advantage. Their geographical situation was chiefly disadvantageous. The Hebrew nomads whose movements are symbolized by the adventures of Abraham, Isaac, and Jacob in *Genesis* were tenders of sheep moving from one feeding ground to another, and they had to negotiate for access to the few precious wells and use of the grazing grounds. They came into a world already parceled out. If we suppose that Abraham and his group left Haran shortly after 2000 B.C. (*Genesis*, chap. 12), one should see him moving up and down seeking a land and finding only places of temporary rest which he and his tribe had to quit because of the uneasy suspicions of the rulers of the land. As testified by the story told in *Genesis*, Chapter 34, about the summary vengeance taken for the rape of Dinah, the suspicions were not groundless. It was only many generations later, during the invasion of the "promised land" by Joshua (*c.* 1250 B.C.) that the Hebrews could begin to settle down in territory they could call their own. The land they began to possess was actually no land of "milk and honey," despite the reports of the spies that had been sent ahead by Moses (*Numbers*, chap. 13).

It was part of the least desirable terrain in the ancient world, in comparison with other, more developed regions.

To the southwest of Palestine, our present name for the land that the Hebrews took over from earlier peoples, lay the rich thread of the Nile. With its yearly floods, it had supported a civilization in Egypt for two thousand years and more. To the north and northwest lay what historians call "the Fertile Crescent," an arch of irrigated, cultivated land following the course of the Tigris and Euphrates rivers and lying between the sands of Arabia to the south and scattered mountain ranges and plateaus to the east, north, and west. Because of its position, exposed to invasion, the Fertile Crescent had supported a succession of city-states—Ur, Accad, and Babylon. Unlike the relatively isolated Nile Valley, the cultivated land around the Mesopotamian temple cities was a permanent temptation to the nomads of the Arabian desert and to the hunters and herdsmen of the mountains and plateaus to the north. At the first signs of decay in a temple city of the Fertile Crescent, the barbarians from without would flow in and take over the city and the profits of centuries of culture. If, in the fashion of more fortunate invading tribes, like the Kassites and the Elamites, the Hebrews had been able to "muscle in" on a rich, settled region, they might have lacked the impulse central to their own achievement: to insist that they were a people apart and that their god was the only god. Thus, their misfortune, which gave them the comparatively poorer land that lay open to them in the twelfth century B.C.—land that was available because both the Egyptian empire and the Hittite empire to the north had lost their grip on this no man's land between them—was a sort of good fortune in disguise. Their inferior position contributed to their persistent effort to assert their own continuity and importance in a territory where petty kingdoms were falling into decay. Thus, Hebrew history with its assertion of continuity has overtones that came from the persistent sense of insecurity created by poor geological and political position.

The land which, little by little, the Hebrews took over from petty city kings was a poor land to begin with. It stretched north and south a hundred miles or more. It lay between two "containing walls" that were to pen in ambitious Hebrew kings for centuries. The wall to the east was nature's creation; beyond the Jordan and the Dead Sea was the Arabian desert. The wall on the west was political and was constituted by the boundaries of the city-states of Philistia and Phoenicia; it cut the Hebrews off from access to the Mediterranean, the "Great Sea." The land that the Lord had promised Abraham really amounted to this: a saddle of territory cut by steep mountains that ran north and south, land that included fertile plains to the north (particularly the Plain of Esdraelon) but that, as it went south, decreased in fertility and increased in rockiness and wildness. South of Jerusalem, a point of diminishing returns is quickly passed. The real disadvantages of a predominantly rocky, mountainous, and barren terrain were only partly balanced by a great *potential* advantage: the land taken up by the Hebrews was a kind of bridge between the rich and old civilizations to the north and to the south. Because trade routes had to pass through the land they controlled, the Hebrews were able, at several times in their history, to build up a great commercial prosperity—a prosperity that would collapse as soon as political conditions altered and took the command of the trade routes from Hebrew control. (An example of this is seen in the history of Judah after the temporary prosperity of Solomon's empire.)

In short, the comparative poorness of the land the Hebrews were able to conquer—the poverty of the land itself and the uncertainty created by the position of the land—contributed to the sense we find throughout the Old Testament: that the chosen people exist on sufferance, and that their continuance as a nation depends on factors beyond their control. To be sure, these are factors that the Hebrew historians locate in "the Other," in the inscrutable will of God. The Hebrew historians found it easy to see past history as a succession of divine interventions. What we should explain in part as economic and military reverses were to them acts of divine punishment, and what we should regard as the results of the intermittent exploitation of the advantages of the Hebrew geographical and political positions are judged to be divine rewards for good behavior. It is a cynical remark, but true, that happy peoples have neither histories nor a desire to seek out gods. The Hebrews were neither happy nor secure; and their history testifies to their constant pursuit of Jehovah, in order either to woo him to do his people's will or, if he will not do that, to understand the divine acts and submit to them.

If the dice were loaded against the Hebrew late-comers geographically and politically, they were loaded *for* them in all other respects. The "old cultures"—the cultures of the very people whom the Hebrew historians present as the eternal enemies of "God's chosen people"—had rich gifts to offer. It does not matter that the Hebrews took these gifts unconsciously and so had no awareness of what their cultural debts were. The important thing, at least for our own understanding of the Bible at this point, is to indicate briefly what had already been accomplished by the old cultures and precisely what advantages accrued to the Hebrews from receiving an already lighted torch from other hands.

Perhaps we can understand this relationship better if we take a trivial example of a similar relationship in our own society. We see quite often that the leaders who are able to take up and continue the work that past generations have done are frequently men who come from the backwoods or the "sticks." They may be crude and naïve, but they have the vigor to continue enterprises that more cultivated persons can no longer control or guide. The Hebrews were, culturally speaking, hillbillies who took over whatever served their purposes from the exhausted Egyptians and the still vigorous Semitic peoples to the north. Because there was much that they did not have to create from the ground up, much that was already fashioned for them, they could expend their energies on refining certain concepts about "the Other" and man which are still a part of modern culture. This act of refining took them centuries; the set of ideas which they finally produced is their one gift to civilization, and it is enough. Plainly, the Hebrews remained in cultural dependence on the older societies in matters of architecture and other refinements of life. When Solomon builds his temple, he calls in Hiram of Tyre and his architects; and, as the prophets tell us darkly, when Israel yearns for the "fine things" of life, she is forced to pattern her luxuries on Egyptian and Babylonian models. The "beds of ivory" (*Amos* 6:4), the "pleasant pictures" (*Isaiah* 2:16), and "apples of gold in pictures of silver" (*Proverbs* 25:11) were all imported refinements like those which "the navy of Tharshish" brought Solomon once in three years—"gold and silver, ivory, apes, and peacocks" (*I Kings* 10:22). Americans should be able to understand this cultural dependence, since it must be obvious that many of our own "fine things" are imported. We get our fashions and perfumes from Paris, our tweeds from England, and many of our wines from Spain. For this sort of thing, older nations have no cause to look to us. Our important creation is, like that of the Hebrews, a way of life that is composed of elements taken, in the first place, from older societies. Our distinction is to have adjusted these elements to each other and to have put the result to the test within the boundaries of our national experience. This was also the Hebrew distinction.

It is incorrect to say flatly that Egypt gave certain gifts and that the Fertile Crescent gave others. (A similar futile debate concerns whether eighteenth-century Americans got their ideas from the English or the French.) The mutual indebtedness of the two cultures of Egypt and the Crescent throughout their histories is sufficiently indicated by the presence of Egyptian vases in Babylonian ruins and the depiction of Semitic mercenaries in Egyptian bas-reliefs. Nevertheless, several precise Hebrew debts to the two separate cultures can be allocated. Were our knowledge fuller we might modify the following remarks, but we would have no reason to modify the initial statement: that the Hebrews started out with certain insights about man and God that they did not themselves create.

As indicated, the civilization of the Fertile Crescent, to the north, was the creation of a series of peoples that had for centuries been flowing into the cities and plains of the Tigris-Euphrates Valley.

Some had come from the desert to the south and, like the Hebrews, were Semitic. Some had come from regions to the north and were Aryan. But though the invaders conquered the dwellers in the temple cities of Accad, Sumer, and Babylon, they were conquered in turn by the sophisticated cities. The older people might perish, but their gods, their systems of city organization, and their legal codes survived. And it is aspects of this persistent mythology and legal code that the later and uncultivated Hebrews, wittingly or unwittingly, took over.

The mythological preoccupations of the people of the Fertile Crescent are not unique. All early peoples face the questions as to how the earth began and how man was created. All early peoples answer these questions in terms of narrative rather than of scientific or philosophical speculation. But it was the explanatory narratives of the Fertile Crescent that the Hebrew historians drew on, and altered in their early narratives. The stories of the creation, the fall of man, and the flood have their parallels in Babylonian story. The use of such narratives provided the Hebrew historians with a firm sense that their later narratives had a real point of departure, that the special destiny of the Hebrew people which they recorded had close connection with the creation of the known universe and its preservation through its first great disaster, a flood. Indeed, a divine plan—even though it seemed to be centered on a certain people and to be indifferent to the enemies ringed about that people—would lack ultimate authority on the imagination unless, somehow, it embraced the entirety of creation and reached back to the beginnings of time. This real need was filled by the common stock of Babylonian narrative explanation of the origin of man, the world, language, and occupational differences.

The second gift of the Fertile Crescent was the outline and (often) the specific detail of the code of law that the Hebrew historians build into their narrative structure when they tell of Moses the lawgiver. The code of Hammurabi (1728-1686), the great ruler of Babylon, is not the only Fertile Crescent law code that has survived, but it is the fullest. Close parallels to it in the later Hittite and

Assyrian laws indicate that the Hebrew adoption of earlier legal codes developed by more sophisticated cultures is but the most famous example of a process as old as history itself. As we know, the process still continues. When we talk of the "American legal system," we speak of a set of social procedures that happen to be American now but that have been, successively, English and Teutonic, or that reach back to the codes of Justinian and Solon, and beyond these to some of the regulations which the Hebrews took over from codes ancient in their day.

The gifts of the Egyptians—to single out two important ones and to ignore the possible models for Hebrew song in Egyptian poetry as well as Babylonian, the parallels between the Egyptian story of the two brothers and the tale Joseph, and the similarity between Hebrew proverbs and Egyptian collections—are of two sorts, one negative and one positive. The negative one was enthusiastically acknowledged by Hebrew historians. The positive gift was not acknowledged and is still a matter for debate. The negative gift is indicated in the fact that the Hebrew historians are always ready to lash out against "the abominations" of the Egyptians, and they mean by this something very specific, the theriomorphic animals, the gods with human bodies and animal heads. These strangely mingled creatures are, some students suppose, the remnants of early Egyptian totemism, the worship of an animal sacred to a particular tribe. What happened to these early totem gods by the time (*c.* 1500) the Hebrews came into contact with them is complex. As Egypt became highly unified, the totem images lost their immediate function of standing for a small group of people in a restricted region, and those gods who survived became the object of general admiration. Some of them survived by dint of taking on the qualities of nature gods, by standing for forces like the sun and the heavens as well as for the collective tribal consciousness to which the totem might refer. At any rate, the Hebrews encountered them in Egypt in those movements into the south that we suspect in the wanderings of Abraham (*Genesis,* chap. 12) and the later adventures of Joseph and Moses.

What kind of religion the Hebrew nomads had is uncertain.

"Abraham" may have carried with him recollections of human-formed nature gods in Babylon, though one must recognize that some of the Babylonian gods also had theriomorphic aspects. Or Abraham's devotion to "the Other" may have been restricted to veneration of the sun and the moon, the two changing features of a monotonous desert landscape. At any rate, the abundant references to *Egyptian* abominations seems to indicate that it was the multiple pantheon to the south that became, for the Hebrew imagination, the loathsome embodiment of the ridiculous and confusing aspects of polytheism. "The Other," whatever its locus, could not reside in a group of grotesquely formed and confusingly presented deities—deities whose deeds were shocking and whose functions overlapped. (The bulls of Ashur, winged and human of head, and the odd composite beasts on the Ishtar gate at Babylon play a quite different role in Hebrew history and make their contributions to the prophecies and visions of a thousand years later, when the prophets are trying to render visible the inexpressible glories of the courts of heaven.)

It is argued by Breasted, Sellin, and other students of Egyptian history that Egypt had another gift to offer the Hebrews: the insight that, behind a multiplicity of gods of places and tribes and functions, there is one god. This deity is related to the many gods as a father is related to his children or as a ruler is related to his subjects. Or, even better, the many gods are but particular aspects of the functioning of the one god. This gift of the monotheistic insight, if actually taken up by the wandering Hebrews, could have helped them in the creation of concepts that have dominated or haunted men's minds ever since. Certainly the Hebrews were the first people in the ancient world to build their culture and interpret their history on the assumption that "the Other" was a single force rather than a multitude of beings tugging and pulling at each other as they shaped their own destinies and man's.

Whence came this insight? It is a recorded fact that, in the years 1375-1358 B.C., at a time when the Hebrews were perhaps servile Egyptian laborers and still lurking in the wings of history, a significant Egyptian figure, the Pharaoh Ikhnaton, initiated a religious reform. Moved by the same objections to the multiplicity of gods later voiced by the Hebrew sages, Ikhnaton regarded the temples of the many gods as so many houses of illusion. He set up a new cult, devoted to one god, Aton, the sun, who was, in abstract language, the source of all created being. The symbol for the god was a sun disk from which extended rays ending in human hands, as if to indicate the beneficent and all-embracing activity of this one god. Ikhnaton's own name meant "he in whom Aton is satisfied." In Biblical phrase, there was none besides Aton.

Ikhnaton's reform met failure in his own society. The enmity of a priesthood whose temples and incomes were endangered sparkled with a surface violence that led to the erasure of the name of Aton from all monuments as soon as Ikhnaton was dead. But it was the inertia of twenty centuries of worship of "the Other" in the guise of the many that offered resistance mute and deep to the worship of a single creative and sustaining force such as Ikhnaton tried to exalt. Indeed, so far as subsequent Egyptian history is concerned, it was as if Ikhnaton had not been. But his insight, some argue, lives on in the views that dominate Hebrew culture and direct the shaping of Hebrew history.

Those who question this theory, and with reason, prefer to believe that monotheism is the creation of the Hebrew prophets (*c.* 850-500 B.C.), who taught the later priestly editors what to see in the old records which they were setting to rights (500 B.C. and onward). If this is the correct story, the monotheism of Ikhnaton is, in the language of genetics, a "sport," as void of consequences elsewhere as it was in the Egyptian land. The figure of this melancholy king may serve to remind us, as we turn to the Hebrew story, that the history of the development of mankind is full of wasteful repetitions and false starts. Nevertheless, it should also show us that the creation of important ideas is not, as assumed by the Hebrews and by many other nations since, the prerogative of one people. The spirit of the Lord, like the wind, blows where it listeth (*John* 3:8); and this is a truth one should keep hold of.

The orthodox view of the origin of monotheism attributes the comparatively late insights of the prophets to the teachings of Moses, who anticipated the prophets although he lived four or five centuries before full-blown monotheism and its ethical and religious consequences were unfolded to man's view.

One other view of this complex matter is worth noting. Those who reject the orthodox account of the origin of monotheism and who do not believe there is evidence to connect the teachings of Moses with those of Ikhnaton feel that the religion Moses revealed to the children of Israel was of a more primitive sort. According to this theory, the Jehovah of Moses—to use the conventional form of the sacred name Yahwe—was no more than a local mountain and thunder god whom Moses took over from his Midian hosts and made into the special patron of the children of Israel. Such a god was far from being the one god of the Egyptian ruler and the Hebrew prophets. In technical language, the followers of Moses were at best practicing not monotheism but henotheism, the worship of a single god who is not, however, regarded as the only deity. According to a good deal of Bible testimony, the early Hebrews recognized the apparent fact that other peoples had gods who worked for them. The images or "teraphim" which Rachel takes from the house of her father Laban are the "luck" of the family, and the narrative in *Genesis,* Chapter 31, regards the theft as a prudent one. The many warnings against bowing down to enemy gods (e.g., *Exodus* 23:24) presuppose evil things rather than—our feeling today—non-existent things. The story of Micah (*Judges,* chaps. 17 and 18) records the setting up, by a Hebrew, of a household god which is presently stolen by a tribe that is in need of a deity.

One other gift should be mentioned, if gift it can be called. The various peoples whom the Hebrews either conquered or opposed in Palestine had their "abominations" also. Though their gods served the functions of Egyptian gods and were related to the confusing pantheons of the successive societies of the Fertile Crescent and neighboring regions, they deserve special mention here; for it was Moloch, Chemosh, Dagon, and Ashtoreth that stood in the foreground of the Hebrew imagination for many centuries. The Egyptian "abominations" were not before the eyes of the Hebrew historians and prophets; they appear in the Bible as recollections cherished but vague and confused. Dagon of the Philistines, Ashtoreth the widely worshiped fertility goddess, and the less famous fertility and nature deities of the "dwellers of the land" were a threat to any nascent monotheism. Thus, the Hebrew opposition to idol worship was, whenever it was flourishing, a practical as well as a theoretical objection. The Hebrews might have learned from their own prophets that the worship of many and grotesque gods was less moving and satisfying than the worship of one god. But it was from the Canaanites, from the "daughters of Heth" (the Hittites), and from the Moabites and the Philistines that they could renew each day their knowledge of the evil results of bowing down to sticks and stones. The ritual prostitution of the temple worship of the fertility goddess Ashtoreth, the sacrifice of children to the fiery jaws of the Ammonites' Moloch, the sacrifice of the eldest son to win the favor of the Moabites' Chemosh—these acts the Hebrews could see around them, could even observe among the children of Israel themselves. The latter wanted their new-taken fields to be fertile and listened to the counsel of the settled population who knew what was involved in tilling the fields. These near "whoredoms," as the prophets called traffic with the local Baals or "Lords," not the distant ones in Egypt, gave passion to the devotion to Jehovah which we see in the histories as well as in the prophets.

The other ancient nations achieved, as a record of their past, chiefly mythology and characterless lists of dynasties. This contrast between other records and Hebrew records may reflect the deeper contrast: between polytheistic and monotheistic views. If past events are but the result of the interplay of a vast number of divine wills, then a record of what has happened is not instructive; divinity is too multiple and capricious for events to teach us much except that they have taken place and that gods as well as priest-kings have been involved in them. But if, as the Hebrews came to believe, a chain of events is somehow the expression of a single divine will, then an inspection of a nation's history must enable one to draw a portrait of the deity that has presided over it, alone and all-guiding. Such a history would be more than a record of what has happened. In Hebrew history lay the secret of what manner of being the deity was, how he had dealt with Israel in times past and how he might deal with Israel in the future. Kings were no longer gods or sons of gods. Man was beginning to see the past as something more than an aggregate of successive events to be set down flatly. Here we can see an early emergence of the conviction that has presided over the writing of history ever since: The facts of history are likely to yield a meaning that men can use for charting and interpreting their own experience. Modern historians keep telling the stories of the Revolution and the Civil War, as though those past sections of history have power to teach us how to face the problems of our own day. The Hebrew historians believed, passionately and perhaps naïvely, that the history of other peoples, entangled as it was with delusions and abominations, was but a morass of error. They judged that their own offered clear lessons in justice and godliness.

CHAPTER III

How the Hebrew Records Were Produced

THE Bible is not, as we have just shown, a book written in a vacuum, nor should it be read in a vacuum. We must be aware of the relation of the Hebrew people to the older civilizations by which they were surrounded and even hemmed in. We must be ready to perceive the various sorts of attitudes toward the past that shape the historical books and, for that matter, the books we shall take up later. There are, in the historical books, effects of discontinuity, inconsistency, and unevenness of tone which no sensitive reader can ignore. Success in reading these books involves an understanding of what produced these effects. We must understand the "inner weather" of the Hebrew world as well as the outer, which we have just discussed.

The Hebrew historians worked with a range of materials that the modern historian does not often employ, and they arranged their materials in patterns that would not occur to the modern investigator of a past era. Both of these circumstances must be kept in mind.

The materials were of two kinds: There was the end product of an orally created and preserved tradition, a collection of loosely connected or unconnected tales that were finally set down in writing after centuries of oral preservation; and there were records made by court scribes and chroniclers. The events recorded in the historical books to the time of David *(I Samuel) tend* to be legends, hero tales, and tales explaining ancient divisions of caste and custom that for many centuries had not been set down at all. Those that survived to be incorporated first into simple chronicles (850-750 B.C.) and then into the more complex structure of the Pentateuch—the "five books" of Moses—are arranged by the priestly editors (500-400 B.C.). The stories had survived because, to begin with, they had appealed strongly to simple tribal imaginations and had given a sufficient account of the origin of the world and of their own tribe. They tell of the garden of Eden, of Cain and Abel, of the tower of Babel and the flood, of the early fortunes of all mankind. They later limit their area of interest and tell us of the founding fathers of Israel—Abraham, Isaac, and Jacob—in whose lives the beginnings of the special destiny of the Hebrew nation might be seen. The tales of Moses and

CHART 2. The Creation of the History Books

Previous to 1000
Oral tradition and fragments of song, proverb, and law
1000-922 Reigns of David and Solomon: the United Kingdom
Oral tradition and fragments of song, proverb, and law
Court histories of David and Solomon
922-842 The divided kingdoms
Court records of the divided kingdoms
J about 850: narrative materials covering the lapse of time contained in the Pentateuch; written from the point of view of Judah
842-722 The divided kingdoms
Court records of the divided kingdoms
E about 750: narrative materials covering the lapse of time contained in the Pentateuch; written from the point of view of the Northern Kingdom or Ephraim
722-587 The time of Judah's survival
J and *E* combined into a single narrative
Deuteronomy written about 650; discovered in the Temple 621
Court records of Judah
587-538 The Babylonian exile
JE combined with *D* (Deuteronomy)
Deuteronomic editing of *Joshua* and *Judges; Samuel* and *Kings* composed from court records and other materials
538-167 Postexilic period
500-400 priestly editing of the Pentateuch; hence, the formula *J E D P* (*P* standing for priestly editing)
300-250 *Chronicles*, employing material from *Samuel* and *Kings* and other material; *Ezra* and *Nehemiah*

Joshua and of the motley crew who jostle each other in *Judges*—these too once had to depend on word-of-mouth transmission. On the other hand, the accounts of David and his successors *(I Samuel* to *II Kings) tend* to be based on court chronicles that were used and then discarded by the men who put the books of history into their final shape. Hence the references, often tantalizing, to books no longer existent. "Now the rest of the acts of Ahab, and all that he did, and the ivory house which he made, and all the cities that he built, are they not written in the book of the chronicles of the kings of Israel?" (*I Kings* 22:39.) "Now the rest of the acts of Josiah, and all that he did, are they not written in the book of the chronicles of the kings of Judah?" (*II Kings* 23:28.) The court chronicles have served the editors' pious purposes. Ahab's wickedness and Josiah's piety have been displayed, and the chronicles are discarded, though presumably they contained accounts of battle and court intrigue that would still delight secular palates.

But, though we may be aware of the existence of the two sorts of materials, the Hebrew historian did not know he was dealing with two different kinds. The modern historian wishes to interview, if possible, men whose memories extend back to the events, or he wishes to have access to written records set down at a time close to when they happened. He is least satisfied when he has to employ rumors and tales that have been handed down for several generations. If he is forced to employ them, for lack of more reliable materials, he is careful to "correct" them, and to excise from them the improbable and the wonderful. He is careful to point out the elements of romance and excitement that fireside narrators habitually introduce to enliven their materials. But the Hebrew compilers lacked a very sharp sense of difference between the wonderful and the possible. The most we can detect, as in *Judges* when Micah's idolatry is excused by the remark, "In those days there was no king in Israel, but every man did that which was right in his own eyes" (*Judges*, 17:6), is a slight uneasiness when ancient material is unorthodox as measured by later standards.

As sympathetic readers who wish to understand the nature of materials we read, rather than to ride roughshod and often contemptuously through the books of history in the style, we might say, of a literal-minded agnostic, we should be aware that one set of "laws" operates in the creation and preservation of orally transmitted material and another guides the creation of records that are written and arranged. Of course, by "laws" we mean descriptive "laws" like the law of gravitation. This latter law does not make the apple fall; it says that the apple has fallen in such and such fashion. No more do we say that oral tradition must behave in special ways; we try to suggest succinctly how Hebrew oral and written tradition did, as a matter of fact, behave or unfold. At the very least, these "laws" should act as shock absorbers as we read older kinds of narrative containing few of the marks that we expect to find in the modern narrative created by a trained, dispassionate observer.

Motives on the Level of Oral Tradition

Three or four laws prepare one to deal with oral tradition on its own terms rather than on our quite irrelevant ones. First, *oral traditional narrative has either a weak grasp on time sequences or none at all.* We need but recollect the stories read to us when we were children, stories that were also created by oral transmission to begin with, to recall that phrases like "once upon a time" and "a little later" and finally "they lived happily ever after" signify the cavalier treatment folk narrative has for time relations. Of course, narratives like those in the Pentateuch were doubtless thought of as constituting with other narratives an account of the forebears of the teller and his audience. In consequence, the treatment of time sequence may have been more respectful and attentive than that which we can observe in the utterly unlocalized folk tale when "once upon a time" in "a kingdom by the sea" lived "a king with three sons." In such narratives there is no grasp upon time nor need there be. But the Hebrew tale-tellers, if we can judge by analogous efforts in other cultures, were telling stories designed to instruct as well as amuse; however, their instruction was the imparting not of exact knowledge but of names and events embedded in a narrative context. (We shall see that the narrative method of conveying information, and ethical thought as well, remains the predominant Hebrew means of instruction. The prophets supplement it by other methods, but they do not discard it. Neither does Jesus.)

How precise was the information thus conveyed? The tale-teller certainly did not have in mind a set of dates such as we can observe in a history book. Still, he would of course make a clear distinction between a tale of origins and a story that concerned more recent forebears. The story of Adam and Eve is one of origins, and so apparently was the tale of Peleg, of which only one sentence survives: ". . . in his days was the earth divided . . ." (*Genesis* 10:25). Comparatively recent ancestors are involved in the tales told of Abraham, Isaac, and Jacob. Between these two groups—the very first people and the fairly recent—would be located carelessly those tales which concern neither ultimate origins nor recent events: accounts of earlier and less important wanderings and, in the Hebrew collection, of the great flood. This sense—that some stories are earlier, some later—certainly does not create a rigid sequence. The rigid sequence is the creation of the later, systematizing Hebrew historians, dominated by their need to establish the continuity that shall testify to the constant interrelation between Jehovah and his people. But this casual arrangement does offer a *basis* for the later working of a sharper time sense. Just how weak the time sense of the tale-teller might be we may learn from comparing our own memories of what we know at first-hand and what we have been told concerning earlier generations of our families. What happened to us and when—this is clear. The *chief* events in our parents' lives are fairly clear, though we are not likely to be very sure about which happened first. But when it comes to narratives told about our grandparents, we assign them to an entirely undifferentiated stretch of time: "in grandfather's day." Beyond that time, unless we are historians or antiquarians, there is something called "the past" to which we assign all the other family legends save those which concern our family's coming to America at a certain date, if that information has been transmitted to us. To be sure, as a corrective to vagueness, *we* have what we remember of formal American history, of which the history of our family is a tiny part. Naturally, where tale-telling is the *only* form in which the past lives on, there is no such check. Vast stretches of time are compressed like an accordion, remote figures become near-contemporaries, and father may have for son a man that belongs to a distant generation.

Some students think that Abraham left Ur of the Chaldees about 2000 B.C., and they suppose a movement of the Hebrews into Egypt—symbolized by the story of Joseph—about 1500 B.C. Yet, according to the sequence of the tale-teller or a later editor, Joseph was the great-grandson of Abraham. The most, then, one can say of the record of time oral tradition preserves is this: *Some kind of sequence may be preserved, but the actual passage of time will be the creation of later minds that systematize earlier records.* It is a tenable hypothesis that the long life of Methuselah and other Old Testament figures was necessitated by the fact that the early stretches of time were both great and sparsely populated; the life span of each hero had to perform yeoman duty. At least, the nearer we come to the time of written record the shorter the life span is.

Another feature of the parts of the Bible where oral narrative predominates is the kind of moral tone or, as some literal-minded persons regard it, the lack of moral tone. Indeed, many nineteenth-century objections to the central position of the Bible in our culture had this basis. It was pointed out that Jacob wins his birthright by cheating his twin brother Esau not once but twice. Later, the same hero cheats his father-in-law by a breeding trick, and his wife Rachel follows his example and steals the family gods as she and her husband depart. The catalogue of such feats, which are now regarded as morally reprehensible, is long. But some cavilers against the early tales forget that we consider them reprehensible because of moral criteria provided in part by later sections of the Bible itself. Certainly it is wrong to impose standards of ethical behavior on a tale from which such standards are bound to be absent, for the simple reason that they did not exist during the time of the tale's creation and transmission. This observation leads us to our second "law." *The standard of excellence in a folk tale is not good and evil: it is "miracle"; it is success.* What the audience demands of a hero is some incredible feat of strength (Paul Bunyan, Samson, Hercules), some deft slyness that outwits a foe (Reynard the Fox, Scattergood Baines, or Jacob), or an outright display of supernatural power (the "fire spell" that rings the sleeping Brünnehilde with flame or Elijah's "fire spell" that puts the priests of Baal to scorn). The common denominator of all the feats of heroes in folk tale is not that they are good by our own best standards. It is the display of mana, the power that comes from a supernatural source and makes a magician or fighter or ruler superior to his fellows. Strength and slyness and power to work miracles are the outward signs that the special favor of some spirit or god is abetting a person in everything he does. (Sometimes, in folk tale, "the Other" is no more august than a cryptic witch or a talking beast from whom the third brother learns a magic word.)

To apply to such stories our own moral standards is not judicious; our moral preoccupations do not have many points of contact with the interests that the old tales gratified. We need to suspend our "instinctive" moral judgment and read these stories for what they are: accounts of strength and guile displayed in a world that put a higher value on strength and guile than do we. This suspension should not be too difficult. We effect such modification when we read detective stories. We put aside the standards by which we measure the good and evil in our acquaintance. We tolerate or even admire the double-dealing of Perry Mason, though we should be the first to cry out against trickery in a lawyer friend. Perry Mason and his tribe display the kind of mana proper to detectives; they have shrewdness, quickness, and ruthlessness. Moral judgment on their activity is irrelevant. So, we should remember, is flat moral judgment on many portions of ancient tale. Either morality is not involved, or it is a morality that is not ours.

A third "law" in folk tale is what may be called the law of assimilation. *Certain favorite motifs or sequences of event are so powerful as to impose themselves on story after story.* Our own culture has motifs peculiar to it. One particularly dear to the popular American imagination is the "log cabin to White House" sequence. No presidential campaign can go by without the discovery of this motif among the real events in a candidate's career. It was easily found in the careers of Herbert Hoover and Calvin Coolidge. When it did not seem to exist in Franklin Roosevelt's life—Hyde Park was no log cabin—a substitute had to be found, and it was; Mr. Roosevelt's serious ailment took the place of the non-existent log cabin.

Certain motifs recurrent in all oral narratives are richly illustrated by Hebrew story. The story of Joseph is, among other things, the Cinderella tale, with the ten wicked brothers in the role of the two ugly sisters. The tragic relation of Jephthah and his daughter—the father's damaging vow must be carried out at any cost, even to the death of a child (*Judges*, chap. 11)—is a more august version of "Beauty and the Beast."

But besides the motifs common to all oral narrative, there were certain sequences of event especially dear to the Hebrew imagination. The reader of *Genesis* must be struck by the recurrence of the situation in which a "hero"—whose mana is clearly that of wile rather than strength—escapes the persecution of a lustful ruler by passing off his wife as his sister, who then becomes a member of the ruler's household, with disastrous consequences. The tale is told twice of Abraham and once of his son Isaac (*Genesis*, chaps. 12, 20, and 26). Another Hebrew motif is seen in the special circumstances that surround the birth of many a great leader. The hero's mother is barren, or she is past childbearing; by special favor of deity, she is allowed to conceive. Sarah, the mother of Isaac, has been barren and is past the age for childbearing; and the mothers of Samson and of the great priest Samuel have had to wait many years to conceive (*Genesis*, chap. 18, *Judges*, chap. 13, and *I Samuel*, chaps. 1 and 2). Under this heading of Hebrew motifs come special numbers, such as the "forty days," that are a narrative element from the time of Noah onward. Why these and other special motifs recur and why, in more general terms, motifs exert their power in folk tale is a problem that Jung and other psychologists have tried to solve. They have suggested that all such motifs are veiled expressions of man's ceaseless quest for physical security and emotional certainty.

One other aspect of folk-tale "assimilation," the reverse of the effect of motif just studied, is the assimilation of the career of a hero to recurrent story patterns. Particular stories or story patterns may be drawn to a hero of great prestige. There are, for example, "cycles" of stories told about Abraham and Samson. The story of Abraham's life is not a biography in any modern sense; it is made up of a succession of somewhat independent anecdotes that have come to cluster around Abraham because of his prestige as a "father" in Israel. A person who tries to draw, from this succession of tales, a consistent view of Abraham's character runs into trouble; in one tale the "hero" is craven, in another devout and obedient, and in still another courageous. It is wise not to seek a consistency that the stories will not support; it is better to let one's perception of Abraham rest thus: since Abraham was a man with a tremendous reputation for mana, he attracted to himself stories in which the central figures have mana to a notable degree, even though the expressions of mana in the various tales are not, in our judgment, logically compatible. With Samson's "cycle" we have less trouble. Samson had a reputation for a special sort of mana to begin with—strength. Thus, the stories surrounding him are less likely to be at odds with each other.

Recognition of the operation of motif and mana is useful in orienting our reading of these tales. But it should be added that the esteem for mana—though it may produce a scale of values at odds with *our* scale—does not come into conflict with the morality consonant with the time and place of the telling. The morality of most of the tales in the Pentateuch we may describe as based on tribal loyalty. We seldom encounter a hero who exercises his mana to the detriment of the small group to which he belongs. Joseph, when he meets his cruel brothers, only seems to; the reconciliation of the family removes this possibility. The hero may, and does, worst his opponent—a person whom we may judge to be just as good as he is or better—but he is bound by the laws that simply organized peoples still observe. Primitive morality places stress on these points: respect for one's parents, recognition of the power of the blood tie (hence the awfulness of the sin of Joseph's brothers), obedience to the letter—if not to the spirit or intent—of a sworn oath. Judah recognizes this when he says of Tamar, who has been strictly faithful to the letter of the contract which Judah tried to ignore: "She had been more righteous than I" (*Genesis* 38:26). These and similar points go to make up a morality that we regard not so much wrong as inadequate. That we find it inadequate is, in part, a result of the criticism and modification of tribal values which is carried on throughout the Bible.

These, then, are the important "laws" governing the creation and transmission of oral narrative. Such narrative is not history in the current sense. It is, however, history in two senses that do not readily come to us. First, as archaeology tells us, popular Hebrew tradition did preserve a record, under names and events reworked in accordance with the principles just explained, of migrations and cultural contacts that are testified to independently of the Bible by contemporary lists of names, by the location of places mentioned in the Pentateuch, and by pottery and buildings and artifacts found at these ancient locations. Archaeologists have not discovered Abraham's encampments, nor are they likely to. But their work provides us with a picture of Palestine that is not at odds with the traditional indications in the *Genesis* stories. On another count these stories have historical value. Although they give only an indistinct record of what happened to Abraham, Isaac, and Jacob, they offer a very clear record of what, in the opinion of later Hebrews, *had* happened to Abraham, Isaac, and Jacob. These views—admittedly incomplete, idealized, and arranged—served as a basis for the superstructure of Hebrew faith, a faith that has made a lasting impress on later ages. To deal properly with this faith, we must start with the conception that the later Hebrews had of their own origins, "correcting" it with other kinds of knowledge by asking: "What really lies behind the stories of the patriarchs?" Very little "correction" is necessary when we ask the other question: "What stories—what revelations of 'the Other' in action—nerved later Hebrews to continue and enrich their religious culture?" The answer is: the stories in the books of history as we have them now. These were the stories that "counted"—that convinced the later Hebrews, during disaster and exile, that nothing could really shatter the continuity of their destiny since, as the early records seemed to show, it was a continuity guaranteed not by man but by the same power that, in the language of the prophets, spread out the heavens like a tent and guided the stars on their accustomed courses.

Motives on the Level of Written Hebrew Transmission

Obviously, whatever we know of the very old Hebrew oral traditions is available to us because of the workings of another Hebrew tradition, the written one. This tradition was made possible by the possession of an alphabet whose appearance is now dated about 1500 B.C.; script was used by the priestly caste. There were two sources of materials: the early oral traditions as set down by earlier scribes and the relatively later records set down by court scribes at no great distance from the events related. The writers of either sort of material may have had intentions differing widely from those of the priestly editor-historians who, after the return from exile (538 B.C. and onward), gave Hebrew history its present form. The earliest arrangers of oral tradition, theory has it, worked to bolster the pride of the separate kingdoms, Israel and Judah; the kingdoms had a common tradition but each wished to use it to assert its superiority. The court scribes set down the deeds of their kings—Northern or Southern—in order to glorify them. The priestly historians, in contrast, were members of a polity that had no king and was instead directed, ideally, by a noble and inspired priesthood.

Thus, conflicting motives lie behind the production of Hebrew history; the product can best be described as a *palimpsest*. This term, at least, can suggest a good deal about the interplay of oral tradition and various written traditions. A palimpsest, strictly speaking, is an ancient document which has had its original text erased to make way for later writing. The medieval monks, in poor supply of writing materials, often erased a classical text from a sheet of papyrus and entered thereon a saint's life instead. The modern classical scholar can by various techniques recover the precious earlier text. In a special sense, the books of Hebrew history are such a creation. They make up not one history but several histories, with the later imposed upon the earlier, the first written versions of oral tradition and the early court records. And it is here that the term *palimpsest* enlightens not only by similarity but by difference. The saint's life which the monk indited took the place of the classic poem and had no relation whatever to it. In contrast, each new telling of the Hebrew destiny is added to the earlier record but does not entirely obscure it. The new telling is, rather, intended only to supplement and interpret that early record. Thus, unlike the classical scholar who discards the saint's life to get at Euripides, the student of the Bible must discard nothing. Instead, he must be aware that he is in the presence of several histories cobbled together at a late date (*c.* 500-400 B.C.) out of materials created in earlier ages. Thus, though the Bible that we read is the final account of the history of the Hebrews, we are often in the presence of the earliest account. For example, we may, in *Exodus* and *Leviticus,* be reading of Moses. But Moses meant different things to successive ages, and these different views all appear in the *one* narrative that we read: Moses is a lawgiver, Moses is a stern critic of a purely legal approach to human behavior, Moses is a mystic face to face with his deity. Today two writers who take different views of, for instance, Napoleon do not combine forces to write a composite life. It would by turns reflect the view that Napoleon was a man who worked for "one world" before his time and the view that the French leader was a man driven by loathsome psychoses that inflicted agony on a whole continent. The reader has to deal with such a combination in the Biblical narratives that present Moses or Saul. Saul, one narrative tells us, was a man of courage and had what we today would call animal vitality; he was a rallying point for a people that badly needed a leader against the Philistines. But another section of the Saul story shows us a bad man, who followed his own impulses rather than God's directions that came from the mouth of Samuel. The priestly editors, as they set in order the records of past eras, took the low view of Saul; but, for reasons soon clear, they allowed traces of the other view to remain.

The conventional formula summarizing how this composite was put together—a formula that applies chiefly to the Pentateuch or the Hexateuch, *Genesis* to *Joshua*—is expressed by the series of letters JEDP. To simplify what is most complex and is still a subject for debate: P stands for the priestly revision (500-400 B.C.) and refers to the final editing and adjusting of the contents of the historical books. This was work done some time after the Hebrews were allowed by Cyrus the Persian to return to Jerusalem (538 B.C.) from the forty- or fifty-year exile in Babylon. The Hebrews were allowed to rebuild their Temple and refound their cult of Jehovah; however, they were not permitted to set themselves up as a politically independent state. The result of Cyrus' generosity was, for more than three centuries, a *theocratic* state: a state governed and directed by a temple priesthood rather than by a secular ruler. This priesthood naturally wished to justify the position of power and prestige it occupied. It drew up, out of the materials at hand, a continuous account of the Hebrew past that would *tend*—it no more than tends—to justify the theocratic *status quo:* a state devoted to God and guided by God's priestly servants.

Throughout the books that are conventionally assigned to Moses' authorship—*Genesis* to *Deuteronomy*—the chief sources the priests had for their use were two connected accounts of Hebrew history, both including much the same narrative material and both ultimately resting on oral tradition. These two narrative collections (J and E in the formula JEDP) were composed during the time of the divided kingdoms (933 B.C. to 721 B.C. for Israel, the Northern Kingdom; and 933 B.C. to 586 B.C. for Judah, the Southern Kingdom). It is thought that the Southern narrative was first; J took shape about 850 B.C. The Northern narrative, E, was given form about a hundred years later, 750 B.C., and not too long before the fall of the Northern Kingdom to Assyria in 722 B.C. The two collections differ at many points. The most obvious ones, which first led to their disentanglement from the Pentateuch, where they mingle, are the following: Deity is referred to in J as Jehovah and in E as El (the Lord). The J compilation reflects a Southern or Judean point of view, and E represents a point of view attractive to the tribe of Ephraim and the other "nine tribes" included in the Northern Kingdom, Israel. In J it is Judah, the "father" of the Southern Kingdom, who protects Joseph; and in E it is Reuben, the "father" of a tribe included in the Northern Kingdom, who tries to temper the violence of the other brothers. Another difference of emphasis appears in the special narratives which tell of the founding of altars. E gives events at Northern shrines like Bethel and Shechem, whereas J mentions Hebron, a Southern shrine. (In the books *I Samuel* to *II Kings* various court narratives and military histories take the place of J and E as "raw material" for the priestly historians to manipulate. The priestly treatment of these books resembles the treatment accorded the more ancient records.)

What in J and E were simple chains or cycles of stories clustering about great heroes have continuity imposed upon them in the final priestly version of the Pentateuch. But it is not such a continuity as one would find in the work of a modern historian who regards some of his materials as naïve and who recasts them carefully so that they are "in tone" with the rest of his work. The recasting conceals what the older material was like when the historian found it. The continuity effected by various Hebrew revisions never concealed completely the variety of materials that had passed through the historians' hands.

J and E, it is thought, were first combined shortly after the fall of the Northern Kingdom in 722 B.C., in a time of peril when all traditions—even Northern ones—might be regarded as precious. This initial combination was gone over and reinterpreted at least twice.[1] The first of these is thought to be a revision necessitated by the laws

[1] In addition to the Deuteronomic Code mentioned in the text, scholars perceive another code, the Holiness Code (*Leviticus*, chaps. 17-21). They date this code of laws, opposed to the "abominations" and endeavoring to set up standards for settled city life rather than nomadic existence, at some time previous to 621 B.C. The point of view expressed in it may have led to revisions of the now-combined JE narratives.

and religious insights expressed in *Deuteronomy* (D, in the formula). If *Deuteronomy* is the book "found" by Hilkiah the high priest during the Temple repairs (621 B.C.), King Josiah indeed had reason to rend his garments. It is as Josiah says in his command to the priests:

> Go ye, enquire of the Lord for me, and for the people, and for all Judah, concerning the words of this book that is found: for great is the wrath of the Lord that is kindled against us, because our fathers have not hearkened unto the words of this book, to do according unto all that which is written concerning us. (*II Kings* 22:13.)

For generations people have been living contrary to what the Lord commanded Moses. *Deuteronomy* gives warrant for the centering of worship of the Lord at one temple where forms of worship can be controlled. Some of the laws are more humane than those which appear in earlier codes. Scholars believe that the tone of D (or *Deuteronomy*) encouraged a revision of the combined JE collections; what had been good enough for other generations had, in part, to be brought into line with the new code that stirred Josiah so deeply.

There is little doubt as to what the final revision (the priestly or P) did. It was the revision to end revisions. The priestly editors did more than cast a stone into the stagnant waters of old narrative; their revision led those waters into a carefully dug channel far removed from the simple fountains of delight in mana where they had first been tossed up. As influential members of a theocratic state, the priestly editors sought to make the various materials that told of Hebrew history fall into some kind of accord with their own view of what that history should be.

This question immediately arises: Why did the priests, who had the strongest of motives to assert a continuity of heavenly guidance that had finally produced the theocratic state, fail to produce a work proving their view up to the hilt? Why does the history they finally produced lack the homogeneity that we may suppose bound these last editors and historians together: a conviction that they were the chosen of a chosen people? Why are the books of the Pentateuch and the other books of history palimpsests, in the sense noted, works that allow us to see a succession of stages rather than only the last stage of interpretation? Certainly it was the last stage that, in the view of the priestly editors, offered the correct interpretation of all Hebrew history. Modern historians arrange their materials to drive home their main point. Many nineteenth-century historians looked at the past and could see it only as a triumphant preparation for the emergence of nationalism. A twentieth-century Marxian historian can look nowhere without discovering apt illustrations of his thesis: the inevitability of class strife. Our question, restated, is: Why did not the priestly editors, urged by the strongest of motives and with all the available material under their control, do likewise? Why does their work preserve religious insights and cultural patterns proper to other ages and at odds with their own convictions?

The answer is this. Just as "laws" described the creation of oral tradition, "laws" also governed the activity of the arrangers of the final version of the Pentateuch. (One imagines that these "laws" also held during earlier revisions.) The "laws" put stern limits to the activity of the priestly editors who wished to illustrate their particular theory of history but had to do so by use of materials that came from times when it did not exist.

The first "law" is a gravely limiting one. Whatever their own intents, the priestly editors were convinced of this truth: *the documents transmitted from the past were sacred.* They had mana just as did the heroes whose deeds they reported, and mana is not to be tampered with. The histories were preserved in the Temple, and their very existence was the chief warrant that the Hebrews were a special people. Meddling with the given records was interdicted; words could not be changed even though they had become archaic and hard to comprehend. (Typical is the trouble we have with the word *ephod.* At times it seems to be a garment worn by a priest [*Exodus* 28:6], at other times an idolatrous image [*Judges* 8:27 and 17:5].) Moreover, if a narrative was to be included, it had to be included in its entirety, however repugnant certain details were to the moral sense of the priests. The story of Noah's drunkenness—valuable because it "proved" why the subjection of the sons of Ham, the Canaanites, was just—was not tampered with or bowdlerized (*Genesis* 9:18-28). Indeed, the grossness of many a preserved narrative is testimony far from mute to the fact that the priestly editors did not alter much of the actual substance of a given story. The sacredness of ancient documents forced on them the faithful preservation of the sharp practice of Jacob, and Judah's disgrace in his dealings with Tamar.

Nevertheless, although the given documents were sacred, an imperative also sacred had to be satisfied. Cost what it might, the priests had to make manifest their special view of Hebrew history. They were forbidden, by their own consciences, to rewrite; but they could manipulate. At point after point, the present books of history testify to the working of the second "law": *the priests were guided by a need to rearrange and systematize.* If they did not do this, they could not illustrate the *continuity* of Hebrew history that had led, without real deviation, from the promises of God to Abraham to the theocratic state. The creators of oral tradition had, at best, a very weak grasp on time. The editors, keenly aware of the chain of events that had placed them where they were, had a better grasp; and in the succession of historical events the priest believed they could make out "one increasing purpose." This purpose was, as stated, the establishment of the priest-directed state for which the last revision was being prepared. The genealogies linking together heroes who, in oral tradition, float vaguely in the undifferentiated past, and the groups of events constituting a succession of periods are props to make rigid and definitive a history that, in its earlier stages, was doubtless casual and unsystematic. That we speak of the age of the patriarchs, of the forty years in the wilderness under Moses, of the conquest, and of the period of the "judges" is a testimony to the success with which the priests imposed a tidy sequence upon traditions that had existed without much order. (The later books—*I Samuel* to *II Kings*—offered an obvious "order" that the priestly editors only needed to underscore. They could point to the "glories" of the United Kingdom under David and Solomon and to the later perils and sins of the divided kingdoms. It did not matter to the editors that the glories of Jeroboam II, the Northern king, actually did not fall short of those of Solomon. He is dismissed with the habitual formula: ". . . he did that which was evil in the sight of the Lord: he departed not from all the sins of Jeroboam the son of Nebat, who made Israel to sin" [*II Kings* 14:24].)

Yet this system had to be built out of blocks which had their natural place elsewhere. Two courses lay open to the editors who found materials recalcitrant. *Material that was irrelevant could be compressed or omitted.* Relevant material, like the drunkenness of Noah, had to be preserved as it was. But material which was to one side of the main line was less sacred and was indeed treated freely. When we read through the genealogies of *Genesis*—a dull occupation—*our* interest is tantalized by cryptic reference to Nimrod the mighty hunter and Enoch "who walked with God," and we are briefly moved by the ballad fragment that sticks out like a shipwrecked spar in tossing genealogical waters (*Genesis* 4:23-24): "And Lamech said unto his wives, Adah and Zillah, Hear my voice; ye wives of Lamech, hearken unto my speech: for I have slain a man to my wounding, and a young man to my hurt. If Cain shall be avenged sevenfold, truly Lamech seventy and sevenfold." But these matters, potentially just as interesting to us as the Noah and Joseph stories, did not contribute directly to the story of the special destiny of Israel; and they were dropped, or almost dropped, by the wayside. *Material that was necessary but repugnant could be interpreted.* To be sure, some stories the priests reproduced without comment. But others they found so objectionable on grounds of morality or religious doctrine that they permitted themselves direct or indirect comment. Though the text is sacred, the editors occasionally allow themselves a brief comment at the beginning or end of a tale that is religiously or morally distasteful. Thus, in *Judges* more than one narrative is prefaced or concluded with the comment: "In those days there was no king in Israel: and every man did that which was right in his own eyes" (*Judges* 21:25). Or if one narrative made a point unattractive to the priests, such as the priest Samuel's tolerations of the institution of kingship (*I Samuel,* chap. 12), another could be included to counter the point; in *I Samuel,* Chapter 8, we have Samuel's prediction of the pains that kingship will inflict upon the Hebrew people.

Further, it is the supposition of scholars that actual sections of narrative and discourse are the creation of the priestly editors—sections giving a direct expression to their view of past history and the godliness of a Temple-centered culture. Such scholars see the more philosophical recital of the origin of the world (*Genesis* 1-2:3) as a late account, different in spirit from the anthropomorphic second account (*Genesis* 2:4-25), where God creates by physical shaping and not by mere utterance. In the same class, though less exalted in effect, seem to be addresses and prayers uttered by kings as well as priests that express a theocratic view of society and the place of the Temple in society. For example, Solomon's address at the sanctifying of the Temple accords more with a priestly than with a kingly view of the occasion (*I Kings,* chap. 8).

Some may ask whether such an addition does not amount to tampering with a vengeance. To a modern view, yes. But to the editors the addition of what a king or priest ought to have said at a certain moment would fill out rather than distort the brief, older narrative. That the priests ended up by having a hero say what *they* would have said should not surprise us. It was a convention of composition employed also by Thucydides a little later in a work meant to be very sober history. The funeral oration of Pericles is not the literal set of words he delivered above the dead Athenians; it is the words that would be suitable for such a man to deliver at such a time. This idea of what a historian may do is not far removed from the priestly afflatus that seems to provide full discourse in contexts often meager or simple.

Furthermore, though the priests had a historical sense notable in their own day, *they made little attempt to allow for change in custom and usage.* Occasionally some old custom is too gross for easy acceptance. The most striking example is the treatment of the marriage of Abraham and his half-sister Sarah. This is treated ambiguously, and that we are able to perceive it at all is testimony to the faithfulness of the priests to the historical record which was given them to reproduce. Occasionally one senses a total bafflement on the part of the priests, as in the narrative which tells how Zipporah throws the foreskin of her son at her husband Moses and says: "Surely thou are a bloody husband to me" (*Exodus* 4:25). We may suspect that the outbreak is a protest against a rite—circumcision—which belongs to her husband's people and not to hers; but our curiosity and ingenuity find little reflection in the priests' dutiful reproduction of this incident and many others like it. They compiled their history to understand and trace the will of God; and they did not suppose that the workings of that will should be at all points intelligible.

These, in short, are the complexities that await a reader of the books of Hebrew history. The books can be a source of pleasure, provided one makes the efforts of comprehension just outlined. Further, the mixture of naïveté and native shrewdness that crops up in many a tale is a manifest delight and will need only incidental underscoring as we turn to the specific books. Abraham's negotiations for the purchase of the cave of Machpelah catch us up and put us down in a very real, though very different, world. The chaffering of Abraham and Ephron the Hittite, who owns the cave, proceeds on the elaborate assumption that Ephron is willing to give his property to Abraham. But this display of generosity is but a necessary convention, as the speech of Ephron shows us: "My lord, hearken unto me: the land is worth four hundred shekels of silver; what is that betwixt me and thee? bury therefore thy dead" (*Genesis* 23:15). We may be misled, but Abraham is not; in the next verse the conclusion of the matter is this: "And Abraham hearkened unto Ephron; and Abraham weighed to Ephron the silver, which he had named in the audience of the sons of Heth, four hundred shekels of silver, current money with the merchants." Here, in this little scene and in scores like it, is the savor of a real world, undimmed by the systematizing labors of the final editors. It does not particularly serve *their* purpose when Hagar's desperation is described thus: "And the water was spent in the bottle, and she cast the child under one of the shrubs. And she went, and sat her down over against him a good way off, as it were a bowshot: for she said, Let me not see the death of the child. And she sat over against him, and lift up her voice, and wept" (*Genesis* 21:15-16). But such details richly serve our purposes. Within the later ambitious framework, Biblical narrative remains homely and direct; it still speaks of the sandy and stony wastes from which it came, and we are able to see the grime and sorrow that, at the outset, mingled with the aspirations employed by the prophets and the priests to make the Hebrew "high religion." Other religions usually present only the ideal realization of certain typical human aspirations; in the Bible, we can see these aspirations running their full course, from their first stirrings, confused and painful, to their final transformation into doctrines precise and detached.

But, as suggested earlier, delight in the naïve, specific texture of these books is not the only pleasure the narratives offer. Excitement also comes from giving attention to the mingling of the various time levels of a culture that had, by the time the historical books were completed, more than fifteen hundred years behind it. Excitement comes from seeing the slow unfolding of ideas that we now regard as obvious and self-evident. The pleasures that the simple narratives stir may be sufficient for the person who regards the enjoyment of literature, ancient as well as modern, as an end in itself. But these books can further evoke curiosity as to what gives them a rather special claim to our attention. Some of their power to dominate man's imagination is due to the aesthetic qualities of simplicity and realism just mentioned. But it is also due to the persistent tensions that make these narratives, early or late, notable expressions of man's pursuit of what lies beyond him. The Hebrews were not curious about man-in-himself, man isolated in his own narrow area of consciousness. This latter curiosity is richly ministered to by modern novels like Proust's *Remembrance of Things Past*, which teach us just how complex—and how horrifying—man-in-himself is. The curiosity that lends wings to Old Testament narrative is concerned with man in his relation to "the Other." There are many books that deal abstractly with this question, and they do not usually take a direct grip on the attention. The Bible does take such a direct grip because its opening historical books constitute a monument to this curiosity, not as thought about and annotated, but as worked out in action; not as an argument but as a series of events.

CHAPTER IV

Genesis to *Judges*

AS NOTED earlier, the traditional terms applied to the early books of the Bible are *Pentateuch,* the "fivefold" collection of books from *Genesis* to *Deuteronomy,* or *Hexateuch,* the "sixfold" collection that groups *Joshua* along with the first five. *Pentateuch* was particularly attractive because it coincided with the supposition that Moses, who is buried in the last chapter of *Deuteronomy,* was the author of the first five books of the Bible. The other Hebrew name for the first five books, the Torah or the "law," indicates that these had special and binding authority over the Hebrew people since a large part of the Pentateuch is taken up by the instructions that Moses received on Mount Sinai. The term *Hexateuch* was also attractive, for it brought the fortunes of the Hebrew people to a definite resting place in the "promised land"; the time of wandering was over. The reason for grouping *Judges* with these six books in this analysis is that in *Judges* also oral tradition bulks large. The range of human experience reflected in these first seven books is fairly homogeneous, except when an insight like the first account of the creation appears, or when blocks of legal regulation belonging to a later age are intruded.

The narrative sections of the seven books are products of a way of thinking which led the tellers of tales to be more concerned with explaining origins or demonstrating the mana of a hero than with those questions of righteousness and the nature of Jehovah which dominate the Hebrew imagination at later dates. But it is well to remind ourselves of the complex mingling of cultural levels in these books. If they were arranged in order of date of composition, certain poetic passages would come first. The brief song of triumph that Miriam utters after the Red Sea is passed (*Exodus* 15:21) and the brutal and amazing ballad chanted by Deborah (*Judges,* chap. 5) are older than the first account of creation (*Genesis,* chap. 1) and the farewell address of Moses (*Deuteronomy,* chaps. 30-33).

Many of the narratives are in themselves unified in texture and rest easily on one time level (e.g., the Samson cycle). But other sections of the Pentateuch, notably the material accumulated around the important figure of Moses, reflect several stages of oral and written tradition.

Though such considerations as these ought to remain in the background of the reader's mind, his first task as he begins the reading of *Genesis* is to orient himself to the chronology and the historical backgrounds of the various narratives. Two steps are necessary here. The reader has to perceive the time periods making up the continuity that is the creation of the later editors. Further, he has to see how far the Hebrew account of what happened in history is in accord with what was actually happening. As was said before, Hebrew history did not happen in a vacuum; there was a constant interplay of Hebrew and non-Hebrew historical destinies that is not very clearly displayed in the Bible itself.

As the Hebrews themselves saw their past history (*Genesis-Judges*), it fell into several distinct sections. Only in the first period (*Genesis*, chaps. 1-11) do we have a presentation which makes no distinction between the Hebrew and non-Hebrew human destiny. The tales of this period do little to define the *Hebrew* fate; they tell of the creation of the world, the beginning of the institution of the family and of pursuits like agriculture and hunting and of arts like music. They tell of certain early disasters such as the great flood and —though this is placed later—of the universal destruction of the "cities of the plain" that leaves only Lot and his two daughters alive upon the earth. These are tales that depict the origin of all mankind.

But all the other periods—from the first appearance of Abraham on—belong to the Hebrews, and the rest of mankind has the role of threatening Israel or is simply beyond the horizon, beyond the "threshold" of Hebrew consciousness. One may say that, by the end of *Judges*, four of these specifically Hebrew periods have passed before us. The first is that of the patriarchs Abraham, Isaac, and Jacob; these three men were "fathers in Israel" and presided over the nomadic destinies of a fairly multitudinous tribe. To this section the success of Joseph in Egypt is a triumphant conclusion. The nomads who have been wandering up and down on the face of the earth are finally given a foothold in the North Egyptian province of Goshen; the curtain of *Genesis* falls on the predictions which the dying Jacob makes concerning the still more glorious future (*Genesis,* chaps. 48 and 49).

The second and third periods—of the wandering in the wilderness (*Exodus-Deuteronomy*) and of the conquest of Canaan, the "promised land" (*Joshua*)—show us Israel taking the first two steps toward the glorious future that the dying Jacob foresaw. *Exodus,* the "outgoing," begins after a considerable and mysterious lapse of time. The Hebrews no longer occupy, as in the time of Joseph, a favored place in the Egyptian sun; rather are they slaves whom Moses stirs to revolt and flight. It is this forty-year flight that occupies the four books of *Exodus, Leviticus, Numbers,* and *Deuteronomy.* During this time the Hebrews camped at various locations on the Sinaitic peninsula. The narrative allows us to see Moses inspiring and chiding a recalcitrant people who "lust after the flesh-pots of Egypt." More important, for the history and speculation that follow, we see Moses in close communication with Jehovah on a mountain peak. Here he receives the complex body of law—the Hebrew Toräh—which becomes the norm of external virtue in the following ages. Finally, we see Moses denied entrance to the promised land, apparently for a curious "disobedience"; he hesitates to work a miracle that the Lord commanded (*Numbers* 20:7-13). Moses dies on Mount Pisgah in view of the land, after the address (*Deuteronomy,* chaps. 30-33) that is more in accord with what the later prophets perceived about God than it is with the view of deity suggested by the complex code of laws distributed through the books from *Exodus* onward. (*Leviticus* is the book of the Levites, the priestly caste; *Numbers* concerns, among many other things, the reckoning of the tribal population; and *Deuteronomy,* which contains the concluding addresses of Moses, is the "second" lawgiving.)

Joshua concerns the third period of Hebrew history. According to the idealized priestly view, Joshua, the general chosen by Moses, leads his people to the Jordan, crosses it, takes Jericho and other cities (but not Jerusalem), and dies. Joshua's successes had their limitation, as the following passage indicates. The "children of Ephraim," an important tribe "drave not out the Canaanites that dwelt in Gezer: but the Canaanites dwell among the Ephraimites unto this day, and serve under tribute" (*Joshua* 16:10). A chapter earlier, we hear of the Jebusites, the inhabitants of Jerusalem, that "the children of Judah could not drive them out: but the Jebusites dwell with the children of Judah at Jerusalem unto this day" (*Joshua* 15:63).

The group of narratives of the fourth period bridge the gap between the "conquest" of the land of Canaan and the rise of the United Kingdom under Saul, David, and Solomon. The tone of this group of tales is a reversion to that of the narratives of the patriarchs in *Genesis;* the purposive, directed accent of the stories of the Moses-Joshua periods fades out and does not revive until we turn to Samuel and Saul. Into the *Judges* period are put a variety of tales—wonder tales and hero tales—and the chief figures are not judges in our sense of the word; they are the kind of leaders that Abraham was in his day, and they exercise their gifts of strength or guile for their own profit and for the profit of their close associates.

To give dates for these five periods—that is, to place them against the succession of events known from other sources—is simply to indicate *probable* correspondence. (In *Samuel* and *Kings* an *actual* correspondence can often be indicated.) The date of creation, traditional chronology has it, was 4004 B.C. It is useless here to do more than add a few details to the picture of the culture of the Fertile Crescent in this great stretch of time that has already been outlined in Chapter II. The characteristic structure of the Fertile Crescent city was the temple, around which the life of the community centered. Erected on the flat river basin land, it was a high, pyramid-like structure with steep steps leading up to it or around it. Recollections of such structures appear in the story of the tower of Babel (*Genesis*, chap. 10) and—in the patriarchal period, our second one—in Jacob's dream in which the procession of the angels up and down the "ladder" is not unlike the splendid processions that honored Marduk, Ishtar, and other gods in the cities of Sumer, Accad, and Babylon (*Genesis* 28:10-22). If we are so bold as to date Abraham's departure from "Ur of the Chaldees" between 2000 and 1800, we do so because in this period a temporary breakup of the Semitic Babylonian civilization took place; an Aryan people named the Kassites invaded from the northeast and may have precipitated such internal confusion and consequent wandering of dispossessed peoples as we may fancy we see in the stories told about Abraham. This comparatively fragile hypothesis leads us to regard Abraham as something more than a desert-dwelling nomad; we can regard him and his followers as people whose tenuous hold on one civilization—the Babylonian—has been shaken loose by invasion and chaos. They may be thought of as carrying with them, in their pursuit of land in Canaan and elsewhere, fragments of the common fund of Babylonian stories: of the creation of the world from the body of the slain dragon Tiamat (who seems to linger as *Leviathan* in the Scriptures), of the tree of life and the tree of knowledge from which man must not eat lest "he become as one of us," and of the flood.

Whatever the background of Abraham, the narratives that concern his wanderings and those of his son and grandson suggest a people without a land who had to bargain with the holders of a well or a pasturage for the right of temporary residence (*Genesis* 21:22 ff.). The persistence of a felt allegiance with the older culture of the Fertile Crescent may be reflected in the tales of Isaac's and Jacob's journeys into the north in search of wives of proper blood; these journeys avoided what were regarded as misalliances with the "people of the land"—Hittites, Canaanites, Hivites, and others. The brutal revenge taken by the sons of Jacob for the seduction of their sister Dinah (*Genesis,* chap. 34) is not defensible by our standards; but once one accepts the tribal emphasis on purity of blood one can comprehend the behavior of the brothers—*any* alliance with Shechem is unacceptable.

But the Hebrews in what we call Period Two, the age of the patriarchs, came into a territory, Canaan, which we should think of as

CHART 3. Events, *Genesis* to *Judges*

EGYPT	THE HEBREWS (and Canaan)	ASIA MINOR AND SYRIA	THE FERTILE CRESCENT
2100 War in Palestine	Abraham?	c. 2000 Hittites in Asia Minor	2130-2088 Hammurabi of Babylon: lawgiver
	Canaanites settle in Canaan		1800 Non-Semitic Kassites in Babylon
		c. 1700 Aramean movement into Mesopotamia	1700 Assyria overlords of the Semites of the middle Euphrates
1680 Hyksos invasion: "shepherd kings"	Joseph?		
	1650 Immigration into Palestine of Israelites, Ammonites, Moabites, and Edomites		
1580-1557 Ahmose I: Hyksos expelled			
1501-1447 Thutmos III: organization of empire in Palestine and Syria			
1411-1375 Amenhotep III: peak of Egyptian power			
1375-1358 Ikhnaton: religious reforms	"Habiru" in Palestine trouble kings subordinate to Egypt		
1292-1225 Rameses II: 1272 treaty with Hittites	Oppression under Rameses II	1272 Hittite treaty with Egyptians: Hittite power curbed	
1225-1215 Merneptah: 1223 suppression of Asiatic revolt	1220 Exodus of Moses		
	1200-1028 Hebrew invasion of Canaan and conquest		
	1190 Settlement of Philistines: people displaced by Greeks from the north		
	1150 Battle of Barak		

existing within the Egyptian "sphere of influence." The kings outside whose city gates Abraham and Isaac pitched their tents were probably subject kings to the Pharaoh. (The great power that Egypt was warding off by a bulwark of military alliance and commercial treaty was the Hittite empire. It had been crushed by Egypt and was in the process of disintegration when, many centuries later, the army of Joshua began its "infiltration.") Perhaps, as the letters these subject kings complainingly tell Amenhotep III and Ikhnaton, some of the sons of Jacob did not follow Joseph to Egypt (*c.* 1500) but remained—the "Habiru" of the letters—to harry the local kings, who got little profit or protection from their Egyptian alliances. And perhaps the sensational success of Joseph in Egypt is at least a symbolic comment on the waning strength of Egypt that we know could not for a century shake off the rule of the alien Hyksos, who to the Egyptians were the hated "shepherd kings"—1675 to 1567 B.C. Joseph's success in Egypt is easier to understand if one supposes he arrived at a time when the Hyksos—possibly Semitic—were in power and were willing to use the talent of a Semite. To be sure, the arrival of Joseph and his tribe takes place peacefully; but, whether under a Hyksos or under one of the Pharaohs that expelled the Hyksos, it was probably watched with resentment and only tolerated; else how explain the sudden reversal of fortunes transforming favored guests into slave laborers whose only hope lies in escaping from their prison and following Moses?

There is a further point to be made about the Egypt that, in Biblical story, seems to play the role of a powerful enemy. By the time of Moses' departure (*c.* 1290 B.C.), modern students tell us, Egyptian culture had shot its bolt; the monuments that were to house dead kings and make the memory of Egypt immortal, the pyramids, had been built more than fifteen hundred years before. In the days of Joseph and Moses, Egypt was merely holding on—holding on with a grip that doubtless seemed to a new, inexperienced people like the Hebrews quite grim and awful. (This death grip showed its last great vigor in curbing the growth of the Hittite empire, an act that incidentally helped clear the way for the armies of Joshua in sections of the land of Canaan. Another help that speeded up the disintegration of both Egyptian and Hittite alliances in the Palestinian region was the invasion of the "sea peoples," the Philistines and the Phoenicians, in the two centuries preceding the times of Saul and David.) Egyptian power progressively weakened until, by the times of the prophets (850-586 B.C.), it was a hollow reed, and the king who sought to lean on this reed, when he was fearful of the new might of the Assyrians or Babylonians, might expect to have his hand pierced.

The dates here followed for the descent of Joseph (*c.* 1500 B.C.) and for the departure of Moses under Rameses (1301-1234 B.C.) indicate a sojourn of something less than the traditional four hundred years of abode in Egypt. But it must be recalled that the Hyksos, the northern invaders of Egypt who may have been favorable toward Hebrew nomads, took over Egypt in 1675 B.C.; from this date onward, Egypt would have been a conceivable setting for the settlements of Joseph and his brothers. Further, it is a Hebrew "habit" to group blocks of history by such easily recalled figures as forty and four hundred. At any rate, we are fairly sure that Rameses built the "treasure-houses" Pithom and "Raamses" (*Exodus* 1:11); we know quite certainly that this Pharaoh was a proud and energetic ruler, though he was unable to crush the Hittite power to the north. He could well be an oppressor who would tolerate no dissidence among resident minorities. His successor, Merneptah (1234-1227 B.C.) even defeated "Israel" in Palestine in 1229 B.C.—a fact that may indicate the arrival of the Hebrews under Joshua (1250 B.C. and onward) or, just as likely, the persistence in Canaan of Hebrew tribes during the time when Joseph and his brothers and their descendants were living in Egypt.

What was the origin of Moses, the man of genius who harried and drove a people toward a "manifest destiny" they often feared and wished to escape? Some scholars are unimpressed by the Hebrew etymology for his name, in which its meaning is "drawn" and would refer to Moses' being taken from the river Nile. They find in the name a repetition of an element that appears in several Egyptian royal names and means "son" or "child" (e.g., Thutmose). On this observation and on other circumstances the theory has been elaborated (by E. Sellin and others) that Moses was not a Hebrew at all, but was rather an Egyptian of royal blood who was intolerant of the time-eroded Egyptian laws and religion. Thus, the revolt of Moses may have been in the name of the religious reform of Ihknaton that had been undone a century before. Seeing no chance for this insight in his own petrified country, the "Egyptian" Moses sought a new god (which he found under the name of Yahwe on Mount Sinai), a new people (a subject population desperate enough to listen to him), and a new land (which he himself never reached.)

This theory about Moses' origin is at odds with two other theories suggested by the Bible itself and other background material. According to the Biblical and orthodox theory, Moses was a child of Israel; he is set apart from the earlier leaders not by what he may have encountered in his Egyptian education but by what was revealed to him on Mount Sinai, that and nothing else. The Hebrew historians were as aware of the growth and change in their past religion as are we. They explained this growth by supposing a series of self-revelations of God to man: a series that began with God "walking in the garden in the cool of the day" in Eden and continued in the interviews between God and Noah, and God and the three chief patriarchs. As the Hebrew historians judged the matter, what had been early learned about the nature of deity was not incorrect, but it was certainly incomplete. Indeed, the successive self-definitions pronounced by the deity in the presence of a favored mortal constitute one of the chief principles of continuity in the books of history; it is a principle that is quickly taken over by the followers of Christ when they need to defend *his* position in the sequence of Hebrew history. God promised Noah that there would be no further large-scale catastrophes; God promised Abraham that his seed would be as the sands of the sea; but what the Lord reveals to Moses surpasses anything displayed to the comprehensions of the others. For Moses as well as for the earlier heroes, the deity of Sinai begins with an impressive show of sheer power; fire and thunder are the tokens of his presence. But Jehovah favors Moses with something more. By offering him the tablets of the law, Jehovah sets himself up as the source of the tissue of custom and exact regulation that was to hold society together. Further, by revealing the name not known to Abraham and Isaac (Jehovah), the deity conferred on Moses power that the earlier worshipers of "El" (the Lord) had not (*Exodus*, chap. 6). A large portion of the mana of a being, man or god, was thought to lie in its name. A reflection of this feeling persists in our unwillingness to be introduced to people whose reputation we do not admire. If these people have been introduced to us, if they possess our "name," they will have—we fear—power over us. Finally, in the expression attributed to God in one of the several confrontations—"I am that I am"—is the assertion that he is not a tribal deity and but one of many such beings (*Exodus* 3:14). It is an assertion of uniqueness that the Hebrews, in the next thousand years, keep rediscovering at the heart of their unorderly speculation about "the Other."

The last theory—also a modern one—can be much more briefly stated. It assumes that Moses, when he fled to Paran and married the daughter of a local priest, came into contact with the special local god of the region, no more than a petty deity, lord of the region cloud, thunder, and storm. The whole experience of Moses, then, led not to the discovery of new aspects of "the Other" (the orthodox view); it but provided him with a deity no different in kind from the other deities that already thronged the ancient world. In this view, an event so important in retrospect was comparatively routine and simple and cannot be regarded as a real step beyond the deity of the patriarchs toward the ethical monotheism of the prophets. All such steps were taken many centuries later by Elijah and the prophets who followed him.

Perhaps the conclusion of the matter is this: Whatever the sources and content of Moses' insight, the important fact for us is that around him and his career there gathered, as the ages passed, a collection of ideas about "the Other" that help organize the Bible and live on as parts of systems of thought both religious and non-religious.

For the third period, the period of wandering recorded in the books from *Exodus* to *Deuteronomy*, we need add little to what has been said earlier. The experience of Abraham in a hostile world is being repeated, though on a larger scale. The armies of Moses encounter the armies of petty chieftains and of rulers of cities of some power. All these, for good reasons, oppose the arrival, the temporary settlement, or the passing through of a considerable group of a strange, landless people (e.g., *Numbers* 21:21-35; 22:1-5; 31:1-12).

Nor is the picture altered by what history and archaeology tell us of the actual Hebrew entrance into the "promised land" in the period of *Joshua,* the period of conquest. The priestly editors, with their own view of history as a succession of events closely watched over by deity and guided for the benefit of the children of Israel, would like to suggest that a complete conquest took place. But the older documents which are incorporated into *Joshua* do not illustrate the editorial comment or tendency. We see the Hebrews advance, led by Joshua, into a loosely organized culture of city-states (Jericho, Ai, Gibeon, and others), free of the recent yoke of the Hittite but unable to defend their freedom against the threat of Joshua's army. We see groups of people bound together by similarities of worship (chiefly a worship of fertility gods, excavations have shown) and often of language, but nevertheless unable to agree on a policy of repelling the invaders from the south. Some cities submit (*Joshua* 9:3-15), some resist singly (*Joshua,* chap. 6), and others seek to set up a league of mutual defense (*Joshua,* chap. 10). Thus, the conquest of Canaan was made piecemeal. It was possible because of the weakness of Egypt and the decay of the Hittite empire; neither any longer imposed a strong unity that would hold off the advances and skirmishes of the Hebrew forces. Certainly, Joshua could not have gone so far had he been trying to penetrate and take over a still unified region like Egypt itself; and he could have made no better headway had he been addressing the growing power to the north, the power of Assyria that in later ages vexed the nation Joshua was seeking to establish. At his hour of death, Joshua reminds his people of the covenant and suggests that the land is already the Hebrews' and will be taken from them only if they go after "strange gods." There is, in this book as elsewhere, a contrast between the idealized view of Hebrew history taken by the priests and the less heartening picture which the older documents provide: Hebrew mastery only of islands of population in a hostile land.

Judges is continued testimony to this reality. Here we see that some cities remain unconquered (Jerusalem is not finally conquered until the time of David). The Hebrews are at a disadvantage when they face the superior weapons and iron chariots of the Philistines along the coast. The Philistines had already moved on to the iron age, leaving the Hebrews, equipped with their bronze-age weapons, at a loss. The Hebrews are also vexed by an obvious internal difficulty which the sweeping view of the priests would like to overlook: the tribes do not compose a nation unified by devotion to the cult of Jehovah. They are a collection of tribes bound by a common tongue and a common stock of recollections. But language and legend do not suffice to bring *all* of them to the aid of Barak in a battle against an enemy who has nine hundred iron chariots (*Judges* 5:15-16); the tribes of Reuben, Dan, and Asshur abstain from the conflict. The story of Jephthah (*Judges,* chap. 12) reveals the even more painful picture of Hebrew tribes battling with each other rather than with the enemies who threaten them. At the end of *Judges,* it is the opportunity to censure and punish the faults of a tribe (Benjamin) that produces unified action among the Hebrew clans with, in the retrospective view of the priests, a common destiny.

In the fragmentary entries of *Judges* we see each of the twelve tribes concerned with consolidating or continuing its little holding of conquered territory and far from eager to go to the defense of the territory of another tribe. This bias persists, tragically, throughout *Samuel* and *Kings*—that is, to the end of the Hebrew story, so far as the Old Testament shows it. A clue to how limited was Hebrew importance in the generations after Joshua is the apparent fact that neither Egypt to the south nor any of the powers to the north shows a sign of exerting itself against the scattered Hebrew tribes. Egypt, as indicated, was perhaps unable to do much. Certainly the children of Israel did not, until the time of Solomon, draw the attention of any of the great states. The chief enemies that the "judges" and Saul and David have to deal with are the Philistines, a federation of five seaboard towns along the Mediterranean; they continue to be harried by older kingdoms of Semitic origin, Ammon and Moab to the east across the Jordan and the Dead Sea, and Edom to the south of the Dead Sea.

The "Laws" of Oral Tradition at Work

We have just given a kind of double summary of Hebrew history in the first seven books: as it appeared to the priestly historians, and as it must appear to us when supplemented by other sources of information.

These summaries are made at a considerable disadvantage. Much of what we work with is oral tradition which behaves in ways that illustrate the "laws" already noted. (He who deals with such material must exercise a high degree of caution.) But, in recent generations, complete skepticism about the historicity of these opening books sometimes discounts too much. A recent example concerns the hypothesis that monotheism was wholly the creation of seventh- and eighth-century prophets and that the Hebrews of the conquest were religiously indistinguishable from the peoples they conquered. Excavation has indicated that tenth-century Hebrew sanctuaries do not have the ritual objects essential to the performance of the native, Canaanitish cults.

A view of Hebrew history as seen by later historians gives us the picture of the past which governed later Hebrew thought and action. The second summary, which supplements the Bible version of Hebrew history with material gathered from other sources, suggests that the Hebrew summary is not entirely out of line with what the ancient history of the Near East reveals. Assyrian records contain independent mention of later kings of Israel; and a king of Moab set up the stone which bears an inscription praising Chemosh, god of Moab, for freeing the country from the oppression of Israel. But of chief value is not the infrequent factual confirmation of Old Testament history that comes from the historians of other nations.

It is the restoration of color and movement to the entire panorama of ancient history which used to present the startling spectacle of Moses and Joshua and David done in hues that, against the dim, uncertain background of Egypt and Assyria, were garish and unreal. Now that the background colors have been strengthened and much is known about cultures the Bible only mentions or often misrepresents, our figures in the foreground, from Abraham onward, take their places in the larger picture.

Yet all this unexpected aid does not cancel the truth that the largest part of the material just summarized obeys the "laws" of oral tradition. So it is well to seek out, in these first seven books, the marks that such tradition has left. In Chapter III the "laws" were stated; here certain illustrations remind the reader of what he may expect to find. The preference that singles out the miraculous rather than the just, already noted in the tales of Esau's loss of birthright, appears at almost every turn. Mana in the form of faith "over and above the line of duty" is displayed by Abraham in his willingness to sacrifice his only child, though the child is his sole material assurance that his "seed" will multiply (*Genesis,* chap. 22). Mana in the form of guile appears in the maneuver that undoes the city of Ai (*Joshua,* chap. 8) and in the misrepresentation which enables the children of Gibeon to win Hebrew protection (*Joshua,* chap. 9). Mana as skill in "testing" the motives of others appears in Joseph's story when, despite his delight at seeing his brothers, he conceals a divining cup in the grain the brothers are carrying back to the north so that he may accuse them of theft and test them still further (*Genesis,* chap. 44).

Mana of every sort appears in the collections of tales we find in *Judges.* All through this Hebrew "book of wonders" some kind of excellence—not always excellence we today admire—keeps appearing. Deborah is a "prophetess" in the old style, loud at the war cry and shameless in her boasts of victory (*Judges,* chaps. 4 and 5). Jael is a heroine on a grand scale, violating the sacred laws of hospitality when she drives the nail through the temple of Sisera, her sleeping guest (*Judges* 4:18-22). Samson, despite his appalling thick-headed-ness in all his adventures with women, is full of the mana of sheer physical strength; and he also has a rural malice that appears in the story of the foxes and elsewhere (*Judges* 15:3-5). Ehud (*Judges*, chap. 3) is a Hebrew Scarlet Pimpernel who frees his people by perpetrating the first "locked room" mystery in literature. And Gideon is a military leader who does not mind putting himself at a disadvantage; he dismisses part of his army simply to show that the favor of the Lord is with him (*Judges*, chap. 7).

And, to turn back to the earlier books, the career of Moses is a veritable glossary of the forms mana may take. Through Aaron, Moses is a wonderworker at the court of the Pharaoh (*Exodus*, chaps. 7-10); he himself is able to draw water from a rock (*Exodus* 17:1-7); and he can assure Hebrew success so long as his arms are uplifted (*Exodus* 17:8-16). (Hur and Aaron hold them up when Moses grows weary.) And on the face of Moses, after he comes down from his interview with Jehovah, is a glow too strong for ordinary eyes to bear (*Exodus* 34:33-35).

The power of the motif to impose itself on various narratives has been sufficiently noted in the discussion (Chapter III) on the recurrent themes of the wife-represented-as-sister and the barren-mother-who-unexpectedly-conceives. But the assimilation of a set of deeds to the life of one hero needs a further word here. Stories of all sorts are drawn to the august figure of Moses, and sometimes they are stories that agree ill with each other. Of this leader it is said: "Now the man Moses was very meek, above all the men which were upon the face of the earth" (*Numbers* 12:3), and we are inclined to agree when we read how he flees from punishment for the crime of killing the overseer (*Exodus* 2:11 ff.). But he is bold when he returns with Aaron to the Pharaoh's court (*Exodus*, chaps. 7 ff.). He smites with death the Hebrews who have revolted in the wilderness (*Numbers*, chap. 16), yet when a curse from God upon the children of Israel threatens, Moses casts his lot with the children and against God.

It is not that such an accumulation of narrative is beyond reconciling. Indeed, the mixture of fierceness and tenderness in Moses' attitude toward the people is a trait found in all religious innovators including Jesus. But a narrative that has accumulated is not to be read in the same way as a narrative arranged according to an *explicitly* stated principle. The priestly editors, at least, did not ask what stories about Moses were consonant with their conception of him and what were not.

A slightly different trouble faces a reader of the Samson cycle. Here the incessant defeat of Samson at the hands of wily Philistine women is incredible. But to read the later stories of the cycle with the supposition that the hero should get some profit from his previous experience is to "psychologize" Samson. To him, if not to us, each encounter with a Philistine woman is a new one. This is grossly apparent in the Delilah story, where he achieves triumphs of obtuseness, allowing himself to be betrayed not once but four times.

Little more need be said of the morality of the tales. The virtues previously mentioned—tribal loyalty, hospitality, and so on—are abundantly illustrated; and frequently details that may strike us as outrageous are but the "defects" of certain primitive virtues. The story of Tamar's triumph over her father-in-law Judah is to the point. The modern person is likely only to see the fact: that Tamar tricks her father-in-law into having sexual intercourse with her. Yet careful reading of the story reveals her as a heroine after an antique style rather than a harlot. Tamar was but claiming from Judah what was hers by right. Her husband, the son of Judah, had died; and Judah was slow about betrothing her to a remaining son. She therefore did no wrong when she led Judah into an unknowing fulfillment of the tribal law. Her father-in-law acknowledges her virtue when he says: "She hath been more righteous than I . . ." (*Genesis* 38:26). All this is not to say that the reader can scan a narrative like that in *Judges,* chapters 19 and 20, with comfort; for it will occur to him that the worst detail, the treatment of the Levite's concubine, is very blithely overlooked by everyone concerned. Perhaps this sampling of ancient ethics can be terminated thus: It is unwise to suppose that the old tale-tellers were familiar with the Sermon on the Mount. They were fully conversant with the moral codes of their own day.

The Role of Myth

We have suggested that early history and moral tale shade off into myth. But the preoccupations of the three forms—history, tale, and myth—are not absolutely identical. Though they cannot be flatly separated from each other, each nevertheless displays a dominant emphasis. The tale concerns the matters just discussed, revolving around mana and simple, limited moral insights. In the tale which is predominantly mythical in interest, the emphasis is on origin. The tale exists to explain certain facts, within limits proper to the comprehensions addressed. Many an explanation involves, as in the tale of mana, the depiction of actions offensive to a later moral sense. The first hearers of the tale in *Genesis* 9:18-27 were not offended to learn of Noah naked and drunk. To them, the story explained why the descendants of Ham, the son who looked on his naked parent, were worthy of censure.

Myth, then, drives the events of a tale toward explaining a fact of nature or a social phenomenon that has its origins in past ages—a phenomenon so strange or arbitrary that an explanation has become necessary. Myths do not have to be invented to explain currently adopted customs; they must render intelligible customs which are rooted in forgotten necessities. In our culture, no one has to explain to a child the origin of the gas station; its social function is self-evident. But when a modern child confronts a hitching post for the first time, he demands an explanation; and if the parent is both uninformed and inventive, he may produce a set of statements that have much in common with myth.

Myth has been called science before the age of science, a partially true definition. Certain myths lose authority when an explanation based on analysis and measurement is advanced. But certain other early explanations preserve their power—as poetry, as imaginative handlings of the inscrutable—simply because such questions as concern the origin of all being and the goal of all being lie outside the scope of strict techniques of investigation and yet remain of deep interest to the general human mind. To illustrate this distinction: The tower of Babel story (*Genesis* 11:1-9) "explains" the varieties of language; and the story of the sexual relations between Lot and his daughters (*Genesis* 19:30-38) explained, to Hebrew hearers, why one was privileged to look down on traditional Hebrew enemies, the Ammonites and Moabites; they were the descendants of an incestuous relation.

Neither of these two explanations any longer has power to satisfy *our* curiosity on the points in question. We can learn about the sources of language variation from philologists, and we have no particular desire to look down on the descendants of Lot, who, ethnology counsels, are now indistinguishable from the other descendants of Adam. In consequence, we regard this sort of myth or explanation as simply quaint.

But not all the myths in the Bible can be so classified. The narratives in the opening chapters of *Genesis* deal with a question on which we have, even now, no fully satisfactory information. True, other sources give us an account of the emergence of man as a physical being, and we hear of the earth as a fragment cast off from the sun. But we have less satisfactory accounts of the growth of human tendencies called variously "rational" or "spiritual." Even in our theory of the development of the universe we run into the problem of "infinite regress." We at least feel that somewhere the explanation of one effect by an antecedent cause must halt; somewhere we would like to find the first link in the chain of cause and effect in which we occupy a late place. Curiosity as to what endowed man with "humanity" or what began and has since sustained the evolutionary process is perhaps "unscientific" since questions of this sort are unlikely ever to be answered. But the human imagination is not altogether inhibited by the word "unscientific." It continues to circle around questions to which there will probably be no very satisfactory answer.

Indeed, if such questions do have a locus, it is in "the Other." Because we continue to feel that, at some points of our experience, we are in a state of dependence, we continue to find very moving those old tales that are early expressions of the sort of curiosity we still have. We do not care too much for the story of how the first herdsman and the first husbandman fell out, an aspect of the Cain and Abel story; but we still are moved by the part of the same tale that seems to take up, in terms of action rather than speculation, the recurrent question: what is violence and how did it come into the world (*Genesis* 4:1-17)? This is not to say that the only questions worth asking are those that cannot be answered. But it is to say that a great many apparently normal objects of human curiosity—what "the Other" is, what good and evil are, whether man is a dependent or a self-subsistent creature—are not handled at all by really strict scientific disciplines and are, instead, handled with some dexterity (if not finality) by art and poetry and the old tales now under consideration. It would be obtuse to argue that such treatment is conclusive and gives us definitive answers. All we need to say is that such handling is an important part of the treatment which questions about deity and good and evil get. Men would be unwise to give up, *The Book of Job* with its image of affliction undeserved, just as they would be unwise to give up a Faustus and his pact with the devil out of a doubt that Faustus ever existed. In the opening books of the Bible there are, though on a smaller scale than *Job* or *Faust*, certain vividly expressed guesses of early man that we should not be overhasty in discarding for our supposedly better-informed ones.

In addition, the brevity and simplicity of these mythological narratives commend them to us. At these points, the Bible is usually an "open book." One does not need a "key" to the Babel story or to the story of Adam and Eve. But a less clear sort of myth remains to be mentioned. One does need, now and then, a "key" to deal with a narrative such as that of Samson and the lion. What is one to make of the incident of Samson's taking honey from the carcass of a lion which he has slain (*Judges* 14:5-9)? If one explanation is entertained, the incident is a confused memory of sun worship. The sun was worshiped under the form of a lion; that the honey can be taken from the lion simply signifies that the summer sun favors the work of the bees. This sort of mythological tale is difficult because it involves us with a forgotten theological account of the framework of the world. When such an explanation has been forgotten, as it certainly was by the time the priestly editors began to put Samson's cycle to rights, we find ourselves in the presence of a closed book into which we are allowed only to glance. Such tales and the later references of the prophets to Leviathan and the fall of Lucifer the daystar are references to matters that have, at the time of recording, nearly dropped beyond the horizon of man's awareness. In their esoteric obscurity, they are in sharp contrast with a tale of explanation like that of Adam and Eve, which has remained in the broad daylight of human consciousness because it is readily intelligible and permanently suggestive.

The Varieties of Awareness of "the Other"

We have indicated previously the various channels through which early man sought to establish contact with "the Other"—that which was greater than man, that upon which man judged he was dependent. The early books of the Bible are fascinating partly because they constitute a full gallery or museum of the various early attitudes of man toward the greater power that haunted his imagination. Animism, totemism, nature worship, and other forms soon to be noted—they are all there. Since these attitudes are not exclusive but are complementary to each other, we should not expect to find (nor do we) any noticeable or orderly progress in these books from one form of apprehension to another. Nor, when we do observe the appearance of the insights characteristic of ethical monotheism—the insights of what is called a "high religion" where theories are complex and the object of conscious manipulation—should we assume that older attitudes will not reappear. They will reappear in the Biblical narrative for two reasons: because of the *palimpsest* method of composition, which presents a record of *accretions* of insight from early to very late times rather than successions of insight; and because of the nature of religious insight itself, in which a new insight does not automatically cancel an older one, and we are offered no guarantee that the human fancy will adhere to a new-discovered attitude and eschew an old one. (The entire course of Hebrew-Christian growth is a rich illustration of this truth.)

Animism, defined as the attribution of spirit or will to inanimate objects and to localities—spirit or will that the wary early man must reckon with—is an element in the attitude of the Hebrews toward the power which they know they must win to their purposes. Sometimes this attitude appears fully; sometimes we must simply sense its guiding presence. We suspect its presence whenever we read of an oak tree or a terebinth under which a person or treasure is buried; we know from other cultures that the *anima* or spirit which makes the oak tree an august object is that of the dead person or—in the instance of the secreted treasure—an unidentified spirit that is able to watch over the secreted jewels. In *Genesis* 35:8 Rachel's nurse is buried under an oak; and when the followers of Jacob put away their "strange gods" and "all their earrings which were in their ears," Jacob takes the collection and puts it under "the oak which was by Shechem" (*Genesis* 35:4). In the story of the burial of the nurse and in the mention of the "pillar" which Jacob puts above the grave of Rachel—a pillar, say the editors, that stands "unto this day" (*Genesis* 35:20), it seems to be the spirit of a dead person that makes a place holy and dangerous. Often, however, as the incident of the buried jewels suggests, a tree or place has its quota of intangible life without any suggestion as to the source of that life. The spirit is *there,* that is all; and its presence is a circumstance that the prudent will reckon with. For this reason almost any oak is a good place to bury treasure, and oaths can be taken under the tree's spreading limbs, for who would be so bold as to risk going back on a vow to which not man but the spirit of a place was the witness?

That animism is not always based on the continuation of the soul of the dead is suggested at least by such incidents as the vision of Jacob at Bethel and the foundation of the cairn or pile of witness rocks at the place called Mizpah. Mizpah, for example, did not exist until Jacob and his angry father-in-law Laban compounded their differences and agreed to part peacefully, after piling up a mound of stones. The formula they utter—"The Lord watch between me and thee, when we are absent one from another" (*Genesis* 31:49)—presupposes that a being is now indwelling in the "mizpah" or watchtower, with power to note and punish the man who is so bold as to go beyond the pile of rocks.

Another encounter of Jacob's with a place spirit puts this point into still clearer relief. Jacob, on his way north to get his bride, rests at a place which, he decides, must be full of mana and power for he has the vision of angels ascending and descending the heavenly ladder or stairs. Upon awakening, he decides that this place is doubtless the house of the Lord (*Beth,* house, and *El,* the Lord); and after arranging rocks to form a primitive altar, he departs with a promise that if it were made to an omnipotent deity would seem both crass and dangerous. For he promises to come back and found a cult at this spot—to set up a regularized, recurrent worship at the altar—*if his affairs in the north prosper.* If not, one supposes, the altar will be allowed to fall down, all because the spirit of the place lacked power to make the distant affairs of Jacob prosper.

For when there are many deities—in every bush or tree or at every level place in the turn of a mountain path—the relation of man to such powers is extremely pragmatic. Man watches shrewdly to see whether the local deity "delivers the goods"; and if the deity does not, man promptly judges it unable to operate at a distance or to go against the power of another localized deity. When (we shall see) deity is monotheistically viewed, this very simple relationship is altered. Then, when man's prayers are not answered, he cannot straightway remove to a rival shrine; he has to inspect more closely the exact nature of his relation to the one all-prevailing deity.

Exactly this is what we shall be able to observe in the speculations of the later prophets when disaster overwhelms Israel. To such prophets, the pragmatic test of deity which we find in the story of Gideon's fleece (*Judges* 6:36 ff.) would seem either impious or incomplete. Gideon has received an order from the Lord, but he hesitates to carry it out, since he is not sure that the deity has sufficient power to back up the project of a battle with the Amalekites and the Midianites. He says to the Lord: "Behold I will put a fleece of wool in the floor; and if the dew be on the fleece only, and it be dry upon all the earth beside, then shall I know that thou wilt save Israel by mine hand, as thou hast said." The Lord obliges. But the hard-headed Gideon is not quite certain that this deity is a top-flight source of mana. Says he to the Lord on the second night: "Let not thine anger be hot against me, and I will speak but this once: let me prove, I pray thee, but this once with the fleece; let it now be dry only upon the fleece, and upon all the ground let there be dew." The anger of God is not hot; deity seems to recognize that Gideon's precaution is legitimate; ". . . it was dry upon the fleece only, and there was dew on all the ground." This calculating extortion of "signs" appears in many places. When the Lord offers to furnish King Hezekiah a proof that he shall recover from his mortal illness—shall the sun's shadow go forward ten degrees, or go back ten degrees?—Hezekiah replies: "It is a light thing for the shadow to go down ten degrees: nay, but let the shadow return backward ten degrees" (*II Kings* 20:10). The Lord immediately performs the feat that Hezekiah judges is more difficult.

The most dramatic encounter of man with such a deity is worth analysis because it lets us summarize the operation of animism. This is the meeting of Jacob with what is euphemistically referred to as "a man" (*Genesis* 32:24). Why Jacob must wrestle all night with this being, we may make a prudent guess: the "man" is the spirit of the place and bars the "ford Jabbok" to Jacob and his followers. The concluding section of the story shows that Jacob is really wrestling with deity embodied with physical form and power that daunt Jacob but do not overwhelm him. As daybreak approaches, the spirit says: "Let me go, for the day breaketh" since he is subservient to the rule that, centuries later, the ghost of Hamlet's father must obey. Jacob demands to know the name of the local being that opposes him since it is often in a being's name that the "secret" of his mana reposes. Once one knows the name, one has considerable power over the being. (Adam has his power over animals because he is allowed to *name* them; God gives Moses special power by revealing a divine name as yet unknown; and, in later days, the king who takes a census is regarded with bitterness because he gains power over all the persons whose names he has on his census lists.) The being at the ford does not give Jacob his name; instead, he gives Jacob a new name—Israel, "prince of the Lord"—and of course new mana. Jacob then allows the "man" to escape and, a curious circumstance to survive but one that lights up the whole obscure tale, names the place of the encounter Peniel, "the face of God." As he says, "I have seen God face to face, and my life is preserved." Plainly, the entire story of a combat with a local deity is distressing on many counts to the priestly historians of the sixth century B.C. From their point of view, deity undergoes the indignity of a physical struggle with a mortal and, further, is nearly worsted; and a new name and new power are wrung from this deity—the "man" is not able to present these to Jacob as a free gift, as does God to Moses. Yet we understand the difficulties faced by the last revisers elsewhere as well as here if we see this as one more story that on some counts they would desire to omit but that on others must be retained. This story explains the origin of a name (Israel) fundamental to the whole Hebrew "frame of reference." Also of some importance, it explains something that persisted in the priests' own day: the idea of the uncleanness of a sinew in the thigh. What the priests try to effect, in their presentation of a picture of deity far removed from theirs, is a veiled and truncated version. The nature of the being at the ford and the occasion of the encounter are not stated; and only the concluding phrase allows us to see the entire story in a proper perspective.

Animism has one other important Biblical expression. Spirits may be present in portable objects—objects that a person can take with him, objects whose supply of mana can be a source of power and good luck wherever one is. The "strange gods" and the amulets that Jacob buried under the protecting oak (*Genesis*, chap. 35) had to be handled with care and respect not only because they were of precious metal; they were the mana-charged Hebrew equivalents of "good luck" rings and mascots of today. They were, it is true, being discarded; but, like atomic waste, they could not be discarded in a casual way, for they were dangerous. Does not Jacob say of Bethel, "How dreadful is this place" (*Genesis* 28:17)? The power of a place or a tree or an image was primarily power pure and simple, just as is the power of an electric arc or the atom bomb in our view. That power is morally neutral until we begin to channel it in directions, humanly speaking, either evil or beneficent. So, to earlier man, the power of "the Other"—dispersed, ubiquitous, and dangerous. The *teraphim,* which Rachel takes from the house of her father Laban when she flees with Jacob, are to be thought of as small, grotesque images which are the abode of the spirits of the dead of a particular family. *Our* morality may censure the deception that Rachel practices on her angry father; she pretends to be ill and does not rise from the pile of luggage where the teraphim are concealed. But in the view of the public that cherished this story for many ages Rachel is praiseworthy, since her shrewdness is to the profit of the tribe to which she now belongs; the teraphim were a source of power, power which her theft turned into channels beneficial to those around her.

Another portable sort of mana exists in the Ark of the Covenant which the Hebrews carry with them through the desert. This oblong box carried on poles is supposed to have contained the "tables of law," the stones which Moses brought down from Mount Sinai. The fortunes of this box allow one to see very fully the workings of the great neutral power that is deity or that emanates from deity. In the first place, regardless of the spirit or deity it proceeds from, it is power and nothing but power. To handle it well requires, several incidents show, continuing tact and wisdom. The Ark is "the luck of Israel," and the temporary loss of it is a catastrophe, and when David brings it finally into Jerusalem, the return is an occasion for dance and festival (*II Samuel,* chap. 6). Yet the power of the Ark does not automatically redound to the benefit of the Hebrews, as one might suspect from the story of how the mere presence of the Ark in the sanctuary of the Philistine enemy lays their god Dagon low (*I Samuel,* chap. 5). For when the Ark is being handled by the Hebrews and is in danger of falling from its cart, "the anger of the

Lord" is kindled against Uzzah, the man whose hand steadied the sacred box. "God smote him there for his error [or 'rashness']; and there he died by the Ark of God" (*II Samuel* 6:7). Additional light on the dreadful workings of the holy is cast by King David's reaction; he is angry with the Lord for causing Uzzah to die, but his fear of the Lord redoubles because of the very anger he has been bold enough to feel (*II Samuel* 6:9).

In light of these stories it is easy to see why the manipulation of this power which is dangerous to all who try to use it was regarded as a full-time job. The stories of Moses, then, devote much time to the setting up of elaborate ceremonials to conduct this power to proper outlets. As early as Moses' first approach to the deity on Mount Sinai, the danger of divine power not properly controlled is clear. Only Moses is to go up to the top of the mountain. His brother Aaron and other holy men may come up the slope a certain distance. But the mass of men, probably unclean and hence not protected against the cracklings of the awful power, are to keep a considerable distance away, as are the cattle, who will likewise perish if they ascend the slopes of the mountain (*Exodus* 19:10-25). "The iniquity of holy things" can be borne only by members of a priestly caste drawn from the sons of Levi, a tribe to which both Moses and Aaron belonged. Men who rashly draw near to the Holy of Holies receive summary justice. Fire darts out from the altar and consumes them (*Leviticus* 10:1-2), or a gulf opens beneath their feet (*Numbers* 16:30 ff.).

Mana, as the last illustrations suggest, is not to be thought of as inhering only in deities of an animistic origin. Thus, the deity which Moses seeks out on Mount Sinai is often judged to have been a *nature deity,* less localized than the "man" at the ford Jabbok and a controller of thunder and storm. It is deity in this aspect—as a controller of storm, as power great enough to hold back the sun for Joshua until a battle is won (*Joshua* 10:12-14)—that appears as the animator of innumerable metaphors in the *Psalms* speaking of storm and sun, of angry wave and quiet sea. One may contrast the two modes of apprehending deity (the mode of animism and the mode of nature worship) in this way: A nature deity is less localized (he may dwell on mountaintops rather than on *a* mountaintop), and man in his wanderings feels his power almost everywhere. Animistic deities exercise power only at their place of residence or near it; and their effects are, when compared to the grand ones of a nature deity, very modest. Plainly, the religious insight which locates deity in a power of nature rather than at a ford or in a pile of rocks is likely to have a longer and more complex life than animistic insights. The latter proliferate on early levels of oral tradition, but they tend to weaken and lose their authority when a people's religious life moves in the direction of speculation and ceremonial. Ikhnaton regarded deity as inherent in *all* nature or beyond the horizon; and similarly it is on nature that the Psalmists of the Old Testament rely when they seek to provide tangible embodiments of deity.

Evidences of *totemism*—the insight that, according to many students, locates the collective "soul" of a people in some animal which is regarded as the "father" or "protector" of the tribe—appear infrequently in the Biblical narrative, perhaps because any theriomorphic (animal-shaped) source of mysterious power would be immediately identified with the "abominations" of the Egyptians, such as the hawk-headed sun god, Ra. But one cannot escape being struck by Nehushtan, the brazen serpent. It appears first as an image fashioned by Moses and held up before the children of Israel to draw out the poison of the snake bites they have just had (*Numbers* 21:4-9). Here the serpent is no more than a tool in the performance of what is called "sympathetic magic." But the image became much more in the later history of Israel. It was preserved as the Ark was preserved; and it became, like the Ark, an object of worship. Not until the time of the reforms of Hezekiah (*II Kings* 18:4) was this serpent broken up because "unto those days the children of Israel did burn incense to it." Here again, the trace of an attitude repugnant to the priests persists because of their respect for the material they have in their hands. The brazen serpent cannot be suppressed because it is associated with an exploit of Moses and has become an essential item in the story of Israel, even though it came to a bad end in the time of Hezekiah, when it was indistinguishable from the totem objects of the neighboring peoples.

This kind of overt idolatry had no place in a temple where there was only one object of worship concealed in an innermost compartment: the Ark surmounted by two cherubim. Between them, on top of the Ark, was the "mercy seat," a brass plate where the power of the deity was specially focused and which could be approached once a year by the high priest of the Temple. That there was a special location of deity's attention in the Temple is shown by King Hezekiah's behavior when he receives a letter from an enemy. "And Hezekiah received the letter of the hand of the messengers, and read it: and Hezekiah went up into the house of the Lord, and spread it before the Lord" (*II Kings* 19:14). Yet evidences of the intrusion into the Temple worship of forms of religion that the priests were determined to exclude—intrusions that had the support of many a king and, sad to relate, the enthusiastic multitude—abound in the history of both the United and divided kingdoms. The necessary implications of worshiping one deity either had not yet been made or—equally possible, the history of religion being what it is, a partially repetitive spiral—had been obscured and forgotten by king and populace alike, who willed to be, like the neighboring kings and their subjects, richly supplied with gods for all occasions.

These indications of the existence of an illogical variety of projections in the early books of history of "the Other" should not be a cause for distress in the reader who accepts the definition of deity he finds in most catechisms. The God of the "high religions" called Judaism and Christianity is conventionally defined thus: He is a being all-powerful, all-knowing, all-just, and all-merciful—a being who is a spirit and yet a person, a being who is not to be known in ways that we come to know many items of knowledge. The section of the Bible we now are dealing with records a variety of efforts to arrive at such knowledge; they move not on the level of definition but on the level of experienced or recollected action, where whatever is strange and inculcates awe is a possible locus of what one cannot control and is yet dependent on. The Bible is, indeed, deeply engrossing because it is an account of how this process of recognizing deity sloughs off many of the initial recognitions until "the Other" is perceived not as having its dwelling and expression in a variety of places and physical forms but as a being and a moving force *not* perceptible to the eye and sense. As Elijah said, the Lord was not in the fire or the storm or the earthquake; he was rather an irreducible minimum that abided when fire and storm and earthquake were past, a still small voice. But this step is a later one and does not concern us here.

Anthropomorphism

Before this step was taken and in the very "climate of opinion" that the first seven books record, the animistic, totemistic, and nature-worshiping recognitions of deity were supplemented by a habit of perception called *anthropomorphism.* This way of viewing deity, which supposes that the god possesses human form, can be regarded as an advance over the other ways of recognizing and isolating "the Other" for imaginative handling. Animism, totemism, and nature worship are chiefly recognitions of "the Other" as undifferentiated power—in the tree or at the ford, on the mountaintops or in the sacred animal. The attribution to the deity of human shape and motive is, at least on the level of action and narrative, an effort to do more than say that mana exists at a certain point. It is an attempt to say what kind of power one is dealing with. This is the importance of the interest *Genesis* and the other books display in the various appearances of deity in human or quasi-human form. It is an attempt to be a little more distinct or precise than one can be about a pile of stones or a tree. God walks in the garden of Eden in the cool of the day (*Genesis* 3:8); God promises to reveal his "back parts" to Moses (*Exodus* 33:23); and God is thought of as shaping the first man by the actual movement of his hands (*Genesis,* chap. 2). This shaping action is in radical contrast to the act of creation recounted in *Genesis,* Chapter 1, where more sophisticated writers presented it as the product of a simple command: "The Lord said, Let there be light; and there was light."

The appearance of God in human form, with the limitation of knowledge and power implied by such form (e.g., God does not know of the fault of Adam and Eve until he makes a "personal" investigation), was doubtless a projection of "the Other" almost as distasteful to some later men as the "man" at the ford Jabbok or the worship of the serpent Nehushtan. The taste of the priestly editors is apparent in the predominance of narratives in which God manifests himself by voice alone, as in many of Moses' interviews with deity and in the call to the young Samuel in the night which he misinterprets as his master Eli's voice (*I Samuel,* chap. 3). *Genesis* is not far advanced when God ceases to appear and makes his will known through angelic messengers. These later narratives do not deny that God is a person, a differentiated being as opposed to the undifferentiated mana of a tree or place. But they do tend to point to what is an important insight with the prophets: Though God is indeed a person, he is also transcendent, mysteriously and awfully removed from what he has created. Perhaps for this reason, the Bible is poor in stories that parallel the habitual descents of the Olympian gods as in the story of the visit of Zeus and Mercury to pious Philemon and Baucis. That the priestly editors were embarrassed by the forthright anthropomorphism of their sources J and E is indicated by the compressed account (in *Genesis* 6:1-4) of the commerce between "the sons of God" and "the daughters of men." That they tried to combine and blend the given narratives to conceal or minimize anthropomorphic tendencies is well illustrated by the story of the visit received by Abraham and Sarah, in *Genesis,* Chapter 18. Verse 1 states: "And the Lord appeared unto him [Abraham] in the plains of Mamre. . . ." Verse 2 tells us, however, that when Abraham lifted up his eyes he saw "three men." Abraham bows to these guests, but his words are, in verse 3, "My Lord, if now I have found favor in thy sight, pass not away, I pray thee, from thy servant. . . ." The confusion continues, with the tale alternating between the singular and plural pronouns (e.g., verses 9 and 10); and the general uncertainty does not lift when, in the following chapter, it is "two angels" rather than "three men" who come to the house of Lot and undertake the correction of the wicked cities of Sodom and Gomorrah.

In any case, the narratives in which the anthropomorphism is either overt or concealed serve as points of departure for the speculations completed in the teachings of the prophets, Jesus, and St. Paul. One may say that the terminus toward which the special Hebrew awareness travels—and beyond which (a modern reproach) it does not travel—is a conception of "the Other" that is able to support an ethical monotheism: the God who is no longer the protecting god of one people only (henotheism) but a universal deity who judges all men by the same standards of righteousness and accords all men the same mercies. One of the great fascinations of these early tales is the alternation between anthropomorphism overt and gross and anthropomorphism more subtly and selectively conceived.

It is the overt and gross presentation of deity in the shape of man that causes—or used to cause—disapproval of the God of the Old Testament. This god, the objections ran, is not only human in shape; he is human in motivation, and with a vengeance. Does he not bear grudges against those who go against his will, play favorites, act on incomplete knowledge? Is not his power sometimes on the verge of colliding with that of another deity? (Reference is to the story of Chemosh and Moabites.) In short, is he anything more than a henotheistic deity, a *particularist* being whose destiny is identical with that of the one people who worship him and whom he tries to favor? To such questions a temporary answer might be that this is not *the* God of the Old Testament, and that to speak so one has to isolate certain views of deity and ignore others. The other views are perhaps less familiar to the casual readers of the Old Testament, who doubtless, like the ancient Hebrews, prefer a good story to abstruse speculation. But it can be pointed out, even within the limits of the narrative material, that to talk about *the* God of the Old Testament is an inaccuracy.

Thus, several notable departures from the kind of deity in question —man-shaped, capricious, and particularist, who does indeed move through many a story—appear in the first seven books. If we are on the alert, we can see, almost before our eyes, the process by which man altered his conception of the deity who walked like a man. We can see the rejection of certain more primitive anthropomorphic conceptions in favor of those that, either to a devout Christian or to an agnostic, approach the more developed, and apparently either better or inevitable, ideas of God. That such ideas are better is not easy to prove; that they are inevitable and are "bound to come" (the agnostic suggestion) is almost axiomatic.

One value of the incident in the second half of *Genesis,* Chapter 18, is its pointing out that what we dismiss as obvious was once far from obvious to men not biologically different from us. Here we see God about ready to "take off" for Sodom and Gomorrah and visit upon them condign punishment; both cities are to be wiped out. This divine act of "justice" seemed acceptable on an earlier level, since the sin of certain men was automatically the sin of their tribe or city. But at this point Abraham begins his series of questions; and we are present as early man rejects an old concept and asserts a new one. Abraham says to God: "Peradventure there be fifty righteous within the city: wilt thou also destroy and not spare the place for the fifty righteous that are therein? That be far from thee to do after this manner, to slay the righteous with the wicked: and that the righteous should be as the wicked, that be far from thee: Shall not the Judge of all the earth do right?" (*Genesis* 18:24-25.) Abraham's questions and the Lords' concessions continue until the Lord has consented to spare the city if there are no more than ten righteous men. Unfortunately, as the next chapter shows, ten such men are lacking; and the destruction of the wicked cities proceeds according to plan. Plainly, what dictates Abraham's questions is a revulsion against one concept of divine justice; the sort of justice that "Yahweh" takes for granted is rejected by Abraham. A god worthy of his devotion must display a justice more exact and discriminating. The "Judge of all the earth" must do right.

A similar important step appears in the much earlier story of Noah, in which the concept of the "covenant" makes its first appearance and automatically imposes limitations on the deity who consents to be bound by it. The "covenant" plays so large a role in the Hebrew-Christian story as to be almost a character; it is simply a promise binding to both parties—in this case, God and man. The bow in the clouds is the symbol of the promise that God has bound himself by. He will no longer take what we call today "unilateral action," as he did when, in his anger, he let loose the waters of the flood. From this point onward, thanks to the concept of the covenant, deity will be less the incalculable power, subject to sudden, retributive anger. He will be, rather, comprehensible within certain limits set up by the contract that he and his people have entered upon. The contract tames the lightning flash of his sheer display of power; a mutually binding promise has been made. It regulates the activity of the people; they will observe the simple code the Lord has given them (*Genesis* 9:1 ff.). But it also regulates the activity of God; so long as the people live up to the set code, so long the covenant must curb deity and direct his power to the benefit of his worshipers.

Often this process of reforming—"purifying" if one will—the anthropomorphic conception of deity is carried out with a breath-taking boldness. When Moses has discovered that his followers have bowed down before the golden calf, a totemistic or fertility deity, he goes up the mountain to face a justly angry deity; the "contract" has been broken, and God's wrath may break forth as in the days of the flood. But the speech of Moses on the occasion is, like Abraham's earlier one, full of instruction. It demands more of the deity than the justifiable anger one might expect from an Oriental potentate whose prerogatives have been ignored. It demands, though obliquely, more than justice. First Moses says to the people, "Ye have sinned a great sin: and now I will go up unto the Lord: peradventure I shall make an atonement for your sin" (*Exodus* 32:30). Then Moses comes to the angry God. He concedes that the people have sinned a great sin and adds these crucial words: "Yet now, if thou wilt forgive their sin—; and if not, blot me, I pray thee, out of thy book which thou hast written" (*Exodus* 32:32). In asserting his solidarity with those who merit punishment, Moses demands of God something over and above justice. Once again, an older view of God turns out to be not good enough. As the later prophets see it: if God is no more than just, what man shall escape punishment? The challenge which Moses offers God resembles a long succession of challenges offered the earlier conceptions of deity. (As a matter of record, God here ignores the challenge by saying adamantly: "Whosoever hath sinned against me, him will I blot out of my book" [*Exodus* 32:32].) As man himself grows in complexity, he demands (or discovers) divine attributes that were totally absent from human imagination when Jacob built his altar at Bethel and said quite crassly: "If God will be with me . . . , then shall the Lord be my God" (*Genesis* 28:20-21). For Moses here, as for the later Isaiah and Ezekiel, a god whose triumphs are based on a display of sheer power is not a worthy object of veneration. To power must be added —slowly and painfully—a discriminatory justice, a universality, and, last, a love for the beings that have been created. These attributes were indeed added, and this is why the Bible is an important "event" in history. On a perception of these attributes hang not only "the law and the prophets" but such modern generalities as "basic human decency" and the brotherhood of man and the importance of the individual. What we must be at pains to see now is that—here, near the start of our long journey in time—these qualities either are absent or flash out intermittently as in the instances noted. "Basic human decency" and the other "self-evident" truths are neither basic in human nature nor, in long sections of history, self-evident. They are the creations of the slow accretion of insight. Perhaps like other accretions, the stalactites and stalagmites of underground caves, these results of long, cumulative processes cannot, once destroyed, be quickly replaced.

One more of these intermittent flashes, a crucial one, must be noted. As indicated earlier, the religious development we follow is no straight-line development; later attitudes alternate with earlier ones. *Exodus* 3:14 ("I am that I am") appears in the midst of stories exhibiting other sorts of deity in action; this does not invalidate what gleams here for a moment. True, the god that moves elsewhere in the Pentateuch is a *particularist* god; he strengthens the Hebrews against their enemies and the gods of their enemies—a "truth" recognized by an alien prophet, Balaam, as the Hebrew wave rolls up from the desert (*Numbers,* chap. 24). He is also a god who demands the observance of certain rigid rules in the commerce his people have with him. But in this brief phrase of self-definition ("I am that I am"), centuries of religious growth are anticipated. God is represented here as rejecting with impatience the obtuse, naïve ideas his followers have had of him. They seem to suppose that he spends his time thundering from a certain mountain range, that Sinai is his special bailiwick, and that an area to the north belongs to another god named Chemosh. Such flashes are brief, and to the unimaginative they seem surrounded by darkness. But they establish the base lines of the vast and sometimes bewildering structures erected by the Hebrew prophets. A point like the one just cited has the power to say to generations that follow: "If God is simply that which exists . . ."

Such *ifs* and their possible consequences, in terms of poetry and of philosophy and theology, lie far beyond our present horizon. They are far away from the deity who walks his special beat like a watchman. But even these books at brief moments suggest that though our consciousness may be preoccupied with the near view, the deeds of Jacob and Joshua, other ranges of experience do indeed await us.

The Creation of Law

One of the great preoccupations of the Pentateuch that draws the eyes from horizons to immediate realities of behavior is the considerable body of law these books contain. Many reader who has plowed bitterly through the dietary regulations and the rules that determine whether a man is "clean" or "unclean" knows this to his sorrow. A beginner should read enough of the collections of law to know what they are like; he should not exhaust his initial enthusiasm for the Scriptures by a prolonged study of them. But he should be aware of their existence, their nature, and their role in Hebrew history—a very important role that determines, both negatively and positively, the teaching activity of the prophets and Christ. For both the prophets and Christ, as well as for generation after generation of orthodox Hebrews, the corpus of law in the books of Moses was a *fact* that one did not ignore, though one dealt with it variously.

Perhaps, for Americans, the Constitution has an analogous position. American speculation on present-day problems necessitating change always recognizes the existence of the Constitution as a fact. Some reformers judge that it is "flexible" enough to admit of change; reformers still more ardent envisage a cleaner sweep and wish to shake off the shackles which it places upon American activity. But neither group dreams of making advances without constant reference to it. Similarly, the prophets and Christ and St. Paul vary in their attitudes *toward* the Torah (the law) and what, in way of commentary, expansion, and interpretation, grew out of the Torah. Some later teachers urged flat conformity, some urged attention to the *spirit* of the law rather than the *letter;* and still others suggested that a "new life" cannot begin until a person has put behind him the old life that was guided by the laws of Moses.

The legal sections are not interesting reading at first encounter. They are irritatingly detailed; many laws reflect ethical attitudes which we now regard as indefensible, and many other laws are moored to customs in which we have not the slightest interest. In fact, we are likely to consider these sections of the Bible a depressing monument to *legalism,* which can be defined as the human tendency to guide the complex flow and interplay of living by a set of cold, calculated rules.

Legalism, in this sense, is certainly present in our own society. Soldiers know it in the rigid protocol of military communications "through channels." All of us know it in the forms we fill out to enable a prospective employer to estimate our merits precisely. We encounter legalism when we pay our taxes or meet—or try to meet—the requirements that "screen" those of us who may wish to move from one social group to another. At most of these points, we are not judged on any intrinsic qualities; we are judged by our college grades, the clubs we happen to belong to, the street address we have, the stores where we buy our clothes.

In the vanished Hebrew day as well as now, legalism is judgment based on external and often superficial signs. It could not operate if we did not assume that one can boil down the variety of human experience into a residue, a set of rules, that applies alike to everyone. For legalism and for the red tape that spins out of it we feel repugnance—whether the red tape regulates "cleanness" and "uncleanness" among the Hebrews or qualifications for owning a driver's license or meriting a government loan among us. Our repugnance is armed by the prophets and Christ and St. Paul when they tell us that the Lord delights not in the burnt offerings commended in *Leviticus* and in the fulfillment of the complex Temple ceremonials (*Leviticus*, chaps. 1-17). A better sacrifice is a broken and contrite heart (*Psalms* 51:17). St. Paul has this kind of sacrifice in mind when he writes that the letter killeth but the spirit giveth life (*II Corinthians* 3:6). Such objections against the life of the letter, law observance and no more, lead us to contrast the Old Testament and the New; we are tempted to speak as though the only spirit known to the "old dispensation" was the *lex talionis*, the law of retaliation which allows taking an eye for an eye and a tooth for a tooth. We may judge, superficially, that this attitude was chiefly superseded by the willingness to turn the other cheek taught by Christ. This flat contrast between the two Testaments is wrong on two counts. First, we shall find that some of the prophets as well as Christ are stern critics of the abuses of legalism. Second, to dwell exclusively on the defects of the legalistic approach to problems of behavior is to underestimate the need for law. It is to miss the significance, in the history of man, of the appearance of any code of law, whether Babylonian, Hebrew, or the Byzantine one promulgated by Justinian (483-565 A.D.). Though to later stages of human development a code of law may seem to offer many barriers to freedom and spontaneity, at the time of its invention or compilation it was a very great support to mankind; it held him up and allowed him to gather together the strength to step forward toward the later attitudes that we say are superior because they are inward and place emphasis on intention rather than deed.

How the collection of laws attributed to Moses was indeed a support to the Hebrews—how, more generally, legalism is an almost indispensable part of human experience—can best be understood if we examine the contribution of law to Hebrew life and see what special shapes it takes in the Torah. Thus far, we have opposed law to a later religious insight—Augustine's "Love and you may do what you will," for example. More justice is done to law as a component in man's life if we try to imagine what experience would be like without law. Actually, it is impossible to imagine a group of people at any stage of society living together without some kind of regulation that sets up standards by which the behavior of individuals is assessed and directed. One of the most fallacious myths in human history is that invented by Rousseau to describe the "state of nature" in which man lived free of law. Civilized man quite frequently pines for life on a carefree South Sea isle where he will escape the trammels of convention. *He* might escape convention there, but the real South Sea Islanders would not. No people, however "primitive," has been discovered that is able to exist without restrictive regulations. In fact, the legal codes to which the naked Australian bushmen submit impose extremely demanding standards of behavior. Only sophisticated civilized man opposes internal spontaneity to external conformity and has the dream of setting up a community with this motto from Rabelais: "Do what you will." The enlightened self-interest of the individual takes the place of imperceptive law. Early societies did not have this dream. Early men looked back with veneration upon some figure, real or fancied, who was the nation's lawgiver, who made life in society possible. The Greeks believed that without the activity of Solon (*c.* 638-*c.* 558 B.C.) there would have been no Greece, and the Hebrews believed that without Moses in the role of lawgiver there would have been no Hebrew society for the later prophets to admonish, reform, and inspire.

From this point of view, the law of retributive justice is better than still earlier sorts of human relation (if, indeed, such can be imagined). To gouge out an eye for an eye gouged is better than to take the life of the first offender; and to take the ox that has gored and put him to death is better than to put the owner of the ox to death. Even the regulations as to what flesh may be eaten and what may not, or as to when a man is "unclean," stand in a more favorable light. These latter regulations we may dislike or regard as limitations upon the free spirit of man. But we should also perceive that no society whatever is constituted until men share a sense of what they may and may not expect of each other. A set of fixed expectations like the Torah has the same merit that even emancipated persons of today find in the rules of etiquette. As soon as it is second nature for a young man to lift his hat to a woman or to open a door for her, or for a woman to say automatically as she leaves a party that she has had a good time, people are free of the burden of making certain choices. If a man had to think each time, he might be disinclined to lift his hat on certain occasions; and a woman might hesitate to say that she had enjoyed a party. But law and custom decide the matter; and if there is tyranny in custom—we feel this tyranny most keenly when we read of alien customs, as in the Pentateuch—there is also beneficence. In large areas of human relations the need for thought or choice does not arise.

In fact, analysis will show that ancient or modern attacks on legalism seldom express a desire to terminate all law and all custom. Instead, they object to the inclusion in the area of legally proscribed or directed activity what, in the opinion of the critic, ought to be the affair of the individual. The modern man who wishes to be "free" wishes to be free in most of his personal relations. He does not say so, but he counts on the continued protection of the laws against theft and violence. In religious history, we see the Quakers revolting against the formalism and ritual of older churches; *legalistic* forms of religion quenched what they called "the inner light," the power within us which effects a direct contact with God. But inspection of Quaker behavior indicates that in many areas of their lives these devout people rely on custom and law as much as do those whom they censure.

In this light, the body of Hebrew law can be regarded as more than a necessary evil. Though the law, as Jesus has it (*Matthew* 19:8), was given by the Lord because of the hardness of the Hebrew heart, it is nevertheless a good, relative to the indecision and tension of a society without law, without a common measure of good and bad. We tend to regard *Hebrew* law as bad because of its role in the story of prophecy and inspiration recorded in the Bible. Hosea, Ezekiel, Jesus, and Paul keep insisting, in opposition to priests and scribes and Pharisees, that in some areas of human experience law operates badly or not at all. How these areas are perceived by these teachers we shall see later. It is well to indicate that such areas do not coincide with those into which our friends move when they suddenly kick over the traces and determine to "be themselves." True, the prophets and Jesus and Paul are eager that people should be free of the law, should be themselves. But they wish to free the self from the law so that it can exist in another relation, not so that it can achieve (a frequent version today) a splendid isolation from all trammels whatsoever.

Hebrew law shares characteristics of law which we can observe elsewhere. It also has certain marks of its own. In our own casual experience, we are aware that some laws on American statute books were passed decades ago, and no one would dream of enforcing them today. We also know that certain laws concern outer trivial aspects of human relations and can be prudently ignored. Other laws concern matters of life and death, kindness and just dealing, and these exercise a superior compulsion on us. Similarly, some of the laws of Moses were framed with a nomadic society in view and could be safely forgotten by later, city-dwelling Hebrews. And one would imagine that dietary laws like those in *Leviticus,* Chapter 9, would yield precedence to the command to protect the "stranger within the gates": "Thou shalt neither vex a stranger, nor oppress him: for ye were strangers in the land of Egypt" (*Exodus* 22:21).

Another feature, doubtless stultifying to the spirit, which Hebrew law shares with all other codes of law is that a workable legal code must be more than the Ten Commandments or any other generalized set of precepts. We today say, "Circumstances alter cases," by which we really mean there is a gap between noble goals and the relating of them to specific human actions. Let a reader scan the passages regulating the punishments ensuing upon the actions of an ox (*Exodus* 21:28-32), the behavior of a man toward his servants (*Exodus* 21:20-21, 26-27), or the degree of responsibility a man has for the vows made by his womenfolk (*Numbers,* chap. 30). If the reader is not familiar with similar collections or if he has not looked into modern statute books, he will protest against the niggling distinctions or against the manifest cruelty inherent in a specific regulation. We learn, for example, that if a slave has married a woman slave, he may—when his bondage is over—go free without his wife or remain with his wife and serve the man who owns the wife (*Exodus* 21:1-6). We ask (and we receive no answer): What if the slave wishes to go free and take his wife with him? Yet any law code shows us that precept, however noble, must be watered down and doled out. Any collection of laws is a record of a kind of casuistry. The lawmakers must do more than contemplate the lofty ideals of their civilization; they must get down to *cases.* Thus, we see the makers of Hebrew law trying to foresee all the *possible* situations in which vows might be made, servitude ended, and oxen gored. But try as they might, they failed to exhaust the possibilities. Willfully or unwittingly, they overlooked the case of the slave who wishes to leave his master and take his wife with him. This is error, but it is the kind of error to which makers of law are congenitally subject.

A final feature of Hebrew law is specially characteristic of Hebrew culture though traces of it can be seen in our society when we hesitate to deal with a novel necessity unless we can find in the Constitution or in the speeches of Washington or Jefferson a go-ahead signal. To the Hebrews, Moses was *the* lawgiver, the sole vehicle of divine utterance in this direction. Therefore, all regulations in successive ages had to be attributed to him. The "Holiness Code" and the Deuteronomic Code, which was discovered as late as the time of King Josiah (621 B.C.), had to be linked up with Moses and Mount Sinai. We should be astounded if a modern jurist discovered in the

Constitution *specific* regulations governing air traffic or outlining building codes for a city like New York. (A jurist does not hesitate to link these new laws with what is called "the spirit of the Constitution.") The Hebrews were under the necessity of attributing laws necessitated by later conditions of society with the leader who tried to direct the behavior of a nomadic or wandering people. (See *Leviticus* 25:23-34 for examples of laws that can apply only to a settled people facing the problem of property ownership.) To us, it is transparent that the regulations for Temple worship apply to a formal temple, like that constructed by Solomon; they do not seem very relevant to worship in a tabernacle of skins that was moved from place to place in the wilderness. Further, because all laws must have the authority of Moses, within the limits of a few chapters one runs the gamut from laws reflecting the harsh, restrictive justice that goes back to Hammurabi to laws tempering justice with mercy. "Thou shalt not suffer a witch to live" is cheek by jowl with "Ye shall not afflict any widow or fatherless child" (*Exodus* 22:18, 22). Even within the limits of one law we find a startling mixture of high and low justice. The following regulation begins well, but it ends depressingly:

> And if a man smite his servant, or his maid, with a rod, and he die under his hand; he shall be surely punished. Notwithstanding, if he continue a day or two, he shall not be punished: for he is his money. (*Exodus* 21:20-21.)

That is, the servant is the property—the money—of the master, whose loss will be sufficiently grievous if he loses the labor of his disabled servant. This is, indeed, cold comfort to the injured servant.

These are considerations that aid a reader who turns back to the laws after he has grasped the Hebrew story in its entirety. Even he who does not choose to hesitate among the laws or return to them cannot read elsewhere in the Bible without remembering that the Torah was a dominating point of reference for the Hebrew imagination.

CHAPTER V

I and *II Samuel; I Kings* (to Chapter 12)

THE break made here between *Judges* and *I Samuel* is, like all such breaks, an artificial one. Contrasts that it permits us to make are true, but it minimizes the elements of continuity. Thus, in speaking of the greater firmness of the historical basis and the lesser role played by tradition of an oral origin, or in noting the advances in conception of "the Other" and of human personality, we are observing changes that should be observed. But they are not sudden changes, and they have their anticipations.

The books considered in this chapter cover a comparatively short period, 1080 to 922 B.C. They center on the activity of four men: the priest Samuel and the three kings Saul, David, and David's son, Solomon. (Dates given for the activity of Samuel are 1060-1010 B.C. The reigns of the three kings are given as follows: Saul, 1020-1000, David, 1000-960; and Solomon, 960-922.) This period, despite its brevity, struck the later Hebrew imagination as a glorious one. Did not the Hebrew tribes achieve their first and only unity under David, and was not Jerusalem under Solomon the equal of any pagan city? Future national consciousness could draw strength from these recollections, could look forward to a return of the glories of David and Solomon. That our own national consciousness is founded upon such uncritical recollections of the American past we can see by inspecting what the man in the street believes about the origin of our country. His story concerns the coming together of various peoples in the name of freedom, the crucial struggle that began in 1776, and the inspired framing of the Constitution. He believes that truly there were giants in those days, and he is annoyed with historians who try to reduce Washington and Jefferson to their actual stature. The early *Life of Washington* (1800) written by Parson Weems gave us an idealized Washington; for many years sober historians have labored to give us the "real" George Washington.

Strangely, the Hebrew accounts manage to do both tasks at once for the four great men they present. They give us a picture that, within idealized outlines, yet preserves bold strokes and precise details revealing in these men a mixture of courage and cowardice, nobility and pettiness. All this is, again, the effect of *palimpsest.* Our priestly editors are building their history out of earlier materials—oral traditions, cycles of narrative preserved by separate tribes, and court records. For reasons already suggested, they work

CHART 4. Events, *Samuel-I Kings*, Chapter 12

ISRAEL: THE UNITED KINGDOM		PHILISTIA AND OTHER KINGDOMS		SYRIA (THE ARAMEANS)	
1180-1013	Samuel	1080-1000	Philistine domination of the Hebrew tribes		
1020-1000	Saul's reign				
1000-1060	David's reign		David's victories over Philistia, Ammon, Moab, Edom, Hamath, Syria, etc.	1000	Aramean occupation of Syria
960-922	Solomon's reign	c. 970-936	Hiram of Tyre	c. 960	Aramean kingdom of Damascus
922	Division of the kingdom				

under a double burden as they labor to make one narrative out of several. They must be loyal to their idea of what God's hand has wrought by means of Samuel, David, and Solomon; but they cannot crudely alter the actual records.

In consequence, one reads best if, for example, he keeps one eye on David's ideal role, as founder of the Hebrew nation, and the other on what David's reported acts add up to: a man with flashes of generosity and moments of malice, a man with his full share of the heroic "virtues" of hating his enemies deeply and rewarding his friends largely. We must remember that David lived at a time not far distant from the sack of Troy, which is the subject of the *Iliad,* and we should not be startled at his displaying the illogical mixture of rashness and timidity to be observed in Achilles and the other heroes of Homer's poem.

The fusing of an idealized with an actual account we can see in the stories of Samuel and Solomon as well as in the story of David. Ideally, Samuel is the inspired servant of God, the last "judge," who wishes to lead the people by issuing a call to righteousness and not by a display of force. Ideally, Solomon is the consolidator of peace, the establisher of a godly prosperity, and the fount of Hebrew wisdom. Yet a careful reading shows that his "peace" was supported internally by the employment of alien mercenaries to keep in check the tribal disunity with which David had been plagued in his last years. The external supports of Solomon's "peace" were commercial treaties and marriage alliances with powerful nations. We may admit that it was a shrewdly contrived peace, but it disintegrated as soon as Solomon was dead (933 B.C.); from this point to the end of the story, we have the divided kingdoms: the ten tribes of "Israel" to the north, and the kingdom of Judah to the south. Further, Solomon's material prosperity can be regarded as the result of his calculation rather than of divine favor. His kingdom lacks seaports, it is poor in natural resources? Solomon gains a seaport of the Mediterranean thanks to the same Hiram of Tyre who provides builders for the Temple—his ignominious repayment consists of Hebrews exported as what we would call "slave labor" (*I Kings* 5:13-14). Solomon gains a seaport on the Red Sea, and the visit of the Queen of Sheba perhaps set up trade routes as well as provided that curious queen with answers to her "hard questions," since her people, the Sabeans, were a rising nation to the southeast. In fact, Solomon's prosperity is based on his performing the comparatively artificial role of middleman. He commands some already existent trade routes and invents others (e.g., from the Red Sea port of Eziongeber to Tyre); and he deals in "luxury articles," in "ivory, and apes, and peacocks" (*I Kings* 10:22). We may see, in Chapters 7 and 8 of *I Kings*, a glorification of Solomon as the godly institutor of the full, formalized worship of God in the Temple at Jerusalem—a worship already long set down in the laws of Moses but impracticable without a fixed center of worship. And yet the editors are forced to include details at odds with this ideal picture. For example, Solomon sets up shrines where his various wives may worship their own gods (*I Kings* 11:1-8); doubtless he had to promise such shrines before he could make his many profitable marriages.

This insistence of the continued effect of *palimpsest* is a necessary one, even though the careers of these figures offer an interwoven continuity rather than the effect of cycle noted in the "lives" of Abraham and Samson. Otherwise, we do not see the function of these narratives in the general collection of historical books; and we are likely to miss a subtle but important shift in the prevailing interest of the books as compared to earlier ones. There, in the materials orally created, the interest was in myth (accounts of origins), in the various sorts of mana displayed by heroes, and in the different forms of the deity's own mana. It is just to say that in the books now in hand myth and other earlier interests are in the process of being subordinated to historical fact. Certainly one feels the succession of the four great men is not cyclic—is not, that is, a series of happenings that would submit to being shifted into quite different sequences, as would the deeds of the patriarchs and their relation to each other. The career of each hero of *Samuel* presupposes the existence and achievements of the earlier men; furthermore, the achievements of each man's later career presuppose those of his former days. The narratives are factual also in the sense of being more circumstantial than many of the earlier cyclic tales. More subordinate figures are named, and journeys are more precisely traced (e.g., the course of David's flight from Absalom in *II Samuel,* Chapters 15 and 16).

We may suspect, then, a closer correspondence to fact, but fact still subordinated to something else. It is no longer subordinated to myth, to man's curiosity about how history began. It is subordinated to man's curiosity as to what history is; the events recounted are in the service of a *theory of history.* From now on, subtly or crudely, the facts of oral tradition and court narrative are viewed through the semi-opaque texture of what the Hebrew priests thought history to be.

But before we turn to this semi-opaque texture, we must make a further attempt to see what the Hebrew history *was*. The world in which the "twelve tribes" existed, during the century before and the century after 1000 B.C., was still very much the world faced by Moses and his successors. The Hebrews face societies culturally superior to them. (When Solomon wishes to build a great temple, he has to rely on the skill of foreign architects; and when he wishes to live in luxury proper to a monarch, he has to import foreign products.) In this period, the progressive decay of Egyptian power spares the Hebrews the necessity of undertaking a task that would still have been overwhelming to a new people, that of meeting the armies of the Egyptians. To face the armies of the allied Philistine kings was all Saul and David could manage. Nor, in this period, is the progressive growth of the Assyrian power to the north a real threat. That this danger was not more keenly present to the imaginations of the early recorders, who represented the Philistines and the Ammonites and Moabites as the real external threats to the emergence of the United Kingdom, was thanks to the temporary dike thrown up against the Assyrian flood by a lesser power to the north. This was the Syrian or Aramean kingdom; it usually appears in the Biblical story as an enemy, but it functions, if unconsciously, as a friend.

Consequently, in this light a study of the historical setting, now and in the period of the divided kingdoms, suggests that the creation of David's kingdom and the continued existence of the two kingdoms, Israel and Judah, following the kingdom of Solomon, is a kind of miracle, dependent on several "ifs." *If* Egypt had been strong enough to exert in this region the sort of energy she could still display in the days of Rameses II and Merneptah (and Moses), when she could halt the expansion of the Hittite empire . . . *If* Assyria had but collected enough power to rush across the retaining wall of the Aramean kingdom lying between her and the Hebrews . . . *If* the peoples whose lands constituted the immediate boundaries of the

Hebrew state, people like the Moabites and the Philistines, had but seen fit to make common cause against Saul and David and their upstart pretensions . . . But none of these things happened in the times we now consider, and David and Solomon were able to patch together an "empire" under sufferance. At its greatest extent, in the days of the "wisest king," it had tributary or commercial relations extending as far south as the Red Sea and as far north as the city of Tiphsah on the Euphrates. This territory was about three times as great as the stretch of land "from Dan to Beersheba," the traditional northern and southern limits of Hebrew control. That it was a jerry-built empire, based on fortuitous circumstances rather than thorough conquest and organization, is indicated by its rapid disintegration. The eighty years from the beginning of David's reign to the end of Solomon's is the peak of the Hebrews' material greatness.

What is of crucial importance for the history of Judaism and Christianity is that this "empire" lasted long enough to become a vivid memory, to suggest to future generations of Hebrews the permanent possibility of a state reconstructed on the models provided by David and Solomon. Hebrew groups quite unlike each other seized upon the glories of David and Solomon as warrant for their actions. Thus, the returned exiles (538 B.C. and onward) erected a theocratic state on ground lines that they judged David had laid down. About three centuries later (168 B.C. and onward) the militant Maccabees tried to set up a nationalistic state that, despite Greek and Roman power, should recover the dissipated glory of Solomon's realm. Even at so late a date as the present, the new state of Israel is haunted by what David and Solomon ideally achieved.

The real achievement of David and the three other "makers of Israel" may be suggested by a running summary of the shifting internal affairs. Throughout our period of history, these offer as great a threat as the power of outside nations. We can see, reading *Judges* thoughtfully, that what we have about the year 1100 is not the materials for a nation. It is, instead, a group of tribes more aware of their separate dignity than of the bonds of race, language, and past history—bonds that, in the eyes of the later priestly editors, ought to have united them. These tribes face common dangers from the Philistines and elsewhere, but their temporary unions dissolve when danger is past. Each tribe struggles for *its* foothold, quite often without much aid from its blood relations. We do, however, see two groupings: Judah to the south and, to the north, the unity composed by Ephraim and Manasseh, the tribes bearing the names of the two sons of Joseph. In fact, in all of *Judges,* the only story that indicates the existence of any strong sense of the previous value of each tribe to all the others is the startling one that concludes the collection. Here the exaction of vengeance for the outrage committed by the tribe of Benjamin is halted with the realization that Benjamin is, as well as greater tribes, a son in Israel; and no son of Israel must be allowed to perish (*Judges,* chap. 21). For this reason, wives are provided the remaining members of the tribe.

It was such a world that Samuel, the great priest, moved through on his judging circuits. Samuel views this world, as do the priestly editors, as not necessarily a *bad* world, for all its lack of political and military unity. There was danger from without, and there was danger from within; and—significantly enough—the danger from within that Samuel feared was not the lack of tribal unity but the Hebrews' persistent tendency to forget Jehovah and slip into the worship of the fertility gods who were, after all, the gods of the land, whereas Jehovah was a god of alien origin. Thus when old Eli accuses Samuel's mother of drunkenness, he is naturally supposing that she has been visiting some nearby temple of Ashtoreth where intoxication was part of the ceremonial (*I Samuel* 1:12-16). Likewise, the "fault" of Eli's sons that makes the old man accept their death may be traffic with the non-Yahwistic religions of the land (*I Samuel* 2:22 ff.). But there were many sanctuaries where the will of the Lord was made evident, and Samuel makes the tour of them, like a modern circuit judge. As the idealizing editors look back upon his day, it was a time when godliness was almost within man's grasp. The covenant of righteousness binding God and man was simple in statement and easy to execute. There was no king to consult: only God and his righteous emissary, Samuel (*I Samuel* 7:15-17).

All these idyllic conditions—if idyllic they were, rather than terribly insecure and unstable—are altered by the movement culminating in the activity of Saul. We are told that the people will to be as other people; they no longer desire to be "judged" by Samuel and others, and they ask for a king—a reasonable request from the point of view of *Realpolitik,* which would point out that the righteousness of a priest would not defend the tribes against the kings of Philistia and Edom. The priestly editors take a dim view of the request for a king (*I Samuel,* chaps. 8 and 10) and are careful to show Samuel anointing and then chiding the first king, King Saul. Samuel may no longer be the chief temporal authority in the land, but he holds God's power in his grasp. He is to Saul what Moses was to Pharaoh (*Exodus* 7:1)—"a god," or, as we would say, "in place of God."

However, it is Saul and David, and not Samuel, who meet the iron chariots and weapons of the Philistines and finally establish security; and they lead a people woefully unequal to their enemies. There was no smith in the land of Israel, and the Hebrews had to go down to Philistia to have implements sharpened. "So it came to pass in the day of battle, that there was neither sword nor spear found in the hand of any of the people that were with Saul and Jonathan: but with Saul and Jonathan his son was there found" (*I Samuel* 13:22). Yet Saul's efforts are presented in an unfriendly light. Doubtless this crude giant who did not want to rule and who "hid himself among the stuff" (*I Samuel* 10:22) was a far cry from the beautiful and poetic David; and Saul's later fits and his fear of David's threat to his royal power do not endear him to us. But we must remember that the priestly editors favored everything concerning the tribe of Judah, David's tribe, since only the tribe of Judah returned from Babylon and populated the theocratic state the editors lived in. Saul came from the recently disreputable and minor tribe of Benjamin. It is he, not David, who, in the eyes of the editors, bears the onus of being the first king and bringing to an end the period of the "judges"; and frequent clashes with the God-instructed Samuel fix him still more firmly in the role of a godless, proud man. (One of the clashes, at least, should win for Saul considerable sympathy. Samuel has, in God's name, demanded the total destruction of the Amalekites and all their possessions. When Saul modifies this command and saves cattle for sacrifice on the altar, Samuel's censure has a discordant sound, even though it contains a noble phrase that we shall later find in a better context: "Hath the Lord as great delight in burnt offerings and sacrifices, as in obeying the voice of the Lord? Behold, to obey is better than sacrifice, and to hearken than the fat of rams" [*I Samuel* 15:22].)

Nor should the similar Saul-David contrast conceal from us the fact that David suffered under the same necessities endured by Saul. Though anointed by Samuel when that priest is out of love with Saul and though a member of an important tribe, David also has to cut and turn, as the narratives illustrate fully. To survive Saul's enmity, David has to live as an outlaw who "shakes down" local magnates in return for "protection" (*I Samuel* 25:1-10); he marries with political intent (*I Samuel* 25:43-44; *II Samuel* 3:2-5); he has to take refuge in a hostile Philistine city and lulls suspicion there by feigning madness and concealing the intent of his small-scale military activities (*I Samuel* 21:10-15; 27:5-12). Only the natural suspicions of some Philistines relieve him from the embarrassment of marching to the final battle against Saul (*I Samuel,* chap. 29).

David's own period of active warfare is capped by his seizure of Jerusalem, until then in the possession of the "friendly" Jebusites. Middle and old age quickly set in. As we can observe in the Anglo-Saxon poem *Beowulf,* heroes fight dragons in their youth or their old age; they seldom have middle years. David's declining years offer him little enjoyment in return for his early hardships. Consider this catalogue: the suppression of Saul's followers and the securing of the throne for David (*II Samuel,* chaps. 3-9); the conquests that establish his kingdom as an empire (*II Samuel,* chaps. 8 and 10); his unrighteous pursuit of Bathsheba (*II Samuel,* chaps. 10 and 11); the revolt of his son Absalom, who is supported by Judean forces that may have felt David did not favor his own tribe sufficiently

(*II Samuel,* chaps. 13-19); the disastrous "numbering" of the tribes and the related purchase of the Temple site from a Jebusite (*II Samuel,* chap. 24); and the ignoble intrigues among the sons of David to achieve the succession to the throne (*I Kings,* chaps. 1 and 2). All this does not compose a particularly glorious picture. And the picture is rich in details ignored by later celebrators of the glorious David, "ruddy, and withal of a beautiful countenance, and goodly to look at" (*I Samuel* 16:12). As in the time of *Judges,* a man's first loyalty is his special tribe, and there are few traces of what we today would call nationalism. In the name of Judah, Absalom has no trouble stirring up revolt against his father, and the name of Israel can easily rouse the northern tribes to disaffection (*II Samuel,* chap. 20).

It is not necessary to point out how Solomon's struggle to win power and keep it offers a continued picture of the same uneasy unity. Solomon as a king of united Israel is suspected by his own tribe (Judah) of making too many concessions to win the support of the northern tribes; but his concessions to tribes not his own are never, as the activities of Jeroboam suggest, handsome enough (*I Kings* 11:26 ff.). This revolutionary is supported by Egypt in his exile, along with an Edomite who promises to be useful against Solomon. (A third "adversary" of Solomon's is Rezon of Damascus in Syria. Of him, *I Kings* 11:25 says: "And he was an adversary to Israel all the days of Solomon, . . . and he abhorred Israel, and reigned over Syria." He ruled the people that, during the time of the divided kingdoms, frequently invade and yet also ward off direct Assyrian invasion.)

With all this in mind, we do not find odd the quick and final breakup after Solomon's death. The tribes, coerced into unity by Saul, dazzled into sustaining unity (as our narratives would like to have it) by the beauty of David and the magnificence of Solomon, soon respond to their "natural" centrifugal impulses. But these impulses have been kept in abeyance long enough for an ideal to be set up—an ideal in part unreal yet quite haunting. It is the image of a united Israel, one that can be thrown on the screen of the temporal future, as with the Maccabees, or on the screen of eternity when, in Christian speculation, "the city of David" merges imperceptibly with "the city of God."

Kingship

Two elements of the theory of history begin to take the place of an interest in origins and sheer mana and preside over the compilation of these books. They are theories, as usual, presented *in action* rather than abstractly stated. First, there is the change in the attitude toward kingship. Second, there are significant alterations in the conception of "the Other" implied by the stories.

Hebrew kingship was, in its world, an institution in a class by itself. This cannot be stressed too much. The kings of Sumer and Accad and the kings of Egypt were divine beings, and their deaths were regarded as crushing catastrophes. When a king fell in battle, the battle was over; and the peaceful death of a king was decently concealed, or it was euphemized as in a mass underground burial at Ur which surrounded a dead ruler with drugged but still living courtiers. A still more ornate euphemism for burial was the magnificent preparation for the ruler's existence beyond death. In these cultures the king, as the living God, was naturally the chief celebrant of religious ceremonials.

It is not strange that traces of this concept of kingship appear in our books. David dances in priest-king fashion before the returning Ark, and we are told that Michal, David's first wife, looked on him and "despised him in her heart" (*II Samuel* 6:16). (Does this enigmatic phrase mean that she is a follower of the priest Samuel and rejects the concepts of kingship common in other lands?) A similar accent appears in the sanctification of the Temple and the part Solomon plays in the ceremony (*I Kings,* chap. 8). But these scanty traces offset the quite different picture of kingship that prevails in Hebrew record. Here is neither the divine king of old Egypt nor the king who, many centuries later, ruled "by divine right" in seventeenth-century Stuart England. Instead, we find a limited monarchy.

True, it is not limited by popularly elected legislators. It is limited by the will of God as revealed to a selected priest or prophet.

Two narratives in *Samuel* have to do with the inception of kingship. One suggests that it is a positive evil. The people ask Samuel for a king, and he seeks to dissuade them by describing the plight of peoples who are in fact ruled by a king. The Hebrews' sons will be taken to be the king's warriors and charioteers; the Hebrews' fields will become the king's fields; there will be a tithe of all produce to support the king and his officers. Samuel concludes his warning: ". . . ye shall be his servants. And ye shall cry out in that day because of your king which ye shall have chosen you; and the Lord will not hear you in that day" (*I Samuel* 8:17-18). The king the Hebrew people will receive will resemble, in his display and use of power, the priest-kings of neighboring peoples who are answerable to no one but themselves. Instead of a righteous "judge" they choose a ruler. Samuel speaks to the people concerning himself:

> Behold, here I am: witness against me before the Lord, and before his anointed: whose ox have I taken? or whose ass have I taken? or whom have I defrauded? whom have I oppressed? or of whose hand have I received any bribe to blind mine eyes therewith? and I will restore it you. (*I Samuel* 12:3.)

Despite this root and branch rejection of kingship, another narrative suggests that a king in Israel can be regarded as a qualified good, though it would be better if the people did not desire that good and were satisfied with the greater good they already possess, the sure guide to righteousness they have in a person like Samuel. He says of Saul:

> Now, therefore, behold the king whom ye have chosen, and whom ye have desired! and, behold, the Lord hath set a king over you. If ye will fear the Lord, and serve him, and obey his voice, and not rebel against the commandment of the Lord, then shall both ye and also the king that reigneth over you continue following the Lord your God. (*I Samuel* 12:13-14.)

A covenant can still be sustained, although the ideal conditions therefor have been rejected by the people. Samuel concludes:

> Only fear the Lord, and serve him in truth with all your heart: for consider how great things he hath done for you. But if ye shall still do wickedly, ye shall be consumed, both ye and your king. (*I Samuel* 12:24-25.)

". . . both ye and your king." This passage sets down very clear specifications about kingship. Plainly, a king is acceptable to God on the same basis that his people remain acceptable to him. The king is good so long as he submits himself to a measure of good and evil external to his own will. What is that measure? The standard of righteousness which, in theory, guided the separate tribes in the times of the "judges." No Hebrew king who wishes his supply of divine support, of effective mana, to continue may ignore this instruction.

The practical result of the denial of divinity and automatic righteousness to a king is important for the rest of the Hebrew-Christian story. Samuel—whatever the positive limitations of his own actual character which the stories of proud, arbitrary action allow us to suspect—is the first of a long chain of priests who differ from the chief priests at Egyptian or Mesopotamian temples. The lives of such priests were bound up with the performance of the rites of their special cult; they lived to enjoy the perquisites of their position. The Bible tells us of several priests who fill their offices differently. Each major Hebrew king has bracketed with him a priest or a prophet. Even the wicked Ahab seems to recognize as an inescapable fact the presence of Elijah, his stern monitor, when he says: "Hast thou found me, O mine enemy?" (*I Kings* 21:20). Sometimes, as in the story which concerns Samuel's anger with Saul for preserving the Amalekite cattle, we may feel that the priest is defending his own dignity rather than a high principle, but at many other times we see the king being brought to heel by a priest who is concerned with moral principle. Nathan is quick to declare to David the heinousness of David's liquidation of the husband of his new mistress Bathsheba, even though the man is not a Hebrew but a Hittite—a circumstance worth noting. David says to Nathan's long and pointed rebuke only one sentence: "I have sinned against the

Lord" (*II Samuel* 12:13). Thus, in terms of action, we see the principle of righteousness being regarded not as purely Hebrew but as something that can be insisted upon in all relations among all peoples.

Another mark of the demotion of the Hebrew king from the august position occupied by his peers elsewhere appears in a later story. When King Hezekiah of Judah requires an answer from the Lord, he does not, as might a priest-king, receive it direct. After he has spread a perplexing letter out for the Lord to read, he receives an answer—but it comes from the priest-prophet, Isaiah (*II Kings* 19:14-20).

In conclusion, it is easy to suspect abuses of priestly power in these distant times. Further, it is easy to suspect how happy the priestly editors were to preserve narratives that represented their class as occupying the absolutely central position in society. But we cannot ignore the much more important fact that kingship as it existed in Israel was a new thing in the ancient world and that the king was always regarded, despite his august position, as a limited, fallible being, subject to the very correction to which his people also bowed. Higher than the people and the king were principles of right dealing.

Whatever the causes, the king was shorn of his divinity and was given instead the demanding task of living and governing in accord with moral principles that had some of the divinity he had lost. These principles were an expression of the will of an entity who was regarded as indeed "other" and beyond the flaws of character and the dangers actually to be seen in the career of any king. This circumstance at least clears the way for the activity of the prophets in times to come (850 B.C. and onward). The prophets might risk punishment when they spoke out, but they were not challenging the very structure of Hebrew religion and society when they did so, as similar critics would in other civilizations of the time. The priests and prophets enjoyed, in fact, the privilege that had been denied the king—the privilege of speaking for Jehovah.

The "Other"

We have said that nowhere in our story are we to erect barriers and say *before* and *after.* This is certainly so in whatever we are able to observe in *Samuel* and *Kings* about changes in man's conception of deity and relation to deity. David is instructed by the Lord not to start fighting the Philistines until he hears "the sound of a going in the tops of the mulberry trees" (*II Samuel* 5:24). Saul feels himself bound to slay his son Jonathan because Jonathan has gone against a vow Saul has made to the Lord (*I Samuel,* chap. 14).

But there are two new emphases. They do not cancel insights that continue from earlier times, but they certainly begin to predominate over the earlier conceptions of Jehovah's operations. The first emphasis dwells on the close link between God's power and God's justice; the activity of God is thought to display the equal yoking of the two, as in the tale of God's protest against David's treatment of Uriah the Hittite (*II Samuel,* chaps. 11 and 12).

The second emphasis represents a shift in the conception of how God is related to his creatures. The equation, for a good many of the earlier narratives, can be stated thus: God takes cognizance of the special hero or tribe that has won his favor or lost it. This attitude receives classic expression in the self-definition God offers Moses: "I will be gracious to whom I will be gracious, and will shew mercy on whom I will shew mercy" (*Exodus* 33:19). That the conception has already been questioned in terms of action, we know. We recall Abraham's censure of the automatic destruction of *everyone* in Sodom and Gomorrah (*Genesis* 18:16-33). It is an element in Moses' casting his lot with the people rather than with the angry god who intends to be avenged upon the worshipers of the golden calf (*Exodus* 33:31-32). But these gestures are exceptions to the predominant accent of the older stories, where, indeed, not so much the hero's own destiny is being decided when he exerts his share of mana as the destiny of the entire tribe to which he belongs. Thus, when Jacob wrestles with the "man" at the ford, he wins not only for himself but, in effect, for his people a new name, Israel (*Genesis* 32:28). But now the exceptional becomes the rule—or, at least, is in process of becoming the rule. The king, the "successor" to Jacob, is no longer divine, and his possession of power does not free him from censure. Further, he is not *the* representative of his people; the "luck of the Hebrews" does not necessarily lie in what he does.

Naturally related to this shift is the growth of the view that God is a respecter of persons rather than an omnibus endorser of tribes or nations. Marks of this growing interest in *all* human beings on deity's part is the brief but often vivid and unforgettable depiction of the minor figures in the story of David. When Saul's daughter Michal is taken away from her second husband to be returned to David, we have this moving detail: "And her husband went with her along weeping behind her to Bahurim. Then said Abner unto him, Go, return. And he returned" (*II Samuel* 3:16). When David is fleeing from his rebellious son Absalom, he is vexed by a follower of Saul, Shimei, who throws rocks and curses David by saying: "Come out, come out, thou bloody man, and thou man of Belial" (*II Samuel* 16:7). The historical narrative can take time, a little later, to tell us of Shimei's discomfort when David is again secure (*II Samuel* 19:16-23). David's captain Joab, Absalom, Ahithophel the plotter. . . . One can make a fairly long catalogue of names that belong to persons, to human beings individually presented. This list is long enough to suggest that an important consequence of moving from a god of the nation to a god capable of judging individuals was an increased sensitivity on the part of the historians. They had discovered–not as a concept but as an emotion–"the infinite importance of the individual." This concept we today believe is one of the chief marks of the "American way."

To be sure, to the very end of Hebrew history such all-embracing phrases as "the people have gone awhoring after strange gods" persist. They are part of the historians' mental furnishings. But added to this older stock is the newer one we are defining: Jehovah is interested in the activity of the individual in and for itself, and individual activity has individual consequences rather than tribal consequences.

True, this insight is one more of those perceptions taken today as self-evident platitudes but actually arrived at by slow, painful stages. How was it that the Hebrews were moved to make this shift?

First, because of the very concept of kingship just analyzed. If a king is not automatically a god (or godhead on earth) his actions are subject to the very kind of scrutiny that Nathan brought to bear on David's adultery: David is not above a standard of justice *external* to him, nor is Ahab in a later age. That standard of justice exists in the will of God or in the interpretations of that will by God's chosen priest. If the king is, in some sense, the god, his actions are right simply because they have been performed. Similarly, if the hero's destiny is the tribal destiny, there are kinds of scrutiny that the hero's behavior will escape. For example, Jacob, by cheating Esau, founds the fortunes of *all* who succeed him. His act is not subject to censure; it has succeeded and by that token comes from God. But David and all the kings after him are neither gods nor the tribe. They are less than either, and what they do—since they are importantly placed—must be assessed. From this act of assessment, carried out in terms of narrative rather than of detached ethical analysis such as we find in Plutarch's *Parallel Lives of Famous Greeks and Romans,* certain concepts begin to grow. We now judge these concepts as self-evident. Today, none of us supposes there is any possibility of confusing what we are and do individually with what is done by the collectivities to which we belong, the family or the nation. Thus, individual Germans who, in 1945, heard about the Nazi concentration camps did not feel a deep guilt for what was done there. Germans do indeed feel responsible—as might we, under similar circumstances—for crimes they have committed as individuals; but they feel they escape judgment for the large-scale activities of the group to which they belong. Our own attitude toward a shocking deed committed by a relative is analogous. We deplore it, certainly; but we do not feel that *our* individuality is hopelessly involved. Instead, we can recover our self-esteem and pursue whatever ideal goals we have set before ourselves.

Another advantage accrues to us, the readers of the Bible, from this altered view of the human being flowing from the central perception that deity is righteous rather than arbitrary and tends to set up relations with individuals rather than with peoples. As we read of Saul and David, we seem to be in the presence of personality, a limited and individual set of marks that enables us to distinguish sharply between one person and another. The priest-kings of Babylonia, Assyria, and Egypt are known to us by means of inscriptions in temples, on cliffs, on public monuments, and in formal records, where the achievements of each ruler are treated as though they were earthly manifestations of divinity. What these priest-kings were as human beings we do not see very clearly. The divinity hedging in a king builds a high barrier that we cannot see over, except to observe the ruler of Egypt or the king of Assyria moving about with the pose proper to public ceremonial or battle. They are like the commanding figures of our own time whom we view only on public occasions or in picture magazines and newsreels. Only certain favorable and august aspects of the characters of our great men reach us. Consequently, it is shocking to read the memoirs of an intimate of some great modern person and realize what he was when he had his slippers on and relaxed with his advisers and friends; the details are at odds with our previous view. What the Pharaohs and kings of Babylon and Assyria were like when they had their slippers on we shall never know. Records which adulate a ruler who was a god do not let us see anything but the living deity; there is a calculated and monotonous display of greatness.

But Hebrew record shows us that, even to the court historians, Saul and David were no divinities. They were passionate human beings, capable of generosity and faithfulness but subject, even as we, to moods of malice and vanity. Can one imagine, in a record devoted to telling of a priest-king, the sort of details that enliven the story of David? David has vowed he will not harm two persons whom he regards as his enemies: his general, Joab, and Shimei the Benjamite. On his deathbed, he instructs Solomon to do away with these two. With an almost incredible effect of malice, David says of Joab: "Do therefore according to thy wisdom, and let not his hoar head go down to the grave in peace." He varies the formula for Shimei; these are the dying father's last words to his son: "Now therefore hold him not guiltless: for thou art a wise man, and knowest what thou oughtest to do unto him; but his hoar head bring thou down to the grave with blood" (*I Kings* 2:6, 9).

The great man, the saying has it, is no hero to his valet. Hebrew history is an early expression of this important insight. In consequence, Saul and David are persons rather than monumental figures carved in granite. To most of us the sacrifice of hieratic majesty is a slight one to make for what we get in return: David the outlaw thirsting for water from Bethlehem but refusing to drink it because three men have brought it to him "in jeopardy of their lives" (*II Samuel* 23:17); David lamenting the death of the son who has given his father every reason to hate him:

> And the king was much moved, and went up to the chamber over the gate, and wept: and as he went, thus he said, O my son Absalom, my son, my son Absalom! would God I had died for thee, O Absalom, my son, my son! (*II Samuel* 18:33.)

This flexibility and variety of presentation give these narratives their continued power over believer and agnostic alike. Time and again, though the presentation is brief, we are forced to admit: "This is true. This is how it must have happened." We do not mean "happened" in a literal sense but as we say it when we are struck by an incident in a great novel. The incident in *Vanity Fair* that tells of the unexpected return of Rawdon Crawley and his discovery of his wife Becky in the company of Lord Steyne has intrinsic vigor and truth. The stories of Saul and David abound in the same vigor and truth. In the experience therein the choice and emotions of the individual occupy the foreground. To be sure, we can ignore the likelihood that such an attitude toward human experience is a consequence of altered attitude toward "the Other." Yet, though we may not agree that a shift in man's idea of deity was the cause of this excellence, we can at least agree that until each being is thought of as having a separate, assessable destiny, personality as we understand it does not exist.

The shifts from a god of power and caprice to a god of power and justice and from a god of a people to a god who has attention for persons as well as collective people have consequences extending beyond our present horizon. What is here revealed in terms of action becomes the chief stock in trade of that modified form of action, prophetic thought—prophetic thought which, in its assertions and aspirations, will be discussed in Chapters X and XI.

CHAPTER VI

The Divided Kingdoms: *I Kings* (Chapter 12) Through *II Kings*

THE remainder of *I Kings* and all of *II Kings* form a unit suitable for consideration. But this section of the books of history is much less a unity than the books just treated. The story that begins with Samuel and ends with Solomon and his glory has a continuous movement, for what we see is the material for a drama if not a drama. It would be an ambiguous drama, to be sure; for we do not know whether to judge the movement that culminates in Solomon's kingdom as sheer triumph or qualified triumph. But we do have a strong sense of the interdependence of the events related.

Such an interdependence is less easy to sense in the section we now take up, for several reasons. The chief one is that there is no longer any political or economic unity behind the events related. In *I Kings*, Chapter 12, this section begins in an atmosphere of confusion and disunity that, if accidentally, sets the tone for all that follows. The northern ten tribes, under the leadership of Jeroboam, have come to Shechem to sue Solomon's son for some relaxation of his father's "yoke." Rehoboam's answer is not conciliatory: "And now whereas my father did lade you with a heavy yoke, I will add to your yoke: my father hath chastised you with whips, but I will chastise you with scorpions" (*I Kings* 12:11). The northern tribes ask, "What portion have we in David?" and they make Jeroboam their king. As the narrative the editors seem to be using has it: "So Israel rebelled against the house of David to this day" (*I Kings* 12:19). This rebellion is straightway signalized by activity that sets the pattern for northern religion: Jeroboam says, "It is too much for you to go up to Jerusalem," and he sets up two calves of gold, makes a "house of high places," and makes "priests of the lowest of the people, which were not of the sons of Levi" (*II Kings* 12:25-31).

CHART 5. Events, *Kings*

ISRAEL		JUDAH	
922-901	Jeroboam I	922-915	Rehoboam
901-900	Nadab	915-913	Abijam
900-877	Baasha	913-873	Asa
877-876	Elah		
876	Zimri (rebel)		
876-869	Omri: founder of a new dynasty, the house of Omri 880 Omri's conquest of Moab		
869-850	Ahab: activity of Elijah 854, 853, 850 Three wars with the Arameans c. 853 Ahab and Benhadad II of Syria allies against the Assyrians in Battle of Karkar	873-849	Jehoshaphat
850-849	Ahaziah		
849-842	Joram: activity of Elisha Battles with Benhadad II of Syria	849-842	Jehoram: married to Ahab's daughter Athaliah
842-815	Jehu: founder of new dynasty 841 Jehu a payer of tribute to Shalmaneser III of Assyria	842	Ahaziah
		842-837	Athaliah, daughter of Ahab of Israel
		837-800	Joash, son of Ahaziah
815-801	Jehoahaz		
801-786	Joash	800-783	Amaziah
786-746	Jeroboam II 760 The prophet Amos 750-735 The prophet Hosea	783-742	Azariah (Uzziah)
		750-735	Jotham
746-745	Zechariah		
745	Shallum (rebel)		
745-738	Menahem c. 738 Menahem pays tribute to Tiglath-pileser of Assyria (Pul)		
		735-715	Ahaz: treaties with Tiglath-pileser of Assyria
738-737	Pekahiah		
737-732	Pekah (rebel) 734 Syria and Israel against Judah		
732-724	Hoshea: placed on throne by Assyria		
722	Sargon captures Samaria		

CHART 5. Events, *Kings*—*(continued)*

EGYPT		SYRIA (ET AL.)		ASSYRIA	
945-745	Sheshonk I: campaign against Israel and Judah c. 918				
		900	Benhadad I of Syria wages war against Israel		
				884-859	Ashurnazirpal commences to draw near to Hebrew territory
				859-824	Shalmaneser III of Assyria
				853	Battle of Karkar
		850	Mesha of Moab revolts against house of Omri		
		844-804	Hazael of Damascus wars against Israel and Judah	c. 841	Shalmaneser makes his fourth campaign against Damascus: Jehu's tribute
				745-727	Tiglath-pileser III
		734	League with Israel against Judah	738	Western campaign: Menahem of Israel pays tribute
		732	Fall of Damascus	733-732	Campaign against the west
				727-722	Shalmaneser V
				722-705	Sargon of Assyria

CHART 5. Events, *Kings—(continued)*

EGYPT		JUDAH		ASSYRIA		BABYLONIA	
		715-687	Hezekiah c. 701 Sennacherib at Jerusalem	705-681	Sennacherib	722-710	Merodach-Baladan of Babylon struggles to conquer Assyria; embassy to Hezekiah c. 711
663	Destruction of Thebes by Ashurbanipal	687-642	Manasseh	681-669	Esarhaddon		
				669-626	Ashurbanipal		
		638	Amon				
		640-609	Josiah 622 Discovery of the law in the Temple 609 Battle of Megiddo: death of Josiah	612	Fall of Assyria to Babylonians	626-605	Nabopolassar of Babylon founds the Chaldean kingdom
605	Defeat of Necho by the Babylonians at Carchemish					605	Babylon defeats Necho of Egypt at Carchemish
		609	Jehoahaz				
						605-562	Nebuchadrezzar
		609-598	Jehoiakim: enthroned by Necho				
		598	Jehoiachin: taken into captivity by Nebuchadrezzar				
		598-587	Zedekiah: enthroned by Nebuchadrezzar				
		587	Destruction of Jerusalem				
		561	Release of Jehoiachin by Evil-Merodach			562-560	Evil-Merodach

Thus, he effectively detaches his tribes from Judah, which is left to go its way alone and, very often, ignominiously. (This is a division that had been promised Solomon for going after other gods. That one tribe remains for Rehoboam to rule signifies God's favor to David and Jerusalem [*I Kings* 11:9-13].)

Historically viewed, this separation is a result of a centrifugal tendency that Saul, David, and Solomon combated with some success; but they did not suppress it. The United Kingdom becomes, for good and all, the two kingdoms. The Northern Kingdom, variously called Israel or Ephraim, has its capital first at Shechem, where Jacob had hidden earrings beneath an oak (*Genesis* 35:4) and Joshua had delivered his final address (*Joshua,* chap. 24), and later at Samaria, which was built (*c.* 870 B.C.) by the founder of a new northern dynasty, Omri, on purchased land (*I Kings* 16:24). This kingdom, with territory that began only a little north of Jerusalem itself, had important sacred places, including Bethel where Jacob had had his vision of the ladder and set up a stone altar (*Genesis* 28:19-22), and Shiloh, where Joshua had set up the tabernacle (*Joshua* 18:1) and Samuel had been dedicated to the service of the Lord (*I Samuel*, chaps. 1-3).

To the south is Judah, with the prestige of its holy city, Jerusalem, supported by less ancient traditions than those surrounding the northern shrines, and with geographic and political handicaps that soon made themselves felt. The land of Judah is rugged and less productive than the land of Israel, which included some productive plains, like that of Jezreel where Naboth had his vineyard. Israel acted as a barrier to the north and could easily disrupt the trade routes which Solomon had set up. Some of this is pathetically indicated in a brief reference to conditions in the reign of the Judean Jehoshaphat who lived about seventy years after the death of Solomon: "Jehoshaphat made ships of Tharshish to go to Ophir for gold: but they went not; for the ships were broken at Eziongeber." The disunity of the two kingdoms, to their mutual harm, is indicated by the following: "Then said Ahaziah the son of Ahab [a Northern king] unto Jehoshaphat, Let my servants go with thy servants in the ships. But Jehoshaphat would not" (*I Kings* 22:48-49). When another king of Judah, Amaziah, challenges a Northern king to battle, this king's answer shows that in the hundred years since the times of Ahaziah and Jehoshaphat relations between the two kingdoms have deteriorated. The Northern king replies by using an insulting parable:

> The thistle that was in Lebanon sent to the cedar that was in Lebanon, saying, Give thy daughter to my son to wife: and there passed by a wild beast that was in Lebanon, and trode down the thistle. (*II Kings* 14:9.)

The Northern king drives his point home to his inferior brother:

> Thou hast indeed smitten Edom and thine heart hath lifted thee up: glory of this, and tarry at home: for why shouldest thou meddle to thy hurt, that thou shouldest fall, even thou, and Judah with thee? (*II Kings* 14:10.)

Sometimes Judah is Israel's ally, and sometimes Judah is Israel's enemy. But in either instance, she holds the short end of the stick. The daughter of Ahab, Athaliah, has married the king of Judah; upon the death of her son, when her position is threatened she does not hesitate to seize power and holds it for several years (*II Kings*, chap. 11). We hear of a king of Judah supporting a king of Israel against Syria and having the bad luck to be involved in the purge of the house of Omri by Jehu; in vain does he flee "by way of the garden house" (*II Kings* 9:27). And we detect not brotherhood but petty power politics in the triple alliance involving Judah with Israel and Edom in a campaign against Moab (*II Kings*, chap. 3). The alliance suggests, behind the bare narratives of *Kings*, the cold opportunism by which, in past centuries, large European countries varied their "commitments" to maintain the "balance of power." In *Kings*, it is very plain that it is Israel which rigs the balance; Judah can only watch her moves with apprehension. One of the worst of these was an alliance with Syria against Judah; it was as if France should make an alliance with Germany to invade Belgium (*II Kings*, chap. 16).

It is not strange, in the light of this, that the division between the two countries was deep, even though they shared a language and a god. The division lasted for more than two hundred years, until the fall of the Northern Kingdom to Assyria (722 B.C.); and it did not provide readily useful materials for the later historians. It provided, in fact, two stories of two nations; out of these the later historians labor to make one story: of God's persisting relation with his one, chosen people. Yet the materials in *Kings* testify to the fact that there are only occasional points of contact in the narrative of the prosperous and proud Israel to the north, prosperous because she is able to continue some of the policies of alliance by marriage and commerce that had made Solomon prosperous, and the narrative of the impoverished and dependent Judah to the south.

These two stories—in substance the sort of court records that contributed to the history of Saul and David—are combined rather awkwardly. The two most obvious editorial methods are splicing or weaving together, and pointing up by direct editorial comment. The last editors were by inclination pro-Judean since Judah was the one tribe that survived the waves of conquest and was able to come back and set up a theocratic state. One would expect the weaving together of the older histories to accrue to the credit of the Southern Kingdom, as does indeed the constant and rather bald commentary. But here the editors ran into a difficulty. Apparently the court records of the prosperous Northern Kingdom were at many points full and explicit, whereas the records of the subordinate Southern state were bare and meager. A rough estimate shows that the proportion of Israel narrative to Judah narrative is three to one. Therefore, though the machinery of the compilation is an effort to keep the lives of Northern and Southern kings running evenly, careful reading shows that the historians are not always able to offer much specific about the reigns of the Southern kings they list. It almost seems as if they are reduced, in trying to fill out their record, to a dependence on chronicles of kings whom they dislike. Jeroboam I (922-901), Omri (876-869), Ahab (869-850), Jehu (842-815), Jeroboam II (785-745)—these are the justly famous names of the two kingdom narratives up to the time of the Assyrian conquest of the Northern Kingdom in 722 B.C., and these men are all Northern kings. As noted, the most famous set of events in the south concerns a resistance to the rule of a queen of Northern origin, Athaliah.

The method of parallel narrative is unable to establish the preëminence of Judah in the period 933-722 B.C. The method of recurrent editorial comment on the religious contrast between the two kingdoms endeavors to put Judah in a good light. The comments strike us as naïve and not strictly in accord with the facts, but their use is quite understandable. The priests choose to make out that Judah, if inferior in other respects, has during these two centuries the preëminence of godliness. The suggestion is that Judah, through these years, has worshiped Jehovah faithfully and has not bowed down to the old abominations of the "people of the land." To create this impression is the intent of the monotonous summary comments on the Northern kings and the Southern kings. Each king of Israel wins a comment like this one on Omri: "But Omri wrought evil in the eyes of the Lord, and did worse than all that were before him. For he walked in all the way of Jeroboam the son of Nebat, and in his sin wherewith he made Israel to sin, to provoke the Lord God of Israel to anger with their vanities" (*I Kings* 16:25-26). The judgment on his son Ahab is not a precise judgment; it is a recurrent formula. After Ahab's specific faults are listed—and they are many—the comment rolls forth: Ahab "did more to provoke the Lord God of Israel to anger than all the kings of Israel that were before him" (*I Kings* 16:33). This persistent bias explains the distressing neglect of the reign of Jeroboam II (786-746), who won a temporary glory and prosperity to which both the prophets Amos and Hosea testify. He "departed not from the sins of Jeroboam the son of Nebat"; the less godly can consult "the chronicles of the kings of Israel" if they wish to trace his material prosperity—chronicles that apparently were discarded after the editors of *Kings* had done their work.

The kings of Judah, who occupy so little space and who appear usually when the Northern king summons them to aid him in battle (e.g., Jehoshaphat's support of Ahab, *I Kings,* chap. 22) are tendered a brief testimonial of which King Asa's is a model. When Asa destroys his mother's idol, this comment is added: "But the high places were not removed: nevertheless Asa's heart was perfect with the Lord all his days" (*I Kings* 15:14). A similar good case is made out for his son Jehoshaphat, who "walked in all the ways of Asa his father; he turned not aside from it, doing that which was right in the eyes of the Lord: nevertheless, the high places were not taken away; for the people offered and burnt incense yet in the high places" (*I Kings* 22:43). Of Joash of Judah and his son Amaziah, and his grandson Azariah (783-742) the same comments are made. Perhaps record was too brief to allow the priests to see the degree of perfection. One suspects that lack of knowledge was filled by this line of reasoning: Judah alone of all the tribes has survived; her kings must have been godly, even though evidence points to the persistence of idolatry in their days.

The transparent bias of the editors is patent when they face a king they feel called upon to censure: Ahaz (735-715), who had dealings with Assyria to defend his kingdom against the coalition of Israel and Syria and who sent back from Damascus the plan of a heathen altar. What is the explanation of his defection from the qualified righteousness of his fathers? What kept him from doing what "was right in the sight of the Lord his God, like David his father"? This is the answer, as the writers of *Kings* see it:

> But he walked in the way of the kings of Israel, yea, and made his son to pass through the fire, according to the abominations of the heathen, whom the Lord cast out from before the children of Israel. And he sacrificed and burnt incense in the high places, and on the hills, and under every green tree. (*II Kings* 16:3.)

Actually, the spiritual adultery of the Northern Kingdom was matched by the spiritual adultery of the Southern, and this from the time of Solomon himself, who was more than tolerant of foreign cults (*I Kings* 11:1-10). When the religious life of the Southern Kingdom undergoes a real housecleaning, under Hezekiah and Josiah, there is a very full stock of abominations. Hezekiah's "purge" is brief enough to quote:

> He removed the high places, and brake the images, and cut down the groves, and brake in pieces the brazen serpent that Moses had made: for unto those days the children of Israel did burn incense to it. . . . (*II Kings* 18:4.)

Josiah's destruction of cults that had been restored or added by Hezekiah's wicked son Manasseh (*II Kings*, chap. 21) occupies many verses (*II Kings* 23:3-14) and amounts to a kind of museum exhibit of ancient belief; present and worshiped in Jerusalem were Baal, the sun, the moon, the planets, and "all the host of heaven."

The books of *Kings*, in their present form, offer us the effect of *palimpsest* in the sense defined in the *Genesis* discussion. One must grasp (as we have just done) what the theocratic editors wished to see and what the narratives they drew on provided them with. On one hand, though much more lamely than in the Samuel-Solomon narratives, we have an ideal version of the history of the two kingdoms. On the other hand, we are able to see quite clearly that the old records do not support this partisan view. What happened in one kingdom happened in the other. The contrasts between them are not those of religion and culture. They reveal the military and political inferiority of Judah, but indicate no great religious superiority.

The actual course of the narrative hints at a state of affairs in Judah that the editors gloss over. It accords with what historical and archaeological research suggests about these two hundred years. We suspect the existence, in Judah, of a considerable practice of polytheism, with Jehovah, at the best, only a "first among equals." Nor is the political situation admirable; both kingdoms exist on "borrowed time." Israel survives until her sometime friend, sometime enemy to the north, Syria, finally goes under the Assyrian flood (732 B.C.). Judah survives a century and a half more, but only by the skin of its teeth. It plays a diplomatic game stigmatized, often quite rightly, by the prophets Isaiah and Jeremiah as useless to avert disaster. Ahaz of Judah plays the same game after the fall of Syria when he goes to Damascus to curry favor with Tiglath-pileser of Assyria (*II Kings* 16:10), and it is a mysterious disaster that keeps Jerusalem from falling before the Assyrian besiegers during the reign of Ahaz' son, Hezekiah (*II Kings* 19:35-37)—a disaster attributed by the old record to "the angel of the Lord" and by modern students to a plague. A century later King Josiah (640-609) tries to play off the rising power of Babylon against the waning power of Assyria and its ally, an enfeebled Egypt, and Josiah "has his reward" when he goes up to Megiddo to oppose the Egyptians on their way north to aid the Assyrians. The wrath of the Assyrians for the devious Judean diplomatic "line" does not descend, but simply because the Babylonian empire has just crushed Assyria (612 B.C.). But this happy event offers Judah a respite of only twenty years, and, as we shall see when we turn to the story of the prophet Jeremiah, Judah uses the interval to seek the help of the "hollow reed," Egypt. In the year 587, Babylon ceases to toy with anything but total submission, and Judah is destroyed. From the spectacle of destruction which terminates *II Kings,* the priestly editors can draw but this cold comfort: Jehoiachin, the next to last king of Judah, is "lifted up" from his Babylonian dungeon and given new garments and decent food (*II Kings* 25:27-30).

Thus, viewed unemotionally, the story of the two kingdoms ends in disaster; it is unlikely to have a continuation. We know that history is full of the "rise and fall" of great empires that have left no large mark on the memory of later men. It is worth emphasizing that, when we deal with the rise of the United Kingdom and the falls of the two kingdoms, we are not dealing with empire on a grand scale but with the total destruction of two petty kingdoms. That this unimportant disaster could have a sequel—that those who felt they preserved the traditions we have been studying were able to produce a literature and continue the cult of Jehovah is at least not a frequent follow-up to total destruction. Indeed, in *II Kings,* Chapter 17, we see that the great conquering nations like Assyria had a definite colonial policy toward the peoples they took over. Holy places were razed, and the people themselves were taken from the regions to which they had religious attachment and were transplanted to till strange, distant fields. Plainly, the theory behind this treatment was that the conquered would cease to be troublesome as soon as they were torn from their god and his local base. This—to all effects—was what *did* happen to the people of the Northern Kingdom. Despite legend which locates them in various places in the world as far apart as Japan and England, they sank without a trace into the welter of tongues and races living in the Fertile Crescent.

That this did not also happen to the people of the Southern Kingdom can be explained, but it should not be accepted complacently. These Hebrews were not dependent upon the continuance of a royal house; they no longer believed their deity was fixed in his existence upon a certain hill or stretch of land; they looked to wise men for instruction in the law that they were able to take into exile with them. All these factors favored the rise of a new institution to take the place of the ruined Temple of Solomon: the synagogue—"the gathering of the people." Here wise men and prophets could rise up and remind the Hebrews "weeping by the waters of Babylon" of past glories under David and Solomon and could promise future glories under some imagined leader.

Thus the external relations of the two kingdoms to the world they existed in. Their internal life exhibits several qualities. One, already mentioned, is the tolerance, in north *and* south, of expedient worship of alien and old local gods. Ahab's worship of the Sidonian Baal is an aspect of his marriage to Jezebel, and when Jehu revolts against Ahab's son, the worshipers of Baal are destroyed for political rather than religious reasons. We read how, after all the images associated with the house of Omri and Ahab have been shattered, reform stops short:

> Howbeit from the sins of Jeroboam the son of Nebat, who made Israel to sin, Jehu departed not from after them, to wit, the golden calves that were in Bethel, and that were in Dan. (*II Kings* 10:29.)

We read also how Ahab's elder son Ahaziah has a serious fall, is sick, and sends outside the boundaries of his own kingdom to inquire of Baal-zebub, the god of Ekron, a Philistine city (*II Kings* 1:2). This story is practically told in reverse when a highly placed Syrian, Naaman, comes to Elisha to be cured by Elisha's god. That such shifting of religious allegiance was normal in Elisha's time appears in Elisha's acceptance of the fact that Naaman must continue to worship in "the house of Rimmon," the Syrian god (*II Kings,* chap. 5). In short, throughout this part of the world, the general feeling was that there was no use risking the anger of a god whose cult was popular; even more, there was no use risking the anger of people who worshiped a god other than Jehovah.

The political history of the more prosperous Northern Kingdom is spectacular and bloody and gives some color to the priestly view of God's dislike for Jeroboam and all who sit in his throne. They sit there as often by right of conquest and palace revolution as by right of descent. It is often captains of the king's army who, like the leaders of the later Roman Praetorian Guard, take over the name as well as the reality of power. The succession of such upheavals is often swift. Zimri ousts the legitimate king (876 B.C.), and is immediately ousted by another captain, Omri. The house of Omri, which includes Ahab and his two sons, Ahaziah and Joram, lasts almost thirty-five years (876-842 B.C.) until there is another break in orderly succession. This time it is Jehu, a captain of the host, who is nerved by Elisha to put a godless house out of power (*II Kings*, chap. 9), but Jehu and his successors are as faithless as his predecessors. The house of Jehu, however, holds its position for a century (842-745 B.C.), and one of the kings—Jeroboam II (786-746 B.C.)—recovers territories that had long been lost to Israel and Judah (*II Kings* 14:28). But this Jeroboam's son, Zachariah, is slain by Shallum, Shallum is slain by Menahem, and Menahem's son Pekahiah is slain by his captain Pekah. Thus ends, or almost ends, a house-that-Jack-built sequence. The last ruler of Israel slays his predecessor, Pekah, but he is spared death at the hand of a fellow Hebrew by the king of Assyria, who shuts him up in prison and conquers his country (722 B.C.).

This must suffice for the Northern Kingdom, with the exception of the concluding section of this chapter, which concerns prophetic activity and its impact on the house of Omri. The story of the Southern Kingdom, despite the manifest similarities to the story of the Northern Kingdom, does offer also striking divergences that, in part, justify the all-over view of the two kingdoms taken by the priests. We have noted the pious general statements with which almost every King of Judah is laid to rest; and although unworthy or unpopular kings are occasionally put out of the way (*II Kings* 12:20; 14:19-20; 21:23), there is no real break in the succession from the son of Solomon to the last days, when Zedekiah (598-587 B.C.) occupies the throne after his nephew Jehoiachin has been carried away to Babylon. The kings previous to the fall of the Northern Kingdom (722 B.C.) are relatively undistinguished, despite the kind words the editors wreathe about the memory of each one. But the four whose lives cover the seventh century—Hezekiah, Manasseh, Amon, and Josiah—preside over events and developments hardly less important than the achievements of David and Solomon. Hezekiah, a "good king," was notable less for himself than for his association with the prophet Isaiah. In the first place, Isaiah, a man of the order of Samuel and Nathan, did not hesitate to demand that his king live up to the will of God. Both king and prophet had seen the startling disappearance of the kingdom to the north and could regard the event as a signal payment for religious evils that were common in Judah as well. To turn aside the wrath of the Lord—and the armies of Sennacherib that were the "rod" expressing that wrath—the cults of other gods were driven out (*II Kings* 18:4). For the first time, if we read our records carefully, we see the god of the Hebrews ceasing to be one among many.

That this was a startling innovation, as startling as were the reforms of the Pharaoh Ikhnaton in Egypt centuries before, the following reigns of Manasseh and Amon indicate. Hezekiah's son, Manasseh (687-642 B.C.), restored all the altars his father had destroyed, added other cults to them—perhaps with the intent of currying favor with hostile neighbors—and "made his son to pass through the fire" (*II Kings* 21:6). Manasseh's activities are the "cause" of the final fall of Judah; so grievous are they that not even the actions of his virtuous grandson Josiah move Jehovah to retrieve his curse:

> Behold, I am bringing such evil upon Jerusalem and Judah, that whosoever heareth of it, both his ears shall tingle. And I will stretch over Jerusalem the line of Samaria, and the plummet of the house of Ahab: and I will wipe Jerusalem as a man wipeth a dish, wiping it, and turning it upside down. And I will forsake the remnant of mine inheritance, and deliver them into the hand of their enemies; and they shall become a prey and a spoil to all their enemies; because they have done that which was evil in my sight, and have provoked me to anger, since the day their fathers came forth out of Egypt, even unto this day. (*II Kings* 21:12-15.)

The "line of Samaria" is the line of utter destruction. It is this curse—a curse not completely fulfilled since the Lord finally did not "forsake the remnant of mine inheritance"—that won for Manasseh his evil reputation and made him a byword for spiritual adultery.

But, important for us, we can observe, in the alternation between the monotheism that Isaiah and Hezekiah enforced and the polytheism and the amalgamation of foreign and native cults that Manasseh worked toward, an example of one of the descriptive religious "laws" phrased in Chapter III of this guide—religion offers us no straight-line sequences of growth, or very few. More frequently, we can see the creation of new forms and ideas, and then a circling back to earlier forms. Only later, in the time of Josiah, after Manasseh and his son Amon have done their evil work, do we see a return to the attitudes that Isaiah and Hezekiah tried to enforce. In the history of religion all is not gain—nor is all loss.

Josiah, whose political maneuvers led to his death at Megiddo (*II Kings* 23:29), renewed the reforms of his great-grandfather, and even more definitely than that ruler centered Temple worship at Jerusalem. It is not cynical but merely realistic to note that by now the old holy places to the north—Bethel, Shiloh, and Samaria the city —were in the hands of the composite "impure" people who were the sons of the few Hebrews the Assyrians had left behind and the new alien populations they had brought in. At these northern shrines descendants of the Hebrew priests brought back to placate the lions of the region might still officiate. But in the eyes of Josiah—and in the eyes of most Hebrews for hundreds of years to come—the cult of Jehovah as practiced in Samaria was hopelessly corrupt, and a Samaritan was looked on with as much suspicion as if he were an outright worshiper of Moloch. (This attitude persists into New Testament times and gives point to the story of the "good Samaritan" [*Luke* 10:30 ff.] who, although a member of a despised sect, befriends the hapless traveler whom the "correct" priest and Levite have passed by.)

Josiah did more than merely center Temple worship at Jerusalem. He gave it a richer content, if we judge that the books "found" during the repair of the Temple (*II Kings* 22:8 ff.) are a creation of his own century and not of Moses' distant era. So viewed, this code, the Deuteronomic Code, appears as an accumulation of the prophetic insights of the last century and a half, woven together with the legal regulations that settled, complex patterns of life necessitate.

Whatever the true account of this book, we can regard Josiah and his actions motivated by the discovery of the book as sources of benefit to the people who were soon to undergo defeat and exile. The exiled generations (597-538 B.C.) had more than the memory of a local deity to take with them to Babylon. In addition to the combination of the Northern and Southern versions of the Hebrew past, by this time fused into one history, they could take with them a code testifying that *their* deity, unlike some Babylonian deities with whom they would come in contact, was concerned with righteousness as well as power.

The First Prophets

The twenty years of disintegration and disaster that followed upon the death of Josiah (608-586 B.C.) is summarily stated in *II Kings*, Chapters 23-25; and we can study this period most profitably by turning to the career of the prophet Jeremiah. But before we leave the interwoven and compromised accounts of *Kings*, we must direct our attention to a kind of activity in these books that is so intense and sustained as to deserve the term "a new thing." Here too, the "new thing"—Hebrew prophetic activity—turns out to be a little less than new. It is a deepening and conscious orienting of an activity we have already seen in Samuel's career. We can draw no harsh lines between the rebuking of their kings by Samuel and Nathan and the rebuking of Ahab by Elijah for taking over the vineyard of Naboth.

Nevertheless, students of Biblical history see the activity of the two men, Elijah (876-850 B.C.) and Elisha (850 and onward)—and of the prophetic schools of the time and minor figures who stand in the background, like Micaiah son of Imlah (*I Kings*, chap. 22)—as a fresh and even novel departure. Those who say "fresh" judge that Elijah and Elisha, in the resistance they offer to Baal and other popular gods of the region, are but recalling the Northern Kingdom to recollection of the one god whom Abraham and Moses in time past worshiped. They are but laboring to revive a memory obscured by many centuries of tolerant living among the gods of the Palestinian region. On the other hand, students who say "novel" consider the teaching of Elijah and Elisha an utterly new thing and suppose that until their day Jehovah had never been regarded by his worshipers as more than a very powerful god—the special protector of the Hebrews—among many other powerful gods. So viewed, worship of Jehovah did not make it safe to neglect the gods that had made the Philistines and Tyrians mighty peoples.

Whether these two prophets returned to an earlier concept that had been languishing unnoticed (the god of Moses) or created a new monotheistic concept which was later projected back to the times of Moses and Abraham is a question not to be decisively answered. That the monotheistic idea existed in Egypt in the general period to which Moses is assigned is a fact. Certainly the priestly historians regard Elijah as a reviver of older views rather than the innovator of an utterly new idea. Whatever view we may take, this minimum agreement is possible: In the career of Elijah is the inception of an activity—prophetic activity—that arises when a man judges his lips to have been touched by the hand of the one true God, with the shattering consequence that the man owes no deference to any authority, not to the king or the nation, nor to an established priesthood, be it of Jehovah himself.

Thus, the prophet, like his prototypes Samuel and Nathan, often seems to be an arrogant man. This judgment is tempered only if we comprehend his precise conviction: that he is being arrogant for something outside himself, the will of God. At least, we can observe as a characteristic mark of all the prophets an alternation of attitude: intransigent pride when they speak for God and utter abasement and timidity when they judge they speak in their own persons. After Elijah has had his triumph over the priests of Baal, mana or a sense of God's support deserts him utterly. He fears for his life, flees to the wilderness, sits under a juniper tree, and laments: "It is enough; now, O Lord, take away my life; for I am not better than my fathers" (*I Kings* 19:4).

The narratives showing us the two early prophets in action—

rather than speculating, as do some later prophets—remind us of several important things. First, our own impression of what a prophet is, though that impression is really the end product of the very activity we here begin to scrutinize, does not give us a very clear idea of how various the activity of early prophets was. Thanks to the greatest of the prophets—Amos, Hosea, Isaiah, and Ezekiel—prophecy means one of two things to us. It means the foretelling of events that are going to happen in the near future. (The sixteenth-century prophet Nostradamus had a revival of popularity among us during World War II; certain of his rhymed verses seemed to apply to the outcome of the war.) It also means—and more importantly—utterance with reference to certain *constants* (as mathematicians would say) in all human experience; it asserts the permanent truth of certain moral and religious insights. Hebrew prophecy has claim on our attention chiefly in this sense. That Isaiah foretold the fall of Babylon seemed to the ancient Hebrews impressive. But from where we stand, Babylon has fallen and cities more mighty than she. What we look to the Hebrew prophets for, the reason we can still read much prophecy with attention, is that they were concerned with the *conditions* under which a people prosper or perish. The prophets, it is true, were obsessively concerned with the chosen of God. But ever since, what they have said of the chosen of God has seemed to apply to other national destinies. American pioneers took the Bible with them, and to their pious (and energetic) hearts the prophets spoke direct. And even in our generation, a sophisticated historian like Toynbee does not find Isaiah on the fall of Tyre inapposite.

This power to predict is the claim of ancient prophecy on our imagination. But this is prophecy purified and dominated by one or two impulses. In the activity of Elijah and Elisha we see "prophecy" as a mixed thing and including activities that we no longer link with prophecy at all. Indeed, we might have trouble in finding a link between the magical feats of Elijah and the "still small voice" that follows upon the wind, earthquake, and fire (*II Kings* 19:11-12).

But a link there is, and it is mana. Elijah is a man marked out for God's favor; in whatever he undertakes, that favor will be displayed. To us, some of Elijah's deeds have almost no connection with his chief task: to establish for his generation the oneness of God, or his superiority to Baal. But in their own day and for centuries thereafter, the variegated deeds of Elijah and Elisha were "proofs" that the two men bore the perilous gift of God's favor; they carried the "iniquity of holy things" (*Exodus* 28:38) and were the dispensers of God's material gifts like full jars of oil and rain in due season, as well as God's wisdom. In this light, even the startling incident in which the offended Elisha curses the children who mock his baldness and seems to summon the "two she bears" who come out of the wood and tear the children to pieces shows to the Hebrew audience, if not to us, the sacredness and the power of God's selected vehicle. The children's mockery has called forth the display of mana (*II Kings* 2:23-24).

Lumped together for a moment, the careers of the two men show feats which display some sort of power beyond ordinary human capacity. The following list is not exhaustive. Elijah has great physical power; he runs from Mount Carmel to the king's city faster than the king's horses can draw the king's chariot (*I Kings* 18:44-46). Both prophets have the power to bring back a dead child to life; we should note that this does not lie simply in the utterance of a word but depends upon a proper use of magical gesture (*I Kings* 17:8-24; *II Kings,* chap 4). Elisha is able to recover—"magically"—a precious axhead and make it float upon water (*II Kings* 6:1-8). His conveyance of power to King Joash to defeat Syria in battle depends upon the king's proper performance of his share in a spell; Elisha is angry with Joash because the latter hits the ground with the bundle of arrows not six times (the proper number) but only three (*II Kings* 13:14-19). Elijah's power extends to all that he touches or possesses; his gift of his mantle to Elisha his successor is not a merely touching gesture, as it would be with us. Elijah's power, or part of it, lies in the garment itself; and the canny Elisha proves this to his own satisfaction by smiting the waters of the Jordan and challenging the Lord to manifest himself with the question: "Where is the Lord God of Elijah?" When the waters part, he is convinced of the mantle's value, just as, immediately after, his followers institute a three-day search to be sure that Elijah was actually taken up into heaven in a chariot of fire (*II Kings* 2:12-18).

Much closer to our own ideas about prophecy than all this display of power in almost any activity undertaken are three poses particularly clear in the life of the older prophet: Elijah's resistance to the worship of Baal, his exposure of injustice in high places, and his power to foretell. In the magnificent contest with the priests of Baal —a contest heightened for those who hear, as they read *I Kings,* Chapter 18, the wild music of Mendelssohn's *Elijah*—we are seeing an exhibit of mana that is, unlike some of the others just mentioned, a display not for the sake of trivial advantage but for the sake of a principle. That the drenched altar blazes at Elijah's command is an *action* establishing what later prophets are content to express verbally: only God exists and only God is holy. The pendant to this incident, moving but less dramatic, comes when Elijah flees to his juniper tree and has the important revelation earlier noted. He discovers the voice of God not in the many displays of sound and power that had once been final signs for Moses and his followers about Mount Sinai. God speaks to Elijah in a still, small voice.

This perception is a moment in Hebrew history much more important than the magnificence of the material triumph on Mount Carmel. That triumph was, after all, an assertion of power. This moment amounts to an assertion about the nature and quality of "the Other." It is as crucial, in the Hebrew-Christian experience, as Abraham's questioning of the deity angry with the wicked cities of the plain (*Genesis* 18:16-33) and as the words that Moses heard from the Lord: "I am that I am" (*Exodus* 3:14). It is, this still small voice, a further refinement upon early presentations of deity in narrative confines. Fire and earthquake and thunder—these once were the awesome accompaniments of God's utterance. But thanks to Elijah's insight, many of the prophets who succeed him can dispense with such displays; they will need only the warrant of a voice to accept a novel conception of deity and the revisions of old habits of thought which the deity may urge upon them. (This does not mean—since religion moves in circles or spirals to create its effects—that the earlier concomitants of divine utterance are gone. Consider but Ezekiel's encounter with deity more than 250 years later; the "wonders" of the Lord return in rich and complicated panoply [*Ezekiel,* chaps. 1-3].)

Finally, this event now in question should have strong interest both for the believer and for the agnostic student of cultures. To the believer, it is a record of a closer approach to the deity he feels himself still in contact with. To the agnostic student of cultures, it marks a definite stage in the growth of the set of ideas that is an important element in the equation called culture-history, an equation he is trying to understand. The agnostic may question the ultimate truth of the set of ideas to which Elijah contributes, but he does not deny that this body of doctrine is an important element in the collection of ideas that guide modern man. He does not doubt, to be specific, that Elijah's "still small voice" is related to what believer and agnostic alike refer to as conscience, that inward commentator upon our outward actions which we all judge we bear with us.

It is this moment that gives Elijah preëminence over Elisha. Elisha, we see, occupies a secure position of much dignity and little danger. The worship of the Lord has been reëstablished, the king seeks out the prophet for charms and predictions, and the prophet has about him a group of younger men who wish to learn the various aspects of his art. Elijah is an outlander from Gilead across the Jordan; he is in constant danger of arrest and death; he speaks to a civilization that does not want to be moved from its comfortable compromises in religion; he speaks to a king who does not want to be reminded just how he has come into the possession of Naboth's vineyard (*I Kings,* chap 21). He is not only Ahab's "enemy"; he is the enemy of the entire society which he addresses, whereas Elisha is its good, stern friend.

This contrast in fortunes would suggest that there is much justice in the circumstance that it is Elijah who is singled out for the special favor of being carried direct to heaven. Elisha—though his corpse manifests singular powers (*II Kings* 13:21)—was doubtless consigned to Sheol along with the rest of mankind, obscure and great. Only Elijah, along with Enoch, had the early pleasure of walking with God.[1]

[1] Our discussion of early Hebrew prophecy has said nothing of the roving bands of prophets whom Saul twice encounters (*I Samuel* 10:10; 19:18-24). Apparently these "prophets" were ill organized and capable of generating mass hysteria. Since they were not readily distinguishable from the poor and social malcontents, they won for prophecy a bad name. "Is Saul also among the prophets?" is a jeering question. It is a bad name or suspicion that prophecy, as a matter of fact, never shakes loose. A prophet seldom speaks unless he wishes to attack some aspect of things as they are. Whatever his particular motives, he is a dangerous, suspect man. Prophets like Elisha, and Hezekiah's guide, Isaiah, occupy a fixed and comfortable social position. That they are in the minority we shall see in the chapters on prophecy. The career of Jeremiah is the career of the prophet *par excellence,* and it has its links with the earlier one of Elijah.

CHAPTER VII

I and *II Chronicles, Ezra,* and *Nehemiah*

IT HAS been said that the only history is "contemporary history." One of the meanings of this statement is that what we see in past history is determined in part by the society we happen to be living in. If it is a democratic society, we look on the past to discover the first stirrings of democracy. We look on the Roman Republic with admiration, though it was hardly a republic in our sense of the word; and we lament the changes that set in at the time of Julius Caesar and Octavius Augustus, shortly before the birth of Christ. On the other hand, historians who write within the confines of a fascistic society will produce a different account; they will see the emergence of Caesar and other Roman "strong men" as a warrant for the existence of the modern dictator-state. Thus a democratically oriented account of Rome and a totalitarian-oriented account will offer many divergences. The two groups of modern historians will share the same body of facts, but it is their own position that suggests what to make of these facts. (Here in our own country, different reports of the American past are offered in southern and in northern schools.)

This consideration must be kept in mind as we seek to explain the existence, in the Bible, of a work of history which retraces hastily the whole stretch of history from Adam to the event of the return from the Babylonian exile. *I* and *II Chronicles* and their continuation and completion in *Ezra* and *Nehemiah,* which tell of the actual return to Jerusalem in the century following 538 B.C., lack the innate vigor and attractiveness of the other books of history we have read. At a few points, as in the account of Nehemiah's secret and nocturnal survey of the ruined city of Jerusalem (*Nehemiah* 2:9-16) and the narrative of the hazardous rebuilding of the city walls (*Nehemiah,* chaps. 4 and 6), occur passages which are the peers of more famous stories in the other books. But from the point of view of liveliness and compulsive force, these three books often have a death-in-life air. The respect with which David is treated in *I Chronicles* results in the suppression of the great king's humanity, and David tends to become a hieratic figure assuming a bas-relief pose proper to the reception of tribute or the direction of an extensive realm.

CHART 6. Events, *Ezra* and *Nehemiah*

EGYPT		ISRAEL		PERSIA	
		538	Return of exiles under Sheshbazzar	538	Cyrus takes Babylon
		538	Altar for burnt offerings rebuilt: foundations for Temple laid	530-522	Cambyses
525	Cambyses of Persia takes Egypt	520-516	The rebuilding of the Temple	521-486	Darius I 490 War against the Greeks
				486-465	Xerxes I 480 War against the Greeks
		458	Return of exiles under leadership of Ezra	465-424	Artaxerxes I
				424-423	Xerxes II
		444-432	Nehemiah's first and second visits	423-404	Darius II
				404-358	Artaxerxes II

For this reason, many readers pass by these books. *Chronicles* seems, and is, a less compelling account of events traced elsewhere; the reconstruction of Jerusalem in *Ezra* and *Nehemiah* is immersed in the sort of legalism, particularism, and ritualism which the Hebrew prophets (among others) have taught us to look on with suspicion. Nevertheless, these books, along with *The Antiquities of the Jews* by the Jewish historian Josephus (37?-95 A.D.), are our sources for a long period of time (538-168 B.C.) that did a great deal to shape later Jewish and Christian culture. In *Ezra* and *Nehemiah* we see the first steps toward the setting up of a Jewish theocratic state. This state lasted, in some form, until the time of the

Maccabees (167 B.C.), and it gave Jewish custom and worship the forms that we encounter in the New Testament.

Before the long dark intermission separating Nehemiah in his last appearance (433 B.C.) from the blaze of day that bursts on us with the opening chapter of *I Maccabees* in the Apocrypha, we can guess from the attitudes of Ezra and Nehemiah, and still more from the tone of *Chronicles* itself, the kind of world that is hidden from us. It is the world in which the Pentateuch and the other books of history quickly took shape (500-400 B.C.); and in it was intensified the legalistic and ritual emphasis of Hebrew religion that, centuries later, Jesus and Paul were constrained to modify and then shatter. It is a period during which the priests and their circles were deciding what Judaism should be and—particularly important for us—how much of the past should filter through to succeeding ages. For these reasons, at least, many a reader will find *Chronicles* and its completing books curious and instructive.

These three books, directly and indirectly, tell us of a kind of society that, in Hebrew history, had scarcely existed before. When the Hebrews first entered Canaan, they were a people with little past or tradition; in this region, by conquest, labor, and trade, they created a tradition and a past. By sword and plowshare and by devious diplomacy, they built a kingdom and then sustained two kingdoms, all under adverse circumstances. For about six centuries, they faced the future with energy if not with wisdom and prudence. Their history, from Saul to Josiah (609 B.C.), testifies to animal vitality. By the time of the conquest of Cyrus (538 B.C.), this vitality was only a wavering flame. Ten northern tribes had disappeared, and so might Judah, the only remaining one. Therefore, when the "remnant" is allowed to return to Jerusalem under Sheshbazzar, a Jewish prince, the Hebrew people are altered. They no longer hope to expand; they wish only to survive. In the small territory assigned to them around Jerusalem they face a future devoid of the promise that Saul and David could see. Persia is a "universal state," and there is no likelihood of carving out another Judah that shall reach from the Red Sea to the Euphrates. In the last three books of history, we can see the Hebrews making a virtue of their necessity. They have been chosen for a special, confined destiny? Well and good. They will set up a state where only descendants of pure blood can live and enter the Temple for worship. In that Temple, it is clear, the Hebrews will worship the *status quo* as well as Jehovah. They will "freeze" their society into one that is ruled by God and God's direct representatives—as, supposedly, were the twelve tribes in the times of the "judges." We can see Ezra and Nehemiah working to peg Hebrew civilization at a certain point; the duty of succeeding generations will be only to keep it there.

Weighing the value of their efforts, we need not conclude that we like the framework Ezra and Nehemiah set up, for it is legalistic and particularist, through and through. But we can do these two leaders the justice of seeing that their solution was almost the only one to the grim problem they faced. They enjoyed the temporary favor of the Persian ruler, Artaxerxes I (465-424 B.C.), and they had to build a society that would not lose them his favor. (Some scholars judge Ezra's return took place under Artaxerxes II, *c.* 397 B.C.)

One may say that the favor of the Persian ruler is assured by a form of government entirely subordinate to the cult of the Hebrew deity. Any foreign observer, at the end of the fourth century, after the work of Ezra and Nehemiah was done, would probably see that all the remaining Hebrew energy went into the ornamenting of the Temple and the elaborate performance of the Temple ceremonies—ceremonies which took up the time of many men. There would be almost nothing to lend color, at a time shortly after the return from exile, to the hints to the Persian ruler that the Hebrews have military ambitions (*Ezra,* chaps. 5 and 6). Moreover, the same stroke—the subordination of all social forms to the direction and the spirit of the Temple—assures the Hebrew people the favor of God.

It is the assumption of Ezra and Nehemiah that the groundlines of the righteous state are laid out in the sacred books of Moses brought back from exile. Once those lines are planned and built on, they need never be altered. The laws of God and the laws of Temple worship are not expected to, in our phrase, "evolve" into something different. Unlike our custom and law, Hebrew custom and law is here thought of as having been given once and for all. It is the function of Ezra to explain and interpret the law, but not to add to it:

> For Ezra had prepared his heart to seek the law of the Lord, and to do it, and to teach in Israel statutes and judgments. (*Ezra* 7:10.)

On a certain day, after due preparations, the people were gathered together, and the leaders–Nehemiah the governor, Ezra the priest and scribe, and others–brought out the books of law and "read in the book in the law of God distinctly, and gave the sense, and caused them to understand the reading" (*Nehemiah* 8:8).

Shortly after this, the work of Ezra and Nehemiah was finished. Their work of restoration had taken a century (537-433 B.C.). It was one thing for "Isaiah II" to greet the coming Cyrus with song: "Every valley shall be exalted, and every mountain and hill shall be made low: and the crooked shall be made straight, and the rough places plain . . ." (*Isaiah* 40:4), and for the first Isaiah to promise of a Hebrew Messiah, the root of Jesse, that it "shall stand for an ensign of the people; to it shall the Gentiles seek . . ." (*Isaiah* 11:10). The Jerusalem that the exiles straggled back to was no glorious city. It was a mass of fortifications and houses in rubble. Hardly less disturbing to Hebrew eyes was the social chaos of the territory, where Hebrews married with the "people of the land" and where, in Samaria near at hand, Jehovah was worshiped in improper fashion by the "impure" descendants of people who had been brought in 150 years before by the Assyrian ruler, Esarhaddon, to fill up the space left by the deportation of the Northern tribes. One might say that the Hebrews took one long look at their confused environment and "settled for" much less than what the prophets had promised them. For several centuries they put away the idea of a triumphant leader who should restore the boundaries of David's and Solomon's empire. Even more significant, they chose to ignore what several prophets had said about burnt offerings. Hosea had represented the Lord as saying: "For I desired mercy, and not sacrifice; and the knowledge of God more than burnt offerings" (*Hosea* 6:6). A Psalm which may or may not antedate the return from Babylon says still more fully:

> For thou desirest not sacrifice; else would I give it: thou delightest not in burnt offering. The sacrifices of God are a broken spirit: a broken and a contrite heart, O God, thou wilt not despise. (*Psalms* 51:16-17.)

The possibilities of material glory and of a religion with an emphasis on interior attitude were both ignored.

Instead, by slow and painful steps the Hebrews restored their city; the events now summarized go very far toward explaining why they lost sight of the various ideal realities their prophets had spoken of. The Hebrews return (*Ezra*, chap. 1). A simple altar is set up (chap. 3), and the foundations of the Temple are laid. Then the "adversaries," people who judge that their worship of Jehovah is as good as the Hebrews', seek to join in the worship. The Hebrew leader, Zerubbabel, replies: "Ye have nothing to do with us to build an house unto our God . . ." (*Ezra* 4:3). Their response is not surprising:

> Then the people of the land weakened the hands of the people of Judah, and troubled them in building, and hired counsellors against them, to frustrate their purpose, all the days of Cyrus king of Persia, even until the reign of Darius king of Persia. (*Ezra* 4:4-5.)

Then, under the stimulus of two prophets, Haggai and Zechariah, Zerubbabel sees to it that the Temple is completed (520-516 B.C.). After this, it would seem, there is a complete halt until the arrival (458 B.C.) of Ezra, "a ready scribe in the law of Moses" (*Ezra* 7:6), who comes at the head of a considerable group of exiles. Ezra takes one look around him and demands a reformation that is shocking to us but also comprehensible: All Hebrews of pure blood must put away their wives and children of impure lineage. True, the scandal is great, and Ezra describes his feelings: "And when I heard this thing, I rent my garment and my mantle, and plucked off the hair of my head and of my beard, and sat down astonied" (*Ezra* 9:3).

Ezra makes the safety of the "remnant" depend on the establishment of Hebrew exclusiveness. A subsequent chapter (chap. 10) records his rigor and success in pushing this reform through.

A little later (444 B.C.) a governor rather than a priest imposes the same kind of destiny. Aside from his important work of rebuilding the walls of the city, he sets up Temple services (*Nehemiah,* chap. 8) and constrains the assembled people to "enter" "into a curse, and into an oath" (*Nehemiah* 10:29) to observe the regulations that Nehemiah puts before them: strict obedience to the regulations of law and Temple worship, avoidance of "mixed marriages," and abstinence from labor and trade on the Sabbath (*Nehemiah* 10:29-39). While the fortifications are being repaired, Nehemiah has occasion to censure Hebrew usury (*Nehemiah,* chap. 5), but when he returns in later years (432 B.C.), it is the violation of the precise oaths that stirs his anger and not the oppression of "the hireling in his wages, the widow, and the fatherless," which is what disturbs Malachi, a prophet of this general period (*Malachi* 3:5). The emphasis or accent of this society has been determined, and it is not surprising that the greatest sin which Nehemiah turns up is the sin of the priest, Eliashib, who has allowed an "impure" relative of his —and an ally of Nehemiah's chief Samaritan enemy, Sanballat, to boot—to occupy quarters in the Temple (*Nehemiah* 13:4-9). Nehemiah orders the Temple to be cleansed because of this impurity, and his sharp eye further discovers neglect of the "portions of the Levites." The Levites and the singers have fled from the Temple, and Nehemiah recollects: "Then contended I with the rulers, and said, Why is the house of God forsaken? And I gathered them together and set them in their place" (*Nehemiah* 13:11). At such tasks as this is Nehemiah busied as the darkness descends and we see the Hebrew theocratic state no more; they are, indeed, tasks that such a state would approve. (From Josephus we hear a little more. Book XI, Chapter 8, of *The Antiquities of the Jews* tells us of tensions between the pure Hebrews and their despised neighbors to the north; these tensions finally lead the Samaritans to erect their own holy place to Jehovah on Mount Gerizim, in 335 B.C.)

Though *Ezra* and *Nehemiah* conclude the "chronicler's" history, it is a comment on *I* and *II Chronicles* that underlines what we have said about the theocratic state set up after the exile. As noted at the outset of this chapter, the point of view from which *Chronicles* is written would satisfy more fully than the Pentateuch and its sequels the view that leaders of the theocratic state were likely to take of past history. In *Genesis* to *II Kings* the concept of Hebrew history is not sufficiently systematized and subordinate to the view of the past acceptable by about 300 B.C. Another "defect" of the older books of history was that the priestly editors had not taken a free hand; though the final arrangement of *Genesis* and the others is theirs, the books abound in incidents and teachings that are uncongenial to a theocratic culture. At the time *Chronicles* was written (300-250 B.C.), the most powerful group in Jerusalem was (if theory is right) the Great Synagogue. This was an organization of interpreters of the law who continued the regularizing and explanatory labors of Ezra. One of the prominent suggestions in *Genesis* to *II Kings,* among a multitude of things, is that kings and nations rise and fall in terms of righteousness—the kind of righteousness that the prophet Amos had in mind and that Malachi did not see about him in the theocratic state. If the Pentateuch and its associated books were complete by 400 B.C., religious extremists to whom ritual righteousness was more important than social righteousness may have weighed the Pentateuch and found it wanting, or inadequate. The troubles with Samaria and the threat of Greek culture from the time of Alexander's conquest of Syria and Palestine (331 B.C.) may have created a demand for a history of Israel that should display the Temple occupying a central position.

Chronicles performs this task. It casts back to the time of David the complex superstructure of fourth- and third-century Temple worship. As a kind of sanction for Temple devotion, David is "done over" so that he emerges as a staid, dignified ruler preoccupied with drawing up Temple protocol. One need only read the two accounts of the entrance of the Ark into Jerusalem to savor how far the purification of David's character has gone (*II Samuel,* chap. 6; *I Chron-*

icles, chap. 13). No longer does David caper before the Ark, and in his company are the priests and Levites that served in the theocratic Temple but have no relation to the religious structure of David's day. David's misdeeds are forgotten, and many chapters (*I Chronicles,* chaps. 22-28) are given over to the lists of families eligible for Temple service. David dies without disgracing himself by the malicious directions that, in the older history, he gives to his son (*I Kings,* chap. 2); and Solomon is worthy of the trust put in him by his father and the writer of Chronicles (*II Chronicles,* chaps. 1-8). He labors at the construction of the Temple even more diligently than in *I Kings.* Solomon indeed marries a daughter of Pharaoh, but the "chronicler's" devotion to correctness and good form creates this remark:

> And Solomon brought up the daughter of Pharaoh out of the city of David unto the house that he had built for her: for he said, My wife shall not dwell in the house of David king of Israel, because the places are holy, whereunto the Ark of the Lord hath come. (*II Chronicles* 8:11.)

Solomon's morals and manners are being corrected at a distance of six hundred years.[1]

The delineation of David as a preparer for the theocratic state rather than a king with faults and dynastic ambitions is the high point of *Chronicles.* Other sections of the book, however, underline the bias of this extremely tendentious history. The stretch from

[1] A curious and characteristic deviation from *II Samuel* concerns David's taking of a census. *Samuel's* account of this evil undertaking begins: "And again the anger of the Lord was kindled against Israel, and he moved David against them to say, Go, number Israel and Judah" (*II Samuel* 24:1). The account in *Chronicles* has a startlingly different beginning: "And Satan stood up against Israel, and provoked David to number Israel" (*I Chronicles* 21:1). It is as if "the anger of the Lord" were an embarrassing phrase by this late date; it is more "seemly" to use Satan as the instigator of that which is evil in David's behavior. We note elsewhere the comparative rarity of reference in the Old Testament to Satan rather than Jehovah as the author of evil. To the writer of *Chronicles,* as well as to the writers of later books in the Bible, Satan is a great convenience. It frees them from the onus of explaining how a good God is the origin of evil; it plunges then, however, into another: If God is omnipotent, how does Satan come by his power?

Adam to David is covered by genealogies that underscore David's importance. It is as if the chief warrant for the structure of Jerusalem about 300 B.C. lies in David's reign; earlier history may be safely overlooked. The account of the kingdoms after the death of Solomon also shows the bias. The writers of *Kings,* it is true, make statements which discriminate the wicked kings of Israel from the comparatively virtuous kings of Judah. But *Chronicles* omits Israel almost entirely. Perhaps by this time it was plain that God was associated only with the destiny of Judah. Israel had not returned from exile; she had disappeared, and her territory was occupied by the Samaritans, the stone in the shoe that Judah now wore. Ignoring the Northern Kingdom, *Chronicles* gives us fuller accounts of the kings of Judah, accounts that often include details and even events that are lacking in *I* and *II Kings.* Whether what *Chronicles* adds is historically valuable and represents traditions that were not drawn on for *Kings* is important. More important for us, however, is that according to this revision the experience of the Northern Kingdom was a blind alley. This emphasis suggests that all that happened to the house of Omri (and not the least of these "happenings" was Elijah) was of little significance to the Great Synagogue and the other successors of Ezra and Nehemiah. Of more interest are the extensively reported reforms of Hezekiah and the great Passover of King Josiah (*II Chronicles,* chaps. 30-32, 35). (The corresponding accounts in *II Kings* are Chapters 18-20, 22-23.) Even the conclusion, which tells us of the generous edict of Cyrus, is in line.

> Thus saith Cyrus king of Persia. All the kingdoms of the earth hath the Lord God of heaven given me; and he hath charged me to build him an house in Jerusalem, which is in Judah. . . . (*II Chronicles* 36:23.)

Here Cyrus' care for the "house in Jerusalem" is a reflection of David's earlier care for such a house. It is an anticipation of the Great Synagogue's care for its compact, well-organized Zion.

CHAPTER VIII

Hebrew Fiction: Pseudo-Historical Narrative

IT IS POSSIBLE to feel that the Bible is an omnibus collection of history, folklore, and poetry. It is even illuminating to do as we are doing at this point and apply the term *fiction* to certain books in the Old Testament and the Apocrypha.[1] But when we apply modern terms like *fiction,* or *poetry,* or *essay,* our use should be regarded as a convenience. It should never blot out the perception that everything we find in the Bible constitutes a unity beneath the surface variety that we now study. This surface variety must not be ignored. As in this chapter, it is well to note that there is a difference between *Esther, Ruth, Daniel* and the historical books just studied. But, in the long run, it is even better to see what the substratum is that connects these books with the historical writings. This substratum is the permanent preoccupation of our writers over many centuries.

[1] The list or "canon" of sacred books that make up the Old Testament was not completely drawn up or closed until the second or third century A.D. This list in its final form excluded books of high intrinsic merit that had circulated among Palestinian and Alexandrian Jews. Among them are four narratives considered in this chapter: *Tobit, Judith, Susannah,* and *Bel and the Dragon.* It is useful to discuss these books along with *Daniel, Esther, Ruth,* and *Jonah,* which were finally included by the Hebrews among the books proper to be read in the synagogues. The process of discrimination that accepted *Daniel, Esther, Ruth,* and *Jonah* and rejected *Judith* and its fellows took several factors into account: the supposed time of the events narrated, the consistency between the events in *Daniel* and the other books and the account of the events in the books accepted by the Hebrews as historical, and the moral and theological accent of the narratives. This winnowing process led to the formation of the Old Testament Apocrypha—a term meaning that certain writings were "hidden" and, later, "unworthy" of religious use. These same writings are included in the Roman Catholic Vulgate among writings suitable for reading in church; the Protestant Bible follows the Hebrew canon or list. This is a discrimination which we ignore. As we shall see later, much of the material in the Apocrypha is useful for bridging the gap between Old Testament and New Testament thought. Further, as our present analysis of Hebrew invented narrative will show, the expression of Hebrew insights in the canonical books does not differ from the expression in non-canonical works. On aesthetic grounds, *Judith* is the peer of any of the narratives included in the Hebrew canon.

They ask what can be said of the Lord; they are determined to see, in the actual texture of event, the workings of deity. The results are patent. No one can have failed to see how, in the books of history, the chief character is likely to be put in a subordinate position to God or to have his dignity only because he is a tool God employs. This insight about history modern historians ignore. In a similar way, whatever the resemblance of Hebrew "fiction" to modern imaginative works (a resemblance that we shall trace), plainly these books too are set apart by a pervasive sense that "the Other" is very close by.

CHART 7. Pseudo-Historical Books

	HISTORICAL EVENTS	DATES OF THE BOOKS: SCHOLARLY HYPOTHESES
538	Return from exile in Babylon	
458	Return of exiles under Ezra	450 *Ruth*
444-433	Nehemiah's first and second visits	450 *Jonah*
331	Conquest of Syria and Palestine by Alexander	
198	Palestine under Syrian Seleucids	
167	Profanation of the Temple: the Maccabees	165 *Daniel* 150 *Judith* 130 *Esther*
103-76	Alexander Janneus: Jewish nationalism	
		100 *Susannah; Bel and the Dragon*
63	Entrance of Pompey into Jerusalem	

As indicated, the term *fiction* would have been abhorrent to the Hebrew scholars who drew up the list of acceptable books. All narratives of events included in the Bible were regarded as true in a literal and strict sense. We need not, however, be guided by their understandable if rigid attitude at this point. Hebrew *fiction*—that is, narrative contrived to resemble reality—can offer us, on a small scale, the sorts of aesthetic pleasure we derive from modern novels. Equally important, it can allow us to see—from a slightly different vantage point—how the "God-obsessed" consciousness of the Hebrew people leaves its mark on fairly free imaginative creations.

Two motives interplay in these stories: the desire to instruct and the desire to entertain. Our own reading of fiction tells us that these are not always a well-matched team. The lead horse (edification or propaganda) pulls too hard, and the off horse (aesthetic satisfaction or delight) refuses to follow. American fiction is full of novels like Upton Sinclair's *The Jungle* or his later "Lanny Budd" series where, quite obviously, social and political propaganda takes precedence over elements of entertainment and over truth to life. To Upton Sinclair the novel seems always to be a soapbox, and effects of possibility and liveliness will always be sacrificed to social message. The impossibility we have to accept in the "Lanny Budd" series is that one young man would be able to "contact" all the great figures of the time, from Roosevelt to Hitler. If we tolerate this impossibility, it is because we feel that Mr. Sinclair's views on the international situation are worthy of attention. We recognize a *doctrinaire* bias and tolerate the imbalance between instruction and entertainment in these novels.

The initial problem we face in reckoning the artistic success or failure of Hebrew "fiction" is the same. Drawing on a variety of materials—fragments of history, legend, folklore, their own invention—the authors seldom overlook their primary duty; at least, there is not an H. Allen Smith among them. More seriously, there is not among them a writer like the great modern French novelist, Marcel Proust. Proust, in his monumental and detailed *Remembrance of Things Past,* showed that he felt his chief duty lay in giving a harmonious, detailed, and aesthetically pleasing picture of the reality he knew. He is plainly not concerned with the "moral" or lesson we may draw from his work. The Hebrew writers of *Esther, Daniel,* and the others were all moralists in the first place and artists only in the second place. In fact, the very elements in these stories that give us pleasure—the brief but sharp pictures of ancient custom, the sudden sense that human motives we still know are fleetingly revealed—are not the chief ones for these old "novelists." Their aim is to urge home a godly point; the other effects are incidental by-products. Thus, in *Tobit,* our delight with the parting comment of the mother to her son-in-law is a delight with something on the periphery of the book. (The mother says, at the end of Chapter 10, ". . . behold, I commit my daughter unto thee in special trust, vex her not.") Likewise, the subtlety in the character drawing of the heroine Judith and the noble colloquy of Ruth and Naomi in the first chapter of *Ruth* can give the reader a keen pleasure. But reactions of pleasure to isolated "gems" ignore the writers' central intent: a drive toward edification. These sections of the Bible offer us not merely a collection of colored stones to hold in the memory. If we but see them so, they have their places in a larger handiwork.

This larger handiwork—the complete narratives and what lay behind their creation—sometimes merits the modern term of praise, "a work of art"; and often it does not. It is not surprising that the least aesthetically successful stories are those in which the lead horse of edification pulls too hard. Tentatively—since this is a matter of personal taste—we may put two narratives in this class, *Daniel* and *Jonah;* and we may add portions of *The Book of Ruth. Ruth* will allow us to see at once the conflict between didactic and aesthetic impulse. A full discussion of its difficulties should prepare us to deal with similar ones in the other narratives.

The Book of Ruth, since it concerns events that are assigned to pre-Davidic times, is printed in our Bibles just after *The Book of Judges.* Yet it is, many scholars suggest, what we today would call "historical fiction." "Historical fiction" may be defined as work which contains a partially invented series of incidents assigned to a past period. That *Ruth* was such a book is suggested by the account of the negotiations preceding the marriage of Ruth and Boaz.

> Now this was the manner in former time in Israel concerning redeeming and concerning changing, for to confirm all things; a man plucked off his shoe, and gave it to his neighbor: and this was a testimony in Israel. Therefore the kinsman said unto Boaz, Buy it for thee. So he drew off his shoe. (*Ruth* 4:7-8.)

We know that a modern historical novel may be written from several motives. The writer's purpose may be to give us a faithful "reconstruction" of the events and manners of a past time; Walter Edmonds' *Drums Along the Mohawk* is such a novel. More often, the modern historical novelist pretends, by use of a distant time, to be writing primarily of past events and past problems. But beneath this pretense moves a passionate desire to say something about his own era and its problems. Margaret Mitchell's celebrated *Gone with the Wind* indeed seems to be concerned with the Civil War; but, as certain shrewd critics pointed out, Scarlett O'Hara and Rhett Butler are not Civil War figures, for their codes and their cynicism place them in the twenties of our own century. Similarly, so careful a workman as Kenneth Roberts uses his mountains of accurate detail to justify rather personal convictions. Roberts is suspicious of the mass of men, and for him the voice of the people is anything but the voice of God; a novel like *Oliver Wiswell* exists to justify his contention.

The Book of Ruth, whatever the great power of the opening chapter, is chiefly a justification of a contention important not in the actual time of *Judges* but centuries later. The problem in *Ruth* is this simple one: what should be the attitude of a Hebrew whose racial purity is beyond question (Boaz) toward the consequences of a "mixed marriage"? Boaz' relative Mahlon has made such a marriage, and with a woman of the hated tribe of Moab. Should the "correct" Boaz be indifferent to the problem that is really more Naomi's than Ruth's—the problem of "raising up" children to Mahlon and grandchildren to Naomi? Should Boaz take Ruth to wife? This is certainly not the kind of problem that appears in the actual *Judges* narratives, whose most notable hero, Samson, is always turning to Philistine women. The problem of racial purity—scholarly hypothesis suggests—was faced by the Jews in the years following their return from exile in Babylon (538 B.C. and later). As they labored to rebuild their ruined Temple, they remembered how jealously they had preserved their own purity in the pagan city of Babylon. What should their attitude be toward the descendants of those "husbandmen and vinedressers" who had remained behind? Doubtless these latter Hebrews had, in the two or three generations after the fall of Jerusalem in 586 B.C., made "mixed marriages" offensive to the pride of race clearly visible in the historical books of *Ezra* and *Nehemiah.* We know that the tension between the "pure" and "impure" racial strains finally led to the permanent division between the Hebrews and the Samaritans. *Ruth,* whenever it was written, was a strong argument against the necessity or inevitability of any such division. It was an argument, as usual, in terms of presented event rather than of manipulated abstraction. The ancient reader was simply urged to observe how Ruth the Moabitess was, after due process of inquiry, taken to wife by Boaz and became the ancestress of that glory of Israel, David himself. What stronger argument could there be for a policy of reconciliation between the racially pure and the impure?

At one other point does *Ruth* necessitate comment that casts light not only on this narrative but on the other tales. Persons who have had their sentiments stirred by the touching first chapter of *Ruth* read on with a sense of shock. Their expectations of what is today called "romance" have been roused, and in the rest of the story they find very little of it. True, Boaz is kind to Ruth in the fields, and he is careful of her reputation when she "lies at his feet" to assert her claim on his attention. But the reader is startled when Boaz seeks to find some other member of the family who will "raise up children" to Mahlon; and it is obvious that Boaz submits to his fate —marrying Ruth—with resignation rather than joy. Here, if we do not reckon with some ancient Hebrew desire for edification, we are quickly confused. We must be willing to admit that "romance" is very nearly a non-existent element in Hebrew culture. The union of the sexes on the basis of sensual desire is an element; but the added cherishing of a person of the opposite sex for idealized qualities one has to look for very intently. Perhaps in the relation of Jacob and Rachel and certainly in the friendship of David and Jonathan there is a "romantic" attachment to idealized qualities. But once again, as with the concept of "personality" discussed in relation to David's life, we see that an attitude regarded by us as a fundamental part of human nature is dormant and absent; its place is occupied by other intense passions. The drive behind the story of *Ruth*, as in the brief narrative of Tamar and Judah in *Genesis*, Chapter 38, is the desire for progeny and a continuation of oneself in the race. If we see, as we read *Ruth*, that it is not concerned with the romantic love which comes to us from the Middle Ages and its stories of deathless lovers like Tristan and Isolde, then accents that seem odd vanish. If we see that all the characters recognize as a high value the continuation of the family and the race, we are able to understand the behavior of Boaz. It is out of respect to his dead relative that he treats Ruth with kindness, and defers to Naomi's "right" rather than shows any special favor for Ruth when he initiates the inquiry in Chapter 4. We also understand why the book ends with mention of Naomi's happiness rather than Ruth's.

Such circumspection—presented at length in order to serve for other narratives as well as this one—is proper to the reading of the Hebrew invented, didactic works. A popular modern novel satisfies its readers and their conventional expectations by telling of success in love and business. In Hebrew story, we may expect to see the pursuit of material prosperity and of progeny; we may expect to see survival of the tribe and obedience to the Lord as the motives for action rather than, as with much of our fiction, the pursuit of either love of prosperity for its own sake.

Thus, *Jonah* has preoccupation with the will of the Lord for its guiding motive. However, aside from having a characteristic Hebrew motive, *Jonah* differs from *Ruth*. *Jonah*, and *Daniel* as well, displays the cyclic or episodic structure that we perceived in the "lives" of Abraham and Samson. This may be the result of an effort to imitate the style of the traditional narratives. It may also result from sheer lack of the adroitness of the authors of *Ruth*, *Esther*, and *Judith* in creating or arranging narratives that are unified and continuous and single in effect. The story of *Jonah* concerns a prophet who is supposedly a contemporary of the Assyrian empire, an empire—as the books of *Kings* tell us—little likely to respond favorably to missionary effort on behalf of the one true God. Actually, *Jonah*, like *Ruth*, is a manipulation of historical details to drive home a point cogent to a later age. The point is that the Ninevites (who stand for the impure peoples round about the Jewish theocratic state set up after the return from exile in 538 B.C.) are as worthy of salvation —and as eager for it—as the self-righteous Jonah, who is unwilling to carry the Lord's message. The eager conversion of Nineveh is analogous to the simple if crude trust in God to be found among the "impure" Hebrews; and the churlish Jonah, unwilling to take God's message to outsiders and angry when they respond to it, stands for the group in Israel that on trivial or legalistic ground wished to exclude large numbers from the community.

So viewed, the story has point if not artistic finish. It can indeed be regarded as employing a method similar to that of the modern political cartoon wherein crude figures of donkey and elephant stand as intelligible symbols for abstract political entities. In such a light the whale's function in the tale would not be misunderstood by those who had the key to the entire tale. The whale is but another item in the story that has been schematized to drive home a doctrinal point. We who have to fumble for the clue can but guess at the symbolic meaning. Does the whale stand for the great exile in Babylon—an exile that was a punishment for past Hebrew misdeeds but from which too many Hebrews returned not in humility but with the sense of self-righteousness and apartness that Jonah displays? Or, more simply, is the whale the wrath of a god whose plain instructions have been ignored? Whatever our answer here, the point to be perceived is that the whale in this story—like many items in the vision literature in *Ezekiel,* in the prophetic chapters of *Daniel,* and in *The Book of Revelation* in the New Testament—was to its audience an understood gambit, an "opening" full of meaning to the initiate. To the initiate, the importance of the whale was not literal but allegorical. Those who allow their energies to be trapped in an argument as to the possibility of the whale episode perhaps resemble the child of today who looks at a political cartoon and judges it a precise picture of something that has actually happened.

The *Daniel* narratives exhibit, on a larger scale, the qualities perceived in *Jonah.* The series of narratives attached to Daniel—a godly youth, a godly man—drive home the following points: the power of the Lord to protect his own, the sin one commits when one bows down to a graven image, the virtue of any kind of resistance to a heathen overlord. The events of the book cover the time of the captivity of the Hebrew people in Babylon and include a prophecy delivered to King Darius, who lived from 521 to 485 B.C.; this permits Daniel a life span of nearly a century. Further, kings are included out of order; and Belshazzar of the famous feast (*Daniel*, chap. 5) was, if real at all, never a king but only the son of a king. Therefore, the occasion of the composition of this historical pastiche would seem to be not the days of actual exile but some later period when Hebrews needed to be encouraged to resist alien pressure to bow down to other gods. The militant resistance to such a pressure in the time of the Maccabees (168 B.C. and onward) suggests to many a suitable time for the composition of this book. It was a time when the Hebrews were stirred by the Seleucid tyrant Antiochus, who had profaned the Hebrew Temple by making sacrifice there to the Greek Zeus. The author of this book—and, one would imagine, the authors of *Esther* and *Judith*, which concern similar resistance—would have a desire not only to locate its events in canonically approved eras but also perhaps to conceal from contemporary oppressors the real intent of his work: to stiffen resistance to tyranny. Only the alien oppressor would be deceived by the trappings of bygone event. Those who groaned under Antiochus would read *Daniel* and understand. (During the Nazi occupation of France, plays were produced and novels were published that had no apparent connection with current French misery. The Nazi supervisers often missed the intent of a work, but the French public did not.)

The events of the episodic *Daniel* are among the most famous in the Bible: the three holy children in the fiery furnace, the handwriting on the wall, and the lion's den. The visions with which these adventures are interwoven are calculated to drive home, in terms of allegory, the points the narratives make in terms of action. (For convenience, discussion of the general significance of Hebrew vision literature is deferred to the section on the Christian *Revelation*.)

Aesthetically, however, *Daniel* with its mixture of separate adventures and vision is what would be called today a confusion of genres or kinds. It is a confusion that did not trouble the creator of the book if he was one man rather than several. His edifying intent was single; he employed whatever artistic forms came to hand. Perhaps because of the absence of such edifying intent three other episodes in the Daniel cycle are found only in the Apocrypha. In the *Bel and the Dragon* stories and in *The History of Susannah,* Daniel appears not as a seer and a defier of pagan authority but in the role of a clever secular man who by his own wit sets matters to rights. His cross-examination of the elders in the *Susannah* story, his trap for the priests in the *Bel and the Dragon* tales may entertain; but they are beside the instructive point of the Daniel narratives contained in the Old Testament proper.

The desire to edify and the desire to amuse both appear in the Apocryphal book, *Tobit,* which is aesthetically more complex if not more successful than the books, like *Jonah* and *Daniel,* that are built on an episodic plan. In *Jonah* and *Daniel* the "fable" or plot is central to the expression of the edifying intent. In *Tobit* edification and narrative are "only coincidental." Tobit, the father who sends his son on an important journey, is, almost incidentally, a pious Jew living in exile under the Assyrians. (Some students suppose the book was actually written in Alexandria about 350 B.C.) The edifying element is Tobit's piety; held up for the imitation of the reader, it expresses itself in two ways: Tobit gives alms to worthy compatriots, and he buries the dead. The story proper owes its start to the fact that Tobit cannot enter the house because he is "unclean" from his tendance upon the dead. He stays outside, and the misfortune that produces his blindness occurs. His blindness puts him in want; want reminds him of the sum of money he has deposited with Gabael in Media. Thus the story gets under way.

The uncertainty of the narrator as to how to go about his task is illustrated by the two points of view from which the story is told. The opening chapters are in Tobit's own words; the later chapters, which leave the suffering Tobit behind, are told from the vantage point of all-seeing knowledge. (There is no such uncertainty in the artistically successful *Esther* and *Judith.*) Tobias, the son, is fortunate to have the company of the angel Raphael in disguise; this being is so assiduous with advice and direction that Tobias comes out of the story with very little credit for what he has accomplished. The angel it is that tells Tobias when to fish, what parts of the fish to save, how to use the heart and liver of the fish to rout the devil Asmodeus on the nuptial night, how to use the gall of the fish to cure his father's blindness. Many of the episodes are handled with skill; the adventure of Tobias is delight without edification. Edification reënters the story when a moral harangue of old Tobit's is quoted (chaps. 12 and 13) and when Tobias dies in the odor of sanctity. Particularly well presented is the trying plight of Sarah, the young woman who has lost so many husbands to Asmodeus; her story is told without any *arrière-pensée* as to moral point. Her loss of husband after husband no more conveys moral instruction than does the sad plight of the wife of Bluebeard as she calls, "Sister Anne, Sister Anne, what do you see?" In short, the adventures of Tobias have their parallels in the tales that folklorists today gather all over the world, tales in which talking animals sometimes perform the functions allotted here to Raphael. Further, Tobit is complex and ingenious in structure. Tobias has *two* errands: to get his father's money and to get a wife. The first duty—more important at the beginning than the courting journey—is finally performed in a sentence in Chapter 9. Furthermore, the dual function of the fish's medicinal parts—to shunt off the devil and to restore the father's sight—is at least an economical narrative arrangement. Despite these merits of ingenuity, *Tobit* errs just as do *Jonah* and *Daniel* in that the two steeds of moral point and aesthetic effect do not pull together, though here the off horse—the tale as source of delight—takes the lead and leaves the edifying animal in the rear.

To a degree in *Ruth* and certainly in *Esther* and *Judith*, structure and moral point are in harmonious relation with each other. For us, *Esther* and *Judith* are superior to *Ruth* on several counts. Female guile employed in defense of one's people and land is a motivation perfectly comprehensible to us, whereas the motivations in *Ruth* require considerable explanation. In the second place, the narratives which display the plottings of the two heroines Esther and Judith are never out of relation with the instructive point, as in *Tobit.* Finally, both narratives are worked out on a scale and with a calculation of effect that would be impossible to the writers of the episodic *Jonah* and *Daniel.* In both *Esther* and *Judith* arrangements of event are as deftly set up as in a competently executed modern novel. If, in *Esther,* the reader regards as anticlimax the last two chapters, which tell of Hebrew vengeance, he should remember that, though the story is Esther's, the triumph must be Israel's. If he considers the first seven chapters of *Judith,* which tell of the gradual advance of the enemy toward the city of Bethulia, too leisurely a beginning, retrospective view will show them as the groundwork of apparent fact that makes Judith's exploit doubly exciting. Persons who see the plot of a story in a rising and falling line will find, in *Esther,* more ups and downs than in *Judith,* where the narrative traces a line from danger to triumph like the flight of an arrow. *Esther* has an exciting alternation of hope and despair; in *Judith,* all depends on the one exploit of the heroine. But it is difficult to see how either story could be more effective in plan.

It is also difficult to see how either could be more effective in execution. On the score of characterization, both give pleasure; there is a full-blown interest in personality and individuality that we saw taking its rise in the accounts of David and Saul. True, the contrasts of character in *Esther* are those of black and white; the vicious and the upright are unalterably opposed to each other. The powers of characterization to be seen in *Judith* are more delicate and mature. The conflict in Judith's heart as to whether she shall continue her ritual mourning for her husband or "do a thing which shall go down to all generations among the children of our race" (chap. 8) gives an added depth to her exploit when it takes place. This perception that human motives are never single appears in the delineation of Holofernes, Judith's victim, whose passion for his visitor is tempered by courtly behavior. In both narratives we can also take pleasure in seeing the writers beginning early to prepare for later, climactic scenes. In *Esther,* the peril of appearing before Ahasuerus unbidden is made very clear by what happens to the injudicious Queen Vashti in Chapter 1. In *Judith,* the heroine's means of escape from the enemy camp with her dreadful spoil is prepared for by her earlier midnight trips to the well outside the camp for prayer and washing. Individual excellences such as these just described are dispersed throughout the Biblical narratives; but the successful use of *all* of them is more than accident. Here are writers who feel a devotion to their craft as well as a devotion to God.

In fact, the writer of *Esther* was so devoted to his craft his book was almost not admitted to the Old Testament canon. God's name is not mentioned save in the supplements contained in the Apocrypha; and Mordecai, Esther's uncle, acts in a self-reliant way that other Hebrew heroes, quick to pray and quick to attribute their triumphs to God's power, do not imitate. That *Esther* was finally included in the canon was not a result of its great aesthetic merits; it was a result of the fact that Esther the woman had become, over the centuries, a national ideal, the female counterpart of David; and the feast of the "lots"—Purim—had become a national festival. All this, rather than the book's literary merit, offset the absence of the holy name and the late, non-canonical location of the events. By the time of Ahasuerus—the historical Xerxes (486-465)—the righteous Hebrews had returned to the Temple, and those who remained in the lands of exile were objects of suspicion rather than respect. Some scholars judge that the entire story of *Esther* is non-Hebraic, and beneath the names of Esther, Mordecai, and Haman they see a legend of the Babylonian gods Ishtar and Marduk repelling the god of an invading people.

For all these reasons, *Judith,* though in the Apocrypha, is a more Hebrew book than *Esther.* Judith is a model of piety as well as courage, as Esther is not. When her exploit is done, she takes up the life of fasting and humiliation that she put aside for a few days; nor is there a "romantic" conclusion provided by some young Hebrew warrior who has been, during her absence, fearfully pacing the ramparts of Bethulia. Further—this is an extrinsic detail like Tobit's almsgiving—Judith is careful to send her spoils to the Temple at Jerusalem: a respect for the holy city less characteristic of the preëxilic times in which Judith is supposed to live than of the Maccabean period when the book was probably composed. Judith is also careful to give the Lord his due credit for her exploit, as Mordecai does not.

Yet, despite all these Hebraic elements, *Judith*—the aesthetic peer of Esther and superior to *Jonah* and *Daniel*—exists outside the canon of the Hebrew and Protestant Bibles. The Hebrews whose opinions shaped the canon would observe, however, that the campaign of Holofernes was not in line with what the books of history revealed. One deviation from literal, accepted truth would outweigh the other sort of "truth" with which we are concerned when we read invented narrative: the truth of plausibility, of insight into human motive.

In conclusion, whatever the pleasure we take in this collection of books, it has to reckon with motivations we do not know as well as those we recognize. Vengeance and courage we understand; but vengeance and courage in the service of specifically Jewish insights may, as we read, give us pause. What we may, at the outset, simply tolerate as elements in a narrative read for its own sake—the almsgiving of Tobit, the careful piety of Judith, the negotiations about Ruth's second marriage—become deeply interesting when related to the longer story which we are following. This story is, of course, the unfolding of a collective religious consciousness from the days of Abraham to the times of Jesus and Paul. What this consciousness concerned itself with, the works discussed in this chapter reveal as clearly as do other books of the Old Testament. The Hebrew virtues and their "defects" appear here as plainly as elsewhere. What are these virtues? They are the courage of Mordecai and Esther that strengthens them under persecution and counsels brutal reprisal, the piety of Judith that nerves her for her one great act and allows her to regard as good a life guided by adherence to a strict ritual, the loyalty to family and tribe that moves Boaz to protect Ruth and strictly limits his display of generosity. One and all, these are aspects of an attitude toward experience which we may judge is incomplete but which we need not scorn. Indeed, as our study of the prophets and the New Testament will show, the motives of these heroes and heroines seem inadequate and parochial because of the gradual transformation of the Hebrew view of the world that takes place in the prophets and, later, in the thought of Jesus and Paul. These are the teachers who have taught us that reprisal produces nothing but reprisal and that only love, on occasion, transforms an enemy into a friend. It is they who have showed us that the ancient loyalties in which *Esther, Judith,* and *Ruth* deal—loyalty to family, tribe, or nation—are incomplete and do not exhaust man's power to love. It is they who have made us feel that outward piety and all other external displays of virtue are less valuable than inner attitudes of immediate trust and faith.

From Hebrew history and from what we have called here Hebrew fiction, we turn to writers who do not employ the framework of invented or historical narrative to support their hopes and fears about deity and mortal man. The writers of *Proverbs* and *The Book of Psalms* and the prophets were, instead, content to put down directly and unsystematically the conclusions to which their passionate meditations led them. They did not need the sanction or aid of event as they recorded what their minds and hearts told them about the Lord. The writers of the books considered in the next chapter produced, in our terms, essay and epigram and poetry. But these books are, in the Hebrew view, all books of "wisdom": they have as their common denominator the desire of writers to contemplate human experience and to draw from it clues to right action.

CHAPTER IX

Hebrew Wisdom and Poetry: "The Other" as Given in Contemplation

AMONG the marks that separate us from the ancient Hebrews and other ancient people is this one: We tend to parcel out our lives into compartments. For instance, we speak of "acting" and "thinking" as though we could, when we choose, separate these two human activities. As the story of the child Samuel indicates (*I Samuel*, chap. 3), the Hebrews had no such view. Samuel hears a voice, and he rises from his bed to answer it. Only at the third call does he realize it is not his human preceptor Eli who is calling to him; it is the father of his people. This realization does not free him to contemplate in quiet the message that comes to him alone. That message, as Samuel's subsequent career shows, is something to be acted upon. The division we make today between "men of action" and "men of thought" is one that the Hebrews would not have understood. Whatever the "men of thought" and vision achieved by way of poetry and prophecy became at once a basis for further action. Elijah hears a "still, small voice," and shortly thereafter he is rebuking Ahab for behavior not in line with what the voice has revealed.

Thus, the Hebrews would have had little patience with a man who lives simply for his ideas, who desires only to perceive them, to clarify them, and to put them in precise order. Such a handling of the materials of vision would have seemed a gross impiety. In their view, whatever was given in thought or dream bore the mark of the divine, had mana, and must be put to use. If vision was put into writing, it was to stimulate action rather than, in our phrase, to be "filed for future reference." Written form was a guarantee that the word of God should not perish along with the man who was singled out to hear it but could survive to be an ever present guide for future generations. We, in contrast, are likely to preserve the speculations of another century because they are historically valuable specimens of how men felt and thought. Our own guidance we expect to come from men who live at our particular moment of history. With the Hebrew, the lapse of time did not outmode wisdom; it only made more precious the "mysteries" that God had revealed in past ages and was not likely to reveal again.

We must recognize that our own approach toward the wisdom of a distant age tends to place the emphasis on the elements of beauty, quaintness, and intellectual oddity to be found in old discourse. Nor can we ignore these elements in *Proverbs, The Song of Solomon,* and *The Book of Psalms.*[1] But we must realize that they were secondary or non-existent for the Hebrews. So primary as to blot out all else was the feeling that each one of the books of wisdom was a cup brimming with the waters of instruction. In these three books, the will of the Lord was revealed, and it was the very same will that the books of history had revealed. Moses faced deity in the burning bush and deity speaking in thunder and lightning, and Samuel received the various messages of the voice in the temple at Shiloh; both experiences were points of departure for action. We should recognize that our emphasis, as we try to understand these books, falls on aspects less important for the Hebrews and so obvious as to need no comment.

Proverbs and *The Song of Solomon* are traditionally attributed to Solomon in his role of wise man and poet. "And he spake three thousand proverbs: and his songs were a thousand and five" (*I Kings* 4:32)—something over the quantity contained in our two books. The collection of poems called *The Book of Psalms* is assigned to David in his role of simple shepherd poet and in his role of king who expends much energy on preparing for worship in the Temple his son was to build (*I Chronicles,* chap. 25).

These attributions of authorship are a by-product of the idealizing

[1] The discussion of one other book of Hebrew wisdom is deferred. *Ecclesiastes* embodies perceptions at odds with those which *Proverbs* and *Psalms* contain. It is better to associate *Ecclesiastes* with *Job.* (See Chapter XII.)

of the two kings. In *I Kings* Solomon's wisdom is shown chiefly in the tale of the quarreling mothers and in the many wise answers which Solomon gave to the Queen of Sheba's "hard questions" and which, alas, are not preserved for us. In *Samuel,* David, during large parts of his career, was busy at other matters than the creation of songs. But in *Chronicles* we find a David and a Solomon who could easily be associated with the books of wisdom.

Both *Proverbs* and *The Book of Psalms* are what we today would call anthologies. *Proverbs* is a collection of "wise saws and modern instances," and *The Book of Psalms* is a repository of the best that the Hebrews over many centuries had created in the way of devotional poetry—the bulk of it to be used in Temple worship. Certainly we do not expect, when we take up Palgrave's *Golden Treasury of English Poetry,* to perceive continuity and homogeneity of quality among the poems included; we simply enjoy the excellence of each separate poem. And no one would pick up Bartlett's *Familiar Quotations* and struggle to find a continuous vein of thought. We know the sort of attention proper to these books: dispersed and intense attention. Similar attention takes us quickly to an enjoyment of these great Hebrew books—books put together and in part created during the theocratic centuries (538 B.C. and onward), but attributed to the great worthies of the Hebrew golden day, David and Solomon.

Proverbs and Hebrew Wisdom

When we open *The Proverbs* and read continuously, the result is often boredom. Here is a succession of sayings, some pithy and famous and others platitudinous and worthy of the obscurity they enjoy. Often we have a sense of observing a laboring epigrammatist at work, trying several times before he achieves the "right" expression of his theme (e.g., *Proverbs,* chap. 4). This one book also contains what we today would regard as different literary forms. We suspect that these are proverbs in the literal sense of the word: sayings invented by some witty, nameless illiterate who has two eyes in his head and whose chance words have been caught up and preserved for generations. "He that troubleth his own house shall inherit the wind" (*Proverbs* 11:29); "Where no oxen are, the crib is clean: but much increase is by the strength of the ox" (*Proverbs* 14:4); "It is better to dwell in a corner of the housetop than with a brawling woman in a wide house" (*Proverbs* 21:9); "A whip for the horse, a bridle for the ass, and a rod for the fool's back" (*Proverbs* 29:3)—all these have an aptness that is spontaneous as well as sharp. In contrast, some of the "proverbs" wear a self-conscious air and are the creation of bookish men eager to convey moral instruction to the many by aping the tone of the popular proverb. Benjamin Franklin's *Poor Richard's Almanac* contains observations that are now the common property of all who speak American English: "God helps them that help themselves"; "Early to bed and early to rise, makes a man healthy, wealthy, and wise." Other observations therein are happily still Franklin's own property. In this latter category of manufactured proverbs that do not come off seem to fall these and the chapter they came from: "He that deviseth to do evil shall be called a mischievous person. The thought of foolishness is sin: and the scorner is an abomination to men. If thou faint in the day of adversity, thy strength is small" (*Proverbs* 24:8-10).

In addition to these two classes of proverbs are more extended compositions to which we today give such titles as "essay" and "character sketch." Proverbs are bandied in the streets. Thoughtful persons wish to follow out the implications of a subject more fully than the give-and-take of ordinary banter permits. In short, they write essays. The essay form is a longer meditation on a topic than the proverb form permits, for the range of a proverb is that of the modern "wisecrack," which loses its barb when it is expanded. The description of wisdom in *Proverbs*, Chapter 3, is more discursive than any real proverbial vein would permit. The sketch of the harlot (*Proverbs*, chap. 7) and the famous picture of the good woman (*Proverbs* 31:10-31) are thorough and imaginative pictures of human types, sketched for didactic purposes.

This perception of the variety of form and tone in *Proverbs* does a good deal for one's grasp of the book; certainly as much pleasure and instruction lie in this book as we get when we put our feet up on the celebrated cracker barrel of the American general store, if we can find one. In such surroundings as in this book, the thread of conversation is tangled but full of shrewd observations on local events and personalities.

But so to regard *Proverbs* is to remain on the aesthetic level of appreciation. It is to ignore what, for the Hebrews who preserved the book, is at the very heart of the collection and its reason for being. The Hebrews saw the sign manual of "the Other" on this book; it contained wisdom not human but divine. For it and for later books continuing and intensifying this vein, we must ask what "wisdom" is. We may find it a way of knowing that, rightly viewed, is one of the chief claims of the Bible on our attention.

To the Hebrews, "wisdom" was a self-evident thing. They called "wisdom" any insight coming apparently from God to guide or rectify the course of man's actions. Its primary authority lay not in its intrinsic excellence—probably our view of such utterance—but in its supposed source. It was the Lord who had granted David or Solomon the power to utter certain songs and sentences. When some of us first encounter Hebrew "wisdom," we are likely to give it an incorrect and even condescending first hearing because we do not distinguish the kind of knowing represented by it from the kind of knowing represented by our modern term *knowledge.* Worse, we may suppose that the latter is the only type of knowing. Such a mistake is natural since, for most of us, education has been a process of acquiring knowledge. We become biologists, chemists, or engineers; we master a special field of knowledge and are then thought to be "educated men." Actually, we are men whose education, whose corner on knowledge, should be defined a little more precisely. Either we have learned a collection of facts observed by past students—we know the phyla of Linnaeus, the stresses of steel, the tables of Mendelyeev—or we have mastered a technique of study, some application of the scientific method, which will lead us to the perception of new facts and laws. If our education has been predominantly practical our "knowledge" consists of the accumulated observations of pas specialists, observations which we shall exploit as we follow our chosen professions. If our education has been "theoretical," we are prepared to set up experiments which will allow us to make a contribution to the fund of knowledge that practical men use every day. Whatever our personal aim, we are impressed by this ever accumulating fund of knowledge which gives a regular, precise, and predictive description of aspects of the world, and we are likely to think it the only sort of *knowing* that deserves respect. We tend to question whether ages that did not know how to produce *this* sort of accumulation of facts have anything at all to offer us; and this attitude is strengthened when we inspect the "science" of early ages. It is either non-existent or the result of trial-and-error procedures hopelessly enmeshed in superstition. The Babylonians had a great deal to say about the revolution of the heavenly bodies, but what they said was tangled up with the supposed influence of the stars on human destinies. The Hebrews simply had no science unless Solomon, in *I Kings* 4:33, made a start at natural history: "And he spake of trees, from the cedar tree that is in Lebanon even unto the hyssop that springeth out of the wall; he spake also of beasts, and of fowl, and of creeping things, and of fishes." However interesting certain early discoveries are, we regard them as harbingers of today's full, systematically arranged knowledge about matter and living tissue. It seems unnecessary for the ordinary college student to go back and study the errors of past "knowledge." He may, if he wishes, glance at them as quaint curiosities on the early spirals of human struggle.

This modern condescension toward early science is extended to the ethical and social thought of past ages. It applies, for example, to the "wisdom" of *Proverbs, Psalms,* and the Hebrew prophets, also to the wisdom of Socrates, Plato, and Aristotle. The temptation is to dismiss what the old Hebrew books have to say as if their insights were of a piece with the more grotesque errors of Egyptian medical books and the process of divination by inspection of a sheep's liver. There are two reasons why such dismissal is hasty. It assumes the kind of progress in all fields of *knowing* that is so obvious and impressive in the recent history of science. It further supposes that the very methods by which science has triumphed—controlled, exact experimentation—can be extended with similar success to problems involving moral values and human relations. If these two suppositions are indeed correct, if we also possess "knowledge" exact and productive in ethical and political realms, then many people are right in considering the "wisdom" of the Hebrews (and of other ancient cultures) quite as outmoded as is a good deal of ancient "science."

But neither supposition about modern ethical and political knowledge should be accepted uncritically. The truly skeptical person, when he looks at history, will question whether the moral and political standards of our own society have the superiority over ancient standards that modern science has over ancient science. He may wonder whether the results of Gallup polls and elaborate modern social studies give us ethical guidance better than that offered by Socrates, Jesus, Marcus Aurelius, and other framers of "wisdom" who did not support their insights by counting noses and drawing graphs. It is, at least, still an open question—not a closed one, as uncritical respect for the progress of science suggests—whether we in our generation are "wiser" than were the sages of past times who could not, alas, "cook with gas." It is an open question whether we see more clearly than they what man is and where his happiness lies. Certainly the honest reader of *Proverbs* is due to have his complacence shaken if he believes blindly in the automatic moral and social superiority of his own age. "He that is slow to anger is better than the mighty; and he that ruleth his spirit than he than taketh a city" (*Proverbs* 16:32). Various schools of psychology still attack the problem of self-control. In professional jargon, they speak of the adjustment of the individual to society and the triumph of the superego over the subconscious; but they put the whole mystery of self-control no more clearly and certainly less winningly than did the person who framed the Hebrew proverb.

The second supposition that we are likely to make unconsciously—that the techniques of science can be applied to human problems as successfully as they have been in the realms of matter (in physics and chemistry)—also tends to make readers impatient of ages making no gesture in this direction. To repeat here: The scientific knowledge of which we are justly proud rests on *exact* measurement and *controlled* experiments. Ethical and social problems involve emotions (which cannot be exactly measured or produced at will). Ethical and social action is based on the preference for one value rather than another; and it is difficult to "prove" that any human preference is "right"; one can only "prove" that iron is heavier than lead. Human problems include so many variables that the psychologist and the sociologist are not able to control to a high degree their investigations into the springs of human action. The chemist has his successes because he can change one factor—and one factor only—in the experiment he has set up; the highly useful work of students of human behavior is done in a realm where intangibles and imponderables forever interbreed and multiply.

This long but necessary analysis of *knowledge* has been made to suggest that in the fields of morals, social ethics, and theology (knowledge of God), the ways of knowing do not conform to the pattern of hypothesis and experiment which we admire. In short, "wisdom" is the product of a way of knowing in matters of ethics that is not *automatically* outmoded by the discoveries of succeeding ages; in fact, "wisdom" and "intuition" go hand in hand.

As to how a person comes to have "wisdom," the Hebrews had no doubt. They said: "The fear of the Lord is the beginning of wisdom." Wisdom was the record of an insight that came directly from the Lord. To some readers today, alternate *accounts* of the origin of such insights occur; and some may suspect that wisdom comes chiefly from the actual process of living in society and reflecting upon that life. All we need to grant, to read much of the Bible with attention and profit, is that men in scientifically "backward" and unprogressive ages can produce observations on ethical, social, and religious matters which continue to be arresting long after the societies they specifically referred to have ceased to exist. We accept and reject the insights of *Proverbs* and of many other books in the Bible by asking whether these fragments of ancient social experience are still valid; this is hardly a test one could call "scientific," but it is one which the wit and sapience of older literature constantly tempt us to make. We read of "turning the other cheek," and know the only way to "test" the truth of Christ's saying is to risk the consequences of such an act. We find the prophets of Israel inveighing against what we today call "power politics" (reliance on displays of force and "connections" and "balance of power") and we know that the truth or folly of what they say cannot be demonstrated in the safety of a laboratory; it must be demonstrated in the world of personal relations, the society of nations. Moreover, what is not true of scientific experimentation is true in human affairs; one course of action makes another course well-nigh impossible, for we cannot retrace our steps to see what would have happened had we followed an insight opposed to the one that did guide us. "Wisdom"—we can suggest—is an uncertain type of knowing yet an indispensable basis to much human action. One need not argue that all the wisdom contained in the Bible is final and binding. One need only say it is a collection of insights that may still quite often cast light on relationships where the technique of science is inept.

"Wisdom," any reader of *Proverbs* will be aware, is not all of a piece. True, all wisdom concerns the activity of man in society or man's relation to deity. To the Hebrews all wisdom was equally compulsive since it came from an august source. But we, in order to handle and understand what is a large bulk of material, can make certain discriminations. For *The Proverbs* the following remarks allow us to recognize that not all wisdom is equally compulsive.

Using the term *philosophic* in a limited way, we may call nearly all Hebrew wisdom pre-philosophic. In our ordinary talk we may say, "John has had many misfortunes, but he's philosophic about them." Here *philosophic* means simply that John is capable of looking at his troubles as though they were another person's; this ability enables him to take them less seriously than most of us take *our* troubles. This is not the sense of the word used here when it is asserted that Hebrew wisdom is "pre-philosophic." We encounter *philosophic* wisdom in the elaborately developed and organized writings of Plato. There each insight is carefully related to other insights that have come to the philosopher; what he says at one point is not at serious variance with what he has said at other points. Indeed, the later points are often deductions from the earlier. Thus, Plato's remarks on the education of children in *The Republic* are dependent on his insights about the universally good and true and beautiful. It all hangs together. In the work of Plato and other philosophers there are certain key ideas. Once we master these, we are well prepared for the philosopher's discussion on a variety of specific topics; the "key ideas" point to the specific observations about love and friendship, education and government.

The mental world that produced *Proverbs* is a very different one, simpler and cruder it is true, but also more direct and vivid. The wisdom we encounter there still crops out in the casual talk of old farmers and elderly women who have seen to it that their children and their grandchildren are twigs bent in the right direction. Such speakers may be uneducated, but their comment on human behavior is penetrating; it is also utterance at random. As in the talk of the sages of our own day, so in *Proverbs*. Certain ideas keep recurring, but they are never treated as key ideas from which less important ideas are to be deduced. Instead, all insights are of equal authority, for they have come in moments of inspiration; it would be impious to attempt to adjust the separate insights to each other. Thus, if we were in a "philosophic" climate, we should do well to be disturbed by the contradictions between the high and low levels of morality displayed in *Proverbs*. But the persons who created and compiled this book and *The Book of Psalms* did not apply the principles of consistency and interrelation that guided the formation of later books of moral or theological speculation. They were not, as was the Roman emperor Marcus Aurelius as he compiled his Stoic *Meditations*, aware that they occupied a certain intellectual position and that, in consequence, there were certain things they might say and certain things that were forbidden them. In a word, they were "pre-philosophic."

Yet as we read the product of this pre-philosophic culture, we find it fairly easy to sort out what the makers of the book collected. We see certain contrasts among the various kinds of wisdom. The contrasts exist in our own spontaneous moral speculation, which is also for the most part pre-philosophic since we, like the ancient sages, are more concerned with "living well" than with "thinking well." That is, as Dale Carnegie has it, we wish to "win friends and influence people"; our attitude toward our social behavior is confused and inconsistent, but very earnest. We wish to establish just and happy relations with our fellows. Nevertheless, shameful but true, we also wish to use the friends we have won for our own specific purposes: to get a better job or consolidate our social position. Those who "think well," who are philosophers, point out that we should not hope to do both. We should be willing either to esteem our friends for the virtues they have or, cynically, to use them for the good they can do us. Our practice is an unconscious mirror of the frequent moral inconsistency in *Proverbs*. Although we say we esteem our friends, we are not averse to using them. This attitude may be illogical, but it is the one most of us act on.

Concealed in this confusion are three levels of wisdom, here stated in order of descending excellence. On one level are precepts with a general application. The next two levels concern precepts that are related to specific instances, that "get down to cases." These are prudential precepts. As we shall see briefly in *Proverbs* and fully in a later book of "wisdom" which is included in the Apocrypha (*Ecclesiasticus*), there is a good and necessary prudence, and there is a bad prudence.

It is useful to observe these three levels in our own casual moral speculation. A precept of *general* applicability is this one: "Friendship is one of the great blessings of life." To this indisputable utterance, we are likely to add prudent codicils. A good one will perhaps take this form: "Friendship and its blessings are to be won only by the use of tact"—and specific examples of tactful approach to persons whose friendship we desire are certain to follow. A less admirable prudence appears in this remark: "Friendship will pay off in dollars and cents to the man who knows how to use it."

Those who cry out against *bad prudence*—in and out of *Proverbs*—and are quick to perceive such canny calculation in the actions of others seem to assume that morality consists entirely of the repetition of general precepts, of noble, irreproachable statements about what human behavior *ought* to be. But observation shows us, just as it once showed the Hebrew moralists, that noble precepts without the skill to apply them to emergent occasions are likely to be hollow. Indeed a large part of the moral life consists not simply of knowing what is right but of doing what is right. It is one thing to know the harbor one wants to drop anchor in; it is another to get into the harbor safely. To do it one must use the winds that happen to be blowing even though one has to follow a crooked course. In fact, the difference between good and bad prudence does not lie in the presence or absence of navigational skill; both sorts require shrewd calculations. One may say that bad prudence consists in forgetting the ideal harbor and taking refuge in a less ideal one. Good prudence tries for the ideal harbor and gives it up only in the face of shoals and head winds.

One must say that *Proverbs,* judged by conventional moral standards, abounds in unobjectionable general moral truths and prudence of a good sort. Christ, when he was instructing his apostles for missionary labors, said: "Behold, I send you forth as sheep in the midst of wolves: be ye therefore wise as serpents, and harmless as doves" (*Matthew* 10:16). The wisdom of doves, one supposes, is general wisdom, which is both harmless and inoperative at times because it concerns only an ideal goal. It is the wisdom of serpents that gets things done, that creates as good a moral life as possible under given circumstances. This is the concern of the majority of prudent observations in *Proverbs;* in the minority are statements that—to follow out Christ's figure of speech—express the wisdom of wolves, of men who ask only: "What's in it for me?"

There is, for example, a prudent caution in this observation:

> He that reproveth a scorner getteth to himself shame: and he that rebuketh a wicked man getteth himself a blot. Reprove not a scorner,

lest he hate thee: rebuke a wise man, and he will love thee. (*Proverbs* 9:7-8.)

This is saying, in our language, "Don't stick your neck out too far." Another proverb uses different words for "Don't tell everything you know": "A talebearer revealeth secrets: but he that is of a faithful spirit concealeth the matter" (*Proverbs* 11:13). Another puts "Don't let anybody take you for a ride" like this: "The simple believeth every word: but the prudent man looketh well to his going" (*Proverbs* 14:15). This famous one is known by every man who seeks to survive or hold his job: "A soft answer turneth away wrath; but grievous words stir up anger" (*Proverbs* 15:1). These two must conclude a list that any reader can prolong: "Hast thou found honey? eat so much as is sufficient for thee, lest thou be filled therewith, and vomit it. Withdraw thy foot from thy neighbour's house; lest he be weary of thee, and so hate thee" (*Proverbs* 25:16-17). This is the common level of proverbial wisdom on which the minds of men move most easily. We know we are asked to come up higher when a saying like this appears: "Who can say, I have made my heart clean, I am pure from my sin?" (*Proverbs* 20:9). And a more rigorous standard of excellence than that on which prudence operates appears here: "The spirit of man is the candle of the Lord, searching all the inward parts of the belly" (*Proverbs* 20:27).

If certain sayings demand, "Come up higher," there are a few that say, with a knowing look, "Come down lower." "Come down," that is, to the level of frank self-interest. Here is a compressed direction for profitable trading: "It is naught, it is naught, saith the buyer: but when he is gone his way, then he boasteth" (*Proverbs* 20:14). This advice might have come direct from *How to Win Friends and Influence People:*

> Put not forth thyself in the presence of the king, and stand not in the place of great men: for better it is that it be said unto thee, Come up hither; than that thou shouldest be put lower in the presence of the prince whom thine eyes have seen. (*Proverbs* 25:6-7.)

The cynical delight in saying, "This is the way things are," and so does proverbial wisdom: "The poor is hated even of his own neighbour: but the rich hath many friends" (*Proverbs* 14:20). A shrewd glance accompanies this remark: "To have respect of persons is not good: for a piece of bread that man will transgress" (*Proverbs* 28:21). And there can be bad reasons for good actions, which the cynical delight to discover:

> If thine enemy be hungry, give him bread to eat; and if he be thirsty, give him water to drink: for thou shalt heap coals of fire upon his head, and the Lord shall reward thee. (*Proverbs* 25:21-22.)

The cynic, Oscar Wilde told us, is the man who knows the price of everything and the value of nothing. From the general moral point of view inherent in the Scriptures, this is the wisdom of a special kind of serpent—an adder.

On all the levels here sampled, one is delighted by the psychological deftness with which human nature is anatomized. There is a single sharp cut, we see what we have not seen before, and the effect is one of truth. "As he that taketh away a garment in cold weather, and as vinegar upon nitre, so is he that singeth songs to an heavy heart" (*Proverbs* 25:20). "Seest thou a man wise in his own conceit? there is more hope of a fool than of him" (*Proverbs* 26:12). "Where no wood is, there the fire goeth out: so where there is no talebearer, the strife ceaseth" (*Proverbs* 26:20). It is hard to see how these could be improved; it is hard to think that they were the common possession of our great-grandparents and are now a closed book to us.

Proverbs is concerned with moral activity. Such activity, it should be noted, is not the sum and substance of what we have delimited as pre-philosophic wisdom. Hebrew wisdom, the prophets will teach us, takes in other territory than that of ethical relationships. Quite as important is a concern with the relations between created beings and their creator. What this region is like, *Psalms* will show us in part and the prophets with indefatigable fullness.

Hebrew Poetry

The Song of Solomon and *The Book of Psalms* are poetry. There is poetry and to spare in books not treated in this chapter. The historical books preserve as their purple passages songs of triumph uttered by Moses (*Exodus*, chap. 15) and by Deborah (*Judges*, chap. 5). *The Book of Job* and the writings of the prophets contain poetry fully the equal of the greatest in *Psalms*. These observations should remind us that the classifications we set up, in order to discuss and understand the Bible, are like the lines of latitude and longitude which map makers impose on the great oceans. The lines are good to sail by, but they are drawn in fancy on the confused and mingling reality of the tossing water.

Before we turn to the separate books, we must give extended attention to what this sort of wisdom is that takes the form of poetry rather than that of epigram and essay, as in *Proverbs*. One should observe the kind of truth poetry does indeed convey and some of the techniques for conveying that truth. Since pre-philosophic wisdom in general is composed of apparently self-evident insights which do not employ the framework of argument and proof, the chief merit of poetry—Hebrew poetry, at least—lies in its power to make an insight as vivid and compulsive for the hearer and reader as it was for the man who first framed the phrases. When the beloved, in *The Song of Solomon*, describes herself, she conveys to us the essence of her nature. "I am the rose of Sharon, and the lily of the valleys. As the lily among thorns, so is my love among the daughters" (*The Song of Solomon* 2:1-2).

Poetry is "true" in that it gives, better than do other forms of expression, the impact of the original insight. The insight may be amorous as in *The Song of Solomon*, or it may be consumed with being face-to-face with deity, as in *Psalms*. We testify to this power when we find ourselves recollecting tags of poetry which we have learned in the past. When Wordsworth describes the beauty of a young woman, he calls her "fair as a star when only one is shining in the sky." We learn no "facts" about the young woman. But no compendium of exact data as to weight, height, and color of hair and eyes could convey the effect of feminine uniqueness suggested. Nor would barometer and temperature readings ever pinch-hit for Kipling's dawn that comes up like thunder "outer China 'crost the bay." Such is part of the excellence of Hebrew poetry. Pope defines excellence in a poem as resting here: "What oft was thought, but ne'er so well expressed." If we alter "thought" to "felt," the formula describes the power of this ancient poetry in its English translation. We have loved, and we felt our immortal longings. This description of the yearnings of one in love—"Stay me with flagons, comfort me with apples: for I am sick of love" (*The Song of Solomon* 2:5)—or this cry of a person who feels that his God has forsaken him—"O my God, I cry in the daytime, but thou hearest not; and in the night season, and am not silent" (*Psalms* 22:2)—shows that the Hebrew poets deal with insights resembling ours. Further, by their choice of language, fresh and naïve, they vivify those insights for us as no generalized and psychological description can do. A book like Denis de Rougemont's *Love in the Western World* can give us an interesting account of the growth of certain psychological concomitants of the emotion of love, and William James's *Varieties of Religious Experiences* offers an exhaustive description of how men have come in contact with "the Other"; but from such works, as is proper, passion and immediacy are absent. Impact is primary and meaning is secondary when "Solomon" writes: "Many waters cannot quench love, neither can the floods drown it" (*The Song of Solomon* 8:7), and when the Psalmist says:

> Save me, O God; for the waters are come in unto my soul. I sink in deep mire, where there is no standing: I am come into deep waters, where the floods overflow me. (*Psalms* 70:1-2.)

To argue that Hebrew poetry has this immediacy is not to promise that it is an open book, ready to yield up all its riches to the hasty reader. Any body of poetry has conventions or ways of expression that we must recognize if we are to get full profit. Conventions that readers of English poetry are familiar with and tolerate, for their own sakes and for their part in the effect of the entire poem, are the sonnet form and blank verse. What these forms are and how they support the poet at his work we are willing to recognize. Often our knowledge of poetic convention directs and cultivates the immediate pleasure we feel in certain phrases.

Hebrew poetry has its set of conventions—some easy, some quite demanding—for the reader to deal with. Some readers, unwilling to reckon with them, assert in effect that everything, even in ancient poetry now living on in an English form, should be self-evident. But these same readers are doubtless quite willing to familiarize themselves with the rules of a game of chance in order to watch it or play it with pleasure, and the "rules" governing Hebrew poetry are really much less arbitrary and more closely related to the bedrock of human nature than are the rules governing movements on the football field.

At any rate, here follows a set of observations concerning the ways in which the Hebrew poets worked as they developed and connected their insights about the beloved or the deity. It is not suggested that there was a *Handbook for Hebrew Poets* with explicit directions for putting Hebrew poetry together. (That there was some awareness of the means by which poetry and prophecy proceeded, this passage from *Hosea* suggests. The Lord is describing his abundant revelation to the Hebrews and he says: "I have also spoken by the prophets, and I have multiplied visions, and used similitudes, by the ministry of the prophets" [*Hosea* 12:10].) What follows is a handbook for the person who would read Hebrew poetry—read it not only for the golden phrases but for a perception of the framework that holds together the golden phrases.

Though certain separate remarks will be made at the end of this chapter about *The Song of Solomon* and *Psalms*, the reading of amorous Hebrew poetry and the reading of the larger collection of religious poetry involve the same problems of apprehension, even to a close parallel of subject matters. Both collections presuppose dramas that run like an endless movie film, offering us a group of scenes again and again. This group of scenes is so familiar to the audiences reached by *The Song of Solomon* and *Psalms* that the poet does not need to explain antecedent circumstances as he begins a particular song. Something like this we detect in our own experience when we enter a movie house in the middle of a feature. So well do we know what Hollywood sends us that one glance at the screen tells us the point the story has reached; the sequence of boy meets girl, boy and girl quarrel, boy and girl "reconcile" is utterly familiar. The ancient Hebrew poets could count on a knowledge of a different sort of succession of events; their audience would know at once what point in the endlessly recurring dramas of human love or pursuit of the deity was being taken up. In the section on *The Song of Solomon,* we shall say something about the "story" presupposed by the poems in that book. The "drama" to which all the Psalms refer is this simple and important one: The play contains three characters—God, the Hebrew people, and the wicked. The second two characters are sometimes thought of as individuals ("I" is persecuted by wicked persons); they are sometimes thought of as collective Israel beset by the heathen. (The actual creation of the play seems to have been the work of the prophets, and in the next chapter we shall see them at their work of fabrication.)

For convenience, we may say that this play has four acts. *Act One:* Deity singles out the Hebrew people (or persons) for divine favor. The clearly defined covenant is established in which God extends protection in return for obedience and righteousness. *Act Two:* The Hebrew people (or persons) break the covenant by disobedience and wickedness. They worship other gods or are guilty of moral faults. *Act Three:* This is the act of punishment. Punishment occurs in three ways. God is angry and expresses his wrath (a) by working natural catastrophes such as famine and storm; (b) by employing some heathen people or simply wicked men to afflict the unrighteous; or (c) simply by becoming the "hidden god" who withdraws his support and leaves Israel or the persons to their own devices. *Act Four:* This is the act of restoration. The covenant is renewed, and God's favor flows forth once more. Since punishment was various, so is restoration. (a) God may "repent" and put an end to famine and storm. (b) God may cease to use the "rod" that the malice of the heathen and the wicked put into his hand, and he "restores" by breaking the rod and once more protecting those who have not lived up to the covenant. (c) God, who has "hidden" himself or turned his face away, may return to those who have been left to their own miserable devices.

This is the recurrent "drama" of the *Psalms* that was elaborately chanted by choirs in the Jerusalem Temple—just as in many Christian churches the succession of events in Christ's life composes the "calendar" of the church years. With a little effort, the modern reader will soon recognize at what point in the Hebrew drama he has "come in."

But once he is in, he must be prepared to make other recognitions. In particular must he recognize how ancient poetic practice draws the web across the woof set up by the drama just summarized. (The problem of reading *The Song of Solomon* is essentially the same. The "triangle" of that poem is lover, beloved, and assorted enemies to the course of true love, rather than deity, the chosen, and the enemies of the chosen.)

1. The most striking poetic device is that of *parallelism*. When the Psalmist writes, "The sun shall not smite thee by day," he quickly adds, "nor the moon by night" (*Psalms* 121:6). Similarly, in the love poems, "Come, my beloved, let us go forth into the field" draws after it the completing element, "let us lodge in the villages" (*The Song of Solomon* 7:11). This is a poetic habit that commends itself for the conveying of deeply felt insights, like the old phrase that says one's heart is too full for utterance; the heart may be too full for utterance, but all the same, what fills the heart must be uttered. The habit of parallel phrasing allows the poet a second chance to utter, and thus to underline, what constrains him. The Hebrew poet conveys not so much an idea, a logical concept, as an impression of physical beauty or divine and awful power. This being so, the repetition inherent in the device of parallelism enables one to try

not once but twice—or more, if he chooses to extend his list of parallel phrases.

In Hebrew poetry, parallelism does not often degenerate into a habit which allows a poet to "grind out" a poem, as did the convention of the heroic couplet in bad eighteenth-century poetry. It is one of the strengths of parallelism as a basic convention that it admits of variations which relieve monotony and remind us that the Hebrew poet was not in the first place a poet, and that his "poem" was not for the sake of art, of isolated aesthetic excellence, but for the sake of the strong, complex insights demanding expression.

The parallelism may consist (and often does) of almost exact repetition of the opening phrase: "Behold, thou art fair, my love: behold, thou art fair" (*The Song of Solomon* 4:1). "Lord, what is man, that thou takest knowledge of him! or the son of man, that thou makest account of him!" (*Psalms* 144:3.) More often the device consists of a repetition of the given insight in different words: "He delighteth not in the strength of the horse: he taketh not pleasure in the legs of a man" (*Psalms* 147:10). The use of different words in the second element leads, perhaps insensibly, to the addition of an aspect of the insight not suggested in the first line: "By night on my bed I sought him whom my soul loveth: I sought him, but I found him not" (*The Song of Solomon* 3:1). "Arise, O God, plead thine own cause: remember how the foolish man reproacheth thee daily" (*Psalms* 74:22). The first statement occasionally begets the exactly opposite insight, though this is a movement of thought that usually takes place within a Psalm rather than within a verse: "My flesh and my heart faileth: but God is the strength of my heart, and my portion forever" (*Psalms* 73:26). Finally, although the usual movement of Hebrew poetry is by means of a succession of paired utterances, each one to a degree a unit in itself, there are many places in *Psalms* and elsewhere where the parallels are allowed to accumulate. A fairly short example of such an accumulation is the address to spring in *The Song of Solomon*.

> Rise up, my love, my fair one, and come away. For lo, the winter is past, the rain is over and gone; the flowers appear on the earth;

> the time of the singing of birds is come, and the voice of the turtle is heard in our land; the fig tree putteth forth her green figs, and the vines with the tender grape give a good smell. Arise, my love, my fair one, and come away. (*The Song of Solomon* 2:10-13.)

The passage just quoted also allows one to see an example of the recurrence of a phrase at some distance from its first appearance; it is something like the refrain in modern song, but its use is not nearly so systematic. Psalm 148 contains a much longer accumulation of parallels; the danger of flatulence that such an accumulation presents is safely avoided.

2. Of aid to parallelism is the *recurrence of phrases* throughout the body of Hebrew poetry, phrases that each poet had in common with his fellows. God is "my rock," one lives in a "dry land," one escapes "the snare of the fowler," and one is in danger of "the horn of the unicorn." In *The Song of Solomon* the figure of a closed garden and a garden entered stands as oblique reference to the pursuit of the beloved. The Hebrew poet was not "original" and did not feel the duty that oppresses many poets today, of inventing new and sometimes strained phrases for well-known insights. One can almost imagine, from certain passages, that there were lists of phrases the Hebrew poet could turn to when he wished to present a familiar insight.

3. Hebrew diction is predominantly *sensuous*. In *The Book of Psalms* one sings praises to a God

> . . . that rideth upon the heavens of heavens, which were of old: lo, he doth send out his voice, and that a mighty voice. Ascribe ye strength unto God: his excellency is over Israel, and his strength is in the clouds. (*Psalms* 68:33.)

To read of God in a theological treatise is to read of a deity who is self-subsistent, self-comprehending, omnipotent, and so forth. This is power in the process of being apprehended. It is a far cry from the power that is primarily felt and that is conveyed in language concerned with reproducing feelings. There is no abstraction in the poet's account of deity; the insight is expressed in terms causing almost as vivid a movement of the sense as that which the poet or prophet felt in the first place when God passed by and his hair stood on end.

4. Hebrew poetry is, one may say, a kind of shorthand used by the poet to keep pace with the succession of sharp insights. The insights seem to come so quickly that the leisurely and connected record we are used to in prose is out of the question. In consequence, another feature (conscious or unconscious on the part of the poet) of Hebrew rhetoric is its characteristic movement, which demands that one be prepared to notice and allow for *abrupt transitions*, for *compressions* and *omissions*. In the song of Deborah, the killing of Sisera flashes before us and is followed by another flash; the juxtaposition is savagely ironical.

> At her feet he bowed, he fell, he lay down: at her feet he bowed, he fell: where he bowed, there he fell down dead. The mother of Sisera looked out at a window, and cried through the lattice, Why is his chariot so long in coming? why tarry the wheels of his chariots? (*Judges* 5:27-28.)

The problem of the poet, from our point of view at least, would seem to be to do justice to the intensity and the rapid succession of insights—as in the Deborah scenes or in the famous Scottish ballad which in one breath tells of the embarkation of Sir Patrick Spens and in the next presents his hat floating on the water. A person who tries to give an account of a ride on a subway express faces a similar problem. He is aware of stretches of darkness and then a sudden passage into light which lets him see, as he shoots through a station, the faces on the platform, the ticket booth, and the magazine stand. His account would have to deal in the first place with a series of vivid visual imprints. It would seem to be outside his line of duty to halt for speculation on the meaning of his mode of travel and of the kind of existence which draws people beneath the earth's surface for their transportation.

The flashing of the Hebrew poets from darkness into the brilliance of the view of God and away again is analogous to the ride on the train. It was not their duty, though in a moment it will be ours, to ask how one insight begets another. Their duty was to put down as many of their intense moments of awareness as they could. The transitions, the compressions and omissions, are the outward sign of this habit of apprehending without analyzing. Though following at a distance, we must be prepared for all the veerings that the wind of the spirit works on the poet. As we read *The Song of Solomon,* we must be ready to turn swiftly from the despondence of the beloved seeking her lover through the night to the logically unrelated message to be conveyed to the lover.

> The watchmen that went about the city found me, they smote me, they wounded me; the keepers of the walls took away my veil from me. I charge you, O daughters of Jerusalem, if ye find my beloved, that ye tell him that I am sick of love. (*The Song of Solomon* 5:7-8.)

In *Psalms* we must be prepared for similar changes of wind. In Psalm 104, all but the last verse is given over to a rhapsodic meditation on the power of the Lord; the concluding verse may seem gratuitous and irrelevant, but it is not unusual.

> I will sing unto the Lord as long as I live: I will sing praise to my God while I have my being. My meditation on him shall be sweet: I will be glad in the Lord. Let the sinners be consumed out of the earth, and let the wicked be no more. Bless thou the Lord, O my soul. Praise ye the Lord. (*Psalms* 104:33-35.)

Such transition would, in prose, take several sentences. Yet this way of presenting impressions is characteristic of Hebrew poetry rather than peculiar to it. The English dramatist John Webster is doing the same thing when he frames words for a man to utter as he looks upon the body of his sister, whose death he has contrived: "Cover her face; mine eyes dazzle: she died young." Perhaps the harsh clash of these blunt statements would be tamed and blended in a setting of prose, but the contorted yet truthful mixture of love and grief would be gone. Similarly, an "arranged" transition in Psalm 23—one that conducted us by easy steps from the green pastures and the still waters to the vindictive close where the Lord sets us a table in the presence of our enemies—would transform a swift race into a platitudinous stroll. The two insights—the peace of green fields, the sweetness of looking down on an enemy—came to the poet. Their relation to each other it is the pleasure of the critic or psychologist to trace. But the Hebrew poet is neither critic nor psychologist. He is a recorder of events and impacts that he must catch quickly in the net of language, lest they escape.

Compressions and omissions are also effects that we, as we read, must think about but that the Hebrew poet created. The poet writes: "The pastures are clothed with flocks: the valleys also are covered over with corn; they shout for joy, they also sing" (*Psalms* 65:13). He is letting the part stand for the whole; and, illogical but true, the part is greater than the whole. Again, there is less effect of awesomeness in an exhaustive list of divine attributes such as one finds in Augustine or Aquinas than in two verses from the *Psalms* like these: "For a thousand years in thy sight are but as yesterday when it is past, and as a watch in the night" (*Psalms* 90:4); and "He shall cover thee with his feathers, and under his wings shalt thou trust . . ." (*Psalms* 91:4). The poet does not merely strike when the iron is hot. He strikes only once or twice and then hastens on to the next insight that demands his attention. But nothing has been lost; his work on the imagination of his hearers and readers has been wrought; if he has worked well, his audience will fill out what he has left blank. His audience adds to the "still waters" of Psalm 23 all that goes with still waters and green pastures. In a modern novel, no such labor and coöperation are demanded of the reader. The novelist is careful to describe the entire lay of the land, the produce that the still waters irrigate, and the breed of cattle—Hereford or Holstein—that crop the green pastures. Such a description produces only passive pleasure, and it is the kind of pleasure the modern reader is most used to. Since the reader has contributed no effort of his own, he is likely to forget the prose description. Those who master the Psalms do not forget what is offered them there.

Persons who admire Oriental art tell us that a Chinese picture of a mountain landscape, composed of ten or twenty brush strokes applied to a neutral background, gives us more of the rocky scene than a Western painting in which every stone and every twisted bush has been carefully indicated by the artist. Similarly, when the Hebrew poet writes, "As the hart panteth after the water brooks, so panteth my soul after thee, O God" (*Psalms* 42:1), the sense of thirst and possible assuagement is presented in two strokes. To add qualifications would be to blunt what the first phrases have accomplished. But—this is the crucial point for the modern reader—none of these strokes does much unless the reader allows the rushing sensitivity of the ancient writer to find completion in his own sensitivity.

5. Edgar Allan Poe once made a celebrated statement—an overstatement—about the length of a poem. No poem, he said, could be longer than twenty-four lines. No poem, an expansion of the statement might run, that concerns the reproduction of immediate experience can be of any very extended length. Poems like *Paradise Lost*, appliers of Poe's dictum would say, attain their great length by providing passages of gray prose texture, sections of narrative verse and of theological speculation, as a setting for the lines to which Poe would award the name of poetry. At least in brevity and intensity, Hebrew poetry satisfies Poe's requirement.

Brevity and intensity are yoked together, as our own experience can tell us. No one can live at the top of his bent for a very long period of time. There are two sorts of escape from an intense emotion: a relapse into the prose commonplace of life, or a shift to another emotion. Shrewd dramatists know this very well and show us people who, facing catastrophe, stop to wonder whether the electric stove was turned off when they left home. Writers of comedy often present us a heroine who cries out to the man who has been quarreling with her, "I hate you! I hate you!" and then, illogically but with an effect of truth to nature, "I love you! I love you!" We say, "How lifelike!"

Naturally, the Hebrew poets do not lapse into prose to escape their intense emotion, though we shall have cause to suspect the prophet Ezekiel of doing so. They either end their poems or escape into another emotion. Black despair, fear that God has cast his people away forever, becomes, in a flash, utter certainty that God has for the Hebrews a future even more glorious than the age of David and Solomon. A prosy reader, a reader used to the orderly mental procedures that enabled him to master "knowledge," is frequently baffled and irritated by the turns which poetic "wisdom" takes. These turns, he should see, are both natural and necessary. There is—to coin a phrase—*a logic of the emotions* as well as what we ordinarily term logic: a set of rules to guide or describe mental procedures. Conventional logic is a discipline by which the mind dispassionately travels from a given assumption to a logically defensible conclusion. *The logic of the emotions* is a term useful to refer to the alternation of emotional states which is the mark of life lived intensely on the level of feeling and insight. "Wisdom," concerned as it is with human relations and relations with God, must move on this level a great deal of the time. This "logic" is as much a part of the Hebrew poetic rhetoric as the obvious aspects of parallelism. It is a fact to be reckoned with as we read the Psalms. We may suspect that it will have to be reckoned with also when we turn to the prophets.

An analysis of the structure of any longer Psalm reveals that the poem proceeds by opposites, after the possibilities of a given theme have been exhausted. There are brief Psalms where only one mood is presented (e.g., Psalms 8, 15, 29, 47, 93, 100, 126, and 142). However, in so short a Psalm as 137, we can see how a mood painful to sustain gives way to a more endurable one. The poem begins with famous phrases descriptive of the exile in Babylon:

> By the rivers of Babylon, there we sat down, yea, we wept, when we remembered Zion. We hanged our harps upon the willows in the midst thereof. For there they that carried us away captive required of us a song; and they that wasted us required of us mirth, saying, Sing us one of the songs of Zion. How shall we sing the Lord's song in a strange land? (*Psalms* 137:1-4.)

In the next verses the mind turns to Jerusalem—"If I forget thee, O Jerusalem, let my right hand lose her cunning"—and, by association of ideas, the writer is drawn on to a more enjoyable prospect: the punishment of Edom and Babylon, who have afflicted Jerusalem. On this startling note the poem ends:

> O daughter of Babylon, who art to be destroyed; happy shall he be, that rewardeth thee as thou hast served us. Happy shall he be, that taketh and dasheth thy little ones against the stones. (*Psalms* 137:8-9.)

How did we get here? By the logic of the emotions, which proceed by association and by opposed attitudes. Downfall and humiliation begets triumph and vengeance as this Psalm disconcertingly demonstrates.

Psalm 10, a somewhat longer composition, allows one to see this process at work. After an opening lament addressed to the "hidden god," the poet gives us ten verses on the wicked man. Then in verse 12—it is as if such wickedness were no longer to be borne—an opposed attitude breaks forth: "Arise, O Lord; O God, lift up thine hand. . . . Break thou the arm of the wicked and the evil man: seek out his wickedness till thou find none. . . . Lord thou hast heard the desire of the humble: thou wilt prepare their heart, thou wilt cause thine ear to hear . . ." (*Psalms* 10:12, 15, 17). Psalm 19 lists fully the various signs of the power of the Lord, but this list finally overcomes the poet; the contrast between deity and himself is too great, and his sense of this contrast finds expression:

> Who can understand his errors? cleanse thou me from secret faults. Keep back thy servant also from presumptuous sins; let them not have dominion over me. . . . (*Psalms* 19:12-13.)

Once this habit of mind is understood, its outward signs—an emotional rather than logical rationale in the songs—should cease to disconcert.

The following observations concern the more minute consequences of the habits of procedures discussed under the first five points. Viewed in relation to the logic of the emotions, to the abruptness of transitions, to the preference of the sensuous to the abstract, each of the following procedures will be seen as a natural consequence of the way of recording insights that we have just defined. Each procedure *in itself* may from time to time be either baffling or irritating, but it should be regarded first of all as an integral part of the poet's effort to sustain the directness and tension of the revelation that has moved him to the "action" of writing.

6. Hebrew poetry is constantly displaying *shifts in person, tense,* and *mode*—at least in the form in which readers of English encounter it. Any conventional guide to effectiveness *in prose* will warn one against unnecessary shifts in person (from *I* to *you,* from *he* to *they*), changes in tense (e.g., from past to present in narrative), or needless passage from indicative to imperative mode. Hebrew poetry as it is made available to us in the King James translation shows a bland indifference to these "rules," and so does a great deal of other poetry for that matter.

In good prose style, each pronoun must be implemented; it must have an antecedent noun or pronoun to refer to. Hebrew poetry abounds in what we may call the unimplemented pronoun, the pronoun without an antecedent; and the reader must acquire skill in providing the antecedent for many a pronoun he meets. Further, in one verse *I* may refer to the poet, and in the next it may refer to the Lord. Fortunately, the *dramatis personae* of the *Psalms* is limited. They are three in number: the Lord, the children of Israel, and the enemies of the children of Israel. Difficulties arise because the Lord may be referred to by all three persons—I, thou, and he—and so may the other two "characters" in the endless drama of sin, punishment, and reconciliation that dominates the minds of the Psalmists. A further complication is introduced by the fact that both the children of Israel and their enemies may be referred to in the singular or the plural.

The shift in pronoun reference is the most complex one.[2] We encounter it in a passage like this:

[2] Indeed, the shift in mode offers us no great difficulty: ". . . for thou beholdest mischief and spite, to requite it with thy hand: the poor committeth himself unto thee; thou art the helper of the fatherless. Break thou the arm of the wicked . . ." (*Psalms* 10:14-15). In our own speech we readily turn from explanation to the more compulsive "Do this, don't do that!"

> He that sitteth in the heavens shall laugh: the Lord shall have them in derision. ["Them" are the heathen.] Then shall he speak unto them in his wrath, and vex them in his sore displeasure. Yet have I set my king upon my holy hill of Zion. (*Psalms* 2:4-6.)

"He" has become "I"; both pronouns refer to the Lord. The cause for this shift? Perhaps it has some relation to the way music was arranged for the different choirs in the Temple, one choir speaking *of* the Lord and the other *for* the Lord. But the matter can also be explained as an intensification of consciousness in the spirit of the poet. The power of the Lord which he has been speaking for suddenly overcomes him, and he gives a record of direct utterance: "I have set my king upon my holy hill of Zion."

A little later in the same Psalm this shift occurs:

> Thou [the Lord] shalt break them with a rod of iron; thou shalt dash them in pieces like a potter's vessel. Be wise now therefore, O ye kings: be instructed, ye judges of the earth. (*Psalms* 2:9-10.)

This is less disconcerting than the earlier one. But here, and in countless other places, the poet suddenly shifts the direction of his address; he ceases to speak to the Lord, he wheels, and he speaks to persons who help to make up the being of the second character in the drama, Israel. (Here too it is a help to think of a choir which, of course, could address certain remarks to the sanctuary and certain other remarks to the assembled people.)

In this passage, the shift is from the Lord, "thou," to "thou enemy," the third person in the drama:

> Thou hast rebuked the heathen, thou hast destroyed the wicked, thou hast put out their name for ever and ever. O thou enemy, destructions are come to a perpetual end: and thou hast destroyed cities; their memorial is perished with them. But the Lord shall endure for ever: he hath prepared his throne for judgment. (*Psalms* 9:5-7.)

Here the shift is from a third-person reference to the Lord to a second-person one:

> The Lord also will be a refuge for the oppressed, a refuge in times of trouble. And they that know thy name will put their trust in thee: for thou, Lord, hast not forsaken them that seek thee. (*Psalms* 9:9-10.)

In Psalm 75, "I" in the first section refers to the Lord, and in the second section it stands for the Psalmist, who has come forward to warn the wicked. In Psalm 79, "the dead bodies of thy servants" suddenly give way to the more intense and direct "we": "We are become a reproach to our neighbors, a scorn and derision to them that are round about us" (*Psalms* 79:4). The change may take place within the compass of one verse: "And let the beauty of the Lord our God be upon us: and establish thou the work of our hands upon us . . ." (*Psalms* 90:17). The shifts, of course, occur in relation to the other two "persons" in the drama, as these verses must suffice to indicate: "I will say of the Lord, He is my refuge and my fortress: my God; in him will I trust. Surely he shall deliver thee from the snare of the fowler, and from the noisome pestilence" (*Psalms* 91:2-3). "I" and "thee" both refer to the second personage, Israel, although "I" means the individual member of the tribe and "thee" means either the individual or the tribe.

The shift of tense is also a source of trouble. The reader will be suddenly aware that the event he and the poet continue to contemplate has lost its moorings in the present and has slipped back into the past or drifted on into the future. The securest aid to dealing firmly with this effect is closely related to the clarification of pronoun reference. There we observed that there were essentially three characters in the drama. Here we may observe that there are essentially four stages to the drama—the "acts" already summarized. There is the time of the covenant, the time of sin, the time of punishment, and the time of restoration. This four-stage drama is the set of events over which the imagination of the Hebrew poet ranges. He causes no trouble when, in Psalm 35, he takes his stance in the time of misery (Act III) and looks back to the time of prosperity before the Lord's punishment began and forward to the time (Act IV) when the human tormentors will be punished and the poet placed in a position where he can enjoy his triumph. Trouble comes when the poet moves from one tense to another without moving from one stage to another, as in Psalm 97:

> The Lord reigneth; let the earth rejoice; let the multitude of isles be glad thereof. Clouds and darkness are round about him: righteousness and judgment are the habitation of his throne. A fire goeth before him, and burneth up his enemies round about. His lightnings enlightened the world: the earth saw and trembled. (*Psalms* 97:1-4.)

Both tenses refer to events in Act III, the act of judgment. The shift from the present to the past is without logical signification although it may have considerable emotional import and suggest a change in emotional distance between the poet and the events he contemplates.

Trouble comes also when the poet does move from one stage to the next *without* changing tenses. Most of Psalm 28 is on the level of the present tense, but the events are those of Acts III and IV. Verses 1-5 concern the misery of the poet when he lacks the support of God; verses 6-9 concern the time of rejoicing consequent on a display of divine power and favor. The reader who keeps in mind the simple sequence of events that lies behind this quicksilver play with time can soon find his own footing. Beneath the vivid imagery, the stages are always very easy to identify.

Such are the shifts. They exist to be met and dealt with because the Hebrew poet is primarily interested in what is immediately given him in vision. He is not concerned with turning his visions into prose—with making sure, for example, that God is represented throughout a brief composition in the third person ("the Lord") and Israel in the first ("we"). Sudden vision gives the poet the very words of the Lord, pronoun orientation changes, and the Lord is *I* and Israel is *you* and Israel's enemies are *they*. And an event allotted at the outset to a future day suddenly becomes—so imperious may vision be—an event that is taking place here and now. All these shifts, then, should be regarded not as inconveniences to be put up with; they are means, very probably unconsciously used, by which the Hebrew poet "steps up" the tension of his record of vision and suggests that the weight of vision is a heavy one, straining him and the language he uses.

7. The "devices" which follow, lumped together, offer less difficulty simply because they are known from one's other reading. But for this reason they deserve note; they are used with a freedom that may catch the reader off his guard. Thus, no one has trouble when, in Western poetry, he encounters the device called *personification.* "Patience on a monument" is conveniently capitalized, and "England" is easily feminized by the pronoun *she.* Our poets "play fair" and let us know when a personification is being brought out. So do the Hebrew poets—sometimes. Often, however, they do not warn us. Orderly personification, to which we are used in poetry, is essentially a *prose* device; it is a studied effort to vivify an abstraction, as in "Patience" and "England." But in Hebrew poetry, a clear line is not drawn between a person and the abstract entity his name stands for. In *Jeremiah* 31:15, Rachel weeping for her children is a fusion of at least three meanings. Rachel is a person in Hebrew history; she is—the point of transition—a "mother in Israel" because she gave birth to some of the men who fathered the separate tribes; and finally she is also *all* Israel weeping for the downfall of the chosen people. And she is these three things almost at once, not in decent and orderly succession. This confusion—confusion from our point of view—enables the Hebrew poet to reproduce the tension of the time of insight. "Rachel" is, to begin with, three sorts of awarenesses that tend to merge. Indeed, we can sometimes see this process of merging taking place. Thus, in a satiric picture of the vain daughters of Zion sketched by Isaiah, what begins as a character sketch in the style of the "good wife" passage of *Proverbs* (chap. 31) is suddenly transposed to another level. The "daughters of Zion" are no longer real women; they stand not even for all Hebrew women. They stand for all Israel, male and female. Isaiah's account of the day of disaster lets us see this transformation taking place.

> And it shall come to pass, that instead of sweet smell there shall be stink; and instead of a girdle a rent; and instead of well set hair

> baldness; and instead of a stomacher a girding of sackcloth; and burning instead of beauty. Thy men shall fall by the sword, and thy mighty in the war. And her gates shall lament and mourn; and she being desolate shall sit upon the ground. (*Isaiah* 3:24-26.)

By the time we reach "her gates," we are concerned with something more than the proper humiliation of vain young women. "She being desolate" is none other than Rachel and stands for the collective entity of the people of Israel.

For the writers of *Psalms,* almost any hero of the past can be used in this wavering but poetically suggestive fashion. The reader of Hebrew history will encounter familiar names, but only in their idealized aspects. It is the David of *Chronicles* and not the David of *Samuel* that appears in Psalm 132. Other frequent names are Aaron, Moses, and Samuel, types of priesthood, and Jacob, the "father" of the twelve tribes.

The names of places are used to stand for a great deal more in poetic discourse than mere geographical points. Thus, in Psalm 108, the list of names is full of significance to anyone acquainted with the Hebrew past, and one cannot miss the note of triumph with which Israel's enemies end the list:

> Moab is my washpot; over Edom will I cast my shoe; over Philistia will I triumph. Who will bring me into the strong city? who will lead me into Edom? Wilt not thou, O God, who hast cast us off? . . . Through God we shall do valiantly: for he it is that shall tread down our enemies. (*Psalms* 108:9-13.)

Edom and Moab and Philistia function both as particular enemies and as all conceivable enemies in time to come. And Babylon the name has, thanks to Hebrew poetry, a longer life than Babylon the city; it has become a poetic "counter" that stands for sin and corruption, just as Zion stands for holiness and righteousness.

8. Metaphor in *Psalms* and *The Song of Solomon* is what it is elsewhere. It is a statement of identity—"You are a pig"—more vivid than the simile—"You resemble a pig." Both simile and metaphor

reinforce the specificity of Hebrew poetry, and when a poet writes a passage like this one, he is beyond reproach:

> Set me as a seal upon thine heart, as a seal upon thine arm: for love is strong as death; jealousy is cruel as the grave: the coals thereof are coals of fire, which hath a most vehement flame. (*The Song of Solomon* 8:6.)

When a poet writes the following passage, he is in danger:

> Thy teeth are like a flock of sheep that are even shorn, which came up from the washing; whereof every one bear twins, and none is barren among them. (*The Song of Solomon* 4:2.)

When a poet writes this last passage, he has been defeated by the device that should aid him:

> Thy neck is like the tower of David builded for an armory, whereon there hang a thousand bucklers, all shields of mighty men. (*The Song of Solomon* 4:4.)

The user of metaphor does well to imitate the hit-and-run driver. The beloved's neck and the tower of David have grotesque dissimilarities that a hasty reference would not call to our attention. This tendency to fall in love with embroidery is, fortunately, little apparent in *Psalms*. *The Song of Solomon* was, many judge, a secular poem, and the poet felt free to linger in a way that offends our taste. In *Psalms*, he speeds on an errand the Lord has commanded; the aesthetic results are happy.

Metaphor serves as the point of departure for an important form, the parable. Some metaphors and similes concern a pair of objects that have a good many features in common. If we say a man has a heart of oak, we may safely linger and think of the slow growth of the oak from a pliant seedling to the rigid giant it later becomes; we may treat the oak as an emblem of man's moral life. The metaphor has been expanded into a parable—a brief instructive story that, though it may concern some moral abstraction, remains as specific as the initial figure of speech. The parable comes to its flowering in the New Testament, but it has its point of departure in the utterance of the prophets. Amos' account of the Lord standing on a wall with a plumb line is a comparison that has not gone very far toward becoming a parable (*Amos* 7:7, 8). Other examples of the parable in the Old Testament are found in *Judges* 9:7-21 and in *II Kings* 14:9, and these in their very opening phrases are not far from metaphor and simile: "The trees went forth on a time to anoint a king over them; and they said unto the olive tree . . ." and "The thistle that was in Lebanon sent to the cedar that was in Lebanon, saying, Give thy daughter to my son to wife. . . ." There are materials for parables in *Psalms,* but a parable too is perhaps an innocent kind of embroidery that the writers of sacred song had no time to execute or judged unworthy of the Temple.

All this goes to compose a sort of handbook for the person who would learn to love the books of Hebrew poetry, to appreciate their temper and movement as well as pick out quotable phrases. Glancing back, one should see that the art of the Hebrew poet is the art of taking short cuts. Only thus could he convey the impact of vision and divest himself of its heavy burden. Our reward for any pains we may take is that we shall be able to follow the swift movements of his spirit, sinuous and startling, various and yet recurrent.

The Song of Solomon

Certain special remarks remain concerning each book here considered. *The Song of Solomon* is a poem toward which various attitudes are possible. The early Church Fathers and the Hebrew commentators chose to regard it as an allegory. Beneath the surface of a series of poems that seem to be concerned with passionate love is a hidden meaning worthy of preservation. The "beloved," for the Fathers, was the Church or the created human soul, and the "lover" was Christ or God. For the term *Church,* the Hebrew scholars substituted the *chosen people,* God's "peculiar treasure."

In recent times, students of this book have recognized that it has most of the marks of the love poetry of all civilizations. This opinion has been developed in two ways. Students have tried to relate the various sections of the book to each other in such a way that a continuous story emerges: the narrative of a simple maid who is taken into Solomon's house of women but is finally returned to her humble lover. This reading of the poem requires more ingenuity than some readers have. The latter are better satisfied with the supposition that *The Song of Solomon* is a loose collection of love poems or perhaps marriage odes sung during protracted nuptial ceremonies. Elements of story are implied, but those elements follow a familiar pattern: the lovers meet, desire to be with each other, but are for a time frustrated by various enemies, such as talebearers and other lovers who can perhaps offer a better collection of gifts to the girl's parents. With this suggestion in mind, one can account for the effects of dialogue between the sweethearts and between the beloved and other women. In short, the poems make reference to a general set of circumstances, just as the Psalms make reference to a generally understood scenario of events.

The Book of Psalms

The Book of Psalms is, as we have already indicated, a collection of poems that effect variations on themes suitable for Temple worship. It is thought that *The Book of Psalms* is not one but several collections, made at different times and, perhaps, for different groups of Temple singers, such as the sons of Korah and the sons of Asaph. Hebrew song is very old, as sections of lyric expression embedded in the books of history indicate. Ancient hymns to other gods, such as the Babylonian Ishtar and the Egyptian Aton, Ikhnaton's deity, have survived and suggest that Hebrew poetic compositions might have existed in David's day. However, the level of religious thought in David's day, as we sample it in *I* and *II Samuel,* could hardly have led to the creation of all the Psalms, for some of them display modes of comprehending deity that, so far as we can judge with certainty, were the creation of the prophets (850-500 B.C.) *The Book of Psalms* was probably given its present form in the centuries after the return from exile (537 B.C. onward to about 100 B.C.). It contains, however, a range of religious poetry that may reach back beyond the time of David.

The poetry of the *Psalms* is poetry in service of "the Other." It amounts to a kind of action rather than a leisurely discourse, and tells us a good deal about the Hebrews' awareness of "the Other," on which they were dependent, or judged they were. What forms this awareness takes we can but note here since the next chapter gives, by means of the prophets, the same story in an easier and more comprehensible form.

The form of the story of Hebrew religious awareness offered by *The Book of Psalms* is difficult for an obvious reason. In this anthology of devotional poetry mingle religious attitudes that the more orderly story of the prophets allows us to classify as early and late. Psalm 68 begins thus, and so continues:

> Let God arise, let his enemies be scattered: let them also that hate him flee before him. As smoke is driven away: as wax melteth before the fire, so let the wicked perish at the presence of God. (*Psalms* 68:1-2.)

It is plainly removed from the kind of religious sentiment that pervades this unwarlike, unparticularist, peaceful Psalm:

> Lord, thou hast been our dwelling place in all generations. Before the mountains were brought forth, or ever thou hadst formed the earth and the world, even from everlasting to everlasting, thou art God. (*Psalms* 90:1-2.)

These and other impressions about deity troop through the 150 songs. What topics are they concerned with? They tell us what God is, without utter unanimity. God is a man-shaped being; he is a spirit. He is the protector of a certain place, Zion; he is the protector of all places since he created all that exists. What is God's character? He is a jealous god; he is a god of mercy. He is a god who holds up before himself and his people a standard of absolute righteousness; he is a god who plays favorites and will permit his chosen people to "get away" with a good deal. How does one please God? By minute observance of all the laws of Moses and by Temple attendance; by turning to him in the quiet of the night and speaking to him without aid of priest and rite. Whom does God favor? His own people and all people.

In the *Psalms,* it is as if an exposed cliffside which had preserved in its strata an orderly account of the successive geological ages had been dynamited and had collapsed into the quarry beneath it. The result? A mass of wonderful and fascinating debris which we can wander over and try to assign to proper places in Hebrew religious history. Indeed, its extreme importance for subsequent Jewish and Christian worship is that it does not record, in terms of poetic wisdom, the religious insights of only one age of Hebrew history—say, of the postexilic theocratic state in which *Psalms* took on its final form. It has, in a popular phrase, "something for everyone." Throughout history, all stages of religious insight persist and are able to find their echo somewhere in *The Book of Psalms.* Less obviously but just as truly, all stages of religious insight are likely at various crises to turn up in the mind and heart of each person. We probably flatter ourselves when we believe that we have put certain religious concepts behind us. Whatever our conscious religious attitudes, there is little in *The Book of Psalms* that at some time does not have power to make us feel that what we read comes not from the collection of songs accumulated around the name of David but from our own hearts.

CHAPTER X

Hebrew Prophecy

WE SUGGESTED that *The Book of Psalms* was a vast quarry which contained, in rich confusion, religious attitudes early and late. A survey of the succession of prophets we choose to treat[1] provides us with material for a fairly orderly account of how later intuitions about deity, human dignity, and good and evil rose after earlier ones had been tried and found wanting. However, as noted in Chapter I, a person gives a false impression of the very nature of man's age-long wrestle with "the Other," and with the social and ethical consequences of such a battle, if he suggests that the later always excludes the earlier attitude. Thus, though we try to observe what upward spiralings there are, it would be untrue to assert that later insights always cancel earlier ones. One prophet, Ezekiel, for example, may present insights that ought to preclude the appearance of other insights but do not. A later prophet may take up again insights that an earlier one has rejected. Further, though we excerpt from specific prophets what might be called their "doctrines," we must continue to be aware that these doctrines exist in the context of "poetic wisdom" described in the previous chapter. They were not advanced as Luther advanced his "doctrines" when he posted on

1 Certain prophetic writers are omitted in this discussion of Hebrew prophecy, chiefly for reasons of clarity of presentation. For example, an exposition of *Micah* would cause us to retrace, for this intrinsically interesting prophet, the moral insights of *Amos* and the Messianic hopes of *Isaiah*. Also, since we are trying to trace the gradual emergence of religious ideas that students of religion ordinarily call "higher," we would complicate our story by giving attention to prophets whose visions repeat particularist and legalistic accents which the prophets here discussed are in the process of rejecting or putting into new contexts. There is much that is characteristic in the cursing of Edom in *Obadiah*, and students of the reconstruction of the Hebrew state after the return from the exile (538 B.C. and onward) cannot neglect the books of *Haggai* and *Zechariah*, and the prophecy in *Malachi* is a useful revelation of the seamy side of the theocratic state. But what we are trying to see in this chapter is the main outline of the growth of Hebrew prophecy. The writers mentioned in this note, as well as *Joel*, *Nahum*, and *Habakkuk*, contribute interesting shadings to that outline, but theirs are not the hands that drew in the bold strokes we admire and now seek to understand.

the door of the cathedral at Wittenberg the ninety-five "theses" that he was willing to debate with all comers. With some confidence one may state Kant's theory of the categorical imperative, and the concepts making up the materialistic dialectic of class strife according to Karl Marx. These and other philosophic concepts have grown in a prose soil, and they are not likely to wither when transplanted into our prose discussion of them. But what we draw from the gardens of prophetic thought has grown in poetic soil. The thought of the prophets is "pre-philosophic" in the sense defined in the previous chapter.

The Characteristics of Prophecy

Though we commence with the prophet Amos, Amos is not a beginning. The beginning of the story we now follow in the prophets is the varied stirring of curiosity which we detected in the Pentateuch, which we have already followed through the activity of Elijah and Elisha, and which we have perceived informing *The Book of Psalms.* It is the curiosity about "the Other" on whom man is dependent. It is "the Other" whom man must bend to his will or, better, whose will man must discover in order that he himself may bend. Seeking to bend deity to one's will is, on the other hand, the activity of medicine men, the "shamans." We have already perceived it in the cures, threats, and spells of "impure" prophets like Elijah and Elisha. It can be summed up under the term *magic.* Elijah extends himself on the body of the dead child and brings it back to life; Elisha uses his mana to make the iron axhead rise to the surface of the stream.

With our modern passion for having things regular and neat, at least in past historical developments, we would like to be able to see that such magical activity is, in the later prophets, left behind and that the men we now take up no longer show signs of wishing to impose their wills on "the Other," to wrest mana or power from God and use it for selfish ends. We would doubtless like to perceive that "prophecy" now becomes an activity in which the ego or self of each prophet disappears and that the prophetic efforts of two and a half centuries (750-500 B.C.) are concerned only with clarifying and purifying the ideas about "the Other" with which Amos begins. But once more, progress in matters of religion and of related "wisdom" follows no straight-line course. In science, in what we today call "knowledge," a successful experiment automatically makes useless the repetition of past experiments. But it is not so in the realm of wisdom and religious speculation. We may see the prophets (and ourselves) achieving insights "better" than those held earlier. But the new insight does not automatically cancel the attractions of the old. Both earlier and later insights respond to or exploit certain natural and permanent human desires or fancies. Although a later religious or moral insight satisfies those desires more fully or in a more balanced way, in moments of passion or distress mankind may circle back to earlier ways of viewing "the Other" or his own moral destiny.

With this warning in mind, we may define the terminus toward which the Hebrew prophets make their collective journey: a conception of deity divested of the "notes" of animism and nature worship that mark many of the appearances of God in *Genesis.* They seek a deity divested also of the obvious marks of anthropomorphism but still possessing what we called personality in the discussion of the presentation of Saul and David in the books of history. God must be more than Aristotle's "first mover" that starts the world and then does not ever intervene. The prophets travel toward a conception that implies, in deity, a love for all beings and one justice for all beings. Such a conception, once achieved, should make unlikely the return of ideas opposed to this view of "the Other." Or so we might argue by analogy with the unfolding of scientific thought. Yet, in the history of Hebrew prophecy, this is not so. The most we can say is that what the prophets accomplish tends to *reduce* the importance of earlier views of deity, but it does not give them a deathblow. They continue to lurk in the minds of the prophets, and for more than twenty-four centuries in the minds of men. Given the opportune circumstance, they will return. In a recent summer, in the American Midwest, there was a long drought, and presently newspapers informed us that prayers for rain were being recited from various pulpits. *In theory*, the minister and his congregation held to a view of God that would tend to inhibit their asking for special favors for themselves and their fields. But their dire need for rain drove them back to a view of "the Other" as a particularist God who controlled the rain clouds which the formal creed of the church had long denied. An agnostic tells of feeling that the force mercilessly tossing his ocean liner was personal and malign; he returned to a view of a natural phenomenon that his intellect had dismissed many years before. In a catastrophe, in a foxhole, persons are likely to discover that a special part of the entire picture of "the Other" constructed by the two Testaments and preserved by the churches is quite attractive; and other parts just as essential will be neglected. At least, lest we become impatient with the prophets for their failure to follow their noses to the goal of universal deity and universal law which to us seems so obvious, we should remember that we too waver. If we practiced prayer during years of war, we no doubt sought to pit "the Other" against our enemy, an enemy that was also the creation of the deity we addressed and probably that deity's worshiper.

The emphasis, consequently, in our present chapter is on two functions, and two only, of the Hebrew prophet: He is a person who foretells events; he perceives the permanent laws that determine how events shall unroll. The prophet uses his gifts to understand the laws of justice and punishment to be perceived in the workings of God; his most important function is to urge the mass of men to understand these laws and bend to them. This does not mean that the later prophets cease to use their insights, their mana in a way we should call magical: the effort to impose the human will or whim on "the Other." Isaiah's curing King Hezekiah of a mortal illness with a poultice is magic (*II Kings* 20:1-7). In a less obvious way, predictions that favor the chosen people are a form of magic; the prophecy of the return to Zion is a projection upon the screen of the future of a picture that the eyes of the prophet can nowhere find in the chaos around him. Thus, that Hebrew prophecy continues "impure"—continues to mingle the act of desiring benefits with the act of comprehending deity—marks the prophets as being men like us.

The great English historian, Arnold Toynbee, has been rebuked for remarking, in a discussion as to whether civilization is going to survive, that if Western culture perishes, perhaps the Pygmies of central Africa will take up the torch. This is a bloodcurdling detachment; most of us are not capable of rising to such passionless estimate. Certainly the Hebrew prophets were not. The horizon, the background of their vision, finally widened to take in all the known world and all known history. But forever large in the foreground bulk the walls and towers of a heavenly or earthly Jerusalem—the haven perhaps of all men, but certainly the special home of a special people, the prophet's own people.

This leads us to state a further descriptive "law" that we should keep before us from *Amos* to *Ezekiel.* It has already been implied, in the previous chapter, in connection with the *logic of the emotions* which we observed organizing the longer *Psalms:* There, the poet sustained one vision until it was no longer bearable, and he escaped it by turning to another, and to us *logically* opposed, vision (Israel in the dust; Israel enthroned). But the prophet—if we may draw a line—is something more than an impassioned singer. He is trying to reshape the future of a nation or an individual. He may be unaware of the demands of logic, but he is deeply conscious of the burden of his responsibility. If so, how can he involve himself in logical contradictions that tend to cancel each other? (We all have heard of the baffling prediction made, during the depression of the thirties, by ex-President Coolidge. Mr. Coolidge remarked that, in the following years, things were going to get either better or worse.) The answer is that the prophet's thought processes are indeed those of the poet. There appear before him deeply stirring images which he may escape but which he may not tamper with to make them logically more compatible with *other* deeply felt images.

As a result, the thought processes of the prophet lead to what we may call *both-and* judgments rather than *either-or* judgments. This is the descriptive "law" that, once we see its implication, prepares us to move with comfort through the prophetic terrain. When we think logically or rationally, when we cease to daydream and settle down to solve a personal problem or to consider a grave social question, we approach our solution by a series of *either-or* judgments. If we are considering the wisdom of inviting a certain stranger to our party, we begin by saying: "Either we do [and face certain consequences] or we don't [and face a different train of consequences]." We then balance one set of consequences against the other and reach a prudent decision by observing which set offers the most good and the least evil. We make our choice between two presidential candidates in the same way. This choice is, of course, easy if the consequences of voting for one candidate are, in our opinion, all evil and for the other all good. Here the problem is quickly solved; and we congratulate ourselves, as we march to the voting place, on being sensible and rational. But suppose we perceive that voting for either candidate is likely to be productive of some good. A Republican president would produce certain benefits and a Democratic president would produce certain benefits—benefits, however, quite unlike those we expect from the Republican. Here we may say impatiently, "If we could only have both of them!" Then, to be sure, we smile indulgently at our lack of logic. We know we cannot have both of them, and we make our *either-or* choice.

Time and again—this is the point of our illustrations—the prophets do determine to have "both of them." That is, alternative visions have risen, each moving and attractive. The prophets do not scuttle one, saying: "You can't have your cake and eat it too." For them, the manifest good of one vision is not undone or thrown out of court by the manifest good of another. Jehovah may at one time appear as a deity specially concerned with the fortunes of Judah; at another time, he may appear as a deity whose interest embraces all humankind. At one time, the prophet may perceive "the infinite worth of the individual" and judge that that worth is fulfilled by a personal, immediate relation to deity; at another time, the prophet may be struck by the importance of the race and the institutions of the race, the Temple and the law, which preserve its satisfactory relations to God. Both sets of perceptions *we* would tend to submit to the *either-or* process of judgment—regretfully, since we perceive excellence or sense in each view. But—this is the *effect* if not the stated intent of Hebrew prophecy—if excellence lies in *both* quarters, must not that excellence be recorded and confessed? The prophets' solution to this dilemma leads to what we have called *both-and* judgments. The visions of two opposed excellences are both preserved. We may continue to say that the two visions are logically contradictory, but at least the prophet's solution—the recognition of the excellence of opposed points of view—is one way of handling contradictions. The prophets, in this treatment, run counter to the behests of logic; but they do little violence to the successive, intense experiences, their perception of a high degree of wisdom in successive attitudes toward God or man. We, on the other hand, can make our *either-or* judgments without many qualms only after allowing the good of the alternate we reject to become blurred in retrospect. The prophet escapes such qualms. Since both possibilities came to him in vision, they are of equal authority; the imprint of the Lord is on both and may not be ignored. So both, in different sections of the same prophet's utterance, are preserved. This is, to be sure, a "pre-philosophic" frame of mind; but it is not subhuman. It is, indeed, very close to that part of our own experience that is spontaneous and unreflective. The prophets are men "of like passions" with ourselves. They arrive at the utterance that is the terminus of their thought by the *both-and* process which, on an unreflective level, is our own way of responding to experience.

The prophets made up a procession of men concerned with a few dominant topics. Their preoccupation with Jehovah and the proper relation of man to Jehovah may produce, for the undiscriminating reader, an effect of grayness or monotony. (The ordinary newspaper offers us a series of contrasting shocks: the "front page," the drama section, the sports column, the funnies.) But to a discriminating reader, the selected procession that now troops past us has a variety both delicate and precise. It is said that God works in mysterious ways his wonders to perform. The lightning, the mana that produces prophetic vision, does not strike twice in the same place. Amos is a rude shepherd. Hosea, his contemporary, is a man of cultivation and even sophistication; and both are secular men, unattached to any official priesthood. Isaiah (the Isaiah of Chapters 1-40 of the collection of prophecy called *Isaiah*) has a secure, important position; he is a priest of the Temple and a court official, the Samuel and Nathan of a later day. Jeremiah is—or comes to be—a social outcast; he turns into what everyone agrees is a dangerous, subversive fellow. And Ezekiel is a Jew in exile, nerving his people to survive. (The marks of "Isaiah II" [*Isaiah*, chaps. 40-55] will be discussed later.)

Thus, our selection of a prophetic company will, in due course,

CHART 8. Hebrew Prophecy

(Bold indicates that the person is discussed fully.)

HEBREW HISTORY		PROPHETS	OUTSIDE EVENTS
869-850	Ahab, Northern king	**Elijah**	Wars with Syria
849-842	Joram, Northern king	**Elisha**	Wars with Syria
786-746	Jeroboam II, Northern king	**Amos** c. 760	Growing power of Assyria: efforts of Northern Kingdom to stave
		Hosea (750-735)	off disaster by an alliance with Syria (see Chart 5)
742-735	Jotham } kings	**Isaiah** (740-701)	Danger from Assyria and narrow
735-715	Ahaz } of		escape by the temporary alliance of Ahaz and by divine aid
715-687	Hezekiah } Judah	Micah (725-690?)	Recognition of the growing power of Babylon

allow us to see not only light from heaven but refraction of that light as it passes through the prisms of quite different personalities and circumstances. It will allow us to see that the appearance, in the history of Hebrew thought, of certain key concepts is conditioned by men who were, they believed, God's chosen vessels.

Amos

The first of these, Amos, is generally agreed to have come upon the stage of Hebrew history about the year 750, some hundred years after the activity of Elijah and Elisha. He resembles Elijah more than he does Elisha—the latter with his comfortable "college" of prophets and his recognized social position. It was Elijah, recall, who came to vex Ahab, the king of the Northern Kingdom Israel, and be his special "adversary." Elijah came from Gilead across the Jordan, and he was a stern, puritanical critic of the sophistication and the mixture of culture in Israel under Ahab and his Sidonian queen Jezebel. Like Elijah, Amos too was an outlander because he came from Judah, which was the subordinate Hebrew nation throughout the time of the divided kingdoms. Like Elijah, Amos, in the opinion of the official priesthood at the "king's chapel" at Bethel, lacked both social position and education. He was, as he tells us, "an herdman and gatherer of sycamore fruit" and lived "among the herdmen of Tekoa," a village some ten miles south of Jerusalem; and he came north on a visit—perhaps drawn by rumors of the magnificence of this northern shrine as well as by the fact that it was a holy place, the spot where, in Jacob's dream, the ladder had rested.

We are to think of Amos visiting the shrine which, like pagan temples in nearby kingdoms, announced not only the glory of a deity but the temporal prosperity and magnificence of a king. That Jeroboam II of Israel (786-746 B.C.) was such a king appears in *II Kings* 14:25 ff.: "he restored the coast [the boundaries] of Israel from the entering of Hamath unto the sea of the plain [the Dead Sea]"; and he "recovered Damascus," a city belonging to the Syrian or Aramean empire that for many years protected the two Hebrew kingdoms from Assyria. We may suspect that Amos as a subject of Judah, the lesser Hebrew kingdom, would have a special reason for resenting what he saw about him in the crowded ways of the popular holy city of Bethel. He saw the wealthy women peeping out of the ivory-mounted, curtained litters, their eyes lined with dark paint, and he called them "the kine of Bashan." He could peer in on luxurious banquets where the most delicate meats—"the lambs out of the flock and the calves out of the midst of the stall"—were served up, and he could see how the food was washed down with bowlsful of wine while music played. He could look with scorn on those sophisticated persons who anointed "themselves with the chief ointments" brought by Jeroboam's caravans from Egypt. Worst of all, he could observe the sacrifices to the Lord as conducted by the chief priest, Amaziah; the temple was crowded with the wealthy, sweet-smelling men and women who, in their turn, cast suspicious glances at the skin-clad, unwashed visitor from Judah. A brief passage—*Amos* 7:10-15—suggests that Amos broke forth in the temple itself against the well-fed priesthood and the modish worshipers, for Amaziah sent to Jeroboam asking to be rid of the plague of Amos; and there is sarcasm and condescension in Amaziah's words to Amos himself: "O thou seer, flee thee away into the land of Judah, and there eat bread and prophesy there" (*Amos* 7:13). Plainly, in the eyes of a comfortable servant of organized, prosperous religion, Amos was a "seer" like those in the ranting rabble that moved Saul to "prophesy"—and fall down in a fit (*I Samuel* 19:24).

Clearly, the worship of Jehovah that had been restored in Israel by Elijah had been taken over and tamed by the prosperous and powerful; a pilgrimage to Bethel and the sacrifice of a lamb without blemish was a part of the smart life. Elijah had cried out against the worship of Baal. Amos cries out against what, in a hundred years, the powerful of this earth had made of the worship of Jehovah. It takes little imagination to see Amos' outburst as analogous to the comment of a man who is wont to worship in a simple frame church and by chance visits a vast neo-Gothic structure on Riverside Drive in New York or on Chicago's North Side. Amos did not have a frame church in his background—only the simplicities of a herdsman's life, in which he and his fellows made their sacrifices on altars of unhewn stone and practiced just dealing in order to survive. The "call"—the impulse to utterance—which later prophets experienced was often quite ornate. Amos' "call" is quite simple. He says: "And the Lord took me as I followed the flock, and the Lord said unto me, Go, prophesy unto my people Israel" (*Amos* 7:15). This call was repeated when he walked along the streets of Bethel and saw the prosperous and then looked in the shadows and saw the poor; ". . . the Lord hath spoken, who can but prophesy?" he asks (*Amos* 3:8). To the poor who heard him, either in the temple or along the streets, he was an asserter of an obvious, suppressed truth. To the wealthy he was uncouth and ignorant; he was in "bad taste" and—as the action of Amaziah indicates—definitely "dangerous." What happened to Amos we do not know. Perhaps he was "escorted" to the Judean border and told not to come back; perhaps, in modern language, he was "shot while trying to escape."

In some way, however, his passionate addresses got set down. What do they come to, what is their essence beneath the bewildering variety of presentation, where vituperation and prediction and parable are strung together? Another comparison with his prototype Elijah clarifies the answer. Elijah spent most of his energy on asserting the preëminence of Jehovah. But what was Jehovah? Thunder, fire, earthquake? No, "a still small voice." But what that small voice said, what it counseled, the activity of Elijah only suggests. If it was the counsel behind Elijah's "line" in the affair of Naboth's vineyard (*I Kings,* chap. 21), it leads directly to all that Amos says about the bond between the Lord and man. Jehovah was not the Lord of Ahab, of the powerful and mighty. He was the Lord of all men and wished to bind all men to observance of the same rules.

True, Elijah's God is also a god of power; and it is Amos who tells us how that power is exercised in the interest of *righteousness,* of a set of simple principles. The power is not, he says, as he takes in the rich and the poor at Bethel, exercised in the interest of those who have money and positions of authority. As we have noted in the *both-and* discussion, one idea does not exclude an opposed one. In *Amos,* the newer concept of a righteous deity does not exclude the older one of a powerful deity ready to act suddenly and arbitrarily; the newer idea is added to the older and from now on co-exists with it. God is still the power of creation (4:13 and 5:8) and there is none else beside him. But to this power, righteousness is added. God is represented as seeking to bind both himself and his worshipers to the simple principles of justice that have struck Amos:

> I hate, I despise your feast days, and I will not smell in your solemn assemblies. Though ye offer me burnt offerings and your meat offerings, I will not accept them: neither will I regard the peace offerings

> of your fat beasts. Take thou away from me the noise of thy songs; for I will not hear the melody of thy viols. But let judgment run down as waters, and righteousness as a mighty stream. (*Amos* 5:21-24.)

By "judgment" Amos means nothing abstract. He means that the poor must have their right at the "gate"—that is, at the place of judgment.

> Hear this, O ye that swallow up the needy, even to make the land of the poor to fail, saying, When will the new moon be gone, that we may sell corn? and the sabbath, that we may set forth wheat, making the epah small, and the shekel great, and falsifying the balances by deceit? that we may buy the poor for silver, and the needy for a pair of shoes . . . (*Amos* 8:4-6.)

To the wealthy, religious observance is a custom and, worse, an inconvenience since its feast days hold them back from their real interest: the exploitation and enslavement of the poor, of those who have no one to speak for them in the gate. No one, that is, except Amos and deity as Amos perceives deity. From his perception of the coincidence of power and righteousness in God follow the other insights of Amos.

Before turning to these consequences, we should note another point. It is thanks to this sort of insight that we today look back on the earlier Old Testament worthies and find them wanting. Isaac and Jacob had power—mana—and to spare. But their destinies unfolded in an era when power had not been qualified; it had not been linked, as in the thought of Amos, with righteousness and with certain other qualities that succeeding prophets make out to exist in deity. Actually, the persons Amos inveighs against—the "kine of Bashan" and the priest Amaziah—are no more unrighteous than Jacob cheating his brother Esau of his birthright. But with Amos, we begin to move toward a time when power itself is not enough and is not axiomatic warrant that the Lord is on one's side.

Amos' judgment, which demands that the power and righteousness of Jehovah coincide, is, like other prophetic judgments, no static thing. Once made, a judgment is seen to beget consequences. The consequences, as Amos sees them, are simple and brief. They take the form of a chain of events upon which later prophets impose variations and elaborations. As Amos views the matter, the fair virgins, the strong young men, and their elders have misconstrued the covenant between God and man; they have judged it as a contract with a god whose power was great but arbitrary—a power that could be won, consequently, to the side of the nation and the persons who, like Amaziah, knew how to flatter and placate an arbitrary deity at his great temple. But the God of the true covenant is not to be sought at a particular place.

> For thus saith the Lord unto the house of Israel, Seek ye me, and ye shall live: but seek not Bethel, nor enter into Gilgal, and pass not to Beersheba: for Gilgal shall surely go into captivity, and Bethel shall come to nought. (*Amos* 5:4-5.)

The contract with this powerful deity is to be kept chiefly in justice and fair dealing with those who are at one's mercy.

Obviously, at Bethel and elsewhere in the Northern Kingdom, the contract has been broken, at least in the eyes of Amos. What happens when the contract is broken? The train of events unrolls thus to the angry, earnest prophet. The Lord commences by measuring all with his plumb line and says to Amos: "Behold, I will set a plumbline in the midst of my people Israel: I will not again pass by them any more; and the high places of Isaac shall be desolate, and the sanctuaries of Israel shall be laid waste; and I will rise against the house of Jeroboam with a sword" (*Amos* 7:8-9). When the Lord says he will not pass by Israel any more, he means that he will not exercise, in relation to them, either arbitrary or special favor; Israel cannot escape justice nor, for that matter, can deity itself. Amos proceeds, with relish, to draw the picture of the coming catastrophe, the visitation of judgment on Israel. There will be "cleanness of teeth in all your cities" (4:6), and those who bury the dead will fear to mention the name of the Lord (6:10).[2] Even mythological vistas

[2] In the discussion of each prophet, the references are, unless otherwise indicated, to the book which bears the prophet's name.

open up as Amos embroiders his spectacle of just retribution; for those who seek to escape may dig down into hell or climb into heaven and all in vain. The Lord will find them out; even if they fly to the bottom of the sea, they will waste their strength. The Lord says: "Thence will I command the serpent, and he shall bite them" (9:3)—"the serpent" in Babylonian myth is the enemy of a god out of whom the earth itself was fashioned. In this time of disaster, remarks Amos with a dark glance at the temple, those who clasp the supposedly protecting horns of an altar will "rejoice in a thing of nought" (6:13); in past years they should have grasped at a more important thing—righteousness.

Thus much is quite clear in Amos picture of the working out of the justice of an offended God. A detail of this justice that later prophets seize on and elaborate appears in the dire promise: "But, behold, I will raise up against you a nation, O house of Israel . . . ; and they shall afflict you from the entering in of Hemath unto the river of the wilderness" (6:14). Isaiah and Jeremiah have more specific ideas about this "nation."

What is far from clear, in Amos, is the end of the drama of judgment. The bulk of his maledictions suggests that he accepted the logical conclusion: the contract of righteeousness has been broken, and the automatic results, a total destruction of the Northern Kingdom, will run their course. But here Amos wavers, and we are in the *both-and* belt of prophetic weather described at the outset of this chapter. An *either-or* judgment would run thus: *either* Israel is righteous *or* she shall be destroyed. We have seen that most of *Amos* accepts this solution. But in three verses (7:1-3), a parable is fleetingly told. A field (Israel) is given over to grasshoppers (the forces of destruction, the anonymous "nation" that the Lord justly calls in to do the work of punishment). But Amos is unwilling to accept the fulfillment of his own prediction.

> And it came to pass, that when they [the grasshoppers] had made an end of eating the grass of the land, then I said, O Lord God, forgive, I beseech thee: by whom shall Jacob arise? for he is small. (*Amos* 7:2.)

Jacob stands for all the Northern Kingdom, and Amos is expressing the hope that somehow the juggernaut of divine justice will not utterly destroy the people who have "asked for" destruction. The third verse concludes the parable: "The Lord repented for this: It shall not be, saith the Lord." This possibility, that a righteous God will at the last pull some of his punches, recurs in *Amos* 9:8:

> Behold, the eyes of the Lord are upon the sinful kingdom, and I will destroy it from off the face of the earth; saving that I will not utterly destroy the house of Jacob, saith the Lord.

The hope finds more extended expression in the rather gentle and ideal vision of an Israel restored to a sight of the divine face which closes the book; some scholars say this passage was not written by Amos. At any rate, it displays with utmost compression the *both-and* kind of judgment. It is as if Amos admits the great attractions of both views: that Israel should be punished to the last man; that the Northern Kingdom, so important a part of the chosen people, ought, despite its sins, to have a continued existence. Since both possibilities are moving, both are recorded. There is no attempt to reconcile them. Both are preserved—the vision of doom, the vision of restoration—with all their intrinsic compulsion. There Amos leaves the matter. Other prophets (we shall see) do not let the *both-and* judgments fall with so resounding a concussion.

Finally—what we should least expect from Amos, whose horizon takes in chiefly Judah and a bit of Israel—one passage indicates that Jehovah is more than the God of one people. The Lord is pleading with Israel to reconsider its wickedness, and the plea takes this form:

> Are ye not as children of the Ethiopians unto me, O children of Israel? . . . Have not I brought up Israel out of the land of Egypt? and the Philistines from Caphtor, and the Syrians from Kir? (*Amos* 9:7.)

The Philistines and the Syrians were, in particular, traditional enemies to the Hebrews. This anti-particularist verse suggests that Amos is concerned with no national or henotheistic deity but with one who has created and who embraces all races. This verse is, however, more than balanced by phrases that fill out the closing picture of Israel's restoration. The restored Hebrews will possess "the remnant of Edom" and other remnants as well.

Indeed, Amos is a fairly naïve person. He is able to state several problems, the ones we have noticed. But he does not see the necessity of pressing onward toward solutions, a necessity that haunts the later prophets. From experience we know how often it is the chance remarks of a teacher rather than his prepared lecture that set our minds to working. The "chance remarks" of Amos were able, for more than two centuries, to vex and stimulate his "pupils," the prophets whom we now approach.

Hosea

As if to demonstrate that the lightning that moves a man to prophecy never strikes in exactly the same way and under the same circumstances, we find that Hosea was a contemporary of Amos but from that point onward quickly parts company with the uncouth gatherer of "sycamore fruit." For Hosea was a subject of Jeroboam II, the Northern king, the same king whose temple Amos attacked. And there are indications that Hosea, the insider, was a man of wealth; he was able to "redeem" or buy back his wife Gomer from her prostitution. Even the range of figures is wider, drawing on sections of experience unknown to Amos. Amos excels with the homely figure; Hosea, quite as direct, refers to the foam of the sea, to battle, and to other matters to put his insights in sharp relief. Even the "calls" experienced by the two men differ sharply: Amos received his "call" when he was in the presence of abuses of worship and justice that he hated; Hosea received his because of a prolonged contact with a sin that he understood and forgave. Amos visits justice, but little more, on a culture that is not his own; Hosea extends mercy toward the same culture, his own, which he comprehends and wishes to redeem. Amos is the prophet of righteousness; Hosea is the prophet of mercy and love.

To see how Hosea became the prophet of mercy and love, how

he extended to his own society a generous second chance rather than offering, grudgingly, the thin opportunity Amos refers to when he speaks to the Lord about raising up "Jacob"—this requires us to turn our attention at once to Chapters 1-3, concerning Hosea's domestic history. Any reader of these chapters is at once aware that the history of Hosea and Gomer is also the history of the Lord and Israel; and to some students of *Hosea* what appears to be a personal narrative is no more than an extended and self-conscious metaphor about the Lord and his wandering spouse, Israel. But, as pointed out in the discussion of the Hebrew use of personification (Chapter IX), the entire "device" of personification was not used as we use it; "Rachel" stands simultaneously for the historical woman, the "mother" of Israel, and finally for Israel itself. And in *Amos* "Jacob" can stand for Israel the nation and then have its meaning narrowed to the single historical personage. Consequently, the narrative of Gomer's adulteries at least has to be read as a story of a person as well as that of a backsliding nation. Hosea writes *as if* his relation to his wife gives him the clue for his entire prophecy; it is from the exercise of mercy rather than strict justice in a personal relation that the clue to the new attribute of the Lord's character comes. So it is convenient to assume, in the following analysis, that the Gomer-Hosea story is a real one productive of an insight rather than a story invented to body forth an insight.

Hosea, prophet that he is, represents each step of his relation with Gomer as presided over by the Lord (all prophets are proud for the Lord and humble for themselves). Following directions, Hosea takes to himself "a wife of whoredoms." The suggestion has been made that Gomer was a temple prostitute whose use was part of the worship of Ashtoreth, goddess of fertility. If so, Hosea would have had to buy her from the priests of the temple of the goddess. At any rate, Gomer bears three children to Hosea; and all are given names ominously symbolic, names which are altered into auguries of good at the end of the story. Presently Gomer leaves her husband for her "lovers" and the many presents they can give her. Hebrew law tells us that Hosea could have had his adulterous wife stoned to death. Instead, he follows her and, we judge, by promises of kindness wins her to return to his house for good. This story, at the very least, Hosea's auditors would recognize as being at odds with conventional behavior. They might even find shocking and disgusting a husband who does not demand condign justice on an erring wife. Hosea's defense of his behavior must have struck a new note: "And I will betroth thee unto me for ever; yea, I will betroth thee unto me in righteousness, and in judgment, and in lovingkindness, and in mercies" (*Hosea* 2:19).

But it is soon plain that the story of Gomer is not being told for its own sake or to defend the behavior of a generous husband. It is, in its present form, a thinly veiled presentation of the prophet's and the Lord's judgment on the present state of Israel. The "triangle" that involves Hosea and Gomer and her anonymous lovers also involves the Lord and Israel and Israel's "lovers." These lovers are of two sorts not clearly distinguished by the prophet: the foreign countries whose "rewards" of gold and wheat and silver tempt Israel from the Lord, and the fertility deities worshiped inside the boundaries of Israel. If the Lord acted justly—and no more than justly—he would do as he seems to threaten in these verses:

> And now will I discover her lewdness in the sight of her lovers, and none shall deliver her out of mine hand. I will cause all her mirth to cease, her feast days, her new moons, and her sabbaths, and all her solemn feasts. And I will destroy her vines and her fig trees, whereof she hath said, These are my rewards that my lovers have given me: and I will make them a forest, and the beasts of the field shall eat them. (*Hosea* 2:10-12.)

Indeed, were Amos telling the story of this adulterous nation, this would doubtless be the end of the narrative. But Hosea is telling it, and, under the figure of Gomer, he shows how Israel is lifted up from her temporary abasement. She will be betrothed to the Lord forever; and the whole matter, on the level of the Lord and Israel, is concluded thus:

> And I will sow her unto me in the earth; and I will have mercy upon her that had not obtained mercy; and I will say to them which

> were not my people, Thou art my people; and they shall say, Thou art my God. (*Hosea* 2:23.)

"I will have mercy upon her that had not obtained mercy." The Hebrews "had not obtained mercy," in the first place, because they did not specially merit to be singled out from all the peoples upon the earth. They "had not obtained mercy," in the second place, because of their failure to keep the contract made long before, which stated that Israel was to worship only the Lord, to rely only on his power, and to live up to the standards of virtue set down in the laws given to Moses by the Lord.

The figure of Gomer is dropped at the end of the third chapter of *Hosea,* but the instruction inherent in it is continued in the eleven remaining chapters of exhortation to Israel. The instruction, we may note, is widened to include Judah as well as Israel, and Hosea does not indicate that the harsh words apply to one kingdom more than the other; here he differs from the less sophisticated Amos, who finds the wickedness of "foreign parts" particularly gross. The political situation faced by the temporarily prosperous Israel is revealed as one which is almost self-evident; the two great powers in Hosea's world were Egypt and Assyria, and the Lord (or Hosea) rebukes the Jews for seeking the support of Egypt, the very land from which the Lord one drew the Hebrews "with bands of love." Hosea prophesies that the Egyptian "lover" shall fail Israel and that the stronger Assyrians shall take over the country—as indeed happens, a generation later, in 722 B.C. Hosea knows that he will not be listened to; despite its dangerous position, Israel is enjoying the external signs of prosperity. But in the prophet's view, true prosperity for both Judah and Israel is more than a matter of winning a temporary security by playing one outside nation off against another and using Israel's geographical position to dominate the trade routes of the ancient world. The continuance of the Hebrew peoples depends on something else: acceptance of the covenant.

But as Hosea sees this contract between God and his people, it is more than a *just* contract; it is a contract full of loopholes for Israel for the weaker contracting member. We have seen, in *Amos,* that the contract is broken by rank injustice, by the rich who sell the poor "for a pair of shoes." As we might expect, Hosea describes the infraction in a more subtle fashion. "Their heart is divided," he writes of his people (10:2). That is, the Hebrew loyalty is divided between the benefits the Lord has promised for the future and those which alliance with a foreign country and worship of Baal and Ashtoreth can apparently deliver at once. With more adroitness than Amos possessed, Hosea diagnoses the ailment of his country in these words: "Israel is an empty vine, he bringeth forth fruit unto himself . . ." (10:1). "Fruit unto himself" consists of the signs of power and prosperity that horrified the visiting Amos. The "fruit" of Israel ought, as a later verse suggests (14:8), to be brought forth to Jehovah. It is true, the experience of love suggests, that a lover does ask, "What's in it for me?" But such love falls short of love that does not bother with this question. At least, the later famous paradox, "For whosoever will save his life shall lose it: and whosoever will lose his life for my sake shall find it" (*Matthew* 16:25), makes the same point. Calculating pursuit of special goals is likely to end in failure, whereas a person not preoccupied with these goals is likely to find that he has arrived at them. This, to be sure, is a point difficult for any group of people, whatever their era in history, to comprehend and act on.

It is interesting to see how Hosea, following his clue, reckons the institutions of his day. He warns Judah not to come up to the holy places of the north, Beth-aven and Gilgal; they have been undone by the behavior of that "backsliding heifer" Israel (4:16). Even more positively—in Amos' own vein—Hosea repudiates conventional religious observances. The Lord pleads with erring Ephraim (Israel): "For I desired mercy, and not sacrifice; and the knowledge of God more than burnt offerings" (6:6). Hosea notes with horror what has happened to many a holy place:

> And as troops of robbers wait for man, so the company of priests murder in the way by consent: for they commit lewdness. I have seen an horrible thing in the house of Israel: there is the whoredom of Ephraim, Israel is defiled. (6:9-10.)

Perhaps one anticipates a later turn of Hebrew thought when one finds an anti-legalistic flavor in these passages. But certainly Hosea is saying that a holy place without love, without the single heart, is both empty and dangerous.

Hosea draws the same picture of the exploiting upper classes that Amos drew; these classes "make the king glad with their wickedness, and the princes with their lies" (7:3). His view of kingship echoes the warning Samuel gave when the tribes demanded a king three centuries before (*I Samuel* 8:7 ff.): "They have set up kings, but not by me: they have made princes, and I knew it not . . ." (*Hosea* 8:4). Hosea is observing the mass of men in his country when he writes: "For they have sown the wind, and they shall reap the whirlwind" (8:7). No group has the integrity that comes from an undivided heart.

Is Israel indeed lost? Amos says yes, and Hosea, in the *both-and* vein, often says yes. "My God will cast them away because they did not hearken unto him: and they shall be wanderers among the nations" (9:17). But, with Hosea, stronger than the vision of God vindicated, his righteous anger expended, is the counter-vision—of a people restored by an act of love similar to the act that brought Gomer back to her house. How, on the plane of God and Israel, is this restoration to take place? The story of Gomer suggests that Israel is unable to do much under its own power. Hosea does, however, include the salutary admonition: "Sow to yourselves in righteousness, reap in mercy; break up your fallow ground: for it is time to seek the Lord, till he come and rain righteousness upon you" (10:12). But in general it would seem that the act of restoration must be staged by the Lord. The act falls into two or three parts—as opposed to the single act of flat condemnation in *Amos.* Hosea does not deny that justice must be done, and justice *is* done. The nakedness of Gomer is exposed, and Israel is left to the misery of its own devices; it must face the consequences, political and social, of its various adulteries. Hosea refers to this stage of imagined future events when he says: "They shall go with their flocks and with their herds to seek the Lord; but they shall not find him; he hath withdrawn himself from them" (5:6). For a time, God has become a hidden God (*deus absconditus* is the traditional Latin phrase applied to deity at this point); and clearly Hosea judges that passive withdrawal, on God's part, rather than active retribution is sufficient punishment for an erring people. To this hidden God—the prophet supposes, pressing the parallel between his personal story and the story of God and Israel—certain thoughts may come. Deity is bound by more than justice; deity is still bound by the "bands of love" even though Israel has struggled to be free of them. "How shall I give thee up, Ephraim? how shall I deliver thee, Israel? . . . mine heart is turned within me, my repentings are kindled together" (11:8). The answer is that the Lord cannot, any more than could Hosea in the Gomer story, give up what he once had loved.

> I will not execute the fierceness of mine anger, I will not return to destroy Ephraim: for I am God, and not man; the Holy One in the midst of thee: and I will not enter into the city (11:9.)

God will not "enter into the city" to work harm among his people. "I am God, and not man." God must be capable of an act that most men would not think of carrying out: the yielding up of what is theirs by rights, the exaction of vengeance and retribution. Here the *both-and* judgments (that God is just, that God is merciful) are not allowed simply to stand facing each other in their simple if contradictory grandeur. Instead, each is allotted to a different point in the sequence of events the prophet imposes upon future ages. The contradictory demands of both insights are satisfied, nor do they, as in logic they might, cancel each other.

All this is a brief sketch or announcement of doctrines familiar to both Christians and Jews. But one must resist the temptation to read into Hosea ideas and aspirations fostered by later prophets and teachers. Christians do just this when they read in *Leviticus* 16:20-22 of the scapegoat upon whose head the Hebrew high priest lays the year's sins of the people before the goat is led out to perish in the wilderness. The Messiah, we know, was later supposed, in recollection of this custom, to bear the sins of all mankind (*Isaiah* 53: 6). But one reads badly if he does not keep separate the original custom—it may have had something to do with placating a demon named Azazel—and its new uses in *Isaiah* and Christian thought. Thus, when the hidden God returns and, in forgiveness, cries out: "I will ransom them from the power of the grave; I will redeem them from death . . ." (*Hosea* 13:14), some readers are likely to suppose that Hosea speaks of the resurrection of the dead. But students of the period insist that the familiar conception of continued existence after death is a late development in Hebrew religious thought. The earlier Hebrews acted on the assumption that there was none (hence the importance of winning the Lord's material "reward" in one's lifetime, as in *Job*) or that existence after death was inferior to present existence and consisted in a cheerless mingling of the spirits of the evil and the good in a vast underground cavern named Sheol by the Hebrews and referred to, in English translations, as "the pit" or even "hell." Thus, when in *Hosea* we read that the merciful Lord will save his people from the grave and from death, what is being saved is not a company of individual souls who, in any case, must descend to Sheol after this life is over. The Lord is promising to save the collective Israel that he temporarily abandoned to its own devices, and he saves it from "the grave" by giving it continuance in the very real and material land of the living. To hear in this verse overtones of individual immortality is to read later ideas into an earlier context. This does not augment the importance of the later ideas, and it keeps us from seeing what is really in the early writing. Thus, to suppose that Hosea is speaking of *individual* immortality is to ignore a fact spoken of elsewhere: that for many centuries the *tribe* or *nation* rather than the *individual* (in our sense) was the unit the prophets labored to put into proper relation to "the Other." The wickedness of kings, priests, and prophets, Amos and Hosea judged, would lead to the just destruction of the *entirety* of Israel—would lead to the wiping out of the social unit. That divine justice and love might come into relation with the performance of the *individual* is a hope still beyond the horizon of Hosea.

It was a "way out" of which no trace appears in either of the first two prophets here considered. The covenant bound God to a people, not to persons; and that was that.

We have now seen two prophets in action. Before we turn to the redoubtable Isaiah, let us draw out from two very different experiences the elements they have in common. We shall encounter these elements the rest of the way; they constitute a yardstick for measuring succeeding prophets. First, all prophets think of themselves as speaking in an age when there is no "open vision." (Were there "open vision," all men would see the truth, and the prophet would have no need to labor.) Each prophet has a "call" and possesses mana to the extent of being bold enough to announce what he is told. God, variously conceived by the prophets, may speak with simplicity or directness, or he may be thought, as in *Ezekiel*, to employ the panoply of ornate vision. But in all cases, the prophet speaks to the people and their rulers. Further, he has a double function. It is his duty to effect refinements upon previous insights. It is also his duty to *affirm* previous and perhaps forgotten insights. We see Amos and Hosea working at both of these tasks. They refine upon previous attitudes toward formal worship, since they assert that more central than ritual is either righteousness or love. They also refine upon popular conceptions of what "the Other" is. And Amos, at any rate, *affirms* previous Hebrew insights about the central importance of the law in so far as it describes righteousness.

As we go on, we shall find that it is Hosea who points to the future. Though Amos is no friend of law perverted to the advantage of the powerful, he seems to say that conformity to the will of God results from outward performance of acts of justice. Hosea says, and so say most of the prophets we now turn to, that conformity to the will of God is the result of some change in *inner* attitude: the single heart that brings forth fruit to God rather than to itself. But certainly the insights of Hosea do not supersede those of Amos. Both live on, mingling or alternating throughout the entire course of religious history.

Isaiah

Our phrase for Isaiah might be "the prophet as a man of public affairs." This man is impelled to speak on the themes which he has inherited from Elijah, Amos, and Hosea—the destiny of the people and of Israel and the nature of Jehovah. But Isaiah's position in the world is unlike theirs. He is, in the kingdom of Judah, no outside agitator like Elijah and Amos, and no private person like Hosea, who sees the drama of his country in terms suggested by a personal drama.[3] He is at the very center of the stage, not because he has thrust himself there but because he stands there by right of birth. He is a member of an important family in Jerusalem, and one might call him the Samuel of the two kings to whom he speaks, Ahaz and Hezekiah. Ahaz (735-715 B.C.) and Hezekiah (715-687 B.C.) occupied the throne of Judah during the time when the growing power of Assyria destroyed Judah's enemies, Israel and Syria, and twice threatened Jersualem itself. The result of Isaiah's position in the midst of these tempests can be seen in the tone of his prophecy. His expression is calculated and ornate; he speaks as one having authority, as one used to being listened to. The result, in terms of doctrine, is the consolidation and testing of old theories and the invention of a new one which, we might say, Isaiah as a man of affairs sees as a practical necessity: the doctrine of the Messiah.

The reigns of Ahaz and Hezekiah saw the shocking defeat and absorption of the kingdoms to the north by the Assyrians. Though the defeat of Judah's immediate enemies, Israel and Syria, was temporary respite, it was obvious that Judah's security would soon be threatened by the attempt of the Assyrian kings to set up a world state. It was a period when Judah had forced on her, by the sheer force of events, the perception that she was the destiny of the entire Hebrew people, something she had not been able to feel since the

[3] The position of Isaiah's contemporary, the prophet Micah, resembles that of Amos. Micah is a villager, and he takes the same view of Judah's vices that Amos took of Israel's. Micah draws near to Isaiah in the doctrine of the Messiah.

division of the kingdoms after the death of Solomon in 922 B.C. Ever since that time and up to the year of her final defeat, Israel, the Northern Kingdom, had been playing a tune to which Judah danced. But after 722, Israel was no longer there to play the tune; her people had been carried away forever by the Assyrians. Therefore, if God's favor to the Hebrews was to be made manifest to an indifferent Egyptian and Assyrian world, that favor would have to be displayed in the fortunes of Judah.

In the time of Isaiah and Hezekiah, Judah could find temporary encouragement in the failure of the Assyrians to complete their siege of Jerusalem where, Sennacherib the Assyrian king boasts in his own royal records, Hezekiah was shut up "like a caged bird within Jerusalem, his royal city" and was freed of his besieger only by giving much tribute. King Hezekiah was the builder of an impressive underground passage that could provide the city with water in time of siege (*II Kings* 20:20); further, he made an attempt to submit his actions to the approval of the Lord and to purify his country of the "abominations" that had been as popular with his ancestors, the kings of Judah, as they had been with the more powerful kings of Israel. But Hezekiah was also playing a game that Hosea, some years before, had described as the seeking of "lovers"; Hezekiah shows his riches to ambassadors from Babylonia, a new-risen power that, a hundred years later, would overwhelm Assyria (*II Kings* 20:12-18). We shall find that Isaiah is as bitter in his censure of these methods as Hosea was or as Jeremiah, on the very verge of Judah's final disaster, will be.

At any rate, Judah had been given a chance to survive; and Isaiah in his prophecies set to work to see that Judah was provided with a clear view of what the chance was and how it should be used. Without mincing words, he describes the plight of Judah in a hostile world, and he is not far from right:

> Your country is desolate, your cities are burned with fire: your land, strangers devour it in your presence, and it is desolate, as overthrown by strangers. And the daughter of Zion is left as a cottage in a vineyard, as a lodge in a garden of cucumbers, as a besieged

> city. Except the Lord of hosts had left unto us a very small remnant, we should have been as Sodom, and we should have been like unto Gomorrah. (*Isaiah* 1:7-9.)

It is to the "very small remnant" that Isaiah's words are directed. If ever a nation had cause to hang on the words of one man, Judah—which, now that the Northern Kingdom has vanished, becomes "Israel" in prophetic speech—was that nation. And Isaiah was a man worth listening to, not only for his intrinsic message but also for the wealth of worldly information he conveyed. What he tells us about the various godless kingdoms, though cast in the form of the elaborate curse he perfected, is more than vague rumor. We can judge that Isaiah functioned as his ruler's secretary of state; he would be present when the emissaries of Tyre and Ethiopia and Babylonia appeared in the court of the king's palace. He speaks of what he has been able to observe.

As is consonant with his experience and social position, Isaiah represents his "call" to be a prophet as a formal interview in which the Lord grants him audience. "In the year that King Uzziah died"—742 B.C., when Isaiah was a young man—Isaiah saw the Lord sitting on his throne, surrounded, like a mighty monarch of Isaiah's own day, with a train of courtiers that filled the temple. The wonders—the six-winged seraphim, the moving of the doorposts—are less terrifying to the Isaiah of the vision than seeing the Lord face to face and suffering, in a phrase from *Exodus* 28:38, "the iniquity of the holy things." It is an "iniquity" that only the favored can hope to stand up under, as the story of Moses on Mount Sinai has shown us. Isaiah cannot forbear crying: "Woe is me! for I am undone; because I am a man of unclean lips, and I dwell in the midst of a people of unclean lips: for mine eyes have seen the King, the Lord of hosts" (*Isaiah* 6:5). At this point, one of the winged seraphim takes a coal from the altar and places it on Isaiah's lips, and says specifically: "Lo, this hath touched thy lips; and thine iniquity is taken away, and thy sin purged" (*Isaiah* 6:7). Henceforward Isaiah will not be as other men. He has been ritually set apart for what shall be his special, lifelong duty. This assurance at the outset removes from the utterance of Isaiah—and of the later Ezekiel—the effect that is pleasing in some of the other prophets: they are proud for God but humble in themselves. Isaiah knows that he is sent, that the heavenly power is with him whenever he chooses to speak. The resulting accent of overweening certainty some modern readers find hard to overlook. They should, at least, recognize that a man like Isaiah acts on the assumption that the source of his unfailing power lies outside himself. He is very different from a man of today whose pride stems from his consciousness of his own achievements. Such a man would not write (as Isaiah does):

> With my soul have I desired thee in the night; yea, with my spirit within me will I seek thee early: for when thy judgments are in the earth, the inhabitants of the world will learn righteousness. (26:9.)

As is fitting, we hear how the prophet went to work to set down what he was told. All that Hosea—the most cultivated of the previous three prophets—has said on this point is this: "I [the Lord] have also spoken by the prophets, and I have multiplied visions, and used similitudes, by the ministry of the prophets" (*Hosea* 12:10). Isaiah, a court official and aware that there is such a thing as proper procedure, begins one of his prophecies with a detailing of circumstances that Amos would have overlooked:

> Moreover, the Lord said unto me, Take thee a great roll, and write in it with a man's pen concerning Maher-shalal-hash-baz. And I took unto me faithful witnesses to record, Uriah, the priest, and Zechariah the son of Jeberechiah. (8:1-2.)

Later, in the throes of denouncing those who sought support from Egypt, Isaiah gives directions, at once imperious and specific, as to how this piece of prophecy shall be treated: "Now go, write it before them in a table, and note it in a book, that it may be for the time to come for ever and ever . . ." (30:8).

Confident of his source of knowledge, Isaiah saw the path the people of Judah would have to follow if they wished to reach safety. It would lead them into a future more carefully worked out than those described by Amos and Hosea. It would, in short, lead Judah into an idealized age of David projected into future days. In two striking passages, Isaiah states what the path is like. He says to the troubled and uncertain leaders of Judah, who wonder whether they should seek support against Assyria: "For the Egyptians shall help in vain, and to no purpose: therefore have I cried concerning this, Their strength is to sit still" (30:7). And to those who ignore this counsel, he adds:

> For thus saith the Lord God, the Holy One of Israel: In returning and rest shall ye be saved; in quietness and in confidence shall be your strength: and ye would not. But ye said, No; for we will flee upon horses; therefore shall ye flee: and, We will ride upon the swift; therefore shall they that pursue you be swift. (30:15-16.)

True, this counsel might today be called *pacifistic*. The important difference is that a great many believers in pacifism think that "sitting still" is all. Isaiah, as the second passage indicates, does not believe "sitting still" is in itself good. It is simply a means of giving free play to the only true power—the power of what Isaiah calls the Holy One. By sitting still, the created do not, as they do when they rush off to Egypt for support against Assyria, interfere with the obscure but certain maneuverings of the Lord that will finally sustain Judah.

Isaiah did not have to suffer for his unpopular sayings, as Jeremiah a century later had to suffer. But he was ignored, as is shown by an incident near the close of Hezekiah's reign and Isaiah's prophetic activity. All his years as king, Hezekiah has been able to hear Isaiah's instructions; yet he does not hesitate to start again the old game that Isaiah says is no good: he shows his wealth to the Babylonian ambassadors (*II Kings* 20:12 ff.). And when Isaiah promises utter destruction in the days of the sons of Hezekiah, the king says, in accents that remind one of Louis XV's "After me, the deluge": "Good is the word of the Lord which thou hast spoken. . . . Is it not good, if peace and truth be in my days?" (*II Kings* 20:19.) If this is typical of the reception Isaiah's words had, the prophet could often feel that his utterance was empty. This explains Isaiah's frequent equivalent to the modern turn of speech: "All right; so you want to do it the hard way."

Such a recognition permeates Isaiah's prophecy. On every hand are the signs that he is not comprehended. The people do not sit still and wait with "fear and trembling" for the Lord to work his will. Their unrighteousness and vanity, burgeoning though they are on the very brink of disaster, show that they are like the people Amos observed at Bethel a generation before; they have no intention of inconveniencing themselves. So Isaiah predicts that ruin will overtake what they take pride in: the high towers, the fenced walls, the ships of Tarshish, and "all pleasant pictures" (*Isaiah* 2:13-16). Isaiah, despite his exalted position, is as stern with the wealthy as was the low-placed Amos. Ruin is indeed invited by the injustice of men who seek to augment their holdings. "Woe unto them that join house to house, that lay field to field, till there be no place, that they may be placed alone in the midst of the earth!" (5:8) The wealthy rise up early to drink and sing. Even though the handwriting on the wall is plain, revelry and other evildoing continue. Sarcastically, Isaiah observes:

> And behold joy and gladness, slaying oxen, and killing sheep, eating flesh, and drinking wine: let us eat and drink; for tomorrow we shall die. And it was revealed in mine ears by the Lord of hosts, Surely this iniquity shall not be purged from you till ye die. . . . (22:13-14.)

What Isaiah sees in the "valley of vision" (22:1) is indeed an echo of what Hosea saw as he assessed *his* contemporaries and judged that they brought forth "fruit unto themselves" and not to the Lord. The energetic, like King Hezekiah, trust in the work of their own hands; they do not see that it is contingent on work beyond their compass.

> Ye have seen also the breaches of the city of David, that they are many: and ye gathered together the waters of the lower pool. And ye have numbered the houses of Jerusalem, and the houses have ye broken down to fortify the wall. Ye made also a ditch

> between the two walls for the water of the old pool; but ye have not looked unto the maker thereof, neither had respect unto him that fashioned it long ago. (22:9-11.)

Here various sorts of pride—some more commendable in modern eyes than others—are put on the same level: pride in Hezekiah's engineering feats, pride of property, pride in the bureaucratic activity of "numbering" or census taking. All this is essentially no better than the transparent and foolish pride that the prophet sees when he passes the "daughters of Zion" in the public ways.

> Because the daughters of Zion are haughty, and walk with stretched-forth necks and wanton eyes, walking and mincing as they go, and making a tinkling with their feet: therefore the Lord will smite with a scab the crown of the head of the daughters of Zion, and the Lord discover their secret parts. (3:16-17.)

These faults are tokens both of external unrighteousness and of the accompanying inner emphasis on self detached from "the Other."

All this tells Isaiah that the "remnant" of Judah will have to have it "the hard way" and eat "the bread of adversity" instead of the milk and honey which is theirs if they will but "sit still." He sees that his people are determined to ape *all* the disastrous habits of the vanished Hebrew kingdom to the north. As we have seen, they set to work to strengthen their armaments. Still worse, they go down to Egypt.

> Woe to them that go down to Egypt for help; and stay on horses, and trust in chariots, because they are many; and in horsemen, because they are very strong; but they look not unto the Holy One of Israel, neither seek the Lord! (31:1.)

Isaiah adds what is crystal clear to him but apparently to no one else:

> Now the Egyptians are men, and not God; and their horses flesh, and not spirit. When the Lord shall stretch out his hand, both he that helpeth shall fall, and he that is holpen shall fall down, and they all shall fail together. (31:3.)

The "stretching out" of the Lord's hand, here and elsewhere, is no gesture of protection; it is the gesture that lets the Lord's mana flow; and of course it will flow against all those who have put their own wills against his. Whether they be Egyptians and "seek to the idols, and to the charmers, and to them that have familiar spirits, and to the wizards" (19:3) or whether they be God's own people, a haughty people who have "transgressed the laws, changed the ordinance, broken the everlasting covenant" (24:5), the same fate will visit them. Isaiah judges that the answer his generation gives him is this: "We have made a covenant with death, and with hell are we at agreement" (28:15); he judges that his performance of his allotted role—his use of the clean lips and the sinlessness given him in the court of the Lord—has played to an empty house. His indifferent audience is a "rebellious people"; they

> . . . say to the seers, See not; and to the prophets, Prophesy not unto us right things, speak unto us smooth things, prophesy deceits; get you out of the way, turn aside out of the path, cause the Holy One of Israel to cease from before us. (30:8-11.)

The "deceits" that they want to hear and that Isaiah will not utter are in terms of their destiny, private and political—that it is in their own hands and may be shaped as they will. He will not say the "smooth things" they want to hear. He will not say, to cast the matter in modern phrases, that each man is a "free soul" and that Israel as a nation should pursue "a manifest destiny" and practice "self-determination."

All this rebellion goes to make up, for Isaiah, a tableau of idiotic defiance of the Lord. On this tableau the first-act curtain descends. When the curtain rises on the second act, nothing can avert the consequences of the pose of defiance in the first act. The Lord addresses the tardy worshipers who think there is still time to do something about their plight:

> Bring no more vain oblations: incense is an abomination unto me; the new moons and sabbaths, the calling of assemblies, I cannot away with; it is iniquity, even the solemn meeting. Your new moons

> and your appointed feasts my soul hateth: they are a trouble unto me; I am weary to bear them. (1:13-14.)

Isaiah's assertions at this point are doubly striking. He was no outsider or private person; he was fortunately placed in his society. Yet he writes: "To what purpose is the multitude of your sacrifices unto me? . . . When ye come to appear before me, who hath required this at your hand, to tread my courts?" (1:11-12.) And so the second act begins; ". . . when ye spread forth your hands, I will hide mine eyes from you; yea, when ye make many prayers, I will not hear: your hands are full of blood" (1:15). The Lord will not be flattered or bribed; rather than look on bloody hands, he will retire from his people and become "the hidden God," in a way that Hosea has already suggested.

Isaiah's great power as a prophet is that he excels in filling out with ghastly detail the second and third acts of his drama, a drama that unrolls ceaselessly and hence confusedly before his eyes. The vigor of Amos is expanded and intensified; it finds play not only in the presentation of the immediate prospects of Israel but in the final doom allotted to those nations which, for a time, the Lord permits to "trouble" Israel. Likewise, the joys consequent upon the third-act restoration of Israel are more than suggested; they are carefully blocked in. One does not need to speak of the "originality" of the prophets. A modern writer may try to avoid the clichés and ideas of previous writers and give his audience the pleasures of novelty. A prophet, in contrast, repeats what previous prophets have said. He does this either because their diction and images have become a part of the general prophetic vocabulary—e.g., "adultery" as a term for unfaithfulness of Jehovah—or because, as the devout person would suggest, they turned their various hearts toward the same flame of instruction, the will of God.

The grisly richness of Isaiah's spectacles of doom must be savored by each reader. Each reader must explore "that day" when the support of the Lord is withdrawn and the appropriate doom expands. One may note that the chapters containing the full-dress execrations upon Babylon, Tyre, Egypt, and other nations offer all the difficulties—and all the brilliant pleasures—that exist in the poetry of *The Song of Solomon* and *The Book of Psalms.* The compressions, the omissions, the flashes of drama (e.g., 21:11-12), the sarcastic addresses to fallen cities, as when Isaiah speaks to Tyre under the "person" of a harlot: "Take an harp, go about the city, thou harlot that has been forgotten; make sweet melody, sing many songs, that thou mayest be remembered" (23:16)—all this ministers to one's taste for Hebrew poetry in all its craggy power. (Good "burdens" or oracles are those which appear in Chapters 13, 17, 19, 21, and 23.)

We must here note the way in which Isaiah, "the man of affairs," implements the last two stages of his drama and suggests just how they will unfold. This interest is a continuation of Isaiah's interest in giving, within the limits of the "valley of vision," a full, exact picture of what was wrong in the society of the times of Ahaz and Hezekiah.

The second act begins, as noted, with the retirement of God. Judah is abandoned to the devices in which she has been confident. A punishment regarded by Amos and Hosea, for the most part, as the simple result of a divine fiat is now shown in operation in ways that would suggest themselves to a man practical as well as inspired. The Lord may "Stretch out" his hand in anger; but the anger achieves its actual effects through human channels. The role of Judah's enemies is specifically worked out, whereas the earlier prophets only suggested it. Isaiah writes:

> O Assyrian, the rod of mine anger, and the staff in their hand is mine indignation. I will send him against an hypocritical nation, and against the people of my wrath will I give him a charge, to take the spoil, and to take the prey, and to tread them down like the mire of the streets. (10:5-6.)

Isaiah can even foresee the results, for Assyria itself, of its success over Judah—a degree of perception that does not cause him to relax his particularist view of history. Assyria will be proud of the lands of Judah; indeed, she will say:

> By the strength of my hand I have done it, and by my wisdom; for I am prudent: and I have removed the bounds of the people,

> and have robbed their treasures, and I have put down the inhabitants like a valiant man. (10:13.)

This Assyrian view of Hebrew misery, Isaiah is sure, is an incorrect one. He asks: "Shall the axe boast itself against him that heweth therewith?" (10:15.) Assyria may flatter itself, but it is no more than a tool; and when the third act begins—that is, when the process of restoration commences—Isaiah promises that the Lord shall kindle from "the light of Israel" a fire that will destroy the rod or ax of which the Lord made temporary use; this flame shall consume the glory of Assyria's forest (10:18).

Since, as this passage suggests, the work of restoration will resemble that of destruction and be something more than the immediate result of a divine fiat, it too has to be thought of as being worked out in terms of recognizable, describable event. The remnant of the chosen people is to be put down and published by a material force, Assyria and perhaps others? So be it. And in continuation, the restoration of Israel-Judah must be worked out in similar terms. The restored realm of Judah, the land of peace where the wolf shall dwell with the lamb and a little child shall lead them (11:6), must be refounded and then protected by a might the equal of Assyria's and Babylon's. Who makes the Assyrians to triumph? The king who leads the multitudes to battle. Who will return the ensign of triumph to the Hebrews? A leader whose power, whose supply of mana, overmatches that of any alien prince or king. Such a leader, plainly, was demanded by the conduct of warfare as Isaiah, in common with all the ancient world, envisaged it. David, ideally or romantically viewed, had been such a leader, and Moses was able to give triumph to his forces by stretching out his arms. For reasons noted in the discussion of Samuel's relation to Saul, the Hebrews tried to fence in the divinity of their kings, tried to make it subordinate to the mana of the priest or prophet. But Isaiah had no such reason for clipping the pinions of a future redeemer or restorer of Judah. The power of the person who lifted up Israel from the dust had to be more than equal to that of the leaders who, unconsciously obedient to the will of the Lord, had cast down the Hebrews.

In trying to sketch the nature of the Messiah as Isaiah sees him, as the anointed or chosen man, we see that the first and essential mark is his power—power to enforce his will on the Assyrians and the possible successors of the Assyrians. Subordinate marks, which will become clearer once the act of liberation is complete and peace has set in, are the righteousness and mercy reflected in the behavior of fierce animals that submit to the little child. These three qualities—power, righteousness, and mercy—localize in the person of the Messiah and on the stage of future history the very qualities which Elijah, Amos, and Hosea had perceived in the deity. Thus, Isaiah's "originality" lies in the perception that somehow the ideal qualities existent in "the Other" must be made operative in the actual course of events; and this is what, to the Hebrew imagination at least, is accomplished by the figure of the Messiah, the counterbalance to God's rod, Assyria.

The Messianic passages in *Isaiah* are insights tossed off in the fire of poetic wisdom. Isaiah may use the word "knowledge," but he always means "wisdom" in the sense previously defined. These passages are not extensive, and because of subsequent religious developments they have had a staggering burden imposed upon them. Thus, in Isaiah's interview with King Ahaz (chap. 7) the famous phrase occurs: "Behold a virgin shall conceive and bear a son." Close reading indicates that Ahaz has despaired of defeating his two confederated enemies, Israel [Ephraim] and Syria—this is previous to 722, of course—and Isaiah, to hearten him, offers him a "sign," which the modest Ahaz tries to reject. But Isaiah thrusts it on him; a virgin (literally a "maiden") shall conceive and bear a son who in his later years shall know good from evil, who shall not resemble the men of Judah "that call evil good, and good evil, that put darkness for light, and light for darkness; that put bitter for sweet, and sweet for bitter" (5:20). But the explicit point of Isaiah's prophecy is that *before* the child "shall know to refuse the evil"—that is, very shortly—both of the enemies of Ahaz shall be brought low by "the razor that is hired," Assyria. The same point is established more fully in the next chapter (chap. 8) by a different story. Here Isaiah speaks of begetting a child of his own; before *this* child "shall have knowledge to cry, My father and my mother" (8:4) Judah's two nearby enemies will fall before Assyria.

Yet those who relate the verses in Chapter 7 to the Messianic Chapter 9 do more than reflect later Jewish or Christian piety. They recognize, if they do not blot it out with the overtones of later orchestration, the first sounding of a melody that has now been repeated for centuries; in its bare simplicity in Chapter 9, it tells us of a child whose birth and adult activity will make "all the difference" for collective Israel. "The people that walked in darkness have seen a great light: they that dwell in the land of the shadow of death, upon them hath the light shined" (9:2). This child will give them joy and, as a military leader, spoil in battle. Nor shall the battles to which he leads be confused and uncertain.

"For every battle of the warrior is with confused noise, and garments rolled in blood; but this shall be with burning and fuel of fire" (9:5)—that is, it shall be decisive. It shall conclude one stage of history and begin another. Who shall this leader be, who teaches the flame of Israel to burn the rod that has punished it? This is Isaiah's answer:

> For unto us a child is born, unto us a son is given: and the government shall be upon his shoulder: and his name shall be called Wonderful, Counsellor, The Mighty God, The Everlasting Father, The Prince of Peace. (9:6.)

What is his descent? Isaiah embodies his suggestion in the following verse. "Of the increase of his government and peace there shall be no end, upon the throne of David, and upon his kingdom, to order it, and to establish it with judgment and with justice from henceforth even for ever" (9:7). That is, this ruler shall be David *redivivus,* born, however, with none of David's defects and carrying easily all of David's virtues, real or fancied. What shall his actual deeds be? Though "The Prince of Peace," he must begin by smiting "the earth with the rod of his mouth"; and in the opening phase of his activity, he is the means by which the Lord recovers the remnant of his people.

In the remaining section of the chapter Isaiah expresses a pious hope that was never realized: that to the standard of the Counsellor shall gather not only the remnant of Judah but the recovered population of Ephraim, the Northern Kingdom. We know that Israel was being, in Isaiah's own day, so efficiently scattered over the world by the colonial policy of Assyria (*II Kings,* chap. 17) that the "ten" Northern tribes sank without a trace. But Isaiah is concerned with an ideal view; he hopes that what has never been true of the relations between Judah and Israel will come to be true. "The envy also of Ephraim shall depart, and the adversaries of Judah shall be cut off: Ephraim shall not envy Judah, and Judah shall not vex Ephraim" (11:13). Nor should one ignore what is promised the happy brothers in Jacob. They shall subjugate the Philistines to the west; "they shall spoil them of the east together: they shall lay their hand upon Edom and Moab; and the children of Ammon shall obey them" (11:14). This is a particularist verse, and it gives a somewhat pinched air to the noble verses opening Chapter 11.

> And there shall come forth a rod out of the stem of Jesse [that is, the house of David], and a Branch shall grow out of his roots: and the Spirit of the Lord shall rest upon him, the spirit of wisdom and understanding . . . : and he shall not judge after the sight of his eyes, neither reprove after the hearing of his ears: but with righteousness shall he judge the poor, and reprove with equity for the meek of the earth. . . . (11:1-4.)

This root of Jesse "shall stand for an ensign of the people; to it shall all Gentiles seek: and his rest shall be glorious" (11:10). The specific context which Isaiah provides suggests that the Gentiles will be seeking in the role of petitioners who hasten to the camp of a successful conqueror. The Gentiles, if accepted at all into the community established by the power and justice of the Prince of Peace, will hold there the position of "second-class" citizens.

Such an observation as the last is perhaps painful. But one reads the prophets badly if he strives to see in each the sum of later doctrine. Isaiah, so far as we can judge, contributed the specific figure of the Messiah. (It is only fair to observe here that Isaiah's contemporary Micah is saying some of the same things. The reader may turn to *Micah,* Chapter 4, for parallels to the triumphs of the restored Israel in *Isaiah,* Chapter 11; and in Chapter 5, verse 2, Micah contributes an important detail as to the birthplace of the deliverer which both Isaiah and Micah awaited. "But thou, Bethlehem Ephratah, though thou be little among the thousands of Judah, yet out of thee shall he come forth unto me that is to be Ruler in Israel; whose goings forth have been from of old, from everlasting.") But Isaiah did not, in contributing the Messiah, suddenly relinquish the particularist emphasis that bulked large in his spiritual inheritance and suggested to him that the Hebrew people had always been a people apart and always would be. His prophecies abound in passages suddenly showing the reverse of the Messianic medal, a reverse that Christianity at least repudiates.

> And it shall be said in that day, Lo, this is our God; we have waited for him, and he will save us: this is the Lord; we have waited for him, we will be glad and rcjoicc in his salvation. For in this mountain shall the hand of the Lord rest, and Moab shall be trodden down under him, even as straw is trodden down for the dunghill. (25:9-10.)

Actually, we should not be disturbed, nor should we read *Isaiah* with our eyes averted to avoid sight of what some would seem to regard as an indecency. Rome, we are told, was not built in a day; and certainly we should not look to find that a concept so complex as that of the Messiah, the redeemer of all mankind, emerged overnight. Isaiah is important for us because his prophecy is the point of departure for the long journey that, in Christian opinion, finds its end in Christ. But it is naïve to expect the point of departure, the sketch of the warrior-ruler in *Isaiah,* to resemble the end of the journey, the figure of Christ.

We do well to recognize that the spectacle of restoration as drawn by Isaiah has its elements of panoply and display as befit a reunited Judah and Israel. But it is not, save for the occasional particularist accent just noted, a display of power inimical to the cherishing of human traits that Isaiah could see were scorned in his own day. In a word, there was room for *reversal.* The poor should be happy, the meek should walk in safety. The Lord has been "a strength to the poor, a strength to the needy in his distress, a refuge from the storm, a shadow from the heat, when the blast of the terrible ones is as a storm against the wall" (25:4). All this change from "the way of the world" cynically tolerated by men is made possible by the activity of the Lord.

> He will swallow up death in victory; and the Lord God will wipe away tears from off all faces; and the rebuke of his people shall he take away from off all the earth. . . . (25:8.)

Here too the accents of material triumph must not be refined away; but it is necessary to make room for that which the societies of Isaiah's own day ignored. Does not the "Branch of Jesse" judge the poor with righteousness and "reprove with equity for the meek of the earth?" (11:4.) And this judgment shall be based on no external measure but on a direct perception of what Hosea would call the direction of the heart—or what we should call, less vividly, intention.

It is important to see that this *reversal*—its need perceived by the Counsellor and enforced by him—becomes a permanent pattern to be followed by the Hebrew imagination. It is a way of looking at the process of change by which evil and injustice are corrected that is exceptionally congenial to the *logic of the emotions.* Rationally and as "men of common sense," we are likely to think of change from a bad to a good condition as an interminable series of steps, compromises, and adjustments; and these changes are made in a middle region between absolute good and absolute evil, a region so gray that we sometimes do not know whether a new adjustment or compromise takes us toward the blackness of evil or the whiteness of good. In the emotional climate of the prophets, the *Psalms,* and the Gospels, all is otherwise. For example, the intermediate area between cruel oppression and kind rule is either ignored or thought not to exist. In "the valley of vision" the tension generated by the sight of cruelty finds its release in the generation of its exact opposite: the spectacle of utter mercy and justice. Christ's beatitudes but continue this frame of mind, this pattern of reversal so congenial to the *logic of the emotions.* "Blessed are the poor in spirit: for theirs is the kingdom of heaven. Blessed are they that mourn: for they shall be comforted. Blessed are the meek: for they shall inherit the earth" (*Matthew* 5:3-5). The prophetic frame of mind is one that the "man of sense" may shake his head over. He may also look at its clear black and white with envy as he wanders lost in the gray realm where compromises are made and horses are traded.

CHAPTER XI

Hebrew Prophecy
(Continued)

BETWEEN *Isaiah* and *Jeremiah* lies a stretch of a hundred years —a hundred years when Judah, as we noted in the *Kings* discussion, was living on "borrowed time"—"protected" by the confusion ensuing upon the decay of the Assyrian power and the rise of the Chaldean or Babylonian empire. But greater than the stretch of time that divides Isaiah and Jeremiah are the differences in their situations and their personal characters. Isaiah was the prophet as public man, who published his prophecies from the comparative shelter privilege and position offer. Jeremiah is the prophet as outcast. In his career we can see fully what we can only suspect when we think of Amos—"what it costs to be a prophet."

Jeremiah's "originality," his unique gift to the accumulating body of prophetic insight, was not a vision or an insight given in vision. (His prophecy repeats, with variations suitable to his own time, the general view that Isaiah takes of history.) Jeremiah's "originality" lies not in what he said but in what he went through. The full savor of the cost—in physical pain, in spiritual isolation—of delivering prophetic instruction taught Jeremiah a great deal. It may be suggested that the recollection of his destiny, his experience of being a prophet, taught those who followed him even more. Thus, if the author of *Isaiah* 53 was looking for a prototype of the Messiah as "a suffering servant," rather than as a triumphant, happy conqueror, he had but to recollect what written record and tradition reported of Jeremiah's career. (Whether the figure in *Isaiah* 53 refers to a person or to Israel personified, one sees it as a figure that records a different apprehension of how the Messiah-entity shall function. To this apprehension, the sufferings of Jeremiah and other prophets may have made their contribution.)

The story of *Jeremiah* takes one to a point in sight of the legendary conclusion: that the infuriated Hebrews who had dragged Jeremiah with them into their exile in Egypt stoned him to death. (See *Jeremiah,* Chapters 43 and 44, for a sufficient motivation for such an act.) The legend, at least, furnishes a conclusion to Jeremiah's story that a sense of aesthetic fitness as well as probability demands. Stoning to

CHART 9. Hebrew Prophecy—*(continued)*
(Bold indicates that the person is discussed fully.)

HEBREW HISTORY		PROPHETS		OUTSIDE EVENTS
687-642	Manasseh			Struggle for supremacy between Assyria and Babylonia
642-640	Amon			
640-609	Josiah	627	Zephaniah	
609-598	Jehoiakim	615	Nahum	Fall of Assyria, defeat of Egypt by Babylon (see Chart 5)
598	Jehoiachin: first captivity	600	Habakkuk	
598-587	Zedekiah	640-585	**Jeremiah,** throughout the reigns of all kings from Josiah to fall of Jerusalem	
587	Fall of Jerusalem: second captivity	598-568	**Ezekiel,** prophetic activity in exile	
538	Return from exile	540	and later **II Isaiah**	Triumph of Cyrus the Persian
520-516	Rebuilding of the Temple	520-518	Haggai and Zechariah	
		460	Malachi and Obadiah	
444-432	Nehemiah's visits to Jerusalem	460-450	III Isaiah	
		400	Joel	

death would be but a culmination to the endless series of physical and spiritual blows that Jeremiah had received all his days from the very people he had judged he was cherishing and protecting.

Jeremiah's career unrolls in the period when Judah's "stay" of an extra century and a half was about done. It was a stay which Hezekiah had used with some profit and which Hezekiah's son and grandson, Manasseh and Amon, had wasted. Amon's son, Josiah (640-609

B.C.), was a conscientious king; whether startled by the divine wrath that the prophets saw in the fall of the kingdom to the north or instructed by Judean prophetic voices, he tried to knit up the raveled texture of the state as left by Manasseh and Amon. For political as well as religious reasons, he made heroic attempts to center worship of the Lord at the Temple in Jerusalem and tried to shape his state in conformity to the books of laws "discovered" at the time of the Temple repairs. But Josiah's attempts were finally in vain. Assyria had fallen (*c.* 612 B.C.), but Babylonia had risen; and the new power approached the walls of Jerusalem by even steps.

It was Jeremiah's very simple message that, at this particular point in the drama of punishment and restoration, all attempts at reform were of no avail, particularly when they were concerned with purifying the externals of devotion to the Lord. He is at odds with the popular prophets who encourage the king. "The prophets prophesy falsely, and the priests bear rule by their means . . ." (*Jeremiah* 5:31). The prophets and priests but flatter the delusions of the wealthy, and Jeremiah must say as much. "They have healed also the hurt of the daughter of my peoples slightly, saying, Peace, peace; when there is no peace" (6:14).[1] Indeed, the act that earlier would have been of use, the creation of a correct internal attitude, is useless *at this point* in the history of Judah, the remnant.[2] The rod of the Lord was lifted, it would descend, and it must be endured for a period as the inescapable punishment for past failures. What use was it—Jeremiah said to the court of Josiah and to the courts of the powerless princelings who followed Josiah in quick succession—to try to win the favor and support of the Lord by ritual correctness and a great display of hostility to the crew of heathen gods? What was the use of tearing down the groves and the high places where the populace

[1] Unless otherwise noted, the references in this chapter are to the prophet whose work is under discussion.

[2] *The Lamentations of Jeremiah* is a collection of "woes" centered upon the disaster that overtakes Judah. Tradition regards Jeremiah as the author of these laments. Modern scholarship does not. Such a judgment has little to add to or detract from the intrinsic power of the poems. They express, in poetic forms already studied in Chapter IX, a very full range of sorrow and terror; they have often been turned to by peoples who are going through a similar collapse of their national hopes and dignity.

was wont to ask favors of the ancient gods of the land? For in a less obvious sense, the highly placed still sought these gods or their like; did they not put their trust in alliances now with Egypt and now with Babylon? Did this act not amount to having trust in the gods of these nations? Their hearts were, in Hosea's phrase, divided hearts. It was too late to do anything to avert the disaster—the destruction of Judah that was the second act of the drama of punishment and restoration which Isaiah and other earlier prophets had worked out. The important thing—this was Jeremiah's message—was for Judah so to conduct herself at the beginning of the second act that she would, at a later date, deserve the glories and peace of the third act: the restoration of the scattered and captive nation. Otherwise, she might expect to receive no more than justice, the descent of the rod that was "hired"; and the Lord, in Isaiah's phrase, would have no occasion to stoop down and wipe away all tears.[3]

This message of Jeremiah's was heard. But it was heard with growing irritation. The leaders of Judah—the factions of court and Temple, the various members of the royal house who were elevated to the throne and then cast down—were distracted and uncertain as the enigmatic wave of the new power, Babylon, hung poised above them. This wave had carried Assyria away; now would it engulf them? They tried to struggle toward the shallows where, they hoped, Egypt might help them; they even sought to dive into the wave and swim with it instead of going under. So occupied, what were they to make of Jeremiah, this fellow from the village of Anathoth and member of a priestly family there? He told them pertinaciously, as Isaiah had told their more fortunate ancestors, that their strength was to sit still. He kept insisting that, though the wave might seem to be Babylon, it was really the anger and justice of Jehovah which no wiles or skill could turn aside.

[3] Jeremiah's was not the only prophetic voice that was heard in the troubled times of Josiah and his successors. Three other prophets—Zephaniah, Nahum, and Habakkuk—made their utterance during this period. Zephaniah predicts the doom of Judah, the brief prophecy of Nahum is concerned with rejoicing over the imminent fall of Assyria, and Habakkuk is stirred by the near approach of the Babylonian power.

Consequently Jeremiah's fate should not surprise us; he was regarded as a quisling, as a creature of Babylon who came through a northern gate of the city to spy and left by that gate to carry information to his masters. Only a few, toward the end, became convinced that his "instructions" came from the Lord and not from the Babylonian king, Nebuchadnezzar. The last governor of Judah, Gedaliah, was one of these. But he was slain by a patriotic hothead, Ishmael; and no one else, among those who remained in Judah, could believe that Jeremiah spoke of the will of the Lord when he told them to stay in the land and not to go to Egypt for a specious safety.

Thus, Jeremiah's effort to convey his message, that Judah must accept the just judgment of God and not struggle against it, ended in spectacular failure. He was "despised and rejected of men" (*Isaiah* 53:3). In fact, only two factors granted him the span of life that he endured: the feeling that any man who put himself forth as a prophet might well be one, even though his supply of mana led him to peculiar utterance; and the disunity within the walls of Jerusalem. A careful reading of *Jeremiah* in an order different from that in the Bible[4] shows how this disunity worked to Jeremiah's

[4] The following order arranges the narrative chapters according to the successive kings and the regent Gedaliah; under all of these rulers Jeremiah was engaged in varieties of prophetic activity. The arrangement attempts to suggest the order of the chapters within each reign, but there are not always decisive guides to this order.

Josiah (640-609)	Chap. 1. The "call" Chaps. 2-12. Prophecies containing historical references but with little direct narrative element
Jehoahaz, son of Josiah (609—three months)	
Jehoiakim, son of Josiah (609-598)	Chaps. 13-20. A mixture of prophetic utterance and prophetic acts Chaps. 22, 23, 26, 27, 25, 36, 35
Jehoiachin, son of Jehoiakim (598) (surrender to Babylon) (also called Coniah or Jeconiah)	
Zedekiah, son of Josiah (598-587) (appointed by the king of Babylon)	Chaps. 21, 24, 28, 29, 37, 38, 32, 33, 34, 39
Gedaliah, regent (587)	Chaps. 40-45

temporary advantage. One group in the city would for a time believe that he was saying something to their profit and would shield him from the anger of another group. This won Jeremiah time to drive home his message in whatever ingenious form he could improvise.

When Jeremiah first comes to Jerusalem from Anathoth, a few miles away to the north in the traditional territory of Benjamin, a northern tribe, he comes as a semi-private person, and as a private person he continues: a person whom the people of his own village quickly abominate because of the bad name he gives to their town. They say to him, "Prophesy not in the name of the Lord, that thou die not by our hand" (*Jeremiah* 11:21). Jeremiah arrives at Jerusalem driven by a "call" that has daunted him from the moment he first heard it. It has come without the panoply of Isaiah's vision; no cherubim bear burning coals from the Lord's altar. Only the Lord himself, with a simple gesture, reaches out and touches Jeremiah's lips. In vain does Jeremiah cry out: "Ah, Lord God! behold, I cannot speak: for I am a child" (1:6). The Lord answers:

> Say not, I am a child: for thou shalt go to all that I shall send thee, and whatsoever I command thee thou shalt speak. Be not afraid of their faces: for I am with thee to deliver thee. (1:7-8.)

Then to this the Lord adds, in capsule form, what Jeremiah's message is to be.

> Behold, I have put my words in thy mouth. See, I have this day set thee over the nations and over the kingdoms, to root out, and to pull down, and to destroy, and to throw down, to build, and to plant. (1:9-10.)

He is to be a prophet, but he is also to be a tool, just as Babylon, the seething pot to the north, is to be a tool, as the second phase advances, the phase of just judgment. Again the Lord heartens Jeremiah, and it is not difficult to understand why he needs heartening.

> Thou therefore gird up thy loins, and arise, and speak unto them all that I command thee: be not dismayed at their faces, lest I

> confound thee before them. For behold, I have made thee this day a defenced city, and an iron pillar, and brazen walls against the whole land, against the kings of Judah, against the princess thereof, against the priests thereof, and against the people of the land. And they shall fight against thee; but they shall not prevail against thee; for I am with thee . . . to deliver thee. (1:17-19.)

Soberly viewed, the "deliverance" of the Lord is no great favor to Jeremiah. Jeremiah savors to the full the pains of social ostracism, and he learns what the filth and hunger of Jerusalem's well-like prisons are. As suggested, it is the indecision and disunity among the great of the Jerusalem world as well as the Lord that permit Jeremiah, for a time, "to save his soul alive." Such a "deliverance" few men, if gifted with foreknowledge, could ask for or wish to endure.

If our rearrangement of chapters is followed—a rearrangement in line with the order of kings and of events set down in *II Kings*—this is the picture that Jeremiah's career of prophecy presents. He is buffeted like a tennis ball from the racket of the priesthood to that of the princes and from the racket of the princes to that of the king himself. So far as the narrative sections show, Jeremiah enjoyed freedom of utterance during the reign of Josiah and spoke as he chose. This is what we should expect under a reforming king, who was ready to be shown how he had offended. However, Josiah's death at the hands of the Egyptian Pharaoh suggests that he may have gone counter to Jeremiah's warnings about alliances and may have established an understanding with Babylon, against whom Egypt, in support of Assyria, was marching. But after the death of Josiah (609) and after Babylon's defeat of Pharaoh Necho at Carchemish in 605, the peril of Judah from Babylon is too great; few will listen in quiet to Jeremiah's grim statements about Judah's future. It is the priesthood that first seems to object to his sayings as delivered in the court of the Temple; and he is at this time rescued by the princes (chap. 26). But as dangers intensify under the last three kings, he no longer has the support of the princes. It is as if they are no longer in a mood to bicker with the Temple priesthood over the division of power and now agree with the priests that

Jeremiah's promises of doom are a threat to the common security. Therefore, they throw Jeremiah into their prison (chaps. 37, 38). Beaten and starved, he is "delivered" by Zedekiah, the last king of Judah, who has been set on the throne by Nebuchadnezzar and who has no power to curb the princes in their plots against Babylon. Plainly, Zedekiah comes to suspect that the Lord may indeed be speaking through Jeremiah when the prophet counsels submission to the rod.

When the city finally falls to Nebuchadnezzar in 586, Jeremiah's story could have had a happy ending had he but chosen. He is offered the comforts of exile and protection; it is as if the Babylonians took the very view of him that the priests and princes did in the last years when they judged he was Babylon's creature. But Jeremiah chooses—and perhaps this is what impressed Gedaliah, the regent appointed by Nebuchadnezzar—to experience a little longer the disunity and the atmosphere of futile hatred and revolt among those who remain behind in the ruined Jerusalem. As noted, Gedaliah, Jeremiah's only protector, is liquidated by a patriot (chap. 40). The few who remain turn to Jeremiah and ask him to speak to them from the Lord; but the "line" he suggests, that they will win final succor by staying in the city and on the land and enduring the tyranny of the Babylonians, is more than they can endure. Instead, they depart for Egypt, which still can offer them a haven even though it can no more come up against the triumphant Babylon. The refugees drag Jeremiah with them, as if they wish to keep an eye on this dangerous troublemaker (chaps. 43, 44).

Such are the "fortunes" of Jeremiah. They constitute a brutal demonstration of what was a foregone conclusion to the prophet early in his activity. His fate was to speak for God to the passionate and willful city of Jerusalem. What other lot than suffering and rejection of his message could he expect? At times, as when the animus of the priesthood has thrown him into the stocks, the touch of the Lord's hand seems to fade from Jeremiah's lips, and he says in his own person, a person deprived of the extension of divine mana that at other times can nerve him to speak out:

> Cursed be the day wherein I was born: let not the day wherein my mother bare me be blessed. Cursed be the man who brought tidings to my father, saying, A man-child is born. And let that man be as the cities which the Lord overthrew, and repented not: and let him hear the cry in the morning, and the shouting at noon-tide; because he slew me not from the womb; or that my mother might have been my grave, and her womb to be always with me. Wherefore came I forth out of the womb to see labor and sorrow, that my days should be consumed with shame? (20:14-18.)

It was plain that Jeremiah was to be cast away and destroyed; that was what his service of Jerusalem was to come to. The bitterness and pessimism of this "chosen vessel" have a famous echo in the cry of Christ at the time of crucifixion: "My God, my God, why hast thou forsaken me?" (*Mark* 15:34.)

Yet despite this frequent sense that divine support is lacking, Jeremiah continues his role of prophet and of doom; he obediently rubs salt in the wounds as the scenes of destruction commence. He can do nothing else. As a limited mortal, he says to himself, "I will not make mention of him [the Lord] nor speak any more in his name." Such a resolution is empty. As he adds: ". . . his word was in my heart as a burning fire shut up in my bones, and I was weary with forbearing, and I could not stay" (*Jeremiah* 20:9).

So part of the fascination of Jeremiah's career lies in his dodges and improvisations; quickly he frames a new method to win the public's attention when a previous method has been forbidden him. This display of ingenuity reminds us that the Hebrew prophet was—or could be—many things. Prophecy is not the product of the pure contemplation of a philosopher; it is the creation of a man of action. With Jeremiah, direct utterance of God's word is but the most obvious form of prophetic action (chaps. 2-12, 31, 46-51). But when such speech is forbidden, there are other avenues that can be followed—avenues in which we should be very startled to find latter-day prophets like Walter Lippmann or John Foster Dulles. Jeremiah can no longer appear in the court of the Temple? He writes a little book and sends it to his temporary friends, the princes.

But then, when King Jehoiakim gets the book and burns it in his winterhouse? Jeremiah redictates the little book—and more—to his faithful scribe, Baruch (chap. 36). Are both direct attacks, those of speaking and writing, denied him? Jeremiah attacks the enemy, those who believe that the consequences of their divided hearts can be avoided, on the flank where they least expect to discover the forces of this one-man army. He invites the priests and people into the vale of Hinnom (the rubbish heap below the east city wall that later becomes, in Hebrew thought, Ge-henna, the "place of burning"). There he breaks a "potter's vessel" and arouses curiosity by his act. He then predicts that this valley of the son of Hinnom shall be called in future times "the valley of slaughter"; he points to the fragments of the pot. Like these shards, the city of Jerusalem will be broken and cannot be made whole again (chap. 19). On another occasion, when he knows that further writings of his will be burned, he takes advantage of a chance circumstance. He has heard that a shepherd people, the Rechabites, have taken refuge in Jerusalem from the Babylonian army. Jeremiah stages a little scene in a room of the Temple. After his audience has gathered, he executes a conventional gesture: he offers the Rechabites wine. The Rechabites refuse; they have been forbidden by their forebear Jonadab to drink wine. Quickly Jeremiah drives home the point this answer suggests to him. The Rechabites are faithful to an *earthly* father. How much greater should be the obedience of the Hebrews to a heavenly father with whom they are linked by the famous covenant? Speaking for the Lord, he says:

> I have sent also unto you all my servants the prophets, rising up early and sending them, saying, Return ye now every man from his evil way, and amend your doings, and go not after other gods to serve them, and ye shall dwell in the land I have given to you and your fathers: but ye have not inclined your ear, nor hearkened unto me. (35:15.)

With an eye to his own people, Jeremiah concludes the scene by saying to the Rechabites: "Therefore thus saith the Lord of hosts, the God of Israel: Jonadab the son of Rechab shall not want a man to stand before me for ever." This is less a promise to the Rechabites than a warning to the Hebrews in the room.

At a later time, at the commencement of the reign of Zedekiah, Jeremiah appears in a public place carrying a wooden yoke on his shoulders. He stands in the presence of a highly placed man, Hananiah. Hananiah, who gets the point, prophesies that the yoke of Babylon will soon be broken; to show this, he takes the wooden yoke from Jeremiah's shoulders and breaks it. Jeremiah now has the opportunity he has been maneuvering for. Acting on instructions coming from the Lord—"Go and tell Hananiah, saying, Thus saith the Lord: Thou hast broken the yoke of wood; but thou shalt make for them yokes of iron" (28:13)—he addresses his rival: "Hear now, Hananiah; the Lord hath not sent thee; but thou makest this people to trust in a lie. Therefore thus saith the Lord: Behold, I will cast thee from off the face of the earth: this year thou shalt die, because thou hast taught rebellion against the Lord" (28:15-16). The chapter ends with characteristic scriptural brevity: "So Hananiah the prophet died the same year in the seventh month" (28:17). It is worth noting that the man who arrests Jeremiah as he seeks to leave the city by the "gate of Benjamin" is the grandson of Hananiah and might have strong personal reasons for suspecting that Jeremiah was going out to communicate with the enemy (37:13). Even when Jeremiah is confined in prison, as if to keep him from giving aid to the Babylonians at the city walls, the prophet's ingenuity turns up a device to assert an aspect of his prophecy: that punishment, though indeed inescapable, would not last forever. In the presence of witnesses in the court of the prison, he buys a field of Hanameel, his uncle's son. The price, "seventeen shekels of silver," is paid; the bargain is signed, sealed, and witnessed. The enigmatic purchase concluded—enigmatic because Judah is on the verge of ruin, when no "man of sense" would think of making a business transaction—Jeremiah turns to his friend Baruch and explains its meaning. It has only symbolic value; certainly Jeremiah did not believe that he himself would live to enjoy it. His instructions to Baruch are these:

> Thus saith the Lord of hosts, the God of Israel: Take these evidences, this evidence of the purchase, both which is sealed, and this evidence which is open; and put them in an earthen vessel, that they may continue many days. For thus saith the Lord of hosts, the God of Israel: Houses and fields and vineyards shall be possessed again in this land. (32:14-15.)

All these examples display Jeremiah as one of the sweating workers in the Lord's vineyard. In contrast, Isaiah has the air of being the overseer who strolls past to see how the buds are filling out.

Indeed, much of Jeremiah's teaching activity is of a pattern with Christ's activity. The formal enunciation of the Christian message waits upon St. Paul. Christ teaches or "prophesies" by means of whatever accident puts in his hand: a field of grain on the Sabbath, the faith displayed by a Roman centurion, or the curiosity of a Samaritan woman beside a well. He tells stories rather than announces doctrines and even, as did Jeremiah when he wore the yoke of wood, acts them out. Christ does not merely censure money-changing in the Temple; he takes a whip to the offenders. Such modes of teaching are highly suitable to the presentation of "wisdom," that body of moral and religious insights that are intensely felt by the teacher but not logically organized and methodically presented.

Jeremiah, though he had to turn a stony face on his people so long as he addressed them in Jerusalem, is not without the *both-and* contrasts of judgment which relieve at last the tension of a terrible view too long sustained. True, it was his limited function to promise that Jerusalem should be destroyed. But he found comfort in the thought that Jerusalem should not be utterly destroyed—that, at a future date, it should exist once again, a market for the produce from the field of Hanameel which he had purchased. He was able to express this compensating insight to those who had been carried away (in 598) with King Jehoiachin or Coniah (reference is to *II Kings* 24:14) to Babylon. Jeremiah, in Chapter 29, has heard that a prophet who has gone with them has been counseling resistance; this prophet—Shemaiah—must not be listened to. And Jeremiah seeks to woo the exiles from their dependence on Shemaiah by speaking not of the doom that has overtaken them but of the happiness that—at the end of "seventy"-odd years—awaits them.

> For thus saith the Lord. That after seventy years be accomplished at Babylon I will visit you, and perform my good word toward you, in causing you to return to this place. For I know the thoughts that I think toward you . . . thoughts of peace, and not of evil, to give you an expected end. Then shall ye call upon me, and ye shall go and pray unto me, and I will hearken unto you. And ye shall seek me and find me, when ye shall search for me with all your heart. And I will be found of you . . . : and I will turn away your captivity, and I will gather you from all the nations, and from all the places whither I have driven you . . . : and I will bring you again into the place whence I caused you to be carried away captive. (29:10-14.)

This promise, already expressed by Isaiah, is one that Jeremiah could not utter in Jerusalem, lest it be misinterpreted and regarded as a reprieve from present disaster. Those in Babylon could expect no such reprieve; therefore, the mercy of this future knowledge could be safely granted them. Fuller statements of this "third act" in the drama of God's judgment appear in the chapters that follow (chaps. 30-31), but they make no addition to this aspect of Isaiah's vision; in fact, they omit reference to a Messiah. Jeremiah seems to suppose—despite his own bitter experience to the contrary—that the people can be trusted to live up to the covenant *this time.* He writes:

> Behold, the days come, saith the Lord, that I will make a new covenant with the house of Israel, and with the house of Judah: not according to the covenant that I made with their fathers, in the day that I took them by the hand to bring them out of the land of Egypt: which my covenant they brake, although I was an husband unto them. . . . (31:31-32.)

The new covenant, Jeremiah perceives, will put the law of God in the "inward parts" of the people; no man shall need to instruct another, for all men shall know the Lord, "from the least of them unto the greatest of them" (31:33-34).

This hope, that the establishment of a new covenant is all that is needed, a later prophet, the author of *Isaiah* 53, who perhaps knew the fame of Jeremiah and what it cost to be a prophet, judges as delusory. True, the people are precious in the sight of the Lord, and they must be saved. But the setting up of a new covenant will not do the job. We might say that the later writer reaches his solution by combining the clues offered by Isaiah in his sketch of the ideal figure of the Messiah and by Jeremiah not in his teachings but in his actual struggle to save the people from their waywardness.

But before we can turn to this anonymous prophet whose utterances conclude our inspection of Hebrew prophecy[5] there is another man who demands attention for several reasons. He is not a prophet who stands in sight of deliverance like the author of *Isaiah* 53. He is a prophet who continues the work suggested by Jeremiah's letter to Babylon, the work of nerving a people, a "remnant," to endure exile in the proper fashion. We may say that he carries out his task in a way Jeremiah would have approved. Certainly, Ezekiel is no Shemaiah (*Jeremiah*, chap. 29) fomenting a revolt of the exiles that would probably persuade their conquerors to exterminate them.

Ezekiel

Ezekiel is to be thought of as a person living among the exiles in Babylon, in a period that extends from 598 to 568 B.C. His visions, the opening chapters of his book tell us, commenced when he was living "among the captives, by the river of Chebar . . . in the fifth day of the month, which was the fifth year of King Jehoiachin's captivity" (*Ezekiel* 1:1-2), or about 593 B.C. He may be recognized by us as a man in whose writing difficulties result when prophecy ceases to be sheer "poetic wisdom" and takes on some of the qualities of

[5] Actually, an exhaustive account of Hebrew prophecy would conclude with a consideration of Haggai and Zechariah, who, as noted, are concerned with the reconstruction of the tiny Hebrew state that was a Persian province not more than twenty miles in diameter; and it would find, in the prophecies of Joel and Malachi, a record of life under theocratic control that lasted until the time of the Maccabees (167 B.C.).

prose. Readers who have developed a taste for the flashing, undeveloped insight, quickly presented and quickly dropped, will find Ezekiel irritating. He says everything the previous prophets said; the trouble is that he says much more and tries for a full, exact statement of what they touched glancingly. Statements that an agnostic and a devout believer can agree upon accepting, in *Hosea* and *Isaiah,* as splendid poetry are, in *Ezekiel,* explicitly developed. In the description of the "call" in Chapter 1, the difference is at once manifest. Ezekiel's "call" resembles the fairly ornate presentation found in *Isaiah,* Chapter 6, but it fills in this courtly scene with details more grotesque than moving. In *Isaiah* 8 the deity is enthroned in magnificence, and that is all. In *Ezekiel* the nature of the throne and the appearance of the cherubim are described. To visualize the actual relation of the wings, wheels, and bodies in *Ezekiel* 1:4-25 is a difficult task. Commentators suggest that what Ezekiel saw of the theriomorphic or animal-shaped men or deities on the gates and walls of Babylon may have contributed to his visions.

Another contrast with Isaiah's account of his "call" appears in Chapter 2. In *Ezekiel* the message is not briefly described as a coal placed on the lips of the prophet. Spread out before the eyes of Ezekiel is "a roll of a book" which is full of "lamentations and mourning and woe" (2:9-10). Then, a grotesque detail, Ezekiel is invited to eat the book: "Son of man, eat that thou findest; eat this roll, and go speak unto the house of Israel" (3:1). So Ezekiel eats the volume; the Lord, who has been described (1:26) as "the likeness as the appearance of a man," says to him: "Son of man, cause thy belly to eat, and fill thy bowels with this roll that I give thee" (3:3). The Lord adds that Ezekiel's task, now he has eaten what is "as honey for sweetness," will not be difficult. He is to deliver his message to a people that speak his own language. Ezekiel is a "son of man"—that is, a mortal being; and what he is asked to do is not above his strength.

Throughout the book of prophecy, Ezekiel's response to vision is what we have seen here. Keats has written: "Heard melodies are sweet, but those unheard are sweeter." The melodies Ezekiel offers us are "heard melodies." We, as auditors, are not asked to contribute harmonies and "resolutions" drawn from our own experience. When Ezekiel shows us the destruction of Tyre (chap. 27) poetry is not altogether absent, but the catalogue of inhabitants and of the social structure of the city is prosy and full. The lightning flash of Isaiah's composition on the same theme (*Isaiah,* chap. 23) is dissipated in the broad light of day which Ezekiel provides for us. And the visions of the rebuilt Temple in Jerusalem (*Ezekiel,* chaps 40-46) approach the exactness and coldness of an architectural drawing.

Another difficulty results from the placing of vision in full daylight, in the atmosphere of explicit statement. The contradictions created by the logic of the emotions, by what we have called the *both-and* frame of mind, tend to become patent, nor can they be excused on the basis that they are successive visions. We feel that Ezekiel is bound to show awareness of the sharp contrasts, whereas prophets who work in the mood of "poetic wisdom" are not. Thus in Ezekiel's proselike prophecy a particularist view of God wars against the idea that God is the only God and thus the God of all men; a God of vengeance and blood lust does not accord so easily, as it does in *poetic* discourse, with a God of mercy and justice. But, though Ezekiel has the soul of a writer of prose, he is no philosopher or theologian; and the contradictions just noted stand out in the glaring light of day, sharply revealed and unadjusted to each other.

If this were all we had to observe in *Ezekiel,* the book could serve the useful if ignoble function of underlining the excellence of the "poetic wisdom" of the other prophets. But Ezekiel makes contributions to the total of prophetic ideas so important in the unrolling of the Hebrew-Christian story that he deserves the patience and attention that some readers, at first glance, may hesitate to provide.

What are these ideas? They are the opposed terms of certain contrasts that, by now, we know are fixed ones for the Hebrews. The Hebrews began by feeling that their God was interested chiefly in the *people* Israel and that what moved deity to action was a desire for the continuity of the tribe of Israel. In *Ezekiel* these hoary concepts come into opposition to concepts so much in the foreground of religious consciousness today that we take for granted that they have always been in man's mind. If we are in some sense religious, we tend to take as self-evident that God is interested in the *person,* the individual, rather than in the group. Believing this, we suppose that the continuance of the individual, in life and after death, is one of the chief concerns of deity. These latter suppositions about the God-man relationship are very nearly absent from our record to date, as we know from our observation of the relatively late appearance in the history sections of what we call personality. The basic concern of the earlier prophets is the survival and restoration of collective Israel. The early Hebrew heroes are representatives of the tribe; they have mana and are the "good luck" of the tribe. The prophets assume that the power, the justice, and the mercy of "the Other" are going to be exercised for the *collective* Israel or Judah; all men will be saved or all will be destroyed together, as God in *Genesis* destroyed Sodom and Gomorrah. Amos may recognize the gap between the rich and the meek, but he gives no indications that the meek will escape the general catastrophe brought on by the behavior of the proud, nor does Hosea in his more developed drama of Israel's punishment and repentance. Even Jeremiah tends to conform to the older view, and if he distinguished between the utter destruction awaiting those who fly to Egypt and the final restoration of the "remnant" that have accepted the Babylonian captivity, he is still thinking of a collective, unitary group. He heartens (*Jeremiah,* chap. 29) those who have already been carried away to Babylon by telling them "they" shall return in seventy years. Practically speaking, "they" will be dead; it is their "seed" that will return. The sins of the collective fathers descend collectively unto the fourth generation and are justly punished—this is usually the view of God's justice taken by the earlier prophets.

Naturally, with our conception of personality as something of our own that detaches us from both nation and family, we are uncomfortable when we encounter this view head-on. So was Jeremiah.

When he comes to think of the days when "Rachel" shall no more weep for her children, he makes out a happy feature of those days.

> In those days they shall say no more, The fathers have eaten a sour grape, and the children's teeth are set on edge. But every one shall die for his own iniquity: every man that eateth the sour grape, his teeth shall be set on edge. (*Jeremiah* 31:29-30.)

(The emphasis should be on "his" in the last line.)

In *Jeremiah,* this insight is not encouraged to burgeon and send forth tendrils. In the prosy and discursive *Ezekiel,* it is permitted to develop so fully that it amounts to a rejection of what, for all previous centuries, has been orthodox doctrine.

> The word of the Lord came unto me again, saying, What mean ye, that ye use this proverb concerning the land of Israel, saying, The fathers have eaten sour grapes, and the children's teeth are set on edge? As I live, saith the Lord God, ye shall not have occasion any more to use this proverb in Israel. Behold, all souls are mine; as the soul of the father, so also the soul of the son is mine: the soul that sinneth, it shall die. (*Ezekiel* 18:1-4.)

Some verses later, after detailing just how a man shall walk in justice, Ezekiel concludes that the man who has kept the Lord's judgments and dealt truly with his fellows shall live (18:9). Such a man "shall not die for the iniquity of his father, he shall surely live" (18:17). Thanks, further, to Ezekiel's legalistic frame of mind—a frame of mind that flourishes in the climate of prose, and recalls the exhaustive catalogues of broken vows and oxen that were wont to push with their horns which we found in *Exodus,* Chapter 21—all the consequences of this rejection of the old proverb are taken up and we arrive at this striking alternative for the wicked man:

> But if the wicked man will turn from all his sins that he hath committed, and keep all my statutes, and do that which is lawful and right, he shall surely live, he shall not die. (*Ezekiel* 18:21.)

There is appended a moving verse that echoes the distress of Hosea's Lord at the near prospect of Israel's destruction: "Have I any pleasure at all that the wicked should die? saith the Lord God: and not that he should return from his ways and live?" (18:23.)

Note this in further justice to Ezekiel. True, the tone of this discussion may be legalistic; the virtue of the individual is to be judged chiefly by his external performance: "Therefore will I judge you, O house of Israel, every one according to his ways" (18:30). But Ezekiel concludes his discussion of the reward of the individual by putting emphasis on the single heart, on the correct intent which Hosea demanded of collective Israel.

> Cast away from you all your transgressions, whereby ye have transgressed: and make you a new heart and a new spirit: for why will ye die, O house of Israel? (18:31.)

The intrusion of the phrase "O house of Israel" is a sign of the *both-and* state of mind. In the rest of the chapter God may be interested in effecting a relation with *individuals;* but that does not mean he is no longer interested in the "house of Israel" and *its* continuation.

Indeed, it is Ezekiel's interest in the continuation of the house of Israel rather than the survival of individual Hebrews that lies behind the famous visions of the "valley of dry bones" in Chapter 37. Ezekiel is carried in vision to a valley where dry bones are scattered, and is instructed to utter words that restore articulation to the scattered bones and put sinew and flesh on them.

> So I prophesied as he [the Lord] commanded me, and the breath came into them, and they lived, and stood up upon their feet, an exceeding great army. (37:10.)

To the hasty reader this vision might appear to concern the resurrection of righteous individuals who deserve rewards they did not receive in life. Careful reading shows that this is not so. The Lord takes pains to explain the import of the vision: "Son of man, these bones are the whole house of Israel." Though the bones—that is, the scattered members of the Hebrew collectivity—may say, "Our bones are dried, and our hope is lost," they are wrong. The prophet is to say to the bones—that is, to the Hebrews in Babylon, under his care and detached from the land of the living which is Jerusalem and the territory around Jerusalem:

> Behold, O my people, I will open your graves, and cause you to come up out of your graves, and bring you into the land of Israel. And ye shall know that I am the Lord, when I have opened your graves, O my people, and brought you up out of your graves, and shall put my Spirit in you, and ye shall live, and I shall place you in your own land. . . . (37:12-14.)

Thus the "valley of dry bones" to sober sight. But one need not deny that from recollection of this kind of insight in a later era when restoration of the group was no longer likely might arise the other possibility, the immortality of the individual. And the triumphant air of the reunited bones might suggest to later prophets and seers that the restored individual might lead a life unlike that which the dead were judged to lead in the cheerless Sheol where good and evil dead mingled indiscriminately.

Ezekiel does not take the step toward belief in personal immortality suggested by the two sections just discussed when they are put into association with each other. When and how this step was indeed taken remains a matter for scholarly debate. Some students see the influence of Persian religion, which had an afterlife divided between the kingdoms of good and evil. Others try to connect the emergence in the Hebrew-Christian story of the idea of a happy immortality with the many "mystery" religions in the ancient world around the time of Christ. But at least, here in *Ezekiel,* we see a prophet poised to take a step that later persons actually take.

Ezekiel's pose of halting lets us see Israel facing a grave possibility. If the chosen people do not soon return to Jerusalem, if they continue scattered in Egypt and the lands of the Fertile Crescent, continuance of the old customs must be on a different basis from that of the Temple worship set up by pious King Josiah. The Hebrew institution of the synagogue, where God was served by the reading and explanation of the law rather than by ritual sacrifice at one holy place, was an invention of this time: an invention apparently preserved when the Hebrews were able to return and resume their Temple worship. It is well to note that synagogue worship places emphasis on individual as well as collective righteousness. The reward of collective righteousness is obvious: a prospering nation. But the reward of individual righteousness is not so certain, as the skeptics of Old Testament days will tell us when we turn to *Ecclesiastes* and *Job*. What are we to conclude when our own eyes tell us that the good are despised and the evil prosper? The concept of a future life, with appropriate rewards made there, is one resolution of this difficulty. Ezekiel does not make this resolution; but he has sketched in the outlines of the difficulty.

We are also in Ezekiel's debt for what he does with the figure of the Messiah, summoned up by Isaiah. The Counsellor, the Prince of Peace, has added to him, by Ezekiel's extended metaphor, the famous aspect of "the Good Shepherd," although in *Ezekiel* the figure is applied to the Lord rather than to an emissary or intermediary. Ezekiel begins Chapter 34 by saying:

> Woe be to the shepherds of Israel that do feed themselves! should not the shepherds feed the flocks? Ye eat the fat, and ye clothe you with the wool, ye kill them that are fed: but ye feed not the flock. . . . And they were scattered, because there is no shepherd: and they became meat to all the beasts of the field, when they were scattered. My sheep wandered through all the mountains, and upon every high hill: yea, my flock was scattered upon all the face of the earth, and none did search or seek after them. (34:2-6.)

This is almost the language of a later book, Plato's *Republic,* where the cynical Thrasymachus argues that the sheep exist for the profit of the shepherd and Socrates counters with the insistence that a good shepherd tries to practice the art of sheep tending, having the well-being of the sheep rather than the profit of the shepherd as its end. Ezekiel retells the familiar story of Hebrew disaster in these new terms; all past shepherds have mistaken their duty and—like Thrasymachus—have eaten the fat of the sheep and clipped the wool for clothes. If the diseased and scattered sheep of Israel are to be reassembled, a better shepherd must be found. But the Lord and Ezekiel—have had full experience of human shepherds; only a shepherd more than human can perform the task. The Lord says to Ezekiel: "Behold, I, even I, will both search my sheep, and seek them out" (34:11). Once, however, the task is begun, it may be delegated to another; and it should not surprise us to discover that this under-shepherd is "my servant David." Under David's care, the flock will enjoy a new arrangement, "a covenant of peace." Evil beasts will be driven away, and the sheep "shall dwell safely in the wilderness, and sleep in the woods" (34:25). This gentle, idyllic view of the act of restoration, presenting the redeemer not as an awful conqueror but as a humble herder of sheep, is qualified by Ezekiel's legalistic description of the successive steps by which the work of the shepherd advances. For restoration cannot take place without judgment, and judgment is executed in those terms of *reversal* dear to the prophetic mind.

> I will seek that which was lost, and bring again that which was driven away, and will bind up that which was broken, and will strengthen that which was sick: but I will destroy the fat and the strong; I will feed them with judgment. And as for you, O my flock, thus saith the Lord God; Behold, I judge between cattle and cattle, between the rams and the he goats. (34:16-17.)

There is justice, and no more, for the cattle that have "thrust with side and shoulder" (34:21); mercy is for the sheep that are lean and meek. This insight is one of Ezekiel's great donations to later imaginations. It charms when it centers attention on the Good Shepherd; it causes uneasiness, particularly in later times, when it speaks of the separation of the sheep and the goats.

At any rate, these steps toward emphasis on the individual and *his* destiny and on the suggestive figure of the Messiah as shepherd put us in Ezekiel's debt. As the sequel will show, they outweigh what seems a return, in the chapters on the Temple (chaps. 40 ff.), to the rankest sort of legalism. As observed in our first chapter, man draws near "the Other" not by a direct line but by circlings. Ezekiel makes well-nigh a complete circle or spiral; he touches, in some way or other, about all the possible attitudes: legal-antilegal; tribalistic-individual; a god of summary judgment, a god of considerable mercy. Moreover, certain of the points he passes through he touches and treats with lasting effects.

Isaiah II

"Isaiah II" is the name which the majority of Old Testament scholars now give, for want of a better one, to the author of *Isaiah,* Chapters 40-55.[6] "Isaiah II," modern speculation suggests, was a person who, toward the end of the Hebrew exile in Babylon (*c.* 540 B.C.), put on the prophetic mantle that had been worn by the man whose name was really Isaiah. If we are truly in the presence of such a borrowing of a past and august reputation to sanction further prophecy, we encounter a frame of mind that is not without its parallels, prophetic and literary. In the old story, Elijah gave his mantle to Elisha, and the younger prophet became, to all effects, the older one. In later Apocryphal Hebrew literature, men draw the folds of earlier persons' fame around them. *The Wisdom of Solomon* is written by a man who feels that what he utters is worthy of Solomon and so deserves to bear his name. Certainly what is ad-

[6] Scholars also distinguish an "Isaiah III," the author of Chapters 56-66. In the interests of clarity, this postexilic prophet who repeats effectively the various themes established by Hezekiah's Isaiah is not treated here. But as a poet he is little inferior to the writers of the other sections of the book called *Isaiah.*

There is still a minority who choose to regard the entire book of *Isaiah* as the work of a single man. The argument for the existence of "Isaiah II" is chiefly based on the alteration in tone of the chapters in question and on the references to the historical figure of Cyrus, the Persian conqueror of Babylon who stirs so many wild hopes in the heart of the writer of these chapters. Cyrus is a leader whom the early Isaiah would have had to foresee at the distance of nearly two centuries. The traditional assumption, that the entire book is the creation of the historical Isaiah, would of course invalidate what is said below about the possible relation between Jeremiah and the concept of the suffering servant; it would not invalidate what is perceived here in the way of change of tone and modification of the prophetic conception of how the last act of the Hebrew collective drama will actually take place. There are clear contrasts between Chapters 1-36 and Chapters 40-55, however one chooses to account for them: as the product of the gifts of two prophets or as the product of one prophetic insight which alters strikingly in the second group of chapters.

vanced in *Isaiah* 40-55 is worthy of Isaiah. In a sense, it belongs to him since it takes the view of the Hebrew future that Hezekiah's minister took; and it differs from that view chiefly because it fills it out with insights stirred by current events. It is as if the writer said: "This is what Isaiah would see if he were alive today." Something like this, certainly, we often say when we read a modern novel that reminds us of what an English master of the novel would write were he alive today; thus: "Dickens, but a little diluted." Certainly we may say of Isaiah II: "The old Isaiah, but suffused with joy and certainty, freed from fear of the day of doom."

One of the great Psalms refers to the Babylonian captivity and begins: "By the rivers of Babylon, there we sat down, yea, we wept, when we remembered Zion"; and the song soon arrives at this plaintive question: "How shall we sing the Lord's song in a strange land?" (*Psalms* 137:1, 4.) Isaiah II plainly had stopped weeping; he had taken a harp down from the willows where the mourners had left it, and he knew exactly how to sing the Lord's song in a strange land. The events he anticipated were indeed encouraging, even if they did not mean all this prophet saw in them. The event that, in the imaginative work of *Daniel,* is predicted to Belshazzar at a feast (*Daniel,* chap. 5) was realized by the descent of the Persian army. The fall of the king of Babylon—whom Isaiah I referred to as Lucifer in Chapter 14—was as sudden as any Hebrew prophet could desire. Cyrus had earlier conquered Media and other states, and he took over the city of Babylon in 538 B.C. Shrewd contemporary observers could have predicted this some time before because of the internal weakness of the Babylonians and the growing repute of the Persians.

Further, the Persians proved to be a different type of conqueror from those the Hebrews had known in the previous course of their history. The policy of the brutal Assyrians toward the conquered was either to exterminate or to assimilate them so completely that no trace was left. The policy of the Babylonians had been one of wholesale transplanting of the subjugated. The policy of Cyrus, at least in relation to the Hebrews, was to restore them to the land from which their conquerors had taken them. This unusual act of the new ruler gave the Hebrews a chance that they crucially needed: the chance to catch their breath, look upon their past, and determine what portions of it were relevant to their present experience. Cyrus furthermore beat down the mountains and filled the deep valleys that lay between the exiled Hebrews and their sacred, ruined city; in sober language, he linked together his new lands with improved systems of communication that assured him political control over outlying places like Jerusalem. But, to the Hebrew imagination, it seemed that the Persian ruler gave back all that mattered—"all that mattered," to be sure, from the point of view of the theocratic priests who, in the following centuries, put together the books that make up the Old Testament. It did not matter that Cyrus did not give the Hebrew people political independence; for that independence, the priestly presentation of past Hebrew history constantly suggests, was one which both king and people had used badly. The heads of the theocratic state that we see in formation in *Ezra* and *Nehemiah,* in the prophets *Haggai* and *Zechariah,* did not mind giving Cyrus and his descendants their tribute. Enough internal freedom remained to allow the Hebrews to labor at setting up and perfecting the theocratic utopia demanded by the closing scenes of Hebrew history as Isaiah and other prophets saw it. As stated, it is in *Ezra-Nehemiah* that we see the leaders of Israel making their actual preparations for setting up this godly state, laying down the firm lines on which, forever after, should repose a changeless civilization, inspirited by Temple and synagogue. And what the leaders of the Hebrew theocratic state took for eternal did indeed survive the fall of the Persian empire before Greek Alexander. It lasted until the Seleucid overlord, Antiochus Epiphanes, profaned the Temple in 168 B.C. and by this outrage ended the state—and set the Hebrew people in motion once more, to seek the kingdom of God in some other quarter than an earthly and theocratic utopia.

The actual theocratic state and its real fortunes lie, of course, outside the vision of the prophet who is heartened by the approach and triumph of Cyrus. What Cyrus actually did is forgotten, and the theocratic state set up by the Hebrews did not survive. What does survive, in Hebrew and Christian forms, is the vision of hope that the moment of emancipation stirred in the anonymous prophet (or stirred, from the traditional point of view, in the breast of the first Isaiah, at a distance of two centuries). The Messiah, variously conceived, and the kingdom he is to set up form the components of a set of visions that have stirred the human imagination ever since. This set of visions stands for a potential experience; for centuries it has spurred mankind to the creation of "kingdoms of God"—all of them impermanent and falling short of what Isaiah II saw, but each one adding facets and details to the ecstatic, imprecise convictions of the prophet that are their point of departure. To seek a Messiah, to enjoy the kingdom he sets up for us—this urge has produced much good and much tragedy in the history of Western civilization. Few utopias are planned which do not echo, strongly or faintly, the words of this Isaiah. Commonwealths set up by revolutions are attended by hopes that at last "the kingdom of God" in some form will be set up for the benefit of actual men. The present Russian state may, on the conscious level, trust to Marxian blueprint; but, on the unconscious level, the age-old conviction that Russia is holy Russia and will be the redemption of the rest of the world moves strongly. In altered form, this conviction lies behind a recent American hope, that this century shall be "the American century." Both Russians and Americans desire, in forms acceptable to a modern age, a temporal kingdom of God; and both are convinced that they are the Messiahs to bring it about.

This section of *Isaiah* opens with an ecstatic outburst:

> Comfort ye, comfort ye my people, saith your God. Speak ye comfortably to Jerusalem, and cry unto her, that her warfare is accomplished, that her iniquity is pardoned: for she hath received of the Lord's hand double for all her sins. The voice of him that crieth in the wilderness, Prepare ye the way of the Lord, make straight in the desert a highway for our God. Every valley shall be exalted, and every mountain and hill shall be made low: and the crooked shall be made straight, and the rough places plain: and the glory

> of the Lord shall be revealed, and all flesh shall see it together: for the mouth of the Lord hath spoken it. (40:1-5.)

Without further preparation we are thrust into the wonders of the last act. If many a modern reader has felt that he has been draped with a shroud as he read the prophetic meditations on the first two acts—the sins of Israel, the horrors of her punishment—he should feel that he has emerged into the light of day: a light brilliant and piercing that sets in sharp relief all the features of the landscape of restoration. Here is none of the prosy leisure of Ezekiel. The rapidity of utterance and the violent mingling and adornment of all the prophetic themes create effects of godly intoxication. The vision of a wilderness breaking into flower, of a people restored to what they lost by their own folly, has for the other prophets lain too far in the future to stir them to joy. But this prophet stands on the very threshold, this future is his to enter upon and walk through, and there is no reason for him to hold back his ecstasy.

To all this rapture we quite properly respond. But since we also desire to see what place this prophet holds in the procession of prophets, we try to note where he repeats older prophets and where he adds to the themes they have provided him. But even the old themes are altered since his stance in relation to them is changed. Older prophets felt that they existed somewhere in the first or second act. Our prophet, watching the curtain rise for the third act, sees what has thus far happened as something to be remembered as a salutary warning or, better, as an almost necessary part of the godly spectacle that rushes toward its magnificent conclusion. He says, for example, something we could not imagine hearing from Jeremiah: Israel "hath received of the Lord's hand *double* for all her sins." Nor is his estimate of the sins and consequent suffering that of other prophets. Sin, for them, is sin, and that is that; and suffering is a grievous evil and an inevitable consequence of violating God's will. The present prophet agrees that all this is true; but he insists that it is not the entire truth. For him, sin is the first step and the suffering of punishment the next step toward the coming of the

Messiah and the glories of the New Jerusalem. Isaiah II does not say, as did some later unorthodox moralist: "O blessed sin by which I fell." But he does say that the three-linked chain—sin, punishment, and redemption—could never have been otherwise. The Lord says: "Behold I have refined thee, but not with silver; I have chosen thee in the furnace of affliction" (48:10). Here, affliction works more than just retribution; when Israel has received "double" for all her sins, she has become an Israel that she was not before. Refined in the fires of affliction, she has become worthy to have revealed to her what she did not know before. Other prophets have suggested that the "hidden God" would return; but it remains for Isaiah II to say what this return will be.

> For a small moment have I forsaken thee; but with great mercies will I gather thee. In a little wrath I hid my face from thee for a moment; but with everlasting kindness will I have mercy on thee. . . . (54:7-8.)

As part of the "great mercies" seen by this prophet, the Hebrews will have a knowledge of "the Other" fuller than it has ever been before. "Behold, the former things are come to pass, and new things do I declare: before they spring forth I tell you of them" (42:9). The "new things" to which a "new song" must be sung include a definition of deity that, the prophet insinuates, was not known to the Hebrews before the exile. "Remember ye not the former things, neither consider the things of old. Behold, I will do a new thing; now it shall spring forth; shall ye not know it?" (43:18-19.) The Hebrews, by their suffering, have earned a right to a new insight, an insight that all earlier men of "wisdom" lacked.

> Hast thou not known, hast thou not heard, that the everlasting God, the Lord, the Creator of the ends of the earth, fainteth not, neither is weary? there is no searching of his understanding. (40:28.)

What does this new insight actually come to? The following three verses are as near explicit statement as the prophet comes.

> Ye are my witnesses, saith the Lord, and my servants whom I have chosen: that ye may know and believe me, and understand that I

> am he: before me there was no God formed, neither shall there be after me. I, even I, am the Lord; and beside me there is no saviour. . . . Yea, before the day was, I am he; and there is none that can deliver out of my hand: I will work, and who shall let it? (43:10, 11, and 13.)

Phrases here will immediately recall God's words to Moses: "I am that I am" (*Exodus* 3:14). This early, compressed definition of deity is filled out by the utterance of Isaiah II. Whatever we suppose the real time was when the utterance of Mount Sinai was conceived and set down, the fact does remain that, in the special history of prophecy we now follow, "Yea, before the day was, I am" is a "new thing." For it amounts to a flat cancellation of the conceptions of God in the historical narratives—a god that works only for Israel, often in the presence of hostile and quite powerful gods. It fills out what Elijah's chief revelation only suggests: that God is chiefly "a still small voice." What is this small voice? Isaiah II tells us: It is that which existed before aught else was made or existed. This small voice is not power or justice or mercy or any other special attribute isolated by a prophet at the cost of ignoring other attributes. The deity perceived by Isaiah II includes, indeed, all the attributes to which the understanding of men can attain. But when man has "understood" that God is powerful or just or merciful, he has not exhausted what there is, in the being of God, to understand. "To whom then will ye liken God? or what likeness will ye compare unto him?" asks the prophet (40:18). God has neither form nor motives that can be *fully* understood by created beings. (Amos and Hosea, isolating a special attribute of justice or mercy, spoke as though God was indeed understood by them in his entirety.) Isaiah II cries: "Woe unto him that striveth with his Maker! Let the potsherd strive with the potsherds of the earth. Shall the clay say to him that fashioneth it, What makest thou? . . ." (45:9.) No, beyond certain points to which the vision of man has reached in the prophets—or so Isaiah II seems to say—exist ranges of power and activity in God that we cannot understand. Yet God's existence in this fashion and no other we must recognize, even though we become involved in that which is difficult to comprehend. "I form light, and create darkness: I make peace, and create evil: I the Lord do all these things" (45:7). This is a "hard saying"—that the Lord is in very fact the creator of "peace and evil." But there Isaiah II lets his efforts at definition halt. This *both-and* judgment, we shall see, creates the skepticism of *Ecclesiastes* and the agonies of *The Book of Job*. But whatever the logical difficulties the vision of Isaiah II may suggest to us, there is no room for either skepticism or agony in the midst of the joys of restoration.

> For my thoughts are not your thoughts, neither are my ways your ways, saith the Lord. For as the heavens are higher than the earth, so are my ways higher than your ways, and my thoughts than your thoughts. (55:8-9.)

(It is the presumption of many a hero of the Pentateuch that the thoughts and ways of the Lord are indeed man's ways, except that the Lord is more powerful and consequently more capricious than man.) In this perception of the gap that exists, Isaiah II allows the matter to rest. The arms of the Lord, he knows, are stretched out toward Israel; for the prophet of the return, that is enough.

The other matter of central importance is what Isaiah II does with the figure of the Messiah and with the position of the Hebrews in time to come. (As to this, the reader will quickly recognize that the restoration is worked out in terms of reversal, of the violent opposites commented on in the discussions of Isaiah's prophecy.) Whether the prophet's remarks on these two points are "true" of the course of human history, the belief and experience of the individual must decide. Yet it must not be ignored that in a very precise sense these two insights about the Messiah and the restored people have indisputable existence. They were *facts* for the imaginations of countless persons—*facts* that conditioned the expectations and the actual deeds of human beings beyond number. On this basis alone it behooves us to delineate precisely what Isaiah II creates and transmits. That it is an integral part of Christianity is patent. That, in altered guise, it is part of the expectation of orthodox Jews is also well known. Aspects of it, however, nerve modern political movements as unlike as Zionism, which has created the nation Israeli in Palestine—a "return" if there ever was one—and the communist state, which regards itself as the result of a "new dispensation," on a materialist, "scientific" basis, to be sure.

The idea of the conquering Messiah we can see in the first Isaiah, and Ezekiel's concept of the Good Shepherd partly opposes and partly fills out the common stock of speculation. Since the *both-and* frame of mind characterizes Messianic speculation and since one conception exists happily in the company of conceptions *logically* opposed, let us list the three or four guises in which the Messiah of Isaiah II appears. In all the guises he is, as he was to the earlier Isaiah, a necessary figure in the historical process by which the fiat of the Lord restoring Israel is to be worked out. All guises but that in Chapter 53 have for a common denominator a Messiah who conquers and who then exercises his power in a benevolent manner. The other Messiahs, then, have been sufficiently explained in other contexts. To understand what, in human terms at least, "produced" the last Messiah, the really novel one at this point in our story, is the chief business of this review of Isaiah II's thought on this topic.

Taking a rapid survey then, we note three slightly different "conquerors": the Messiah as a mythologically conceived deliverer; the Messiah as a historical, time-located personage (Cyrus himself); and the Messiah as an ideal restorer, David come to life again and more glorious than the historical David probably ever was.

The mythologically conceived deliverer is displayed only once and would not deserve note except that this is a conception running parallel to much speculation elsewhere in the ancient world.

> Awake, awake, put on strength, O arm of the Lord; awake, as in the ancient days, in the generations of old. Art thou not it that hath cut Rahab, and wounded the dragon? (51:9.)

Here, as in *Psalms* 74:12-17 and elsewhere, we seem to encounter a champion like Marduk who, in ancient Babylonian legend, triumphs over primeval chaos in the form of Tiamat the serpent and creates an ordered world from his victory. This concept has a long life, extending far beyond the times with which we deal. The triumph of the god Mithra over the bull and, better known to us, that of St. George over the dragon testify to the attraction of the notion of a hero who confronts "darkness and Old Night" on behalf of the helpless. Sometimes, as in the St. George story, the helpless is no more than a maiden bound to a tree; more often, the helpless includes all mankind, as in the Mithra story, or, as in the *Isaiah* reference, an entire people. To later expectations of what the Messiah will do, such timeless battles have seemed to make a contribution. That is, the Messiah must be man's champion not only in terms of historically contained event but also in terms of events that are performed outside of or above history. The Messiah must succor the defenseless forever and continuously, not just at a certain date in history.

The second guise of the Messiah as conqueror identifies him flatly with Cyrus—who, historical record indicates, showed no *special* interest in the Hebrew people and their God. The Lord of Isaiah II describes Cyrus as follows: "He is my shepherd, and shall perform all my pleasure: even saying to Jerusalem, Thou shalt be built; and to the temple, Thy foundation shall be laid" (44:28). He is the rebuilder, in a sense, of the material Jerusalem. Some aspects of his actual course of conquest find reflection in the three verses that follow:

> Thus saith the Lord to his anointed, to Cyrus, whose right hand I have holden, to subdue nations before him; and I will loose the loins of kings, to open before him the two-leaved gates, and the gates shall not be shut; I will go before thee and make the crooked places straight: I will break in pieces the gates of brass, and cut in sunder the bars of iron. . . . For Jacob my servant's sake, and Israel mine elect, I have even called thee by thy name: I have surnamed thee, though thou hast not known me. (45:1, 2, 4.)

The phrase "though thou hast not known me" acknowledges the real state of affairs; the Lord has permitted all the conquests of Cyrus, even though Cyrus remains in ignorance as to the source of his power and probably attributes his victories to the Persian gods he brings into the Fertile Crescent with him.

The third guise, which moves from Cyrus toward an *ideal* conqueror, repeats what the first Isaiah has said about the Prince of Peace; and in many passages it is not important to distinguish between Cyrus and this being.

> I have raised up one from the north, and he shall come: from the rising of the sun shall he call upon my name: and he shall come upon the princes as upon mortar, and as the potter treadeth clay. (41:25.)

This seems to refer to Cyrus. But what follows this declaration moves on, by an easy association of ideas, to an ideal conqueror. (Even the phrase "from the north" was judged in later centuries to refer to Christ, who came from Galilee to the north of Jerusalem.) The important note added to the picture of the ideal conqueror and ruler comes from the firm view that the Messiah does the work of a God who is the one creator of all existence and, hence, inevitably the God of all men. The Messiah whom God raises up cannot escape exercising his justice for all men. There are still particularist passages (e.g., 43:14-22) that assert Hebrew preëminence. But such descriptions are more than counterbalanced by the descriptions of the Messiah's all-embracing rule. The act of conquest will be followed by a justice and exercise of power that will make further conquest needless. The Lord announces:

> Behold my servant, whom I uphold; mine elect, in whom my soul delighteth; I have put my Spirit upon him: he shall bring forth judgment to the Gentiles. He shall not cry, nor lift up, nor cause his voice to be heard in the street. A bruised reed shall he not quench: he shall bring forth judgment unto truth. He shall not fail nor be discouraged, till he have set judgment in the earth: and the isles shall wait for his law. (42:1-4.)

In such a declaration, socially viewed, the delineation of the Messiah might find its completion. Indeed, these three guises, though not the same, are not deeply opposed to one another. The fourth guise, if we desire chiefly clarity and tidy exposition in the prophets, will strike us as being at odds with the mood of delight and triumph that guides the hand of the prophet as he sketches the killer of the serpent and Cyrus and the ideal David. In such designs, what room is there for a Messiah who is described thus: ". . . his visage was so marred more than any man, and his form more than the sons of men" (52:14). Nevertheless, it is for this figure, for this "root out of a dry ground," that the following task is reserved. "So shall he sprinkle [or *startle*] many nations: the kings shall shut their mouths at him: for that which had not been told them they shall see; and that which they had not heard shall they consider" (52:15). One judges that "the kings" would not "shut their mouths" when they saw a glorious, conquering Messiah, at least if they knew the Hebrew prophets. Such a Messiah had become a familiar prophetic article. But a Messiah who lacked all the marks of glory—physical presence and material power—would indeed amaze.

What need, what perception about the destiny of the Hebrews exacted the framing of this different conception of the Messiah, opposed at almost every point to the older, more popular view? It is an insight that dominates a very small portion of the vision of Isaiah II. What suggested to him that it was after all not a conqueror who could lead the Hebrews back to Jerusalem but a person "despised and rejected of man; a man of sorrows and acquainted with grief" (53:3)? Such a man, naturally, would not be received with rejoicing; people would turn from him in disgust. Why then does Isaiah trouble the all-over consistency of his prophecy of rejoicing by the introduction of this figure?

We have already suggested that the career of Jeremiah showed to all thoughtful men of the Hebrew nation "what it costs to be a prophet." The following verse, Christians believe, looks forward to Christ's earthly career; but it also seems to look back to careers like Jeremiah's: "Surely he hath borne our griefs, and carried our sorrows: yet we did esteem him stricken, smitten of God, and afflicted" (53:4). From the point of view of Isaiah II, everything Jeremiah had said to his own generation about the drama of the Lord's judgment had actually happened. Yet Jeremiah's message—and, in a sense, the messages that various other prophets had delivered with discomfort if not with pain—had been ignored. Jeremiah, at least, had been regarded as a dangerous man and a fool. Isaiah II adds, of the "suffering servant" concerning whom we only suggest that Jeremiah may have been the type: "He was taken from prison and from judgment: and who shall declare his generation?" (53:8.) It is the lot of this sort of Messiah to suffer the gravest of catastrophes—from the Hebrew point of view, poverty and lack of offspring. This catastrophe was in itself a kind of adverse judgment upon the man whom it overtook. Yet, it might well seem obvious, the Lord in the days of Jehoiachin and Zedekiah worked through none of the great of the world but through the man who was scorned and beaten and cast into prison. In that career there was no outward sign of luck or popular recognition. To the end—or so far as we can follow his fate—Jeremiah served his people by being out of step with them. Seldom did he have the cold comfort of hearing the people to whom he spoke confess to a suspicion that it was they who were out of step rather than the prophet who harangued them early and late.

A general question is posed by this meditation upon Jeremiah or, more inclusively, by any meditation upon the process of "saving" a people who often seem not to care to be saved. Perception of this question and a possible answer to it are essential for an understanding of Isaiah II. They are crucial if we are, later on, to make sense of Paul's descriptions of other of Christ's relations to the people he wished to benefit. The question may be put thus: Why is the Messiah as suffering servant judged to be a necessary supplement to the Messiah as some sort of conqueror?

A passage that is not Messianic but is concerned, rather, with the Lord's own immediate relation to his people gives a clue. "Jacob" (or Israel) has ceased to call on God, nor has God called on him for offerings.

> Thou hast bought me no sweet cane with money, neither hast thou filled me with the fat of thy sacrifices: but thou hast made me to serve with thy sins, thou hast wearied me with thine iniquities. (43:24.)

"Serve" here is in the sense of enduring the consequences of the unrighteousness of Israel. The next verse describes a "response" of deity to the ingratitude of the people in terms that Amos would not have understood, since it offers much more than justice. "I, even I, am he that blotteth out thy transgressions for mine own sake, and will not remember thy sins" (43:25). "For mine own sake" of course refers to the need for sustaining the reputation of Jehovah among the Gentiles. But this note of vanity fades when to this verse is added: "Put me in remembrance: let us plead together . . ." (43:26). God or his emissary, a conquering Messiah, is not likely to "plead together" with those who are to be benefited. Such an emissary, at any rate, offers his benefits "on a platter," to be taken or left. Yet the Hebrews do not deserve their benefits on a platter. They have sinned before, and they will sin again; they may have put aside one sort of "adultery," but they will discover another—that is certain. Thus they will never "deserve" the mercies of the Lord; they will not merit the restoration that Cyrus or a second David is to bring about. Consequently, if these mercies are to be extended to the Hebrew people, if the Hebrews are not to be plunged anew into further consequences of further sins, some way must be discovered by which the demands of justice may be made subordinate to the stirrings of mercy. The demands of justice cannot be dismissed as, say, they are by an indulgent human parent. They must be worked out in some other destiny than that of the Hebrew people so that the unending process of sin, exile, and restoration that the Hebrews are committed to can be cut across. The people cannot terminate the process? Then this is an additional task the Messiah must take upon himself. His role as a representative of God's *just* relations with the people is, for reasons that we have seen, that of conqueror. But his role as a representative of God in his *merciful* relations to a recurrently erring people requires him to take upon himself the punishment that the people have merited but can scarcely endure; they have survived one Babylonian exile, but is it likely, Isaiah II seems to ask, that they would survive another? The Messiah demanded by mercy is no Cyrus, no ideal adjudicator of right and wrong. Instead, he carries our griefs and sorrows; and we, who judge misfortune as a sign of divine displeasure, feel that we are better than he is. In this, however, we deceive ourselves. Isaiah II writes:

> . . . he was wounded for our transgressions, he was bruised for our iniquities; the chastisement of our peace was upon him; and with his stripes we are healed. All we like sheep have gone astray; we have turned every one to his own way; and the Lord hath laid on him the iniquity of us all. (53:5-6.)

"The chastisement of our peace"—this phrase suggests that any peace which the Hebrew people will enjoy in the future they will have not because they have earned it but because the chaos and destruction headed toward them are deflected, are absorbed by a Messiah who accepts what he has not deserved.

It should be noted here that much qualified modern scholarly opinion regards this "suffering servant" as a personification rather than a person like "Cyrus." It is a personification of the order of "Rachel weeping for her children"—Rachel who may begin as a historical personage but quickly is understood to refer to all of Israel. If the Messiah as "suffering servant" stands for some collective entity, it must have reference to Israel or a portion of Israel. Some students consider that this "servant" stands for all Israel and is "bruised" for the "iniquities" of all mankind. Others judge that the personification has reference to the spiritually elect of Israel. Their misfortune and humiliation are to instruct or redeem collective Israel; these men are, in Biblical language, the leaven that leavens the whole lump. Such interpretations vary from the traditional view just developed, but they still center on a Messiah, whether personification or person, whose "routine" is what we have described. It is a "routine" involving unmerited adversity which is to the benefit of those, the majority, who have merited adversity. Modern criticism, as suggested, notes the tendency in Isaiah II toward universality and infers that the majority that has merited punishment and receives mercy is not collective Israel but mankind, all "the nations."

That such a variety of opinion exists about a passage that came to be interpreted very precisely by Christians should not surprise the reader. Imprecision and what semanticists would call "multiple referents" are inevitable concomitants of insight which expresses its apprehension of "the Other" in poetic rather than philosophic terms. One may recognize the variety of suggestion this crucial passage makes. One should also recognize that these differing suggestions grow from one central seed or tension. This tension is the felt need to relate unworthy created beings to a deity who is merciful as well as righteous and full of power. The "servant" can be thought of as a person or as a spiritual elite of Israel or as Israel in its entirety; and those who are vicariously saved may be the unworthy of Israel or all mankind. But there can be no doubt—and here is the important minimum area of agreement—that the "action" of the "drama" of sin and repentance has taken a new turn. Whatever or whoever is to be saved will be saved not by his own efforts but by the efforts of another being or entity.

This new turn is one that later centuries have never forgotten, though admittedly they have read different meanings into this prophesied "action." To Christians this "servant" is Christ, and to mystical Judaism, the "servant" is Jewry itself, suffering across the centuries and becoming an atonement for the rest of mankind and an instruction to it. It is the Christian meaning that necessarily will occupy the foreground as we turn to the New Testament: the "servant" as a certain sort of person rather than as a personification of a people. Even so, the reader of the New Testament should recall the other possibilities, among other reasons for the purpose of understanding the "rejection" of Christ by those to whom he came. The "servant" passages and the other Messianic passages of the Old Testament prophets had stimulated a variety of hopes rather than one precise hope which the career of Jesus satisfied. Too narrow a reading of these passages constricts their meaning to a small area; we may be sure that those who are wise after the event will probably distort the initial appeal of a passage. As to what that initial appeal was, we are likely to remain in uncertainty. "The identity of the Servant, whether representing the nation of Israel personified or an individual, is again a matter of divided opinions . . ."; so remark Oesterley and Robinson in *An Introduction to the Books of the Old Testament.*

Isaiah 53 is rounded out with a legalistic statement of the whole matter. Though the Messiah was guiltless,

> Yet it pleased the Lord to bruise him; he hath put him to grief: when thou shalt make his soul an offering for sin, he shall see his seed, he shall prolong his days, and the pleasure of the Lord shall prosper in his hand. (53:10.)

". . . When thou [Israel] shall make his soul [the servant's] an offering for sin, he [the Messiah as suffering servant] shall see his seed." The Messiah who suffered, among many disgraces, the disgrace of having no children of his own shall have prolonged existence when the guilty, the collective Hebrew people, have profit from his lack of guilt. Isaiah II does not mention the "scapegoat," the sacrificial ram on whose horns the Hebrew high priest placed the collective sins of the past year before the beast was led into the wilderness (*Leviticus,* chap. 16). But it is possible to say that he sees a need and a solution analogous to the ancient function of the scapegoat; he perceives that the Messiah must become not a glorious leader but the least of those he serves. The scapegoat, by being driven forth, balanced the books for the past year; he enabled the Hebrews to get out of the red and into the black. The Messiah as suffering servant can be thought of as balancing the books once and for all. By his acceptance of punishment, he made certain that past sins should be canceled and that in the future those who lived in the restored Israel should lack power to destroy it by their foreseen sins and willfulness.

This—or something like it—is what Chapter 53 of *Isaiah* comes to in the context in which it appears. It brings into focus a set of ideas that is presupposed by the writers of the New Testament as they endeavor to assign meaning to an existence that was, from an external point of view, as devoid of reward and as disgraceful as that of Jeremiah. The importance of these ideas as they are later put into relation with the life of Christ seems a self-evident fact to a believer.

To other persons, who do not find this fact self-evident, who do not judge that the link between Chapter 53 of *Isaiah* and the New Testament is an absolutely necessary one, this chapter may be thought of as springing from a recognition of tendencies that are a permanent part of human nature. Through the centuries there are variations in the language which expresses these tendencies; but man's sense of inadequacy in face of "the Other"—or society or his job or his future—remains intense. Man still seeks out "many inventions" to bridge the gap between what he is and what he hopes for. He desires some kind of "best" for himself; in his sober moments, he knows that he scarcely deserves this "best." How, then, is he to put his hand on it if the law of justice, or what we call the law of cause and effect, continues to operate? Our answer is that luck must somehow intervene in our favor and give us what we do not entirely deserve; we must keep counting on somehow "getting the breaks." Humanly speaking, the Messiah as suffering servant is an effort, on the part of our prophet, to provide the collective Hebrew people with the assurance that the Lord is going to see to it that they, whatever their demerits, "get the breaks." That this insight continued into New Testament times and burgeoned there is a testimony to its essential attractiveness to men who, weak and limited, are trying to put themselves into a secure, effective relation to whatever they judge is greater than themselves.

Whatever the uncertainty as to the true picture of the Messiah, the writer of the chapters now under discussion had little doubt about the results of his activity. The Hebrew people would quickly come into the enjoyment of a position of preëminence. They would savor all the pleasures of a glorious restoration, and they would go on to be "a light of the Gentiles" (*Isaiah* 42:9). These are high hopes. As a matter of fact, when the Hebrews' theocratic state was established on the return to Jerusalem, one of the chief springs of action was the priestly desire to exclude not only the "full Gentiles" but Hebrews whose forebears had "remained on the land" and were of impure ancestry. All this we have noted in the discussions of *Ruth* and *Jonah.* We also have noted earlier the supposition of the scholars that still another writer draped around his shoulders the cloak of old Isaiah. Chapters 55-65, in the judgment of a good many students, record a postexilic protest against the priests who have captured the reins of power in the restored state and restrict a generous application of the world-embracing visions in Isaiah II and instead are faithful to the particularistic, excluding accents of *Isaiah,* Chapters 1-36. Hence the important threat in these last chapters that God will, if his plan is circumvented by the people in power in Jerusalem, choose a "new people." The full significance of this threat is not worked out until New Testament times, when the Hebrew "rejection" of Christ as a Messiah inspires Paul to act out what "Isaiah III" held only in theory.

CHAPTER XII

Hebrew Skepticism and Drama: *Ecclesiastes* and *Job*

ECCLESIASTES and *Job* are ordinarily assigned to fairly late dates. Of the two, *Ecclesiastes* is regarded as the later; it is usually dated shortly before the Maccabean uprising against the Seleucid power or about the year 200 B.C. (See next chapter.) *The Book of Job* concerns, on the surface, a hero living in a time like Abraham's when a man's wealth lay in his flocks and herds. But specific references to settled conditions of life and the veins of thought indicate that *Job* was written long after the Hebrews had had a full experience of urban life and the national disappointments of defeat and exile in the sixth century B.C. These experiences made the Hebrews far from secure in Zion; the thoughtful could not escape scrutinizing the covenant that was supposed to exist between Jehovah and his people. For these reasons and others, much of *Job* is judged to reflect the uncertainties and heart-searchings of the Hebrew people after the return from exile—that is, after 538 B.C.

But it is not for these reasons alone that these two books serve to close our study of the Old Testament and point toward the New. The writers of both books seem to recognize another set of answers to the predominant Hebrew questions than those which are the stock in trade of the writers of *Proverbs* and *The Book of Psalms* and of the prophets themselves. God is power and justice and mercy, and human righteousness is life in conformity with these divine qualities—these, completely or incompletely stated, are the answers we have become accustomed to. In *Ecclesiastes* and *Job* we encounter another set, a pessimistic and skeptical set. Both books work out these answers with the brilliance we are accustomed to expect of "wisdom"; and *Job* differs from *Ecclesiastes* in that skepticism is finally rejected—on grounds that do not seem to be as compelling as the reasons advanced earlier in the book for being certain about God and his plan for mankind. To the tellers of the tales of *Genesis,* it was a self-evident fact that the exploits of their heroes had the support and sanction of some deity; and the career of Moses, figuratively speaking, unfolds in the shadow of Mount Sinai where the previous covenant between God and Noah was affirmed and made explicit. The skepticism running through these books is, one might say, a springboard that sends one toward the further developments of Hebrew and Christian insights. It is we may predict, a vein of "wisdom" that opens up into two further veins. He who has become skeptical as to the plan of God for mankind will be answered by a sustained and logical argument, an argument which tends to leave behind the "pre-philosophic" climate of the Old Testament; or the doubter may be answered by a revelation fuller and more complete and detailed than that which reached the prophets and satisfied them. But *Ecclesiastes* and *Job* do not explore these veins; they only make exploration necessary.

Ecclesiastes

Ecclesiastes is a Greek expression meaning "a member of an assembly"; it is the equivalent of the Hebrew term *koheleth,* "the master of the assembly." The English often suggested is "the preacher." If "preacher" is the term we apply to the author who borrows the name of that prototype of all Hebrew wise men, Solomon, we must recognize that he is far from the typical preacher with his message of hope and inspiration. Rather is the author of *Ecclesiastes* a worthy forerunner of the famous English poet-preacher John Donne (1573-1631), who posed for his last portrait decked in his shroud, to remind all who saw it of the vanity of human effort and the certainty of man's last end. Metaphorically, the "preacher" in *Ecclesiastes* writes dressed in *his* shroud. That does not mean he does not have a keen recollection of the pleasures and hopes of this life; indeed, he is able by a sharp phrase to revive the excitement of wine and singing men and women. But he knows that the last end of all pleasure and joy is dust; and so he reduces all the multiplicity of life—love, ambition, even righteousness and godly action—until it is small enough to be covered by the key phrase in the book: "Vanity of vanities, all is vanity."

We have but to recall the sections of the Bible we have read to know that there were other times in Hebrew thought when all was not vanity. In the eyes of the old tellers of tales, the efforts of the heroes were not in vain; their bravery and cunning won the material rewards of position and wealth. In the eyes of priestly historians who took a fairly long view, the course of Hebrew history was not in vain, for one could see—if not always clearly—the hand of God in the ups and downs of the fortunes of the chosen people. This second insight is shared, of course, by the prophets. It is true that, in the sight of different prophets, different bands linked God to man. Sometimes the bands were those of legalistic contract and at other times those of simple, direct love. But the prophets did not question that one could perceive the workings of "the Other" in the course of human events. The "rewards" which God accorded man were various, ranging from the crudity of flocks and herds to the intangible pleasures enjoyed by the hero, like Jeremiah, who has seen the will of God and has done it. But so far we have not encountered the unsettling suspicion that there *is* no divine reward for human action or that, if there is, human eyes are unable to make it out. So it is a "new thing" when "the preacher" asks: "And how dieth the wise man? as the fool" (*Ecclesiastes* 2:16). If this is so, what is the use of pursuing any human good, even the distinctly rarefied good of "wisdom"? True, "wisdom" excels folly "as light excelleth darkness" (2:13).[1] But does that give the wise or righteous man any reason to congratulate himself?

> The wise man's eyes are in his head; but the fool walketh in darkness: and I myself perceived also that one event happeneth to them all. (2:14.)

The wise man, at "the latter end," is no more secure than the fool.

[1] Unless otherwise noted, the references in this chapter are to the work which is being specifically discussed.

"The preacher" has a kind of vision of the time of final judgment, where the wicked face the righteous. Does he see the sheep and the goats of Ezekiel's vision? Distinctly not. There is no certainty that the evils and frustrations which one cannot escape observing in the life of the righteous man will be redressed by an act of justice after the man is dead. So far as the writer's knowledge goes, ". . . that which befalleth the sons of men befalleth beasts; even one thing befalleth them; as the one dieth, so dieth the other; yea, they have all one breath; so that a man hath no pre-eminence above a beast; for all is vanity" (3:19). Flatly he states the matter: "All go unto one place; all are of the dust and all turn to dust again" (3:20). And he concludes, as if inspecting a theory of consolation generally advanced in his day: "Who knoweth the spirit of man that goeth upward, and the spirit of the beast that goeth downward to the earth?" (3:21). That the human soul goes upward has been rumored, but the man who is truly wise and who does not abandon his skepticism will not put absolute faith in such rumors. He will rest on what he can perceive: ". . . that there is nothing better, than that a man should rejoice in his own works; for that is his portion: for who shall bring him to see what shall be after him?" (3:22). The answer to the concluding question is, of course, *no one*.

So comments "the gentle cynic," as some have called this writer, on the Hebrew habit of thought that for many centuries had linked righteousness with material prosperity and more recently had sought to find the reward of just and upright dealing in some kind of life and judgment beyond the grave. To the other Hebrew habit of thought—which saw the hand of God not so much in the life and rewards enjoyed by the individual as in the continuation and well-being of the Hebrew collectivity—the writer gives an answer that is no more cheering. He looks upon the chain of events so full of meaning to the prophets: the establishment of the covenant, its infraction, and what can be regarded as punishment and restoration. He sees only a fraction of what Hosea and Isaiah and the prophet of "Cyrus" see. He certainly is unable to discover the drama of national sin and restoration in which God and his chosen people are the chief performers. He sees only this in past history: "The thing that hath been, it is that which shall be; and that which is done is that which shall be done; and there is no new thing under the sun" (1:9). Does that which, with labor and tears, is performed "under the sun" have even the ideal value of instructing the generations to come? Scarcely. "There is no remembrance of former things; neither shall there be any remembrance of things that are to come with those that come after" (1:11). Rather is each generation bound to repeat the fruitless struggles of past generations. History does not allow us to make out, in it, a drama where tensions arise and then are resolved by a freeing vision and peace. Instead, we are allowed only the sight of cycles, of an endless recurrence of events. Whether these cycles are stage-managed by "the Other" or simply unroll accidentally or of their own power, human knowledge cannot say.

> To every thing there is a season, and a time to every purpose under the heaven: A time to be born, and a time to die; a time to plant, and a time to pluck up that which is planted; a time to kill, and a time to heal; a time to break down, and a time to build up. . . . (3:1-3.)

This long catalogue is ended by the question: "What profit hath he that worketh in that wherein he laboureth?" (3:9.) The only "profit" that the "preacher" can extract in this: History repeats itself and only the fool acts as if his own deeds will cause it to cease repeating itself and bring forward "a new thing." The mood that irradiates the fourtieth chapter of *Isaiah*—that what follows the act of Israel's restoration shall in no way resemble what preceded Israel's fall—finds no echo in the breast of "the preacher." Rather does he think that the possibilities of existence open to man are limited in number and fully known, and the wise man does not suppose that he or mankind can go beyond these limitations.

The wise man, then, will study to live in accord with things as they are; he will stifle foolish hopes that things may be otherwise. His motto will be the "nothing too much" which we later encounter in Greek and Roman philosophy.

> Be not righteous over much; neither make thyself over wise: why shouldest thou destroy thyself? Be not over much wicked, neither be thou foolish: why shouldest thou die before thy time? (7:16-17.)

The wise man will, in our phrase, have the good sense not to "stick his neck out." He who excels in either vice or virtue is "asking for trouble." The virtues that "Solomon" holds up to us are those of a gentleman which exist to create the maximum of comfort and the minimum of inconvenience. We all recognize that, in college, a student who is a "gentleman" aims at a "gentleman's grade"; he will pass his work, but he will not inconvenience his fellow students by setting too high a standard. Similarly, in business, a "gentleman" conforms to "good business practice"; he avoids dishonesty if possible, but he does not suppose that he can always avoid it. This, at least, is the mood behind the specific advice that "the preacher" offers. He does not speak of the "high impossibilities" that prophets and saviors traffic in. He speaks—and in comfortable accents, too—to the "ordinary sensual man" when he says: "There is nothing better for a man than that he should eat and drink, and that he should make his soul enjoy good in his labor" (2:24). To the good judgment of the same man he appeals: "Better is an handful with quietness, than both the hands full with travail and vexation of spirit" (4:6). True, he sometimes contradicts himself. In one place he says (5:18) it is a good thing for a man to enjoy meat and drink, the fruit of his labors; and in another he says: "The heart of the wise is in the house of mourning; but the heart of fools is in the house of mirth" (7:4). But this is the kind of contradiction all of us can observe in our own catch-as-catch-can thinking. We want to have a good time; we also know that there can be "too much of a good thing." We recognize our inconsistency; we do not try to expel it from our lives and our thinking. Further, when we are in the mood of *Ecclesiastes,* we know that we are not heroes. We do not imagine we can live up to the high standards visible in the careers of saints and prophets; and we are inclined to think no one really expects of us such high performance. Our virtue is of a lower sort;

it is the prudent virtue already noted as the concern of a good many of the wise sayings in *Proverbs*. The prudent man knows this: "He that diggeth a pit shall fall into it; and whoso breaketh an hedge, a serpent shall bite him" (10:8). The prudent man also approves the shrewdness of such a verse as this: "Dead flies cause the ointment of the apothecary to send forth a stinking savor: so doth a little folly him that is in reputation for wisdom and honor" (10:1).

This, then, is a prudence that echoes the canniness of *Proverbs*. But that book was a collection; this book is at pains to provide *reasons* for living prudently. These reasons, we must not fail to perceive, are certainly at odds with the reasons for human action that the total of Old Testament history and prophecy urge upon one. The counsels of prudence studding *Ecclesiastes* reflect this central conviction: that man dwells in nearly complete darkness and he had better move cautiously. This is a far cry from the conviction of many a prophet: that past history sheds a clear light on the present and tells us the path we should follow.

If all this is so of *Ecclesiastes*, what led to its inclusion in the canon or list of sacred books? First, the august reputation of its supposed author, Solomon. Second, certain pious passages which counsel submission to the will of God rather than submission to the darkness in which man walks. (The most famous of these begins: "Remember now thy Creator in the days of thy youth" [11:9-12:7]. It is a passage at odds with the book's general skepticism as to man's immortality.) But, as we read, we are likely to feel that whatever piety *Ecclesiastes* contains is the piety of a person who regards it as bad form to be too skeptical. True, the book ends thus:

> Let us hear the conclusion of the whole matter: Fear God, and keep his commandments: for this is the whole duty of man. For God shall bring every work into judgment, with every secret thing, whether it be good, or whether it be evil. (12:13-14.)

But this conclusion does not really cancel the skeptical inspirations that commit man to the dust and human history to cycles. It is a decent gesture toward a possibility which cannot after all be disproved: that God may well be working in history, favoring his people and rewarding individual virtue, even though one searches in vain for clear signs of such divine labor.

Job

The Book of Job is often a rich record of skepticism as to our power to see, in human history, the marks of divine labor and guidance. But it is not content, as is *Ecclesiastes,* to remain in the "climate" of skepticism. Despite the many barricades in the way, the human soul must manage a return to the attitudes of the historians and the prophets. In Job's struggle to reconcile the contradictions with which he was faced, his righteous life at odds with the afflictions which had overwhelmed him, lies the chief drama or tension of the book. This struggle has haunted the imagination of mankind along with the struggles central to other great tragedies. Sophocles' Antigone, uncertain whether to observe the king's order and leave her brother's body exposed outside the city wall or to ignore the king's will and tend her brother's body; Hamlet, burdened with indecision; Goethe's Faust willing to barter his immortal soul for knowledge—these figures seem to sum up certain conflicts that all human beings face. Antigone's clash of duties, Hamlet's struggle between action and thought, and Faust's obsession are all attitudes that we can understand because we have felt them. And so with Job. We know his misery. When we look upon our own lives and see that our good intentions and actions sometimes win us the "reward" of disaster and heartbreak, what are we to conclude? Are we to rest content with the supposition of clear-eyed skeptics like "the preacher" who tell us there is no plan or, if there is, our eyes can never make it out?

That this is a conclusion which disinterested common sense supports is obvious. That it is a conclusion which a human being overwhelmed by disaster is willing to accept—or, indeed, can endure to accept—*The Book of Job* denies. Instead, Job is displayed going backward and forward over his past years and asking: What did I do that was wrong? Does this disaster make sense? Does it, that is, bear fingerprints from the divine hand rather than the marks of what Thomas Hardy calls "crass circumstance"? Rationally, we may judge that Job is wasting his time. But we know, from our own experience, that he is doing what he has to do. For us, then, the "drama" of *Job* lies in the hero's exploration of the various answers to be given to his dilemma: Is God just? If so, how has all this come to Job, a just man? It is unimportant that the final answers are a little less than satisfying. What counts is that, by the end of the book, Job has exhausted the possible alternatives. That, alas, is all he or we can ever do.

This canvassing of possible answers is what makes *Job* haunt the imagination. To be sure, the narrative that frames the search gives an answer. The apparently traditional story tells how a worthy of the time of *Judges* or earlier is made the subject of a wager between God and the devil. Job, a just man and enjoying all the material rewards of justice, is not—Satan asserts—really the Lord's man. Indeed, he can be made to curse God if all the "rewards" are taken from him. The Lord accepts the wager and imposes only one restriction on Satan: he shall not take away Job's life. In Chapter 42 (verses 7 to 17) the wager is apparently won by the Lord; there is no further mention of Satan, and the Lord says that Job has spoken of him as he should. Job's affairs are set right in a way that must strike readers of the great probings and searchings in the body of the book as too trivial to constitute a real resolution of the "drama." The Lord makes things up to Job by giving him "twice" as much as he had before" (42:10). He provides the hero with "seven sons and three daughters" in place of those children on whom the house fell (1:18-19). All this restitution of what was taken away does, on the level of folk tale, of *Genesis*-like narrative, indeed set matters right; the divine favor is reasserted, and that suffices.

But this last scene does not suffice for what is the heart of the book and makes it great; the poetry and the soul-searching debate are not on a *Genesis* level. As soon as Job and his three visitors set to work on the problem (chap. 3), they are out of touch with the opening two chapters and the concluding one. These three chapters which "frame" the book belong to the simple world of folk tale where—for example—the moral sense of the hearers does not object when the lordly husband of poor Griselda throws her into a dungeon for twenty years in order to "test" her patience and prove to himself that his peasant wife is worthy of him. Job and his companions are in touch with the world of more mature and complex experience where definite answers do not come easily, if at all.

For the purposes of convenience and clarity, one may divide and outline *The Book of Job* thus. Part I (chaps. 1 and 2) states the wager between God and Satan and tells of the disasters which overtake Job in consequence. Part II (chaps. 3-31) contains the conversations between Job and his three "comforters" in which the enigma posed by Job's disaster is viewed in many lights; it is easily the most fascinating section of the book. Part III (chaps. 31-37) contains the admonitions of a younger man, Elihu, who rebukes Job for trying to discover the meaning of the disasters. Part IV (chaps. 38-42:6) continues the rebuke, except that the speaker is no longer Elihu but God himself. This part concludes with Job's total submission. Part V (chap. 42:7-17) rounds out the wager story that opens the book; Job's goods are restored, but the Evil One does not—as one might expect—reappear. But one should realize that Parts I and V move mostly on one level of experience—a level that finds in the wager of God and Satan sufficient explanation of what happens to Job. But Parts II, III, and IV proceed without any indication that a divine wager could be the answer to the question, Is God just or is life but a chain of happenstance without meaning? The answer to this question cannot lie in the magnanimous restoration of cattle and children. It lies in the answer Job gives after the Lord has spoken "out of the whirlwind" in Chapters 38 and 39.

> I know that thou canst do every thing, and that no thought can be withholden from thee. Who is he that hideth counsel without knowledge? Therefore have I uttered that I understood not; things too wonderful for me, which I knew not. Hear, I beseech thee, and I will speak: I will demand of thee, and declare thou unto me. I have heard of thee by the hearing of the ear: but now mine eye

> seeth thee. Wherefore I abhor myself, and repent in dust and ashes. (42:2-6.)

Things "that I understand not, things too wonderful for me, which I knew not" cannot refer to information about a secret wager or test. Such a test is not hard to understand, once it has been divulged. In the concluding speech of what we have called Part IV, Job is speaking of the entire problem of the relation between a creator and created beings. The answer to this problem lies, wholly or in part, beyond the limits of Job's understanding.

There has been an effort or two to put *Job* on the modern stage. But the director of such a production is saddled with essentially static material. The "action" is simply the exhaustion of alternate answers; Chapters 3-37 make up a debate, a symposium of views, on the question of divine providence. We should note that this debate is conducted on two levels: the level of human apprehension (Part II, chaps. 3-31) and the level where moves some sort of divine revelation (Parts III and IV, chaps. 32-41). The debate remains on the human level throughout the alternating addresses and harangues of Job and his three not very helpful friends and contemporaries, Eliphaz, Bildad, and Zophar (chaps. 3-31). It moves to the level of revelation when the three comforters cease "to answer Job because he was righteous in his own eyes" (32:1). At this point begin the monologues of Elihu, a much younger man. As Elihu says, he has been silent in the presence of his elders; but he has decided that their wisdom is poor in comparison to the wisdom he now discovers in himself. He speaks by "the inspiration of the Almighty" rather than by the light of prudence and the law that has guided the debate of Job and his friends. He says:

> For I am full of matter, the spirit within me constraineth me. Behold, my belly is as wine which hath no vent; it is ready to burst like new bottles. (32:17-18.)

Refusing to "accept any man's person," Elihu speaks. What he says must be regarded as uttered to Job "in God's stead" (33:6). After Elihu has spoken—he has held the floor without any interruption from his elders—the Lord sets his seal on the man who has spoken "in his stead." Actually, the Lord's speech (chaps. 38-41) is simply a compendium of crushing references to the *power* of the Lord; it is to this address that Job makes the submissive reply already noted (42:2-6). And we should not fail to note that to this double revelation from Elihu and from the Lord himself Job bows his head. Not involved at all is the final news that the disaster has been all in jest and that now matters will be put to rights.

It is, of course, Job when he is *not* silenced, Job when he engages in bitter debate with his smug friends, who interests and moves the reader. Elihu says—magnificently, to be sure—that God is beyond knowing; and God's own address suggests that power like his—power that created "behemoth" and "leviathan"—need not submit to human question. This Job admits before the final self-revelation of God begins.

> Behold, I am vile; what shall I answer thee? I will lay my hand upon my mouth. Once have I spoken; but I will not answer: yea, twice; but I will proceed no further. (40:4-5.)

It is before revelation has asserted itself that the full gamut of *human* answers to the question of evil and suffering has been run. Here lies the section with the greatest power to stir us (chaps. 3-31).

The attitude represented by the three friends in this section is fairly static. They keep asserting, with a pertinacity infuriating to Job, that the legalistic, external measure of virtue is the right one. Job is suffering. He has boils; his children and flocks have been wiped out by the Sabeans and Chaldeans and a whirlwind. To Job's friends, his suffering is obvious proof that he has done something wrong. True, his reputation for virtue is widely known; but Eliphaz, Bildad, and Zophar judge that it must be a hollow reputation. Have not all these disasters taken place? God is a righteous God, they know, and his punishments of men who are not righteous take the simple, self-explanatory form of the visitations Job has just suffered.

These conventional views of his friends are the toils in which Job struggles. He admits that their views are the accepted ones; indeed, they were his own in his days of prosperity. But that they are not the right ones he now knows by direct experience; at no time in his life did he fall short of what the law requires of a just and prosperous man. Consequently, the platitudinous remarks of his friends enrage him. Eliphaz intones: "For wrath killeth the foolish man, and envy slayeth the silly one" (5:2). Bildad asks: "Doth God pervert judgment? or doth the Almighty pervert justice?" (8:3.) Job too knows the conventional theories and does not need to have them recalled to him. Zophar's comment caps the climax when he says:

> Oh that God would speak, and open his lips against thee; and that he would shew thee the secrets of wisdom, that they are double to that which is! Know therefore that God exacteth of thee less than thine iniquity deserveth. (11:5-6.)

Job replies:

> No doubt but ye are the people, and wisdom shall die with you. But I have understanding as well as you; I am not inferior to you: yea, who knoweth not such things as these? (12:2-3.)

From this point onward, though the friends still intervene, they are no longer Job's adversary. Job's adversary is God himself. Job's suffering—suffering that has made him, like Jeremiah, curse the day he was born (3:11 and 6:9)—has freed him from his friends. "What ye know, the same do I know also: I am not inferior unto you" (13:2).

Instead, he would speak to the Almighty, though he is frequently aware of the dangers of such an interview and is finally silenced by those dangers. Job's attitude is complex, full of contradictions that he recognizes. In the mode of poetic and prophetic *both-and* judgments, the opposed insights are usually separated widely enough not to be recognized and become a source of distress. In many a verse, the complexity of Job's attitude toward God flashes out. "Though he slay me, yet will I trust in him; but I will maintain mine own ways before him" (13:15). Absolute trust and sufficient dignity to assert his own virtue—these coexist as they cannot in the minds of the friends, who are safe, whose withers are unwrung. In what follows, Job pursues in monologue various veins of thought horrifying to his friends. (Eliphaz rebukes him: "Should a wise man utter vain knowledge, and fill his belly with the east wind?" (15:2). Undeterred, Job takes up and gives classic expression to themes provoked by his predicament: man's weakness as a created being (chap. 14); the injustice inherent in any man's judgment of the evil fortune of another man (chap. 16); the fragility of the hope that seeks to look for restitution beyond the "pit" where "our rest together is in the dust" (17:16).

As Job twists and dodges—and his battle is with God's inscrutable justice, not with his friends' transparent platitudes—he at times admits that he may have had secret faults; yet these very faults are his own and not to be reckoned in the open market. "And be it indeed that I have erred, mine error remaineth with myself" (19:4). In fact, his friends should have the humility to admit that what they censure in him they could find in themselves did they but look. "But ye should say, Why persecute we him, seeing the root of the matter is found in me?" (19:28.) They are one with Job, and their fate cannot be detached from his (chap. 21). Occasionally, as in Chapter 30, it occurs to us—but not to Job and his friends—that a fault he overlooks is pride in the many virtues he possessed; and we may see a remainder of that pride in his anger that people once inferior to him may now look down upon him. But even this trait is one we understand. Job is not composing a textbook on how to endure adversity; he is simply enduring adversity, and we should at least see that the pride we object to is the same pride that nerves Job to say to his friends:

> God forbid that I should justify you: till I die I will not remove mine integrity from me. My righteousness I hold fast, and will not let it go: my heart shall not reproach me so long as I live. (27:5-6.)

All else the Lord may wrest from him, but not this sense of having done well, of having not deserved what was overtaken him. Here he will not submit to the judgment of his friends, the popular judgment on disaster.

Thus we see integrity becoming an inner awareness rather than an outward display. This is, if any, the solution that comes nearest to satisfying Job before he falls silent in the presence of Elihu and God (chaps. 32-41). The Lord can shake us badly by removing the "rewards" of virtue which all men can see. But the sense of having done well no one, not even the Lord, can remove. It is with this sense that one should connect a famous verse: "For I know that my redeemer liveth, and that he shall stand at the latter day upon the earth" (19:25). Christian connotations suggest the idea of immortality. But a "redeemer" or vindicator was simply someone who fulfilled a contract or paid a debt by which another person (here, Job) was bound. Job's inner certainty that his motives have been pure and have not merited punishment finds this "projection." The conviction that is so strong within must be matched somewhere in the exterior world. The "redeemer" is simply the external counterpart of the certainty that nerves Job to stand up under the blows of God and face the snap judgments of his friends. He adds:

> And though after my skin worms destroy this body, yet in my flesh shall I see God: whom I shall see for myself, and mine eyes shall behold, and not another; though my reins be consumed within me. (19:26-27.)

In terms of the argument Job and his friends have been having, Job here insists he will face up to God and God's justice—a justice that he cannot see now but that he is determined to discover; the phrase "and not another" is his repudiation of all second-hand contact with deity, whether it be the contact of traditional law or traditional piety. Both crumble away into dust before Job's passionate conviction as to his own purity of intention and rectitude of behavior. All the garments woven by custom are stripped away; whatever the penalty, Job stands naked before his God and on those terms demands judgment.

Here the "drama" of Job's experience of adversity halts; and here, in a sense, the development of the much longer and more various drama of the Hebrew people face to face with their creator comes to a pause. The early stages of the story have allowed us to see the Hebrew historians divesting the "power" on which they depend of its variety of location and aspect and narrowing "the Other" down until it has a form quasi-human and a nature resembling and responding to the human nature that we see taking shape in the stories of David and Saul. We have seen the accompanying inspiration of the prophets that takes these insights and limits them still more. They tend to deny to deity a quasi-human form but affirm deity's possession of certain key qualities. But all this activity has been carried on in terms of "action"—something actually done and consequences suffered, or (what the Hebrews regarded as the same thing) a vision experienced and then uttered. All this experience created a body of examples and belief that has animated Jews and Christians ever since, as the history of future time shows us. That this same various and unorganized body of belief was capable of plunging the thoughtful person into skepticism or into the agony of uncertainty and incomprehension, the books we have just looked at clearly suggest.

From such uncertainty and incomprehension there are several escapes. Some, like "the preacher," are not too unhappy in their skeptical Zion. But Job—and persons like him in their desire to feel they have traffic with a deity who possesses the qualities made out by the prophets in their flashes of vision—are not satisfied.

To list the possible escapes from a position producing skepticism or a feeling that God is a "hidden God" for all time is to indicate the further developments of religious experience. These we shall trace briefly in the writings included in the Apocrypha and quite fully in the New Testament. The first escape is what some would call a regression, and traces of it appear in Job's final submission. It consists of saying that God's nature precludes comprehension; the best thing for an individual or a nation to do is to be satisfied with what *has* been revealed. Practically, in Hebrew history, this acceptance found expression in an unwavering dependence on the laws of Moses, the Torah. This attitude places great stress on correct performance of ritual and an exact observance of all that can be found in or drawn out of the law. An analogy for it in our society we can observe when people, troubled by the apparent social chaos of our times, declare that we ought to go back to the "good old days" of horse-and-buggy and homespun virtue.

Objections to an exclusive adoption of this point of view are two, at least in terms of Hebrew history. First, the good old days—the days of David and Solomon—were never really good. Second, conformity to the rituals set up by one's forebears tends to produce an external conformity to law rather than inner virtue; it ignores the need for the single heart commended by Hosea, that heart that gave Job courage in his unequal contest with God's justice. When we turn to the book in the Apocrypha entitled *Ecclesiasticus,* we shall be in the company of a persuasive advocate of the Hebrew "good old days." When, in the *Gospels,* we encounter the Pharisees and the Sadducees, we shall see the danger of trying to "freeze" a living society into molds that have come down from distant ages.

But this is not the only way to move away from the trouble of Job. There are two others. One is to move from the level of pre-philosophical "wisdom" to a level on which "wisdom" tends to become philosophical—tends, that is, to recognize the contradiction set up by the *both-and* judgments and to try to put them into some sort of comprehensible order. Such an escape from the dilemmas of *Job* we can see being attempted in the Apocryphal book, *The Wisdom of Solomon,* and in the speculations of St. Paul.

Another way remains, the way of a revelation that shall seem fuller than those given before. Hebrew literature of the Apocryphal period is full of visions which in explicitness of promise pass beyond what we have seen in *Isaiah* and *Ezekiel* (e.g., *Enoch* and *The Testament of Moses*). And the early Christians judged the records they preserved of Christ's life and utterances to possess material that resolved, for them, whatever was unclear in the Old Testament. Viewed in this relation, *The Book of Job* indeed stands at a kind of mid-point in Hebrew-Christian development. It puts certain beliefs about God and man to one side; it seems to look toward answers that Job, the character in the drama, does not actually reach himself.

THE APOCRYPHA

CHAPTER XIII

The Hebrew Insights in the Hellenistic World

THE Apocrypha are a collection of fourteen books contained in the Greek translation of the Old Testament (the Septuagint) and the Latin translation (the Vulgate). They are usually omitted in Protestant translations which follow a Hebrew tradition at this point. These books, composed at a late date—250 B.C. and after—are of great intrinsic merit, as our study of *Judith* has suggested. The following books in particular—*Maccabees, The Wisdom of Solomon,* and *Ecclesiasticus*—help us to build a firm bridge from the Old Testament to the New. Much speculation in the New Testament may be "new" in relation to the Old Testament, and the complexity of the social picture in the New Testament surpasses that of Old Testament times; but neither thought nor social conditions will come as a great shock to readers who have paused in the Apocrypha at the points we indicate.[1]

The Maccabees

We had to relinquish the thread of Hebrew history at the time (*c.* 433 B.C.) when the work of Ezra and Nehemiah was done. These two men established the Persian-protected theocratic state, which tried to "freeze" Hebrew ritual and social regulations for good and all. Then began what we have called a long intermission that is not

[1] Four of the fourteen books—*Tobit, Judith, The History of Susanna,* and *Bel and the Dragon*—were considered in the chapter on Hebrew fiction. The canonical book of *Esther* has a supplement in *The Rest of Esther,* and *Daniel* has a supplement in *The Song of the Three Holy Children. I* and *II Esdras* retell the events of *Ezra,* with abundant addition of prayer and vision. *Baruch* concerns the times of the fall of Jerusalem before Babylon, and *The Prayer of Manasses* purports to be the utterances of the wicked king of Judah, Manasseh, after his repentance—an event which *II Kings* does not mention. The reader of *Maccabees* does well to concentrate on *I Maccabees,* since *II Maccabees* retraces much of the ground well covered in the first book.

CHART 10. Events in Apocryphal Times

EGYPT (PERSIAN PROVINCE)		ISRAEL		PERSIA	
		433	Nehemiah's last visit to Jarusalem		
				423-404	Darius II
411	Destruction of Jewish temple at Elephantine			404-358	Artaxerxes II
				358-338	Artaxerxes III
		335	Samaritan temple built on Mt. Gerizim	336-331	Darius III
THE CONQUESTS OF ALEXANDER					
		331	Syria and Palestine mastered by Alexander		
PTOLEMIES: RULERS OF HELLENIC EGYPT		323	Death of Alexander: partition of his empire	THE SELEUCIDS: RULERS OF HELLENIC SYRIA	
321	Ptolemy I takes Jerusalem	323-198	Palestine under the Egyptian Ptolemies		
285-246	Ptolemy II (Philadelphus): traditional sponsor of Septuagint translation			223-187	Antiochus the Great
		198-164	Palestine under the Syrian Seleucids	175-163	Antiochus IV (Epiphanes)
		167-160	Revolt against the Seleucids under the leadership of Judas Maccabaeus		
		160-142	Jonathan Maccabaeus leader		
		142-134	Jews under Simon Maccabaeus gain political independence		
		134-104	John Hyrcanus: great territorial extension; treaty with the Romans		
		104	Aristobulus: first Hebrew ruler styled "King of the Jews"		

CHART 10. Events in Apocryphal Times—(continued)

103-76	Alexander Janneus
76-63	Hyrcanus II and Aristobulus II: contest for power
63	Entrance of Pompey the Roman into Jerusalem
40	Herod the Great established as king: supported by Rome

terminated until shortly before the activity of Maccabees begins (168 B.C.). An old saying has it thus: Happy the land that has no history. Whether the Hebrews throughout the theocratic centuries were happy we do not know, but certainly they had no history in any obvious sense of the word. They gave themselves over to the perfecting and complicating of the structure of the state in which they lived. More important, they devoted themselves to the collection and preservation of the works that make up the Old Testament. We know, from a fifth-century collection of Hebrew papyri found in Egypt, that the community at Jerusalem was regarded as something like a court of appeal in matters of ritual. We know also, from various sources, that Jerusalem continued to oppose the Samaritans to the north of them who had built a rival sanctuary to Jehovah.

A train of outside events forced the inhabitants of Jerusalem to give up their position of protected, isolated worship of their chosen god. Apparently there was no great desire to alter the *status quo;* one imagines it was the belief of many in Jerusalem that, whatever the chaos and change outside, growth and alteration had been banished from Hebrew experience. Persia, that had protected Jerusalem and its priestly forms for two centuries, went under before the great Greek conqueror, Alexander; Syria and Palestine were mastered by Alexander in 331 B.C. In 323 B.C. Alexander died, after weeping his celebrated tears when he found there were no more worlds to conquer. His new empire was too large for one man to administer, and it was divided by his generals into three sections; there were Greek, Syrian, and Egyptian areas. At first (323-198 B.C.), the city of Jerusalem was part of the Egyptian or Ptolemaic empire, and the policy of this state toward the Hebrews was much like that of Cyrus and his Persian successors. Indeed, there seems to be some truth to the story that credits Ptolemy Philadelphus (283-246 B.C.) with encouraging the Alexandrian Jews to make the translation of the Hebrew Scriptures that is now known as the Septuagint—loosely called the "Seventy" because it was supposedly the work of seventy-two scholars who completed their task in seventy-two days.

All this atmosphere of peace was terminated in 198 B.C. when Palestine was taken over by the Seleucids, the ruling house of the Syrian section of Alexander's empire, the middle Hellenistic state. The policy of the Seleucids was to assimilate all subject peoples, to dissolve their traditions and make them Greek in language, custom, religion, and thought. After several preliminary threatening moves, the direct attack on the worship of Jehovah in the Temple was made by Antiochus Epiphanes in 167 B.C. When he desecrated the Temple by the introduction of the worship of Zeus, he touched off the revolt led by a Jewish family, the Hasmoneans—better known as the Maccabees, a name which probably means "hammer" in reference to the energy of the famous Judas of the family. In the following years of struggle the Hebrews, for the first time since the material successes of some of the kings of the divided kingdoms five hundred years or more previous, tasted the intoxicating wine of military victory and political importance.

It is true that, to our eyes, this thirty-year struggle for political independence owed its success to factors resembling those which favored the temporary survival of the divided kingdoms. In the days of Ahab and Jeroboam II of Israel and Jehoshaphat and Azariah of Judah, the "enemy" to the north, the Syrian or Aramean kingdom, really served as a dike to keep back for a while the Assyrian flood; at least, the Arameans did not have sufficient *extra* energy to curb the pretensions of Hebrew rulers to the south of them. Similarly, the Seleucids did not have the surplus energy necessary to put an end to the trouble that Antiochus had stirred up in Jerusalem. Antiochus and his successors have more than the "Jerusalem question" to trouble them. They must alternately negotiate and battle with the Egyptians, who are eager to win back what was lost in 198 B.C.; they must work out their own tangled internal problems of succession and finance; and they must keep an eye on the advances of Rome, with whom Judas has made a league of confederacy (*I Maccabees*, chap. 8).

What the reader of *I Maccabees* finds is an extremely vigorous account of the priest Mattathias and his five sons in their attempts to cleanse the Temple of pollution and to keep it cleansed. *I Maccabees* is the most circumstantial book of history that the Hebrews have left us, if we except portions of the historical works of Josephus, who tells equally fully of the final destruction of the Jewish state by the Romans (70 A.D.). *I Maccabees* is not a simple story. The writer lets us see the divisions among the enemies without: the struggle between the Egyptians and Seleucids, the interior troubles of the Seleucid state. We also see the division within: the Maccabees are hampered and betrayed by Hebrew "Greeks" who bear such names as Jason and would rather forget the whole Hebrew past than risk losing the favor they win by Hellenizing and playing the Seleucids' game. The Maccabees, as leaders, seem near to us; they themselves and not the Lord are the chief workers of the victories which they win. The arts of both warfare and diplomacy are done justice. Nor is the older historians' skill at singling out and presenting individual persons and incidents lacking. This one account must stand for many such in this history. It tells of the death in battle of one of the sons of Mattathias. The Seleucid forces, whose weapons and armored elephants blaze "like torches of fire," move toward the Hebrews. The son Eleazar sees his opportunity.

> And Eleazar, who was called Avaran, saw one of the beasts armed with royal breastplates, and he was higher than all the beasts, and the king seemed to be upon him; and he gave himself to deliver his people, and to get him an everlasting name; and he ran upon him courageously into the midst of the phalanx, and slew on the right hand and on the left, and they parted asunder from him on this side and on that. And he crept under the elephant, and thrust him from

> beneath, and slew him; and the elephant fell to the earth upon him, and he died there. (*I Maccabees* 6:43-46.)

The energy of the Maccabees showed itself in force sufficient to keep the nation going until the Roman conquest in 63 B.C.; and it was force uncritical enough of itself to impose the Hebrew code and worship on the Samaritans to the north and the Idumeans to the south. In other words, the Hebrews, once they were able, did not hesitate to play the part that Antiochus Epiphanes had played; as long as they could, they Hebraized as energetically as their one-time oppressor had Hellenized. The Maccabees were willing to carve out for themselves an empire, if that might be. But they were not really divided from the priests who had allowed themselves to be slain on the Sabbath; Maccabees and priests had a single goal before them, though they did not pursue it in the same way. Both groups were determined that the Hebrew people should continue to live as an enclave, an island of righteousness in a sinful world. Either by force or by the more subtle guile of legalism and ritualism, the Greeks were to be kept out and (what was more important) the Hebrews were to be kept in. Both groups were endeavoring to stop the clock forever, to establish a pure state commendable to Jehovah.

The Diaspora

But all the time—during the era of the theocratic state and during the militant period of the Maccabees—the clock was ticking on. The maintenance of Hebrew purity had been an impossible goal ever since the scattering, the Diaspora, of the Hebrews that began when Jerusalem fell in 586 B.C., and that had continued ever since. Greek-speaking Jews might occasionally make pilgrimages to the holy city of Jerusalem, but their real religious life centered in the synagogue where they went to have the law read and explained.

The diaspora was, then, a fact which the Jerusalem priests and the Maccabees might ignore but could not undo. The Jews of the Hellenistic Diaspora—those of the Babylonian do not concern us here—sought to live in peace by following a formula that has later served the Jewish people well. As traders or entrepreneurs they traveled throughout the known world, from the Black Sea to the Pillars of Hercules, and founded "quarters" in all the great cities. (One of the means of the rapid expansion of Christianity was these communities; Christian missionaries could use them as points of departure for their activity.) Each Jewish "quarter" would have its synagogue and its teachers to instruct the young in the laws of Moses. But the "purity" of Jewish custom was modified so that the traders and learned men could move easily through the streets of Rome, Alexandria, and Marseilles.

There were perils in these streets, to the soul as well as to the body; this was well recognized by conservative Jews. In all important forums or marts of trade stood temples to Zeus and other popular gods. And, a more subtle peril, in all the great Hellenistic schools and libraries like the famous one at Alexandria were teachers of the various systems of philosophy that had first been worked out when Athens was the center of Greek culture. Greek culture was spread out very thin; but wherever one was, it was good form to ape Greek ways of thought.

One may say that the temptations confronting a young Jew of the Diaspora were almost identical with those faced by today's young Jew if he has been reared in a strict orthodox family. The business, social, and intellectual rewards of American society await the young man if he will but "go whoring after strange gods"—to use the prophetic phrase. If he will give up the links that bind him to a "peculiar people" and let himself be assimilated by the culture in which he finds himself, he will find life comparatively easy and painless. We should note—as we seek for parallels to the conditions faced by the writers of *The Wisdom of Solomon* and *Ecclesiasticus*—that this is a temptation faced by other religious minorities in America. Members of "peculiar people" like the Dunkards and the Amish certainly discover that their dress, custom, and strict morality draw down many penalties on them that they can easily escape by discarding their sectarian clothes and taking a job in a distant place.

For the Jews of the Diaspora there were three solutions to this problem. They could undergo complete assimilation. Spiritually and mentally, they could discard the habits of thought cherished by the fathers and be more Greek than the Greeks and, later, more Roman than the Romans. That this was what the great Jewish historian Josephus had done was the charge of his enemies among the Hebrews; he tried to write about *his* people's past as elegantly as the Roman historians dealt with their past, and it is a fact that Josephus was with the Roman armies that razed Jerusalem in 70 A.D.

But the way of Josephus was not the only one. Jews could, and did, cling to the ways of their fathers with especial fervor simply because they were keenly aware of outside pressure. This is a policy we shall find recommended when we turn, a little later, to the wisdom of Jesus, son of Sirach in *Ecclesiasticus*.

Finally, the Jews of the Diaspora could follow a *syncretistic* line of thought. *Syncretism* is the name applied to the process by which religious and philosophic elements of unlike origin and nature are put into effective relation to each other. A passable biological analogy for syncretism is the process of "budding" in which the blossom of a superior peach tree is grafted onto the branch of an inferior but more vigorous tree. We all practice a mild and personal form of syncretism when we move from one part of the country to another and, perhaps unconsciously, adjust our accent and customs to those of our new environment.

The Wisdom of Solomon

The Wisdom of Solomon, written in Alexandria about 50 B.C., is above all else a syncretistic book. It manifests, at least by omission, that the more minute ritual and legal regulations of theocratic Jerusalem cannot be observed by the Hellenistic Jew. It admits specifically that many of the early Hebrew narratives are, by Hellenistic standards, crude and naïve, and so are no longer binding upon a Hellenized Jew. On the other hand, the essential Hebrew insights —this is the contention of *The Wisdom of Solomon*—are not at odds with the noblest insights of the Hellenistic world. The pagan insights, moreover, are not so much wrong as incomplete; pagans have lacked the revelation available to all Hebrews in the history of their past and in the words of their prophets.

At many points in *Wisdom,* this collection of insights "worthy" of Solomon and bearing his name, we are likely to feel that we have moved on from the world of the direct, concrete historians and prophets into a different sort of world. Perhaps our sense of strangeness in these altered surroundings is the result of an emphasis, in *Wisdom,* on thought rather than action. Throughout the Old Testament the important thing was to "do well." Even prophecy is a kind of action rather than thought. In contrast, *The Wisdom of Solomon* is shot through with the more sophisticated Hellenistic attitude: "As a man thinketh, so he is." An emphasis on thought—an assertion that thinking well is primary and doing well a "reflex" of correct thought—can be a dangerous emphasis, as we have seen in our study of *Ecclesiastes* and *Job.* In those books, the emphasis induced either skepticism or a complete confusion and uncertainty as to what constitutes good and what God and his justice are. But in the world which the writer of *Wisdom* knows, philosophic thought is so routine an article that the Hebrew assumption of the primacy of doing well over thinking well is no longer a self-evident truth. For the writer of *Wisdom,* a certain course of action must be studied and compared with other courses of action. The writer's religious point of view must be defended much as various moral systems were defended in the Greek schools. Assertion, the mood congenial to poetic and prophetic wisdom, must be subordinated to something resembling demonstration and argument.

As he weighs and measures the traditional insights of his race, the writer of *Wisdom* has three Hellenistic systems of philosophy in mind.[2] It is valuable to remind ourselves with some fullness of the main outlines of these familiar systems. It is not only "Solomon" of

[2] He also has in mind the popular religion of the Hellenic world. The worship of the forces of nature the author of *Wisdom* pardons as a natural mistake. Through delight in the beauty of fire and wind and air, men take these to be their gods. "But for these men, there is but small blame, for they too peradventure do but go astray while they are seeking God and desiring to find him" (*Wisdom* 13:6). He is less patient with worshipers of idols. "But miserable were they, and in dead things were their hopes, who called them gods which are the works of men's hands, gold and silver, wrought with careful art, and likenesses of animals, or a useless stone, the work of an ancient hand" (*Wisdom* 13:10).

Wisdom who writes aware of Hellenistic points of view. Paul in his letters and the writer of *The Gospel of John* draw freely on Greek philosophies as they seek to explain the mysteries which, in the first place, were revealed to them.

The three systems that contribute, positively or negatively, to *The Wisdom of Solomon* are Epicureanism, Stoicism, and Platonism. Epicureanism is the whipping boy. It is regarded as the source of the grossly sensual vices of the pagan world that the Jew of the Diaspora must avoid. On the other hand, Stoicism and Platonism are recognized as containing acceptable insights not hopelessly at odds with truths which have been given the Hebrews by revelation. Further, since the Stoic and Platonic philosophers handle their particular insights fully and continuously, they provide the writer of *Wisdom* a good deal of artillery to use in the long battle that here begins as a contest for the soul of the Hellenized Jew but that ends, in the first three Christian centuries, as a fight for the soul of the Hellenic-Roman world itself.

As stated, Epicureanism is the whipping boy. As a philosophy, it is blamed for the secular vice abundant in Alexandria and elsewhere. (Idol worship, as in the days of Ashtoreth and Tammuz, was the occasion of santurnalian revels; with these, of course, the Hellenic Jew can have no traffic.) Defenders of Epicureanism as a philosophy of conduct would point out the great gap between refined and discriminating pursuit of pleasure (what Epicurus himself advocated) and brutal, immediate gratification of every lust, which appears in the life of crass, insensitive persons. But it is not a discriminating pursuit of pleasure that one sees in the accounts by Petronius (died *c.* 66 A.D.) and others of the life of the wealthy and powerful. No doubt their banquets and debauches were no worse than the celebrations of Egyptian and Assyrian monarchs many centuries before. But in the times now considered, excessive indulgence marched under the banner of Epicurus even thought it was a stolen banner.

But the express theories of Epicurus are that there are no gods of any sort, that what we see and touch are but chance collections of atoms, and that, consequently, one's behavior should result not from a fear of divine wrath and judgment in the life to come but from one's estimate of what will give the most pleasure and the least pain. All these theories *can* be used to justify the life of careless sensual pleasure sketched by the writer of *Wisdom* in his second chapter. Because by mere chance we have come to exist, we waste our time when we act as though some divine purpose animates the universe.

> For they said within themselves, reasoning not aright, Short and sorrowful is our life; and there is no healing when a man cometh to his end, and none was even known that gave release from Hades. Because by mere chance were we born, and hereafter we shall be as though we had never been: because the breath in our nostrils is smoke, and while our heart beateth reason is a spark, which being extinguished, the body shall be turned into ashes, and the spirit shall be dispersed as thin air; and our name shall be forgotten in time, and no man shall remember our works. . . . (*Wisdom* 2:1-3.)

This is one of the "crooked thoughts" (*Wisdom* 1:3) that separate us from God. This attitude is wrong in itself, and its ethical consequences are disastrous. Epicureanism tempts men to say:

> Come therefore and let us enjoy the good things that now are. . . . Let us fill ourselves with costly wine and perfumes; and let no flower of spring pass us by: let us crown ourselves with rosebuds, before they be withered: let none go without his share in our proud revelry: everywhere let us leave tokens of our mirth: because this is our portion, and our lot is this. (*Wisdom* 2:6-9.)

No reader of English poetry can fail to recall Robert Herrick's treatment of this theme:

> Gather ye rosebuds while ye may:
> Old Time is still a-flying . . .

Another form of Epicureanism that would be popular with the powerful is the attitude shown in modern expressions like "Might makes right" and "It's all right if you can get away with it." *Wisdom* 2:10 11 puts the matter thus:

> Let us oppress the poor righteous man, let us not spare the widow, nor reverence the ancient gray hairs of the aged. Let our strength be the law of justice: for that which is feeble is found to be nothing worth.

To such a view the righteous man is opposed. He believes there is a fixed, unaltering measure of justice in a world that is not a chance mixture of shifting atoms but is rather the handiwork of a planning and orderly deity.

There were two popular Hellenistic philosophies, Stoicism and Platonism, that say the world is a planned, orderly place, a place where one may see signs of purpose. These philosophies, consequently, are useful to the writer of *Wisdom.* They enable him to say with some fullness what the order is; they enable him to understand what the "action" of the Old Testament has already revealed to him. To be sure, neither Stoicism nor Platonism is taken over whole. The Hellenic Jew who speaks wisdom worthy of Solomon picks and chooses.

In the Stoic view there was one god or "soul" in the world, and the many gods of popular worship were but ordinary men's imperfect apprehensions of the one god. This one god or "soul" was not anthropomorphically conceived; it was simply the "reason" of things, the inevitability and interdependence that held all the universe together. The consequence of this insight is an ethical or moral attitude quite different from the sensation seeking of popularized Epicureanism. The behavior of the wise man should be an expression of his perception that things cannot always be obedient to *his* will; for he is but a part of a vast whole. When things go wrong, he is in the presence of a necessary aspect of the plan or is watching, as a related Stoic concept has it, the spinning wheel of the blind goddess Fortune. Therefore, he must suppress all spontaneous feelings of disappointment or grief. A passivity, a readiness to accept what the indwelling order of the universe presents is the wise attitude toward life. Hence our sense of the word *Stoic;* a Stoic is someone who can "take it on the chin."

The writer of *Wisdom* finds Stoicism powerfully attractive. He is attracted by the pantheistic Stoic god as a principle of order identical with all created being and coextensive with it. With a Stoic accent, the writer observes that we should be attentive to the Lord "because the spirit of the Lord hath filled the world, and that which holdeth all things together hath knowledge of every voice" (*Wisdom* 1:7). Hebrew revelation has taught the writer that Jehovah created the world and sustains it; thus far would the Stoic seem to be right. But revelation has also taught that God's existence is not involved with the existence of the world. The God that said to Moses, "I am that I am" (*Exodus* 3:14), must be thought of as existing apart from the world which he created. Nevertheless, the Stoic idea that the world we see and touch and encounter in our moral experience is some aspect of deity is attractive to "Solomon." If this indwelling order and regularity is not God, might it not be a subordinate principle, related to deity as, say, a human daughter is related to her father? This, at least, is the figure of speech that the author of *Wisdom* catches up and transforms into an important stone in his arch of speculation.

The writer, in the character of Solomon, introduces his principle with care. "Solomon," like all men, is but a son of Adam; "all men have one entrance into life, and a like departure" (*Wisdom* 7:5). How does he differ from other men? Only in that the Lord has permitted the "spirit of wisdom" to come to him. What this spirit revealed, "Solomon" has no wish to conceal. This "Wisdom" is more than the "wisdom" of *Proverbs*, Chapters 1 and 9. The latter, we say, is "horse sense" moving on various levels of man's ethical experience; when it is personified, the personification is casual and intermittent, as in the passage in *Jeremiah*, where we hear of Rachel "weeping for her children" (*Jeremiah* 31:15). Jeremiah's invention met a sudden need of poetic vision. The "Wisdom" revealed to "Solomon" deserves, if ever a personification did, a capital letter. She is a sustained personification of the order and justice that God has infused into all created things. (The staying power of this concept in human thought is testified to by the name of a great church; Santa Sophia in Constantinople is but the Church of Holy Wisdom.)

What Wisdom, this daughter of God and worker of his will, is, our writer first defines in a passage differing, in its effort to be exhaustive and consistent with the writer's basic assumption, from anything in the Old Testament.

> For there is in her a spirit quick of understanding, holy, alone in kind manifold, subtil, freely moving, clear in utterance, unpolluted, distinct, unharmed, loving what is good, keen, unhindered, beneficent, steadfast, sure, free from care, all-powerful, all-surveying, and penetrating through all spirits that are quick of understanding . . . ; for wisdom is more mobile than any motion; yea, she pervadeth and penetrateth all things by reason of her pureness. (*Wisdom* 7:22-24.)

Yet she is not merely coextensive with the world which she directs and orders, as is the Stoic deity.

> For she is a breath of the power of God, and a clear effluence of the glory of the Almighty; therefore can nothing defiled find entrance into her. For she is an effulgence from everlasting light, and an unspotted mirror of the working of God, and an image of his goodness. (*Wisdom* 7:25-26.)

Even the paradoxes that conclude this description differ from the unconscious contradictions of the *both-and* prophetic judgments. Here the conscious association of violently contradictory elements suggests that the writer is multiplying paradoxes—statements that do not make sense to the superficial view but that, upon longer study, prove to be both true and clear. Wisdom

> . . . being one, hath power to do all things: and remaining in herself, reneweth all things: and from generation to generation passing into holy souls she maketh men friends of God and prophets. . . . For she is fairer than the sun, and above all the constellations of the stars: being compared with light, she is found to be before it. . . . (*Wisdom* 7:27-29.)

How this entity can remain herself and yet be in all things, how she is "above" and "before" the order of stars and lights itself—all this the author of *Wisdom* labors to explain.

A good deal of his explanation seems to reflect the third sort of Hellenistic thought, Platonic speculation. But Wisdom as a "world-soul," to a degree detached from the being of Jehovah and making it unnecessary for him to perform certain functions, is speculation in accord with Stoic models. Further, Stoic prudential morality—its emphasis on self-control, its underwriting of justice and decency—is immensely congenial to one who wants to practice the virtues advocated by Moses and *Proverbs*. Indeed, Stoic ethical precept was so close to Hebrew and Christian ethical thought that in later centuries Christians could borrow freely from the great Roman Stoic, the Emperor Marcus Aurelius (121-180 A.D.). Righteousness in the Hebrew sense—behavior in conformity to the behests of God—is not in practice very different from Stoic virtue, which is behavior in conformity with what reason perceives about the order of the universe.

However, despite these points of meeting between Hebrew thought and Stoicism, the Platonic vein of Hellenistic philosophy has the greatest gift to make to religious thought that was trying to put old habits of flat intuition behind and become philosophical. One great Platonist was an Alexandrian of Jewish origin, Philo Judaeus (*c.* 20 B.C.-*c.* 50 A.D.). In early Christian centuries, it was Plato and his interpreters who aided a Christian champion like St. Augustine as he struggled to defend, to the cultivated world, the crudities and the bluntness of holy record. If Wisdom or Sophia seems to have been suggested by the Stoic conception of deity, it is Platonism that helps the writer of *Wisdom* to see precisely in what ways Sophia differs from God and how she operates.

Students of the history of philosophy are careful to make sharp distinctions between what Plato said and what his many followers in the Hellenistic world read into what he said. Plato is, naturally, the source of Platonism; and his followers in later centuries who modified and developed his thought are often called Neoplatonists. This latter sort of Platonism is judged to be the teaching of Plato worked over and confused with religious beliefs and aspirations current in the ancient world. The beliefs now to be summarized are perhaps more Neoplatonic than Platonic; but they are the beliefs with which our writer and the author of *The Gospel of John* seem to be in contact.

This set of beliefs can be likened to a ladder reaching from the lowest sort of excellence, a very poor sort, to the highest. The highest excellence, of course, is God himself and the ideas of perfection —the Good, the True, and the Beautiful—which have their existence in the mind of God. All excellences inferior to this highest kind rest on lower rungs of the ladder of perfection, and each is excellent not because of any virtue inherent in itself but because it contains some reflection of the perfection of God and his ideas. A good moral act is not good in itself. It is good because it contains some suggestions of the perfect idea of good in the mind of God. Any human perception of truth is good not absolutely but because the human knower feebly imitates the act by which deity knows truth. As the Platonists have it, human acts are good by "participation"; a man "participates" in an activity that is perfect only in God himself. Indeed, since man stands on a rung of the ladder far below the top rung, his knowledge of good and truth is a rather poor replica of the good and the true in the mind of God.

It cannot be otherwise. At least, no other possibility struck the Neoplatonists. In Platonic language, the top of the ladder rests on the level of God; it rests on that which has "being." The bottom rests on Nothing, on that which does not exist and which is called "non-being." That we exist at all is a result of the act of divine creation by which the visible, material world was formed; deity effected a mixture of various proportions of being and non-being. Thus the created world, to eyes that have been opened, is the ladder which extends from a point near nullity to a point some distance short of deity.

This account of creation differs widely from the account given in *Genesis* 2:2 ff. Here the Lord seems to find matter already at hand and kneads it to suit his fancy. Neoplatonists would like better the account which opens *Genesis,* where the Lord creates by fiat rather than by actual shaping: "And God said, Let there be light: and there was light" (*Genesis* 1:4). But of course the *Genesis* story does not allow us to predict the Neoplatonic comment on the ancient narrative—suggesting that non-being or the non-existent acquires its share of being, little or much, by *participation* in the being of the One. This participation, flatly stated, is a result of the divine imposition of form on non-being; and "form" is but the order and perfection of ideas in the mind of God. Just as the human good act participates in God's goodness (but is never identical with it, as Stoics might say), so do the beauty and order which we perceive in nature imitate divine beauty and order. Nature and we can no more than imitate, since both we and nature are a mixture of nothingness and form. Orthodox Christian theology distresses some when it speaks of "original sin," that basic human imperfection created by Adam's disobedience to God. More easily comprehensible is the Neoplatonic original sin, which is simply the imperfection that is part of everything that has been created from nullity. In consequence, there must always be a great gap between the rung on which human beings stand and the rung which is on a level with deity.

This gap must be bridged. How is one to set about doing it? How may that which is imperfect effect contact with that which is perfect? Though couched in philosophical terms, this is but a restatement of the question Job asked. How may man wrest protection and justice from that which is entirely "Other"? How may man "justify" himself to God? As Job says:

> If I justify myself, mine own mouth shall condemn me: if I say, I am perfect, it shall also prove me perverse. (*Job* 9:20.)

The only answer that Job got was: submit to the powerful and inscrutable deity. It is an answer in accord with the older Hebrew emphasis on right *action*. The Neoplatonic answer underlines the preëminence of the need for right *thought*. Before a man commences to act, let him see where he *is* on the ladder. Let him see that he is the most complex of created beings, but still a being immeasurably separated from the uncreated, the One. To perceive this gap is to be well on the way to what religious persons call "salvation."

But here a difficulty intervenes. It would seem impossible for man ever by his own power to scramble from his rung to the distant rung that stands for the One, "the Other" in our phrase. The success of the scramble, for the Neoplatonist, continues to depend on "right knowledge." When man turns from illusions to Truth, his task is nearly done. It is enough to prefer light to darkness, to prefer the being of God to the non-being which the worshipers of pleasure pursue.

But the Hellenistic world, which had preserved Plato's thought and had made it available to the writer of *Wisdom*, contained not only the cults of the old gods and the systems fashioned by human beings. It contained what are called "mystery religions." These bore their name because their rites were secret; the obscure initiations at Eleusis and elsewhere offered "salvation" consisting not primarily of right knowledge but, in the first place, of an emotional experience which only later was explained to the initiate. Thus, the person initiated into the mysteries of Eleusis was encouraged to believe that, by the favor of the goddess Demeter, he had been reborn and was a new man. His appearance was, of course, what it had been before, but his inner nature—his "heart," in the phrase of the Hebrew prophets—was something new. Consequently, his existence could never be the same. He was cut off from the man who had sought out the "mysteries" at Eleusis. Further, the "miracle" of rebirth that had taken place there was not thanks to the merit of the person who had come to the shrine but thanks to the generosity of the deity.

This insight helped many Neoplatonists to bridge the gap in the ladder between the imperfect mortal and the perfect deity. (It was a gap that Plato himself believed could be bridged intellectually; but this was not the belief of many who followed in his wake.) Man was by nature imperfect and separated from the One. Knowledge of the gap and its significance was necessary but would not take a created person up to the level of deity. Some kind of gesture or aid must come from the One. The writings of the Neoplatonists try to state what this aid was. It was akin to the aid that had already seen to the actual creation of the earth and man. Now it would give man the necessary boost up the ladder toward perfection. Aeons, demiurges, etc.—these are the names that Neoplatonists give to the messengers of the One, and the names need not concern us. We need only recognize that such go-betweens existed; they were intermediaries helpful to men seeking salvation in the "climate" of thought that determines much of the activity of Sophia as described in *The Wisdom of Solomon.* This same "climate" later makes contributions to the conception of Christ's role held by St. John. Wisdom may be—as noted—the rational principle, the structure of the world, in Stoic style. But what she specifically does for man, how she is needful to him, is fully intelligible only in terms provided by the system of thought just sketched.

In Chapter 9 of *Wisdom* the plight of created man is described in terms that reflect the Neoplatonic world of thought:

> For what man shall know the counsel of God? Or who shall conceive what the Lord willeth? For the thoughts of mortals are timorous, and our devices are prone to fail. For a corruptible body weigheth down the soul, and the earthy frame lieth heavy on a mind that is full of cares. And hardly do we divine the things that are on earth, and the things that are close at hand we find with labor; but the things that are in the heavens who ever yet traced out? (*Wisdom* 9:13-16.)

Plainly, a "corruptible body" bears with it the dross of non-being that keeps man from comprehending that which has complete being. The final question in the passage points to the necessity of Sophia's existence as an intermediary. "And who ever gained knowledge of thy counsel, except thou gavest wisdom, and sentest thy holy spirit from on high?" (*Wisdom* 9:17.) The writer answers his question: "And it was thus that the ways of them which are on earth were corrected, and men were taught the things that are pleasing unto thee; and through wisdom were they saved" (*Wisdom* 9:18).

As "Solomon" continues his exposition of this point, he shows that every stage of Hebrew history was witness to the to-and-fro movement of Wisdom. The "facts" of Hebrew history are reinterpreted. Adam and Moses may seem to be the doers of an act, but the real agent is the unseen daughter of God. God, as the writer of *Wisdom* conceives deity, is still the God who created all things by his word, and he continues to watch over them—but not by "walking in the garden in the cool of the day" (*Genesis* 3:8). "Solomon's" deity watches at a distance, and it is his agent Wisdom who intervenes and guides man and the material world—Wisdom "that sitteth by thee on thy throne" (*Wisdom* 9:4).

What kind of existence has this entity had?

> And with thee is wisdom, which knoweth thy works, and was present when thou wast making the world, and which understandeth what is pleasing in thine eyes, and what is right according to thy commandments. (*Wisdom* 9:9.)

That is, Sophia is eternal, she existed before the world was created, and she possesses what man cannot possess: a direct view of the ideas of excellence in the mind of God. It is a set of ideas that man cannot have, but if he fails to measure up to them, he will be "judged." Man's ignorance imposes difficulties, yet the writer is not overwhelmed by fear as Job was. He can hope that Wisdom, the intermediary and aid, is at his side. Why need he fear? For Wisdom "knoweth all things and hath understanding thereof, and in my doings she shall guide me in ways of soberness, and she shall guard me in her glory" (*Wisdom* 9:11). With the knowledge that Wisdom pours out, "Solomon" or any other man may hope to bridge the gap between himself and deity. "For she is unto men a treasure that faileth not, and they that use it to obtain friendship with God, commended to him by the gifts which they through discipline present to him" (*Wisdom* 7:14).

One striking result of this insight is that righteous activity is regarded as centered in the choices of each person, not on a tribe's observance of a fixed code and elaborate ritual. We have seen that, with the exception of Ezekiel, it was the moral destiny of Israel rather than the moral choices of Israelites that bulked large in prophetic thought. Certainly this alteration in emphasis was congenial to the Jews of the Diaspora who were not likely to see the holy city of Jerusalem very often. "Solomon" tells them they can do the will of God with the aid of Wisdom rather than be, in theory, dependent on the ministrations of a Temple priesthood in a distant city. Also attractive to Jews who had to rub elbows with "unclean" pagans every day of their lives was the teaching that the moral life was not a matter of careful observance of ritual and dietary precept; it was a matter of following out the simple clues the writer provides. Evil was not the infraction of specific laws. Evil lay in turning away from Wisdom and the deity she served; good consisted in putting non-being behind and drawing near to absolute being. All the special prescriptions of "Solomon" have this simple distinction in view. Misfortune is not a visitation from an angry deity or a temptation from the devil. In *Wisdom,* man's greatest source of darkness is in himself. We see this in Wisdom's commentary on the Egyptians of Moses' time. Their great misfortune was their lack of knowledge, and their "wickedness" toward the oppressed Hebrews was not, as *Exodus* has it, consequent upon the Lord's ceaseless hardening of the Pharaoh's heart. Their evil was the natural product of the inner darkness in which they lived.

> For wickedness, condemned by a witness within, is a coward thing, and, being pressed hard by conscience, always forecasteth the worst lot: for fear is nothing else but a surrender of the succours which reason offereth. . . . (*Wisdom* 17:12-13.)

Instead of "reason," we might permissibly read ". . . the succours which Wisdom offereth . . ."—the light that shines for those, whether Egyptian or Hebrew, who will turn to it. Exaggerating to be sure, the writer underlines the plight of the Egyptians for the benefit of his Jewish readers in Alexandria.

> For the whole world beside was enlightened with clear light, and was occupied with unhindered works; while over them alone was spread a heavy night, an image of the darkness that should afterward receive them; but yet heavier than darkness were they unto themselves. (*Wisdom* 17:20-21.)

The writer says in effect to his audience, "Man's last enemy is man."

Man and not Satan is the producer of moral evil, of the kind of activity that makes the entrance of Wisdom impossible.

In such a context, virtue depends quite simply on a change of one's orientation. Man, by turning from the dark and non-being, permits Wisdom to lead him toward the light and being. Dante said of God: "In his will is our peace." *Wisdom* states the matter thus:

> But thou, our God, art gracious and true, long-suffering, and in mercy ordering all things. For even if we sin, we are thine, knowing thy dominion; but we shall not sin, knowing that we have been accounted thine: for to be acquainted with thee is perfect righteousness, and to know thy dominion is the root of immortality. (*Wisdom* 15:1-3.)

Virtue, in this book and unlike the pure contemplation which seems to be the terminus of life Platonically conceived, keeps in touch with the Hebrew emphasis on "doing," even though it is admitted that correct knowledge must precede doing. True, in *Wisdom* salvation receives the support of a kind of knowledge which the prophets did not deal in; but salvation after all implies activity rather than passivity. One must make part of the journey, although Wisdom meets more than halfway those who seek her. "She forestalleth them that desire to know her, making herself first known. He that riseth up early to seek her shall have no toil, for he shall find her sitting at his gates" (*Wisdom* 6:13-14). Wisdom will complete the human desire for good, but she will not come unless the desire is stirring, unless the mortal has faced toward her. In the language of the love poetry of *The Song of Solomon*—language constantly used by the devout and mystic when they speak of holy matters—"Solomon" writes of Wisdom: "Her I loved and sought out from my youth, and I sought to take her for my bride, and I became enamoured of her beauty" (*Wisdom* 8:2). In this whole relation of the mortal and Wisdom appears a contrast with Neoplatonic systems. There the demiurges that emanate from deity emanate automatically; Wisdom, the daughter of God, must be sought with desire as well as intellect.

The results of this conception are far-reaching. One need not insist that later thinkers are in touch with *The Wisdom of Solomon.* But they are in touch with veins of thought richly illustrated by this book. In altered forms, we shall meet again the following concepts: Wisdom in its function of intercessor between God and created man; the "free gift" that man may take from Wisdom; and the new nature that results from life in contact with Wisdom. All these are markers on the philosophic avenues leading out of the impasse faced in *Ecclesiastes* and *Job,* where perception of the moral life in terms of external activity and external and material "rewards" leads to either skepticism or frustration.

That the author of *Wisdom* has traveled far from the views of his fathers, a single point will summarize. In other ages, one of God's chief rewards was thought to be prosperous old age and gray hairs. The writer of *Wisdom* says pointedly: "For honorable old age is not that which standeth in length of time, nor is its measure given by number of years: but understanding is gray hairs unto men, and an unspotted life is ripe old age" (*Wisdom* 4:8-9). Early death is no longer a source of grief. The wise man "being made perfect in a little while, he fulfilled long years; for his soul was pleasing unto the Lord: therefore hasted he out of the midst of wickedness" (*Wisdom* 4:13-14). The rejection of the closely related Hebrew "reward" of posterity is sharp:

> And happy is the eunuch which hath wrought no lawless deed with his hands, nor imagined wicked things against the Lord; for there shall be given him for his faithfulness a peculiar favor, and a lot in the sanctuary of the Lord more delightsome than wife or children. (*Wisdom* 3:14.)

Ecclesiasticus

Ecclesiasticus—the title means "church-book" and comes from the Latin Vulgate—is also known as *The Wisdom of Jesus the Son of Sirach.* It is "wisdom" far removed from what we have been observing in *The Wisdom of Solomon.* One cannot call the "wisdom" of

Ecclesiasticus a return to orthodox Hebrew ways of thought. For one thing, it was written in the early part of the second century B.C. and antedates *The Wisdom of Solomon* by more than a hundred years. More importantly, it is the work of a Palestinian Jew who had never thought of leaving Judaism for the Hellenistic patterns that, in the day of Jesus Ben Sirach, Antiochus Epiphanes was urging upon the Hebrew people. But *Ecclesiasticus* is, in its own way, as useful a book to us as we approach the New Testament as is *The Wisdom of Solomon.* It holds up before us, in an unflinching fashion, the response to Hellenistic thought that is neither submission nor compromise and adjustment. This is an attitude continued into New Testament times. What we see of it in the portraits the Gospel writers draw of the Sadducees and the Pharisees is not flattering. When we read of these groups, when the Gospel writers tell us of their intransigence and blindness, we do well to remember Jesus Ben Sirach and the sterling qualities of the book he wrote.

The prologue, written in Egypt by the grandson of Jesus, includes several remarks that deserve note. The grandson speaks of the difficulties of translation from Hebrew into another tongue, and he indicates that his translation will find a ready audience among the Hebrews "who in the land of their sojourning are desirous to learn, fashioning their manners beforehand, so as to live according to the law." Not all the Hebrews in Alexandria were eager to Hellenize or find some easy *modus vivendi.* Some wished to intensify their Jewishness, just as British colonials at present make a great point of tea and crumpets in darkest Africa. The translator goes on to justify his presentation of a book that is by a "modern" rather than a canonical author.

> . . . my grandfather Jesus, having much given himself to the reading of the law, and the prophets, and the other books of our fathers, and having gained great familiarity therein, was drawn also himself to write somewhat pertaining to instruction and wisdom; in order that those who love learning, and are addicted to these things, might make progress much more by living according to the law. (*Ecclesiasticus,* Prologue.)

Plainly, the writer of this book holds up to his readers the value of persisting in old ways. Nor does he suggest that the Hebrews may expect further revelation. All has been given; now one needs only to understand. In fact, he flies in the face of tradition at only one point; he presumes to add to the collection of wisdom under his own name. He does not, like other people in his age, write "in the spirit of" some one of the famous dead. If there is any book in the Old Testament canon in whose spirit he composes, it is *The Proverbs.* His accent often suggests that he judges he is as full of meat as the ancient writers and that it is the same meat.

A person fresh from *The Wisdom of Solomon* might judge the "wisdom" in Chapter 1 of *Ecclesiasticus* to be the same entity as that which he dealt with in the other book. For one reads: "All wisdom cometh from the Lord, and is with him for ever," and "Wisdom hath been created before all things, and the understanding of prudence from everlasting" (*Ecclesiasticus* 1:1, 4). The Lord "created her, and saw her, and numbered her, and poured her out upon all his works. She is with all flesh according to his gift, and he hath given her to them that love him" (*Ecclesiasticus* 1:10-11). But later encounters with this personification show that the resemblance to the *language* of *Wisdom,* whatever the cause, is not equivalent to a resemblance of theory. Jesus Ben Sirach's "wisdom," other passages show, is not a precise theological concept; it is but the sort of personification that "poetic wisdom" in the Old Testament has made familiar to us. Like Rachel weeping for her children and the daughters of Zion sitting in the dust and Jacob cast out by an angry Lord, this personification is expandable and collapsible at will. As this writer says simply, "The fear of the Lord is the beginning of wisdom" (*Ecclesiasticus* 1:16); and this wisdom is not an item in an ambitious reinterpretation of ancient record, as is *The Wisdom of Solomon.* It is but our old friend wisdom from *Proverbs,* garbed as always in various sorts of detached moral odds and ends—noble or prudent or canny—and all in accord with the general Mosaic precepts. Sometimes this "wisdom" is personified (e.g., in *Ecclesiasticus* chap. 6), but often it is not so treated (*Ecclesiasticus* chap. 16).

Jesus Ben Sirach works within the limits of traditional Hebrew culture, and he works well. He deserved the attention of those who read the translation of his work in Alexandria, and he deserves the attention of all men who care to lend an ear to what the Jewish-Christian tradition has to say. Here, wisdom is nine parts correct and prudent action and one part theology. (Reverse the formula and you have *The Wisdom of Solomon.*) For most men, this is the correct proportion, since we live aware of special problems rather than of the social and religious presuppositions that underpin our society. We are, we say, "practical men," and there is much to delight us in the practical, unsystematic, and psychologically acute observations of Jesus Ben Sirach. His book is more attractive than *Proverbs* because the lack of system is not accompanied by the brevity that makes *Proverbs* as distracting for continuous reading as Bartlett's *Dictionary of Familiar Quotations.*

The mode of this book, one may say, is often the mode of the familiar essay—a form often suggesting to us that we and the author have settled down by the fire for a chat. To be sure, Jesus Ben Sirach differs from a master like Montaigne, whose divagations have for their center a skeptical "What do I know?" Jesus does not doubt that there is something he does know. Yet his style of conveying it has something of the great Frenchman's slippered charm. When he writes of the misery of dining always at other men's tables, it is, one feels, from direct observation:

> Better is the life of a poor man under a shelter of logs, than sumptuous fare in another man's house. With little or much, be well satisfied. It is a miserable life to go from house to house: and where thou art a sojourner, thou shalt not dare to open thy mouth. Thou shalt entertain, and give to drink, and have no thanks: and besides this thou shalt hear bitter words. Come hither, thou sojourner, furnish a table, and if thou hast aught in thy hand, feed me with it. Go forth, thou sojourner, from the face of honor: my brother is come to be my guest; I have need of my house. These things are grievous to a man of understanding; the upbraiding of house-room, and the reproaching of the money-lender. (*Ecclesiasticus* 29:21-28.)

His acute description of the "winking man" brings to mind a type that is still with us:

> One that winketh with the eye contriveth evil things; and no man will remove him from it. When thou art present, he will speak sweetly, and will admire thy words; but afterwards he will writhe his mouth, and set a trap for thee in thy words. I have hated many things, but nothing like him; and the Lord will hate him. (*Ecclesiasticus* 27:22-24.)

What he says of the "gifts of a fool" is true, as we know from our own experience:

> He will give little, and upbraid much: and he will open his mouth like a crier: today he will lend, and tomorrow he will ask it again: such an one is a hateful man. (*Ecclesiasticus* 20:14-15.)

And his commendation of the married state is truthful and shrewd rather than romantic:

> He that getteth a wife entereth upon a possession; a help meet for him, and a pillar of rest. Where no hedge is, the possession will be laid waste: and he that hath no wife will mourn as he wandereth up and down. For who will trust a nimble robber, that skippeth from city to city? Even so who shall trust a man that hath no nest, and lodgeth wheresoever he findeth himself at nightfall? (*Ecclesiasticus* 36:24-26.)

But despite this acuteness, the psychologist is subordinate to the moralist. (In modern culture, it would seem to be the moralist who is subordinate to the psychologist.) The theoretical moralist can move on the level of discourse where only perfection is discussed. Jesus Ben Sirach is a practical moralist, so he must get down to cases. He must become involved in prudence; prudence must enter one's calculations if the ideal good is to be served while one struggles in the mesh of circumstances. Much oftener than in *Proverbs,* we encounter prudence that is on the verge of becoming canniness and using moral precept as a cloak for selfish action. It is noble to say, "A faithful friend is a medicine of life"; it is prudent to say, "Sweet words will multiply a man's friends; and a fair-speaking tongue will multiply courtesies"; it is canny and more than canny to say, "Separate thyself from thine enemies; and beware of thy friends" (*Ecclesiasticus* 6:5, 13, 16). The prudence sometimes becomes an overt nudge when Jesus Ben Sirach remarks, "Be not slow to visit a sick man; for by such things thou shalt gain love," after saying decently, "Be not wanting to them that weep; and mourn with them that mourn" (*Ecclesiasticus* 7:34-35). "Gaining love" is a different thing from "mourning with them that mourn"; it is a descent, and an apt one. A chapter beginning with an observation that has appealed to generations as permanently true—"He that toucheth pitch shall be defiled"—can give way to these sharp-sighted instructions to a young man who wishes to rise in the world:

> If a mighty man invite thee, be retiring, and so much the more will he invite thee. Press not upon him, lest thou be thrust back; and stand not far off, lest thou be forgotten. (*Ecclesiasticus* 13:1, 9-10.)

In these mixed gardens of wisdom most readers will delight to wander and cull choice flowers.

If, in addition, we wish to observe the continuity of Hebrew tradition, we must note what happens to the traditional themes. First, any expansion of these themes is not, as with *The Wisdom of Solomon,* traceable to Hellenistic suggestion. It is a development of what is already given by the Hebrew tradition. Whereas in *Wisdom* fear was the stigma of darkness, in this book it is the predominating note of the proper attitude toward deity. Death is the sentence of the Lord upon all flesh. If it is a sentence that the Lord qualifies for the virtuous—"For it is an easy thing in the sight of the Lord to reward a man in the day of death according to his ways" (*Ecclesiasticus* 11:26)—Jesus Ben Sirach does not have much to say of the reward. He warns:

> Number not thyself among the multitudes of sinners: remember that wrath will not tarry. Humble thy soul greatly; for the punish-

> ment of the ungodly man is fire and the worm. (*Ecclesiasticus* 7:16-17.)

But he can hold out no great assurance to the virtuous: "All flesh waxeth old as a garment; the covenant from the beginning is Thou shalt die the death" (*Ecclesiasticus* 14:17). In short, we are still in the "climate of opinion" where the good and evil alike go together to the pit or Sheol. The writer is sure of "fire and the worm" for the ungodly. But what for the godly? The most that our moralist can suggest appears in this passage:

> Desire not a multitude of unprofitable children, neither delight in ungodly sons. If they multiply, delight not in them, except the fear of the Lord be with them. Trust not thou in their life, neither rely on their condition: for one is better than a thousand, and to die childless than to have ungodly children. For from one that hath understanding shall a city be peopled. . . . (*Ecclesiasticus* 16:1-4.)

He goes so far as to minimize the value of offspring. This says little about what the childless righteous may expect after death. The glory of having founded a city? This is as far as we come toward the doctrine of immortality that even in the era of Jesus Ben Sirach was being debated at Jerusalem.

If a certain generosity frequently lights up an observation, at many points we are in the presence of utterances that we have met often. "Good things and evil, life and death, poverty and riches, are from the Lord" (*Ecclesiasticus* 11:14). How God can be the author of both good and evil tests the ingenuity of teachers to come; it is no challenge whatever to Jesus Ben Sirach. An unbridled legalism appears in this chance comment on Eve: "From a woman was the beginning of sin; and because of her we all die" (*Ecclesiasticus* 25:24).

All this reliance on long-fixed habits of thought is hardly balanced by recognition, in a passage in Chapter 24, that the first Fathers may not have known all. Wisdom was not known perfectly by the first men, but the caution is that neither will the last men know it. Therefore, one had better abide by the certainties of tradition and custom. The writer says: "I will yet pour out doctrine as prophecy, and leave it unto generations of ages" (*Ecclesiasticus* 24:33). His "doctrine as prophecy" will but confirm against outside attack the certainties that bind the Hebrews to their Lord. Even when he sighs for "new signs" and "divers wonders" (*Ecclesiasticus* 36:6), he is not asking the Lord to turn the world upside down, as would an ideal conqueror or a "new Jerusalem." He is but asking for a slight display of power that will strengthen the *status quo,* the theocratic state.

Suitably the book ends with a section beginning, "Let us now praise famous men, and our fathers that begat us" *(Ecclesiasticus* 44:1). The men he lists are "famous" in the writer's eyes for the same reasons that they deserved fame centuries before. Abraham and the others bore the marks of divine favor, and they did God's will. They are not worthy of fame for the recondite reason that the author of *Wisdom* makes out: that Sophia has been always at their side, invisible but supporting.

The Dead Sea Scrolls

Out of such materials may a bridge be built from the Old Testament to the New: a bridge that is an assertion of continuity between the world of the prophets and the theocratic state of post-exilic times and the world of the New Testament, the world of Jesus and the early church. To this bridge, already impressive, strengthening girders have been added in recent years. The world in which Christ walks in Gospel narrative is sufficiently real; there (see Chap. XIV) we already have a sufficient sense of tension and counter-tension among social groups and ideas. What those tensions express we have seen in the Apocrypha: the coexistence of opposed ways of following God and pleasing him. Now, thanks to the discovery of the Dead Sea scrolls, we have other valuable testimony to the nature and the texture of the world which Jesus knew at the beginning of our era.

In 1948 the whole Western world was excited to hear of a discovery that equaled the tales of writers of popular fiction in color and suspense; it surpassed those tales in intrinsic importance. In a cliffside cave near the north end of the Dead Sea were discovered elongated clay jars that contained rolls of Hebrew books that had been deposited there many centuries before. Some Arab boys had been playing in the vicinity, and one of them had tossed a stone through an opening in the hillside. There was a sound of breakage, and investigation revealed the jars and their precious contents, decaying rolls of leather. The boys' elders, herdsmen simple yet shrewd, saw a chance of gain and offered these first Dead Sea scrolls for sale in nearby Bethlehem; from the hands of antique dealers, the scrolls passed to various persons and organizations. Some were bought by the Syrian Orthodox metropolitan bishop of Jerusalem, and others by the Hebrew University. For many months the various purchasers were not able to compare their treasures since they lived on different sides of the line that separated the state of Israel from the state of Jordan. Moreover, because of this division, further exploration of the caves did not go forward, and even the age and significance of these ancient manuscripts gave rise to hot debate. For example, was the very complete copy of *Isaiah* a medieval copy or—and this is the majority judgment—a precious record of the text of *Isaiah* as it existed in the first century before Christ? (If it was, it was many centuries older than tenth-century versions of the Massoretic or traditional Hebrew text on which, until 1948, modern Bible study had had to depend.) Another question soon asked was this one: what group of people had put the rolls into a cave for safekeeping? What community had preserved, as of equal importance, the text of *Isaiah* and Hebrew works that modern man had never seen or heard of? (These other books were soon called, for convenience, *The Habakkuk Commentary*, *The Manual of Discipline*, and *The Wars of the Sons of Light with the Sons of Darkness*.)

These questions have now received answers—answers to which the majority of scholars assent, thanks to further evidence that has accumulated in subsequent years. Moreover, exploration has penetrated the barrier between Israel and Jordan and has found a whole series of caves in the hillsides near the north end of the Dead Sea. There are few caves with manuscripts as well preserved as those in the first cave; but there are many caves where the fragments of ancient documents are scattered amid dust and clay like forest leaves. And no leaf is without value; cleaned and carefully handled, each fragment testifies that the ancient library which is dispersed among these caves contained a copy of a certain Old Testament book or of an unknown book which recent men have never seen.

Of almost equal interest is the fact that near the caves are ruins of buildings that housed a community that is often called the Wadi Qumran community since near the ruins is the water course of a stream known as the Wadi Qumran. The ruins date to Roman times in Palestine (63 B.C. to 70 A.D.), and archeologists have identified meeting halls, a dining room, a writing room (scriptorium), arrangements for the storage of grain and water, and provisions for washing. This was in all probability the community that multiplied copies of the books of the Old Testament and lived by the precepts of the previously unknown *Manual of Discipline*. This was the community that at its breakup stored its only precious objects—words of truth, a sharp contrast to the treasures of furniture and jewels that encumbered Egyptian tombs—and then vanished from the stage of human history. Who were these people and under what threat did they leave behind, in the safety of the caves, what has turned out to be a gift to the people of the twentieth century?

The prevalent answer develops thus. This was the chief community of the Essenes—the "pious ones"—that for about two centuries (*c.* 167 B.C. to 68 A.D.) lived separated from the city of Jerusalem on its distant hills and from Jericho in the nearby plain; further, it was the "mother house" of several similar communities scattered through Hebrew land. If an Essene community, the Qumran group was a protest—as we learn from the Jewish historian Josephus and others—against the adulteration of Jewish law and rite by contact with the Hellenistic world where power and sophistication took precedence over godliness. The Essenes lived together—preferably in celibacy—and devoted themselves to cherishing the pure ancient traditions and to writing books of their own in which they expressed their own sense of what these traditions meant in their own day. (Their own books are books of law, hymns of praise, and works of apocalyptic vision. No explicit history of the community has been found, and vague references to contests between wicked priest-kings and teachers of righteousness are chiefly tantalizing.)

The Essenes, at least, judged that living in the Hellenistic world meant withdrawal from a world in which revived Jewish nationalism, under the Maccabees and their successors, was once more trying to set up a kingdom of this earth. Withdrawal meant commitment to a simple and even grim life of ritual purity and obedience to the laws of God and to the direction of the master of the community. The chief hope of the community looked forward to a time, not far distant, when some sort of Messiah would appear and when there would be a final battle between the children of light, who followed the Lord with true understanding, and the children of darkness who, in Essene eyes, could be either the Roman conquerors or the Hebrew ruling families. (This last hope clearly works a vein of religious aspiration that we find in Jewish apocalypse like *Enoch* and in the Christian vision of "last things," the book of *Revelation.*) They were, in short, a community animated by some of the convictions that led, in America, to the creation of the Shaker communities and the Rappites of New Harmony in Indiana; the only way to live in an evil world was to withdraw from it and practice a rule of life that was pleasing to God, however offensive to man.

The actual history of the community was one of isolation and yet danger. *The Habakkuk Commentary* speaks of a contest between the head of the community, "the teacher of righteousness," and a wicked priest. Here students suspect a contest, perhaps ending in death, between the "teacher" and one of the successors of Judas Maccabaeus, perhaps Alexander Jannaeus, early in the first century before Christ. Later, the community was struck down by earthquake (31 B.C.), abandoned, and then reinhabited until the Romans arrived (68 A.D.). The Romans were stirred to anger by the nationalism of the Jews in Jerusalem; ironically, they wiped out a group of people that was as critical as were the Romans of Hebrew aspirations toward establishing an earthly kingdom. (To be sure, there was a difference. The Romans assumed that only Rome had a right to such a kingdom; the Essenes were certain that any such pursuit was a turning away from God.) It was at the time of the Roman attack, scholars think, that the manuscripts were probably deposited for a safe-keeping more than temporary.

This discovery that has required many years to complete—if it is complete—is sensational and exciting. It has offered magazine readers the sort of excitement that other generations found in *King Solomon's Mines*. But as the opening of the rolls and the cleaning of the fragments progresses in Jerusalem, something more solid than sensation is offered persons who are curious about the period between the two Testaments and also about New Testament times themselves. The scrolls offer facts and diminish the need for certain scholarly hypotheses. To be sure, we may never know precisely what contest, for example, took place between the "teacher of righteousness" and the wicked priest. But the Essene "library," which includes these writings, has answered many questions that are important to Biblical scholars and to readers who wish to see the Old and New Testament in the clearest light possible.

The various "answers" that the collection gives fall under two headings; they answer one sort of question for readers of the Old Testament and another sort for readers of the New.

The "answers" that concern the Old Testament amount to an assurance of the reliability of the texts of the Old Testament which we possess. The oldest Hebrew text, previous to 1948, went back only to the tenth century A.D. The much older translation of the Old Testament books into Greek (the Septuagint) was made two or three centuries before Christ. Since these two versions are in some disagreement, scholars have supposed that one text—usually the Hebrew, the one produced by early Hebrew scholars, the Massoretes—represented a pure tradition and the other a corruption. The scroll of *Isaiah* seems to support this view since there are only slight disagreements between it and the text that is a thousand years younger. But an equally old text of *Samuel* from another cave contains, *in Hebrew,* readings that support the variations that for centuries have been observed in the Greek translation of the Old Testament, the Septuagint; the translators who created it, then, worked faithfully and not loosely as much modern theory has suggested.

The cumulative effect of such scrolls is a double one. It underlines the faithfulness of those involved in the transmission of the text. It denies that, at the time of the Essenes, there was one tradition that was the pure tradition. Instead, the Essene community knew, accepted, and cherished more than one version of the Pentateuch and other Old Testament books. If there was, in an even dimmer past, one "pure" text from which both the Greek Septuagint and the Hebrew Massoretic texts stem, that text underwent variations long before the Essene community collected its library. Twentieth-century theories that assumed a constant change and perhaps adulteration of what had been presented by tradition are less secure now; a high degree of conservatism has been witnessed to by the scrolls themselves. (The scrolls, because of their antiquity, are also invaluable to scholars who wish to study the development of Hebrew language and handwriting.)

If certain of the scrolls testify to the continuity of the Old Testament tradition, others like *The Manual of Discipline* give us what is certainly just as valuable: a closer view of the Hebrew world—or part of the Hebrew world—at the time of the New Testament. To be sure, the Gospels and *Acts* already enable us to peer into that world. But there is much that remains enigmatic. What, for example, was the administrative structure of the early Christian community? *Acts* does not allow us to say surely. Were the characteristic and novel assertions about the nature of Jesus and his place in Hebrew tradition unique insights?

The special scrolls in question, at the very least, let us rephrase our queries, although they make no mention of the Christians. (The New Testament makes no explicit reference to the Essenes and *their* teaching.) It is true that the view that the "teacher of righteousness" is flatly a Messiah or "suffering-servant" figure whose persecution and possible sudden martyrdom have been "projected" into the career of Jesus is now regarded as eccentric and goes far beyond what can be proved. But it is not regarded as unlikely that Essene teachers, with their emphasis on purity and observance of the law, with their firm opposition to the powers of this world, and with their keen sense of the nearness of the end of man's history, prepared discontented masses of people to listen to Christ and his followers when they made some of these points. The Essene emphasis on a sharp contrast between two ways of life, the way followed by the holy ones and the way of uncleanness followed by the mass of men anticipates remarks in *John.* The Essene *Wars* testifies to a general expectation that, in some way, the time drew near when the Lord would intervene in the structure of human history and once more manifest himself. On such ideas the Christions had no copyright: a fact already visible to careful readers of *Wisdom* and other intertestamental books.

Some students find that there is more than a dependence of idea upon idea. They see in the organization of the Essene community in the desert a clue to the Christian community's organization as it commenced to take shape in *its* desert: a suspicious Jerusalem, an unfriendly Roman world. The Essene community was ruled by a council composed of twelve laymen (a fact that at the least testifies to the persistent importance of this figure in Hebrew history) and three priests. Above these was an overseer or shepherd, a sort of bishop, who perhaps continued to direct the "Many," the male adults, as the rather nebulous "teacher of righteousness" had once done. Perhaps from the experience of the Essene community the later Christian one, also faced with the necessity of living thrust apart from the Jerusalem Temple, drew useful lessons; it too had to make practical adaptations and applications of an ancient heritage.

Further, it was with the Essenes and their purified versions of Judaism that, as some suppose, John the Baptist had illuminating contact. The crowds that came readily to listen to him at the side of the Jordan near Jericho had perhaps learned a habit of attention to wandering critics of the Jerusalem *status quo* from traveling Essenes who had spoken in similar terms and who even practiced among themselves a kind of baptism. And, it is strongly argued, it was the teaching of the Essene community that may have been decisive for the view of Christ that we have in *John* (see chap. XVII) rather than Greek philosophy and oriental religion.

But cautious students of the scrolls warn us that it is uncritical to regard the great religious movement, Christianity, as the teaching of the "pious ones" projected on a world screen. Rather do the scrolls like *The Manual of Discipline* illustrate the Apostle Paul's saying: "The whole creation groaneth" (*Romans* 8:22). The kind of awareness that aspired to listen to Christ and to those who spoke of him already stirred among the Essenes as well as in many other places. Because of this expectation, this "groaning," it is not surprising that Christianity is built with stones that come from many quarries. To this truth, the Dead Sea scrolls along with many of the books of the Apocrypha offer rich testimony.

But how the stones are arranged is in part a new thing. Study of the scrolls and of much of the apocryphal material surveyed in this chapter help us to name the novelty of the "new thing." Echoing various sources, Christianity in the long run addressed itself not to one race or a portion of one race; it addressed itself to all men and offered all men salvation and strength to face the Lord on terms that minimize the value of birth and law, or—as with the Essenes—a secluded observation of the law. The wisdom and necessity of such an offer may have appeared doubly clear to Christ and his followers because they knew of a way that was separatist and legalistic: the way of the Essenes. It was a way that achieved, in intenser forms, the modes of righteousness already visible in a book like *Ecclesiasticus.*

In a great apostrophe addressed to Hebrew religious consciousness at the end of *Ecclesiasticus* there is a kind of summation of the uneasy balance that we have observed in the Apocrypha and, in a way, in the previously unknown books from the Qumran caves.

> When ye glorify the Lord, exalt him as much as ye can; for even yet will he far exceed: and when ye exalt him, put forth all your strength, and be not weary; for ye can never go far enough. Who hath seen him, that he might tell us? and who can magnify him as he is? There are yet hid greater things than these be, for we have seen but a few of his works. For the Lord hath made all things; and to the godly hath he given wisdom. (43:30-33.)

The Hebrew imagination in the Hellenistic world was indeed aspiring to "greater things"; but it would not take these things from the hands of their conquerors who, in some respects, were their cultural superiors. Instead, they scrutinized again and again what the Lord had already given them, as in *Wisdom* and *Ecclesiasticus*. Or they withdrew to the stony wastes near the Dead Sea to serve the Lord in purity and await vision. In Paul's word, they "groaned." The events which are displayed in the New Testament are, to the Christian imagination, these very "greater things"; they are vision and the fullfillment of vision.

Thus, in the apostrophe to God in Chapter 43, we find all the themes provided in Old Testament thought summed up. There is nothing about the One and the Many, about being and non-being. Jesus Ben Sirach and the little state lying around Jerusalem have enough wherewith to live godly lives. The uncertainties faced by Job are ignored or dismissed. The prophecies about the Messiah have been fulfilled or satisfactorily explained. Against this point of view, the New Testament is a protest. It asserts, in effect, that the writer of *The Wisdom of Solomon* was striking out in the right direction; it asserts, most definitely, that conservative, legalistic Judaism should not ignore the paradoxes of *Job* and should not reject the possibility of fuller revelation.

THE NEW TESTAMENT

CHAPTER XIV

The World at the Time of the Gospels

THE birth date of Christ is calculated in different ways, and the dates range from 7 B.C. in the reign of Herod the Great (who died 4 B.C.) to the census of Quirinius, 6 A.D. But despite this initial uncertainty, one can say that the events in the New Testament and the recording of them embrace roughly a hundred years. Knowledge of what was happening elsewhere during the time from the birth at Bethlehem to the revelation imparted to John on the Isle of Patmos in the last decade of the first century of our era contributes to our mastery of the New Testament. Christ, his followers, and his opponents all lived in a world that not only was Hellenistic but was becoming Roman. In 63 B.C. the great Roman general Pompey took over the city of Jerusalem, and this step was but one of many by which the Romans "moved in" on a world that had, for more than a century and a half, been ruled by the successors of Alexander.

After a period of experimentation, the Roman power put on the throne at Jerusalem a family whose name later—and with some justice—became a byword for cruelty and vice, the Herodian family. What commended this family to the Romans was not their cruelty and vice; it was the willingness of most of the members to curry Roman favor and do the will of Rome. It was a bad house from the Hebrew point of view because, although Semitic, it was not Hebrew; it had its origin in Idumea to the south of Judah, a territory peopled by the descendants of Israel's traditional enemy, Edom, and but recently forcefully converted to Judaism. Nor was its origin the only thing wrong with the house of Herod; if not in Jerusalem, the Herodians went so far in their mimicry of Roman amusements and vices that suspicion of them became deep-rooted and could not be torn up by the attempts of a Herodian like Agrippa I (died 44 A.D.) to be more Jewish than the Jews when he was in residence at Jerusalem. To the Romans too the Herodian house eventually proved to be a bad choice; they could neither keep order among their subjects nor govern their own suspicious and often libidinous natures. The Romans throughout the time preceding the final destruction of Jerusalem had to redraw boundaries and reassign territories to various members of the numerous descent of Herod the Great. The

CHART 11. Events in the Time of Christ

CHRIST'S LIFE	JUDEA	ROMAN EMPERORS
Born 7 B.C.-6 A.D.	9-6 Roman census under Saturninus, governor of Syria 4 B.C. Death of Herod the Great: Philip, tetrarch of Iturea and Trachonitis, 4 B.C.-34 A.D. Herod Antipas, tetrarch of Galilee and Perea 4-39 (the "Herod" of Christ's mature years) Archelaus, ethnarch of Judea, 4 B.C.-6 A.D. (After 6 A.D. Judea is ruled by Roman procurators and is part of the Roman province of Syria.) 6 A.D. Census of Quirinius, governor of Syria	31 B.C.-14 A.D. Augustus
		14-37 A.D. Tiberias
Baptized 26 A.D. or later	26-36 A.D. Pontius Pilate, procurator	
Crucifixion 29-33 A.D.		
	36 A.D. End of Caiaphas' term as high priest	

New Testament demonstrates this incidentally. If the birth of Christ precedes 4 B.C., he was born while Herod the Great ruled over Judea. But by the time of Christ's crucifixion (*c.* 30 A.D.) Herod's son Archelaus had been discarded as ruler of Jerusalem and nearby territories; there was a Roman governor, a procurator, who had his residence at the town of Caesarea on the Mediterranean but who came to Jerusalem—as at the time of Christ's apprehension and trial—to keep watch on the religious enthusiasm of the Jews at times of festival. A later event, the trial of Paul at Caesarea in the time of the procurators Felix and Festus, allows us to see a Herod ruler (Agrippa II) playing the part of a rubber stamp to the Roman will. By the year 70 A.D., the Herods had demonstrated their inability to create a reasonable facsimile of order. The Roman power said, in effect, "Enough is enough!" and destroyed the Temple and the holy city of the stubborn race that would not be assimilated to the Roman pattern for conquered peoples.

What was the Roman pattern, the last in the considerable series of patterns that were imposed upon the Hebrew people? It had some harsher features than did the old pattern of Cyrus the Persian, but it was much less arbitrary and cruel than that of the earlier conquerors of the Northern Kingdom, the Assyrians. The Romans chiefly wished to "cash in" on their conquests; an Assyrian-like uprooting and wholesale disruption of a culture was likely to lead to diminishing returns. But, on the other hand, what we seem to see in the relation of Cyrus to the Hebrews of his day—a considerable deference to the culture and religion of the people who had come under his yoke—was no part of the official Roman attitude. The Roman troops and governors felt only indifference toward the claim of the Jews that they were a "peculiar people"; and they were finally roused to anger and destruction because these claims kept interfering with the profitable operations of this particular section of the Roman empire. As the century wore on, persecution of recalcitrant Jews and recalcitrant followers of Christ was often the prevailing custom. Two notable persecutions were those of Nero (64 A.D.) and Domitian (93 A.D.).

When such display of force was not needed, the Roman order of the day—the "day" that includes Christ and St. Paul—was simply the consolidation of the Roman conquests and a profitable if not efficient exploitation of the regions that Julius Caesar, Pompey, and Antony had brought within the boundaries of the empire. Two striking forms that this exploitation took were taxes and levies on man power. In the Gospels, the Roman eagerness for money is clear; the necessity of paying a tax is the occasion of the journey of Mary and Joseph to Bethlehem. Less clear, in the Gospels, is the Roman need for man power; but other records show us Rome transforming large portions of the conquered populations into slaves who were shipped off to work on the great farms of Italy or in the salt mines of Sicily. Thus, Rome's display of order and power was made possible by a calculating and often wasteful use of what subject regions had to offer. We seem to see in the empire of Cyrus an awareness that the health of the entire empire depends on the well-being of every part: a well-being, furthermore, with religious and cultural as well as economic aspects. Such an awareness was not a striking element in the Roman colonial policy. The Romans extended from Egypt to Gaul the web of their roads, their law, and their order; and there is little question of the effects of this web that covered the civilized world. A modern traveler who visits the ruins of Roman temples and aqueducts is struck by their monotonous sameness. A Roman aqueduct at Segovia resembles a Roman aqueduct at Nîmes, and a Roman theater at Arles resembles similar structures hundreds of miles away.

These identical aspects of Roman remains and even of less tangible things like legal and literary forms enable us to see how the Roman world differed from the one it endeavored to swallow up, the Hellenistic world. Politically, Roman centralization was effective rather than, as with the successors of Alexander, intermittent and often inefficient. The Hebrews had been able to continue their theocratic state under the Egyptian Ptolemies, and they were able, by force of arms, to set up a nationalist state in the time of the later Syrian rulers, the Seleucids. But quite as important as this political contrast are the cultural differences that separate the Roman from the Hellenistic world. When Paul scornfully cuts short his address to the men of Athens, when John dips his pen in the fire of prophecy and writes of what he sees at Patmos, both men are, in their separate ways, estimating the price the world has had to pay for Roman law and order. It was the price that any society pays for the comforts of mass production and centralization, for the use of mass-produced architecture and artifacts from the Bosporus to the Pillars of Hercules. Modern critics of societies see similar dangers in standardized conveniences that, in our country, extend from New York Harbor to the Golden Gate.

On dictated terms that demanded conformity and submission, the Romans offered their subject peoples their version of the "good life." The people in the provinces had a chance to imitate the pleasures of the wealthy citizens of Rome and to build cities (as did Herod I) that were copies of the second-rate architecture of Rome; and they could watch "Roman" spectacles: the gladiatorial battles or Roman vulgarizations of the great Greek tragedies.

It is easy, once all this is called to mind, to see why Rome, in the minds of the writers of the books now included in the New Testament, easily stood for "the kingdom of this world." In their eyes, the Roman world is one in which man is encouraged to rely on power alone and to enjoy the pleasures that power is skillful at providing. Such a kingdom is, as the New Testament writers viewed the matter, indifferent to the life of the spirit. The life of the spirit is erratic, unpredictable, and individual, whereas the amusements and tastes of masses of men are dreadfully predictable. For many reasons, Rome chose to govern by offering the masses bread and circuses. This emphasis was sufficient to call forth the remark of Christ, that man does not live by bread alone.

The man who, in the Roman world, was concerned with his mind or his spirit—who, for some reason, was unable to find satisfaction in the routine pleasures of his fellows—had two courses of action open to him. He could keep quiet and hug his distress to his own breast: a Stoic solution. Or he could speak out against the crassness and vulgarity of the world and try to alter it. In their own ways, this is what both Jesus and Paul did. Both men, from the Roman point of view, attempted to modify the Roman *status quo;* and they had, for their deaths, only themselves to blame.

It can be said, in favor of the "world order" that Augustus Caesar set up, that it did substitute for the political chaos of the Hellenic world a legal uniformity; one knew where one was. It made available to all people both law and a *version* of Hellenistic culture. But the *kind* of version is part of the price that the world paid for Roman order. What happened to the variety of philosophies that had existed to challenge the Hebrew who lived in the Hellenistic world? It is the complaint of Juvenal (a Roman satirist *c.* 60-140 A.D.) that every "successful" Roman hastened to buy a Greek slave who could give him some smattering of philosophy, who could talk to him of Plato and the Stoics when no other diversion offered. Juvenal was, as a matter of fact, pining for the old Roman days when the Romans were too simple and busy to import foreign fashions. But his complaint is left-handed testimony to the fact that the Romans had nothing in the way of philosophy to offer the world they had taken over. The best they could do, when they wanted to *think* about the "good life" instead of live it carelessly and thoughtlessly, was to take up one of the systems already popular in the Hellenistic world and rework it. This is what we see in the great poem of Lucretius (96-55 B.C.) *Concerning the Nature of Things* which reflects the Epicurean point of view, and in the moral essays of Seneca (4 B.C.-75 A.D.), who had for some years tried to inculcate in the young Nero the principles of Stoicism.

Finally, Roman religion—the religion, say, that the Roman troops brought to Asia Minor and Palestine—was a shoddy, unsophisticated export. The *popular* Roman religion, as St. Augustine pointed out centuries later, is nothing but a collection of weak personifications of the forces supposedly encountered in daily living. There is a god of the threshold, a god for each step of the agricultural processes of sowing, cultivating, and reaping; there is even a goddess who presides over the Roman sewers. In the term we have used, popular Roman religion is animistic in the extreme since it attributes mana to external physical objects and concrete human functions. It is routine, businesslike, and mechanical, and much less attractive and poetically moving than the Hebrew animism of the Pentateuch that located "the Other" at a river crossing or on a high mountain. The Romans came to have, to be sure, a pantheon of gods modeled on what they observed of the Greek Olympians. But by the time the Roman armies had come to Palestine, this nature worship had, in official circles, been superseded by what seems to us a worship of the state itself rather than the forces of nature or the mana inherent in special places, objects, and activities that had had their day in popular Roman devotion. In practice, from the time of Augustus (63 B.C.-14 A.D.) the ruler of the Roman state was himself regarded as divine; in 27 B.C. distinctly divine titles were awarded this ruler by the Roman Senate. This led to making the sum and substance of official Roman religion consist of a very simple act: a sacrifice at the altar of the divine ruler, the emperor-god. Formal religion began and ended with this one act that acknowledged the divinity of the person in whose hands all power in the state was centered. The only ethical consequence of this religion was acceptance of whatever the divine emperor willed. Louis XIV said, "I am the State." In the words of the French "Sun King," the Roman emperor was indeed the state. Since he was the state, whatever he did was a divine act and—in theory if not in practice—not open to censure. This attitude repeats ideas that the prophets had tried to eject from Hebrew culture: that the chief mark of deity is power rather than power close linked with justice and mercy. It is also a repetition of ancient Egyptian and Babylonian ideas about the divinity that doth hedge a king; the Pharaoh and the kings of Babylon and Assyria were, unlike Saul and David, beyond control or reproach.

The actual lives of the first-century emperors offer rather depressing spectacles of vanity, calculation, and pursuit of distraction along with some efficiency. Yet—and this explains in part the Jewish and Christian refusal to make the sacrifice to the divine Caesar—the official Roman doctrine was that a fallible human being was a fount of divine mana, *the* fount, in fact. Jews and Christians alike insisted that higher than Caesar was the moral law which enabled one to censure what the ruler at Rome did; and higher than the moral law was the deity which the Roman ruler impiously pretended to be. The early Christians refused to sacrifice to Caesar. This sacrifice was an act that, to worldly and cynical Romans, had no meaning or importance whatever. But to the Jews and Christians, it was a denial of the order that governed their lives. (Modern parallels to this ancient conflict flock to the mind. The *Führer* or *Duce* who was regarded as the personification of the state and whose acts, in consequence, were above the laws of decency and justice which ordinary men obey was, with some differences, the divine ruler come to life again. Those Germans and Italians who refused to acknowledge the aspects of divinity in such leaders reënacted the roles of the Jews and Christians who would not sacrifice to Caesar.)

Actually, this state religion did not suffice for the Roman people and the multitudes they had conquered. At best, such a religion as this amounts to a vote of confidence in the activity of the leader or the importance of the large social unit to which one belongs. There are other psychological needs or demands on "the Other" that state worship does not satisfy and that other forms of religion seem to minister to. Veneration of the divine Caesar was impotent to teach the mass of men how to live. It did not create for them an imaginative universe in which the life of each man, whether enslaved or free, had significance. There were, indeed, in the world into which Christ was born bodies of belief that satisfied these desires. Along with the cargoes of wheat and furs traveling the Roman roads and sea lanes came these religions. They seemed to offer to men in all parts of the empire a way, a path, as the temple sacrifices of the emperor did not.

These bodies of belief were the "mystery" religions, whose celebration and significance existed only for the initiated. We have already spoken of the Greek rites at Eleusis that seemed to give individual man rebirth and a sense that his existence had meaning. The Eleusinian mysteries were but one of many that Juvenal the Roman deplored. When Juvenal said, "The Orontes River is flowing into the Tiber," he meant that religions and customs belonging to the shores of foreign rivers like the Orontes in Asia Minor were invading Roman life along the Tiber and polluting it. He believed that the worship of Janus and Cloacina and Caesar was all the religion one needed anyhow. But the conventional Roman rites could not offer any assurances of security, except to the wealthy, whose houses and horses and lands made a visit to the temple a superfluous and modish gesture. The rites of Isis from Egypt, the worship of the

"Great Mother" of Asia Minor, the Greek mysteries—all these offered assurances of security that today we would call psychological. These assurances were created by secret rituals of initiation, in contrast to the empty public rites of Roman religion. In an atmosphere of excitement and stress, the person initiated had acted out for him a "mystery" explaining for him, as nothing had explained before, the real meaning of human existence. In the "mystery" of Isis and Attis, for example—a religion which Egypt exported along with its wheat—was told the old tale of a goddess of love and fertility (Isis) who falls in love with Attis, a man who is slain but who, by the devotion and power of the goddess, is brought back to life. The "meaning" of this divine drama was that each human being can, if he will, reënact the role of Attis and become worthy of the support of the goddess.

In vain did Juvenal and others protest against the excitement generated by the mystery religions of Isis and others—against the excitement of the Roman proletariat as it ran along the streets shaking the sistrum of Isis and shouting about rebirth. In vain were protests, because such a mystery gave each person a sense that his life mattered. (And what did his life matter to divine Caesar?) It made him feel that, in the sight of Isis, there was neither slave nor free.

This aspect of religion in Roman times was, humanly speaking, to the profit of Christianity. Christianity too offered its devotees a fresh start, a rebirth; and of course the phrase "neither slave nor free" is St. Paul's (*Ephesians* 6:8; *Colossians* 3:11). For a time official Roman religion had the power to persecute Christianity and drive it underground into the catacombs. But interestingly enough, Christianity received really strenuous and dangerous spiritual opposition not from the state religion of Rome but from the mystery religions of Asia Minor that offered, in terms of another story than that of the life and death of Jesus, some sort of rebirth and some sort of individual freedom and dignity. The mystery religion most dangerous from the Christian point of view was Mithraism, which was based on the deed of a legendary Persian hero who redeems mankind from evil and death by killing a monstrous bull. (This should remind us of the suggestion that the Messiah saves his people by killing a serpent, a suggestion offered by Isaiah II.)

In *John* 4:35 Christ is quoted as saying: "Lift up your eyes and look on the fields; for they are white already to harvest." The statement is a literal description of the religious condition of the ancient world after it had been put to rights by crass Roman energy. It is true that Romans and non-Romans of wealth and cultivation could still find comfort in the various Hellenistic philosophies still available. But, except for the protected and cultivated, a philosophy is not a way of salvation. What the great bulk of mankind seeks is not an intellectual demonstration of the excellence of some set of values. The bulk of mankind seeks salvation, and this usually consists of a set of examples and precepts that move the heart or emotions rather than win the assent of the mind. To the neglected and desperate men that suffered in the Roman world, a philosophical system was a mockery; it did not offer a way out. They needed a path or way to take them past the frustrations of an existence in which power was abused and gentleness and virtue were not rewarded.

The Palestinian Foreground

Thus is composed the not-too-distant scenery against which the action of the Gospels and *The Acts of the Apostles* is performed. Of the scenery in the foreground, of the political conditions in Palestine, something has already been said at the beginning of this chapter. The "Roman peace" was peace only if a subject people accepted all its conditions and regarded Roman law and order as a benefit and Roman taxation and exploitation as a just exaction in return for it.

This order was enforced variously in Jerusalem and other Jewish regions. Sometimes it was the rule of a Herodian, sometimes it was the power of a Roman procurator that attempted to keep the Hebrew population in line. The presence of Roman soldiers in the holy city of Jerusalem was an especial offense to the pious since the soldiers bore "images" on their standards and were housed in a stronghold called the Antonia which, sacrilegiously, looked down on the sacred area of the Temple.

But the reaction of the Hebrew people to their latest servitude was not unified. Some accepted and some resisted, and the modes of acceptance and rejection were various. The group whose acceptance of the Roman "new order" was looked on with contempt by all other classes was that called in the Gospels the "publicans." These men—and among their number was Matthew the apostle—were the most overt of the "collaborationists." The tax money must be collected; the levies on export and import must be imposed; and Jewish citizens were found who were willing to do this work. It was regarded as dirty work, as work that made the laborers "unclean," and for several reasons. The tax collector was, obviously, the tool of the conqueror and the exploiter of his Jewish brothers; and, from the point of view of the pious, he was "unclean" permanently since every day he handled the coins which bore the image of Caesar, the Roman god. The publicans were often prosperous—one of them is able to offer Christ and his followers a banquet—but from the conventional point of view, they were regarded as "sinners" and "lost souls." A Jew who was pious, moreover, a Jew who was educated, would find some other career than that chosen by Matthew. Christ is, for these reasons, reproached for his association with publicans. His answer to those who accuse him is this: "I came not to call the righteous but sinners to repentance" (*Luke* 5:32). It was, indeed, often the "sinners"—those who were somehow excluded from the "righteous" and the correct—who had ears for the unconventional interpretation of righteousness that Christ advanced.

There were other "collaborationists" whom Christ was not able to stir, except to enmity. These were the *Herodians*, the members of Herod's court and the hangers-on. The publicans could regard Christ as a person who offered them a substitute for their lost respectability. But the Herodians could only consider him a dangerous fellow, an instigator of the mass resentment that was always simmering against the alien Herodian family. The misfortune of the Herodian family would be the misfortune of those who followed it. To these men,

Christ appeared as one more troublemaker who would convince the Roman overlords that the Herodians were not capable of ruling. The Herodians do not play a great role in the Gospels. They do seem to be connected with the opposition to St. Paul in the later chapters of *Acts*. At any rate, they animate one of the contradictory currents through which Christ and St. Paul steer fragile crafts.

In the Gospel story, Christ's greatest enemies are represented as being the Sadducees and "the scribes and Pharisees." These two groups can be distinguished from each other, but they had as a common denominator their special brands of piety and their attitude toward the Roman power. This attitude represents an effort to revive the happy relation between the leaders of the theocratic state and the Persian conquerors (538-331 B.C.). But we have already pointed out that, whereas the Persian princes were more than tolerant of the religions they found among their new subjects, the Roman officials simply endured the strange faiths of Asia Minor and Palestine without trying to respect them; and this endurance could be abruptly suspended when a religious faith led to political and administrative difficulties. We see this in the contemptuous attitude of Pilate toward the Sadducees in all four Gospel accounts; nor did the Romans distinguish between a group that asked only to be allowed to practice its traditional religion and other elements that opposed the traditionalists. To the Roman eye, these various groups were all of a piece; and of this dullness of perception the Sadducees and Pharisees were painfully aware. Their attacks on Christ were in part motivated by the fear that the Romans would confuse this popular leader with respectable persons like themselves and that possible Roman action against a growing popular movement would harm all Jews.

These grounds for enmity against Christ the Romans could have understood. There were other grounds which they could not have had much interest in; yet these are grounds that we must also understand as we follow the story the Gospels present to us. The Pharisee and Sadducee resistance to Christ and his followers was less effective because the two groups took somewhat divergent views of the

Hebrew past. The Sadducees were an aristocratic party and members of the Temple priesthood. Their name *Sadducee* is thought to be derived from Zadok, one of David's priests (*I Kings* 1:34 and 2:35). They labored to preserve Hebrew religion—particularly the cult of Temple worship—in the forms that had been, supposedly, established by Moses. They admitted as binding upon the conscience only what could be found explicitly in the sacred books of the Old Testament; they denied the validity of religious practice that could not find warrant there. Particularly did they challenge religious doctrines such as life after death and the interference of angels and demons in human affairs, for these doctrines could not be fully supported by Old Testament statement.

The Pharisees (literally "the separated ones") had their origin about two centuries before Christ as a group of persons in a teaching function. Much of their teaching took place in the popular meeting places, the synagogues rather than the Temple in Jerusalem. They were "separated" from the more conservative on grounds that we have already seen in the activity of Jesus the son of Sirach (*Ecclesiasticus*). It was this man who, after a study of the law and the prophets, judged his own utterance to be as full of meat as were the ancient holy books. The Pharisees did not doubt that whatever they taught was in the law, the Torah, in spirit if not literally. But to the conservative Sadducees, the abundance of new truth and new law that the "separated" adduced from the ancient books must have seemed fantastic and presumptuous. Both of the greatest teachers and commentators on the Old Testament in the period when Jesus and Paul lived were Pharisees; the teaching of Rabbi Hillel anticipates the liberality and antilegalism of Christ's own teaching, and Hillel's grandson Gamaliel is famous because he was the teacher of Paul and tried to moderate the Jewish enmity toward the early followers of Christ. (See *Acts* 5:33-40.) The best of the Pharisees struggled to bring the masses of men back to the Lord, the fountain of living waters of which Jeremiah had spoken. Their new doctrines —those which concerned angels and demons, those which spoke of death and judgment and all "last things"—were a result of a desire to make the worship of Jehovah a living rather than a dead thing.

If this is the divergence between the Sadducees and the Pharisees, a question arises: Why did the Pharisees oppose Christ? Christ also wanted to remove the dead hand of legalism from Hebrew religious life; Christ also preached immortality and judgment. The Gospels, though they do not give us a balanced view of Christ's enemies, do suggest a partial answer. By the time of Christ, many of the Pharisees had come to regard themselves as the official interpreters of God's will to the masses of the uneducated, and they had fallen blindly in love with their special interpretations. Customs and teachings that had been advanced as useful additions to the written traditions had, by the time of Christ, become—in the opinion of the Pharisees—as binding as the regulations explicitly stated in the laws of Moses. The length of fringe on a man's prayer shawl, the wearing of phylacteries (small wooden boxes tied to the forehead and containing parchment inscribed with sacred verses)—these and other religious customs seem to be the creation of the Pharisees. Thus, to the writers of the Gospels, the Pharisees were just as legalistic, authoritarian, and unbending as were the Sadducees. Paul can set the two groups at odds by mention of life after death (*Acts* 23:6); but in the Gospels we see them united by their bitter opposition to the attempts of Jesus, this prophet without credentials, to continue the process of interpreting and altering "the law and the prophets." In their eyes, no good could come from Jesus, an uneducated man and—worse—a citizen of a recently settled area, "Galilee of the Gentiles": an area where traditional learning must be vastly inferior to the rich deposits of wisdom and commentary preserved in Jerusalem and constantly being interpreted there.

The Sadducees and the Pharisees as seen in the Gospels resemble each other, then, despite their differences. The teachings and practices of each group represent an effort to "freeze" Hebrew religion at a certain point. The two groups differ as to where the point is, but they agree that it has been reached and that there is no need of further unconventional and dangerous teaching. Christ begins by speaking in the synagogues; but soon, because of the pressure of the

Pharisees, he is teaching at the seaside and along the public way. That the Pharisees' faith had become frozen like that of the Sadducees explains the overtones of our adjective "pharisaical." The Pharisee says, "I thank God I am not as other men"—not, that is, ignorant of the precisely correct form of doctrine and worship that is pleasing to God.

The Sadducees and Pharisees were the shepherds who had gone astray and who could no longer lead the sheep: the Hebrew masses. Christ regards them as his chief enemies. He says: "Think not that I am come to destroy the law, or the prophets: I am not come to destroy, but to fulfil" (*Matthew* 5:17). His opinion is that neither group in power any longer struggled to "fulfill" the law and the prophets; and their actual negation of the law and the prophets was worse because they seemed to be piously at work preserving them. They are detestable to Christ not because of their subtle coöperation with Rome but because of their effort to "freeze" the worship of God, to make the Temple and the interpretation of the law their sinecures, their "rackets." Again and again the teaching of Christ suggests that the Temple as presided over by the priests and the moral life as presided over by the Pharisees had become complex and confusing to the ordinary man. The man in the street gave up hope and became a "sinner," since the truly godly life was a full-time job and left no time for earning one's bread by the sweat of the brow; or he looked elsewhere for his religious and political guidance.

In looking elsewhere, the ordinary man found such guidance among a succession of men called Zealots. These lone-wolf teachers had no official status in Hebrew society, but they performed a very real function in protesting against corruption and smugness in high places. On the other hand, their agitation for a restored Hebrew nation led to useless revolt and final defeat. John the Baptist, the forerunner of Christ, is often placed among the Zealots. At least he resembles a fairly long list of "wild men" of whom other records tell us. Gamaliel mentions two such men, Theudas and Judas of Galilee (*Acts* 5:36-37); and the captain who arrests Paul supposes that he is "that Egyptian, which before these days madest an uproar, and leddest out into the wilderness four thousand men that were murderers" (*Acts* 21:38). These men lived in the wilderness "on locusts and wild honey"; and they appeared from time to time in places beyond the reach of the respectable Sadducees and Pharisees. They harangued any people who would listen to them; they ranted much in the style of Amos at Bethel, and they did not lack for topics. They could point to the corrupt Herodian family, whose chief—but not only—crime was incest. They could point to the inert and supine Hebrew leaders in Jerusalem who were not ready to oppose to the death the servants of Satan: the Herodian family and the power of Rome. These Zealots called the masses to resistance on two grounds: They reminded the people of the promises made by Isaiah and other prophets concerning a conquering Messiah, whose advent the priests would doubtless find upsetting. They referred to the recent glories of the militant Maccabees, glories temporarily extinguished by the Roman armies. To be sure, the Zealots were uncouth fellows who could not conceive any kind of compromise with the alien ways that had come in with the Greeks and the Romans. But just such preaching would find willing hearers among those who felt that the official priests and teachers neglected and ignored an obvious duty: to minister to all men. So the followers of the Zealots set up their tents and stayed to listen to the harangues; and they went after the leader when things became too hot for him and he had to flee to a more lonely fastness. This describes the fortunes of John the Baptist, who finally uttered his death warrant by his censure of Herod's private life.

It is not strange that the viewers-with-alarm at Jerusalem saw the Zealot pattern in the life of Christ. That his doctrines were opposed to some of the typical Zealot doctrines—he did not preach "a kingdom of this world," and he was more concerned with the salvation of individual souls than with the restoration of the national state of Israel—might not be perceived by his persecutors. It was not, as a matter of fact, perceived by his disciples. In one verse Peter recognizes who Christ is—"the son of God"—and in the next breath he offends by supposing that the "son of God" has come to earth to break the yoke of Rome and set up a new Jewish state on the Maccabean model (*Matthew*, chap. 16). And the defection of Christ's popular following is notorious. The Jerusalem populace welcomed Christ when he entered the city; and it quickly hated him when it was clear that he did not will to, or was unable to, play the role of popular champion against Rome and against the repressive Sadducees and Pharisees.

A complete picture of the Jewish society under Roman rule demands the mention of one more group, the *Essenes*. This group is nowhere mentioned in the New Testament, but their existence has been regarded by some students as "conditioning" the teachings of John the Baptist and Christ. The Essenes, a group whose name may mean the seers or the mysterious ones, were members of the monastic or semi-monastic community near the Dead Sea, the community that preserved for us the Dead Sea scrolls. This group of devout Jews was much more "separated" than the Pharisees had ever been and withdrew from the society they deplored rather than—as did the Pharisees—remain in it for purposes of reform. From the second century B.C. onward, the Essenes formed communities of persons who withdrew from society to cultivate purity and godliness—a purity and godliness that discounted the ritual aid to the good life which was centered in Temple worship; Essene piety—as the "libraries" of the scrolls themselves suggest to us—found a sufficient support to piety in meditation upon the laws of Moses and the behests of such a prophet as Isaiah.

Such a group would be equally impatient with the worldly leaders of Jerusalem; to them, the coöperation of Sadducees and Herodians would seem an unholy alliance: a secular and religious betrayal. But they would be equally impatient with the Zealots who might plan to unseat the masters of Jerusalem by force and take their places. Instead, only God was holy, and only the Essenes sought him "in spirit and in truth." Indeed, the elaborate arrangements for communal living which archeologists have studied at Wadi Qumran, the Essene community, suggest that here is expressed a conviction that only by radical separation from the world did one begin to approach deity. To the ears of such persons the "hard saying" of Jesus Ben Sirach—"He that toucheth pitch shall be defiled" (*Ecclesiasticus* 13:1)—would have a congenial ring. Some of the "hard sayings" of Christ—such as that which demands that his disciples give up father and mother and "let the dead bury their dead"—are thought to parallel the ascetic, world-scorning spirit of these Jewish monastics. Certainly, it is well to remember that Christ's hearers knew of this way or "solution" to life in an evil world—knew that certain men from the time of Judas Maccabaeus onward had made the best of an evil world by retiring from it. They would know that, though it might be difficult to give up all for the life of the soul, it was not impossible: the Essenes had already effected the sacrifice.

This then—the Roman background and the Hebrew foreground—made up the world in which Christ moved and had his earthly being. His life was not lived in a sterile vacuum and does not consist of a leisurely stroll toward its end, the cross. Instead, Christ walked in a tumultuous world which the writers of the Gospels knew so well—and which they judged their readers would also know—that they felt no need to sketch it in explicitly. They, the Gospel writers, were interested in Christ, not in the society he struggled with. We too—after our several fashions—are interested in Christ. But our interest will not be deep and complex unless we are aware that his life, humanly speaking, was more deep and complex than the Gospels sometimes suggest. The purpose of this chapter is to insist that the figure with which the Gospels are concerned is no immaculate, posed form in a stained-glass window. It wears soiled garments and moves along dusty roads. It is as beset by the miscomprehensions of ardent followers as by the outright persecution of enemies. What friends as well as enemies did not see, it repeats and relates to each other preoccupations that in the Old Testament are intense but dispersed. What is holiness? How can God be just as well as merciful? How can man, who is imperfect, be put in relation to God, who is perfect? All these questions and related ones cross each other in their separate courses in the career and teaching of Christ. As we shall see, Christ is not consistently "original"; no more were the prophets. His power over human imaginations, to be sure, rests in part on what he did teach. But it rests also on these teachings, some new, some old, as they come into relation with a real life lived under the conditions just analyzed. The whole is greater than the sum of the parts. It is the "configuration" constituted by word and deed that moved the early Christians and that has moved Christians and non-Christians in succeeding centuries.

CHAPTER XV

The Gospels: Their Creation

O*UR IDEA* of Christ rests chiefly on the first four books of the New Testament. They are "good news"—the meaning of both the Greek-derived "evangel" and the Anglo-Saxon "gospel." History is full of accounts of persons who opened these books and found utterances that they had been waiting to hear. To such devout men it was sufficient that these books seemed to give direct and plain accounts of the life, teachings, and death of Jesus; to them the Gospels offered a way of life and a pattern of heroism. Such a reaction still lies at the center of a person's reading of the Gospels; and an attempt to answer other questions about these four books—how they came to be, how they differ from modern records of notable lives—is no attempt to shift the center of a reader's interest from Jesus to other questions.

But involved in one's admiration for Jesus, one's response to the impact of his teachings, is the necessity to understand for oneself and to be able to explain to other persons what manner of record the Gospels are. As with Amos and Hosea, so with Jesus—a reader's first impression of power and authority must receive the aid that can come from historical insight into the literary forms which preserve the fame of prophet and Messiah.

To some readers, there is an element of strangeness in the accents of the Gospel records. Let such readers also recall that when we look through family photographs, those that come to us from decades ago seem stiff and unnatural; only when we realize that both photographers and sitters were subject to limitations that modern photographers have put aside do we see that the stiff poses, the staring eyes, and the garish illumination are necessary elements in the old pictures. We cannot demand of them the "lifelike" gesture, the "natural" play of light and shadow. At the center of the Gospels, with an analogous stiffness, stands Jesus. But the writers of the Gospels do not take candid shots for the picture magazines. That is, they do not use methods of biographical presentation that our readings of modern accounts of great men accustom us to. Modern biographers, moreover, usually let us see by footnote and incidental comment that they are fashioning their books from memoirs, newspapers, diaries, and eyewitness accounts. They also obligingly build up for us all that we need in way of background explanation. The Gospels are not, in this sense, biographies. We have no more right to read them as we read lives of modern heroes than we have to look at daguerreotypes and tintypes as if they "ought" to be action photos. The old photograph is a "true" picture of the sitter; but we must learn not to be thrown off by the rigid pose and the artificial background of balustrade and garden. Likewise are the Gospels a vivid record of the impact the figure and career of Jesus made on several generations.

This contrast between ancient and modern methods should not be too startling to us. We have already seen that the Old Testament "life" of King David was written subject to limitations that a modern biographer of a king does not know. The Old Testament account tells us chiefly of a man who was expected to exemplify justice and be obedient to God's direction. David as administrator of a growing kingdom and encourager of international commerce we can suspect; but we cannot see him very well. Similarly, the Gospels are records of a being who offered mankind a unique gift. They overlook matters of chronology that would concern a modern biographer. They take for granted customs and social groupings that have, as in the previous chapter, to be explained. And they organize the narratives in line with suppositions about Jesus that, for a modern reader, must be made explicit.

Contrasting Views of the Gospels

Such problems were not ones that came to the minds of the mass of readers in past centuries. These readers lacked what we call an "historical sense." Instead, they cherished stained-glass windows which showed Christ riding on his donkey through a medieval portcullis; they revered pictures of the Virgin in Renaissance garments. We, on the other hand, have a sense of shock when we see a modern picture of the Nativity in which the virgin has bobbed hair and St. Joseph wears a leather jacket. This is our awareness of history at work; it is an awareness that, sooner or later, leads us to put questions to the Gospels. It is an awareness that lies behind more than a century of careful study of the Gospels, a study that is detached and analytical and that would seem impious to men who cherished anachronistic images of Jesus in stained-glass windows.

These latter men also accepted the authorship of the four Gospels as transmitted by centuries of tradition. They did not question that *Matthew* came from the hands of the tax gatherer whom Jesus called from his lowly, despised task (*Matthew* 9:9). *Mark* was a book fashioned by the follower of Peter, John Mark—sometimes identified with the young man who loses his garment at the time of Christ's arrest (*Mark* 14:51). *Luke,* along with *Acts,* is the creation of Paul's Greek-speaking companion, Luke "the beloved physician" (*Colossians* 4:14). And *John* was accepted as a book written very late in the life of the disciple who, at the Last Supper, "leaned on Christ's bosom" (*John* 13:23). When one accepts this view of Gospel authorship, one ignores such circumstances as the fact that Jesus likely spoke in Aramaic, a Hebrew dialect, whereas the four Gospels survive in Greek (it is debated whether all of them were written in Greek); one ignores other difficulties that we shall touch at once. Instead, one thinks of each Gospel as a record of contact with Jesus—first-hand contact in *Matthew* and *John* and almost as direct a contact in *Mark,* whose author had the advantage of whatever Peter recalled. Only was the writer of *Luke* at a greater distance from Jesus and the events of his life.

Finally, for many centuries devout imagination suggested that these writers had the additional advantage of guidance from the Holy Spirit. Old engravings show us pictures of the Evangelists at work; the writer holds a pen in his fingers, but its upper end is guided by a disembodied hand, all that was visible of the Holy Spirit.

These were the views that centuries of Christian devotion took of the composition of the Gospels. But, since many readers added thought to devotion, difficulties began to appear. No longer was the disembodied hand quite so visible; and men began to ask whether the human hands were truly those of the historical Matthew, Mark, Luke, and John. They also began to ask what relations existed among these books.

Such curiosity was stimulated by the question of factual consistency. As the reader moved from *Matthew* to *John,* he could observe that in *John* the cleansing of the Temple, the expulsion of the money-changers, takes place early in Christ's ministry (*John* 2:14) and that in the other three Gospels, the act is deferred to the last weeks of Christ's life (*Matthew* 21:12, *Mark* 11:15, *Luke* 19:45). The reader could see that, though all four accounts of the last week follow the same general pattern of events, there are variations in detail, in Jesus's utterances and the judicial procedures. *John* seems to suggest a last meal on the evening *before* the day of Passover, and the other Gospels place the event on the evening of the Passover itself (*John* 18:28; c. *Matthew* 26:17-19). And the empty tomb is discovered in different manners and under slightly different circumstances (*Matthew* 28, *Mark* 16, *Luke* 24, *John* 20).

Variations like these certainly would not occur in modern "lives" of one man. At the least, modern biographers would subject the varying accounts to analysis and argue the superiority of the one they elected to follow. Such critical awareness is certainly at a minimum in the Gospels; and for many readers, at any rate, the existence of varying accounts of the same events is a fact about the Gospels that must be dealt with.

This is a question of inconsistency. Strangely enough, three of the Gospels—*Matthew, Mark,* and *Luke*—aroused questions because of a certain kind of consistency they displayed. These three Gospels had indeed for many centuries been called the synoptic Gospels because they took a common view of the events of Christ's life, as opposed to *John,* where a different sequence is followed. It is not simply that the writers of these Gospels, like three modern students of Jefferson, have gone over the same body of reference material and consequently produce works that have the same factual outline. Rather do the synoptics suggest a dependence of two of the Gospels on the ordering of facts established in the third. Indeed, it is usually thought that *Matthew* and *Luke* accept the somewhat arbitrary arrangement of events established in *Mark* for the major portion of Christ's life.[1]

From perceptions like these, scholars have moved forward to tentative solutions that seek to explain the factual incoherence easy to observe and also the pecular relation of dependence among the synoptics. These explanations certainly amount to severe corrections of the view that the four Gospels are lucid and self-evident presentations of the person of Christ. Yet these scholars all agree that the Gospels offer us our only chance to view Christ. But they all insist—whatever their own view of Christ's nature—that seeing Christ involves seeing those who see Christ. As we read the Gospel records, we must realize that, though we are in the presence of the light that comes from Christ, it is light that is refracted through four prisms—or, as we shall see, through a good many more prisms than four. Had there not been a presence, a being named Jesus, there would be no light to be refracted by the prisms. But the light that reaches us has been shifted in color and direction—sometimes trivially, sometimes not—by the prism it has passed through. Those who saw Jesus, those who were dependent on those who saw Jesus, were men with strength and limitations of perception. An acquaintance with modern study of the Gospels and some of the theories that this study has framed will help us to see the perceivers of Jesus and, finally, Jesus himself.

Indeed, scholarly theory about how the Gospels came into existence enable us to witness a process that is a continuous and deeply unified response to a person of overwhelming stature and force. Man, as the saying has it, is the measure of all things. But when certain august matters—in this instance, Christ—are measured by

[1] *Matthew* and *Luke* have accounts of Christ's birth that do not appear in *Mark;* their accounts of the last week and the day of resurrection display variations from *Mark's*. Hence, the question of inconsistency among the accounts is not limited to the contras between the Synoptics and *John.*

men, the measurements differ. This difference should not lead us to doubt that there was an object which was being measured.

It is not to be expected that modern theories about the creation of the Gospels should have reached a settled account. The books are not closed; and competent scholars continue to challenge the outlines previous students have traced. But there is a large body of shared opinion that suggests that what we have called the process of refracting the light that comes from Jesus was not a simple act of the writing of four books by four persons at special times.

The process, rather, falls into two main periods, difficult to set first-century dates to, but certainly existent; these are the period of oral transmission of information about Jesus, and the period when this information was written down. Further, both oral transmission and writing took place under influences of two sorts. First—and of course most telling—was the influence which the memory of Jesus exerted on the minds of successive generations. But another sort of influence was overlooked by generations of devout Christians whose imagination was not "historical." It was the influence on the Gospel writers of events *subsequent* to the death of Jesus. These writers belonged to a church, and the church had had a history. It had had varied relations with its parent Judaism; there had been periods of Roman toleration and Roman persecution; and there had been intense missionary activity. This later history as well as the recollection of Jesus left marks on both oral tradition and the Gospels themselves.

Influences of the Historical Situation

The shaping effect of the experience of the early church on what it recollected about Christ is the first point to grasp. If ever any books in the world were animated by a desire to speak the truth, the books are the Gospels. But from our own experience we know that "telling the truth" is always done at some later date, and we are separated from the event we wish to relate faithfully by other events which have also left their marks. In varying ways, the Gospels—written at a considerable distance from the time of Jesus' death—are colored by various "adult" experiences: the experiences of writers who had been growing older in a church that was growing older. We see in *Acts* 1:12 ff. that immediately after Christ's ascension his followers were, in a sense, children. Marvel was experienced but not understood; when Peter was delivered from prison, some thought that it was not he who stood before them but his spiritual "double" (12:15). The power of the Holy Spirit was already felt (*Acts* 2:2ff.), but its continuous workings had not yet been experienced and weighed. The community faced a dubious future and hardly knew how to take the first steps toward it.

But by the time the Gospels took their final form—by the end of the first century or a little later—the Christian community had become "adult." It still had the memory of Jesus. But united to that were many subsequent memories that, at their best, encouraged a deeper and more subtle assessment of what the meaning of the memory of Jesus was. A community that is "adult"—that has survived persecution, experienced the growth of religious forms, has been threatened by distortions of its founder's image and by "false teachers"—such a community will judge that it has a deeper understanding of Christ's teachings and intentions than did the distraught Jerusalem community at its outset. The "infant" Peter had to be taught by vision that there was no difference between clean and unclean (*Acts* 11); yet such a perception was an easy part of the insight of the "adult" community which retold Peter's story. In this sense, each of the Gospel writers was "adult." Each one colored the facts and sayings of Jesus by what his "adult" experience of following Christ had taught him.

Our explicit records of such experience appear in *Acts*, the letters of Paul, and in a veiled form in *Revelation* (see chaps. XVIII-XX). But, since these experiences were a kind of further revelation to the writers of the Gospels—showed them with great precision what faith in Jesus meant—a brief inspection of its impact must be made here. The writers of the Gospels were not writing and compiling their books in a sterile vacuum; they had what the Germans call a *Sitz im Leben,* a position in life, in a world.

Since the Gospel writers all worked at more than a generation's remove from the death of Jesus, they were aware of the shifting—indeed, the deteriorating—relation between Christians and the Jewish community. At first Christians were not sure what the following of Christ involved them in. But, as the events in *Acts* and Paul's letters indicate, the followers of Christ soon saw that they could not cherish the image of Jesus *and* remain full members of the Jewish community. At the outset, they attempted to carry on their preaching in the synagogues (*Acts* 13:14-52, 18:4); they attempted to perform their Temple duties (*Acts* 2:46, 21:27). But, for reasons that twentieth-century students can understand—but that the early Christians could not—the men who were preaching "Christ crucified" were thrust out of the synagogues and the Temple by acts of overt hostility. Sometimes these acts amounted only to a severance of relation between Jews and Christians. Sometimes they came to what the Christians could only regard as a "betrayal" of Christians to the Roman power.

The consequence is that the Gospel writers felt set apart from their spiritual forebears. They do not give the Pharisees the credit they deserve; they tend to put the entire weight for the crucifixion of Jesus on the Jews; and they tend to maximize the religious and intellectual gaps that existed between them and their "parent" community. The Gospel writers became doubly sure, because of the wall that was rising between Jews and Christians, that all that Jesus had uttered was a "new thing." We can be reminded of the recurrent tensions between the United States and England. Actually, the two nations share a language, customs, and a body of law. But this does not preclude the flare-up of bitter suspicion on both sides of the Atlantic. As an old saying has it and as accents of the Gospels illustrate, family quarrels are the bitterest ones. To the writer of *Matthew,* for example, tension with the Jews gave a recollected saying of Christ added and grim force: "He who is not with me is against me" (*Matthew* 12:30). Such "adult" experience would carefully preserve Jesus' assertion that he would set son against father and that he came not to bring peace but a sword (*Matthew* 10.33 f.).

Relations between the church and the wider world also thrust themselves on the attention of the writers. Bitter relations with the Jews had focused Roman attention on the Christians as a dangerous minority who could be regarded as "atheists"; they refused to participate in the routine cult of emperor worship, and they denied that the older gods were gods at all—they either did not exist or were demons. This helped to stir the Romans to persecuting action (Nero, 64 A.D. and Domitian *c.* 92 A.D.). Even when actual persecution did not rage, the early communities had every reason to cherish the saying of Christ: "My kingdom is not of this world" (*John* 18:36); and there must have been few days when they did not have to distinguish what they owed to Caesar from what they owed to God (*Luke* 20:25). Further, by cultural standards, the Christians could feel themselves an inferior group. Instead of strolling through great libraries and great baths and temples, all ornamented by works of art, the Christians met in obscure rooms, read to each other from the sacred books that they shared with the Jews, listened to exhortations by men like Peter and Paul, cherished the memory of Jesus, and had a simple sacrament involving bread and wine. They had every reason to feel that the world that had "rejected" their leader continued to reject them. This sense left marks on the Gospels; it deepened the melancholy colors of Christ's destiny, centered the attention of Gospel writers on the problem of personal salvation, and made doubly attractive to them the redress that heaven contained for those who had suffered as they followed Christ.

Because of this double pressure, Jewish and Roman, the bewildered group at the time of the resurrection had become a church—that is, a widely dispersed group of people who shared a faith and were bound by certain fairly flexible arrangements. Thus, the Gospel writers looked back from a position *within* a church. It was a church that had grown by missionary activity, a church that had endured scorn and adversity. Some scholars judge that Christ's instructions to the disciples on what is often called the "first missionary journey" (*Matthew* 10) are more an embodiment of the church's own missionary experience than a recollection of Jesus' instructions. Or—which seems preferable—if the chapter contains Jesus' directions, they are directions that, once again, were colored and refracted by the Christian experience of a generation or more. Many a Christian missioner had taken no thought as to how he should speak and had awaited the incitement that came from God's spirit (*Matthew* 10:19) and, when a mission failed, had shaken the dust of a house from his feet (*Matthew* 10:14).

Finally, one of the Gospels—*John*—was certainly written by a man who was aware of intellectual complexities created for members of a church who lived in a wide, sophisticated world: a world already so old, so mature, that it was full of philosophical systems that offered men reasoned plans of behavior or mystery religions that provided obscure but thrilling ways of gaining some kind of rebirth. Here too the problem was that of creating a record of Christ that would brace a Christian to face tensions and know that, in Christ, he had more than the powers and dominions of his world could offer him.

Oral Tradition

This was the first-century world in which all the writers lived. But, as we know, they did not write one and the same book. In the first place, they were dependent on the collection of materials that happened to be at hand in their city—Antioch or Rome—and in their decade. But before they wrote, there was a time—at least more than a generation, scholars agree—when there *was* no writing about Christ.

At first glance such a lapse of time is startling to a modern reader, accustomed as he is to a rush of biographies from the presses within a year or so of the death of a great man. Why this profound silence on the part of the followers of a man who was regarded not only as great but more than man? The answer is that the followers were not silent; they simply were not writing. Instead, they spoke without ceasing of the leader who died and rose again from the dead; and from their speaking grew a church with a belief and a ceremony.

But writing was delayed. To the unliterary mind, speaking is action, and writing is inaction. (We see this in the pioneers who opened up our Midwestern prairies and often left no record of their adventure.)

There were other reasons why the Christian community did not write. The followers cherished sayings of Jesus that promised an early return (*Matthew* 24:44; *Luke* 12:40). There is little need to make a record of a life that has been interrupted rather than ended. Only after years had slipped by and many of the "saints" had "fallen asleep" was it clear that the return was delayed; instead, Jerusalem, the obvious locus of Christ's return, had been razed (70 A.D.). At this time, groups of Christians existed in Antioch, Ephesus, Corinth, and elsewhere—even in far-off Rome. Works had to be created that would serve to speak for Christ when all the first speakers were gone or, at the least, widely scattered.

Some such need lies behind the creation of the four Gospels and the numerous others that are now lost but that ancient writers quote. But we must remember that the Gospels did not fill a silence or a void. The world—the Christian world, that is—was full of speaking about Christ, and the Gospels were but an extension of this speaking. There was, before the Gospels, a period of oral tradition. For several decades word of mouth preserved not a formal life of Jesus extending between fixed dates for birth and death. It preserved instead the essence of Jesus: what he was, what he offered man. This was the Gospel before the Gospels, the "glad tidings" that dusty travelers carried along the Roman highways.

What was this unwritten Gospel that was the common property of Paul and Silas and Barnabas and those others whose names even we do not know? Twentieth-century students of the Bible like Rudolph Bultmann and Martin Dibelius who practice what is called "form-criticism" have been able to make illuminating suggestions. They inspect the letters of Paul and the "sermons" of Peter and Stephen in *Acts* (chaps. 2 and 7) and point out that none of the early preachers narrated the *life* of Christ in a coherent way. They had more important matters to convey. Peter was constrained to speak of the sheer power that Jesus offered those who believed, Stephen incurred stoning by speaking of Christ as the completion of Hebrew history, and Paul was not concerned with the "historical Jesus"—his task was to speak of "Christ crucified" (*I Corinthians* 1:23).

From these samples of what the oral tradition must have been, "form-criticism" builds a bridge to the written Gospels, which were continuations of such declarations. "Form-criticism" suggests that—as Christianity spread, as men from Macedonia and elsewhere appeared in night vision to apostles and said, "Come over into Macedonia and help us" (*Acts* 16:9)—preachers and missionaries had to be trained so that they could recreate the work of the waning twelve and the others who actually had known Christ. What, in way of intellectual luggage, did such men carry with them?

According to "form-criticism," items like these: First of all, the tremendous fact of Christ's resurrection from the dead and the narrative of the last week which lent support to the resurrection event. (Variations, as noted, exist in the passion-week accounts. But the various days are linked in a coherence, a progression, that is absent from the anecdotal sections that concern the ministry.) Then, such stories as those about Christ's relations with John the Baptist and the transfiguration on the Mount which also testify to the divine nature of Jesus. Likewise, stories of miracles that witness to the mana, the power, at the command of Jesus. Also, particularly useful to men speaking to congregations still predominantly Jewish, collections of "proof" texts—texts from the Old Testament that pointed to and "proved" the validity of Christ's claims to being the Son of God and the Messiah (*Matthew* 1:23, 2:6, 2:15, 2:18, 11:10). Also "controversy" texts which display Christ in argument with the Pharisees, matching their appeals to Old Testament tradition either with other appeals or, shockingly, with pronouncements of his own (*Matthew* 12, 15, 16; *Luke* 20:27). (". . . for he taught them as one that had authority, and not as the scribes" [*Mark* 1:22] was the slander Jesus aroused.) Also, collections of moral sayings in the vein of *Proverbs*, and tales fashioned to make a point. And—these are regarded as comparatively late since Paul, who knew of the resurrection stories, did not mention these—self-subsistent tales which tell of the birth of Christ.

As these materials passed from mouth to mouth, pattern and motif—forces we discussed in Chapter III—had a chance to begin their work. "Form-criticism," at least, sees pattern in the many stories of miraculous cure: the ailing person approaches Christ, he solicits a cure, Christ asks a question that tests faith, and then the cure is effected, often with the additional remark: "Thy faith has made thee whole" (*Luke* 8:48). The "controversy" stories with their sequence of quotations from Hebrew scriptures and the usual conclusions in which Christ makes a citation that is final and overwhelming display a regularity that would be an aid to oral transmissions. So also do stories in which things happen by threes, as in the temptation of Christ by Satan (*Matthew* 4) and the agony in the garden, during which Christ turns to his sleeping followers three times (*Mark* 14:32-42). All such organization of material is familiar to any reader of the Old Testament. The infant Samuel heard the voice of the Lord three times (*I Samuel,* 3); the prophet aids his own memory and startles the consciences of his hearers by working forward from "For three transgressions of Damascus and for four . . ." to "For three transgressions of Israel and for four, I will not turn away the punishment thereof . . ." (*Amos,* 1:3, 2:6).

Perhaps even before the writing of our Gospels some of these materials were put in writing as well as committed to memory. The itinerant preacher might have traveled provided with a collection of "proof" texts from the Old Testament by which he supported his claims about Christ's nature. He might have possessed a collection of the sayings of Christ with some brief indication of the circumstances under which they were said; such collections would naturally make no attempt to indicate day and month for each saying. Such collections, along with the still-vivid oral tradition, existed to be drawn on when the time finally came and the writing-down of the Gospels began.

The Making of the Gospels

When did men commence to write Gospels?

Some say that *Mark,* the earliest Gospel, was written at the time of the Neronian persecutions (64 A.D.) when the Christians were represented as a threat to the Roman state. Such a Gospel as *Luke,* along with *Acts,* has been regarded as an attempt to give the Christian communities a clean bill of political health in Roman eyes (just as *Matthew* seems a resolute attempt to reconstruct a bridge between Christianity and Judaism). Some scholars, however, think that the fall of Jerusalem before the angry troops of the Emperor Titus (70 A.D.) initiated the writing of the Gospels; truly, with the destruction of the ancient city and the desecration of its holy places, the geographical center of Christianity (as of Judaism) received an almost mortal blow. Judaism regrouped its forces, at Jamnia and elsewhere, and trusted to the synagogue, the law, and the interpretations of the law. Christianity, as one of *its* strategies of survival, began the writing of the Gospels. There are some scholars, however, who put the Gospels even later than this; they see in all the Gospels such distinct marks of the work of a long oral tradition and such clear signs of the assimilation of thought-forms and religious patterns of the Roman world that they suppose that the writers of the Gospel tarried a very long time indeed before they set to work. Because of this delay, the recollections of Jesus were merged with other streams of religious thought and feeling running strongly in the ancient world.

This uncertainty we have sampled appears when we look at the dates suggested for the composition of the Gospels. (In parentheses appear the names of the cities regarded as the most likely locations where the various Gospels were composed.) *Mark,* 64-85 A.D. (Rome). *Matthew,* 75 A.D. or later (Antioch). *Luke,* 75 A.D. or later (Ephesus or elsewhere). *John,* 95-105 A.D. (Ephesus). The range of dates does not indicate an act of composition taking many years; it indicates the uncertainty among qualified persons who weigh the evidence for the various dates.

CHART 12. The Creation of the Gospels

HISTORICAL EVENTS		FORMATION OF THE GOSPELS	
29-33	A.D. Crucifixion	29-33 to 60	Period of evangelistic preaching and oral transmission of narratives concerning Christ's life. First tentative written collections of material relating to Christ's teachings and deeds. One of these is thought to have been the source Q (for German *Quelle*) of the teaching sections in *Matthew* and *Luke*.
36	Conversion of Paul		
			Q
61-63	Paul in Rome		*Mark* (65 or later) (Addressed to a Gentile audience, perhaps a Roman one.)
66	Revolt of the Jews		
70	Fall of Jerusalem		*Matthew* (c. 75) (Written at Antioch (?); addressed to a Hebrew audience.) — *Luke* (c. 75) (Written at Ephesus (?); addressed to a more cultivated audience than that reached by *Mark*.)
93	Persecutions of Domitian		*John* (95-105 A.D.) (Written at Ephesus; biographical framework independent of *Mark* and teachings independent of Q; possibly dependent on a non-Marcan oral tradition.)

The range of dates indicates disagreement as to the time of writing. The student will find wide disagreement as to dates of composition, but he will find much agreement as to the methods of composition and the relationship of the Gospels to each other.

Thus, on the question of dating, there is strong difference of opinion. But there is less difference when the question arises as to the *sequence* in which the Gospels were written. First came *Mark*; then, resting on the course of events established in *Mark, Matthew* and *Luke*; and then, after these two and after a considerable gap of time, the non-synoptic Gospel of *John*. That is, modern students must display uncertainty in dating the Gospels—a result of the indifference of the writers, who were composing their books to aid mankind and not just analytic students of the New Testament—but the same students tend to relate the same story of the "emergence" of the Gospels from the period of "silence" when only oral tradition was at work. Their opinions offer tentative answers to the questions that most readers ask: questions about factual inconsistency and the opposite curiosity stimulated by the obvious interdependence of the three synoptic Gospels. That the Gospels are factually inconsistent—for example, in the relation of the circumstances of the discovery of the empty tomb—can be explained in part by word-of-mouth transmission in different sections of the Mediterranean world (the crucial fact did not alter; the tomb was empty.) But attendant facts could vary—who it was who first came, to whom they spoke. That the synoptics display interdependence finds an explanation in the hypothesis now widely held by scholars.

This hypothesis is called the "two-document" hypothesis; it clearly refers to the synoptics and not to *John*. According to this theory, the writer of *Mark* provided one of two basic documents when he combined what was available to him in the traditions of the Christian communities. He had a starting point in the baptism of Christ and a terminus in the tightly knit accounts of the passion week and the resurrection. Between these crucially important blocks of material, the writer of *Mark* wove together a loosely chronological narrative of Christ's ministry, a narrative that linked the separately existing tales of miracle and controversy and teaching by such expressions as: "And again he entered into Capernaum after some days . . . ," "And he began to teach by the sea side . . . ," and "And he went out from thence, and came into his own country; and his disciples follow him." (*Mark* 2:1, 4:1, 6:1). This may be far from the rigidly established framework of a modern biography. But it is hard to see how Mark could have gone beyond this; he was depending on the general recollection of the church, which knew of baptism, ministry, and passion. He did not have the newspapers, congregational debates, and private diaries that make the task of the modern biographer relatively easy.

Mark, at any rate, is the first of the two "documents" that the other two synoptics rest on. It is his succession of event that they reproduce in their account of Jesus. But the reader of *Matthew* and *Luke* sees that these books reproduce at great length materials absent from *Mark. Mark,* like so many Old Testament narratives, is a Gospel of action, of things done, wonders witnessed, miseries endured. To their compressed reproduction of these Marcan matters, the other two writers add birth stories (each seems to be in contact with fairly independent strands of oral tradition at this point); and they add passages that represent the teachings of Jesus. There are wise sayings in the vein of *Proverbs.* There are parables or allegories that recall the plumb line and the basket of summer fruit in *Amos* (7:7, 8:1). There are discourses that hint of the "last things" (*Matthew* 24), the rolling up of the scroll of human history which riveted the Hebrew imagination from the time of Isaiah onward (*Isaiah* 34:4).

These materials too once likely existed in oral form. But since what the writers of *Matthew* and *Luke* present is, in many instances, identical, scholars have supposed that Matthew and Luke supplemented what the first "document" (*Mark*) gave them by drawing on another written source: a manuscript that contained teachings and sayings of Jesus. This document is called Q; the German word for source is *Quelle.* It was a collection that, in its compression and lack of logical order, in its effect of miscellany, was not unlike what we read when we scan *Amos* or *Jeremiah,* where exhortation follows upon vision, and vision yields place to explicitly contrived parable.

But instead of reproducing this hypothetical second document as they found it, Matthew and Luke made it their quarry from which they dug large blocks of material. It was material which they located as they saw fit in their reproduction of the chain of events provided by *Mark*. Thus, what Matthew locates in one place, the Sermon on the Mount, Luke regards as having been delivered on a plain (*Matthew* chaps. 5, 6, 7; *Luke* 6:20-49). The writers produce a few of the same parables (e.g., the parable of the lost sheep, *Matthew* 18:12-14 and *Luke,* 15:3-7); and each presents several that do not appear elsewhere.

All this is possible, the "two-document" hypothesis unfolds, thanks to the existence of the second source, Q, this collection of utterances that enabled the writers of *Matthew* and *Luke* to supplement the Marcan picture of Christ's deeds with a record—sometimes full, sometimes hauntingly enigmatic—of Christ's thoughts.

This is the majority report on a complicated and important topic, the synoptic problem. There are many minority accounts for which scholars argue cogently and brilliantly.[2] But, almost without exception, the attack is addressed to the theory just summarized; the ancient views of the Gospels do not enter the modern discussions. Beyond the horizon of serious scholarly interest are such matters as the ancient symbolism, derived from *Ezekiel* 1:10, which provides for each evangelist a mysterious token: for Matthew a man, for Mark a lion, for Luke an ox or bull, and for St. John an eagle. The association of the lion and St. Mark, famous in Venice, would be regarded by expositors of the "two-document" hypothesis as an irrelevance.

[2] There is, for example, the "four-document" hypothesis which accepts the majority report but refines it by suggesting that *Luke* and *Matthew* each rest on additional documents which provided the nativity narratives and the unique parables. There is a further supposition that *Mark* itself rests on an earlier work, of course lost but referred to as "proto-Mark." Moreover, there are reworkings of the "two-document" hypothesis that suggest that *Matthew* was the Gospel first to be composed, and that the writer of *Mark* excised the teaching material and embellished the factual narrative. Of such sincere labors, the ordinary reader is likely to say: "The simplest explanation is the best." At any rate, the "two-document" hypothesis and "form-criticism" in combination cast light on many of the striking synoptic difficulties.

The Fourth Gospel

When modern scholarship comes to *John* it finds problems unlike the synoptic ones. *John*, any reader will see, stands alone, with the exception of the opening baptismal story (1:19 ff.) and the concluding events. It represents the ministry as centered in Judah and not in Galilee. It provides the Gospel story with an interpretive preface (1:1) that briefly spreads philosophic wings—wings that are extended again in some of the discourses of Christ on his own nature (e.g., chap. 10). It weaves in incidents that the synoptists do not include: the marriage at Cana (chap. 2), the visit of Nicodemus (chap. 3), the extended miracle narrative in Chapter 5, and the raising of Lazarus from the dead (chap. 11). Further, these narratives and those which exist in altered form in the synoptics (chaps. 4 and 6) use the stories for a very different purpose; the stories are no longer self-subsistent entities but become occasions for the very sort of extended and philosophical analysis that the opening verses of the Gospel foreshadow.

There is general agreement that the author of the book drew on a body of tradition—perhaps oral, perhaps written—with which the synoptists were not in contact. The *John* problem, as we shall indicate more fully in the chapter that deals with the image of Jesus in this Gospel (chap. XVII), concerns not so much what the sources of the book are as what the attitude of the writer was toward his sources and, in the last analysis, toward Jesus. Was "John" an Essene who brought to his viewing of Jesus insights related to secret Hebrew lore, the sort of lore that we are becoming familiar with in the Dead Sea scrolls? Was he a Hellenist who wished, like Philo Judaeus of Alexandria (30 B.C.-A.D. 50), to allegorize the story of Christ and thus add intellectual stature to the faith? Was he a follower who saw in the death and resurrection of Jesus analogues to the mystery religions that spoke of a dying and rising God? Was he touched by the esoteric ideas of the Gnostics; did he see in Jesus an insubstantial emanation of the One? None of these questions is perverse; they are legitimately aroused by the Prologue (1:1 ff.) and by the many discourses of Christ which dwell on the opposition between light and darkness, on the contrast between Jesus and the "prince of this world" (12:31), and on the peculiarly close relation between the Father and the Son, of which the synoptics say comparatively little (chaps. 10, 14).

The Gospel of John is judged to have been composed at Ephesus at the end of the century; if so, it is at the greatest distance of all four narratives from the events concerned. Harsh judgment—too harsh, some feel—regards John (whether the apostle or some follower of the apostle) as a writer who transforms the teacher and leader of the three synoptics into a theological symbol, a term in a Platonistic "demonstration" of how the world is to be saved. Such a judgment ignores the vivid narratives like the wedding at Cana and the account of the crucifixion, narratives that are circumstantial and direct. This judgment also seems to assume that all viewers of Christ ought to see the same object. But we have already perceived that, though the synoptic writers see in much the same way, each has his peculiarity of vision and leaves the mark of his personality on his book. To Matthew, Christ is in the succession of the Hebrew prophets, to Mark he is a healer and wonder worker, and to Luke he is a being peculiarly respectful of the rights of each individual. The varying aspects made out by these writers should suggest that what they tell us does not necessarily exhaust the being or nature of Christ. What *John* tells us of Christ certainly supplements what we see elsewhere; but this Gospel is not as hopelessly at odds with the other three Gospels as some students of the "Johannine problem" like to insist.

Perhaps the whole problem of psychological variation among the four portraits may be summed up by a rough analogy. The accounts that a wife, a close friend, an acquaintance, and a chance viewer would give us of a great man of our own period would not be identical, nor would we expect them to be. The numerous viewers are not the same person, nor did they stand in the same relation to the man. But what they say of him is all rather useful for filling out the final and complete portrait. That the wife and the close acquaintance tell us different things—contradictory things indeed—does not mean that either the wife or the acquaintance is, by this fact alone, untrustworthy. Rather, are we put in possession of two pieces of evidence that allow us to perceive contradictions in the man's character—contradictions to be recognized and dealt with. Readers of the Gospels are sometimes disturbed at the contrast between the curt Christ who drives the moneychangers from the Temple and the gentle Christ who talks with Martha and Mary. But moneychangers and simple, devout women are scarcely the same sort of company and are not likely to call forth the same sort of treatment. In fact, this very variety of impression recorded in the Gospels should suggest to the reader that he is in the presence of a person and not a walking myth or a theological abstraction.

CHAPTER XVI

Christ in the Synoptic Gospels

THOSE who speak of "the Christ of the synoptics" and "the Christ of *The Gospel of John*" as though the two were utterly dissimilar beings transform what is confessedly a rift between the two accounts into a gulf that can scarcely be bridged. These critics suggest that the Christ of the first three Gospels is a healer and teacher; they assert that, in so far as he has "immortal longings," he has them in a thoroughly Jewish fashion, entirely consonant with the culture that cherished the visions appearing in *Ezekiel* and *Daniel* and in the pseudepigraphic book of *Enoch.* They assert that *John's* Christ is a non-Jewish figure which is hardly more than a term in an argument philosophically and theologically conceived, a term deprived of the rich and perplexing humanity apparent at every turn in the first three Gospels.

An alternate view—that this contrast presents us aspects of the same being but aspects differently perceived and presented—is the one taken here. But clarity and full comprehension are both served if one takes up the simple task first, mastering the views taken of Christ in *Matthew, Mark,* and *Luke.* Then a person should be in a position to decide whether John's idea of Christ is near to what the other writers see or far from it.

The synoptists, as the writers of the first three Gospels are called, differ among themselves in ways indicated in the previous chapter on the creation of the Gospels. Nevertheless, they tend to allow us to see very much the same person acting as healer, leader, and teacher. He acts, for the most part, as our acquaintance with Old Testament prophets suggests such a man should act.

Little needs to be said here concerning the common biographical framework of the first three Gospels. The birth of Christ with its omens and signs, the persecution and perils of his early years, the prophetic baptism by John the Baptist, the fortunes of the first teaching work (success always qualified and tainted by the suspicion stirred up by the agents of the Sadducees and Pharisees), Christ's gradual acknowledgment to his disciples of the secret that he is more than another in a long series of teachers and reformers, the final journey to Jerusalem and his judgment there—these touching and familiar elements meet us at every turn of the synoptics.[1]

Simplicity and directness commend the books. No reader misses the mounting tension of the three accounts: the early triumphs in Galilee and the early obstacles; Christ's announcement of his special destiny and his recognition that it is likely to entail death rather than glory; the temporary success in Jerusalem of moral victory over the Sadducees and Pharisees that is, in effect, a death warrant; and the final doom, deeply moving to all readers because in it is a grim promise of the treatment the world allots those who offer it the greatest gifts. The life of Christ as it is reflected in the synoptics arouses "pity and terror" as do the greatest tragedies. In the theater, watching the career of a tragic hero, we shudder, and we may

[1] The trial of Christ, told with variation of detail in the four Gospels, is intelligible if the following circumstances are held in mind. Since Jerusalem is the capital of a difficult Roman province, it is under the direct supervision of the Roman procurator, who resides in Caesarea on the coast but who comes to Jerusalem at times when there are likely to be patriotic outbreaks. Pilate is in Jerusalem because of the Feast of the Passover. Jesus, after his arrest, is brought before a Jewish court, the Sanhedrin, which the Jews were permitted to hold. This court finds him guilty of blasphemy, and the Hebrew penalty for this was death (*Leviticus* 24:16). However, the Romans did not allow the court of a subject people to inflict the death penalty. For this reason, Jesus is sent to Pilate. Pilate is unwilling to pronounce the penalty of death on "this just man." He is indifferent to the religious preoccupations of the members of the Sanhedrin; blasphemy of any god but the divine Caesar was no great offense. Further, Pilate is represented as finding no link between Jesus and the politically dangerous Zealots who agitated revolt against the power of Rome. (*Luke* here furnishes an extra step. Christ is sent to Herod Antipas, who was in Jerusalem for the Passover—Herod Antipas, the son of Herod the Great and tetrarch or petty king of Galilee, Jesus' native province. The interview with Herod ends in mockery (*Luke* 23:6-13), and Jesus is returned to Pilate.) Pilate offers to release Jesus as part of the Passover celebration; but the people, acted on by the priests, choose Barabbas, described by Luke as an inciter of sedition and a murderer, and described by John as a robber. After this, Pilate finally pronounces the sentence for which the chief priests and the people have been clamoring, and Jesus is led out to his crucifixion.

murmur: "There, but for the grace of God, go I." But the majority of tragic heroes—Oedipus, Hamlet, Macbeth—become involved in their tragic doom because of ignorance or blind chance or some inherent weakness. Christ, the Gospel writers suggest, was not ignorant of his fate; it did not overwhelm him unaware. Nor did he "fall" because of a flaw of character. He "fell" with full knowledge; he "fell" because of his merits, not because of his defects. So our shudder as we read the Gospels is not like that which we have for tragic heroes in whom we recognize our ordinary selves. Instead it is for the disaster that would apparently overtake us even if it were possible for us to be perfect. Two utterances of Christ haunt our imaginations: the address to God in the garden of Gethsemane—"O my father, if it be possible, let this cup pass from me: nevertheless, not as I will, but as thou wilt" (*Matthew* 26:39)—and the cry reported by Mark as being uttered on the cross: "My God, my God, why hast thou forsaken me?" (*Mark* 15:34). They are as poignant as the famous cry of Job which anticipates their accent: "Though he slay me, yet will I trust in him: but I will maintain mine own ways before him" (*Job* 13:15). They are not the contrivance of poets but are words that simple men have kept in memory, and express the enigma at the root of all existence. Job's enigma was a fairly simple one: Why is virtue unrewarded? Christ's is more complex: Why does the performance of our manifest best seem to produce the fate that overwhelms us? A part of the great power of these three narratives lies in the enigmas which the career of Christ suggests and which, in less august form, every human being encounters in his own life.

But Christ is more than a tragic figure. On him a great religion was based. So we must proceed soberly to an analysis of what the synoptic Gospels reveal concerning him. The synoptics have not only the common biographical framework noted. They have also, with allowance for the differences of emphasis mentioned already, a common view of Christ's activity. That activity was, in the first place, a rough and unsystematic blend of doing and saying, like the blend apparent in the career of the earliest of the great prophets, Elijah, and in the career of Jeremiah, the prototype of the "suffering servant" of *Isaiah*, Chapter 53. Like Elijah's, Christ's activity is "impure" or mixed; miracles of healing mingle with expressions of "wisdom" of a moral or eschatological sort. And like Jeremiah, Christ is represented as forever alert to what chance opportunity presents. Many an instruction of Christ comes into being as did Jeremiah's when he seized upon the presence of the total abstainers, the Rechabites, in the city of Jerusalem or when he arranged for the purchase of the field of Hanameel and thus asserted the continuance of Israel.

Some persons who have a passion for order look with regret on these recrudescences of what they regard as "earlier" forms of religious activity. If they had the manipulation of the Hebrew-Christian story, they would construct a direct, rising course from the "impure" or mixed activity of Elijah to the prophetic, single, and almost depersonalized rejoicings of Isaiah II. They would certainly not allow, if this were in their power, the return of the varied arts of the primitive Elijah in the activity of the teacher who succeeds Isaiah II. These critics would like to be able to say that, in the days of Jesus, the time is past when a teacher of ethical insights "doubles in brass" and heals and foretells events as well as preaches. But, as suggested early in this book, the development of a religion moves not in a straight line but in a circular fashion or, better, a spiral one. Thus, when we come to the synoptics' presentation of Christ, we have come full circle and seem to see Christ resting on a point on *his* section of the spiral directly above the point where we saw Elijah working miracles and defying natural law. This is not to say that Christ's wonderworking in the synoptics is no more than a repetition of Elijah's in *Kings*. One should recognize that it occurs on a spiral whose arc does not coincide with Elijah's. At least, we should sense, in whatever Christ does, the accumulated force of later prophets' declarations about Israel and individual man—declarations that Elijah did not know. That Christ raises the daughter of Jairus from the dead, is able to cure illness by touch and word, and can even work his wonders at a distance (*Luke* 7:1-10)—all this takes place in a different context from that which surrounds Elijah's wonders. This context has been built up by the insights and problems provided by the great prophets and posed by the authors of *Ecclesiastes, Job,* and *The Wisdom of Solomon.* Elijah's kindling the fires on Jehovah's altar asserted the superior power of the god of Israel and the inferiority of the gods imported by Jezebel. The wonders performed by Christ assert more than the power of God; they assert his justice and righteousness. These miracles are judged, by his followers, at least, to be the outward and visible signs that in this man are gathered up and fulfilled everything the prophets have said about righteousness and mercy, about the Messiah and the kingdom of heaven.

When, as *Matthew* has it, Christ at the mid-point of his ministry asks his disciples: "Who do men say that I the Son of man am?" their answer is: "Some say that thou art John the Baptist: some, Elias [Elijah]; and others, Jeremias, one of the prophets." There was not wanting a belief that the future deliverer of the Hebrews should be the avatar or embodiment of an earlier hero: a John the Baptist or Elijah—or David, for that matter. But Peter's answer repudiates these possibilities: "Thou art the Christ, the Son of the living God" (*Matthew* 16:13-17). Peter's answer is, in its own way, an assertion that Jesus' feats are no stale repetition of the feats of Elijah. As we have said, they are performed in a different context. It is a context in part provided by the utterances of the prophets whose activity is "purer" and less mixed than either Elijah's or Jesus'.

Miracle

The writers of the synoptic Gospels do not, then, present miracle for its own sake (though John Mark has a strong inclination in this direction). They present it as a warrant of the correctness of Christ's assertions about the nature of virtue and the process of redemption. The ancient world was full of narratives of miraculous healing; for example, the Greeks were fond of stories of Apollonius of Tyana and the wonders he performed. Therefore, Christ's acts of healing were, in the eyes of his followers, useful supports to his central assertions; but they were not without their parallels elsewhere. But the most the

Gospel miracles count for is what is called ancillary or aiding proof of the declarations that Christ finally makes about himself and the future course of events. That the miracles had such a secondary role and they did not lead automatically to the discovery of Christ's identity, the course of events in the synoptics shows plainly. When Christ asks the question about his identity, only Peter gives the proper answer. The rest have taken the "signs and wonders," the acts of healing that are oblique and incidental announcements of Christ's identity, for the deeds they would expect of many a wandering teacher who challenged the power of the Sadducees and the Pharisees.

The synoptics often indicate this role of miracles. *Mark* tells us of a prediction of Christ's: "For false Christs and false prophets shall rise, and shew signs and wonders, to seduce, if it were possible, even the elect" (*Mark* 13:22). More often than not, the miracles are performed grudgingly, and their efficacy seems to stem from the laconic words: "Thy faith hath made thee whole" (e.g., *Matthew* 9:22). In only one instance—and this is in *John,* Chapter 9—is a miracle performed with any show of gesture and the complexity of magic spell which is so large a part of the wonders told of Elijah and Elisha. In the incident in *John,* Christ does apply spittle-moistened clay to the eyes of the blind man. But when he is faced with the task of bringing back to life the daughter of Jairus, he imitates none of the techniques of Elijah and Elisha; he does not lean on the body of the child, he does not breathe into her mouth. He merely takes her hand and says, "Damsel, I say unto thee, arise" (*Mark* 5:41).

In fact, persons who endeavor to "explain" the miracles as comprehensible and natural events point out that a great many of them can be regarded as "psychological"—i.e., the ailments are what today would be called "mental" or "psychosomatic." The symptoms of madness cease as soon as faith in the power of the healer sets to work in the mind of the ailing person.

But, naturally, this is not the view of the "signs" that Mark and his peers take. Therefore, a modern reader makes a mistake if, at the outset, he tries to purge the career of Christ of what he regards as the dross of ancient mistaken belief. He must recognize that, for the Gospel writers, whatever was set down about miracles was pure gold. True, the reader who seeks to thread his way through the synoptic Gospels by picking and choosing among the miraculous may be able to construct a figure of Christ "the great psychologist"; but "great psychologists" do not found religions. To understand Christ as the central figure in a religion that took command of the decaying Roman world, we have to labor to see him, in the first instance, as he moved the imaginations of those who recorded his life. He may well have been what our judgments imply when we call him "a great psychologist" and a great teacher. But these merits were, to the early Christians, but by-products of the central truths announced by Christ himself and elaborated by St. Paul and others: that he was also a unique being who offered what no other teacher, healer, or secular leader could offer. In short, one loses grasp on the central spirit of the Gospels if he commences to handle the miracles in the fashion just now indicated. A person may say of the cure of the man suffering from "devils" (*Mark* 5:1-20), "This is possible; his ailment is plainly psychological." He may say of the woman who is cured of her "issues of blood" merely by touching the hem of Christ's garment (*Mark* 5:24-34), "This is less possible. Her ailment is either psychosomatic or entirely physical." And he would say of the raising of Lazarus from the dead, "This simply could not have happened."

A similar waste of time is the effort to reduce the miracle of feeding the five thousand to the creation of generous attitude among all present by the act of Christ and his disciples when they open their own scrips. The attempt to give a reasonable explanation of other incredible feats of Jesus may preserve a faith that is offended by the miraculous. (E.g., Christ was not really "walking on the waters" in *Matthew*, Chapter 12; he was walking through moonlit shallows and only seemed to those who saw him to be walking on the sea.) But such efforts, which extend to the events of the crucifixion, have one bad and immediate effect. They detach the modern reader from the "climate of opinion" in which the Gospel writers lived; and what was essential in the narrative from their point of view evaporates. Lost also is much chance to understand why Christianity has been able to exercise its power. This act of primary comprehension should not be confused with the secondary and very important question: Was this power the Gospel writers attribute to Christ actually his, or was it a "projection" of the peoples' hopes into the career of a human teacher? Yet this secondary question is not likely to be answered very well if the reader neglects to see what kind of books the Gospels are. A perception of the early Church's view of Christ must take precedence over a precise weighing of that belief. Similarly, in Old Testament history, a perception of the effect, among the Hebrews, of the belief that the Red Sea had parted for them by divine command does more to illuminate one's comprehensions of the later course of Hebrew history than concentration on the ingenious suggestion that the children of Israel actually walked across sandy shallows temporarily cleared by a strong wind.

One risks, furthermore, failing to see that Christ is presented as no more than tolerating these demands on his power. He offers the "bread of life," but the "generation of vipers" keep asking for something else. They ask for wheat loaves, for relief from physical pain, for the establishment in Jerusalem of a state that can resist the power of Rome. All these desires are, in the phrase of *Ecclesiastes*, "vanities"; and they are vanities for reasons which Christ has explicitly described to his followers.

Christ the Teacher

The constant struggle of Christ to "get things straight"—to assert to the masses of people and his intimates the significance of his outward deeds—involves him in informal teaching. As we should say, he has to reëducate persons who are ignorant or ill informed. The term that hails this activity of Christ—"the great teacher"—is of older standing than "the great psychologist" and takes us closer to the heart of Christ's effect on those who saw and heard him.

As we analyze the "methods" Jesus used to shake his hearers from their apathy, we shall recognize fashions of utterances met previously in the prophets. They were far from unique in his own day; some of them had already won the locust-eating John his followers. Even the crucifixion can be seen as a final act clarifying, to the eager and mistaken apprehension of his contemporaries, the truth that Jesus was something else than a Zealot who was gratifyingly critical of those in high place and something other than a conquering Messiah who would bring back the glories of David and the Maccabees.

And the crucifixion is a concrete event, not an abstract statement about the identity of Christ. All of Christ's teaching, in the synoptics, follows this pattern. As with the prophets, Jesus' words are a form of doing, often no less violent in effect than his purging of the Temple. If what he conveys is doctrine, it is doctrine always closely united to the rich and various personality of the teacher. Thanks to the framework of narrative put together by Mark or some nameless earlier writer, the effect of his instruction is constantly that of being delivered in motion. It is "wisdom" not spun out in the silence of a cell by a monk or in a forest by a Hindu guru or wise man who condescends to instruct those who seek him out. It is "wisdom" that flashes from a struck flint. No secondary treatment, as here, can create this effect; but one can insist that the sparks burst out unpredictably rather than systematically. The great "saint" of Hellenic history was doubtless Socrates. But the position in which the imagination catches Socrates, in life and at the point of death, is a sitting one; and the atmosphere is one of leisure. Socrates hears a chance comment, he leans forward, he asks to have it repeated; and soon he and his friends are closeted for a long discussion of justice or love or truth in a thoroughly philosophic atmosphere. There is no room for leisure in the synoptics. Christ is on the move, pursued by his admirers no less than by his foes.

Many of Christ's most telling remarks are the result of chance encounters. The Pharisees observe him eating with publicans and protest. Christ answers them: "They that are whole need not a physician; but they that are sick" (*Luke* 5:31). It is an answer created by a specific situation; further, like many of Christ's other remarks, it has an element of careless sarcasm—here for the men who presume they are "whole," the Pharisees—that says, "If this shoe fits, wear it." Another saying, the one that caps *Luke's* story of the pious centurion, is another such spark from the flint of the moment. The Roman sends a message asking Christ not to take the trouble to visit the centurion's ailing servant; a word spoken at a distance will be enough. When Jesus hears this, he "marvels"; then he turns to the Hebrew sensation seekers in his train and says: "I say unto you, I have not found so great faith, no, not in Israel" (*Luke* 7:9).

Remarks like these are doubly suggestive because they are presented in utter nudity of style and circumstance. What in a more sophisticated culture would be a point of departure stands decisive and alone. Indeed, Christ's style of teaching is close to the type of instruction Nathan offers David when he says: "Thou art the man" (*II Samuel* 12:7). It is less close to the developed modes of discourse in *The Wisdom of Solomon.* The synoptics contain not truth as contemplated; they present truth as experienced, as acted out.

Such teaching necessarily implies a rather large dependence on what the moment offers the teacher. A physicist has to set up his experiment carefully if his students are to profit by his instruction. Christ "sets up" his experiments carelessly. In the realm of moral instruction a quick, unexpected buffet is more memorable than a planned course of persuasion. One recalls Cellini's anecdote: how his father cuffed the boy Cellini on the ear, not because the boy had done wrong but because the father desired him to remember the salamander before them in the fire. The Gospels abound in such quick strokes. Christ walks with his disciples in the Sabbath fields; as he walks there, he plucks grain and is rebuked by the Pharisees. After a reference to David and the "shew-bread" (*I Samuel* 21:6), Christ concludes the matter: "The Sabbath was made for man, and not man for the Sabbath" (*Mark* 2:27). Often these blows have an effect of intolerable harshness as when he says, in reply to the request of his mother and his brethren to speak with him: "Who is my mother? and who are my brethren?" Before the shock of this cruel question is gone, he gestures to his disciples and says: "Behold my mother and my brethren. For whosoever shall do the will of my Father which is in heaven, the same is my brother, and sister, and mother" (*Matthew* 12:46-50). A blow associated with a pregnant saying is, as Cellini's story suggests, worth more than a disquisition on the brotherhood of man. In another anecdote, Jesus flouts another Hebrew taboo. A disciple makes the excusable request: "Lord, suffer me first to go and bury my father." Jesus replies: "Follow me and let the dead bury their dead: but go thou and preach the kingdom of God" (*Luke* 9:59-60). This underlines, as could no formal discourse on lower and higher duties, the painful sacrifice that Christ intends to demand of his followers.

Indeed, he rebuffs them as often as he encourages them. To a man who says, "Lord, I will follow thee; but let me first go bid them farewell, which are at home at my house," Christ replies somewhat coldly, "No man, having put his hand to the plough, and looking back, is fit for the kingdom of God" (*Luke* 9:61-62). As in the tale of the rich young man (*Matthew* 19:16 ff.), he erects hurdles that must be taken in "good form" by those who think they wish to follow him.

Even when, on occasion, Christ does not go counter to the taboos most men accept, the effect is still one of shock. Speaking of God's answer to prayer, he exploits what is called "the parental instinct": "If a son shall ask bread of any of you that is a father, will he give him a stone? or if he ask for a fish give him a serpent?" Doubtless at this point his bearers who were also parents were congratulating themselves. Then Christ adds: "If ye then, being evil, know how to give good gifts unto your children: how much more shall your heavenly Father give the Holy Spirit to them that ask him?" (*Luke* 11:11, 13.) The phrase "If ye then, being evil" transforms an easy platitude into something new. It is as if his hearers had suddenly found they were on a breath-taking express elevator—not on one that moves gently from floor to floor. All of these illustrations suggest that truth harshly conveyed remains. Further, much of the "wisdom" hat Christ dealt in was intrinsically harsh, for it challenged fixed and often very comfortable modes of thought. Those who followed Christ had to be willing to sever all of their ties with family and community, and this is not done without a painful wrench.

There are refinements upon Christ's methods of instruction and argument. Some of these become intelligible and pointed if we see them against the Old Testament background. This is particularly apparent when Christ trades blows with the learned of his culture. Particularly in *Matthew*, "the Gospel to the Hebrews," is Christ's activity presented in relation to the Hebrew cultural background. This background was made up of a set of beliefs and customs that were no longer, as in the days of *Genesis*, a new thing in an old world; they were an old thing in an old world. Christ spoke to the learned of this world as well as to the ignorant, making reference to topics crucial to them and using methods or argument habitual in learned circles. It is well to be aware that "proof" in the arguments between Christ and the "vested interests" (the Pharisees and Sadducees) was not a matter, as we flatter ourselves it is with us, of testing our assumptions and the links by which we go from valid assumption to conclusion. "Proof" among the Hebrew learned consisted in showing that one's assertion had the warrant of some passage in Scripture. Scripture could not be mistaken; whatever was in line with it could not be mistaken. Disagreement in argument arose chiefly as to the interpretation that could be placed on various inspired passages. (And that interpretations could indeed differ, the strife between the conservative Sadducees and the "separated" Pharisees indicates.) One got a verbal adversary on the run not by demonstrating the weakness of his basic assumptions and his logic but by discovering impiety in his interpretation of a sacred verse or by capping his "proof text" with an even better one.

We can suspect that Christ was an adept at both methods. When he desires to "prove" his own divinity, he quotes the enigmatic opening of Psalm 110: "The Lord said unto my Lord, Sit thou on my right hand." The meaning of the enigmatic text, Christ asserts, has not been clear until this time, when the "Son of God" actually exists on earth. But now the passage clearly means that David foresaw the birth of a unique being, a "Son of God" (*Matthew* 22:41 ff.). Jesus' opponents cannot give an answer; at least, the Gospel writers delight in presenting Christ's arguments in such a way that the opponents appear stunned. The writers suggest that their only effective answer is use of force and, finally, appeal to the power of Pilate.

In passage after passage the author of *Matthew*—like the authors of the other two synoptics, to a lesser degree—reflects this frame of mind in his own thinking. Christ's divinity and Messiahship are "proved" by references to *Isaiah,* to *Micah,* and to other prophets. Thus, the flight into Egypt during the persecution of Herod the Great is regarded as preparation for the fulfillment of a saying in *Hosea:* "Out of Egypt have I called my son" (*Matthew* 2:15). The mission of John the Baptist fulfills a saying of Isaiah: "For this is he that was spoken of by the prophet Esaias, saying, The voice of one crying in the wilderness, Prepare ye the way of the Lord, make his paths straight" (*Matthew* 3:3). The early ministry in Galilee also has the warrant of a text of *Isaiah* (*Matthew* 4:14). Even Jesus' manner of entry into Jerusalem is referred to in a confusing verse in the prophet Zechariah (*Matthew* 21:4-5). This method of thought does not perhaps carry proof for us, but it was common to the society in which Christ lived.

This habit apparently characterized Christ's own thought about himself and his destiny. Thus, when the Pharisees seek a "sign," Christ first says: "An evil and adulterous generation seeketh after a sign, and there shall no sign be given to it, but the sign of the prophet Jonas [Jonah]." Then he adds in an enigmatic style that all present, even the Pharisees themselves, would judge to be a proper use of the old story: "For as Jonas was three days and three nights in the whale's belly; so shall the Son of man be three days and three nights in the heart of the earth" (*Matthew* 12:39-40). A parallel between Jonah's fate and Christ's death and resurrection that a modern person might dismiss as "purely coincidental" would to the Hebrews who looked back on this interchange be convincing in the highest degree. From interviews like this one, the Pharisees, the "blind leaders of the blind" (*Matthew* 15:14), can only retire with their hands over their mouths, a traditional sign of defeat. They bided their time until Jesus "asked for it" by entering Jerusalem. *Luke* shows Christ justifying his Temple cleansing by his words to the moneychangers as he drives them out: "It is written, My house is the house of prayer: but ye have made it a den of thieves" (*Luke* 19:46). And *John*, who least of all represents Christ as resting on this sort of support, presents him as defending to Nicodemus the "scandal" of the crucifixion by a reference to the beneficent use which Moses made of the brazen serpent in the wilderness:

> And as Moses lifted up the serpent in the wilderness, even so must the Son of man be lifted up: that whosoever believeth in him should not perish, but have eternal life. (*John* 3:14-15.)

The method of capping a text opposed to one's point of view by a text supporting it is implied by many of Christ's interviews with the Pharisees, but the fullest example appears in the early exchange between Christ and that prince of Pharisees, Satan, who demonstrates his proverbial power to quote Scripture. The three temptations—the devil works on Christ's physical hunger, challenges him to test God's care for him by leaping from a high place, and offers him all the kingdoms of this earth—are all rejected by Jesus by means of words quoted from Scripture. But it is the second temptation that allows us to see fully this kind of interchange.

> Then the devil taketh him up into the holy city, and setteth him on a pinnacle of the temple, and saith unto him, If thou be the Son of God, cast thyself down: for it is written, He shall give his angels charge concerning thee: and in their hands they shall bear thee up, lest at any time thou dash thy foot against a stone.

Jesus replies: "It is written again, Thou shalt not tempt the Lord thy God" (*Matthew* 4:5-7). Here—as doubtless in many debates in the Temple area—the victor's palm goes to the speaker who offsets the pretensions of the previous speaker. This kind of argument informs much political debate, where the past is a quarry from which each speaker picks up rocks to throw at his opponent.

Another method of debate that Christ uses once with skill does not involve manipulation of Scripture. (St. Paul also used it, in *Acts* 23:6 ff.) It is a complex argument that involves two common debating feints, the dilemma and the "red herring." The dilemma is a question to which there are only two answers, both of them painful or inexpedient to give. (Consider the embarrassment of a man who is required to answer this question: "Have you stopped beating your wife?") The chief priests and the elders inquire by whose authority Christ is teaching in the Temple. He parries that question with this one: "The baptism of John, whence was it? from heaven, or of men?" Christ's opponents "reasoned with themselves, saying, If we shall say, From heaven; he will say unto us, Why did ye not then believe him? But if we shall say, Of men; we fear the people; for all hold John as a prophet" (*Matthew* 21:25-26). Further, the painfulness of the John query acting as a "red herring" turns Christ's enemies aside from their real purpose: to discover his own estimate of his identity.

Finally, Christ can take refuge in a statement so ambiguous—and impious from the conventional point of view—that discussion is broken off. At his trial, he is reported as having said, "I am able to destroy the temple of God, and to build it in three days" (*Matthew* 26:61). Such claim to divine power is sheer blasphemy, and the hearers can do no less than tear their robes. That the saying was also perplexing and ambiguous appears when one notes the differing interpretations of it given by two Gospel writers. One, the writer of *Matthew*, accepts the remark at face value, as a reference to the power that Christ has and refuses to use. The bold saying is judged by the author of *John* to conceal a meaning that the future was to reveal to the faithful: "this temple" was the temple of Christ's own body, which was, in the space of three days, to be destroyed and lifted up (*John* 2:18-22).

In conclusion, it is plain that the frame of mind enjoyed by the Gospel writers is not easy for us to reproduce. When the writer of *John* reports that Christ said he would be "lifted up" as Moses lifted up the serpent in the wilderness, he is saluting a marvelous correspondence between past and present events. He is not likely to remark that there is also a considerable difference between the lifting up of a redeemer and the erection of a serpent fetish to offset the results of snakebite. Nor does he recall that this same fetish had finally to be removed from the Temple in the days of King Hezekiah because it had become the object of "adulterous" worship. A reader is right to have these various perceptions; he is not right when he supposes it was the business of the Gospel writers to have them.

Parables

One famous element in Christ's skill as a teacher remains to be commented upon: his use of parable. Parable, we suggested elsewhere, is in origin but an expanded and exploited metaphor, and it is an especially attractive vehicle for popular instruction. After-dinner speakers battle the digestive torpor of their listeners not with abstract defense of a point but with an anecdote illustrating their main contention. The parable has, as Christ sometimes uses it, the charm of the riddle. The narrative element in Christ's parables wins attention; a sense that its meaning is not fully revealed prolongs attention after the story is done.

Christ exploited both these attractions of the parable to the full. The Gospel writers regard the element of riddle as especially important. Thus, they judge Jesus' revelation of his identity and function to be a gradual process, and it was the parable that allowed him to make partial reference to ethical and eschatological doctrines without committing himself too soon. Indeed, the following pattern of instruction often occurs: The parable is delivered to the multitude, and its meaning is later explained to the curious disciples.

Yet, as a matter of fact, the meaning of many of the parables is self-evident. Though the parable of the sower is "explained" to the disciples, its lesson is evident within the limits of the narrative as first given (*Matthew* 13:1-17). When Christ concludes his public deliverance of the story with the formula, "Who hath ears to hear, let him hear" (*Matthew* 13:9), we often judge that the meaning is complete, without the painstaking explanation Christ gives to his followers. But we must recognize that the Gospel writers regarded

Christ's use of the parable as intended to stir the curiosity of the masses rather than to gratify it.

One other quality of the parable form must be kept in the foreground of our minds whenever we encounter this sort of narrative, which is less prevalent in our society than it was in Christ's. That it is not entirely absent a pseudo-folk tale like Benét's *The Devil and Daniel Webster* indicates. The real meaning of the story lies not in the mere rescue of the luckless Jabez, who has bartered his soul; it lies in what Webster says about the glory of having lived, of having been a human being. But it is true that most modern fiction entertains by creating an illusion of reality, though it may incidentally convey some moral insight. In the parable, the emphasis swings in the other direction: little care is given to the illusion of reality; much care is taken to build up to a moral point. Christ's parables produce the illusion of reality very hastily, as a few opening passages show: "For the kingdom of heaven is like unto a man that is an householder, which went out early in the morning to hire labourers into his vineyard" (*Matthew* 20:1). "The kingdom of heaven is like unto a certain king, which made a marriage for his son" (*Matthew* 22:2). "A certain man planted a vineyard, and set an hedge about it . . ." (*Mark* 12:1). The famous parable of the prodigal son begins thus simply: "A certain man had two sons; and the younger of them said to his father, Father give me the portion of goods that falleth to me. And he divided unto them his living" (*Luke* 15:11-12). In brief, the events happen somewhere, to certain people. But everything in the tale is in strict servitude to the moral or eschatological point.

If a parable made any claims to being a transcript of life, we would be bewildered by the foolishness of the father (*Mark*, chap. 12) who sends his "well-beloved" son to collect the rent after two servants who have gone on the same errand have been beaten; and the foolishness of the father is matched by that of the servants who kill the son to get the inheritance. But we should rather ask: What teaching point does this strange story make? Clearly, the point is that God—the "certain man"—has sent his prophets, who have been rejected; and now he sends his son, who will be rejected still more brutally by the husbandmen, the mass of humanity or, possibly, the Hebrew people, who believe that rejection of the son will make their place more secure. In reading the parable in *Matthew*, Chapter 25, of the ten virgins who await the arrival of the bridegroom, the modern reader who has the habit of regarding fictitious narrative as a transcript of life may feel a good deal of sympathy for the foolish virgins who used up their supply of oil; and he may stigmatize as churlish the refusal of the prudent virgins to share their supply. But this is to misread the very nature of a parable. Here, the entire narrative is manipulated to make this one point: "readiness is all," and those who are not forever ready to welcome the coming of Christ the bridegroom may expect to weep and wail and gnash their teeth. All other considerations are sacrificed. Considerations of mercy and justice that occur to us and that are, indeed, in part the creation of Christ's own teachings must be suppressed.

The censure, in still another parable (*Matthew* 25:14 ff.), of the servant who does not imitate his fellows and put out at interest the one talent his master left with him but instead hides it does not lead us to consideration of whether Christ was commending the taking of interest. The master's concluding remarks should unlock the riddle for most readers:

> Take therefore the talent from him, and give it unto him which hath ten talents. For unto every one that hath shall be given, and he shall have abundance; but from him that hath not shall be taken away even that which he hath. (*Matthew* 25:27-28.)

It is miscalculation to feel indignation for the feckless servant. The story is invented to drive home an ethical point which, in this instance, Christ does not explain to his attentive circle. But the point—we should be able to see—is that the Lord gives spiritual gifts for use and exercise, not to be hoarded. Viewed in this light, the treatment of the servant is not at odds with Christ's general preaching about the kingdom of heaven.

Guesses of this sort are needed to make sense of the double-barreled parable in *Matthew*, Chapter 22, concerning the wedding of the king's son. In the first section, chance guests (the Gentiles) take the place of the guests (the Hebrews) who receive the invitation rudely (verses 2-10). In the second section (verses 11-13) an entirely different point is made—again, that "readiness is all"—when the king casts out the guest who does not wear a wedding garment. Useless is it to inquire in a literal spirit: "But if the guest was picked from the passers-by, how could he have had a garment ready?" This is a question we might address to a modern psychological novel; but we have no business asking it of one of Christ's parables, which were conceived and executed in quite another cause.

All this is to say more precisely what was stated at the outset, that the parable is expanded metaphor. It draws out to their full the potentialities perceived in the similarities between a natural object, a grain of mustard seed that grows into a huge plant, and the growth of Christ's kingdom from its small, unimpressive beginnings. A poet usually drops a metaphor quickly since, too long cherished, it is likely to produce effects of grotesqueness. The reader of the New Testament parables must overlook the grotesque or the improbable and seek the moral enlightenment intended.

Ethical Doctrines

A "great teacher" is great not only because he has command of a technique flexible enough to sway a variety of audiences. He is a great teacher because he has something great to teach. Our account of Christ as seen in the first three Gospels is not complete until we see what he was deeply concerned to drive home. Beneath the variety of epigram, argument, and parable are two main topics: Man must see his ethical behavior in a new light; man must recognize Christ for what he is—a certain kind of Messiah rather than another popular teacher or wonderworker.

Christ's ethical doctrine appears in the Sermon on the Mount (*Matthew,* chaps. 5, 6, 7) and in the same remarks differently distributed in *Luke.* It appears also in the chance remarks that are the fire struck from the flint of emergent circumstance. It is an ethical doctrine that Christ likens to "new wine" (*Matthew* 9:17); but this phrase represents justifiable overemphasis of an educational sort, since a quick about-face is an easy movement to execute. But there is continuity as well as novelty in all of Christ's teaching. Christ himself said:

> Think not that I am come to destroy the law or the prophets: I am not come to destroy, but to fulfill. For verily I say unto you, Till heaven and earth pass, one jot or tittle shall in no wise pass from the law, till all be fulfilled. (*Matthew* 5:17, 18.)

It is well—perhaps with the sanction of this passage—to begin by looking at the Old Testament ethical insights which Christ continues or "fulfills." We see at once that Christ is a reformer and critic of the type of Amos and Hosea. His vantage point is unofficial and ambiguous. Though his ethical doctrine combines the laws of righteousness and love found in the two prophets, his situation is more nearly that of Amos. He is an outlander, and he presumes to level his spear at the fortress where authority and tradition live in comfort. The fortress (to his view) is occupied by men bent on distorting the relation between the Father-God and his created children; they are set on placing hurdles on the course that all men must run—hurdles that only the expensively trained (the Sadducees and the Pharisees) will be able to surmount. The bulk of the children of Israel become discouraged and decide that righteousness is not for them. In truth, righteousness is not for them if it entails residence in Jerusalem and the daily performance of observances costly in time and money. But there is another way, and this "way" is, one might say, the stick of dynamite which Christ uses to break up the log jam created by centuries of legalism and tradition worship. It is a way that Hosea, if briefly, has already pointed out. It is the placing of righteousness not in the external act but in the intent preceding the act.

What made so novel, in Christ's day, utterances that are to us—perhaps dangerously—a few moral truisms? A sufficient answer is to say that Hosea's insistence on intent, on the heart that brings forth fruit to God and not to itself, had been lost in the 750 years of Hebrew history that separate him and Jesus. In the generations terrified by Assyria and Babylon, it was the sheer material continuity of the nation that counted. If the rod of Assyria fell, it fell for the sin of collective Israel, a very overt and tangible thing. Israel was being punished for its outward and notorious deeds, the spiritual whoredom it had committed; it was not being punished for anything so intangible as the intent that had preceded the act. Nor did Hosea's insight about the primacy of intent establish effective contact with Ezekiel's perception that the teeth of the individual should be no more set on edge even though the father had eaten sour grapes (*Ezekiel* 18:2 ff.). How could it, when the bulk of Ezekiel's prophecy is legalistic in tone and is concerned with the setting up of a theocratic state rather than with the separate person and his moral life?

In the following centuries there were voices—ardent in *The Book of Psalms,* troubled in *Job,* and self-assured in *The Wisdom of Solomon*—that suggested that what must count most in the eyes of God was the moral life of the individual. But these voices made less noise than the shouts of the militant Maccabees, concerned with the nation, and the measured utterances of the Sadducees and Pharisees, concerned with Temple purity and the externals of morality.

"I am not come to destroy but to fulfill." This expresses the view taken in the synoptics of Jesus' function as an ethical teacher, as a divine being also. The laws of Moses are fulfilled when they are made binding on the heart as well as on the overt activity of the flesh.

> Ye have heard that it was said by them of old time, Thou shalt not commit adultery: but I say unto you, that whoever looketh on a woman to lust after her hath committed adultery with her already in his heart. (*Matthew* 5:27-28.)

To the obtuse Peter, Christ explains his doctrines very fully. He cancels the "shadow" of the laws because he would have man be faithful to their "substance."

> Do not ye yet understand, that whatsoever entereth in at the

> mouth goeth into the belly, and is cast out into the draught? But those things which proceed out of the mouth come forth from the heart; and they defile the man. For out of the heart proceed evil thoughts, murders, adulteries, fornications, thefts, false witness, blasphemies: these are the things which defile a man: but to eat with unwashen hands defileth not a man. (*Matthew* 15:17-20.)

Law is to be rejected because it seldom goes deep enough to get at the heart of the matter. From the point of view of this "new" teaching, the truly "unclean" man was the hypocrite, who kept himself ritually pure but from whose lips words devoid of charity and comprehension came. They are the subjects of the famous outcry:

> Woe unto you, scribes and Pharisees! for ye are like unto whited sepulchres, which indeed appear beautiful outward, but are within full of dead men's bones, and of all uncleanness. (*Matthew* 23:27.)

The many vivid sayings of the Sermon on the Mount are variations on this one simple theme: Virtue must be driven inward. The knowledge that men have of virtue must send down deeper roots.

All Jesus' "new" ethical teaching asserted a truth that isolated Hebrews already seen or felt the need of. Among the prophets, whom Jesus found congenial, he could observe that the prophetic mind displays a preference for what we have called "reversals." The only change that will count is a full change. The Beatitudes—and many other sayings of Jesus—envisage a complete upsetting of the *status quo* as part of the encouragement and vindication of the interior sort of virtue.

> Blessed are the poor in spirit: for theirs is the kingdom of heaven.
> Blessed are the meek: for they shall inherit the earth.
> Blessed are the merciful, for they shall obtain mercy. (*Matthew* 5:3, 5, 7.)

Obviously, these promises moved the humble to wild hope and gave unfriendly hearers grounds for supposing that Christ might be working in Zealot fashion to provoke a political upheaval. To such a suspicion, Christ's answer—"Render unto Caesar the things that are Caesar's" (*Luke* 20:25)—is an enigmatic reply in isolation; but taken in the context of his cumulative ethical utterance it is sufficiently clear. His crafty foes ask this question to trap him into a declaration of revolutionary import that they can report to Pilate. But Christ's answer outpaces their question. As long as we live, the kingdom of this world—Caesar's or some other ruler's—will be with us. The reversal of which the Beatitudes speak will be complete only in the kingdom of heaven. Only there is the intent behind a course of action accurately recognized. Though Christ is capable of facing up to evil with vigor and harshness, he is no revolutionary of recent model who intends to create utopia overnight. His ethical teaching suggested that, though one might try on earth for the reversal that is complete only in heaven and even turn the "rogues" of Sadducees and Pharisees out, other rogues would take their places. Rogues, like the poor, are always with us.

No castigation of thieves and hypocrites will ever transform this world into a place where virtue and humility are fully and properly rewarded. Here, indeed, Christ parts company with Old Testament prophets who had supposed that their hopes for a restored Israel would be realized in "the kingdom of this world"—that is, in history and time. For example, Isaiah II supposes that an Israel that has suffered "double" for its sins will have a restoration entailing a political reversal; the Babylonian rogues will be cast out, and the Israelites, instructed by their sorrows, will regain power and all the pleasures of power. It is not such reversal that Christ holds up as the culmination of the ethical life pure of intent *and* act. Perhaps the picture which Jewish history of the past century and a half offered was destructive of a faith that Israel restored to power could also be a righteous Israel. The nineteenth-century Englishman Lord Acton said: "All power corrupts, and absolute power corrupts absolutely." Judas Maccabaeus' family had used its power to impose its ways on weaker groups of Hebrews within the nation and on weaker outside nations. (Among these were the Idumeans, from whom the Herodians came.) The inconclusive result of the Hebrew possession of earthly power was that the oppressed peoples were ready to welcome the Roman conquest and its "new order."

Whatever the cause, Christ teaches that purity of intent cannot be worked out in terms of national prosperity or in terms of individual prosperity and well-being. It was the loaves and fishes that the mass of Christ's followers were won by. (Modern missionaries speak of their "rice Christians," who flock to a pastor so long as he can feed them.) The "bread of heaven" is a tougher bread, on which teeth could be broken, for it had the leaven of such "hard sayings" as this: "For whosoever will save his life shall lose it: and whosoever will lose his life for my sake shall find it" (*Matthew* 19:24). Christ is not saying that virtue is its own—and only—reward. But he is saying what is scarcely more attractive to the mass of men: The rewards of virtue, though certain and sure, are deferred rewards, not the immediately restored prosperity of Job, the new cattle, the new set of children. The rewards of pure intent await one (Christ teaches in *Matthew* and *Luke*) in the "kingdom of heaven."

If Christ's teaching is called the "new dispensation," it is not always an arrangement that softens or liberalizes earlier standards observed by the Hebrews. Christ's whole attitude toward the past and the heavy hand of the past is ambiguous. In one breath he may dismiss the complexities of "clean" and "unclean." But in another he makes certain legal regulations more binding than they had been before. When he denies men the right to put away their wives (*Matthew* 19:7 ff.), he is challenged by reference to the permission to divorce in the laws set up by Moses. His answer is that Moses gave the children of Israel this privilege because he knew the hardness of their hearts. It would seem that, at this point, purity of intent abrogates the old law only to substitute a more demanding one. Perhaps a virtue resting in externals is only an approximation to true virtue. Thus, many things were allowed the Hebrews that cannot be allowed the followers of Christ, whose virtue is of a more developed and integrated sort. (We allow a child certain deviations in behavior that we do not tolerate in an adult. We say that the child is imperceptive in certain directions, and much must be forgiven him.)

The almost impossible demands of the integrated sort of virtue receive direct expression in the saying: "Be ye therefore perfect even as your Father which is in heaven is perfect" (*Matthew* 5:48). This is manifestly a counsel of perfection that many may imitate but none achieve. Men, in "the hardness of their hearts"—which "being translated" is perhaps the weight of habit as much as that of perversity—will often fall short of "the way"; and whenever they do, they return to the realm of law. We do not see this difficulty so clearly in the synoptics as we shall when we turn to the apostle Paul and his dealing with backsliding Christians.

Eschatology: the "Last Things"

Christ's ethical teaching, interpreted by some followers as a flat challenge to the *status quo* dear to the hearts of Sadducees and Pharisees, is but one important aspect of the radiation set up by his having existed at certain times and places. Quite as important as the ethical attitude—though not so immediately attractive to many a modern reader—is the estimate of himself that Christ, by deeds and words, gradually encouraged to take shape in the minds of his intimates. Many an agnostic indicates that he can "take" Christ in the guise of moralist but not in the guise we now turn to: that of Messiah and establisher of a new world. One is free, to be sure, to excerpt from the Gospels the elements one finds attractive. But there is more than an accidental connection between the ethical system and the Messianic suppositions now to be taken up. For the writers of the Gospels, certain loose threads in the ethical speculation of Jesus are tied up firmly only in the Messianic speculation. The evangelists' picture of Christ, as asserted before, is not a thing of "shreds and patches," however richly colored and shifting; it possessed unity for those who first drew it, and we should try to see what this unity was.

What are the loose threads that need tying? They are the ones already noticed in *Job*—not in the framework chapters, 1, 2, and 42, but in the real matter of the book that lies between. Job, recall, was aware (if a little proudly) of an interior righteousness; he did not allow his "friends" to state that secret evil deeds were an explanation of his material misery. Job's real contest is with God. If God is righteous, how are we to explain the earthly lot of many a righteous man? The greatness of *The Book of Job* lies in the statement of this question. Both obvious answers—the speech of Elihu (chaps. 32 to 39) and the thunderclap (chaps. 39 and 40)—seem unsatisfactory. Submission to an inscrutable and even arbitrary power is no "solution"; nor is Job's nearest approach to one altogether satisfying to us —his inner awareness of his virtuous intent.

The prophets too, in terms applicable to the nation rather than to the individual, had posed a similar problem, though it was the reverse of Job's in an important respect. Job was manifestly virtuous; the Israel of the prophets was manifestly sinful. Job asks for a "redeemer" who shall work justice and restore him. Israel's problem posits the need of a "redeemer" who shall supersede justice and lift up Israel from the dust in which it deservedly sits. In both instances, a need was felt for some sort of readjustment of things as they are. (It is a need that led to the perfecting of the figure of Sophia in *The Wisdom of Solomon.*) This need is met—for some persons successfully, for some persons not—by the aspect of Christ's activity which we now consider. In his definition of himself given to his disciples, Christ solves the problem raised by Job and the prophets.

Christ, whose ethical teaching concerns not the righteousness of Israel but the righteousness of individual men, is displayed in the synoptics as the "redeemer" that Job hoped would vindicate him against the judgment of his friends. But, though Christ is represented as having the function of vindicating the individual, it is the individual as envisaged in Christ's ethical teaching. Is there any man who is perfect, as Job judged he was? The answer is: No, not one. (This phrase comes from Psalm 14 and is used by Paul, in *Romans* 3:10, to make this very point.) All men are, instead, in the position of the collective Israel, which deserves stern justice (Amos) and receives mercy after the time of testing and punishment (seen as a grim necessity in *Hosea* and worked out rather precisely in *Isaiah* Chapters 40 ff.). Whatever the purity of the individual, it is a tarnished purity, flawed with the malice and indecision that make the law necessary. In the eyes of the Gospel writers, Christ is more than a teacher. He does for his pupils what teachers, unfortunately, cannot do: he performs a task that is beyond the strength and persistence of his followers. In short, the drama of restoration is no longer one in which the chief characters are God, Israel, and the "rod" (Assyria or Babylon). It now involves these three: Christ (as emissary of God), individual man, and Satan. The "formula" touches both *Job* and the prophets, but it also differs. Unlike *Job*, it is the unrighteous and imperfect man who finds his "redeemer." Unlike the prophets in general, it is no longer a question of saving and restoring a chosen people; it is a question of saving and restoring each created being.

The two formulas run thus: for the prophets, God or his Messiah, the chosen people, and the rod; for the synoptic writers, the Messiah, the individual, and Satan. The shift of emphasis from God to the Messiah and from the chosen people to the individual has been foreshadowed. But the third shift—from Assyria or Babylon, the rod, to Satan, the "adversary"—is, in the Old Testament, foreshadowed only in *Job*, where God gives Satan the power to torment Job but not to destroy him. It also receives a kind of treatment in the passage in *Isaiah* which tells of the fall of the king of Babylon (*Isaiah* 14:4 ff.). Some students of the Bible feel that in passing from the later prophets to this aspect of the New Testament (the emphasis on Satan and the fiery kingdom where he rules over sinners) one passes from a plain, economically stated ethical monotheism to a world in which demons and angels are needlessly multiplied. That such is indeed the effect of the transition again rests with the individual judgment. But in the emergence of Satan and his crew against God, Christ, the angelic army, and man we can—in the figure we use—see one more example of the spiraling movement. Attitudes once relinquished are taken up anew but not in the same context of event and thought. That a world surrounded by beings of light and darkness has been at many times in religious history an attractive, plausible concept is a fact. That this view became attractive to the Hebrews between the close of the Old Testament and the opening of

New Testament days is a special example of this fact; and it merits brief comment.

Where the devils came from was, in Christ's day, no secret. They were the angels who resisted God and were cast from heaven to become, in form of serpent and man-beast composites, the relentless foes of the realization of God's plan. Where the angels came from is, from a literary point of view, a more vexing problem. There are good angels who are messengers for God in *Genesis* and other books of history, but the only hint of evil immortal beings appears in the reference to "the sons of God" who possessed the daughters of the children of men and begat a race of giants (*Genesis* 6:2 and 4). Many trace the demonology of the New Testament and of the Apocryphal Jewish books like *Tobit,* where the demon Asmodeus appears, to contact of the Hebrews during exile and later with another religion, popular in the Persian empire: the religion of the prophet Zoroaster. In this religion the soul of man is seen as a battlefield on which the powers of light and darkness clash. Other persons suppose that Hebrew demonology had its origin in indigenous animism; the gods of streams and hills, denied their meed of worship by the growth of monotheism, became the malicious but unsuccessful enemies of the triumphant Lord and his Messiah.

Just why the existence of such an adversary is attractive is an easier question to answer. When God is the only supernatural being, he must be regarded as the author of evil as well as of good. It is the Lord that must harden Pharaoh's heart and keep the people in Egypt; Job has to ask: "What? shall we receive good at the hand of God, and shall we not receive evil?" (*Job* 2:10.) Such a conception does not trouble people who delight chiefly in narratives displaying the power or mana of a deity. But it is increasingly a source of distress when the pursuit of "wisdom"—philosophic and pre-philosophic—becomes common. How can a deity who is regarded as all-just and all-merciful be the author of that which seduces the will of man and corrupts it? We have seen the writer of *The Wisdom of Solomon* broaching the Platonic solution: that evil is not something positive; it is simply a lack of *being* in those who are at the foot of the ladder which rises up toward perfect being, God. But other Hebrew writings of this same period indicate that this was not a popular solution, and it has not been since; it appears in the thought of detached, contemplative men. In most men, the experience of evil is sensed as something positive, not simply as the negation of all that is good. To most men, then—certainly to the Jews in the period being discussed—the concept of Satan satisfied both an emotional and a logical need. For ordinary people, Satan is emotionally satisfying because the author of evil is to be resisted as a person, just as one, if devout, loves God and Christ as persons. Further, one escapes the shocking implication of the early narratives, that Jehovah is the immediate author of evil. Belief in the power of the Evil One as a solution of the problem of evil raises difficulties of its own; but they do not occur to the author of the synoptics.

This is sufficient to explain the status of Satan in the first-century Jewish imagination. Satan was now master of Gehenna or hell. Gehenna, in the first instance a rubbish heap or place of burning outside the city walls of Jerusalem, is not the same as Sheol. Sheol, remember, was a place where the souls of all the dead went, whatever their virtues or vices when alive. Apparently as a consequence of the Pharisaic contention that the dead were lifted up, a region had to be found for the good dead to exist separate from the evil dead. Belief in two areas where life continued after death—hell and heaven—solved this difficulty. They were areas "known of old" to the followers of the Persian Zoroaster.

Satan, as we see him in the New Testament, had his wiles of direct or indirect assault. He had become, the important point for us, the permanent opposer of God and Christ and was a fixed protagonist in the drama involving God and the Messiah, man, and the "adversary." Dramatically speaking, Satan was more acceptable to the imagination than the "rod" of Assyria or Babylon, which was, after all, simply a tool in the hands of an angry God. He is the foe of all men; more especially, he is the foe of Christ.

In the last hundred years, persons who could still accept Christ as a teacher rejected Christ as the arch-enemy of Satan. All that such a crude contest implied belonged, the rejection ran, to an earlier stage of human history. This fairly recent judgment is understandable; but it does not follow that the Gospels are whole when this struggle between Christ and Satan is cut out or ignored. That the Gospels without Satan are *Hamlet* without Hamlet is not true; but they are certainly *Hamlet* with King Claudius, Gertrude, and Polonius left out—*Hamlet,* that is, with most of the opposing forces omitted. When Jesus is taken to the top of the mountain and offered earthly power, when he is perched on a Temple pinnacle and invited to test God's care by throwing himself down, he is in the presence of a real being; he is not thought of as being tempted by a metaphor for evil or non-being. When, at the end, Jesus tells his disciples that the time has now come when he belongs to "the prince of this world" (*John* 14:30), the Gospel writers do not mean that abstract evil or non-being was now free to work its design on him. They meant that, in their opinion, Christ would immediately face the tools of Satan—the high priest and the Roman procurator—and would presently descend into hell itself and "harrow" it and would bring back from his three days' journey the souls of the patriarchs who did not merit a gloomy asylum.

This was the immediate confrontation of Christ and Satan. That a later confrontation would take place—a final one—is suggested in the so-called "little apocalypse" or revelation of Christ which appears in *Mark,* Chapter 13, *Matthew,* Chapter 21, and *Luke,* Chapter 21. The promise of this apocalypse, which serves as a kind of preliminary sketch of *Revelation,* is that after a time of disaster and persecution, Christ will return in glory to confront Satan and his cohorts, and it will be a meeting to the utter profit of the righteous. Thus the future career imputed to Christ by the synoptists puts into orderly relation two functions of the Messiah that existed illogically side by side in the *both-and* perceptions of Isaiah II, who felt the Messiah must suffer and must also triumph. How he was to do both within the framework of history, Isaiah II does not say. He only knows, by successive flashes of insight, that he is right. To these old insights about the Messiah, the synoptic Gospels contribute the suggestion that there are two stages. The first stage is one in history, in time; and it was terminated by the crucifixion and resurrection. The second stage is one that exists at the end of time and in eternity. (The distinction between time and eternity has been before us ever since God said to Moses, "I am that I am" [*Exodus* 3:14].) The Messiah who appears in history is to be the "suffering servant," the being who is utterly defeated by "the prince of this world" as well as rejected and ignored by the mass of people to whom he, in the first place, came. The Messiah in his other role, that of conqueror and Prince of Peace, will appear only at the end of history. Such a conqueror is also a judge—"Wonderful, Counsellor," as Isaiah has it (*Isaiah* 9:6) —and will distinguish the good men from the evil men, the rams from the he goats in Ezekiel's phrase (*Ezekiel* 34:17). This Messiah will not resemble the Messiah of the first Isaiah at one point; he will not labor to separate a chosen people from all other peoples. Instead, he will come to all peoples. Once the act of judgment is performed, the reign of eternity will begin.

There are subtle consequences of this view of Christ as more than prophet, as the Son of God and the foretold Messiah, that exercise the intellects of Paul and the writer of *John*. But this account suffices for the synoptic writers, the first tellers of the story of Jesus. They but suppose an interim between the first confrontation with Satan, in the time of Herod Antipas and Pilate, and the second and last. It is supposed to be a brief interim during which it will be the duty of the "saints" of the Church to reveal to men the true significance of the death and resurrection of the "prophet" from Galilee. As Christ tells his followers, there will be, in this period, "wars and rumors of wars" (*Mark* 13:7). It will be the duty of the steadfast to bear witness. When their witness is rejected, they may shake the dust of a house or a city from their feet and depart elsewhere.

Any further plan for the founding of a Church that shall testify to Christ during this interim is but sketched in one bold stroke. Christ says to Peter:

> And I say also unto thee, That thou art Peter, and upon this rock I will build my church; and the gates of hell shall not prevail against it. And I will give unto thee the keys of the kingdom of heaven: and whatsoever thou shalt bind on earth shall be bound in heaven: and whatsoever thou shalt loose on earth shall be loosed in heaven. (*Matthew* 17:18-19.)

These statements about Peter's position have, for obvious reasons, been the occasion of dispute and bloodshed in centuries that the Gospel writers, with their expectation of Christ's early return, had no curiosity about.

Nor does the writer of *The Gospel of John* have much curiosity about the prolonged, time-contained history of the Church which was founded on Peter, "the rock." His indifference, we shall see, has another source than the synoptists' lively expectation of an early return. That source is, in a sense, a philosophic one.

CHAPTER XVII

Christ in *The Gospel of John*

IN THE synoptics we have seen Jesus speaking to the multitudes by proverb and parable; we have seen him impressing his intimates by gesture as well as word; and we have seen him fighting on their own grounds and with their own weapons the champions of legalism who are the unconscious allies of "the prince of this world." These views have been through the portals of sight opened by *Mark*, *Matthew*, and *Luke*. There is one portal of sight remaining, provided by *The Gospel of John*. It offers us a view so unlike what we have been observing that many scholars of the "Johannine problem" call it an entirely different one.

Some of the contrasts that lead them to this assertion are these. There is a difference in the arrangement of events leading up to the last week. (There is, however, a considerable agreement among the four Gospels as to what happened during the last week.) As noted, Christ's ministry in *John* is more Judean than Galilean; and it is more exclusively devoted to the disciples and attentive individuals like Nicodemus the Pharisee than in the synoptics, where Christ often addresses large groups of people. Another contrast is the comparative lack of specific detail. *The Gospel of Mark* seems to show us Christ in actual Galilean surroundings, *Matthew* shows us Christ in conflict with various classes of Hebrew society, and *Luke* permits us to see a teacher who needs support and comfort as well as obedience and attention. In comparison, the atmosphere of *John* (up to the last week) lacks these marks. The stage is quite bare; and at its center we see Christ discoursing rather than Christ teaching and acting. And, say the perceivers of difference, the discourses are concerned not with the ethics and eschatology of the synoptics but, first to last, with developing a view of Christ's identity and function that has links with Hellenistic Platonism rather than with traditional Hebrew thought that is direct, "pre philosophic," and naïve.

All these differences indeed exist and must be studied; but the gulf separating *John* from the synoptics is perhaps not so wide and deep as some make it out to be; and it should be remembered that all gulfs and ravines have bottoms and that the terrain they divide is, on a deeper level, still continuous.

The stage is properly set for this Gospel by the opening fourteen verses. "In the beginning was the Word, and the Word was with God, and the Word was God" (*John* 1:1) announces the preoccupations of this writer as clearly as the nativity story announces Luke's accent and the opening genealogy Matthew's. As the first fourteen verses suggest, the "drama" of *John* is, when compared to that of the synoptics, a static one. There is no mounting tension. There is reiterative exposition of the key ideas.

Early in the book Christ is visited secretly at night by the Pharisee Nicodemus and reveals to him in essence all there is to know about his nature and destiny. Their interchange allows one to savor the characteristic tone of *The Gospel of John.* Nicodemus begins by greeting Christ in no uncertain terms: "Rabbi, we know that thou art a teacher come from God: for no man can do these miracles that thou doest, except God be with him" (*John* 3:2). Nicodemus is certainly a Pharisee unlike those we met in the synoptics; he is eager for instruction, and he seems to know already the outlines of the instruction that he is seeking. The ensuing dialogue between Christ and his visitor follows a course that is novel if we read it immediately after *Matthew* or *Luke.* Christ presents his respectful caller with a series of enigmatic remarks which he explains when he is prompted by Nicodemus' questions. He says: "Verily, verily, I say unto thee, Except a man be born again, he cannot see the kingdom of God." Nicodemus asks the indicated question: "How can a man be born when he is old? can he enter the second time into his mother's womb, and be born? Christ gives a more developed explanation:

> Verily, verily, I say unto thee, Except a man be born of water and of the Spirit, he cannot enter into the kingdom of God. That which is born of the flesh is flesh; and that which is born of the Spirit is

> spirit. Marvel not that I said unto thee, Ye must be born again. The wind bloweth where it listeth, and thou hearest the sound thereof, but canst not tell whence it cometh, and whither it goeth: so is every one that is born of the Spirit. (*John* 3:5-8.)

On these lines of initial enigma, question, and instruction the rest of the conversation unfolds. It is the first of several such conversations and the connected discourses of Christ which make up a large part of this Gospel. They are full of difficult remarks, but these remarks differ from the "hard sayings" and the sudden verbal blows that abound in the synoptics. These sayings—like "Let the dead bury their dead" (*Matthew* 8:22)—are usually "hard" because they affront habitual ways of thinking and acting; they demand a response that the majority of men can scarcely make. In the majority of instances they do not baffle one; they simply demand a great deal of the hearer. (There are enigmatic sayings in the synoptics, but these have to do with Christ's gradual unveiling of his identity and purpose; they may even be feints to put his enemies off the scent.)

The difficult remarks in *John* are hard sayings in a very different sense. They are difficult because, almost from start to finish, Christ is presented as concerned with a certain rather specialized sort of meditation on the process of redemption. Since it is not primarily a redemption in terms of "last things"—a redemption that a Jewish audience, after all, was well prepared to grasp—Christ's speculation is expressed in often long and connected discourses. They are discourses that lack the vehemence, the wry humor, and the homely touch of his remarks in the synoptics. In *John*, there is an approach to the mood of the lecture room, though the actual scene may be the tomb of Lazarus or a dining chamber at Bethany. It is the mood of the lecture room because Christ's friends often play the role of helpful, intelligent pupils who raise their hands when a point is not clear and by an apt question enable their teacher to develop his theory. In *John*, however, the "pupils" often give their clues inadvertently.

A person who wishes to savor at its sharpest this variation in emotional temper between the synoptics and *John* should read two stories that have a basic situation in common: *John* 4:1-42, and the synoptic accounts in *Matthew* 15:21-28 and, slightly differently, in *Mark* 7:24-30. The stories are not identical. *Mark* tells of a "Syrophenician" woman whose daughter has a devil, and *Matthew* calls this person "a woman of Canaan." To her plea for help, Christ returns a brutal answer: "Let the children first be filled: for it is not meet to take the children's bread, and to cast it unto the dogs" (*Mark* 7:27). The "children" are the Jews, and the "dogs" are the outsiders, among whom the woman is numbered. From acquaintance with the synoptics, we see that the remark is directed at the comprehension of the disciples, not at the woman's. The woman persists; she catches up Christ's words with dexterity worthy of a Pharisee debating in the Temple area and says: "Yes, Lord: yet the dogs under the table eat of the children's crumbs" (*Mark* 7:28). Christ's relenting remark, as *Matthew* has it, is brief and ties the final knot on the whole story: "O woman, great is thy faith: be it unto thee even as thou wilt" (*Matthew* 15:28). This remark points to the lack of belief among the "children" for whom the banquet is spread, but it does not expatiate on that lack of belief.

The story in *John* concerns a Samaritan woman who, though a believer in God, is in Jewish eyes almost as much an outsider as the woman of the other tales. But Christ does not dwell on her origin (though the woman does); and he performs an incidental wonder, that of knowing the woman has had five husbands. It is wonder that leads to her conversion. The reader who comes from the synoptic treatment of similar material will certainly note how the *John* anecdote is encrusted with material representing the constant tendency of Christ in this Gospel to read a hidden, specialized meaning into whatever chance presents. Thus, Jesus says of the water which the woman offers him:

> Whosoever drinketh of this water shall thirst again: but whosoever drinketh of the water that I shall give him shall never thirst; but the water that I shall give him shall be in him a well of water springing up into everlasting life. (*John* 4:13-14.)

When the woman hails him as a prophet and remarks that she does not worship at Jerusalem but at the Samaritan holy place, Jesus launches out on an address directed, one may say, more at the thoughtful, devout reader of the Gospel than at the simple woman beside the well.

> Woman, believe me, the hour cometh, when ye shall neither in this mountain, nor yet at Jerusalem, worship the Father. Ye worship ye know not what: we know what we worship: for salvation is of the Jews. But the hour cometh, and now is, when the true worshippers shall worship the Father in spirit and in truth: for the Father seeketh such to worship him. God is a Spirit: and they that worship him must worship him in spirit and in truth. (*John* 4:21-24.)

The same tendency appears in Christ's reply to the simple command of his disciples: "Master, eat." He answers, again with the effect of directing his remarks to the cognizant readers of the Gospel rather than to the simple men who have returned with provisions for a meal: "I have meat to eat that ye know not of." The disciples ask confusedly, "Hath any man brought him aught to eat?" (This question is parallel to the initial confusion of Nicodemus.) Prompted, Christ delivers a careful explanation of his remark that begins: "My meat is to do the will of him that sent me, and to finish his work" (*John* 4:31-34).

In such a book, the excitement of a gradual and even grudging revelation is absent. Recall how, in *Matthew,* the knowledge that Christ is something more than a teacher or a Zealot is first possessed by the disciples; recall how failure to grasp the truth about him leads to the confusion of the masses on Palm Sunday and the enmity of the important Hebrews. In *John,* even the impetus of the concluding chapters is diminished by the extended instruction (chaps. 13-17) which Christ gives his disciples on the eve of his arrest. In lieu of the tension of the synoptics, the writer offers one the full satisfaction of his curiosity as to Christ's identity. "Who do men say that I the Son of man am?" In the synoptics, the answers to this question are, as we have seen, glancing, ambiguous, and suggestive;

and they are usually made in language and images drawn from Hebrew life and tradition. The answers in *John* are full, explicit, and (by comparison with the synoptics) exhaustive. Especially is the language employed not the "pre-philosophic" language used by Christ in the Temple arguments and along the highways. Instead, it is often a reflection of a collection of terms that lived on, in Roman days, in the centers of Hellenistic culture. The writer of *John* draws on the *lingua franca* of Platonic or Neoplatonic converse; he makes use of coins of philosophic interchange that passed easily from hand to hand.

Further, the discourses of *John* are not concerned with satisfying a variety of needs. It is as though the writer judged that Christ's ethical teaching had been fully enough presented in the other three Gospels; it is as though he judged that Christ's estimate of himself as a savior in terms and images supplied by the Hebrew tradition had also been sufficiently rehearsed. Indeed, it is as if one task remained at the late date at which he wrote, somewhere between 90 and 115 A.D.: the description of Christ's nature and function in terminology that would illuminate a group of readers ignorant of the Hebrew discussions of "last things." If this group was to be touched, it would have to be by manipulation of words and phrases already in their minds.

This task was not, by the year 90, an unrecognized one. Ever since the "gift" of Christ had been—to use a traditional phrase—"rejected" by the Jews, Paul and many other missionaries had moved outward from the Palestinian world and into a pagan one. Paul, who boasted that he was "made all things to all men" (*I Corinthians* 9:22), did not hesitate to jettison strictly Jewish cargo that would keep him from sailing into foreign harbors. By the time of the writing of *John*, Paul was long dead; but, because he and other teachers had brought their essential cargo into many ports, the Roman world was full of men who were, *in some sense*, followers of Christ. Two persecutions (64 and 93 A.D.) had already tried to stamp out the people whose "mystery" did not permit them to sacrifice to Caesar, the living divinity. It had already been seen by

Peter as well as by Paul that converted Gentiles could not be Christians in a Jewish sense, either in custom or in the terminology they employed. The language that commended Christ to potential Jewish converts would not move the hearts of potential Gentile converts. The language that would stir these hearts had to be sought out; and in a later chapter we shall see the apostle Paul at work on this task. It is the same task, many years later, that concerns the writer of *John*. The ethical precepts of Christianity were plain enough and did not call for further reworking; they would not fall strangely on ears that had heard Stoic instructions. But the problem of exposing properly the nature and function of Christ, of finding a substitute for the passionate and disorderly Hebrew eschatological speculation of the synoptics—this problem remained.

And it was a problem that required immediate solution. Paul's explanations had not "pegged" the value of Christ's sacrifice. Other valuations were being set up; and whether inflationary or deflationary, all were beside the true mark. The Jews denied that Christ had been, at best, more than a traditional Hebrew teacher, a mortal. Christians of pagan origin were developing the theory that Christ had never really been a created mortal—that he was a celestial simulacrum that passed before the eyes of his followers. Thus, what Paul's letters had not permanently offset, this final narrative of Christ's life tried to offset: the danger that the figure of the real Christ who was at once human and divine would be "captured" and exploited by the various philosophical sects in the world to which Christ's story and example had been brought.

One of the most dangerous sects was, as later Christian history tells us, that which told or reinterpreted the story of Christ in terms provided by Platonic or Neoplatonic philosophy. This philosophy contributed to the terms employed by the writer of *John* when he reports the discourses of Christ. Platonic terms, as the writings of the orthdox St. Augustine show, were highly attractive to Christians who felt the need of supporting the structure erected by faith with buttresses of a philosophic sort. Indeed, Platonic language was as attractive to the writer of *John* as it had been, two or more centuries before, to the Hellenistic Jew who used it, in *The Wisdom of Solomon,* to explain and defend his traditional faith. But as with that earlier writer, so with the writer of *John,* and to a higher degree. Use of Platonic language does not mean automatic acceptance of the full Platonic comment on the religious questions being handled. The full Platonic comment on the Christian story was the very comment the writer of *John* wished to deny: that the material world is not real and that God or the One projects into the visible world one more shadow who talks, suffers like a man, and is called Jesus, but who is really no man at all—who is, instead, only an "emanation" of the divine One. At the end of the first century, those who possessed secret or special knowledge were called Gnostics. Some of these, apparently, judged that the projection of the appearance of Jesus into the visible world took place simply to draw the fancies of simple men away from their gross dependence on illusion, matter tainted with non-being. The effect of the phantasm of Jesus was to fix human fancies, if possible, on the Real: the One that has absolute being. This explanation does not provide the writer of *John* with the meaning of Christ's existence. It does give him terms which can be substituted for the Hebrew eschatological terms and images which were inoperative at places in the Roman world.

Despite similarity of language, *The Gospel of John* denies, in its opening verses, what Platonizing Christians were probably saying about Christ. *John* has it that Christ the Word was "in the world" actually (*John* 1:10); his coming was not a magic-lantern projection that deluded men into believing they had seen a being who spoke to them of matters that had been secret or unknown before. Christ does indeed speak of such matters. But he was no emanation of the One, as indeed does the "word," the Sophia, of *The Wisdom of Solomon* sometimes seem to be. He, the Word, was "made flesh and dwelt among us" (*John* 1:14). No insistence could be more flat, and thus is rejected what Platonism would be likely to teach us about Christ's identity and mode of existence. Indeed, this taking-on of humanity that ended in an actual crucifixion is, in Paul's language, "unto the Jews a stumbling-block and unto the Greeks a foolishness" (*I Corinthians* 1:22); nevertheless, for the writer of *John* as well as for other Christians, it is an irreducible fact. Christ lived and breathed; whatever the insinuations of Platonizing Gnostics, the death he suffered was actual.

But also actual is the existence of Christ in eternity, an existence that the synoptics touch briefly when they see the end of history and time at the second coming of Christ, and which they also presuppose when they speak of Jesus as "the son of God." As the verses of *John* have it: "In the beginning was the Word, and the Word was with God, and the Word was God. The same was in the beginning with God" (*John* 1:1-2). For this Gospel, the contemplation of the Word as a permanent element in the framework of things is as important as study of what Christ did when in human form. Such contemplation does not cancel what the other Gospels present (Christ as mortal man or Christ as Messiah in triumph); but it completes. To express the relation of *John* to the other Gospels, one might borrow Christ's own words: "I come not to destroy but to fulfill."

Because *The Gospel of John* is concerned with the eternal, abiding aspect of Christ's relation to man, it has sometimes been called "the spiritual Gospel." It ignores, in part, the temporary bonds set up in Galilee between Jesus and special human beings. It seeks to underline the relationship that exists—or can exist—between Christ and all human beings, at all times. *John's* reports of the discourses display recurrent figures of speech that describe this unaltering relation. Christ is the Door, he is the Way, he is the Water of Life. The concern of this "spiritual Gospel" is not with the immediate drama involving the historical Christ, the people to whom he in the first place came, and the "adversary" Satan. It is the same drama viewed "under the aspect of eternity," with the emphasis not on the drama as it took place in Galilee and Jerusalem (with the exception of the last chapters) but as it always takes place, or *can* always take place. The "persons in the drama" (Christ, man, and the devil) are still the same; but our perception of them is altered. Perhaps that altered perception led in the first place to the terminology and the figures of speech peculiar to *John.* Christ the Word, who aided in the shaping of the world and who was physically a man at one time, is a being as available to men of a later day as he was to the comparatively small number who knew him well. We are in the place of the Samaritan woman at the well and can drink of the Water of Life whenever we wish. *John* suggests that Christ waits eternally to be found by Nicodemus or other seekers, whether they come by night or day.

Since Christ is the bread, the water, the light (all metaphors indicating that Christ has being and is contrasted to that which does not have being), salvation in this Gospel is not so closely tied to a set of specific events in history. Here there is a contrast to synoptic eschatological speculation where, at a certain point in time, hell is "harrowed" and, at another certain point in time, righteous and just men receive their dues from the Messiah as judge. In *John,* salvation is a process possible at any point in history, once the identity and function of the Word have been revealed and accepted. Each man has, at any time, the opportunity to be "born again." Christ said to Nicodemus: "Except a man be born again, he cannot see the kingdom of God" (*John* 3:3). Here "the kingdom of God," though the possibility of a "latter day" is not excluded, is conceived of as present. This suggestion, as a matter of fact, has its parallel in *Luke.* Luke, for all his interest in "last things," reports this interchange.

> And when he [Jesus] was demanded of the Pharisees, when the kingdom of God should come, he answered them and said, The kingdom of God cometh not with observation: neither shall they say, Lo here! or lo there! for, behold, the kingdom of God is within you. (*Luke* 17:20-21.)

If this kingdom is "within you," it is supposedly a state of being potential in each man at each moment of his existence. By an act of will or by suddenly gaining access to proper knowledge, each man can call this "kingdom of God" into actual existence.

Such an event must be what, in *John's* language, is called the rebirth of the water (baptism) and the Spirit. It is an about-face little dependent on the reversal of material conditions involved in the advent of the kingdom of heaven that are presupposed by the Beatitudes (*Matthew* 5:3-11). There it is suggested that the meek and the poor in spirit need not look for any striking adjustment of their fortunes in this world; only in eternity, or at the second coming of Christ, can they expect a merited reward. The entrance into the enjoyment of the kingdom of God is not, in *John,* dependent on any set of striking external events. The writer is chiefly concerned with a quiet reversal carried on within each man. This reversal is, one may say, the conclusion of a line of thought that begins with Hosea. If right intent is all, then the results thereof will not be found in external activity but will be interior to each person; and the "rewards" of virtue for which Job pined in vain and which, in *Matthew,* are deferred till the final battle with the "adversary" are in *John* immediately available to each man. In the winking of an eye a man is reborn of the water and the Spirit, and his rebirth requires the confirmation of no outward token or material prosperity. The last judgment will but set the seal on an act already long performed and profited by. "It is the spirit that quickeneth; the flesh profiteth nothing . . ." (*John* 6:63). Life after the manner of the flesh is life according to the law—or, as Platonists would say, life that looks toward the foot of the ladder and not toward the top rung. Life according to the spirit is life stirred by the knowledge of what Christ is and what he offers.

"And ye shall know the truth, and the truth shall make you free" (*John* 8:32). Forms of the verb *to know* appear without ceasing in this Gospel, an emphasis central to its view of Christ's teaching. To *know* the identity of Christ is the essential human act. Once men "know," they are "free"—free of the law and free of the attractions of that which is not of the highest excellence. The keynote of the legalistic version of the good life is: "Thus do." For the sake of contrast, one may say that the keynote of the synoptics is: "Thus desire and will." The burden of *John* is: "Know, and the rest shall be added unto you."

Perhaps we can define the kind of knowledge the writer of *John* has in mind, and distinguish it from what passed for knowledge among the Gnostics, by noting another saying in this Gospel. Christ says: "A new commandment I give unto you, That ye love one another; as I have loved you, that ye also love one another" (*John* 13:34). "Love," we recall, is also the term which sums up the fairly complex ethics of *Matthew*. The knowledge conveyed so extensively in *John* does not, like certain kinds of Gnostic or Platonic teaching of which we hear, draw a man away from the world of human contacts and ordinary occupation. The issue of that knowledge is not contempt for men and the world or indifference to them; it is this "new commandment," love of one's fellows. In the dubious but useful language of one school of psychology, this is but the "reflex action" of ethical activity that follows upon the knowledge of what Christ offers every man at every moment.

Those who wish to Hellenize *John* have, it is plain, a case. Christ offers rebirth and a consequent state of inner peace to every man. Did not the "mysteries" offer something like this? And did not the pagan sages insist that the clue to the good life they were offering was knowledge which would be able to end desire (Stoic) or regulate it (Epicurean)? Hebrew "ways" can be divided between doing right (legalistic) and desiring aright (the purity of intent); and both ignore the primacy of knowledge in ethical activity. But to differentiate the knowledge in *John* from the *gnosis* offered by Hellenic philosophies is part of the justice we owe the Fourth Gospel. The teachings of Plato himself are supported by invented myths, explanations accepted by both Socrates and his hearers as short cuts to knowledge and no more. The speculation available in *John* is immersed in a different context. At one point the writer insists: "And he that saw it bare record, and his record is true: and he knoweth that he saith true, that ye might believe" (*John* 19:35). The Christ who offers his followers special knowledge is not, in the opinion of the one who reports the discourses, a Platonic myth, a contrivance that helps clarify an intellectual point. He is one with the good shepherd sketched by Ezekiel (*Ezekiel* 34:11 ff.), he is the door, he is the "true vine" (*John,* chap. 15). And it is not with the accents of a Socratic mythmaker that Christ speaks of his approaching "glorification," his crucifixion.

> Verily, verily, I say unto you, Except a corn of wheat fall into the ground and die, it abideth alone: but if it die, it bringeth forth much fruit. He that loveth his life shall lose it; and he that hateth his life in this world shall keep it unto life eternal. (*John* 12:24-25.)

Here ideal conceptions mingle in an inextricable way with the regret that "glorification" is only thus attainable. This declaration is more detached than the analogous one in the synoptics: "O my Father, if it be possible, let this cup pass from me: nevertheless, not as I will, but as thou wilt" (*Matthew* 26:39). But the declaration in *John* is not utterly detached. Marks of the strong human personality we know more vividly in the synoptics remain.

Indeed, such marks, neglected in our analysis of the approximations to theology in *John,* are fairly abundant. Narratives peculiar to *John* sometimes affirm qualities of character displayed in the synoptics. Christ is a doer of works as well as a purveyor of ideal knowledge. He ekes out a waning supply of wine at Cana (*John* 2:1-11); as we have seen, he reads at a glance that the Samaritan woman has had five husbands; he cures the man who is not able to enter the "troubled waters of Bethesda" (*John,* chap. 5). At moments, the reader will feel himself surrounded by the aura he knows well from the synoptics. But, to be judicious, he must also recognize that the similar material exists not for its intrinsic interest (as in the synoptics) but as a point of departure for a discourse urging upon him once more the identity of Christ: he is the eternal, ever-present "Way" or "Door." The healing of the lame man on the Sabbath introduces a prolonged dispute between Jesus and the legalists that permits Christ to expatiate on the relation between himself and his father rather than offer some epigram on purity of intent, as we should expect in the first three Gospels (*John* 5:17 ff.).

Even the most celebrated "act" peculiar to *John,* the raising of Lazarus from the dead, is not presented primarily for its wonder but as one more occasion for inculcating a lesson on the nature of Christ. When Christ hears of the death of Lazarus, he says: "This sickness is not unto death, but for the glory of God, that the Son of God might be glorified thereby" (*John* 11:4). The conversation before the tomb is opened gives him the chance for the following assertion:

> I am the resurrection, and the life: he that believeth in me, though he were dead, yet shall he live: and whosoever liveth and believeth in me shall never die. (*John* 11:25-26.)

What Mary is finally led to is a confession of faith: "I believe that thou art the Christ, the Son of God, which should come into the world" (*John* 11:27). Yet, in justice to the real complexity of the record of such matters in *John,* one must note, even in the midst of this clear exposition of doctrine, effects that insist on the humanity of Christ (e.g., *John* 11:33-38). Jesus here is no master conducting an abstract exposition; he is in the midst of bereaved mortals and he himself is bereaved.

Finally, the collective crucifixion story would be poorer if we lacked details that *John* presents (*John* 19:25-27). The human imagination always sees, at the foot of the cross, Mary the mother of Jesus supported by the disciple John; this Gospel has placed them there.

In the long run, one must perceive that *John* is joined to the other books as well as set apart from them. With some justice it has been said that this Gospel is not so much another "life" of Jesus as a meditation on that life. It is a meditation that lets its full knowledge of Christ's identity appear at every turn of the story. It is a meditation that often subordinates the humanity of Christ to his divinity. The results of this meditation should not be minimized. But no facile conclusion, such as that here we have a Hebrew Zealot or Essene Platonized, is judicious. The language of Platonism is used, but it is used to depict, for non-Hebrew eyes, a being who did not know Plato and whose knowledge, humanly speaking, came by other channels. These channels, we have seen, take their rise in the sandy wastes across which the Hebrew nomads drove their flocks or on the sides of the mountain where Moses saw the burning bush and listened to the thunder. Christ could be made comprehensible to the Hellenic-Roman world, but he did not come from that world. He came from the world through which we have been finding our way. The paths we have gone along are strange to some tastes, and we have seen them finally lead to the figure that was able to move the wills of the Greeks and the Romans and those who remained when the Greeks and the Romans were gone.

The effects of the figure of Christ are involved in the "complex of ideas" which we call Christianity and, to an extent, Western culture. They are understood badly without knowledge of their cause. We know that our knowledge of their cause is incomplete. But we can say with assurance that the cause is the being who brought into a single focus many aspects of Hebrew traditions. To suppose that Christ was merely an ethical teacher with no Messianic hopes or that he was a Zealot whose career was "adopted" by Paul and worked over to suit that apostle's tastes is not to come nearer the "historical Jesus." It is but to substitute other hypotheses about Jesus for the ancient hypotheses held by the Gospel writers. Their ideas, it can be shown, are not developed with the rigor that some readers would desire. Plainly, also, one set of hypotheses (the synoptists') takes a fairly literal and traditionally Jewish view of Christ's identity and function, whereas the other approaches knowledge of Christ through channels of apprehension that are called either "mystical" or philosophical. But the person who wishes to subscribe to modern unfavorable criticism of the Gospels should at least bear in mind that the hypotheses of the Gospel writers about Jesus are those that have "made the difference"—or a great deal of the difference—between two periods of the civilization to which we belong. This difference is a fact that any student of Western culture has to reckon with. Certainly we who live in Western culture and hope it will be prolonged must reckon with these hypotheses. We do well to try to see them and their shaping work clearly, with the marks it has left on our society and, even though we may not be aware, on our own habits of thought. What we expect of existence and look for in the future is often a prolongation of the Gospel hypotheses, even though the language we use to express our hopes may conceal their origin. But the kingdom of God is still the kingdom of God, though we seem to be talking, at various points on the globe, of New Deals, Five-Year Plans—though we discuss our personal happiness in terms of socially adjusted egos rather than those of the "single eye" and Christian love.

The writer of *John* concludes his book more truly than he knows; or perhaps it is some commentator who adds the last two verses of the book:

> This is the disciple which testifieth of these things, and wrote these things: and we know that his testimony is true. And there are also many other things which Jesus did, the which, if they should be written every one, I suppose that even the world itself could not contain the books that should be written. Amen. (*John* 21:24-25.)

The world is "full of books" that venerate Christ or study him as an enigma. But of all these books, the Gospels present—not altogether clearly, not altogether consistently—the image that has "taken."

CHAPTER XVIII

The Acts of the Apostles

THE *ACTS OF THE APOSTLES* is a fairly continuous narrative which begins with the ascension of Christ. It falls into two parts. The first concerns the Church or the community of believers as it existed in Jerusalem (*c.* 30-44 A.D.). The second concerns the Church as its contacts were widened by the missionary efforts of Paul and many others (44-*c.* 60 A.D.). *Acts* is a story, the second volume of a work by Paul's disciple, the Greek-speaking "beloved physician" Luke, written to show what manner of men these Christians were whom Nero in 64 A.D. thought worthy of torture and death. The events related have, like the four Gospels, the Roman world for their background and, in the first part, the Palestinian world for their foreground.

Acts is a work of history. But, as with the other sections of history in the Bible, it is history without the paraphernalia that we today need for a ready understanding of a distant period. It is history without more than incidental reference to the contemporary world and its events and customs of thought and action that help explain the movements of events actually recorded. This story, which belongs to Peter at first and which is then transferred to Paul, is still very much history as the priestly editors of the Pentateuch understood it: a collection of narratives dovetailed to make a sequence covering the extent of time involved and, much more important, illustrating a certain view of history.

Modern students try to gain a rounded, fuller view of what the early Christian community was and how the early missionary effort won its successes—successes great in regions that Paul did not visit as well as in those he did. Such students regret the restricted view of the early Church that Luke takes. They would like to hear more about Apollos and other persons who merely lurk in the background of this collection of narratives. This regret resembles that felt by readers of Old Testament history who are moved to lament the priestly bias which may reduce the account of historically important periods to a few verses (e.g., the account of the prosperous reign of the Northern king, Jeroboam II, in *II Kings* 14:23-29). In conse-

CHART 13. Events, *The Acts of the Apostles*

THE CHURCH		PALESTINE		ROME	
29-33	A.D. Crucifixion				
37-38	Conversion of Paul			37-41	Caligula
39	Paul's first visit to Jerusalem	39	Deposition of Herod Antipas		
39-44	Paul in Syria, Galatia, and Antioch	41-44	Judea an independent kingdom under Herod Agrippa I, grandson of Herod the Great	41-54	Claudius
44	Paul's second visit to Jerusalem				
45-47	First journey				
48	Jerusalem council				
49-51	Second journey (Greece)	50	Herod Agrippa II: king over a small portion; dependence on Rome	50	Expulsion of Jews from Rome
51-54	Paul in Asia	52	Felix procurator		
55	Winter in Corinth				
55	Arrest in Jerusalem			54-69	Nero
55-57	Imprisonment in Caesarea	57	Festus procurator		
57-58	Voyage to Rome				
60	End of first Roman imprisonment				
64	Traditional time of the deaths of Peter and Paul in Rome			64	Burning of Rome: persecutions

quence, a fuller account of the first decades of the Christian Church has often to rest on the shaky props of inference and parallel. Moreover, *Acts,* like Old Testament books of history, has its special bias. It is history not for its own sake—the kind of history that Roman historians were approximating—but in the service of demonstrating a religious awareness, of pointing out the workings of the Holy Spirit in certain events singled out from a multitude of events. It has, then, some of the strength and limitations of Old Testament history.

The similarities cannot fail to strike the reader. In *Acts*, the concern is with Peter and Paul and other men less prominent as instruments of the Holy Spirit. This Holy Spirit was the Paraclete or Comforter which Christ had promised his followers when they were disturbed by the thought of his departure (*John* 14:16 ff.). The second chapter of *Acts* tells us how this Spirit descends in the likeness of cloven flames on the heads of the members of the community in Jerusalem. Its first "wonder" is to work the miracle of the "speaking with tongues"; later and more importantly, it furnishes the ardor for the far-flung missions. This concern of *Acts* with the working of the Holy Spirit leads to this understandable result: Events are retold if they help to answer the question, How, precisely, did the Holy Spirit work? The book concerns chosen heroes in relation to this moving force, just as Old Testament history is concerned with chosen heroes in relation to the power of Jehovah as it moves them to various sorts of action. In reading Old Testament history, persons who have a variety of curiosities about the past are often irritated by the proportion they find there. For example, the account of the reforming king of Judah, Josiah, is full-blown when it tells of the "discovery" of the books of law in the Temple, and niggardly when it tells of the political and military aspects of Josiah's reign: "Now the rest of the acts of Josiah, and all that he did, are they not written in the book of the chronicles of the king of Judah?" (*II Kings* 23:28.) Such dismissals teach the reader that there are things which he would like to know but cannot expect the priestly editors to present to him; their interests are intense, but they are also narrow.

So, to a lesser degree, are the interests of Luke. Human curiosity would like to be better informed as to the actual setting up and organizing of the Church as a temporal institution. Such curiosity would probably be willing to sacrifice the summary of Israel's history that is Stephen's last address (*Acts*, chap. 7) and Peter's repetitious account of the animals let down in a sheet (*Acts*, chap. 11). But one's irritation can be checked if he realizes what Luke's principle of selection is. It is a principle that makes him regard the address of Stephen as central to his tale and the appointment of the deacons (*Acts* 6:1-4), about which we would like to know more, as incidental. Stephen's address and Paul's various addresses at Antioch, Lystra, and Athens are, for Luke, testimonies to what Christians are and what they offer to the Jewish and Roman worlds. Luke judges that Christians are, first and foremost, a group of people in whom the Holy Spirit works. Much less important to him are the particular forms of church organization which that Spirit has set up in one place or another. Nor is there a need to cover all missionary activity once the nature of that activity has been displayed in the career of Paul.

Along with this view which limits and guides the historian, there is a naïveté of presentation that continues the directness and simplicity of Old Testament historical narrative. Luke presents a narrative without either apology or preparation. The colors of his stories resemble Old Testament colors; they are fresh and strong, and they do not create the effects of blending and shading found in the work of more sophisticated historians. Such a story as that in *Acts*, Chapter 14, which tells of the encounter of Paul and Barnabas at Lystra with a pagan population, is told flatly. Paul restores to life a man apparently dead, and the grateful pagans wish to honor the two Jews as gods—as Jupiter and Mercury who, in Greek legend, were wont to visit men and benefit them unawares. Paul denies these honors passionately, and the story is done. To it, as to other narratives in *Acts*, the mind of the reader is busy supplying overtones, seeing this encounter of the new religion and the old pagan faith as but another incident in the very complex and confused development and interplay of religions in the ancient world. But whatever the comment one adds, the accent of Luke's narratives always insists on the crucial importance of the exploits of Paul and his companions since they contributed to the expansion of the one true faith. Likewise, Paul's exploits are not simply samples of fascinating and typical encounters between a new faith and older modes of thought—

encounters which are legion, as the student of comparative religion knows. Yet, if one is to read *Acts* with both sympathy and comprehension, it is well to recall the discrimination made in other eras, between "sacred history," which dealt with the long chain of events having the life of Jesus for its central link, and all other sequences of events that might unfold in Greece or Italy or France or our own country. Today we tend to minimize this difference, and some doubt that the Hebrew-Christian story is a record utterly different from the other records we know. But we must see, whatever our own judgment at this point, that the writer of *Acts* would reject the modern conception with all his energy. The deeds he is telling of were not, to employ the phrase of his hero Paul, "done in a corner" (*Acts* 26:26); and these deeds are, in his estimation, more important for mankind than any events that Greek and Roman historians can narrate. Luke's Lord was like no other god, and the records of the Lord's dealings with his chosen followers could not resemble any other records. In consequence of this certainty, the tone of *Acts* frequently reminds a sophisticated person of a small-town man asserting the merits of his village. It is an attitude vulnerable to satiric criticism, but it has an air of clarity and conviction that satiric criticism cannot re-create.

For these reasons, the religious preoccupations and the tone of *Acts* prolong those of Old Testament history. But *Acts* at two points is a different kind of work. It is not the end product of the tortuous process of accumulation and arrangement in the Pentateuch to which the letters JEHDP refer. It is not a blend of oral tradition centuries long and several varieties of early written record. Instead, the *materials* with which Luke worked resemble those used by a modern historian. For the deeds of Paul, Luke had Paul's own account or the accounts of Paul's early companions. He even had the testimony of his own eyes and ears, as the pronoun "we" in the second half of *Acts* indicates (e.g., *Acts* 16:11 and 20:14-15). For the earlier events in Jerusalem, he had—his own position in early Christian activity would suggest—the opportunity to speak with and know the important actors. Luke's association with Paul began about 50 A.D., and the paths of the early missionaries often crossed and certainly led them back to Jerusalem, where the Christian community was presided over by James, the brother of Jesus. Thus, though what Luke makes of his materials offers to view the similarities with Old Testament history already noted, his book is, one may say, his own creation. Plainly, he repeats narratives that modern historians would be critical of; but they are narratives less distant in time from the events they concern than the stories contained in the Gospels, and certainly than those appearing in the Pentateuch. This nearness to the events aids Luke and gives an effect of unity to the two-section history that has Peter and Paul for central figures. Naturally, such an effect of unity was not within the grasp of the editors of the Pentateuch. The final insights about God and Israel held by the priestly editors were at odds with the tone and point of the hero tales which they had to work with. An easy accord exists between Luke's conception of the role of the early Church and the materials he had to present.

Development of the Church

The Acts of the Apostles points plainly to aspects of the Roman world that have changed. But certain things have not changed. The political and religious state of the Roman world remains as sketched in Chapter XIV. The Roman rulers are determined to consolidate the "peace" that ended the Roman civil wars at the time of Augustus, and they will not take no for answer. They make little distinction between the Jews and the followers of Christ who, unwillingly at first, separate themselves from the Jews. The Roman rulers have no interest whatever in the doctrinal disputes that thrust Jew and Christian farther and farther apart until any sort of reunion is unthinkable. In *Acts*, most of the Romans we encounter stand silent and watchful, with their eyes seeking to find out trouble. This is particularly their pose in Jerusalem where the Jews keep remembering one conquering deliverer, Judas Maccabaeus, and are eager for the appearance of another. As noted, the Romans finally cleaned out this trouble spot in 70 A.D. When they did, they set up two sorts of Diasporas or "scatterings." The scattered Jews sought substitutes for the national integrity that could never be reconstituted. Their subsequent history shows that the people found a substitute for the Temple in the observance of the law and a study of the law and the prophets. Such observance and study supported the conviction that the Jews were a "peculiar people" even though their promised land was now occupied by other races. The scattered Christians, whose dispersion, enforced sometimes and sometimes desired, had begun about thirty years before the fall of Jerusalem, soon transformed a bitter necessity into a golden opportunity. Unlike the Jews, they set to work evangelizing wherever they had to flee. But the Roman power did not distinguish between these two scatterings; when fear drove, the Romans scourged Jew and Christian alike. Did not Jew and Christian, in the city of Rome and elsewhere, set up communities that stood apart from conventional custom and religion? (Among Paul's earliest converts at Corinth were two Jews, Aquila and Priscilla, who had fled from persecution at Rome.) Not until a later day were hostile Roman rulers able to distinguish between the lesser threat of Judaism and the greater threat from Christ's followers, who did not modestly ask, as did the Jews, the chance merely to exist apart in a hostile world but who were determined to convert that world. This determination led to events lying outside the time range of the New Testament; but the mixture of humility, constancy, and martyrdom that forms a large part of the history of Christianity in its first three centuries is not at odds with what *Acts* shows us.

Important as it is to be aware of the pressure of the "Roman peace" on the early Christian community, we must also reckon with the pressure of the immediate Jewish community. In the period covered by *Acts*, the Herodian family continued to be an offense to many of the Jews over whom they ruled. Agrippa I or "Herod Agrippa" governed the city of Jerusalem and other large areas from 41 to 44 A.D. and is the "Herod" under whom the persecution mentioned in *Acts*, Chapter 12, took place. He was eager to please both his Jewish subjects and his Roman overlords. He observed the externals of

Jewish piety and incited a persecution of the hated followers of Christ; he acted as a Hellenizing ruler should by presiding over games in honor of Caesar. His death as described in *Acts* 12:20-23 resembles an account of the same event given by the famous Jewish historian Josephus 37?-95? A.D.) and is at least an indication of the light in which the early Christian viewed him. His son, Agrippa II, is the ruler who, along with the Roman procurator Festus, hears Paul's defense at Caesarea (*Acts,* chaps. 25 and 26) and who says to Paul: "Almost thou persuadest me to be a Christian" (*Acts* 26:28). The remainder of this man's career—his association with the Roman armies that moved on Jerusalem a few years later—indicates that his comment was ironical; he would take no step that would endanger his standing with his Roman supporters or unnecessarily affront his touchy Jewish subjects.

The social groups in Jerusalem and throughout the country prolong the divisions of Christ's day: in the large city the Herodians and Sadducees and Pharisees; roaming up and down the land, the Zealots. Most of these opposed the new sect, for it had no gifts of either profit or power to offer them. But in the background of *Acts* we see shrewd men who regard the new sect as something to be exploited. Thus, the Samaritan Simon Magus tries to purchase with money the power of the Holy Ghost. But the Christians did not pass beyond the opposition of orthodox Jewish teachers when they left Jerusalem behind them. Wherever the Christian missionaries went—the experiences of Paul suggest—men zealous for the law and the prophets lay in wait to argue and create danger.

In this Roman and Jewish world, the Christian Church began its existence. The early chapters of *Acts* show us that the community was scarcely aware that it was a church. Disorganized by the loss of their leader and his ignoble crucifixion, the disciples and the others pulled themselves together only with difficulty. Clearly, Luke believes it was the descent of the Holy Spirit that created for that community a destiny beyond disgrace and destruction. But the Holy Spirit did not bring with its courage a clear vision of what this future was. Peter and his companions knew they were to be a community of faithful witnesses to Christ as the Messiah; but the kind of effort entailed they learned gradually. Their own inclinations led them back to the Temple—a direction that Jewish hostility and the destruction of the city finally closed to them. At first they did not think of themselves as practicers of a new religion and builders of a new church from blueprints already at hand. Instead, they supposed—perhaps naïvely—that they could accomplish what their leader had failed to do: convince the Jewish leaders that Christ's claims about himself were correct. We see Peter going to the Temple and sharing in the religious observances, as Paul still does some twenty-five years later; and only the Jewish opposition reminds the disciples that their leader Jesus had spoken of a wider destiny.[1] Nor do they "catch on" quickly. Peter is *twice* thrown in prison, Stephen is stoned to death, and the first work outside Jerusalem is taken up only because the community has been temporarily ejected (chap. 8) from the city. Indeed, it takes a vision (chap. 10) to convince Peter—the "rock" upon whom the Church is to be built—that the "field" that is ripe to harvest and in which the community must labor is not Jerusalem but the world. The vision is precisely the kind that would have to be addressed to a man who, emotionally, is a Jewish particularist; it is of a sheet where mingle animals clean and unclean. The voice in the vision says, "Kill and eat." Peter resists the command (10:15) and wins the stern reply: "What God hath cleansed, that call not thou common" (*Acts* 10:15). It takes Peter, according to the narrative of *Acts,* some time to reach the conclusion of the matter; but after he has said, "Of a truth, I perceive that God is no respecter of persons" (10:34), he does not hesitate to associate with Gentiles and eat with them. The instinctive temper of the early community is displayed by their anger at what Peter has done. His defense (chap. 11) is to tell of the vision of the sheet which has reminded him (11:16) of instructions given by Christ but till now overlooked. He ends by saying: "What was I, that I could withstand God?" (11:17.) His inclination led him toward the Temple;

[1] The references in the remainder of the chapter are to *Acts* unless otherwise noted.

but both he and his community must obey the command of the vision.

That Christians with a strict Jewish background found this command painful to obey; that many of them obeyed the letter of the command and at the same time ignored the spirit by making Gentile converts observe dietary regulations and the rite of circumcision—all this is quite clear from subsequent events in *Acts* and from the letters of Paul. The persecutions of Agrippa I ("Herod") (chap. 12) drove them forth; but many of the ejected followed the example of Daniel and his prayer and preached facing Jerusalem. As the disputes over circumcision and diet in *Acts*, Chapter 15, indicate, many early followers of Christ regarded the continuation of traditional Jewish rites as necessary to the spiritual health of the new communities which they were setting up. Even though Gentiles often outnumbered Jews in these new communities, the import of Peter's vision of the sheet was ignored as long as possible. The Pharisees who had joined the community wanted to impose their codes upon it, and Peter protests: "Now therefore, why tempt ye God, to put a yoke [i.e., the law] upon the neck of the disciples, which neither our fathers nor we were able to bear?" (*Acts* 15:10.) But the mood of the Pharisees finds a reflection in the apostle James's own resistance to full acceptance of the Christian vision. True, we can make little complaint when James directs the converted Gentiles to "abstain from pollutions of idols and from fornication" (15:20), for these are two obvious habits of the pagan world that did not square with following Christ. But when it is added that the converted Gentiles must abstain "from things strangled and from blood," the emphasis falls upon what are called "indifferent matters." Deference is being shown a very ancient Hebrew conviction—that the blood of an animal was, mysteriously, the "life" and could not become an article of diet. Blood remained in an animal that had been strangled; naturally—to the Hebrew—it could not be eaten. Doubtless this conclusion to the discussion was expedient since the prohibition would avoid disputes between Gentile Christians and Jewish when they met at a common table. But it was nevertheless a compromise favoring the traditional culture of the first missionaries; it was opposed to what St. Paul was preaching: that there is neither Gentile nor Jew.

Paul

Because of this special insistence, and for other reasons, Paul is called "the apostle to the Gentiles." What Peter and his associates were unwilling to do or did only grudgingly, Paul did gladly. He put Judaism behind him because he was convinced, as other early missionaries were not, that the good news of "Christ crucified" was sufficient and did not need the supports that others tried to carry over from the faith they had put behind them. In this connection the eclipse of Peter by Paul in *Acts* has a poetic rightness. It was Paul's kind of missionary activity, if not his activity unaided, that created the Christian Church. It drew the simple group of believers and preachers from their hiding in the Jewish community where they were trying to survive by assuming a kind of protective coloration. It made necessary the transformation of their simple community where they practiced a primitive form of communism—based on non-Marxian premises, to be sure—into a more complex and flexible organization that could function though the various communities were separated by the great distances of the Roman world. In the Jerusalem community had been neither master nor servant; those who had known Christ preached and those who had not had this privilege took care of the group. The community that Paul did so much to construct extended over the Gentile world (tradition has it that Paul traveled as far as Spain before his death); means of communication among the multiplying groups had to be set up, and principles of order and administration had to be decided on. These principles found a model not in the small, close-knit arrangements at Jerusalem but in the efficient arrangements by which Rome held its empire together. The actual setting up of a hierarchy in which the duties of bishops and presbyters became fixed and differentiated lies outside New Testament times. But Paul's letters to the Corinthians chide them for disorders and battles which, ideally, would not exist among those who, in all simplicity, "loved one another." A stronger rein than that of love was needed to keep communities like the Corinthian one in order and in accord with Christian practice elsewhere.

From the time of the Protestant Reformation onward, Christian sects have been inspired by the ideal aspects of the picture *Acts* draws of the primitive Christian community. Neither *Acts* nor the letters of Paul give one a strong warrant for believing that early Christianity was ever "primitive" in the romantic sense. The scanty records suggest that, from the outset, it was composed of normal human beings who, though they responded to the figure and the teachings of Christ, responded also to the stirrings of the flesh, of what Paul calls "the old man" (*Ephesians* 4:22). Vanity, bickering, and self-righteousness, these marks which give modern agnostics ammunition when they wish point to the gap between what Christians say they believe and what they actually do, were all present in the early communities. It was to combat these persisting marks of Satan's power over the early Christians that the framework of the Church began to rise. When Paul took the Church into the wider Gentile world, he imposed on it necessities that the Jerusalem community did not know—necessities of administration and policy shaping and compromise with Caesar that have been with Christianity ever since. Christ and Christ's Church are—perhaps tragically—two different things. Christ's life and teaching offer mankind counsels of perfection; a church, to survive, must reckon on the imperfection surrounding it in the outside world and likely to appear among the "community of saints" itself. Christ, one may say, announced that the Church would come into being; it was Paul's task to bring it into being. (The task of others also, to be sure.) It is hardly fair—the habit of some hostile critics of Paul—to regard the apostle as the villain in the story of Christianity. Paul was a man, with limitations that appear clearly in his letters. But he did what had to be done, and the second half of *Acts* shows him doing it well.

What the community and its needs were up to the time of Paul was often determined, as suggested, by "various and emergent occasions." Paul, *Acts* lets us see, changed all this. He too was an opportunist often enough. But, unlike Peter and the others, he searched for opportunities, and differed from the early group of devout and reluctant men who often give one the impression that they hope opportunity will not find them out.

What sort of man was Paul? What made him the effective apostle to the Gentiles that he was? Paul's answer is quite simple and quite correct; it is the vision that came to him on the road to Damascus, a vision that may have drawn some of its strength from the resolution the first martyr Stephen displayed. Paul's visions are described, with considerable variation of detail and circumstance, in *Acts,* Chapters 9, 22, and 26; in *II Corinthians,* Chapter 12, and in *Galatians,* Chapter 1. It has been suggested that Paul was subject to epileptic seizure, and that this affliction brought about the vision on the highway from Jerusalem to Damascus. If so, it is the impression accompanying this seizure—the sight of Christ, whom Paul had never seen in the flesh—and not the seizure that led to the entirely interior reversal of values of which Christ speaks in *John* 3:3 and that made Paul a "twice-born man." Paul's outward effectiveness stemmed, he tells us in *II Corinthians* 12:9-10, from this moment. But it is an effectiveness with a longer history than the moments and hours in which he lay in trance or, a little later, which he spent in the Arabian desert near Damascus (*Galatians* 1:17) meditating on the consequences of Christ's question, "Saul, why persecutest thou me?" This longer history does much to suggest why Paul would be willing to attempt what others drew back from—the carrying of the "good news" to the four corners of the earth. It suggests, further, why his efforts had success.

Paul was by birth a member of the Jewish Diaspora. He was born in Tarsus in Cilicia, a seacoast region to the north of Palestine. Thanks to some circumstance (perhaps his parents were Roman citizens) he was a Roman citizen and enjoyed two privileges: the right to appeal to Caesar and freedom from degrading punishment. His profession, by which he often supported himself during his missionary journeys, was that of tentmaker. One may imagine that in his early years at Tarsus he had the chance not only to learn a trade but to acquire the familiarity with Stoic and Platonic thought displayed in the letters. He had also, certainly, a chance to observe what the prophets called "the abominations": the rites and revels of popular pagan religion. From Tarsus, Paul was sent to Jerusalem to sit at the feet of Gamaliel the great teacher; and when he makes his first appearance in *Acts,* he has become more of a Pharisee than many Jerusalem Pharisees. He has become more stern and demanding than Gamaliel his master. Londoners are often struck by the passion with which colonials and Americans take up British ways; and in our own country, we note the eagerness with which persons from beyond the Alleghenies take up an accent that they judge is better than their own. Paul displayed his deep orthodoxy by taking a part in the early persecution leading to the death of Stephen and the flight of some of the followers of Christ into nearby Samaria.

All this passionate orthodoxy was shattered by the vision on the road to Damascus. One can suppose, in the emotional and mental history of Peter and the other disciples, a gradual development: a growing attachment to the person of Jesus that does not necessarily cancel the claims of orthodoxy. At least, this is what the behavior of Peter and the others suggest. But in the mind of Paul, there would be a clear opposition between Judaism and admiration for Christ; there could be no middle ground, only a gulf. When the vision established for Paul the rightness of Christ's views, Judaism was no longer worth defending. What was good in it lived on in the teaching and the deeds of Christ. To others, Christ's declarations about the cancellation of the law by a "new dispensation" might appear to be enigmatic statements to be piously preserved. To Paul, they were a program for action. It was a waste of time to try to find a middle ground on which followers of the law and followers of Christ could live together. There was only one thing to preach, and that was "Christ crucified" and the consequences of that fact as Paul saw them.

If we are just in saying that Paul had been more ardent than the Jerusalem Pharisees, we may well go on and say that in his missionary activity he was determined to outstrip, in devotion and achievement, the men who had known Christ in the flesh. Three effects of this determination appear in the second section of *Acts.* (The ethical and theological results can be deferred to the chapter on Paul's letters.) Here we are allowed to see the radiation of Paul's energy in his systematic planning, in his attitudes toward Judaism and the pagan world, and in the consummate generalship with which he conducts his own defense as well as his missionary campaigns.

In *Acts,* Chapter 13, we see the first step of his systematic plan: the offering of the gospel to the Jews—a gift that Peter and his companions could not believe would be rejected. When Paul sees this rejection, he "shakes the dust of the place from his feet," in the words of Christ's instructions to the apostles (*Matthew* 10:14). Henceforth, his effort is directed to the Gentiles, and his three missionary journeys take him into territories beyond the ken of most Palestinian Jews. In the first he travels through a section of the hill towns in Asia Minor. But, at the behest of another vision in which a Macedonian Greek appears and says, "Come to us," he embarks on the first of two journeys that opened up regions untouched by other preachers. Yet the encounter with Apollos, *Acts,* Chapter 19, is a reminder that what Paul had done, others soon set about to do. Apollos knows only the baptism of John the Baptist, that of water, rather than the baptism of Christ, the baptism of water and Spirit; and it is pleasant to note that Apollos and Paul quickly reconcile their differences.

One is able to note Paul's generalship in this circumstance: though he is driving toward the Gentiles, he drives through a channel immediately accessible to him—the synagogues in the various Jewish towns where he, as a trained interpreter of the scriptures, had a right to a hearing. The narratives suggest that what he said was delivered with fire, enough fire to stir resentment and persecution. But they do not justify a modern accusation, that Paul was a "rabble rouser." The majority of Jews at Thessalonica reject him and cry to the magistrate: "These that have turned the world upside down have come here also" (*Acts* 17:6). But this was not always Paul's reception, and the good effect of his teachings at Berea is noted by Luke. The Jews there are "more noble than those in Thessalonica, in that they received the word with all readiness of mind, and searched the Scripture daily, whether those things were so" (*Acts* 17:11). This indicates, as part of Paul's method, an appeal to evidence and individual judgment that has no place among the techniques of the street speaker who hopes to drive men mad. Further, Paul can practice the arts of expedience as well as those of courage. The circumcision of Timotheus (*Acts* 16:1-4) indicates that he would not arouse enmity when other courses were open to him. He is "all things to all men" when the satisfaction of the whims and prejudices of factions costs only what is "expendable"; he is intransigent (as we shall also see in his letters) when the satisfaction of the convictions of others involves the sacrifice of convictions that, in his opinion, are central to Christian belief. Example: The picture in *Acts* of Paul's relation to the Greeks and to the Gentiles in general indicates that not only in the presence of the Jews does Paul know how to be—in the sense explained— "all things to all men." He draws on those elements in his own background that establish a link with his Gentile hearers. He mentions his Roman citizenship; he displays those aspects of the Christian belief which he knows they are prepared to hear; and he is not averse to letting his Jewish foes "hang themselves" by a show of traditional doctrines that in pagan eyes will seem barbarous and unimportant.

The most notable example in *Acts* of Paul's skill in exploiting his knowledge of Greek and Roman culture appears in the address delivered in Athens, at the invitation of "certain philosophers of the Epicureans and Stoics" (*Acts* 17:18). Paul shows himself to be more than the "babbler" they name him; and his failure to win them is properly explained by Luke's editorial comment: "For all the Athenians and strangers which were there spent their time in nothing else, but either to tell, or to hear some new thing" (*Acts* 17:21). Athens was no longer the intellectual center of the pagan world; the seat of Hellenic culture had shifted to Alexandria and now was being drawn toward Rome. We see Paul's audience on the Areopagus as a very different one from that Socrates had spoken to. The men who there condemned Socrates to death were full of prejudice and were determined to resist the impact of philosophy on their traditional ways. Paul's audience had made a repast of all the philosophies of the past four centuries, and now their palates were jaded, they counted on this Jewish barbarian to amuse them. There is no question of their condemning Paul to death, and the sympathetic say: "We will hear thee again of this matter" (*Acts* 17:32); so saying they condemn not Paul but themselves, in Luke's opinion. For Paul's address, of which *Acts* 17:22-31 is a condensed report, is shrewd in its chosen approach and in what it omits. Paul startles the cultivated Athenians by accusing them of being "too superstitious"; and he turns an inscription he has noticed on an altar—"To the Unknown God"—to his own uses. An altar raised to avert the anger of some god to whom specific rites cannot be offered because no one knows his name gives Paul his chance. "Whom therefore ye ignorantly worship, him declare I unto you" (17:23). The ensuing description which links the inscription with the Lord would probably make the Stoic listeners nod their heads in agreement. (Recall that in *The Wisdom of Solomon* the writer could make considerable use of Stoic outlooks.) Paul clinches his argument—and incidentally displays his own cultivation—when he says:

> That they should seek the Lord, if haply they might feel after him, and find him, though he be not far from every one of us: For in him we live, and move, and have our being: as certain also of your own poets have said. (17:27-28.)

Nor would many of his Stoic hearers challenge Paul when he ridicules the folly of worshiping idols made with hands.

> Forasmuch then as we are the offspring of God, we ought not to think that the Godhead is like unto gold or silver, or stone, graven by art, and man's device. (17:29.)

It is the conclusion to all this that arouses the mirth of his hearers or sends them wandering away.

> And the times of this ignorance God winked at; but now commandeth all men every where to repent: because he hath appointed a day, in the which he will judge the world in righteousness by that man whom he hath ordained; whereof he hath given assurance unto all men, in that he hath raised him from the dead. (17:30-31.)

The Stoic, with his view of the eternal recurrence—that which has been shall be—would be indifferent to the "new dispensation" which ends the times when God was willing to "wink" at the mistakes of the non-Hebraic world. The doctrines of the Just Judge and the resurrection from the dead were not "reasonable"; at least, they had the sanction of none of the systems which Paul's hearers knew. Thus, Paul's case on the Areopagus was lost, by default rather than by condemnation. But we shall see Paul in his letters returning to retrieve the defeat of this day, to insist to the Gentiles that their religion at its best was not wrong but incomplete. (The author of *Wisdom* had said the same thing in his day.) Paul's strategy when faced with the Gentiles was the same one he employed with his previous followers.

Paul has, in addition, a shrewdness in grasping at momentary opportunities that appears most notably in the concluding chapters of *Acts,* at every turn of his defense of himself after he is arrested in Jerusalem (chaps. 21-26). He escapes the untender mercies of the Sanhedrin and is taken to the comparative safety of Caesarea. To be sure, he overshoots in insisting on his Roman citizenship and his right to go to Caesar (*Acts* 26:32). But he is fertile in expedients from the moment the mob goes for him in the Temple to his final interview with Agrippa II and Festus. But his cleverness is not at war with his dignity. He does not falter when the odds are against him; he never "speaks small" of the religion he preaches. Though in danger, he will not accept the taunt of Festus: "Paul, thou art beside thyself; much learning doth make thee mad." He makes the sober but firm reply that ends with the famous words: ". . . this thing was not done in a corner (*Acts* 26:24-26).

Acts reaches its completion rather abruptly, with Paul's successful arrival at Rome. Why the book terminates so suddenly has caused much speculation. According to one theory, both *Luke* and *Acts* were written to show that the activities of Christians, and especially of Paul, offered no political threat to Rome; this theory also suggests that "most excellent Theophilus," who is addressed at the beginning of both books, was an important Roman official and, if persuaded, would defend Paul before Nero himself. Whatever the cause, our last view of Paul displays him teaching "those things which concern the Lord Jesus Christ . . . no man forbidding him" (*Acts* 28:31). Whether Paul was released and was able to make a journey to Spain which he had mentioned in a letter (*Romans* 15:24) and then was imprisoned a second time in Rome, Luke does not say. And it is tradition that tells us how Paul died—by beheading at the time of the Neronian persecutions (64 A.D.). (Tradition also tells us something of the death of the other hero of *Acts:* Peter, during the Neronian persecutions, was crucified head downwards since—the apostle contended—he was unworthy to die with his head upwards, in the manner of his master.)

Whatever its imperfections and omissions, *Acts* does what its composer intended. We see in it enough of the growth of the early Church to understand what is not included but is a matter of general knowledge: that thanks to beginnings at Jerusalem and the activities of Paul and others, meager indeed in comparison with the task they set themselves, the teachings of Christ and his example gained access to the ancient world and to our own.

CHAPTER XIX

The Letters of Paul

IF PAUL were known to us only as he is presented in *Acts,* we would know the essentials of the man's nature which enabled him to fulfill the behest of Christ and take the gospel to those who had no expectations concerning it. We would recognize in the figure drawn by Luke how an irresistible force made Paul able to surmount barriers that other early Christians hesitated to approach. We would see (and do see) how believable it is that this man could take a new religion to an alien world, even though the religion bore with it a weight of doctrine unpleasant or incredible or unnecessary to the members of the Gentile world. We see Paul doing this by sloughing off much of his ancestral Judaism: the mass of rites and customs like circumcision and diet and habits of prayer and Temple sacrifice. We also see him insisting on the preservation of other traditional Jewish insights that (as we saw in the Gospels) were gathered together and focused by the activity of Christ.

We are able to see all this not only in *Acts* but also thanks to the letters of Paul which were preserved by the churches and the persons who received them. It is well to observe at once that the letters of Paul fall into two groups: letters of instruction addressed to specific churches and letters addressed to individuals *(Timothy, Titus,* and *Philemon).* The letters to persons are often called the "pastoral" epistles since they concern the duties of the leaders of the Christian flocks. Of the epistles to churches or groups of churches (like *Galatians*), modern scholars question Paul's authorship of *Ephesians* and *Colossians.* There is also some question as to whether the "pastoral" epistles are, in their entirety, Paul's creation. As for *Hebrews,* modern scholars but repeat the words of Origen, who in the third century said: "Who wrote the Epistle to the Hebrews, God only knows." At any rate, we are by now accustomed to the process by which the prestige of a great leader creates pieces of writing which are not composed by him but are written in his spirit or temper.

The ancient "letter" was something quite different from what, in our days of cheap postage and paper and easy modes of transportation, it has come to be. The letters of Cicero (106-43 B.C.) and Pliny (61-*c.* 113 A.D.) as well as those of Paul show how means of transmission had to be found; and Paul, unlike these highly placed Roman letter writers, did not have a special messenger waiting for his call. He had to watch for the good fortune of encountering some journeying fellow believer who would carry his messages from Caesarea or Rome to one of the churches that Paul had founded and pined to revisit. Moreover, because of the cost of materials, the occasion for the writing of a letter had, for a poor man like Paul, to be one of some moment. In sharp contrast are Collected Letters of some modern person. There, most of the letters, compositions dashed off at odd moments, are a substitute for the friendly, lively, and often aimless conversations that would take place if the writer were in the company of his friends. It is the unusual modern who thinks of his letters as being addressed to a wider audience than that composed by his friends and perhaps his friend's household. The nearest modern parallel to the ancient attitude toward letters is the attitude of Alexander Pope (1688-1744) toward his correspondence. In his lifetime, Pope retrieved his letters, polished them, and then had them printed. However grotesque, this practice has its ancient equivalent. Cicero and Pliny did not regard their letters as the least considerable of their literary products, and in them are developed veins of meditation that modern writers would exploit in essays and articles meant only for print.

In this light St. Paul's letters should be viewed. It is true that his styles of expression are various, rather than uniform and formal like the style of Cicero's letters; but no topic is too weighty for him to investigate. Thus, *The Epistle to the Romans* reflects an effort to produce a connected and developed argument that will commend Paul to a community he has not yet visited. In contrast, the Corinthian letters have all the variety of tone and change of pace that Paul doubtless employed when he was able to address this vexatious congregation in person. In these latter letters to a community he knew well (as in *Galatians* and *Philippians* likewise) Paul chats about himself, harangues the vicious and backsliding members of the congregation, and then—almost without warning—rises to levels of insight that leave the controlled and orderly analysis of *Romans* far behind. The style of the "pastoral" epistles is still closer to modern letter style. In the letters to Timothy, expressions of affection and "items of interest" mingle with the spiritual advice that was the only largesse St. Paul had to scatter.

The audience envisaged by St. Paul as he wrote or dictated a letter —to his dictated letters he would affix his signature in a "big round hand" (e.g., *II Thessalonians* 3:17)—determined the degree of formality and the conduct of the argument at hand. It is stupid to suggest that Paul's letters are "modern" (dubious praise!), for they are written in a world at many points unlike ours. They are "ancient" and have family resemblance to other ancient letters in being occasioned usually by matters of moment and in treating topics that we look to find handled elsewhere. Whereas Wendell Willkie wrote *One World,* Paul could but—lacking our printing presses or the ancient equivalent, an expensive corps of copyists—write *The Letter to the Romans.* But it is incorrect, as the reader would find out at once, to suggest that most of the letters of Paul have the elegance and polish and impersonality of other ancient correspondence. Beneath the variation of the styles already noted in this common mark: vehemence. The deeds on which Paul bases his faith were not "done in a corner"; and Paul has no intention of speaking low and going softly. The tone of the letters is frequently that of a man speaking at the top of his bent; it is a tone by turns attractive and unattractive. Thus, the Corinthian letters and those to the churches in Galatia offer startling contrasts of gentle pleading and flat, almost bullying command. In some moods Paul might seem to be saying, "Come, let us plead together," as God says to the second Isaiah (*Isaiah* 43:26). But soon, such is his vehemence and conviction, pleading gives way to statement, and statement leads on to command. A "great theme"—God's love, the doctrine of atonement—can be put out of the way by Paul's sudden recollection of the bad news he has had about specific abuses. He has heard that the Corinthian Christians practice the vices for which their city is celebrated; it is reported that the Galatian churches are listening to other and unworthy teachers, now that Paul is gone. These abuses, as Paul's exclamatory, broken style suggests, must be put to rights, and no time wasted either! One is reminded of the old-time preacher who did not mind breaking off his sacred descant to chide an inattentive person in the congregation.

All this variation of style and subject matter makes for impatience in reading, particularly in *Corinthians, Galatians,* and *Philippians,* which are letters addressed to communities that Paul knew well. But such life and variety are testimonies that the letters continue the ancient Hebrew emphasis on "action." Paul is no university lecturer who delivers at the same time each year the same remarks. He is one of those who "are turning the world upside down"; and when he cannot do this in person, he does it by means of his letters.

The story is told of a modern woman who destroyed or preserved letters from an intellectual friend in accordance with a simple rule. The letters that were lively and full of gossip she preserved, saying, "For me." The letters entirely preoccupied with a "great theme" she tore up and threw into the wastebasket, saying, "For posterity." Paul's letters have reached posterity, but they were not addressed to posterity. They were aimed at specific groups so directly that what is said to his friends is not, to us, always clear and connected. We are often in the presence of something like what we call "family jokes"; Paul refers to circumstances that only he and the recipients of the letter can actually know.

In short, whatever consistency the body of correspondence has is a reflection of the consistency in the personality and thought of Paul; it is not calculated. Paul did not, in the phrase of T. S. Eliot, take any pains "to prepare a face to meet the faces that you meet." It is doubtful that he ever speculated much as to the fate of his letters, which were often answers to specific queries or attacks on immediate problems. The letter to Colossae has, near its end, this remark: "And when this epistle is read among you, cause that it be read also in the church of the Laodiceans; and that ye likewise read the epistle from Laodicea" (*Colossians* 4:16). But this sort of direction—whether Paul's or an imitator's—is very close to the directions that, in family correspondence today, indicate a forwarding sequence for a "round robin" letter. Various remarks in the letters to the Corinthians suggest that Paul wrote them other letters which have not been preserved. But, because Paul was a man of great reputation and because of the contents of many of his letters, his communications were preserved by the churches that received them not because of Paul's pride but because of their own pride at having been singled out for a communication.

Further, when it became plain that the "interim" between Christ's ascension and his second coming was going to be long and that the Church would have to work out a painful existence in a hostile world—a world that assaulted believers with the guile of argument as well as the brutality of crucifixion and boiling oil—Paul's letters were sought out and collected, for they offered arguments by which the persuasion of both Jew and pagan Gentile could be turned aside. (The canon or list of acceptable books was, for the followers of Christ, still uncertain in the second half of the second century after Christ.) Nor were the collectors of the letters finicky about authenticity. The soundness and usefulness of the doctrine expressed told more heavily in a letter's favor than *prima facie* evidence that Paul had actually written it.

Of course, along with Paul's letters were collected letters that bore the names of other important leaders in the early Church: Peter, John, James, and Jude (or Judas). Some of these letters bear marks associating them with the historical personage; for example, there is much that unites the letters of John and *The Gospel of John*. Some of the letters, however, reflect persecution and doctrinal troubles that did not arise in the lifetime of the supposed authors. Since most of these letters are addressed to no particular church or person, they are often called the "catholic" or general epistles, in contrast to Paul's specifically directed letters. The topics treated—Christian morals, the nature of Christ, the proper attitude toward persecution—are variations upon what we shall be able to note in our reading of Paul's letters or have already noted in *The Gospel of John.*

Paul's Personality in the Letters

The range of interest is, like the range of tone, very wide in these letters of Paul. The collection contains Paul's own estimate of himself (*II Corinthians,* chaps. 11, 12, and 13; and *Galatians,* chaps. 1 and 2) and much that is *logically* irrelevant to the central theme of his thought: that the law of Moses is canceled since Christ's sacrifice and love make unnecessary the legalistic, external handling of ethical problems. But this central theme is what is called a counsel of perfection. We soon see that Paul is a believer in perfection who nevertheless has a clear view of what men actually are. Thus, though he believes in the law of love, his letters contain passages as legalistic in tone as the laws of Moses. In these passages, he seems to reduce virtuous action to external observance of rules rather than to an inner attitude antecedent to all overt action. Finally, and most importantly for the history of Christianity, the letters express fully St. Paul's solutions of the intellectual problems that faced him as "an apostle to the Gentiles."

Paul's self-portrait, in *II Corinthians,* is a passionate explosion of recollection touched off by a danger to the congregation at Corinth. The people there will receive—or have received—the visits of other missioners; and these missioners may not be like Apollos, submissive to the authority and doctrine of Paul. They may challenge his position in the ranks of teachers; they may subvert his doctrines. Other churches could boast that they had been founded by one or more of the "twelve," those who followed the Christ when he had human form, whereas Corinth had for its founder a man who had not known Christ in the flesh and who had even been a persecutor of Christians. At the outset of his defense, Paul says: "For I suppose I was not a whit behind the very chiefest apostles" (*II Corinthians* 11:5). He says more violently, with the effect of using paradox when prose fails: "I am become a fool in glorying: ye have compelled me: for I ought to have been commended of you: for in nothing am I behind the very chiefest apostles, though I be nothing" (*II Corinthians* 12:11). Since, in experience of Christ, he is not behind the very chiefest apostles, churches of his foundation are not behind churches founded by Peter and James and John. What he underwent on the road to Damascus, when he "was caught up into paradise, and heard unspeakable words, which it is not lawful for a man to utter" (*II Corinthians* 12:4) puts him on a level with those who knew and followed the earthly Jesus for many months. This "glorying" into which the childishness of the Corinthians has forced him is a "glorifying" not in his own strength and merit but in the strength which was given him in vision. Paul confesses he is an inadequate vessel for the play of this strength. He even has "a thorn in the flesh"—some say epilepsy, some say malaria—that renders him inadequate to the imposed task.

> For this thing I besought the Lord thrice, that it might depart from me. And he said unto me, My grace is sufficient for thee: for my strength is made perfect in weakness. Most gladly therefore will I rather glory in my infirmities, that the power of Christ may rest upon me. (*II Corinthians* 12:8-9.)

Measured by the strength of the Lord, all men are weak—a truism ever since the time when Jeremiah cursed the day he was born to carry a burden above his own abilities. Paul, however, rejoices in his weakness: "Therefore I take pleasure in infirmities, in reproaches, in necessities, in persecutions, in distresses for Christ's sake: for when I am weak, then am I strong" (*II Corinthians* 12:10). Only by such a paradox can he assert, to the Corinthians, what kind of authority he has. It is an authority, he reminds his bad-mannered flock, that he has not used to his own profit, nor has Titus whom Paul sent to them when he could not come himself. He has used his gift for their benefit. "And I will very gladly spend and be spent for you; though the more abundantly I love you, the less I be loved. But be it so, I did not burden you: nevertheless, being crafty, I caught you with guile" (*II Corinthians* 12:15-16). This "guile" is the wisdom of the serpent which Jesus commends (*Matthew* 10:16); it is the prudence which, in *Proverbs,* is a necessary aid to achieving virtuous goals. The Corinthians (and others) had to be caught despite their own indifference and bad habits. To make this catch, Paul does not hesitate to do what has to be done. And all that he has done gives him a right to regard the Corinthians as his own, to defend them against the unhealthy winds of doctrine blowing from other quarters. Some of the interlopers who have come to lead the Corinthians astray vaunt themselves upon their Hebrew origin. "Are they Hebrews?" Paul asks. His answer to this question leads him to passionate, compressed autobiography.

> So am I. Are they Israelites? so am I. Are they the seed of Abraham? so am I. Are they ministers of Christ? (I speak as a fool) I am more; in labours more abundant, in stripes above measure, in prisons more frequent, in deaths oft. Of the Jews five times received I forty stripes save one. Thrice was I beaten with rods, once was I stoned, thrice I suffered shipwreck, a night and a day I have been in the deep; in journeyings often, in perils of waters, in perils of robbers, in perils by mine own countrymen, in perils by the heathen, in perils in the city, in perils in the wilderness, in perils in the sea, in perils among false brethren; in weariness and painfulness, in watchings often, in hunger and thirst, in fastings often, in cold and nakedness. (*II Corinthians* 11:22-28.)

It is chiefly in relation to the Corinthians that we see Paul abandoning the high ground from which counsels of perfection are happily uttered and plunging into the swampland of inherited custom, habit, and inertia where most men live. When he is on the heights, he can view the ideal prospect composed by Christian earth and Christian heaven and speak of it in accents that are without rival: "Though I speak with the tongues of men and of angels, and have not charity, I am become as sounding brass, or a tinkling cymbal" (*I Corinthians* 13:1). He sees an ideal brotherhood bound together by the easy cords of love. But when Paul descends to the swamps to deal with the Church as it is rather than as it ought to be, he does not draw back from all the hacking and hewing required to get through the rich second growth of pagan custom, vanity, pride, and indifference that has filled the clearing he once made in Corinth. As he chops away he sometimes distinguishes between what he tells them in the name of the Lord and what he tells them in his own name. "But to the rest speak I, not the Lord" (*I Corinthians* 7:12). Yet, whatever the source, the instruction quite often takes the flat prescriptive form dear to the legalistic mind: this do, this do not do. It was a form supposedly made unnecessary by the gospel of love. "Love and do what you will," said St. Augustine in a kind of echo of Paul's central insight. Without relaxing his grasp on this ideal truth, Paul sees the reality: that men soon cease from loving and, though nominally still a part of the "true vine," return to all the vices they had known before and go on to invent new ones. When Paul writes to his friends

> Therefore let us keep the feast, not with the old leaven, neither with the leaven of malice and wickedness; but with the unleavened bread of sincerity and truth. (*I Corinthians* 5:8.)

he is speaking of the ideal community. But he faces up to his duty, which is to list the actual behavior that has been reported to him.

It is a list shocking to the godly and certainly amusing to the pagan Gentiles who have heard of the high assertions made by the followers of Christ. The Christians, it has been told Paul, are guilty of incest; here they are worse than the Gentiles, who do not so much as name the sin (*I Corinthians* 5:1). The Christians quarrel with each other and air their grievances in the pagan courts of law rather than to the community of the faithful. Christians continue the attitude toward marriage prevailing in the Gentile world, regarding it as a contract and not as—so Paul urges—a sacrament that is an earthly counterpart of the relation between Christ and his Church. These are old sins springing up. But the new-made Christians appear not to be content to sin in the ways of their fathers but must discover new sins: sins that were not possible until they became Christians, sins that display (one must admit) a considerable perversity. Thus, the Corinthians have transformed the agape, the "love feast," a meal which began as a continuation of the common evening meal of the community in Jerusalem to which all persons made what contribution they could, into an occasion for pride and bitterness. The wealthy come with their baskets of "vittels and drink" and gorge in the faces of the poor brothers elsewhere in the room. In his censure of this, Paul shows himself no slave to a holy tradition. The common meal was once a good custom, but since it has been perverted, it must now be suspended.

> What? have ye not houses to eat and to drink in? or despise ye the church of God, and shame them that have not? What shall I say to you? shall I praise you in this? I praise you not. (*I Corinthians* 11:22.)

Only the essential aspect of the old meal need be preserved—the sacrificial meal that in Jerusalem followed the actual meal; and he goes on to describe the Lord's Supper.

Another "scandal" possible only for Christians has arisen from the fact that most of the meat available for purchase has, as a matter of routine, been offered to idols. Actually, Paul points out, meat can neither defile not exalt; actually, there is no reason to abstain from such meat. But some sophisticated Christians make a display of such a meal of meat and shock and unsettle weaker brothers. He asks: ". . . through thy knowledge shall the weak brother perish, for whom Christ died?" (*I Corinthians* 8:11.) As he says a little later:

> All things are lawful for me, but all things are not expedient: all things are lawful for me, but all things edify not. (*I Corinthians* 10:23.)

This is the contrast, in a new context, between wisdom and prudence, the contrast with which *Proverbs* and *Ecclesiasticus* are shot through. It exists in the very nature of things, and Paul cannot be expected to escape it. If one has charity or love, all things are lawful to that person; but to decide what is "expedient" at a given time, under given circumstances, requires the exercise of prudence or the holy "guile" with which Paul "caught" the Corinthians in the first place. We may regret that experience offers us the paradox of the desirable opposed to the possible. But this is so, and Paul does not deserve charges of insincerity and hypocrisy because he recognizes this paradox and tries to deal with it.

Christ said to those who should form his church: "Be ye therefore perfect as your Father which is in heaven is perfect" (*Matthew* 5:48). One may suppose that the perfection of the Father does not have to be reduced to a variety of minute and tedious special rules. From the ideal view, such rules should not be called for in a community that is imitating the perfections of the Father. History is full of human communities that have tried to get along without such rules, and the results are often tragicomic. Whether the community of the perfect is Christianly or philosophically drawn up —whether we have to do with monks or with socialists on the banks of the Wabash—the vision of perfections fades, the "old man" puts in his ugly appearance, and rules must be laid down or the community disintegrates. Paul's letters are full of such rules; and—whether they are presented as his own opinion or the Lord's—they are meant to be binding. Women must wear head covering at the sacred gatherings and men must not (*I Corinthians,* chap. 11). The celibate life is more pleasing to God than the married, but since it is "better to marry than burn," the state of marriage is acceptable (*I Corinthians,* chap 7). Prophesying, intelligible preaching, is better than speaking with tongues, which is here apparently no more than excited nonsense babble (*I Corinthians,* chap. 14). All these rules and observations do not consider the goal, perfection, but suggest *expedient* ways of approaching that goal. The modern reader is free to feel that certain regulations record very old superstitions. (A woman without head cover was thought to be without defense against evil spirits.) He is free to observe that Paul's own enthusiasm for celibacy set up an emphasis that has "told" very strongly indeed in subsequent centuries. But, the point to be stressed, a person is not free to censure

Paul for being concerned with details. He could no more escape them than can any parent. A parent cannot commend an omnibus conception of virtue to his children; he has to water that conception down into specific rules so that his children can drink of it even though to the scandal of the vintner, who is likely to feel that wine should be drunk only as it comes from the cellar. St. Paul was in place of a parent to the Corinthians. He writes:

> And I, brethren, could not speak unto you as unto spiritual, but as unto carnal, even as unto babes in Christ. I have fed you with milk, and not with meat: for hitherto ye were not able to bear it, neither yet now are ye able. (*I Corinthians* 3:1-2.)

In consequence, his ethical precepts are not free of the strain, the heavy emphasis on isolated points, that makes unattractive all special prohibitions, whether those of parents or those found in the laws of Moses.

Theological Doctrines

But the ethical aspect of Paul's teaching is balanced by his accounts of what he saw when he had the leisure to stroll on higher grounds. He saw the Messiah as atoning victim for the sins of created being; he saw the kingdom of God, the resurrection of the dead; he perceived that God is a person as well as a creative force, and he announced the doctrine of the Trinity. These doctrines were all consequent upon Paul's act of faith—an act that drew strength from what he saw when he was "caught up to the third heaven" (*II Corinthians* 12:2).

His doctrines, we saw in the previous chapter, struck the Athenians as outlandish and foolish. Paul's teaching was not "rational" as the Stoics, Epicureans, and Platonists understood the word. A "rational" system was one that explained the universe by a chain of argument drawn from initial assumptions self-evident to the man whose eyes were open. To be sure, the initial assumptions of the Stoics were not those of the Epicureans or Platonists. The Stoic open eyes took in the obvious *order* of the physical universe; the Epicurean open eyes took in the obvious *disorder* and lack of plan in the universe; and the Platonist open eyes saw the obvious order that was a reflection of the One and the obvious disorder that was produced by the taint of non-being in all created objects. Pauls' speech at Athens (*Acts,* chap. 17) was an effort to profit from the ground common to Stoics and Christians. (We have seen how a later explanation, in *John,* was an effort to profit from what was similar in Platonism and nascent Christian philosophy.) But Paul's attempt to play the game the philosophers wanted to engage him in ran into trouble. Halfway through it—or so it must have seemed to his hearers—he announced a change of rules. The "rational" must give way to what is not rational at all, to what does not necessarily follow from any of the initial philosophical assumptions about the world. Paul, at least, could not slough off revealed truth along with Jewish rites and custom. Instead, he resolutely carried it, despite the anger of the Jews and the quick laughter of many Gentiles. He understood quite well the Stoic and Platonic "rules of play," and he knew they had no room for the introduction of new postulates halfway through the game. The inconvenient assumptions Paul had to carry were the Jewish insights that had been caught up and blended by the deeds and teachings of Christ. The Greeks could believe in a god that was a "first mover" of the universe (Aristotle) or an indwelling principle of order keeping the universe on the track (Stoic), or a pattern of order that existed for the material universe to imitate (Platonic). They could not believe in a God that was all these things and yet something more; a person and a redeemer like this, from their point of view, was irrational and ridiculous. What the Greeks had drawn from their various contemplations of the created world was called, in later centuries, "natural theology"; and from natural theology could never be drawn what was given to Paul by Jewish and Christian revelation: that God is a father and redeemer as well as a source of power and order. This was quite irrational. Perhaps, in this connection, Paul would prefer a word of fairly recent coinage; it was *super*rational. Reason could not have predicted this turn of events in the drama involving deity, man, and Satan. But it is Paul's insistence that, once the crucifixion has taken place, reason can make it out as a necessary event. It was necessary because the Gentile philosophies of salvation do not really save and because the old Hebrew covenant has not worked. Hebrew history demonstrated to the prophets as well as to Paul that the covenant of righteousness will always be broken. If man is to live in accord with God, it must be by means of some other relation. This relation was suspected by the prophets when they spoke of the Messiah. But its exact nature was certainly not foreseen, if we except the single passage in *Isaiah* 53 on the "suffering servant."

This is the chief burden of the letters which Paul wrote to early churches. It was a burden, some commentators on the history of Christianity suggest, which he need not have carried. Would it not have been enough, they ask, if Paul had been content to represent Christ as a teacher of ethical truths that were in accord with the intellectual tenets of enlightened Hellenes and Romans? Is it not Christianity's tragedy that Paul saddled the new religion with the paradox, with the *both-and* habits of thought found in the "pre-philosophic" prophets? No wonder, this line of criticism suggests, the Athenians did not listen; no wonder the elegant philosophic game they were willing to play with Paul was called off when he talked of God as a person and spoke of resurrection from the dead.

An answer to this gloomy estimate of Paul's achievement cannot be simple; nor will it be, perhaps, decisive. But if we recall what the Roman world was—a semblance of peace and order hiding a reality of misery and injustice—we can say positively that if Paul had chosen to have his little triumph with the philosophers he would have lost the rest of the Roman world. That world had heard of the various philosophic ways of salvation for many generations, and large portions of the population—particularly the poor and the miserable—could make no use of them. It is not likely that the Syrian slave grubbing on a Calabrian plantation would take heart when his Stoic master told him he must try to feel detached toward his labors and low social position: all passed and so would this. The Platonic teaching that all physical sensation was an illusion and a snare probably would not much aid the slave to endure the lash of the whip. If Paul had let fall from his shoulders the burden of revelation, the masses would have had no cause to distinguish him from other strollers in academic groves.

To be sure, the burden of revelation—the doctrines of rebirth and the savior—resembled the Oriental "mysteries" of Isis and Cybele the "great Mother" that already had a large following. Many of those who turned to Christ did not bother to make a nice distinction between the atmosphere of myth and legend draping the rites of Isis and the assertion of Christ's human and historical existence that is part of the Christian message. Christianity offered a "way out" for the illiterate and socially lost as well as the powerful and cultivated. Indeed, if Paul had not been intransigent, if he had not insisted on his interpretation of the crucifixion, his message would have lost its distinctive marks. They are marks that appear not only in Paul's letters. They appear clearly in many of Jesus' observations reported in the Gospels. Paul was not alone in the estimates he had formed about Jesus. He was simply a vigorous and effective articulator of impressions that were widespread. What was the precise articulation between one idea and another that he effected?

The answer to this question leads us, more than any other topic we have had to consider in our study of the Bible, into what is called theology. This is a region which some students will not care to investigate; perhaps for them John's discussion of the nature of Christ has been a sufficient sample of the sort of complexity that theology involves—theology defined as knowledge of God and the supernatural. Such readers may say that the "whole duty of man" is a purely human one performed between the limits of birth and death. They have found the Bible's accounts—in narrative and in "wisdom"—of how early men conceived and performed this duty illuminating or curious or even deeply moving.

There are, on the other hand, two sorts of readers who would find a sketch of Paul incomplete without an outline of his doctrine. Devout Christians are likely to regard Paul's account of Christ as an indispensable commentary on the direct narratives of the synoptics and a necessary supplement to the teachings in *The Gospel of John*. Persons less devout but nevertheless concerned with finding out what makes Western man tick are not likely to pass by Paul's theological discourse. For it announces themes and poses problems that have dominated the human mind for nineteen centuries. To what degree is the human being in control of his fate? To what extent does deity intervene in that fate? Students of exact sciences dismiss these questions as unanswerable and therefore not profitable for investigation. But they are questions that have exercised the ingenuity and talent of innumerable artists and thinkers even though they—in the words of FitzGerald's Omar Khayyam—often come out by the same door they went in. In short, persons who have left St. Paul behind or who have never known his thought encounter in modern intellectual activity and in their own estimate of their own actions distant echoes of the phrases he hurled at the members of the early churches. It has been observed that the only questions highly worth asking are those that cannot be answered. Perhaps the people who judge this statement contains an element of truth will find Paul's struggles highly interesting.

The "New Dispensation"

Telling phrases that point up the opposition between earlier paths of salvation and the one which Paul indicates are "the old man" and "the new man." (The phrases appear in *Ephesians*, Chapter 4, but the implications of the contrast are worked out in *Romans*, Chapter 6, an epistle that most scholars judge was written by Paul.) The "new man" is he who has had the profit of Christ's sacrifice on the cross, if he wishes to draw on that profit. The "old man" is man, or human nature, before the time of Christ, when Christ's sacrifice had not yet taken place.

How the "new man" may set about drawing on this deposit to his credit must wait. First we must try to see how the "old man," not in touch with any such deposit, might live. In Paul's judgment, he could live according to one of two patterns. If he was a Jew, he lived by the law. If he was a Gentile, he lacked even the partial illumination which the Jews enjoyed and could live only by his natural lights. (The reader who recalls *The Wisdom of Solomon* will see how the writer of that book worked out, for his own age, this portion of Paul's problem. The Gentiles, in his view, were often not far wide of the mark which the Jews could see in the light of revealed truth.) The "old man" who was a Jew had desires such as pride, self-will, and lust, and he kept them in order by more or less blind submission to the laws of Moses. The "old man" who was a Gentile had the same set of desires and, in so far as he was not sunk in gross idolatry and its consequences, made efforts to discover and apply rules. These were rules based on his own observation; often—Paul does not deny—they had a measure of excellence. In both cases, virtue consisted of *works,* deeds performed by the Jew out of fear of God's anger if the rules were broken, deeds performed by the Gentile out of recognition that some acts produced pleasure or calm and others pain and mental unrest. As Paul saw the matter (and his vision is subject to some question if we recall the prophets on these topics), whatever of virtue and comfort the world possessed previous to the crucifixion of Christ worked itself out in externals: a succession of deeds imposed on the Jew by his fear of a jealous God, and on the Gentile by his own intellectual perceptions, his calculus of pleasure and pain. Thus, the centers from which "good works" radiated were very near the periphery of man's nature.

Neither fear nor intellectual perception of good lies deep, like the radiating center of virtue in the "new man"; neither exists at the core of man's being where, Paul is certain, the faith of a Christian exists. The "new man" has faith that he has been redeemed by Christ's sacrifice. His virtuous actions are not a product of external submission and willing (the Jewish "old man"); and they are not a product of an act of intellectual perception (the Gentile "old man"). Not that the faith of the "new man" parts company entirely with either of the other paths of the good life. Faith, like the Jewish submission to divine fiat, is a kind of willing; but it is will on a deeper level where love and confidence in deity move one rather than fear. Faith resembles the best Gentile perceptions and has an admixture of knowledge. But, we have pointed out, it is knowledge that rests not on assumptions which the unaided intellect can make about the nature of existence. Instead, it rests on a set of extraordinary events that the intellect could not have foreseen. But once the "new man" believes the events have occurred, his intellect can make them the framework of the better life. The will of the reborn man is animated by a new emotion—love, not fear. He has a knowledge that in the first place was revealed directly to the heart rather than coldly demonstrated to the five senses.

Paul, like the other prophets and teachers, employs the telling antithesis. He likes to regard the career of Christ from the point of view of *reversal,* of turning the world upside down. But we can seek for elements of continuity. As we now turn to Paul's specific belief that Christ and his death have made all the difference, we can do justice to Paul and still remember that Hosea and other prophets actually anticipated things Paul has said and set models for his frame of mind. Yet Paul's strategy which opposes the "old man" to the "new" one is defensible; the only good break is a clean break. Paul, in working to effect a clean break with old habits of thought, ignores the gradual shifts of opinion extending over centuries that have made his thought acceptable. The oppositions he dwells on are not new; the opposition between the "old man" and the "new" is not unconnected with Isaiah II's vision of how the restored Israel will, in purity of custom and righteousness of action, differ from the old Israel which God cast down. The contrast between salvation by works and salvation by some kind of faith is one pondered by several prophets as they attempt to weigh the value of Temple sacrifice to the moral health of Israel. And Paul's opposition of "the oldness of the letter" to the "newness of the spirit" (*Romans* 7:6) should bring to mind Hosea's emphasis on purity of intent, on the need to produce "fruit unto the Lord."

But these older oppositions were simple and clear. Paul's oppositions have ceased to be simple. He has to fight a battle on two fronts.

He has to define and assert a middle position between Jewish salvation by "works" and Gentile salvation by "knowledge." In *The Epistle to the Romans* we see how he charts a mid-course between the contrasting assumptions of the Jewish and Gentile "old men." The Jews failed because they sought righteousness "not by faith, but as it were by the works of the law. For they stumbled at that stumblingstone . . ." (*Romans* 9:32) The Gentiles faced another sort of difficulty. They had no law to bow to; instead, they were "tossed to and fro, and carried about with every wind of doctrine . . ." (*Ephesians* 4:14) Only Christ causes these "winds of doctrine" to cease from blowing. Only Christ can, by the same act, relieve the Hebrews from the burden of the law and lift from the Gentiles the "vanity of their mind" (*Ephesians* 4:17). Particularly is it the Gentiles who have "the understanding darkened, being alienated from the life of God through the ignorance that is in them, because of the blindness of their heart" (*Ephesians* 4:18). What is this sin of the Gentile "old men," "the blindness of their heart"? It lies, Paul indicates, in the Gentile conception of truth as a body of knowledge that one can arrive at by means of one's own powers of observation and analysis. Paul says, "For with the heart man believeth unto righteousness" (*Romans* 10:10). The mind on which the Gentiles set store will reach conclusions that are valid for thought but not for action. It is the heart which can be touched by love and convey, in action, that emotion to other persons.

If Gentile knowledge and Hebrew law observance are alike in their need of supplement and if this supplement is the unforeseen event of the crucifixion, Paul is justified in saying, "For we know that the whole creation groaneth and travaileth in pain together until now" (*Romans* 8:22). And for both "old men," Jew and pagan, the death of Christ comes to the same thing and creates a common ground between these two ancient extremes. We need follow no farther Paul's varying efforts, struggling as he does to be "all things to all men," to correct the myopia of both audiences. For what there was for both audiences to see in Christ was a single, unified vision. It is a vision that has been central in traditional Christianity. It is a vision that has only in recent times become subject to the "correction" of students who endeavor to reduce the figure of Christ to that of an ethical teacher on whom, ill-advisedly, St. Paul cast the cloak of greatness that, at this point, we scrutinize. This cloak is one which the devout Christian will believe is Christ's by right. Even the skeptical may question whether, at this late date, it is possible to distinguish what Paul saw in Christ from what Christ was—to separate, in the phrase of W. B. Yeats, the dancer from the dance. At any rate, the pattern which Paul traces out in the cloak of Christ's greatness reflects what Paul has seen in the nature of created man and the demands it makes on "the Other."

It should be plain that what follows is an effort to isolate certain key ideas in Paul's thought. When, as here, we ask: "Is mortal man ever righteous by his own power and his own works?" it is in order to trace, in brief compass, Paul's speculation at a certain point.

Paul's answer to the question just advanced—whether man can save himself by deeds and moral excellence of his own—is this:

> There is none righteous, no not one: There is none that understandeth, there is none that seeketh after God. They are all gone out of the way, they are together become unprofitable; there is none that doeth good, no, not one. (*Romans* 3:10-12.)

This pervasiveness of moral evil presents God with two courses of action. (Paul qualifies what he advances here with this phrase: "I speak as a man" [*Romans* 3:5].) Operating within the framework of the law which he gave Moses, God has only one choice: he must judge and punish all of mankind. This solution of righteous judgment and punishment is the one of which Amos spoke, we can recall. The other course of action presents the Lord as operating outside the existing framework of the law, "the old dispensation." The Lord can set up a new arrangement; he can abrogate the law, he can supplement justice with mercy, he can intervene in history and effect what, from Paul's view, no one but God can effect ;"for all have sinned, and come short of the glory of God . . ." (*Romans* 3:23). God can become a human being, capable of suffering and death. Such a death all mortals are worthy of suffering, but not deity. It is this death which creates what Paul calls "grace" and what may be called, loosely, mercy available to all mankind, Jew and Gentile. Since all men are "gone out of the way," there is no created being who truly deserves this gift. Thus, it is a "free gift." Whoever has faith that such a gift is, by the crucifixion, made available to him may, by that one movement of the will, seize upon it and enjoy it.

The fruits of faith are, to Jew and Gentile, quite simple. The reborn man has a sense of security—of having been lifted to a level of moral experience where the exactions of the law and the scruples of the intellect no longer are galling.

Prudence breaks in on Paul's ideal statement of what he sees as he stands on the heights. He points out two consequences that do not come from this "free gift." It is true that the occasion of the crucifixion, of the gift of grace, was human sin. "Shall we continue in sin that grace may abound?" With horror Paul exclaims, "God forbid" (*Romans* 6:1). (It was a variation of this gratifying doctrine that, nineteen centuries later, the monk Rasputin imparted to the ladies of the czarist court.) And shall those who are aware that they have grace—which ends the law, which undoes the burden of sin carried by man—feel that they can now do with impunity what Moses forbade? "Shall we sin, because we are not under the law, but under grace?" Again Paul says: "God forbid" (*Romans* 6:15).

Philosophers have pointed out that what diminishes one tension is likely eventually to produce others. The allied doctrines of grace and salvation by faith have led to exaggerations. Thus, the eighteenth-century sect called the Quietists advocated an utterly passive religious attitude. They judged that *works*—i.e., good deeds, attacks on evil—had no connection with the advent of the gift of faith in the individual soul. A reading of all of Paul's epistles should show that the advent of grace did not diminish Paul's own good works or his expectation of them in his followers. He judged, however, that the good works of believers were no longer the product of fear or calculation. They were the spontaneous overflow of what he calls charity or love.

Foreknowledge

Two other gifts of St. Paul to the corpus of Christian belief are the doctrine of God's foreknowledge and, along with what *The Gospel of St. John* contributes, speculation as to the Trinity. These are facets of Christianity that have bruised many palms; and various emery wheels have gone to work on them. What progress these have made does not concern us. We are concerned with winning a clear, succinct view of what Paul offered the Jews and Gentiles.

When Paul is speaking of those who "love God" or will in future times love God, he makes a crucial statement about their identity:

> And we know that all things work together for good to them that love God, to them who are called according to his purpose. For whom he did foreknow, he also did predestinate to be conformed to the image of his Son, that he might be the firstborn among many brethren. (*Romans* 8:28-29.)

"Predestinate" is, in more gentle translations, "choose." The implication of this act puts a serious strain on the description that St. Paul has otherwise given of "the Other." "The Other," he has said in considerable accord with earlier prophets and seers, is righteous; and "the Other" tempers his righteous demands by mercy even to undergoing incarnation in the form of the "suffering servant" in order to provide grace for mankind.

Paul asks:

> What if God, willing to shew his wrath, and to make his power known, endured with much longsuffering the vessels of wrath fitted to destruction: and that he might make known the riches of his glory on the vessels of mercy, which he had afore prepared unto glory, even us, whom he hath called, not of the Jews only, but also of the Gentiles? (*Romans* 9:22-24.)

And Paul quotes with approval the arbitrary deity who spoke thus to Moses: "I will have mercy on whom I will have mercy, and I will have compassion on whom I will have compassion" (*Romans* 9:15).

Is this not a return to a previous attitude without an improvement on that attitude? Is not this power of God utterly to foretell what turns the human will shall take but a slightly more subtle statement of the arbitrary justice that God once meted out to his chosen people at the expense of their enemies? And since God foresees whether the will of each person will accept or reject the gift of grace, is this not a return to the phrase in Exodus: "The Lord hardened Pharaoh's heart, and he would not let the people go"? We have noted, in Christ's teaching activity, a return to some of the offices of Elijah in the way of miracle and dramatic instruction. But in Christ's activity, one sees also the manifest profit of the ages that separate Elijah from Christ. Those who judge harshly Paul's doctrine of "foreknowledge" call it, in effect, a return to earlier attitudes *without* the profit of all that has occurred in intervening centuries; they suggest that by this doctrine the loving Father of the Gospels is made once more into the arbitrary deity worshiped by the early Hebrews.

In explanation of Paul's choice, one may say that Paul insists on attitudes that are painful—particularly when they later flower in Calvin's doctrines of infant damnation, the "elect," etc.—for philosophic reasons as well as intuitional ones. It was easy for the writers of the synoptic Gospels to tell the story of the God-man-Satan relation with a direct, naïve attribution to Satan of all that hamstrings the human will: Satan tempts Christ, he presides over the region where men will weep and gnash their teeth. It was less easy for the writer of *John* to handle the problem of the origin of moral evil. Although he too speaks of "the prince of this world," his mind dwells on the ladder of perfection reaching, in Platonic wise, from nullity to the absolute being of God. It is extremely difficult for Paul to provide a large role for Satan. Too large a role assigns to Satan real power that can inconvenience deity as well as man. Such a role for "the evil one" suggests, in fact, the kind of dualism that Persian religion offered its believers. To take this role from Satan, to make him into a stage supernumerary and not a real character in the eternal drama of sin and restoration, Paul had to strip him of his power over man. True, the devil and his tools live on in Paul's letters, but they operate only with the permission of God while man is under the law of Moses; in theory, they can no longer touch the man who has had the gift of grace. Further, the man who has *not* taken the gift of grace fails not because of the devil but because of the constitution of his own will and intelligence, which have been fashioned by God rather than the devil.

Some such necessity as this urged the framing of the concepts of "foreknowledge." If for no other reason, the pinions of the devil had to be cut back; they had grown too long during the centuries when he had been a person of some importance in Jewish story and apocalyptic. God, in consequence, seems to harden the heart of the man who is not "elected" to enjoy grace as he once hardened Pharaoh's heart. But one should do Paul the justice of seeing that the attribute of deity has been created differently. The act in *Exodus* is the "projected" attribute of a monarch of absolute power. The act of deity is, in Paul's thought, forced upon Paul by his own definition of deity. God may be merciful; but he is also by definition the one being that is the source of all other being. To put the matter flippantly, Satan may not even function as a third vice-president. And if Satan is deprived of all initiative, then the hardness of men's hearts is once more dependent on the divine act of creation. St. John is not forced into a position so painful to contemplate. For him moral evil is but a failure to perceive the good, a kind of fall in the direction of nullity and emptiness. But Paul is a better psychologist; evil is felt as a presence, not an absence; and it is evil as a presence, a power that moves us, that Paul's theory endeavors to account for. What moves us to sin—or to antisocial action, as we say at present—is sensed by us to be a force, not a vacuum, as the Platonists have it.

The second reason that urges Paul to accept the theory of God's foreknowledge is one much more easily explained. To say that God, whose own existence is in the dimension of eternity—Christ said: "Before Abraham was, I am" (*John* 8:58)—could not know what is to take place in a sequence of events is to admit a radical imperfection on the part of deity. A man sitting on a high hill can watch the road that curves around it and can foresee that the load of hay on his left hand is presently going to bar the highway to the red convertible on the right. A deity to whom all history is a kind of eternal present could scarcely, by the philosophically aware Paul, be denied complete knowledge of all that is to take place.

One need not deny that Paul's speculation on this topic leads to the qualification of what, in the synoptics, is as open and simple as the sun. There a man simply follows Christ and puts Satan and his works behind. How a man becomes able to effect this reversal of old habits and what the consequences to him are—these questions did not trouble the synoptists. In Paul's experience and in the experience of many men since, they did arise.

The Doctrine of the Trinity

The last doctrine to be considered here—the doctrine of the Trinity—has left its mark on the history of Western thought, whatever modern estimates of it may be. It is far more explicitly stated in *John* than in the letters of Paul; but with John it is but part of what one contemplates and with the letters of Paul it is a presupposition of the action of grace and for that reason finds its place here.

As John has it: "For there are three that bear record in heaven, the Father, the Word [Christ], and the Holy Ghost: and these three are one" (*I John* 5:7). The Holy Ghost—or Spirit—is represented in *The Gospel of John* as the "Comforter" that Christ promises his Church when he is on the verge of departure. The refinements of definition of the relation among the three persons were forced on Paul and John (as with the other doctrines to which Paul had to commit himself and the synoptists did not) by both the Jews and the Gentiles, converted or unconverted. The Jews, who regarded themselves as strict monotheists, accused the Christians of being polytheists and worshiping three gods. The pagan Gentiles had no great objection to a number of deities—three, indeed, was modest. But the pagan man in the street had to be reminded that the three aspects of Christian deity were not three deities separately revered.

And if a Gentile convert were a Platonist, he had to be kept from regarding Christ and the Holy Spirit as mere subordinate emanations that did the unpleasant work of creation and redemption which Platonists considered unworthy of the unalterable, self-contained One. Such views, historians judge, cropped up with some frequency in the early Christian era; they constitute what is termed the *Gnostic* heresy—because of the secret, superior *knowledge* which the teachers of these views maintained they had from this apostle or that. To offset these Platonic and Gnostic views, an orthodox Christian apologist had to make two assertions, both offensive. He had to say that Christ was, at a definite time in history, a real man and not a simulacrum untouched by the apparent sufferings of the physical shape of Jesus. He also had to insist that Christ was—outside of time and in eternity—utterly identical with God rather than, as heretics had it, an emanation of deity. If this *both-and* paradox had not been put up against the logical *either-or* that the Gentiles had suggested (either Jesus was a mortal man and died on the cross *or* he was a deity and did not really suffer there), Gentile philosophy would have taken over the interpretation of the story of Christ, and the uniqueness and peculiarities of Christian teachings would have been lost. As they would have stated it (and did state it in future disputes) either Christ was merely a man, and hence incapable of performing a role resembling that of the saving being in a mystery religion, or he was a god only or a member of some god's bureaucracy, and so no more real than Hercules and his fabled labors. This was a dilemma, and the Christians could sacrifice neither horn of it, as a cultivated Gentile—aware of Aristotle's "A thing cannot be and not-be at the same time"—would feel impelled to do. Both alternatives, however logically opposed, had to be preserved because either one (the manhood of Christ, and the godhead of Christ) was regarded as true and essential to faith not only because of theoretical necessities but because of what the apostles of Christ recalled concerning his life, his utterances, and his death.

Similar is the dilemma closely involved with that concerning Christ's own nature: the unitary deity who displays himself in three aspects or "persons." To the ironic Gentile, it must have seemed that in settling for one god or three gods lay the solution. But instead John and Paul—and masses of other Christians—were forced by what they regarded as revelation into the *both-and* position of insisting that God was one *and* three. They were forced into this position by a sensed reality as real as the humanity of Christ. Christians who were Jewish in origin knew that God was one; yet they had "proof"—Christ's assertions about his nature and his miraculous return from the dead—that Christ was also God. They also had traditions about the spectacular descent of the Holy Spirit at Pentecost and its less spectacular but constant aid in the years that had followed. To the early Christians, in the Old Testament lay the "proof" of the oneness of God; but recent events had presented them with two new aspects of deity that the Old Testament did not reveal, or reveal fully: the Son or the Word, and the Holy Spirit.

A plain—and doubtless insufficient—parallel to the "mystery" of the Trinity as understood by John and Paul is the fairly transparent mystery of the relation of one good man to three different demands: as a father he is just and merciful to his children; as a son he is dutiful, deferential, and perhaps even in maturity obedient to his parents; as a businessman he is firm, skillful, and honest. These three "personalities" involved are not entirely alike, nor—unless the man's life be hopelessly divided into compartments so that he is a sentimental father and son and a ruthless competitor in business—are they absolutely different. At least, we see that the good man among his children or talking to his elderly parents is essentially the same man that we first met in his office. We soon come to allow for differences in language and tempo in each newly perceived relation in which a friend is involved. In the Trinity, this inadequate analogy suggests, the activity of Christ the Word redeems the world, the activity of God created the world (with, according to *John*, the aid of the Word), and the activity of the Holy Spirit preserves the world. These are crude distinctions that later theology refined; but they suffice to explain why *The Gospel of John* returns to this theme again and again. When, in *John*, Philip says to Christ: "Lord, show us the Father, and it sufficeth us," an interchange begins which concerns this mystery. What can rest as simple Sonship and Messiahship in the synoptics has to be defined. Christ says to Philip:

> Have I been so long time with you, and yet hast thou not known me, Philip? he that hath seen me hath seen the Father; and how sayest thou then, Show us the Father. Believest thou not that I am in the Father, and the Father in me? the words that I speak unto you I speak not of myself: but the Father that dwelleth in me, he doeth the works. Believe me that I am in the Father, and the Father in me: or else believe me for the very works' sake. (*John* 14:8-11.)

Christ, for John—and for Paul—is "the way," "the water of life," because he is identical with the Lord of Israel himself. The signal difference between John and Paul at this point is that Paul perceives Christ in the mode of action rather in the mode of happy contemplation that pervades a good deal of *John*. For John, Christ is "Christ the Word"; for Paul he is "the saving victim" because—and only because—he who is sacrificed is identical with the being who creates and legislates. If Christ were not God, there would be no gift of grace; the death of Christ upon the cross would be but the death of one more good man misjudged and disposed of by the proud and ignorant. Only this estimate of what Christ was can justify the bold assertions which Paul flings out at his followers.

> Purge out therefore the old leaven, that ye may be a new lump, as ye are unleavened. For even Christ our passover is sacrificed for us. (*I Corinthians* 5:7.)
>
> The first man is of the earth, earthy: the second man is the Lord from heaven. (*I Corinthians* 15:47.)

It is the Stoic view of God that at this point draws near to the Christian "folly." The Stoic, who told us that God was indwelling in the world, would not be daunted by the Christian conception of the function of the Holy Spirit. But here too St. Paul would insist on a distinction; he would insist that his God was not simply the indwelling order of the world and indistinguishable from it. He would return to the old Hebrew view, naïve as it might seem, that God created the world out of nothing and is, so long as he wills, independent of his handiwork, and that he becomes, in the incarnation, involved in it not of necessity (as with the Stoic deity who is no more than the order of the universe) but by free choice.

The most famous passage in Paul's letters (*I Corinthians* chap. 13) does not deny the elements in his thought framed in defense of a religion that the Jews refused to countenance and that the pagans either hesitated to accept or were eager to capture and distort into a likeness of other faiths. But this chapter in *Corinthians* passes beyond his speculations just as does the thought of St. John when he leaves his rather formal discourse to give us a passage joining his Christ to that of the synoptics.

> A new commandment I give unto you, That ye love one another: as I have loved you, that ye also love one another. By this shall all men know that ye are my disciples, if ye have love one to another. (*John* 13:34.)

Paul's passage seems to suggest that, in his own phrase, he has elsewhere been at work providing his churches with "milk for babes," and that here is his final declaration of humility in the midst of much that does not seem like humility. Paul specifically confesses that "prophecies," "tongues," and "knowledge" shall pass away, even though it is "knowledge" as a basis for action that he has been busily fashioning.

> Though I speak with the tongues of men and of angels, and have not charity, I am become as sounding brass, or a tinkling cymbal. And though I have the gift of prophecy, and understand all mysteries, and all knowledge; and though I have all faith, so that I could remove mountains, and have not charity, I am nothing. (*I Corinthians* 13:1-2.)

For all his brave words elsewhere, he now confesses he knows "in part"—no more:

> For now we see through a glass darkly; but then face to face: now

> I know in part; but then shall I know even as I am known. (*I Corinthians* 13:12.)

It is this passion—to be known of God—that was central in Paul's journeys, scourgings, and dangerous escapes. It was central in his no less demanding mental travels. Paul is, in this passage, speaking of a kind of knowing that lies in the heart rather than in the mind and is, in its operation, indistinguishable from "charity" or love. The order in the last verse of the chapter suggests that faith receives its completion in love. "And now abideth faith, hope, charity, these three; but the greatest of these is charity" (*I Corinthians* 13:13). This is a great concession from a man who has placed in so elevated a position faith and his specific, binding glosses on faith. It is, a believer would feel, the power of the specific living figure of Christ at last clarifying—for Paul as for John—the partial and struggling apprehension of a created being.

CHAPTER XX

New Testament Apocalyptic: *The Revelation of St. John*

THE REVELATION OF ST. JOHN, which closes the New Testament, was for many centuries regarded as the inevitable and right conclusion to the collection of books that made manifest the "new dispensation." To devout imaginations, this book was the rounding out of all that one could perceive imperfectly in the history of the Hebrews and in the times of Christ. The author of the book identifies himself quite flatly:

> I John, who also am your brother, and companion in tribulation, and in the kingdom and patience of Jesus Christ, was in the Isle that is called Patmos, for the word of God, and for the testimony of Jesus Christ. (*Revelation* 1:9.)

This "John" conventional judgment identified with the author of the Fourth Gospel, with "the disciple whom Jesus loved." Corollary information that the Roman emperor Domitian commenced large-scale persecution of the Christians in Asia Minor in the year 93 has added details to this traditional picture of the creation of *Revelation.* It has been suggested that the author was sent along with other Christians to the penal colony which is known to have existed on the island of Patmos in the Aegean Sea, not far from the city of Ephesus on the mainland.

The Book of Revelation resembles a large body of Hebrew literature written in the previous two or three hundred years and called "apocalyptic"; it reveals or uncovers matters that for many ages had been concealed to man. Hebrew apocalyptic, as well as this Christian example, was concerned with "last things," with those grand but horrifying events that should terminate human history. It may not be a form of writing immediately congenial or intelligible to modern readers, but it was immediately intelligible to first-century Christians of Jewish origin. These readers, at least, would not find themselves in a strange country when, in *Revelation,* they read of the following matters: the Day of the Lord which, in some way, is a day of judgment and retribution for evil and injustice; the return of Christ in the role of conqueror and judge; the first encounter with Satan, who is tied up until the time of the final battle between good and evil; the setting up of the kingdom of earthly peace which lasts for a thousand years or a "millennium"; the second encounter between the hosts of light and the hosts of darkness at Armageddon, near the historical Megiddo on the plain of Esdraelon where the ancient Hebrews had met many of their enemies in times past; and the end of all earthly, time-contained existence when the "new Jerusalem"—Jerusalem as it shall exist in eternity—descends from heaven. A modern person may find this pageant of "last things" confusing; the first readers—and many readers for centuries thereafter—found it thrilling and heartening.

The writer of *Revelation* perhaps indicates that he knows his book of vision is one of a popular genre, for he is careful to assert that his particular revelation is holy and inspired, even though its materials —the images of punishment, disaster, and glory—are the stock in trade of many writers. At the conclusion of *Revelation* this assertion appears:

> And if any man shall take away from the words of the book of this prophecy, God shall take away his part out of the book of life, and out of the holy city, and from the things which are written in this book. (*Revelation* 22:18-19.)

This declaration resembles one in *The Gospel of John:* "And he that saw it bare record, and his record is true: and he knoweth that he saith true, that ye might believe" (*John* 19:35). We know that the early Christian world saw many prophets who transformed the Christian teaching into forms that departed very widely from what Paul, for example, judged was the essence of Christianity. When the writer of *Revelation* warns against those who would tamper with his vision to make it prove their special points, he is but taking a precaution that his audience would understand.

Other reasons as well as assertions about the importance of what vision presented gave this book the hold that, in many ages, it had on the popular imagination. The interest of the book is intense but narrow; it ignores the moral questions that are recurrent in history. It is concerned with events which will happen only once, events

CHART 14. Events to the End of the First Century

CHRISTIAN EVENTS		JUDEA		ROME	
	Creation of the synoptic gospels (see Chart 12)	66	Revolt of the Jews	69-79	Vespasian
		70	Fall of Jerusalem: destruction of the city		
				79-81	Titus
				81-96	Domitian
		70-135	Jewish council at Jamnia, to set up a basis for the continuance of Judaism without Jerusalem		
93	*Revelation*			93	Persecutions of Domitian
				96-98	Nerva
90-100	*John*			98-117	Trajan

which will bear unquestionable marks of what they are. In ages when devout belief was general and also when the very framework of society seemed to topple, *Revelation* was as timely as a modern syndicated column with its "predictions of things to come." For example, such a period was that just before the year 1000. The round number 1000 and the political chaos of the time combined to suggest to men that the seals of the book of judgment would soon be broken and the vials of God's wrath emptied on a guilty mankind. Another such period is our own, the first half of the twentieth century, when frequent wars and international chaos suggest to devout and literal readers of *Revelation* that the Day of the Lord is at hand. In our times as well as others, ingenious persons have manipulated the numerals that appear in the predictions of *Revelation;* they were able to find, for example, that the First World War was to cease on November 11, 1918; and, more recently, devout persons supposed that the beast with seven heads and ten horns was Hitler and his puppet regimes. Certainly the thought may occur to all of us, when we look on the succession of peace and war in our time, that the tangle and conflict of national and economic interests is never going to be untangled by men. We may say, despondingly, that only some kind of "miracle" can draw us from the center of the tempest to waters that are peaceful and still.

The writer of *Revelation* believed, of course, in the literal possibility of such a miracle; he expected a flat intervention of the divine that would terminate the agonizing ups and downs of human history. Whatever came to him in vision only made more precise this expectation that he shared with the early Church. If the early Church was to have its promised triumph and survive further persecutions like those of Nero at Rome (64 A.D.) and Domitian in Asia Minor (93 A.D.), it was a triumph that would have to be brought about by divine and not by human power. In John's view, the "seven churches" of Asia Minor—the churches to whom the account of the vision is addressed—have not weathered the perils of the first century too well. In the first three chapters of *Revelation* John tries to commend these churches when he can, and he praises those that have produced martyrs, men who have not compromised with their pagan rulers. But some of the churches are in a bad way. Thus, the members of the church at Pergamos "eat things sacrificed unto idols," and some of them hold "the doctrine of the Nicolaitanes," which apparently encouraged compromise with pagan culture all along the line (*Revelation* 2:13-14). Again, after the "angel"—the guardian or guiding spirit—of the church of Thyatira is praised for "works, and charity, and service, and faith," the sad truth has to be admitted:

> Notwithstanding I have a few things against thee, because thou sufferest that woman Jezebel, which calleth herself a prophetess, to teach and to seduce my servants to commit fornication, and to eat things sacrificed unto idols. (*Revelation* 2:20.)

In more temperate language, the pressure of persecution has produced teachers who argue that compromise and syncretism are no great harm when judiciously practiced. Henry IV of France said, when he renounced his Protestantism for the Catholic faith: "Paris is worth a mass." "Jezebel" and her kind argued that one's life was worth more than a foolish consistency that made one draw back from participating in an empty pagan sacrifice or so. But this is not John's view; one is either a Christian, or one is not a Christian. Indeed, worse than the churches which he first censures is the church of Laodicea, where there is neither positive good nor positive evil. Of this church he writes:

> I know thy works, that thou art neither cold nor hot: I would thou were cold or hot. So then because thou art lukewarm, and neither cold nor hot, I will spue thee out of my mouth. (*Revelation* 3:15-16.)

Humanly speaking, *The Book of Revelation* must have had the immediate effect of stiffening the backbones of the members of the "seven churches" and churches elsewhere. To them, many a figure of speech that John employs would have had immediate meaning. "The woman on the beast," Babylon (chap. 17),[1] would be no other than Rome, that had become intoxicated and now maddened the world with the wine of her cruelty and idolatry; and Rome likewise would be the beast to whom the dragon (Satan) gives power.

> And I stood upon the sand of the sea, and saw a beast rise up out of the sea, having seven heads and ten horns, and upon his horns ten crowns, and upon his heads the name of blasphemy. (*Revelation* 13:1.)

Though it is not the aim of apocalyptic to attain clarity, the early Christians could recognize other elements in their religion and the account it gave of the world. "The great wonder in heaven" (*Revelation* 12:1)—a woman who, in her birth pangs, rouses the ceaseless enmity of the dragon—some would recognize as Israel personified or

[1] The references in this chapter are to *Revelation* unless otherwise noted.

even as the mother of all mankind whom Satan was bound to undo. And the Laodiceans and the wavering Christians at Thyatira could draw strength from what John says of the breaking of the sixth seal:

> . . . I beheld, and lo, a great multitude, which no man could number, of all nations, and kindreds, and people, and tongues, stood before the throne, and before the Lamb, clothed with white robes, and palms in their hands. . . . (*Revelation* 7:9.)

John asks who these are, and he is told: "These are they which came out of great tribulation, and have washed their robes, and made them white in the blood of the Lamb" (7:14). This is the portrait of the faithful in the "latter days"; it is intended to hearten the indecisive and fearful.

As indicated, much of the early power of *Revelation* was due to its being the culmination of a kind of composition that had been, for several centuries, vastly attractive to the Jews. The style of apocalyptic writings seems to stem from the over-literal and precise development of the metaphors by which the old prophets were wont to refer to their insights about "the Other." (Another expansion of the metaphor, that which led to the parable, remains attractive today. There the only sensed effects of grotesqueness are the sort we perceived in the parable of the wise and foolish virgins, where the psychological effect of the narrative, the expanded metaphor, is at odds with the teaching point which it serves.) Hebrew apocalyptic does not employ to any degree the aid of ordinary narrative or homely detail. It is concerned with the wonders of the Lord's eternal realm and the grandiose plans which the Lord has for mankind. Still moving to the majority of modern readers is a compressed or undeveloped metaphor that refers to this area of interest. The metaphors with which the vision of Isaiah II begins are ecstatic rather than systematic (*Isaiah*, chap. 40). The coal of fire that touches Isaiah's lips is a good reference to what is difficult to convey by any means: the sense we often have of being possessed by a painful and burning task. But the book that Ezekiel eats (*Ezekiel* 2:9-3:3) is a step toward the traditional Hebrew apocalyptic, in which trenchant and fleeting insight is pinned down, embroidered, and made very precise.

To some tastes such literary needlework is aesthetically painful. Manifestly, persons who feel this way could not take delight either in *Revelation* or in the Old Testament apocalyptic in *Daniel.* Yet a glance at a passage or two in *Daniel,* where the technique is less bewildering, helps the reader who intends to persist with *Revelation.* In *Daniel* 2:24-45 we can observe how the future course of history is minutely linked with an explanation of the composite image that has appeared to Nebuchadnezzar in sleep. What would be acceptable as a brief simile that compared Israel's enemies to a monstrous figure is made to serve as the clue to Daniel's long prophecy of the successive falls of Israel's enemies and the final triumph of Israel. The explanation ranges from the "head of gold" (Babylon) to the feet where clay and iron are mixed (the politically heterodox kingdom of the Seleucids); and such an explanation certainly would fascinate the Jews who were resisting Antiochus Epiphanes, a Seleucid ruler, particularly when Daniel explains that the stone "cut out of the mountain without hands" (*Daniel* 2:45) and destined to shatter the image is none other than Israel itself. Daniel's reading of the monarch's dream—like many of the conclusions which *Revelation* urges upon us—leads to a very specific promise. Whether the promise is aesthetically moving is beside the point; from the point of view of a beleaguered people, the promise implicit in Daniel's explanation was heartening. Similarly encouraging, in *Daniel,* would appear other flat statements of a Messianic cast that involves the "Ancient of days" and the "Son of man" (*Daniel* 7:9 and 7:13).

Literal promises as to future events, exhaustively described visions of the day of the Lord, pictures of the last battles and of the palaces of heaven—from the time of *Daniel* onward, such panoramas heartened and comforted the Hebrews as they struggled to survive. *The Testament of Moses* and *The Book of Enoch* were later works that purported to be accounts of the revelation granted Moses and Enoch in former times. These books—"presumed writings" or pseudepigrapha—borrowed the authority of an ancient name. (Enoch's authority is fragile indeed; all we are told of him in *Genesis* 5:21-23 is that he "walked with God" and that "God took him.") They continued into New Testament times the kind of development of insight offered by *Daniel* and by *Revelation.* A good deal of the prophetic emphasis in *Amos, Hosea,* and *Isaiah* falls on ethical perceptions that immediately commend themselves to us; and if "last things" are touched, they are touched glancingly and movingly as if these prophets were aware, along with Job, that there are some things too high for mortal man to study. The mood of apocalyptic is, needless to say, the mood of close study; the writers do not hesitate to detail the stones that make up the heavenly pavements and the armaments of the legions which the Messiah leads against Satan. To most modern readers, a phrase like that of Christ—"The kingdom of heaven is within you"—is full of power and suggestion because it is imprecise and incomplete. But to some minds such a phrase is unsatisfactory. They desire a blueprint of the kingdom. *Revelation,* like apocalyptic in general, is concerned with furnishing that blueprint.

Thus, in *Revelation,* the breaking of the seven seals of the book in the hand of God (*Revelation,* chap. 5 ff.) and the seven vials that pour out on the earth the various pestilences that betoken God's anger (chap. 16) advise one just what forms judgment will take. And the description of heaven (chap. 21) fills out, for some minds, Christ's own imprecise statements, which often leave one free to suppose, if he will, that heaven is a state of mind rather than a region to be sensed physically in vivid, raw colors. Full and explicit is the description of the court of the Lord in Chapter 4, with all the abundance of detail that appears in *Daniel* and elsewhere. We are told "there was a rainbow round about the throne, in sight like unto an emerald" (*Revelation* 4:3) and that the Lord is fully attended by "four and twenty elders." (Some suggest that these are simply angels, and others that they are a group made up of twelve Old Testament patriarchs and the twelve apostles.) Near the throne are four beasts which chant, "Holy, holy, holy, Lord God Almighty, which was, and is, and is to come"; and the beasts are so wonderful or at least so complex that the visual imagination is strained by them almost as much as by the wheeling creatures in the first chapter of *Ezekiel.*

These items and others suggest that the very grand is always in danger of becoming the very grotesque. The woman in Chapter 12 who brings forth the man child, the enemy of Satan, is given "two wings of a great eagle" to escape her enemy the dragon (*Revelation* 12:14); and the portrait of the "Son of man" which combines elements appearing in *Daniel* 7:9 and 7:13 is thus drawn:

> And in the midst of the seven candlesticks one like unto the Son of man, clothed with a garment down to the foot, and girt about the paps with a golden girdle. His head and his hairs were white like wool, as white as snow; and his eyes were as a flame of fire. (*Revelation* 1:13-14.)

Such pictures are as likely to disconcert as to impress. Particularly is the visual imagination strained to the breaking point by a detail toward the end of this description: ". . . out of his mouth went a sharp two-edged sword . . ." (1:16). It is one thing to say, in glancing metaphor, that the words of a speaker were two-edged swords; but the images in *Revelation* demand precise visualization at every point.

Whatever our aesthetic judgment of this book, we cannot ignore the circumstance that in it are certain statements which, for many centuries, filled out the Christian revelation. Scruples of taste should not keep readers from getting a clear grasp on what *Revelation* does indeed assert. Further, *Revelation* can suggest certain concluding observations about the long train of religious experience which we have been following.

First, the figures and visions we have commented on compose, for John, a continuous vision, with each separate and strange image a step toward the final unfolding. In the courts of the Lord, the seven seals of the book of judgment are broken, and their spell lets loose on the world, to begin with, the famous four horsemen: conquest, slaughter, famine, and, upon a pale horse, death himself. The three last seals permit us to see the saved with the mark of the Lord on their foreheads (later, we learn of those who bear the mark of the beast); we hear the angelic trumpets that bring on the great plagues. Perhaps Chapters 12-14 may be regarded as a symbolically stated history of what *Genesis-Acts* covers more soberly: the events that have placed mankind on the verge of the concluding act of man's story. For we see the woman (the mother of mankind); and we hear of the "war in heaven" between the good and bad angels that enmity to her and her seed has stirred up (12:7). And under the figure of the beast from the sea (chap. 13) and, somewhat later, the woman of Babylon, the recent march of Roman power is seen as the final earthly display of the powers of evil. Mingled, however, with this retrospective account in *Revelation* are the imminent plagues and destructions that are to overtake man as the vials of divine wrath are emptied. Babylon, the power-state that has oppressed the seven churches John addresses, at last falls; and with her go down "the kings of the earth."

There follows upon this fall the concluding sequence of events in which Christ the conquering Messiah, the rider upon a "white horse" (19:11), is the chief wonder of wonders. This "Word of God" (19:13) or "King of Kings" (19:16) makes possible the savage invitation to the "supper of the great God" (19:18) where all the fowls of the air feast on the slaughtered and where, at the same time, the beast is taken.

> And the beast was taken, and with him the false prophet that wrought miracles before him, with which he deceived them that had received the mark of the beast, and them that worshiped his image. These both were cast alive into a lake of fire burning with brimstone. (*Revelation* 19:20.)

(It is interesting to see that when this event is restated at the outset of Chapter 20, the angel's conquest of the Evil One employs figures that are as old as Babylonian mythology. "And he laid hold on the dragon, that old serpent, which is the Devil and Satan, and bound him a thousand years" [20:2]. This figure, in Isaiah II, contributed a detail to the sketch of the redeemer.) At this point, in our far from simple story, takes place "the first resurrection," which is for those who have shown plainly by martyrdom that they do not have the "mark of the beast." Those who were not martyrs—so John encourages the feeble-willed—must wait a thousand years for the second resurrection. After Satan, who has been loosed from his thousand-year imprisonment to stir up temporary trouble, is cast into his lake of fire and brimstone, the members of the general resurrection are to be lined up before "the great white throne."

> And I saw the dead, small and great, stand before God; and the books were opened: and another book was opened, which is the book of life: and the dead were judged out of those things which were written in the books, according to their works. . . . And whosoever was not found written in the book of life was cast into the lake of fire. (*Revelation* 20:12-15.)

At this point time will end, and all those men who are worthy will be absorbed into eternity. As John writes:

> And I saw a new heaven and a new earth: for the first heaven and the first earth were passed away; and there was no more sea. And I John saw the holy city, new Jerusalem, coming down from God out of heaven, prepared as a bride adorned for her husband. (*Revelation* 21:1-2.)

God will greet his people and will ". . . wipe away all tears from their eyes; and there shall be no more death, neither sorrow, nor crying, neither shall there be any more pain: for the former things are passed away" (21:4). This verse, poetic and unexplicit and thus a touching picture of the meeting between God and his chosen ones, is quickly succeeded by the exact description of the "new Jerusalem" which occupies sixteen verses and is, among other things, a catalogue of stones the ancients regarded as precious.

This chain of events has become "classic" in the sense that it has, for many generations, established certain expectations that people in Western culture have had of the future; these often repeat the attitudes that the Jews of the New Testament period had concerning their own future as a race. Some critics of Christianity charge that *The Book of Revelation* has provided Christian sects with a warrant for self-righteousness that one does not find in the catholic spirit encountered in the Gospels and St. Paul. Three examples of the sort of sectarian interpretation to which *Revelation* is subject will suffice. At the time of the separation of Protestants from the Church of Rome, the Protestants were ready to believe that they were the martyrs whose white robes had been washed in the blood of the Lamb and that the woman on the beast was none other than the Church of Rome which oppressed them. *The Book of Revelation* has also been meat and drink to Russian Christians who believed—as we see in Dostoevski and elsewhere—that their country was "Holy Russia" and should precede all other countries on the path to salvation. (This belief is not absent from present Russian speculation, though the language in which it is couched is no longer that of St. John.) Finally, *Revelation* lends itself to use by the evangelists who, throughout the last seventy-five or a hundred years have begged their hearers to "hit the sawdust trail" and write themselves a through ticket to Jerusalem the Golden.

That such special uses do *The Book of Revelation* less than justice is already plain. *Revelation* must be understood in the first place as a member in a long series of Jewish Messianic, eschatological works, works concerned with "last things." It is separated from these others because it incorporates the Christian insight that finally forced Peter to turn to the Gentiles: that salvation and "last things" concerned all men. The eschatological frame of mind is misrepresented by the fairly recent interpretations and uses we have just mentioned. *Revelation* is an effort to sum up, in the sort of language and imagery that the Jews had been using for several centuries, what the meaning of Christianity was to all mankind. The language of vision is not the language of literal statement; it moves *toward* prose (hence the abundant misinterpretations or simplifications of a book like *Revelation*), but the reader does well to recall that the point of departure for whatever is painstakingly worked out in *Revelation* was deeply felt insight rather than dispassionately observed fact.

Among the Gentiles whom it reached John's book made a special appeal which it is well to understand. To them, this prophecy would indeed seem *sui generis*. It offered the pagan world not only a savior but a theory of history unlike that which most people accepted. A common Greek and Roman theory of history was that events moved in cycles and that, with the certainty of clockwork, the "Great Year" would return and, thereafter, all the other years. (Something like this theory finds expression in the phrase from *Ecclesiastes* 1:9: "The thing that hath been, it is that which shall be; and that which is done is that which shall be done: and there is no new thing under the sun.") When the Greeks and Romans were distressed with contemporary chaos, they sought mental and imaginative relief in thinking of the distant simplicities of a golden age when (say) Rome had just been founded or when all men lived a simple pastoral life; and they endured the bitterness of the present point in the cycle of years by hoping that the "golden age" would ensue upon the age of chaos and moral corruption in which they lived. More generally, the classic imagination was time-contained; it did not attempt to suppose that either the gods themselves or mortals could escape the unvarying revolutions of the cycles of years. Thus, to Gentiles of cultivation, the fresh raw colors of the message in *Revelation* would be new things. For the "golden age" of which the Christian book spoke was one that had never occurred in the historical past and would not come to pass in a purely historical future. To establish it—to bring down the "new Jerusalem"—deity put an abrupt end to the wearisome processes of history. If there is no end to the ups and downs of history, perhaps the Epicureans and Cynics of the pagan world and the "Solomon" of *Ecclesiastes* were right. The writer of *Ecclesiastes* has it that to everything there is a season: "A time to weep, and a time to laugh; a time to mourn, and a time to dance" (*Ecclesiastes* 3:4). The consequent course of action? One is wise to eat and drink and be merry, for tomorrow—if we are completely involved in the time process—we all die. But the intrusion of eternity into history alters this. In the kingdom which the Messiah sets up beyond the limits of time—a first-century reader might judge—the alternation of weeping and rejoicing, of good and evil rulers and societies would cease. As John seems to point out to the revelers and fornicators (22:15), in a universe that is scheduled to come to an end and that is not a series of cycles which man's behavior cannot affect or alter for himself or others, man should give some thought to how he eats, drinks, and revels. For tomorrow he lives—"lives" through the events of which *Revelation* speaks or (more generally) comes face to face with an existence which has a dimension in eternity as well as the familiar one in time. It was this latter non-Hellenistic conception that, in the later centuries of Western culture, nerved persons and societies to face bloodshed, barbarian invasion, and the breakup of old social forms. The "city" that was Rome, the "city" of the time-contained world, was not the only city. It was—the city of this world—in fact bound to decay and give way, in St. Augustine's phrase, to "the city of God" which John had seen descending from heaven. That there is for man an existence outside the limits of time as well as within is a conception that has been qualified or scornfully rejected by many persons in the last three or four centuries of our culture. Even so, the concept of a "new Jerusalem" operates in our thinking still, though often under other names. Those who are dazzled by the golden temporal future toward which "progress" is leading mankind are closer to John than they are to his pagan contemporaries who believed in the "eternal return." These modern persons, unlike John, locate their new Jerusalem of increased comfort and distraction in the next decade rather than outside time; but they continue to think of human history as something driving toward events without parallel in the past, events that will lift from man's shoulders the burdens he has previously carried. Of course, to these modern hopes, the worker of the great change is no longer a conqueror Messiah, the "royal Christ" who rides on a white steed; this role has been, in the popular mind, allotted to the technicians and planners who are presently to offer us a new society. But in such present attitudes does *The Book of Revelation* continue to be an unacknowledged leaven in modern man's attitude toward the future. That tomorrow will be better is something that *Revelation* suggested to its world; it cut across the pessimism that a belief in recurrent cycles feeds.

The author of *The Book of Revelation* specifically identifies himself as John. A crucial aspect of the discussions generated by the "Johannine problem" is this: Can the man capable of this vision and this expression of it be also the man who opens for us the portal of vision on Christ's life we find in *The Gospel of John*?

Those who say that one author could not have written both books point to wide variations in vocabulary. *John* is simple and abstract; *Revelation* is detailed, sensuous, and specific. These same critics point to the Hellenized frame of mind which the author of *John* uses when he employs Platonic concepts for his not exactly Platonic purposes, and to the strictly Hebraic frame of mind that the traditional apocalyptic "machinery" of *Revelation* displays, where spiritual matters are not treated abstractly but are treated by the method either of poetry or of expanded, specified metaphor. But this argument against John's authorship of both books is based on the assumption that a man cannot brood in unlike styles on "the water of life" (*Revelation* 22:1). If we listen to tradition and add to it reasons of our own, we may state an opposed view thus: It is true that *The Gospel of John* presents the "water of life" as a stream which the individual may at any time in his life approach and drink from; and the supposition of *Revelation* is that the "water of life" is not accessible at every moment of our present life or, at any rate, will flow fully only at a future time. But both books are concerned with the activity of "the Word." The task of the Gospel is to show what "the Word made flesh" offers men so long as history and time shall last, and the task of *Revelation* is to show us how the Word incites eternity. This contrast in the intents of the two books—one should at least suggest—might create some of the contrasts that make them very different.

At any rate, the contrasts are familiar to a person who has followed the Hebrew-Christian awareness to the end. To put the matter descriptively, one may say that the growth of religion is not directed by logic; it seeks to be in accord with the variety of needs that obsess men when they turn to "the Other." *The Gospel of John*, for example, satisfies one set of needs, the impulse to see the process of salvation in a philosophical light; but the existence of this book does not preclude the appearance of another book to satisfy needs that, though not philosophic, are certainly just as exigent. *Revelation* and *John* stand side by side just as do, in the Apocrypha, *Ecclesiasticus* and *The Wisdom of Solomon*. The first of each pair is traditional and Hebraic; the second (by comparison), syncretistic and non-Hebraic. Let us conclude with a kind of *both-and* judgment of our own: Though what such contrasting books say of "man's fate" varies in substance and accent, all are true records of how various human desires seek fulfillment. All are books that have been produced because their authors chose to wrestle with an angel: not the physically realized deity that met Jacob at the ford Jabbok but the dimly perceived aspects of deity which lurk in shadows and on which—so it seems to these writers—the well-being of man, in the long run, absolutely depends.

CONCLUSION

CHAPTER XXI

What the Bible Is: Descriptive Estimate

THERE was once a young man of considerable taste and little faith. His faith, whatever it was, was not that of his ancestors. He had had courses in biology that told him of the gradual emergence of the primates from other classes of mammalian life; he had had courses of philosophy which told him that all truth is relative to the person who holds it and the culture he lives in; he also found the prohibitions that his elders linked up with the will of God restrictive, and he wanted to kick over the traces. Many other young men of his views do not bother to retain on their bookshelves the Bible: the book that, as they see it, stands for all they wish to put behind them. But our young man believed that literature was important even though he had decided that revelation was not. His highly developed literary taste told him that sections of the Holy Scriptures were aesthetically moving and had left an indelible mark (in the King James translation) on the English language. His problem was this: "How was he to keep the Bible on his shelves without causing people to suppose that he shared his ancestors' views about it?" Our young man had ingenuity as well as taste. He purchased a copy of the Bible, removed the covers, and had it rebound in red leather. He caused to be stamped on the binding, in letters of gold, this alternate title: *Among Other Good Books.* And this is a true story.

That the Bible is indeed "among other good books" no one would deny. That this description is, however, an inadequate one might be urged on two grounds: those of faith and those of sober estimate of what the Bible is and has brought about in Western history. Faith, of course, says that the Bible is a collection of writings directly inspired by the Holy Spirit and offers what no other book offers: a sufficient description of what a man must do to be saved. The sober estimate of the position occupied by the Bible throughout many centuries of our culture is not in utter accord with what the man of faith believes about the Bible; but, on the other hand, it goes far beyond the approval of aesthetically pleasing elements that led our young man to place the Bible "among other good books." A sober estimate, it is true, does not overlook the power of many passages in the Bible to charm and intoxicate with words in the fashion of all great poetry. But it does not allow the case for the Bible to rest there.

As the reader of the Bible looks back through the collection of books—each of which he has read, in the first place, for its own sake—he may be able to sense a kind of unity underlying the great diversity to which he has given his attention. History, "fiction," poetry, "drama," theology—beneath this surface of variety is a certain guiding preoccupation that commands the many literary forms employed. What this is and how it sets Hebrew-Christian literature apart from other bodies of literature with which we are familiar is, by now, an open secret. The Hebrews were—to employ a barbarous phrase—a god-conscious people. They were certain that in all human experience there was more than met the eye; they were sure that this "more" was the essential part of experience. Other literatures—particularly those that have grown up since the Renaissance—are full of works whose authors considered that to write history or poetry or fiction is a self-containing activity. To this view, history is a judicious arrangement of what happened, poetry is an expression of individual emotions, and fiction is a made-up story that seems to have happened. One can name innumerable authors who would treat with scorn the suggestions that a historian's chief duty is to show the marks of "the Other" on past human events, that the poet's chief duty is to speak not of his isolated emotions but of the impact on his heart of that which lies beyond him, and that the task of a fiction writer is so to frame his story that he makes some point about the relation of man to God. That all the Hebrew writers, consciously or not, accepted these suggestions and acted on them is the source of the unity beneath the diversity. That the Bible is an inspired collection of books cannot be proved by argument; this is a conviction that is in part a product of faith. That the Bible does display an amazingly persistent orientation of Hebrew curiosity and creative energy—one that extends over more than fifteen hundred years—we have seen. In this sense, the Bible has a strong claim to being a unique collection of literature. Oriental literature offers some rough parallels, but Western literature none.

One other point can be affirmed in a summary description of the claims of the Bible on the attention of modern readers. This "library," with its persistent narrowing and centering of interests, has fostered a certain set of ideas which are part of the framework of Western culture. The framers of the Declaration of Independence said: "We hold these truths to be self-evident," and then set down a list of "truths" which are not self-evident at all: that each person has a right to life, liberty, and the pursuit of happiness, and so on. Many societies exist or have existed to which these "truths" did not once occur. To these other societies, it was "self-evident" that the subject existed to help build a king's funeral monument or to be a useful but not indispensable cog in the machinery set up by the collective state. Perhaps because we are today painfully aware that the self-evident truths we act on are ignored or denied by millions of other human beings, we can have an attention for the Bible that some of our emancipated ancestors did not have. To many of the Founding Fathers of the United States, the Bible had become "expendable" because they believed the ideas it had produced would, in any case, be produced by "human nature" and, moreover, without the concomitants of the supernatural that eighteenth-century deists and rationalists found regrettable in the Bible. Precisely because we are aware that there are no inevitable "patterns of culture" and that the one we prefer is but one of many, our curiosity as to how our particular pattern was created is keener than it once was. As one act of self-defense and self-preservation, we turn back to the study of the sources of the various ideas constituting our "way of life." Naturally, we find, in our way of life, ideas and modes of sensation that come from non-Hebraic sources. Thus, for the sources of our aesthetic sensitivity, our scientific method, and the formal philosophic disciplines we must look elsewhere. And what the narrow, focused consciousness of Hebrew culture does offer us has, in succeeding ages, received support from other cultures. To state the matter at its minimum rather than to seek a maximum, the Hebrew-Christian tradition endowed the culture to which we belong with these self-evident truths: the uniqueness of the individual, the importance of the *intent* of an action, a certain attitude toward past and future history, and a group of speculations about the nature of deity that has played a large part in the growth of Western thought.

Some of these conceptions are still regarded as "self-evident," and others have drawn, in recent times, a barrage of objection. The uniqueness of the individual is still a tenet on which all Americans agree although they do not agree on how that uniqueness is to be preserved. Most champions of the theory that each man has a special dignity that secular arrangements should cherish are not aware that this idea, this basis for modern political and social action, had its origin in a religious context. The individual was precious in the eyes of Jesus and Paul because each man had a destiny outside history and time as well as within it. To the devout Christian today, this "self-evident" truth is still rooted in religious soil; to the agnostic, it is also true though it grows in secular surroundings. The individual no longer is thought by an agnostic to have an immortal destiny but must realize himself and his potentialities within the framework of time and history.

Similar questions might be asked about the other Hebrew-Christian contributions to ourselves. The preference of *intent* to *act* as a better basis for judging another's behavior presupposes a Judge who is able to read intent truly. We all read intent imperfectly when we "size up" the actions of another. Christ said: "Judge not lest ye be judged." Few of us are close enough to a person to read his intent truly. Consciously or unconsciously, we fall back on the kind of external judgment that is an aspect of the legalism the prophets and Christ tried to put an end to.

The idea that history and time lead us toward a new goal not previously experienced by mankind and that history is more than cycles monotonously repeated is an idea nourished by *Revelation* and other books. We again are not aware of what we are doing when we remove the "new Jerusalem" of *Revelation* from its proper position in eternity and make its locus the next year or the next decade; we do not see that our unconscious efforts to streamline an ancient religious idea may lead to bitter disappointment. True, we can see the mote in the Russian eye that looks toward the Marxian "new Jerusalem," but only an awareness of the actual origin and history of this concept is likely to make us see the beam in our own eye when we look forward to a secular American utopia where there is a chicken in every pot and two cars in every garage.

The group of ideas about the nature of God and his providence has bulked large in the history of Western civilization. "Modern" concepts which represent a revolt against this group of ideas are in a way products of these ancient ideas and should be so understood; this is a perception that needs underlining. A revolt—even if it is played out in terms of words and ideas rather than in terms of barricades and paving stones—is always *against* something. The person who has followed the history of what men have thought about God sees that a new conception of God is conditioned by the old idea that is being rejected. This certainly is plain in the history of the idea of God that we have traced throughout the Bible. The "new dispensation" is not a gradual modification; it is an attempt to reverse, to turn upside down, all that the Sadducees and Pharisees taught concerning deity and the ways of deity toward man. A similar reversal of conventional religious attitudes in our own period determines in part what men may tell us of their new ideas about "the Other" that are to take the place of outmoded ideas. One example must suffice. What the great German novelist Thomas Mann tells us about God in his *Joseph* novels is this: God is simply the sum total of all being and realizes himself within the limits of time as he moves from one age of history to the next. An unwary reader is likely to regard Mann's concept of deity as engrossing and self-contained. A more cautious reader is likely to see that a desire to reject and discredit conventional ideas about God plays as great a part in shaping Mann's novelized philosophy as do the original insights of the novelist. Recall that the Hebrew-Christian God is *not* contained in time and is not dependent on the historical process for self-realization. Mann's "theology"—thus barely stated—reveals itself as a determined reversal of what for centuries was commonly accepted. His "new" ideas, then, are "conditioned" by the necessity of being the opposite of the ideas that were for many centuries regarded as both obvious and true.

The point of this illustration and of what has preceded it is this: What the Western world has become cannot be understood without some grasp of what the Hebrew-Christian element offered. It is on this basis, rather than on the basis of faith alone, that the need for some kind of mastery of the Bible persists. To recommend this sort of study in no way prescribes the individual reader's judgment on the value of the role played in Western history by Hebrew-Christian ideas. It does insist that our grasp on what our present civilization is and "how it got that way" is open to error if we have not made an attempt to understand what that role was. Just how beneficial were the results of the Hebrew-Christian ideas in past history and how necessary is their continuance—this is an assessment that must remain the prerogative of the individual reader after he has learned to be at ease in the Bible, from *Genesis* to *Revelation.*

APPENDIX

English Translations of the Bible

As we have noted elsewhere, at the end of *The Gospel of John* (21:25) appears the comment: "And there are many other things which Jesus did, the which, if they should be written every one, I suppose that even the world itself could not contain the books that should be written." What the writer of *John* promised concerning the multiplication of books *about* Jesus has also come to pass with translations of his own Gospel and all the other books in the Bible: the world is full—perhaps full to overflowing—of translations of the Bible into modern languages.

It would, for example, be possible to write a somewhat illuminating history of English literature in terms of the sorts of translations or paraphrases of the Scriptures which successive ages have produced, from the direct, simple Anglo-Saxon of the *Lindisfarne Gospels* (*c.* 687 A.D.) through the triumphs of the sixteenth century that came to a last focus in the King James version of the Bible (1611), and on through stilted products of eighteenth-century piety to—finally—twentieth-century translations with their various merits.

But that is a story which is told fully and well in several books.[1] What the reader of the Bible who is not a specializing student of literature wants to know is something simpler. What are the merits of various translations current and available to a person at bookstores and in libraries? What gains and what losses will a person experience if he chooses a twentieth-century translation rather than the King James version?

The choice is not a simple one. Each version came into existence under special circumstances and, often, was made in order to meet rather specialized demands. Thus, the person who turns to a certain translation should not judge that his choice is a "better" translation on all counts. He should be content to recognize why it is "better" for him. Much, if not all, translation of the Holy Scriptures into English has gone forward under special historical conditions and has, naturally, employed the language in its then-current state. (And we may doubtless feel content that *our* current variety of English allows us to say "apostle" instead of an Anglo-Saxon "fro-sent.")

All translations of the Old Testament into English chiefly rest on an

[1] *The Bible Today*, "described by Christian Scholars," London, 1955; Charles C. Butterworth, *The Literary Lineage of the King James Bible*, Philadelphia, 1941; David Daiches, *The King James Version of the English Bible*, Chicago, 1941, H. Wheeler Robinson (ed.), *The Bible in Its Ancient and English Versions*, Oxford, 1940.

ancient Greek translation, the Septuagint, that dates from about two hundred years before Christ and on the Massoretic text, which achieved its final form about the year 1000 A.D. Roman Catholic modern translations assign preëminent value to the translation into Latin, the Vulgate, made by St. Jerome toward the end of the fourth century A.D.; they also represent, however, a careful study of the old Greek and Hebrew texts. In general, modern translations are perfected by scholars who are relatively free of doctrinal and religious pressures. But the great century of Bible translations that extends from Tyndale's New Testament (1525-1526) to the King James or Authorized Version (1611) was a century when translators labored under both doctrinal and material difficulties. They did not have the wealth of ancient manuscripts that modern scholars may consult. Among the Dead Sea scrolls, for example, is a Hebrew text of *Isaiah* about a thousand years older than the Massoretic text; mastery of the transmission of the Greek text of the Gospels is now a full-time scholarly career. The sixteenth-century translators did not have before them the idea of scholarly detachment which reminds modern translators of the need for absolute faithfulness to the literal, historical sense of the old Greek and Hebrew texts. They were, instead, blown about by "every wind of doctrine" (*Ephesians* 4:14) of which St. Paul spoke. In fact, the bitter divisions of Christendom into Protestant and Catholic led to the production of the King James and the Reims-Douay (1609-1610) versions. (The latter Catholic version was extensively revised by Richard Challoner, 1749-1750.)

For modern readers, barriers to ready comprehension exist in all the early English translations. Thus, the Reims-Douay version, which rests chiefly on Jerome's Vulgate, was made by translators who were understandably suspicious of the Protestant emphasis on the Bible as the one rule of faith, open to the more or less private interpretation of each man. (This, be it recalled, was a Protestant ideal rather than a reality.) The Reims-Douay translators met this challenge by producing a translation that abounds in Latinisms and Greekisms that, in general, preserve a sacerdotal air and often lend Scriptural confirmation to doctrines that arose in later centuries of the Church. *Matthew* 6:11 reads: "Give us today our supersubstantial bread," and *Ephesians* 3:8 begins: "To me the least of all the saints is given this grace, among the Gentiles to evangelize the unsearchable riches of Christ . . ."

The King James version—"authorized" by the King of England but, alas, not paid for by him—seems, in contrast to the Reims-Douay version, clear, direct, and non-controversial. If this is so, it is so because the King James translation terminated a century of controversial translating activity. The men who produced the work felt under pressure from "left-wing" Protestant translators who refused to say "church" and said "congregation" instead, as well as under pressure from the Reims-Douay emphasis just noted. So, like the Anglican Church which sheltered the fifty-odd translators, the King James version speaks in accents of a doctrinal *via media.* More importantly, it represents felicitous translation on the part of the translators, who worked together as collaborators have never worked before or since. It also represents conscious and continuous borrowing from previous translations into English, from Tyndale and Coverdale (1535) onward.

The King James translation supplanted, in Protestant use, all previous translations, possibly because it avoided extremes but, most likely, because it was adequate to the poetry and inspiration of its Hebrew and Greek originals. At any rate, it was the channel through which the Hebrew and Christian insights took up habitation in the English-speaking, English-writing world; and students of English and American literature whose ears have not been attuned to the King James translation fail to see how the language of the Authorized version flows in the lifeblood of literature in English.

But not all readers of the Bible are students of literature and Anglo-Saxon culture. Many readers are religous and turn to an English translation because it is the "word of life" (*Philippians* 2:16), a fountain of everlasting truth. They find that the Jacobean accents of the Authorized version blur the clarity of the word of life; antique idioms become leaves that clog the fountain of everlasting truth. For such readers—and for other readers who just wish to come quickly and conveniently to "what the Bible says"—translations into modern English offer direct satisfaction. For many of these translations have been made free of the doctrinal pressures of a more fiercely religious time; they employ "plain English" in place of an English that—for us, at any rate—is archaic (and different readers find archaism of idiom quaint or poetic or, simply, irritating). It is only fair to observe that readers brought up on the cadences and the apt diction of the King James version will name most modern translations with the name which Eli's daughter-in-law applied to her child: Ichabod—"The glory is departed" (*I Samuel* 4:21).

There have been, in the last century, numerous attempts to modernize the English of the King James version and to embody, in the interests of greater accuracy, the efforts of generations of Biblical scholars. The Revised Version executed in England (1881-1885) and an American revision of this version (1901) were attempts to cope with the changes in English usage and the growth of knowledge about Biblical matters.

Present readers of these translations will feel that the phrasing of the King James version exerted a pervasive authority over the nineteenth-century revisers; some readers see that, however, the great cadences are gone.

American readers, in recent decades, have become familiar with the translation of Dr. James Moffatt (New Testament, 1913; Old Testament, 1924). It is the work of a translator whose English is direct and colloquial; such Authorized version enigmas as the "dark sayings" of Saint Paul acquire considerable clarity. Almost as popular as Moffatt's work is the New Testament translated by Edgar Goodspeed (1923) and the accompanying Old Testament translated under the editorship of J. M. Powis Smith (1927); these translations are clear, popular, and a little flat. Much more successful—at least, from an esthetic point of view—is the Catholic translation by Father Ronald A. Knox (New Testament, 1944, and Old Testament, 1948); it is a translation that successfully ignores the powerful ghosts of the King James translators and yet avoids the flat chattiness of Goodspeed and others. Knox's translating style is balanced and dignified; it puts an end to the tradition of Latinism in Catholic translation.

But probably the Revised Standard Version that appeared in 1952, the work of committees of scholars appointed by the International Council of Religious Education, has, for Protestants who wish to read a modern version of the Bible, superseded the previously popular works of Moffatt, Goodspeed, and others. Its sales have been wide, and justly so. The growth in Biblical knowledge is well represented, archaic grammatical forms have nearly all disappeared, and the translators have not plunged toward the colloquial simply to avoid echoes of the King James version. For the reader who wishes the "plain sense" of the Holy Scriptures as well as some of their dignity, there is not a better modern translation.

Thus, the choice rests with each reader and his estimate of his taste and needs. Before he purchases a Bible, he would do well to read, among the translations offered him, the following passages: *Genesis* 1 and 2; *Deuteronomy* 32; *Judges* 5; *Psalms* 19 and 23; *Isaiah* 53; *Ecclesiastes* 12; *Matthew* 5 and 6; and *I Corinthians* 13.

BIBLIOGRAPHY

A List of Books Useful to the Reader of the Bible

A. Commentaries and Reference Books

The Abingdon Bible Commentary, edited by F. C. Eiselen, Edwin Lewis, and D. G. Downey, New York, 1929.

A Commentary on the Holy Bible, edited by J. R. Dummelow, New York, 1909.

A Commentary on the Bible, edited by A. S. Peake, New York, 1920.

A Dictionary of the Bible, edited by James Hastings, 5 vols., New York, 1903-1905.

A Dictionary of Christ and the Gospels, edited by James Hastings, 2 vols., New York, 1906-1908.

A Dictionary of the Apostolic Church, edited by James Hastings, 2 vols., New York, 1916-1918.

Harper's Bible Dictionary, Madeleine S. Miller and J. Lane Miller, New York, 1952.

The Interpreter's Bible, 12 vols., 1952-1957, Nashville, Tenn.

Nelson Atlas of the Bible, L. H. Grollenberg, London and New York, 1956.

Oxford Dictionary of the Christian Church, edited by F. L. Cross, New York, 1957.

Rand-McNally Bible Atlas, Emil G. Kraeling, New York, 1957.

Westminster Historical Atlas to the Bible, G. E. Wright and F. V. Filson, Philadelphia, 1956.

B. Books Generally Useful

Baly, Denis, *The Geography of the Bible,* New York, 1957.

Barton, George A., *Archaeology and the Bible,* 7th ed., Philadelphia, 1937.

Bewer, Julius A., *The Literature of the Old Testament in Its Historical Development,* New York, 1924.

The Cambridge Ancient History, 12 vols., Cambridge, England, 1925-1939.

Cook, S. A., *The Old Testament: A Reinterpretation,* London, 1936.

Creelman, Harlan, *An Introduction to the Old Testament,* New York, 1917.

Driver, Samuel Rolles, *An Introduction to the Literature of the Old Testament,* New York, 1800.

Enslin, Morton Scott, *Christian Beginnings,* New York, 1938.
Finegan, Jack, *Light from the Ancient Past,* Princeton, 1946.
Fowler, Henry T., *A History of the Literature of Ancient Israel,* New York, 1927.
Fowler, Henry T., *The History and Literature of the New Testament,* New York, 1934.
Keller, Werner, *The Bible as History,* New York, 1956.
Moulton, Richard G., *The Literary Study of the Bible,* New York, 1895.
Neil, William, *The Rediscovery of the Bible,* London, 1954.
Oesterley, W. O. E., and Robinson, T. H., *An Introduction to the Books of the Old Testament,* New York, 1934.
Pfeiffer, Robert H., *Introduction to the Old Testament,* New York, 1948.
Riddle, D. W., and Hutson, Harold H., *New Testament Life and Literature,* Chicago, 1946.
Rowley, H. H., *The Faith of Israel,* London, 1956.
Scott, Ernest F., *The Literature of the New Testament,* New York, 1932.
Smith, George Adam, *The Historical Geography of the Holy Land,* London, 1906.
Wild, Laura H., *A Literary Guide to the Bible,* New York, 1922.
Willoughby, Harold H. (ed.), *The Study of the Bible Today and Tomorrow,* Chicago, 1947.

C. Collateral Reading

Date and place of publication are omitted when the book is listed under Section B of this Bibliography.

Chapter II

Albright, W. F., *The Archaeology of Palestine and the Bible,* 3rd ed., New York, 1935.
Albright, W. F., *From the Stone Age to Christianity,* 2nd ed., Baltimore, 1946.
Barton, George A., *Archaeology and the Bible,* part i, chaps. 1-5.
Breasted, J. H., *A History of Egypt,* New York, 1909.
The Cambridge Ancient History, vol. i, chap. 5 ("The Semites" by S. A. Cook) and *passim.*
Cook, S. A., *The Old Testament: A Reinterpretation,* chaps. 2 and 3.
Finegan, Jack, *Light from the Ancient East,* chaps. 1 and 2.
Frankfort, Henri, *et al., The Intellectual Adventure of Ancient Man,* Chicago, 1946.

Frankfort, Henri, *The Birth of Civilization in the Near East,* Garden City, 1956.
Gurney, O. R., *The Hittites,* London, 1952.
Jastrow, Morris, *The Civilization of Babylonia and Assyria,* Philadelphia, 1915.
Kent, Charles Foster, *Biblical Geography and History,* New York, 1911.
Langdon, Stephen H., *Semitic Mythology,* vol. v of *The Mythology of All Races,* Boston, 1931.
Pritchard, J. B., *Ancient Near Eastern Texts Related to the Old Testament,* Princeton, 1950.
Pritchard, J. B., *The Ancient Near East in Pictures,* Princeton, 1954.
Steindorff, George, and Seele, Keith C., *When Egypt Ruled the East,* Chicago, 1942.
Wilson, John A., *The Burden of Egypt,* Chicago, 1951.

Chapter III

Bewer, Julius A., *The Literature of the Old Testament . . .,* chaps. 4-6, 15, 18, 23.
Eiselen, F. C., *Biblical Introduction Series: The Pentateuch,* New York, 1916.
Frankfort, H., *Kingship and the Gods,* Chicago, 1948.
Hahn, Herbert F., *The Old Testament in Modern Research,* London, 1956.
Herklots, H. G. G., *How Our Bible Came to Us,* New York, 1954.
Oesterley, W. O. E., and Robinson, T. H., *An Introduction to the Books of the Old Testament,* "The Pentateuch," p. 22.
Pfeiffer, Robert H., *Introduction to the Old Testament,* part i.
Price, Ira Maurice, *The Ancestry of Our English Bible,* New York, 1949.
Roberts, B. J., *The Old Testament Text and Versions,* Cardiff, 1951.
Robinson, H. Wheeler, *The Old Testament: Its Making and Meaning,* Nashville, 1937.

Chapter IV

Barton, George A., *Archaeology and the Bible,* part ii, chaps, 1-16.
Buber, Martin, *Moses,* London, 1946.
Burrows, Millar, *What Mean These Stones?* New York, 1956.
The Cambridge Ancient History, vol. ii, chap. 14.
Golding, Louis, *In the Steps of Moses the Conqueror,* London, 1938.
Hooke, S. H., *Myth and Ritual,* London, 1933.

Meek, Theophile J., *Hebrew Origins,* New York, 1950.
Oesterley, W. O. E., and Robinson, T. H., *An Introduction to the Books of the Old Testament,* "Joshua," p. 68; "Judges," p. 75.
Pfeiffer, Robert H., *Introduction to the Old Testament,* parts ii and iii.
Robinson, H. Wheeler, *The History of Israel, Its Facts and Factors,* New York, 1938.
Rowley, H. H., *From Joseph to Joshua,* London, 1950.
Smith, W. Robertson, *The Religion of the Semites* (reprint), New York, 1956.
Woolley, Sir Leonard, *Ur of the Chaldees,* London, 1929.

Chapter V

Cook, S. A., *The Old Testament: A Reinterpretation,* chaps. 6-9.
Creelman, Harlan, *An Introduction to the Old Testament,* pp. 55-84.
Finegan, Jack, *Light from the Ancient East,* chap. 3.
Oesterley, W. O. E., and Robinson, T. H., *An Introduction to the Books of the Old Testament,* "Samuel," p. 85.
Pfeiffer, Robert H., *Introduction to the Old Testament,* part iii.
Wallis, L., *God and the Social Progress,* Chicago, 1935.

Chapter VI

Barton, George A., *Archaeology and the Bible,* part ii, chap. 19.
Creelman, Harlan, *An Introduction to the Old Testament,* pp. 85-169.
Finegan, Jack, *Light from the Ancient East,* chap. 3.
Oesterley, W. O. E., and Robinson, T. H., *An Introduction to the Books of the Old Testament,* "Kings," p. 93.
Pfeiffer, Robert H., *Introduction to the Old Testament,* part iii.

Chapter VII

Barton, George A., *Archaeology and the Bible,* part ii, chaps. 20 and 21.
Bewer, Julius A., *The Literature of the Old Testament . . .,* chap. 18.
Creelman, Harlan, *An Introduction to the Old Testament,* pp. 200-251.
Fowler, Henry T., *A History of the Literature of Ancient Israel,* chap. 21.
Oesterley, W. O. E., and Robinson, T. H., *An Introduction to the Books of the Old Testament,* "Chronicles," p. 109; "Ezra-Nehemiah," p. 120.
Pfeiffer, Robert H., *Introduction to the Old Testament,* part v, chap. 11.
Rowley, H. H., *The Servant of the Lord,* London, 1952.
Welch, Adam C., *The Work of the Chronicler,* London, 1939.

Chapter VIII

Charles, R. H. *The Apocrypha and Pseudepigrapha of the Old Testament,* 2 vols., Oxford, 1913.
Dougherty, R. P., *Nabonidus and Belshazzar,* New Haven, 1929.
Fowler, Henry T., *A History of the Literature of Ancient Israel,* chap. 26.
Oesterley, W. O. E., and Robinson, T. H., *An Introduction to the Books of the Old Testament,* "Esther," p. 131; "Daniel," p. 330; "Ruth," p. 83; "Jonah," p. 372.
Olmstead, A. T., *History of the Persian Empire,* Chicago, 1948, pp. 107-288.
Pfeiffer, Robert H., *Introduction to the Old Testament,* part v.

Chapter IX

Bettan, Israel, *The Five Scrolls,* Cincinnati, 1950.
Bewer, Julius A., *The Literature of the Old Testament . . .,* chaps. 19 and 20.
Buttenwieser, Moses, *The Psalms,* Chicago, 1938.
Fowler, Henry T., *A History of the Literature of Ancient Israel,* chaps. 24 and 25.
Gordis, Robert, *The Song of Songs,* New York, 1954.
Macdonald, D. B., *The Hebrew Philosophical Genius,* Princeton, 1936.
Oesterley, W. O. E., *The Psalms,* New York, 1939.
Oesterley, W. O. E., *The Wisdom of Egypt and the Old Testament,* New York, 1927.
Rylaarsdam, J. Coert, *Revelation in Jewish Wisdom Literature,* Chicago, 1946.
Wild, Laura H., *A Literary Guide to the Bible,* chaps. 5, 7, and 9.

Chapter X

Baab, Otto J., *The Theology of the Old Testament,* Nashville, 1949.
Bewer, Julius A., *The Literature of the Old Testament . . .,* chaps. 7 and 8.
Burrows, Millar, *An Outline of Biblical Theology,* Philadelphia, 1946.
Cook, S. A., *The Old Testament: A Reinterpretation,* chap. 10.
Guillaume, Alfred, *Prophecy and Divination Among the Hebrews and Other Semites,* New York, 1938.

Lods, Adolphe, *The Prophets and the Rise of Judaism,* New York, 1937.
Mowinckel, Sigmund, *Prophecy and Tradition,* Oslo, 1946.
Pfeiffer, Robert H., *Introduction to the Old Testament,* part v.
Robinson, H. Wheeler, *Inspiration and Revelation in the Old Testament,* Oxford, 1946.
Scott, R. B. Y., *The Relevance of the Prophets,* New York, 1944.
Wright, G. Ernest, *The Old Testament Against Its Environment,* Chicago, 1950.

Chapter XI

Bewer, Julius A., *The Literature of the Old Testament . . .,* chaps. 11-14.
Fowler, Henry T., *A History of the Literature of Ancient Israel,* chaps. 17 and 18.
Mowinckel, Sigmund, *He That Cometh,* Nashville, 1957.
Oesterley, W. O. E., and Robinson, T. H., *An Introduction to the Books of the Old Testament,* "Jeremiah," p. 288; "Ezekiel," p. 318; "Isaiah; chs. xl-lv," p. 262.
Pfeiffer, Robert H., *Introduction to the Old Testament,* part v.
Skinner, John, *Prophecy and Religion,* Cambridge, 1922.

Chapter XII

Barton, George A., *Archaeology and the Bible,* part ii, chap. 26.
Fowler, Henry T., *A History of the Literature of Ancient Israel,* chaps. 23 and 24.
Gordis, Robert, *The Wisdom of Ecclesiastes,* New York, 1945.
Jastrow, Morris, *A Gentle Cynic (Ecclesiastes),* Philadelphia, 1919.
Oesterley, W. O. E., and Robinson, T. H., *An Introduction to the Books of the Old Testament,* "Ecclesiastes," p. 209; "Job," p. 166.
Pfeiffer, Robert H., *Introduction to the Old Testament,* part v.
Ranston, Harry, *Ecclesiastes and the Early Greek Wisdom Literature,* London, 1925.
Wild, Laura H., *A Literary Guide to the Bible,* chap. 7.

Chapter XIII

Burrows, Millar, *The Dead Sea Scrolls,* New York, 1955.
Charles, R. H., *The Apocrypha and Pseudepigrapha of the Old Testament,* 2 vols., Oxford, 1913.

Charles, R. H., *Religious Development Between the Old and the New Testaments,* New York, 1914.
Fowler, Henry T., *A History of the Literature of Ancient Israel,* chap. 26.
Gaster, T. H., *The Dead Sea Scriptures,* Garden City, 1956.
Goodspeed, E. J., *The Story of the Apocrypha,* Chicago, 1939.
Guthrie, W. K. C., *The Greeks and Their Gods,* Boston, 1955.
James, M. R., *The Lost Apocrypha of the Old Testament,* London, 1920.
Metzger, Bruce M., *An Introduction to the Apocrypha,* New York, 1957.
Pfeiffer, Robert H., *History of New Testament Times, with an Introduction to the Apocrypha,* New York, 1949.
Riddle, D. W., and Hutson, Harold H., *New Testament Life and Literature,* chaps. 1-3.

Chapter XIV

Case, Shirley Jackson, *The Evolution of Early Christianity,* Chicago, 1941.
Dill, Samuel, *Roman Society from Nero to Marcus Aurelius,* London, 1920.
Enslin, Morton Scott, *Christian Beginnings,* part i.
Fowler, Henry T., *The History and Literature of the New Testament,* chaps. 1 and 2.
Glover, T. R., *The Conflict of Religions in the Early Roman Empire,* London, 1909.
Guignebert, Charles, *The Jewish World in the Time of Jesus,* New York, 1939.
Klausner, Joseph, *Jesus of Nazareth,* New York, 1943, bk. 2.
Latourette, Kenneth Scott, *A History of the Expansion of Christianity,* New York, 1937, vol. i, chap. 1.
Moore, George Foot, *Judaism in the First Centuries of the Christian Era,* Cambridge, 1927.
Morton, H. V., *In the Steps of the Master,* New York, 1934.
Wolfson, Harry A., *Philo: Foundations of Religious Philosophy in Judaism, Christianity, and Islam,* Cambridge, Mass., 1948.

Chapter XV

Bultmann, Rudolph, *Form Criticism: A New Method of New Testament Research,* Chicago, 1934.
Dibelius, Martin, *From Tradition to Gospel,* New York, 1935.

Dodd, C. H., *The Apostolic Preaching and Its Developments,* London, 1936.

Easton, B. S., *The Gospel Before the Gospels,* New York, 1928.

Farrar, Austin, *St. Matthew and St. Mark,* London, 1954.

Goodspeed, E. J., *The Formation of the New Testament,* Chicago, 1927.

Jones, Geraint Vaughan, *Christology and Myth in the New Testament,* London, 1956.

Knox, Wilfred L., *The Sources of the Synoptic Gospels, Cambridge, Cambridge,* 1953.

Riddle, Donald Wayne, *The Gospels: Their Growth and Origin,* Chicago, 1939.

Scott, Ernest F., *The Validity of the Gospel Record,* New York, 1938.

Streeter, B. H., *The Four Gospels,* London, 1924.

Taylor, Vincent, *The Formation of the Gospel Tradition,* London, 1933.

Chapter XVI

Cadoux, C. J., *The Historic Mission of Jesus,* New York, 1943.

Dodd, C. H., *The Parables of the Kingdom,* New York, 1936.

Enslin, Morton Scott, *Christian Beginnings,* chaps. 39-41.

Fowler, Henry T., *The History and Literature of the New Testament,* chaps. 20-22.

Goguel, Maurice, *The Life of Jesus,* London, 1933.

Montefiore, L. G., *The Synoptic Gospels,* 2 vols., London, 1927.

Otto, Rudolph, *The Kingdom of God and the Son of Man,* London, 1943.

Riddle, Donald, and Hutson, Harold H., *New Testament Life and Literature,* chaps. 14 and 15.

Schweitzer, Albert, *The Quest of the Historical Jesus,* London, 1943.

Scott, E. F., *The Kingdom of God in the New Testament,* New York, 1931.

Scott, Ernest F., *The Literature of the New Testament,* chaps. 3-5.

Chapter XVII

Dodd, C. H. *The Interpretation of the Fourth Gospel,* Cambridge, 1953.

Enslin, Morton Scott, *Christian Beginnings,* chap. 44.

Howard, Wilbert Francis, *The Fourth Gospel,* London, 1945.

Riddle, Donald, and Hutson, Harold H., *New Testament Life and Literature,* chap. 18.

Scott, E. F., *The Fourth Gospel,* Edinburgh, 1908.

Scott, E. F., *The Literature of the New Testament,* chaps. 25 and 26.

Chapter XVIII

Deissmann, G. Adolf, *Paul: A Study in Social and Religious History,* New York, 1926.

Dibelius, Martin, *Studies in the Acts of the Apostles,* London, 1956.

Enslin, Morton Scott, *Christian Beginnings,* chaps. 12, 13, and 42.

Fowler, Henry T., *The History and Literature of the New Testament,* chaps. 3-6, 9, 13, 14.

Klausner, Joseph, *From Jesus to Paul,* New York, 1943.

Latourette, Kenneth Scott, *A History of the Expansion of Christianity,* New York, 1937, vol. i, chaps. 2 and 3.

Lietzmann, Hans, *The Beginnings of the Christian Church,* New York, 1937.

Morton, H. V., *In the Steps of St. Paul,* New York, 1936.

Riddle, Donald, and Hutson, Harold H., *New Testament Life and Literature,* chaps. 9 and 10.

Schweitzer, Albert, *Paul and His Interpreters,* London, 1912.

Weiss, Johannes, *History of Primitive Christianity,* New York, 1937.

Chapter XIX

Dodd, C. H., *The Epistle of Paul to the Romans,* London, 1932.

Duncan, G. S., *St. Paul's Ephesian Ministry,* New York, 1930.

Enslin, Morton Scott, *Christian Beginnings,* chaps. 15-36.

Goodspeed, Edgar J., *The Meaning of Ephesians,* Chicago, 1933.

Kirk, K. E., *The Epistle to the Romans,* Oxford, 1937.

Moffatt, James, *The First Epistle of Paul to the Corinthians,* New York, 1938.

Riddle, Donald, and Hutson Harold H., *New Testament Life and Literature,* chaps. 9 and 10.

Scott, Ernest F., *The Pastoral Epistles,* New York, 1936.

Chapter XX

Case, Shirley Jackson, *The Revelation of John,* Chicago, 1919.

Enslin, Morton Scott, *Christian Beginnings,* chap. 37.

Fowler, Henry T., *The History and Literature of the New Testament,* chaps. 25 and 26.

Kepler, Thomas S., *The Book of Revelation,* New York, 1957.

Index of Passages Quoted from the Bible

Index of Names and Subjects